THE SPEARLESS LEADER

THE
SPEARLESS
LEADER

Senator Borah
and the Progressive Movement
in the 1920's

LeROY ASHBY

UNIVERSITY OF ILLINOIS PRESS
Urbana Chicago London

For my mother and father,
Mildred and Sam Ashby,
and my brother Larry

© *1972 by The Board of Trustees of the University of Illinois*
Manufactured in the United States of America
Library of Congress Catalog Card No. 74-170963

ISBN 0-252-00220-2

CONTENTS

PREFACE

❦

THIS study attempts—through the career of Idaho's Senator
William E. Borah—to focus on significant aspects of the internal history of the progressive movement in the decade following World War I. Borah, who after entering the Senate in
1907 emerged as one of the major figures in American reform
politics, reached the peak of his prestige and influence during
the Twenties. That he figured so prominently in key progressive struggles, aspirations, and disappointments throughout the
decade revealed not only much about his own personality and
political methods but also a great deal about the visions,
strengths, and weaknesses of progressivism itself. Although by
the end of the Twenties he had developed the reputation of
being a "spearless leader," in important ways he illustrated how
spearless much of the progressive movement had become. Borah
did not speak, of course, for all reformers. But he was unquestionably representative of a significant type of progressive and
he was never more than a few steps away from his liberal colleagues in the Senate.

Although I have not written a biography of the Senator, I
have attempted to provide insights into his attitudes, ambitions,
and political style. I have not treated in detail Borah's involvement in matters of foreign policy, but have tried to sort out
some of his major assumptions and activities regarding American diplomacy and to suggest certain links between them and
his reputation as a leading progressive spokesman.

The word "progressive" has appeared in so many forms in
recent historical literature that it sometimes adds to confusion
rather than understanding. Nonetheless, it remains useful as a
general descriptive label for the major outburst of reform zeal
in the early twentieth century seeking primarily to salvage traditional American values and ideals of democracy and oppor-

tunity in the new industrial order. As Robert H. Wiebe has
written, most historians agree that the progressives accepted certain broad social, economic, and political tenets: to bring government closer to the wishes of the general public, to protect
the general public interest through some form of government
regulation, and to divide more equitably the national pie so
that the underprivileged could gain a fairer share. Progressives
thus adhered to cultural standards which, as Richard M.
Abrams has pointed out, included the ideal of disinterested
public service, placed private property rights within a context
of social responsibility, and justified greater government participation to effect conditions beneficial to the general welfare.

Any discussion of progressivism must not, however, ignore
the tremendous diversity of programs and participants. There
is a danger, for example, that a label such as the "progressive
movement" may suggest a monolithic quality that belies the im-
mense variety of the reform efforts of the early twentieth century. Indeed, after reviewing recent interpretations, Peter Filene has concluded that progressive groups and programs were
simply too diverse and contradictory to fit under the general
rubric of a "movement." I have decided, nonetheless, to continue speaking about the "progressive movement" and have
done so simply because it is the term that progressives themselves used and with which they identified. A host of reformers
—including John R. Commons, Ray Stannard Baker, Frederick
Howe, Robert M. La Follette, and George Record—spoke often
of the "progressive movement" and did so in contexts that had
nothing to do with third-party efforts.

This study first took shape under the guidance of Professor
Horace Samuel Merrill of the University of Maryland, to whom
I am deeply indebted. His constant encouragement, his friendly
but astute counsel, and his willingness always to be of service
are qualities to which all his graduate students will attest. Moreover, the warm hospitality and company that he and Mrs. Merrill are always willing to offer provided additional aid. Professor
Robert H. Zieger of Wisconsin State University, Stevens Point,

read numerous drafts of the manuscript, offered insights based upon his own deep research into Republican politics in the Twenties, gave numerous suggestions regarding style and organization, and was always a source of encouragement and friendship. Professor Wayne S. Cole of the University of Maryland took an interest in this project that went far beyond the courtesies of scholarship; his advice, especially regarding Borah and foreign policy, was noteworthy both for its insight and the tolerant spirit in which it was offered. Others who deserve thanks for reading parts of the manuscript in its various stages are Professors Paul W. Glad of the University of Wisconsin and David A. Shannon of the University of Virginia. Professor John M. Cooper, Jr., of the University of Wisconsin provided a critique which was most helpful in writing the final revision.

Numerous librarians and their staffs furnished invaluable aid. Especially important were those of the Manuscript Division of the Library of Congress. Other help came from the libraries of Yale University, the University of Pennsylvania, Harvard University, the University of Virginia, Duke University, the University of South Dakota, the Western Manuscripts Division of the University of Missouri, the University of Chicago, the University of California at Berkeley, the University of Colorado, the Herbert Hoover Presidential Library, the University of Maryland, and the state historical societies of Wisconsin, Minnesota, and Ohio.

Generous grants from the Penrose Fund of the American Philosophical Society, the University of Bridgeport's Special Committee on Research, and Illinois State University were indispensable in allowing me to complete the research. Beth Ann Freedman typed one complete draft and Pat Clemens and Pat Farrens typed revisions. I wish also to thank the editors of the *Pacific Northwest Quarterly* and *Mid-America* for allowing me to quote from materials originally published in those journals.

I owe extra debts of gratitude to Professor Norma Peterson of Adams State College, Professor William R. Steckel of the University of Wyoming, my grandparents Mr. and Mrs. Fay

Hooker, my parents, and Mr. and Mrs. Bryan G. Gross. Of incalculable importance was the understanding, encouragement, and advice which my wife Mary consistently offered; she helped this book grow from the beginning, hearing about Borah, reading about Borah, and talking about Borah while still keeping up her spirits and raising two boys. And to Steven and Eric, a very special thanks, too.

THE SPEARLESS LEADER

I

Introduction

❧

IN 1925 the *Survey* magazine held what H. L. Mencken dubbed "an inquest" concerning American reform by asking a short but pertinent question: "Where Are the Pre-War Radicals?" There was a variety of responses, but to Mencken it was clear that the progressive movement was "now down with the wasting disease." [1]

Mencken's *American Mercury* subsequently took aim at one source of the problem: "the so-called Progressives in the Senate" —for the most part "a sorry bunch of weaslings and time-servers" who practiced "a Progressivism of face-saving devices." The article singled out Idaho's William E. Borah as "the Great Sham" among progressive Senators and the man especially responsible for enervating the cause of liberal reform. According to Senator Peter Norbeck of South Dakota, the article attracted much attention because it was largely true. In the early Twenties, Norbeck had linked himself with the progressives and had admired Borah for being "honest and fearless—a master mind and a wonderful debater"; but as the decade unfolded, he too bemoaned the lack of progressive unity and voiced growing doubts about Borah's commitment to reform.[2]

[1] "Where Are the Pre-War Radicals?," *Survey*, LV (February 1, 1926), 556–66; Mencken's quote in Robert C. Bannister, Jr., *Ray Stannard Baker, The Mind and Thought of a Progressive* (New Haven, Conn., 1966), p. 237.
[2] "The Progressives of the Senate," *The American Mercury*, XVI (April, 1929), 385–93; Norbeck's reaction to the article quoted in Richard Hofstadter, *The Age of Reform* (paperback ed.; New York, 1955), p. 285n.; on Norbeck's "progressive affiliations," see Norbeck to E. L. Senn, January 13, 1923, Peter Norbeck Papers (University of South Dakota Library), and on Borah, Norbeck to Kent E. Keller, March 9, 1922, Peter Norbeck

By the end of the 1920's, there were a number of such expressions of disappointment regarding both the dispirited condition of progressivism and Senator Borah. Since Borah had entered the Senate in 1907, he had figured prominently in discussions among and about liberals on Capitol Hill. During the decade following World War I, he had emerged as a possible "Moses" to reformers. Eloquent, with an extraordinary knack for capturing publicity, colorfully rugged in appearance, superbly talented as a politician who could placate opposing factions, and openly committed to reshaping politics along more liberal lines, he had offered postwar progressivism a major source of hope. By 1930, however, progressive editor Oswald Garrison Villard concluded that "No man has muffed a greater opportunity." Villard was not alone in his disappointment. To Harold Ickes, a participant in the earlier Bull Moose movement and a man who throughout the Twenties lamented the sorry state of reform, it was obvious why "the progressive associates of Senator Borah in the United States Senate, with their eyes at last opened, refer to him as 'our spearless leader.' " [3]

Ickes undoubtedly had in mind Borah's tendency to become "regular" at the moment of truth, to prefer solitude and secretiveness in the Senate, and to lose interest in causes for which he had previously expressed zeal. What Ickes perhaps did not realize was that in major ways Borah reflected many of the strains, tensions, and ambiguities that rendered much of progressivism itself quite spearless in the 1920's. Borah's weakness as a progressive leader was due not only to his habit of "shooting until he sees the whites of their eyes," as Senator George

Papers (Western Manuscripts Division, University of Missouri), Folder 2; for one example of Norbeck's revised views, see Norbeck to G. J. Moen, January 11, 1932, Norbeck Papers (South Dakota).

[3] Villard to William E. Sweet, February 28, 1930, Oswald Garrison Villard Papers (Houghton Library, Harvard University), Folder 3766; copy of memo from Harold Ickes regarding Borah in George Peek Papers (Western Manuscripts Division, University of Missouri), Box 85, Folder 2776. The memo is undated, but apparently was written during or shortly after the 1928 election campaign.

Norris put it, but more fundamentally to the extent to which he mirrored many of the dilemmas of prewar progressivism. These dilemmas sprang from problems of social vision, of the proper basis of politics, of the role of the state, and of the place of the individual in an increasingly organized world. Such matters had plagued progressivism from its beginnings, but for a while they had been overshadowed by the reform consensus of the early years of the century. For Borah and others who wished to continue shaping America along progressive lines, the fundamental task in the "new era" of the 1920's was to recognize and cope with these concerns. The need to adapt prewar reform goals and values to the demands of postwar America was formidable enough without the added factor of unpredictability which Borah brought to it.

The remarkable characteristic of prewar progressivism—indeed, the key to its legislative triumphs—had been a general reform ethos which had overcome the era's internal tensions and contradictions, making possible the forging of political coalitions out of quite diverse groups. At the turn of the century, the growing demands of industrialization, urbanization, and the new immigration had combined with the severe economic crises of the 1890's to weaken class divisions and confront all groups with a common sense of emergency. The appearance of an activist generation—committed to a strenuous, open life and to functional thought—had combined with a growing confidence in human possibilities to inspire hopes of almost millennial proportions. The result had been a prewar consensus, notable for its optimistic faith in an imminent future of brotherhood and righteousness.

In this period of high expectations, lines tended to blur: lines between radicalism and reform, between religious fundamentalism and liberal protestantism, between intellectuals in the academic world and practical politicians on the stump, between moral and economic reform, between the forces of labor and the forces of capital, between those reformers seeking to preserve traditional individualistic values and those anticipating the general benefits and greater efficiency of increased organization. Quite different groups, linked however loosely by an optimistic faith in progress and by an idealism charged with revivalistic fervor, had moved in and out of reform coalitions, leaving behind an impressive array of legislative achievements. For example, the Pure Food and Drug Act (1906) had emerged from the joint efforts of doctors and pharmacists attempting to strengthen their professions, of prohibitionists who opposed the alcoholic content of cure-all medicines, of drug companies seeking national protection against potentially more radical local laws, of muckraking journalists in search of sensational exposés, and of politicians—such as Theodore Roosevelt—hoping to strengthen governmental powers. Similarly, workmen's compensation statutes had resulted from a coalition of judges weary from the emotional weight of cases involving injured workers, of laborers seeking more on-the-job protections, of industries tired of the unpredictability of courtroom judgments and searching for ways to place the issue of compensation on an efficient, orderly basis, and of social justice groups concerned with gaining more rights for the little man in the face of the industrial onslaught.[4]

[4] For an important discussion of the unifying spirit so central to pre-war progressivism, see Clyde Griffen, "The Progressive Ethos," in Stanley Coben and Lorman Ratner (eds.), *The Development of an American Culture* (Englewood Cliffs, N.J., 1970), pp. 120–49. John D. Buenker, "The Progressive Era: A Search for a Synthesis," *Mid-America,* 51 (July, 1969), 175–93, stresses the temporary and practical coalitions of diverse groups inspired by industrial, urban, and immigration changes. On the millennial expectations of the progressive period, see David Noble, *The Progressive Mind, 1890–1917* (Chicago, 1970); on how the crises of the 1890's blurred class lines and provided the necessary impetus for the formation of reform coalitions, see David Thelen, "Social Tensions and the Origins of Progressivism," *Journal of American History,* LVI (September, 1969), esp. pp. 335–41; on how divergent groups combined to change industrial accident laws and produce workman's compensation laws, see Lawrence M. Friedman and Jack Ladinsky, "Law and Social Change in the Progressive Era: The Law of Industrial Accidents," *Columbia Law Review,* LXVII (January, 1967), 50–82; and for an excellent overview

But by the Twenties this prewar progressive consensus was in shambles. As the unifying spirit and confidence of the earlier years dissolved, the internal weaknesses of progressivism became all too apparent. One agonizing problem—and one which Borah symbolized so vividly—was the need to square the basically rural and agrarian social vision of progressivism with the demands of an ethnically and racially diverse urban nation. Although many progressive leaders were urban residents, their roots and biases tended to be overwhelmingly rural. Their penchant for individualism, their hostility to special privilege, and their Protestant faith comprised the intellectual and cultural baggage which they carried with them from their village backgrounds. Even an urban reform mayor such as Brand Whitlock, who celebrated the city as "one of the fundamental forms of human association" and who looked to the "free city" as the hope of the future, held curiously romantic views of the working class and remained much closer to the rural Ohio of his youth than he realized. Jacob Riis, famous for his probing explorations into city slum life, tended to define suitable urban conditions in pastoral terms. And many of the social settlement workers, distinctive for their willingness to come to grips with urban problems, were often concerned with bringing the country into the city.[5]

---

of the emerging activist generation see John Higham, "The Reorientation of American Culture in the 1890's," in John Weiss (ed.), *The Origins of Modern Consciousness* (Detroit, Mich., 1965), pp. 25–48.

[5] Wayne Fuller discusses "The Rural Roots of the Progressive Leaders," *Agricultural History*, XLII (January, 1968), 1–13. On Whitlock, see Jack Tager, *The Intellectual as Urban Reformer: Brand Whitlock and the Progressive Movement* (Cleveland, Ohio, 1968), esp. pp. 33–34, 84–86, 131, 146, 165–82; on Riis, see Roy Lubove, *The Progressives and the Slums: Tenement House Reform in New York City, 1890–1917* (Pittsburgh, Pa., 1962), pp. 59–61, 74, 79; on the settlement workers and agrarian America, see Allen F. Davis, *Spearheads for Reform: The Social Settlements and the Progressive Movement, 1890–1914* (New York, 1967), pp. 60–61. Herbert Janick notes that a severe limitation on "The Mind of the Connecticut Progressives," was the fact that these reform leaders

Borah's roots similarly went deep into agrarian America. Born and raised in rural Illinois, he had felt the profound cultural influences of the Middle Border—its faith in progress, its "missionary impulse," its stress on good conduct instead of theological doctrine, its moralism, and its paradoxical emphasis on the need for conversion and the essential goodness of man. Evangelical Protestantism, the homilies of the *McGuffey Reader,* and the fervor of the Chautauqua circuit had all been central to his early experience. His brief stay in Kansas, where he attended the state university for a year before illness forced him out, and several decades in Boise, Idaho, hardly challenged his earlier views. Not until he was elected Senator at age forty-two did he move to Washington, D.C., where he lamented on a number of occasions the "fatal trek" to the cities.[6]

The growing divergence between the facts of urban life and the rural sentiments of progressives such as Borah had critical implications. It hampered the formation of broad-based political coalitions. It tended to shift reform questions to cultural matters—involving issues of manners, morals, and life styles. It drew lines between agrarian liberals and city reformers on questions of prohibition, immigration restriction, and the place of hyphenate groups in American life. Ultimately it raised questions as to how relevant prewar progressivism was to a nation which by 1920 lived more in the city than in the country. Significantly, Borah's progressive colleagues in the Senate were

---

lacked "personal, intimate contact with urban conditions." *Mid-America,* 52 (April, 1970), 99–100. For a case study of the problem, see Fred Erisman, "L. Frank Baum and the Progressive Dilemma," *American Quarterly,* XX (Fall, 1968), 616–23; Erisman writes (p. 616) that the dilemma "of the Progressive leaders was their inability to adapt essentially rural ideals to a complex urban society." For comments regarding some of the dangers in focusing on the rural-urban dichotomy, see the bibliographical essay.

[6] For Borah's background, see Claudius Johnson, *Borah of Idaho* (New York, 1936), and Marian McKenna, *Borah* (Ann Arbor, Mich., 1961). On the social and cultural patterns of the Middle Border, see Lewis Atherton, *Main Street on the Middle Border* (Bloomington, Ind., 1954), esp. chaps. 1–7, and Paul W. Glad, *The Trumpet Soundeth: William Jennings Bryan and His Democracy, 1896–1912* (Lincoln, Neb., 1960), pp. 1–20.

invariably from western states and, like the Idahoan, had a social vision that was predominantly regional and agrarian.

While emerging cultural divisions thus weakened progressivism by the 1920's, so too did the problem of how to square
individualism with organizational effort. Borah's struggle with
this dilemma placed him on common ground with other reformers who, although not necessarily agreeing with him, also
felt the tug of traditional individualistic ideals and the countervailing demands of technology and mass industry. Progressive
intellectuals attempted to explain the problem away with the
hypothesis that technology would free man from artificial re-
straints and thus allow him to be his natural self. Convinced
that the solution of human problems rested with society, social
scientists such as Charles Horton Cooley, John Dewey, Thor-
stein Veblen, and religious reformers such as Walter Rauschen-
busch emphasized that man was a social animal and that
nineteenth-century competitive individualism had been unnat-
ural; they concluded that natural man was cooperative and that
the new technological order would provide the setting in which
the individual and the group could once again live in harmony.
But the extent of their intellectual adjustment to the facts of
organization and technology was not as complete as it seemed.
Quite often the end result was a definition of community which,
rather than restricting individual autonomy, instead expanded
the range of individual possibilities and liberated man from
artificial institutions and forms. Moreover, when a leading progressive sociologist such as E. A. Ross spelled out the need for
individual adjustment to discipline and order, he did so at
great psychic cost; basically he was torn between the apparent
need for social control to prevent chaos and the individualism
which he preferred. After Ross published his classic *Social Control* (1901), he spent the rest of his life trying to refute the arguments of his earlier book and defending the individual against
society.[7]

[7] Hofstadter, *The Age of Reform*, esp. chap. 6, and Otis L. Graham,
Jr., *An Encore for Reform: The Old Progressives and the New Deal* (New

Despite the realization among many progressives that organization had become a predominant factor in modern life, the pull of old individualistic values was simply far too strong for most of them to overcome. The marked concern for the strong, unsullied individual during the progressive era had manifested itself in a variety of ways: in the desire for personal adventure, in the respect for the virile man "with bark on," in the popularity of a novel such as *The Virginian* (written by Theodore Roosevelt's close friend, Owen Wister), and in the wilderness cult which offered a contrast to the machine order.[8]

The overwhelming technological revolution of the 1920's increased this tension between the individualistic ethic and organization—a fact that manifested itself clearly in the ambiva-

---

York, 1967), pp. 66–69, stress the tension between organization and the individual during the progressive era. Noble, *The Progressive Mind*, esp. pp. 23–80, 117–36, R. Jackson Wilson, *In Quest of Community: Social Philosophy in the United States, 1860–1920* (New York, 1968), and Jean B. Quandt, *From the Small Town to the Great Community: The Social Thought of Progressive Intellectuals* (New Brunswick, N.J., 1970), treat the intellectual efforts to confront the problems of industrial organization and community; on E. A. Ross, see Wilson, pp. 87–113. Bannister, *Ray Stannard Baker, The Mind and Thought of a Progressive*, is a sensitive and perceptive study of one progressive's attempts to come to grips with the implications of the organizational revolution of the period. Alfred Kazin points out that important aspects of the cultural revolt that occurred at the turn of the century and into the 1920's had a similar individualistic thrust; pioneer modernist writers such as Ezra Pound, Hemingway, and Gertrude Stein reflected the nineteenth-century entrepreneurial tradition with its emphasis on "the self-affirming and expansive 'self.'" Review of Margaret Anderson's writings in *New York Times Book Review*, August 16, 1970, pp. 1, 29.

[8] On the desire for personal adventure, see Graham, *Encore for Reform*, pp. 47–48n., 84–88; on the virility cult, G. Edward White, *The Eastern Establishment and the Western Experience* (New Haven, Conn., 1969), and James R. McGovern, "David Graham Phillips and the Virility Impulse of the Progressives," *The New England Quarterly*, 39 (September, 1966), 334–55; on Wister's *The Virginian*, see White, *The Eastern Establishment and the Western Experience*, and John A. Barsness, "Theodore Roosevelt as Cowboy: The Virginian as Jacksonian Man," *American Quarterly*, 21 (Fall, 1969), 609–19, and Noble, *The Progressive Mind*, 154–64, 172–74, 178; on the wilderness cult, Roderick Nash, *Wilderness and the American Mind* (New Haven, Conn., 1967), esp. chap. 1.

lent treatment of Henry Ford as technological genius and rugged individualist or, likewise, in celebrations of Charles Lindbergh's trans-Atlantic flight as the great triumph of both private, lonely effort and the combined talents of American industry.[9] This could only place additional strains on the crumbling progressive ethos. In the Senate, Borah's reputation as a loner plainly illustrated the predicament. His famous lone-wolf qualities made him an archetypical progressive hero, while at the same time these same maverick tendencies limited his effectiveness in leading or working with other reformers.

Closely linked to the problem of self-reliance and group effort was the equally thorny question of government's proper role in the economy and society. Throughout the progressive era, the problem of the methods and ends of state intervention had besieged American liberals. Although rhetoric often exaggerated differences among reformers, the debates between advocates of Theodore Roosevelt's New Nationalism and Woodrow Wilson's New Freedom clearly pointed up the issue. Despite Roosevelt's political appeal, however, his support in 1912 was probably due more to his personal charisma than any overwhelming commitment to his "new liberalism" with its blending of nationalism and reform. Most progressives were deeply suspicious of political power, a fact which would become clear in the 1930's when many former Bull Moose Progressives expressed dismay and bewilderment at New Deal "planning"—something which they had not had in mind when they first endorsed enlarged state responsibility. The pervasive distrust of a strong government among prewar liberals was quite evident in their approach to an explosive subject such as social security; here they evinced their aversion to any state-imposed program and their continuing faith in individual self-sufficiency and voluntarism, which was private, voluntary, nonbureaucratic, and noncoercive. When

[9] See, for example, John William Ward, "The Meaning of Lindbergh's Flight," *American Quarterly*, X (Spring, 1958), 3–16, and on Ford, Roderick Nash, *The Nervous Generation: American Thought, 1917–1930* (Chicago, 1970), pp. 153–63.

Senator Borah inveighed against consolidation of power—
whether politically through the growth of bureaucracy or eco-
nomically through monopolization—he may have struck Theodore Roosevelt as a "rural tory," but he nonetheless echoed a
major sentiment in early twentieth-century reform.[10]

By the Twenties the skepticism with which many progressives
regarded government had deepened. The disappointments of
war and the Red Scare discouraged even dedicated New Nationalists and social reformers. Initially they had seen the war as a
means, however undesirable, of achieving important victories
for social justice; but the war, as Randolph Bourne had warned,
quickly proved much more beneficial to the state than to reform. Even some of the most enthusiastic New Nationalists—
men such as Herbert Croly and Walter Lippmann—began to
have reservations about their earlier commitments to strong
leadership and started wondering about the "new liberalism"
itself. As Frederick Howe realized, "The war had changed an
abiding faith in the state into questionings of it." [11] By the
1920's after several decades of wrestling with the problem, progressives appeared more divided than before in their own minds
and among themselves over the matter of government's proper
role. Before reformers could hope to reshape a powerful national movement, they faced the major task of agreeing upon a
viable program which met the needs of postwar America; and

[10] Graham, *Encore for Reform*, pp. 36–41, discusses the progressive
suspicion of power and the opposition of former New Nationalists to the
New Deal; Roy Lubove, *The Struggle for Social Security 1900–1935* (Cambridge, Mass., 1968), esp. pp. 1–44, analyzes the commitment to self-
reliance and voluntarism; George E. Mowry, *The Era of Theodore Roosevelt and the Birth of Modern America, 1900–1912* (New York, 1958),
p. 55, contains Roosevelt's quote on "rural toryism"; Charles Forcey,
*The Crossroads of Liberalism: Croly, Weyl, Lippmann and the Progres-
sive Era, 1900–1925* (New York, 1961), is a superb analysis of the "new
liberalism."

[11] Allen F. Davis, "Welfare, Reform and World War I," *American Quarterly*, XIX (Fall, 1967), 516–33, discusses the social workers' responses;
Forcey, *Crossroads of Liberalism*, pp. 273–91, analyzes the changing mood
of Croly and Lippmann; Frederick Howe's comment is in *The Confessions
of a Reformer* (New York, 1925; paperback ed., Chicago, 1967), p. 317.

central to any such program had to be at least some consensus on the desired role of the state.

The treacherous assignment of defining the powers of government became even more complicated, however, because of the progressive tendency to believe that the "general interest," rather than "special interests," formed the proper basis of politics. The rubric of the "public interest" had been instrumental during the prewar era in molding the coalitions of diverse groups. It had encouraged the view among varied factions that, together, they represented the "general welfare" against, for example, the arrogance of self-seeking corporate interests. This emphasis on the "public interest," by stressing common bonds over factional distinctions, had thereby allowed each group to associate its own cause with some larger public good.[12] But the concept of the "public interest" proved an early victim of the dissolution of the progressive ethos. Any efforts during the 1920's to advance progressive causes could no longer hope to succeed by relying upon the idea of the general good. That idea, and the moralistic rhetoric that had surrounded it, had struck common chords in the generally confident years of the early 1900's. But in the Twenties, deeply rooted cultural antagonisms had surfaced, dividing wets and drys, town and country, old-stock and new-stock Americans. Since the stakes in these conflicts seemed to involve the very future and quality of the nation itself, the political atmosphere became so emotionally charged that it proved exceedingly difficult to agree upon what comprised the general good. And few progressives seemed willing to accept the conclusions of Herbert Croly or, for a while, Frederick Howe, that only by working directly with special in-

[12] Richard M. Abrams and Lawrence W. Levine (eds.) write that opposition among progressives to "all measures that they could not fit within the 'general interest' rubric" is the characteristic that "above all distinguishes the progressive from the reformer of other eras and other causes." *The Shaping of Twentieth Century America* (Boston, 1965), p. 346. Thelen, "Social Tensions and the Origins of Progressivism," p. 341, and Michael Rogin, "Progressivism and the California Electorate," *Journal of American History*, LV (September, 1968), 311–14, point out the unifying aspects of the "general interest" appeal.

terest groups such as labor was there any chance of reinvigorating American liberalism.[13]

When leading progressive politicians continued to reject self-interest as an acceptable reason for political action and to support only those programs which were purely principled and which ostensibly benefited all groups, they placed impossible demands upon themselves. For one thing, the business of politics required choosing among competing claims; and all such choices invariably aided some groups more than others—indeed, often at the expense of others. Progressives who interpreted their reform efforts as battles for simple integrity, for unquestioned morality, and for good against evil ignored a fundamental fact: their own struggles, priorities, and values very much reflected the needs and desires of interest groups—sectional, political, economic, and cultural. Part of the early thrust of progressivism, for example, had been an expression of late-developing economic regions striving through tariff reform and other legislative acts to overcome the economic advantages which a state such as Massachusetts had long enjoyed. And, within Massachusetts, progressive spokesmen for good government hailed the "public interest" and attacked "fomenters of class hatred" while at the same time actually representing a particular class and generally neglecting the aspirations of labor or the new ethnic groups.[14]

Following World War I the main source of progressive

[13] Croly outlined this approach in several *New Republic* editorials; see for example, "The Progressive Direction," XLIII (July 15, 1925), 192–94, and Forcey, *Crossroads of Liberalism*, pp. 303–4. On Howe, *Confessions of a Reformer*, pp. 317–38. Lawrence W. Levine, *Defender of the Faith, William Jennings Bryan: The Last Decade 1915–1925* (New York, 1965), pp. 179–81, and Arthur Mann, *La Guardia: A Fighter Against His Times, 1882–1933* (New York, 1959), pp. 182–83, stress that the conflicts of the Twenties were cultural and involved ends, not just means.

[14] Abrams and Levine (eds.), *The Shaping of Twentieth Century America*, pp. 233–34, astutely dissect the problem of the "general interest"; Abrams brilliantly analyzes the geographical and class bases of progressivism in *Conservatism in a Progressive Era: Massachusetts Politics, 1900–1912* (Cambridge, Mass., 1964), esp. chap. 1, and pp. 132–33, 243–44, 160–68.

strength on Capitol Hill was the west. The concerns of progressive-minded Senators were not limited to their particular region, but their perspectives and interests were nonetheless much under the influence of parochial rather than national needs. This was not surprising, nor did it automatically render them failures as national reformers. The problem was that, insofar as they tended to place themselves in the camp of the "general interest" and against the narrow exponents of "special interests," they oversimplified politics and limited their abilities to come to grips with major, complex problems of social policy.[15]

Moreover, the attempt to reject self-interest as the proper basis of politics brought out even more the moralistic qualities of the Senate progressives. Almost desperately seeking to place themselves on the high ground of principle and in opposition to self-seekers, they constantly invested their causes with righteous attributes. Hiram Johnson, for instance, apparently took considerable pride in being among "the outlanders, pariahs and outcasts": such was the price of courage. The smugness and lack of self-criticism among progressives such as Borah, La Follette, and Burton K. Wheeler of Montana disturbed Fiorello La Guardia, himself a leading reformer of the Twenties who usually was much in sympathy with the westerners. Senator Peter Norbeck believed that George Norris also tended toward self-righteousness. Although Norbeck had much respect for Norris, he wrote that the Nebraskan was "just the material that martyrs are made of. He would dearly love to be a martyr, but he would want a very good stage setting, or it would not be worth while."[16]

[15] "In relying on 'the people' to promote national reform," asks Eric Goldman, "wasn't the progressive asking special interests not to act like special interests?" *Rendezvous with Destiny* (New York, 1952; paperback ed., 1956), p. 230. Robert K. Murray, *The Harding Era: Warren G. Harding and His Administration* (Minneapolis, Minn., 1969), pp. 204–6, 294–95, stresses the parochial views of the Senate blocs, including the progressives.

[16] Hiram Johnson to Harold Ickes, November 7, 1924, Harold Ickes Papers (Library of Congress), Box 2; Howard Zinn, *LaGuardia in Congress*

Borah similarly took much pride in his own rectitude. He sometimes revealed an overwhelming egoism about his own moral correctness. "I do claim," he wrote, "that I shall leave this post of service without ever having compromised upon a single fundamental political belief which I entertain"—a viewpoint that stirred Harold Ickes to refer to him as "Saint Borah." Seldom susceptible to doubts about his own position, Borah in the Senate resembled a person who a century earlier would have been a "circuit-riding minister of the gospel."[17] He talked in terms of "moral courage to do what the morals of the situation require," and of the need for "a tremendous moral movement." When a fight was for "the people's salvation," he was ready for it.[18]

But, although Borah mirrored many of the strains, problems, and weaknesses that plagued the progressive movement by the end of the war, he nonetheless stood in a pre-eminent position to influence reform achievements and aspirations in the Twenties. For one thing, he was superbly adept as a politician who could keep himself acceptable both to reformers and those suspicious of reform, to progressive insurgents and party regulars.

(Ithaca, N.Y., 1959), p. 83, for La Guardia's impressions of the western progressives; Norbeck to John H. Kelly, July 28, 1922, for Norbeck's respect for Norris, and L. E. Camfield April 18, 1928, for his comments on Norris's martyrlike qualities, Norbeck Papers (South Dakota). David Thelen, "La Follette and the Temperance Crusade," *Wisconsin Magazine of History,* XLVII (Summer, 1964), 299–301, notes La Follette's moralistic personality and self-righteousness.

[17] Borah to J. Ward Arney, February 15, 1922, William E. Borah Papers (Library of Congress), Box 212; Ickes to Hiram Johnson, September 21, 1929, Ickes Papers, Box 3. Gerald Johnson, reviewing Marian McKenna's *Borah,* believes Borah's major weakness was "a moral certainty so colossal as to touch, if not to cross the verge of psychopathology." "Gentleman from Idaho," *The New Republic,* CXLIV (June 12, 1961), 18. The comparison of Borah to a circuit rider is from John W. Owens, "Why They Love Borah," *The New Republic,* XXXIX (May 28, 1924), 13.

[18] See, for example, Borah to Byron F. Forbes, February 3, 1923, Borah Papers, Box 227; to Herbert Croly, March 31, 1923; press statement, November 15, 1923, Box 228; and to H. A. Lawson, November 15, 1922, Box 218.

He not only offered a much-needed bridge between various factions but, as many journalists observed, he could help make Senate progressivism respectable and free of taints of radicalism. He could, as Harold Ickes noted, bask under attention from the White House and, simultaneously, receive constant acclaim as "the outstanding progressive" from reform journals such as *The New Republic* and *The Nation.* Hiram Johnson was always amazed at the protean ability by which Borah could "scowl with Wheeler and La Follette" while pleasing other opposing groups. Indeed, Johnson believed that the Idahoan offered "a most remarkable spectacle. He is able to run with the hare and hunt with the hounds in a fashion that I believe no other man in politics has ever equaled. . . . He has been the constant adviser of Coolidge and the beautiful child of the New Republic and other parlor liberals." [19]

While Borah thus was an important key to progressive respectability in the 1920's, he also was able to gain headlines for liberalism when few others could. He had, according to Herbert Hoover, "a positive genius for newspaper publicity." Borah astutely cultivated a good press and worked carefully with reporters. Starting in 1919, he held regular press conferences—a tactic that inspired Coolidge's alleged comment that "Senator Borah is always in session." These meetings began during the debates over the League of Nations. Some reporters, finding Borah affable and informative, gathered outside his office each afternoon, catching him as he came from the Senate dining room. The meetings soon became customary. "Shortly after three o'clock each afternoon," the *Christian Science Monitor* said in the mid-1920's, "all press trails about the Capitol lead to the office of Senator Borah." The conferences were completely informal, without invitations and open to any reporter. On occasion more than twenty of the "merry villagers," as Borah's secretary sometimes greeted the newsmen, gathered around Borah's cluttered desk, some standing, others sitting on

[19] Ickes to Hiram Johnson, July 17, 1925; Johnson to Ickes, November 7, 1924, June 10, 1924, and July 2, 1925, Ickes Papers, Box 2.

the window sill, and some finding chairs. A relaxed and cordial
Borah, seated in his swivel chair, discussed topics with utmost
freedom, answering questions about subjects ranging from politics to the Hall-Mills murder case or the adventures of Aimee
Semple McPherson. No direct quotes came from these conferences without the Senator's permission, but reporters acquired
news leads and Borah, in turn, obtained information from
them. If he had anything for quotation, he rushed from the
room, dictated it, and had his secretary produce a minimum of
twenty copies. Never, unless Senate activity so demanded, would
he dismiss the newsmen. According to one participant, "Always,
when it becomes apparent that all leads have been exhausted,
it is a member of the press, and not the senator himself, who
rises and suggests to his fellows that they have taken enough of
his time." Usually the conferences lasted from thirty minutes
to an hour, during which time Borah's stenographers were
under orders not to disturb him.[20]

Such meetings, as columnist Raymond Clapper observed,
placed Borah's press relations "on a parity with the White
House" and provided him with more attention than any other

[20] Herbert Hoover's typed manuscript on Borah, June 4, 1933, Hoover
Papers (Hoover Presidential Library, West Branch, Iowa), Box 1-K/14;
Coolidge's quote in letter from Arthur Krock to author, April 6, 1965.
For descriptions and assessments of Borah's news conferences, see clippings
of Raymond Clapper's article in the *Washington News* in March, 1927;
Robert B. Smith in the Philadelphia *Public Ledger*, May 6, 1928; the
Christian Science Monitor, November 10, 1926; *Providence Journal*,
December 1, 1928, Borah Scrapbooks (Library of Congress), Reels, 2, 5,
6. See also "Back Stage in Washington: Butter, Eggs, and Borah," *The
Independent*, CXVII (December 25, 1926), 740; Claudius Johnson, *Borah
of Idaho*, pp. 325–28; Frederick William Wile Scrapbooks (Library of
Congress), December 3, 1926, and April 27, 1927, Scrapbook 25; and
article by Warren W. Wheaton, Philadelphia *Public Ledger*, July 31, 1929.
Herbert Hoover wrote that Borah's press conferences became "one of the
institutions of the city, for he was a fruitful source not only of dramatic
first page statements himself but as he gathered the gossip of the city he
gave many tips to newspaper men as to where they might find stories."
Hoover's typed manuscript on Borah, June 4, 1933, Hoover Presidential
Library, Box 1-K/14.

Senator or Congressman. Senator Norbeck found that Borah was "the center of attention here, for the newspaper fraternity," and Hiram Johnson commented enviously on "the ease with which he directs the moronic members of the press." [21]

Indeed, so newsworthy was the Idaho Senator that the unfriendly *Independent* magazine groaned in late 1927: "the diet of breakfast reading is Borah on page one, Borah in the editorials, and Borah with the bacon and eggs." Or, as a Massachusetts paper complained in 1930, "Borah this and Borah that, Borah here and there, Borah does and Borah doesn't—until you wish that Borah wasn't." [22]

Obviously Borah's careful efforts to establish good rapport with newsmen and his skillful use of the news media helped make him a well-known figure. One leading journalist concluded that the reputation of "the incurably dramatic Borah" rested largely on the fact that he was unquestionably "the ablest and most adroit manipulator of personal publicity" in public life.[23]

But, while a good press was important for Borah's own politi-

[21] Peter Norbeck to Guy F. Barnes, March 30, 1931, Norbeck Papers; Hiram Johnson to Sons, September 23, 1921, Hiram Johnson Papers (Bancroft Library, University of California), Part IV, Box 2; to Sons, December 11, 1926, Box 3; and to Hiram, Jr., December 27, 1935, Box 4. That Johnson resented his own lack of favorable publicity is clear. Writing his sons about his declining prestige on the national scene, he blamed in part the "constant newspaper abuse." Johnson to Sons, March 26, 1922, Part IV, Box 2.

[22] *The Independent*, CXIX (Nov. 26, 1927), 513; editorial from *Fitchburg Sentinel*, February 6, 1930, Borah Scrapbooks, Reel 6.

[23] Frank Kent, "The Reconstruction of Herbert Hoover," *Scribner's Magazine*, XCI (May, 1932), 258–59. For an example of Borah's cultivation of newspaper contacts, see Borah to James O'Donnell Bennett of the *Chicago Tribune*, March 20, 1925: "I must suppose this will be an admission of vanity. Nevertheless, I must take the chance to thank you for your very generous reference to me several times of late. . . . I appreciate it deeply. I should like some day when you are at leisure to have a visit with you." Borah Papers, Box 256. According to Hiram Johnson, Borah also had "the fixed purpose never to quarrel with a newspaper." See Johnson to Sons, September 23, 1921, Johnson Papers, Part IV, Box 2.

cal stature, it was no less valuable for progressivism. His talent
for publicity was a much-needed boon to reform in the 1920's.
Hiram Johnson had little use for what he felt was the Idahoan's
too obvious quest for headlines but, in the mid-Twenties, he
pointed out that Borah had "the greatest forum of any man in
Congress" and was "the only man in the Senate with any pretense to Progressivism who can get great publicity now." [24]

Borah, moreover, was openly committed to using this forum
in behalf of progressivism. He viewed himself as a spokesman
for reform and constantly asserted his intent to liberalize the
Republican party. He brought with him impressive credentials.
Wisconsin's Robert M. La Follette had no difficulty including
him among the small group of Republicans who had been progressive from the beginnings of their terms in office. During his
first years in the Senate, Borah had urged a vigorous antitrust
policy, sponsored a bill calling for an eight-hour working day
for government employees, played a significant role in the struggle for the constitutional amendments providing for a graduated income tax and the direct election of Senators, and campaigned actively for La Follette's re-election in 1910. Since he
did not bolt the Republicans in 1912—even though he had supported the candidacy of Theodore Roosevelt within the G.O.P.
—he was among those to whom former Progressives looked,
once they decided to abandon the third party and reshape the
Republican party in the progressive mold.[25] By the 1920's Borah

[24] Johnson to Sons, November 27, 1926, Johnson Papers, Part IV, Box
3; and to Ickes, July 20, 1925, Ickes Papers, Box 2.

[25] For Borah's record, see the summary of his activities sent by his
secretary, Cora Rubin, to Salmon O. Levinson, June 23, 1931, Borah
Papers, Box 324. Regarding the 1910 Wisconsin election, La Follette
wrote, "Had it not been for the good work of our friends—Senators Cum-
mins, Dolliver, Bristow, Clapp, and Borah . . . it would have been impossible to roll up the great popular majority." La Follette to Albert K.
Beveridge, September 22, 1910, Albert K. Beveridge Papers (Library of
Congress), Box 176. For mention of Borah in discussions about infusing
the Republican party with progressive principles, see for example, copy
of William Allen White to Harold Ickes, December 16, 1916, and Ickes

was unquestionably one of the best-known liberals on Capitol Hill and, partly because of his much-publicized opposition to the Versailles Treaty, had become a national figure.[26]

As America entered the postwar period, Borah expressed his desire to help move the nation in a progressive direction. "I am frank to say," he wrote, "I am utterly tired and disgusted with the reactionary trailing and loitering attitude of some of our party leaders. It is time to be up and doing, to put our face unflinchingly toward the dawn. . . ." Apparently ready for bold steps, he told one constituent that if he were writing the platform for the Idaho Republicans, he "would undertake to outline a real, constructive State program. . . . I would declare for the principle of public ownership of utilities. I would favor government and State or municipal ownership of such natural monopolies as power plants, etc. I would make a live, progressive, constructive platform." He stressed his intention "to build up the Republican party along broad, progressive lines," and gave assurance that he had "no other purpose than to work along these lines." [27]

Borah thus brought to postwar progressivism a reputation for and a commitment to reform. He was well established in national politics and indisputably linked to the progressive wing of the Republican party. His knack for publicity and his politi-

to James R. Garfield, December 1, 1916, James R. Garfield Papers (Library of Congress), Box 115; Ickes to Raymond Robins, May 29, 1919, Raymond Robins Papers (Wisconsin State Historical Society), Box 15; Frank Knox to Theodore Roosevelt, February 8, 1915, Frank Knox Papers (Library of Congress), Box 1. References to Progressives are specifically those who officially left the traditional parties in 1912 and in the 1920's, as distinct from progressives who worked within the two-party framework.

26 Charles W. Toth, "Isolationism and the Emergence of Borah: An Appeal to American Tradition," *The Western Political Science Quarterly,* XIV (June, 1961), 555, writes that the League fight placed Borah on the national political map. From 1919 through the adoption of the Kellogg-Briand Pact in 1929, he was at the peak of his influence.

27 Borah to M. J. Sweeley, June 12, 1918, Borah Papers, Box 192; and to D. W. Davis, May 22, 1918, Box 186. See also Borah to S. D. Taylor, June 17, 1918, Box 195.

cal capacity for making himself respectable to diverse groups seemed to provide key elements necessary to rebuild the liberal ethos of the prewar years.

Yet events would require almost superhuman effort from the Senator. For one thing, there was the overwhelming fact that reform enthusiasm had waned sharply. For another, American reform itself was undergoing a subtle but profound shift from the earlier evangelical progressivism—with its basically rural values and perspectives—to a new-style liberalism oriented more to the problems and views of the urban masses. This transition had started before the war. In California after 1914, for example, new urban voters of varying ethnic origins were dramatically transferring the social bases of progressivism from its original middle- and upper-class foundations toward a working-class, immigrant-based coalition foreshadowing that of the New Deal. Similarly, the impact of the city on manners and morals was imbuing the newly emerging liberalism with a greater permissiveness on questions of life style, while leaving older progressives such as Hiram Johnson sadly contrasting their "younger days, when no woman would have dared either drink or smoke, to this era, when there is scarcely a young girl who dare not both drink and smoke"; an "old fogey" he might be, but Johnson explicitly preferred "the womanhood of old to the non-childbearing, smoking, drinking, and neurotic creature" who symbolized one of the cracks in "the thin veneer of civilization." [28]

Hence, if Borah hoped to provide America with liberal leadership, he needed carefully and sensitively to adjust his prewar

[28] "The 1920's," writes William E. Leuchtenburg, "marked a time of transition within progressivism from the old-style evangelical reformism, under leaders like La Follette and Bryan, to a new style urban progressivism. . . ." *The Perils of Prosperity, 1914–1932* (Chicago, 1958), p. 137. Michael Rogin, "Progressivism and the California Electorate," pp. 297–314, and John Shover, "The Progressives and the Working-Class Vote in California," *Labor History*, 10 (Fall, 1969), 584–601, chart the shifting social base of California progressivism. Johnson's quote is in Johnson to Sons, July 2, 1921, Johnson Papers, Part IV, Box 2.

attitudes to new national exigencies and to the changing demands and nature of American reform. An important requirement for such a task was clearly flexibility and adaptability. It was also a matter of sustained effort, of how tenaciously, unflinchingly, and consistently he would put his own face "toward the dawn."

Political Guerrilla in the
Harding Administration

❦

"I DO believe the world is getting better," wrote Newton D. Baker in November, 1918, echoing the view of many progressives. Such excitement about the reform possibilities of the "new era" ahead was short-lived, however. The enthusiasm so pervasive in liberal discussions in the immediate postwar period received a terrible bludgeoning from the great strikes of 1919, the Wilson administration's growing reaction, the Red Scare, and Theodore Roosevelt's death. Former Bull-Mooser Amos Pinchot—expressing the same discouragement that marked the pages of the leading liberal journals—sadly welcomed the Twenties by noting that "The Old Order Changeth Not"; although the world had changed, the politicians remained "unshaken, though shrunk," and in the control of "the money and brains of our privileged governing class." During the early months of the new decade, the progressive cause reached a nadir.[1]

During these bleak days when progressives were searching for leadership and unity, Senator Borah was one of the few bright lights on the reform horizon. He was, moreover, undoubtedly a key source of the new vitality that began to infuse progressivism by late 1922. Never before had his progressive sympathies, his willingness to battle courageously for reform principles, and his ability to capture national attention been more clear. Through

[1] Baker quoted in Daniel R. Beaver, *Newton D. Baker and the American War Effort, 1917–1919* (Lincoln, Neb., 1966), p. 212; Amos Pinchot, "The Old Order Changeth Not," *Facts* (January, 1920), p. 1. A progressive group, the Committee of 48, issued this monthly. Copy in Amos Pinchot Papers (Library of Congress), Box 40.

24

a series of scattered forays—all evincing the independence and righteous indignation that characterized his political life—the Senator demonstrated his readiness to take a "firm stand" for liberalism. As the country emerged from the suffocating atmosphere of the Red Scare, he spoke forthrightly in behalf of civil liberties. He tried to modify the Supreme Court's power to declare laws unconstitutional at a time when the judiciary was rigidly conservative on economic issues. He joined "the roll of honor" in his fight against the seating in the Senate of Truman H. Newberry, whose campaign expenditures created a national scandal. During the 1922 coal crisis Borah demonstrated sympathy for labor and advocated the formation of a coal commission to investigate the problems of that industry. By the end of 1922 he was vigorously challenging Old Guard Republicans in Idaho and calling for the reinstatement of the direct primary. In December when progressives from across the country gathered in Washington to discuss future strategy, he was a leading participant. Although caution blunted some of his efforts, and although his progressivism was not as effective as some thought it would be, his conduct clearly attracted much praise and respect from liberals.

The Harding administration, which always had to reckon with the Senator, was steadily less enthusiastic about him. Initially Harding, in the name of party unity, had tried to secure Borah's support and actively courted the progressive-isolationist wing of the G.O.P. He confided to Hiram Johnson, for example, that he would be in close consultation with both Johnson and Borah. At one point, after summoning Borah to the White House, he reportedly suggested that the Idahoan handle administrative matters in the Senate.[2] Such efforts to placate the

[2] For Harding's emphasis on party unity see Harding to Raymond Robins, July 26, 1920; to Gus J. Karger, July 26, 1920; and to Henry Cabot Lodge, September 6, 1920, Warren G. Harding Papers (Ohio State Historical Society). For Harding's efforts to demonstrate his sympathy for progressivism, see Oscar Straus's diary description of a June 22, 1920, conference with him, Oscar Straus Papers (Library of Congress), Box 24, and revealing letters from Hiram Johnson to his Sons, December 7, 1920, and

Borah-Johnson faction of the party at first made some of the more regular Republicans apprehensive that the President would not accord the Republican majority sufficient consideration. Ultimately, however, Harding privately conceded that he was giving up on the "Johnson-Borah group" because of the pressure it had been placing upon him, especially in matters relating to foreign policy. By mid-1923, he was convinced that Borah, although talented and brilliant, was "utterly lacking in practicality, stability and fidelity." A cartoonist aptly captured the strained relations between the President and the Senator by portraying Harding and several other administration leaders glumly singing, "Day by Day, in Every Way We Are Getting Borah, and Borah." [3]

To a progressive such as Oswald Garrison Villard, on the other hand, Borah was "the only man who continues to give me much hope." Indeed, in mid-1921 when progressive spirits were touching bottom, *The Nation* described him as "the most effective and virile leader in the Senate" and a man who was "steadily winning the support of liberal groups." The muckrak-

---

August 13, 1921, Johnson Papers, Part IV, Box 2. Harding, according to Johnson on August 13, 1921, "made a very interesting statement to Borah. He said there was no real leadership in the Senate now, that what leadership there was . . . was afraid of Johnson and Borah, and because of this fact, he was most anxious to have us come along with the administration." On Harding's alleged offer of legislative leadership to Borah, see Harry Hunt, "Borah—A Pen Picture," *La Follette's Magazine*, XIV (February, 1922), 23, copy in La Follette Family Papers (Library of Congress), Series B, Box 274. Murray, *The Harding Era*, pp. 49, 59, 125, describes Harding's campaign and postelection efforts to conciliate the various Republican factions.

[3] Clarence B. Miller, Secretary of the Republican National Committee, pointed out the Old Guard's apprehensions to Harding, December 13, 1920, Harding Papers. Newsman Gus Karger, Washington correspondent for the Cincinnati *Times-Star*, talked with Harding and then described the President's dissatisfaction with the progressive-isolationists to William Howard Taft. Karger to Taft, May 14, 1921, William Howard Taft Papers (Library of Congress), Box 487. Harding's quote is in Andrew Sinclair, *The Available Man, The Life Behind the Masks of Warren Gamaliel Harding* (New York, 1965), p. 275, and the unidentified cartoon clipping is in the Borah Scrapbooks, Reel 4.

ing *Searchlight on Congress* believed that he had recently come "to occupy a position and possess a power, at least over public opinion, which has no parallel in recent times." "Borah, today," wrote Hiram Johnson, "is the biggest figure in the Senate, by far, and I believe his words carry to a much greater extent than those of any other man in Washington, save the President." [4]

On December 15, 1919, Lincoln Colcord of *The Nation* had talked with Borah about the awesome challenges which progressives faced. The journalist had found him "more frank and friendly than ever," speaking "as if he felt himself to be one of the Nation crowd." According to Borah, the Senate insurgents had lately ignored important domestic matters because "we were caught in the toils of this [Versailles] treaty fight. But with the beginning of the year, we must take a firm stand." One such "firm stand" concerned civil liberties. Borah was convinced that a prerequisite for reform was free discussion and, to that end, progressives must "fight for the right to say anything at all." [5]

It was thus at a time when public opinion was still hypersensitive about radicalism in America that Borah emerged as a leading spokesman for civil liberties. The hysteria that had swept the Red Scare to its peak in 1919 and early 1920 had subsided but, as *The New Republic* angrily observed, a "phantom army of shibboleths" continued to rush forward "to attack any and every program, squeaking and parroting sounds about 'socialism' and 'bolshevism' and 'business enterprise.'" Moreover, some individuals were still suffering from the denials of liberties which they had experienced during the war. Borah was certain that the situation required immediate federal attention. He wondered if Villard and *The Nation* might help by starting "something in the nature of a real organization dedi-

4 Villard to Borah, May 21, 1922, Borah Papers, Box 218; "Senator Borah at the Front," *The Nation*, CXIII (July 20, 1921), 61; "Borah," *Searchlight on Congress*, VI (July, 1921), 11; Johnson to Sons, September 23, 1921, Johnson Papers, Part IV, Box 2.

5 Lincoln Colcord to Oswald Garrison Villard, December 16, 1919, Villard Papers, Folder 655.

cated to the protection of our civil liberties." Although the Civil Liberties Bureau had accomplished "magnificent work," the Senator believed that too many people viewed it as the agency of conscientious objectors. "We need," he said, "an organization of old-fashioned respectable Americans to bring a heavy pressure to bear on Congress at once." [6]

In early 1921 Borah worked closely with The National Popular Government League for "A Bill to End 'Palmerism.'" At his behest the league prepared legislation to stop lawless government officials from invading civil liberties. The organization reported that "Senator Borah is anxious that we should put the conservatives on the defensive at once, and we all agree that he is right." On February 24, 1921, he introduced a bill calling for a five-year imprisonment, a $10,000 fine, or both, for any federal employee "who injures, threatens, or intimidates any person" exercising his constitutional freedoms. Although Borah's proposal did not become law, it helped to block Senator Thomas Sterling's attempt to secure the passage of a peacetime sedition law.[7]

The Idaho Senator also allied with the American Civil Liberties Union in the struggle to pardon political prisoners from World War I. Despite the government's release of most of the conscientious objectors, thousands of military offenders, and about 235 persons accused of "political" crimes, there were still several hundred prisoners. These included Socialist Eugene Debs, who had received almost a million votes for the Presidency in 1920 while he was in jail. Attorney General

[6] "Into the Doldrums and Out," *The New Republic*, XXV (January 12, 1921), 181–82. Borah expressed his views on the need for more civil liberties groups to Lincoln Colcord. Colcord to Villard, December 16, 1919, Villard Papers, Folder 655.

[7] "Palmerism" was synonymous with the infringements of civil liberties which occurred during the Red Scare under the direction of Attorney General A. Mitchell Palmer. For Borah's work with the National Popular Government League, see the league's bulletin, January 22 and February 12, 1921, and the confidential release from the league to weekly newspapers for use after February 26, 1921, in Judson King Papers (Library of Congress), Article and Book File 70.

Harry Daugherty was adamantly against clemency; to him the prisoners were worse than murderers. Harding refused to grant total amnesty but finally, on December 25, 1921, he pardoned Debs and some of the other prisoners. For Borah, as for many liberals, the President's action was inadequate. The Senator had urged amnesty for all, rather than singling out individual cases such as Debs. The issue, as Borah defined it, was whether men should at any time suffer punishment for their opinions. The answer seemed clear: "I believe at all times in freedom of speech, in a free press, in the right for peaceful assemblage. . . . no government, no class of men, and no views are so sacred that they ought not to be subject to criticism." Until an individual urged immediate violation of the law, Borah believed that he should have the right to express his views, despite their unpopularity.[8]

At a massive Chicago rally in 1922, Borah suggested that "instead of persecuting men with ideas to express we should hire halls for them," and that "the real master under the United States flag is public opinion, and when we try to curb that we try to destroy our government." He inveighed against the "vicious doctrine that when war comes Congress can violate the Constitution in the heat of passion and deny Americans their rights"; such foolishness was "treasonable and diabolical and leads to anarchy and despotism." After listening to him, *The Nation* could but wonder at those who doubted "that Senator Borah has never been so powerful as today." Following Harding's death in August, 1923, Borah continued to aid the American Civil Liberties Union in the successful effort to effect the pardon of the approximately thirty-five remaining prisoners.[9]

[8] See Donald Johnson, *The Challenge to American Freedoms* (Lexington, Ky., 1963), pp. 192–93; Sinclair, *The Available Man*, pp. 225–28; Borah to Harding, June 6, 1922, and to Dan L. Lindsley, January 17, 1922, Borah Papers, Box 212.
[9] Borah to the President, September 29, 1923, Borah Papers, Box 212. On December 15, 1923, Coolidge commuted the sentences of all the remaining prisoners except one insane fanatic.

Throughout the New Era, Borah spoke as a devoted civil libertarian. In one ringing appeal for free speech, he observed that "everybody believes in the right of peaceful assemblage— but the test comes when you are looking upon the gathering of those who hold a different point of view." On another occasion he noted that "when you drive men from the public arena where debate is free, you send them to the cellar where revolutions are born." He also congratulated Justice Louis D. Brandeis for his concurrent opinion in the Supreme Court's decision in *Whitney* v. *California.* To Borah, Brandeis's argument that the Fourteenth Amendment protected a political party which desired a far-distant proletarian revolution was "a classic—in style, in substance, in the unanswerable presentation of free government." [10]

Despite the Senator's praise for Brandeis's opinion, the general posture of the judiciary as a spokesman for special economic interests and as an obstacle to social legislation had long troubled Borah and other progressives. In 1921, he strenuously objected to the appointment of William Howard Taft as Chief Justice. Charging that Taft was not equipped for the Supreme Court, he joined La Follette, Hiram Johnson, and Georgia Democrat Tom Watson in registering the four votes against confirmation. *The New Republic,* sadly interpreting Taft's move to the Court as an indication of "the present temporary triumph of reaction," saw the small number of negative votes as a woeful sign of the status of progressivism. Reformers a decade earlier would have furiously contended the Taft appointment but, in 1921, "of the Progressive group only Borah, Johnson and La Follette recall the ancient days. . . . " Certainly, for Borah and the other opponents of Taft who remembered those "ancient days," the confirmation of the new Chief Justice seemed to bear solemn tidings for the

[10] Borah, "Free Speech: The Vital Issue," *The Nation,* CXV (June 4, 1923), 8; Borah statement, October 14, 1925, sent to *Liberty* magazine, Borah Papers, Box 259; Borah to Louis D. Brandeis, May 20, 1927, Box 281.

future. Hiram Johnson, viewing the appointment as "the most sinister thing that has come to us thus far in the administration," walked home the evening of Taft's confirmation "as low in spirits as I have ever been before. . . ." [11]

There was good reason for progressive concern about the Court and Taft's place on it. The new Chief Justice looked upon the bench as the last bulwark against progressivism, as the defender of private property from the incursions of legislative "experimentation," and as the crucial check on popular action. Hence he opposed possible Court appointees such as Learned Hand, "a wild Roosevelt man and a Progressive" who "would almost certainly herd with Brandeis and be a dissenter." [12] He disregarded the votes against his confirmation, noting that "if one had to be opposed, one could not select more happily the opponents." Observing the Taft court in late 1923, H. L. Mencken wrote sardonically that "the general tendency of all the recent decisions of the sapient and puissant Nine is toward shoving the man down and lifting the dollar up." And, by the end of the decade, Harvard law professor Felix Frankfurter declared that "since 1920, the Court had invalidated more legislation than in fifty years preceding," and had done so by resurrecting "views that were antiquated twenty-five years ago." [13]

The Court's obstruction of reform renewed the old progressive ire against the judiciary. In December, 1922, the second

[11] George F. Sparks (ed.), *A Many-Colored Toga, The Diary of Henry Fountain Ashurst* (Tucson, Ariz., 1962), pp. 141–42; "Mr. Chief Justice Taft," *The New Republic*, XXVII (July 27, 1921), 230–31; Johnson to Sons, July 2, 1921, Johnson Papers, Part IV, Box 2.

[12] Alpheus T. Mason, *William Howard Taft: Chief Justice* (New York, 1964), pp. 15–16, 163–64, 170, 170–75, 236–66, 289–93.

[13] Taft to Otto T. Bannard, July 21, 1921, Taft Papers, Box 495. Taft's brother Horace believed the opposition of Borah, Johnson, and La Follette "seems to make the thing more unanimous, so to speak." Charles Dewey Hilles of the G.O.P. National Committee told the Chief Justice that people "love you for the enemies you have made." Horace to William Taft, July 6, 1921, Taft Papers, Box 495; and Hilles to Taft, July 5, 1921, Box 493. H. L. Mencken in Baltimore *Sun*, November 19, 1923; Frankfurter quoted in Mason, *William Howard Taft*, pp. 292–93.

Conference for Progressive Political Action (CPPA) berated it and, the following month, Congressman James Frear of Wisconsin denounced the concept of judicial review.[14] La Follette, the most vociferous critic, advocated that Congress should be able to nullify the Court's action by re-enacting laws which the judiciary had invalidated.

Although Borah disliked the Court's position, he adamantly rejected La Follette's proposal and sought a more moderate remedy. He had always opposed suggestions that threatened the concept of a government based on separation of powers. Since he objected to legislative or executive invasions of the judicial power of review, he launched a flank attack on the Court. He would not, as La Follette advised, undermine the Court's power to declare laws unconstitutional; instead, he would simply modify this power and require seven of nine justices to concur in such rulings. "It is not clear to me," he explained, "that the majority rule in the rendition of an opinion is a 'Judicial power'." He could not understand why five judges should be able to overrule the action of Congress, the President, and four other justices. A two-thirds vote was necessary to impeach a member of the Court and to override a presidential veto. Only a unanimous vote of a jury could convict a man. Hence Borah found "nothing dangerous or unprecedented in requiring something more than a majority vote of a Court composed of only nine men in overriding a law solemnly passed and approved by the other departments of the government." Thus, on February 5, 1923, he introduced a bill requiring seven of nine votes in the Supreme Court to invalidate an act of Congress.[15]

14 Zinn, *LaGuardia in Congress,* p. 71.

15 Borah to C. C. Moore, November 12, 1923, and to the editor of the Spokane, Washington, *Spokesman Review,* October 29, 1923; to Ira J. Williams, September 24, 1923; and to Hazel Johnson, February 26, 1925, Borah Papers, Box 235. Copy of bill S. 4483, *ibid.* For a critical analysis of Borah's proposal, see the pamphlet *Borah and La Follette and the Supreme Court of the U.S.,* by Charles Warren, former assistant attorney-general, published by the National Security League in 1923. Copy in

Borah was obviously aware of the current division on the Bench. As Taft himself wrote, "There is a great deal of dissent in the Court, which I deprecate. Three of the nine are pretty radical, and occasionally they get some of the other brethren, which is disquieting." [16] With such a situation existing in the Court, the Senator's bill would reduce the judiciary's role as an opponent of social legislation without damaging the principles of judicial review and separation of powers.

"Powerful propaganda," according to Borah, provided "hard sledding" for his proposal. "Practically all the conservative papers have felt the necessity of attacking it. This leads me to believe that I am correct." Although his suggestion did not receive Senate approval it held a prominent place in the opposition to the judiciary that marked the resurgent progressivism of the early 1920's. Liberal Congressmen such as New York's Fiorello La Guardia and Michigan's Roy Woodruff offered to introduce the measure in the House. And ultimately, when La Guardia presented Borah's bill, he described it as "one of the first steps the progressive group in Congress intend[s] to make." [17]

Borah failed to modify the power of the Taft Court as an obstacle to reform but, as a member of the Senate Judiciary Committee, he continued to irritate the Chief Justice. This committee distressed Taft, who viewed its "wretched personnel" as "mainly . . . radicals and progressives," most prominent of whom were "Borah and Norris, both of them enemies of the Federal Judiciary, willing in every way to obstruct its usefulness." Norris was among those "gentlemen of communistic and socialist tendencies who are opposed to any en-

---

George Wharton Pepper Papers (The Charles Patterson Van Pelt Library, University of Pennsylvania), Box 48.

[16] Taft to Sir Thomas White, January 8, 1922, Taft Papers, Box 507.

[17] Borah to Arthur E. Anderson, November 16, 1923; La Guardia to Borah, October 31 and November 9, 1923; Borah to La Guardia, November 1, 1923, Borah Papers, Box 235. Copy of La Guardia statement for newspaper release, November 12, 1923, in La Guardia Papers (Municipal Archives, New York City), Box 2521.

forcement of the law at all." And Borah, whose judgment Taft described as worth less than "two cents on any subject," had great ability but was "the most unstable man" the Chief Justice had met. In early 1922 when Taft supported a bill to enlarge the district courts, he predicted much opposition from the progressives; resignedly, he said, "I always have Borah, Norris, La Follette and Johnson against anything I wish—for my sins I suppose." Several years later Taft was still bemoaning "those yahoos of the West" on the Judiciary Committee.[18]

While Taft grumbled about progressive opposition to the Bench, Columbia University President Nicholas Murray Butler was aghast at the failure of Senate leadership which "practically invited political guerrillas like La Follette and Borah to take the leadership out of Lodge's hands and they do so at intervals in ways that are most distressing." It seemed to Butler, who associated with many Republican leaders, that "within twelve months after the greatest electoral victory in history, we see the Republican Party disintegrating before our eyes." National Committeeman Charles Dewey Hilles agreed that congressional leadership was "appallingly and indescribably bad; the tide is already running against us, and deservedly so. . . ."[19] G.O.P. weakness of command was particularly apparent in late 1921 when Borah and other "Republican Progressives—Who Fought Their Reactionary Colleagues on Everything"—harassed the Old Guard repeatedly. According to one

[18] Taft to Henry W. Taft, May 18, 1926, Taft Papers, Box 600; to Harlan Fiske Stone, January 27, 1925, Box 573; to Thomas W. Shelton, January 8, 1925, Box 572; to Judge Frank H. Hiscock, April 12, 1922, Box 513; to Calvin Cobb, February 12, 1923, Box 533; to Horace Taft, March 30 and April 3, 1922, Boxes 512–13; to Robert Taft, April 5, 1924, Box 556.

[19] Copy of letter from Nicholas Murray Butler to James R. Sheffield, December 15, 1921, in James W. Wadsworth Papers (Library of Congress), Box 19; Charles D. Hilles to Nicholas Murray Butler, April 13, 1922, Charles D. Hilles Papers (Yale University Library), Box 203. According to Hiram Johnson, Harding personally told Borah that the Senate had no leadership and that the supposed leaders were fearful of both Borah and Johnson. Johnson to Sons, August 13, 1921, Johnson Papers, Part IV, Box 2.

observer, in 1921 "an Aldrich, or a Penrose in his prime, could have made a very different story of the special session." But Penrose was enfeebled and dying, and "the new leaders haven't any brains." [20]

The Senate insurgents were not in control, but the absence of strong Republican leadership unquestionably provided them with unexpected leverage. Peter Norbeck, after a few months in his new Senate seat, happily reported back to South Dakota that the "old Eastern leaders . . . don't know where they are. . . . some of the fellows who have been in the saddle during this Republican administration don't know now whether they are afoot or on horseback." The result was that "for the first time in my memory a few of the Northwestern Republican Senators find it easy to get together, agree on a program and have much of it accepted very readily although under protest." Part of the Old Guard's problem rested with the White House, where Harding's achievements as the head of his party had been, in the words of journalist Mark Sullivan, "practically zero." Even Vice-President Coolidge, hardly a man of fast pace himself, asserted that Harding's tardiness in reaching decisions was damaging White House prestige and urged Senator Frank Brandegee of Connecticut to speak to the President about the need for prompt action. Certainly it was in part the frailty of G.O.P. leadership which provided the newly formed farm bloc, seeking to win a more proportionate share of national prosperity for agriculture, with the opportunity to "terrorize" Congress.[21]

[20] *Searchlight on Congress,* VI (November 30, 1921), 3, 19. Nelson W. Aldrich of Rhode Island had been one of the strong men in the Senate in the late 1800's and early 1900's. Pennsylvania's Boies Penrose was a well-known political boss who served in the Senate from 1897 until his death in late 1921.

[21] Norbeck to M. P. Beebe, November 23, 1921, Norbeck Papers (University of Missouri), Folder 1; Mark Sullivan, "One Year of President Harding," *World's Work,* XLIII (November, 1921), 32. Frank Brandegee to Taft, June 14, 1921, Taft Papers, Box 489. Gus Karger to Taft, July 21, 1921, Box 495. See, also, Murray, *The Harding Era,* pp. 125, 127–28, 314, on Harding's lack of decisive leadership.

Borah never openly joined the agrarian bloc, but he usually voted with it and supported it when, for example, it sent Harding a letter endorsing William S. Culbertson of Kansas as chairman of the Tariff Commission. He also defended the group by noting that a manufacturing bloc had long sought to extract favors from Congress. Since farmers simply wanted "equal treatment in the matter of legislation and governmental favors," the stories about the "menacing aspect" of the farm bloc were "the sheerest kind of rot." Borah allied with the agrarians in support of the 1921 emergency tariff bill for western agricultural interests. To the Senator, since tariff schedules for years had benefited only business, higher duties for farm products were only fair. Borah not only backed the emergency measure but also claimed that his role in its passage was significant. Democratic Senators Oscar W. Underwood of Alabama and Furnifold M. Simmons of North Carolina would confirm, he wrote, that "it was through my initiative that an agreement was finally reached for the vote upon the bill at a time when it looked like there might be an indefinite delay." [22]

Unlike most members of the farm bloc, however, he refused to let his support for the emergency scheme commit him to a general high-tariff program. In 1922, he objected to the Fordney-McCumber measure, which contained the highest tariff schedules to that date. He seriously doubted that the need for increased agricultural protection was such as to justify endorsing the 1922 proposal. In his estimation, the only way to obtain genuine agrarian relief was by restoring trade relations

[22] Borah to William Lambie, May 7, 1924, Borah Papers, Box 241, regarding his connection with the bloc, and to E. H. Dewey, March 25, 1921, Box 209, and S. W. McClure, February 5, 1921, Box 210, on the tariff. Technically the 1921 emergency tariff bill was not a farm bloc measure, but most of the agrarian Senators supported it. See Arthur Capper, *The Agricultural Bloc* (New York, 1922), p. 153. On the series of votes, June 16–17, 1921, regarding the Stockyards and Packers Act, when Borah consistently joined the agrarians, see *Congressional Record,* 67th Cong., 1st Sess., 1921, LXI, 2662, 2673, 2675–76, 2680, 2712–13. For the endorsement of Culbertson, see William S. Culbertson Diaries, August 25, 1921, Culbertson Papers (Library of Congress), Box 4.

with the world, not by boosting tariff rates. Moreover, he opposed a high tariff policy in principle because of the resulting unfairness to the American consumer. "The protection system . . . as announced by Hamilton and magnificently expounded by Clay is sound," he reasoned, because it stimulated and diversified "the genius of a whole people." But when protection became a special privilege it was "intolerable and indefensible." Borah thus opposed the Republican majority "on at least 95 per cent of the amendments and provisions presented" during the tariff debates. On August 19, 1922, when the Senate adopted the Fordney-McCumber bill, 48 to 25, he was the only Republican to vote nay, although La Follette and Norris said that they too would have been in opposition if they had been present.[23]

While Borah was splitting from his party during the tariff debates, he likewise flaunted Republican leadership during the fight over the seating of Michigan's Truman Newberry in the Senate. In January, 1922, in what was otherwise a straight party vote, Borah and eight other insurgents broke from the G.O.P. to join the Democrats in opposition to seating Newberry—a growing "symbol of money in politics." Four years earlier, Newberry's excessive campaign expenditures had produced charges that he had violated the federal corrupt practices act. Although the Supreme Court had overruled a lower court's decision against him, suspicions remained that he had in effect bought his way into political office. In early 1922, when the move to bar Newberry from his seat shook the upper house, Harding threw the prestige of the Presidency

[23] Borah statement to the press in June, 1929, Borah Papers, Box 308; Borah to E. H. Dewey, March 25, 1921, Box 209; to F. G. Swanson, August 12, 1921, Box 206. Unlike Borah, the other agrarians, by "accepting the principle of protection in the emergency tariff . . . became enmeshed in a policy of economic nationalism to which they drew closer with further insistence upon protection in the new permanent tariff." James Shideler, *Farm Crisis, 1919–1923* (Berkeley, Calif., 1957), p. 183. For analysis of the votes, see the *Searchlight on Congress*, VII (August 31, 1922), 6. See also, "A Profiteer Tariff," *World's Work*, XLIV (October, 1922), 574–75.

behind him. He expressed his high regard for the Michigan Senator, welcomed him as a guest in the White House box at a Washington theater, invited him to a private White House dinner, and played golf with him.[24] A vote against Newberry would thus be, in effect, a blow at Harding.

During the Senate clash, which the Baltimore *Sun* described as "possibly the bitterest fight waged in a generation over the title of a seat to that body," Borah emerged as "a mountain of strength against Newberryism." He joined La Follette, Norris, and Iowa's William S. Kenyon to lead the insurgent attack. On January 10, before packed galleries and approximately half of his colleagues, he delivered a speech that one journal hailed as "perhaps the best ever heard in the Senate." Using no manuscript, he spoke for an hour, contending that Newberry's participation in "this shameless [1918 election] debauch" was certainly reason enough to deny him his seat. Indeed, the discouraging prospects of allowing Newberry to sit in the Senate moved Borah to comment that "we have travelled further over the road of money in politics in 100 years than Rome travelled in 500 years." For a few minutes after he sat down, the Senate was conspicuously silent. No one rose to rebut him.[25]

G.O.P. regulars, who earlier had predicted a victory margin of five to ten votes in favor of Newberry, became more cautious after Borah's speech and admitted that the majority might now be as small as three. The reason for the reduced optimism was a fear that the Idahoan's performance had influenced the doubtful voters. Certainly the Newberry supporters took no chances. They actively courted the favor of Pennsylvania's George Wharton Pepper, the recipient of the chair left vacant by Boies Penrose's death. Harding entertained Pepper as a guest at the White House and flattered him with the

[24] John D. Hicks, *Republican Ascendancy, 1921–1933* (New York, 1960), p. 88; Frederick L. Paxson, *Postwar Years: Normalcy, 1918–1923* (Berkeley, Calif., 1948), pp. 199, 271; Baltimore *Sun*, January 7, 1922.

[25] Baltimore *Sun*, January 7, 1922; *Searchlight on Congress*, VI (January 31, 1922), 4–5, 16–18; *The New York Times*, January 11, 1922; *Congressional Record*, 67th Cong., 2nd Sess., 1922, LXII, 989–93.

unusual honor of a personal introduction to the Cabinet. On January 10, just prior to Borah's speech, the Pennsylvania Senator took his oath of office. When Borah rose to speak, several G.O.P. standpatters—James E. Watson of Indiana, Selden P. Spencer of Missouri, and Charles Curtis of Kansas—rushed Pepper out to a lunch party. On his second day in office, Pepper presided briefly over the Senate, and he was also the only outsider present at a dinner meeting of the Republican Steering Committee at Illinois Senator Medill McCormick's home. "Whether in response to or in spite of this surplus of food and flattery," the new Senator voted for Newberry, who retained his seat, 46 votes to 41.[26]

The crusading *Searchlight on Congress* grouped names according to "The Newberry Senators" and the "Roll of Honor"—those who opposed him. According to *The New Republic*, the Senate had established a "Pay as You Enter" clause, and those who had supported Newberry reflected greater fear of party retaliation than of the public's anger. There was no doubt that the issue had become a test of progressive principles —a fact that Hiram Johnson made clear when, after missing the vote and opening himself to charges of "trimming," he felt compelled to request the Pennsylvania Railroad to verify his explanation that his train had been caught in a blizzard, causing him to arrive more than an hour after the roll call.[27]

While the Newberry and tariff controversies were in process,

[26] *The New York Times*, January 11, 1922; *Searchlight on Congress*, VI (February 28, 1922), 8. One Senator commented sadly afterwards that Pepper could have made his mark after only two days in the Senate; he failed the test on the Newberry vote, however, and merited nothing more than recognition as "Penrose's successor."

[27] *Ibid.*; "The Senate: Pay as You Enter," *The New Republic*, XXIX (January 25, 1922), 239. In the few days after the vote, a much-embarrassed Johnson cranked out letters on his new Corona, explaining that he had not realized "the bitterness or even the importance of the Newberry contest," had dallied in California assuming there was plenty of time to reach Washington for the showdown, and had been caught in a blizzard. "I have but myself to blame. I'll take my medicine as best I can." See, for example, Johnson to Alexander McCabe, January 14 and 20, 1922; and to Charles K. McClatchey, January 15, 1922, Johnson Papers, Part III, Box 4.

events occurred in the nation's coal fields that were soon to engage the Senate's attention, casting Borah into a central role. For years the overdeveloped coal industry had suffered from labor unrest. The industry's fundamental problems were painfully evident in the 1920's when wartime demands for coal had ended. Throughout the winter of 1921–22, the Harding administration attempted to avert an impending strike in the coal fields; but, on April 1, when bituminous operators slashed wages, 400,000 soft-coal miners left their jobs and hard-coal miners soon joined them. The administration adopted a policy of inaction, except for maintaining order and urging conciliation. Secretary of Labor James J. Davis explained that "the President and myself have had neither legal right nor personal desire to dictate any program" regarding a coal settlement. The Secretary of Commerce, Herbert Hoover, was more concerned with possible coal shortages for consumers than he was with effecting a strike settlement. He urged production in non-union fields and awarded government coal contracts to producers who would cooperate in keeping prices down. In effect the administration concerned itself only with keeping order and encouraging production; it apparently gave little consideration to the impact of its policy on labor organization in an industrial society.[28]

A few days prior to the miners' walkout, Borah assumed chairmanship of the Senate Committee on Education and Labor, a position that Iowa's William S. Kenyon had vacated to become a federal circuit judge. The Baltimore *Sun* believed that the Senator thus had a significant opportunity to turn his chairmanship into "a power that may profoundly affect labor and industrial policies and interests not only in the sphere of coal mining but indirectly in many others." Apparently Borah was prepared to follow a positive program. His initial response

[28] Robert H. Zieger, *The Republicans and Labor, 1919–1929* (Lexington, Ky., 1969), pp. 109–29, 142–43, discusses the economic background of the coal problem and the confused efforts of the Harding administration to cope with the 1922 bituminous and anthracite strikes.

to the coal crisis was an unequivocal call for the reorganization of the industry in the public interest. He believed that "one thing is very clear and that is that the government must take over in some way the management and control of the coal fields of the United States. Under present conditions, the public is at the mercy of the coal operators and employees." On June 7, the Senator challenged Hoover's reliance on voluntary price agreements among coal operators and invited him to propose legislation to restrain rises in the cost of coal. The Secretary answered that prices had retreated since the beginning of his efforts to obtain cooperation among responsible coal operators against profiteering. He warned Borah that the threat of congressional action might undermine the present program and replace it with legislative delays, extended court fights, and an increase in federal bureaucratic control. Hoover saw no "more effective or practical manner of controlling the price" than that which he was following.[29]

On the evening of June 9, Hoover stopped at Borah's apartment for an hour to discuss the question of coal prices. Borah warned him that a congressional investigation would begin if the price scale on which Hoover and the operators were working encouraged profiteering. Hoover reportedly gave assurances that he would strive to obtain price adjustments that were in the public interest. Senator David I. Walsh of Massachusetts, who had joined Borah in questioning the Secretary's policies and in threatening a congressional investigation of the coal operators' prices, learned that Borah had found a basic difference between himself and Hoover during the interview. As

[29] Baltimore *Sun*, April 3, 1922; Borah to Miss Merriam Oliver, April 7, 1922. In mid-February, six weeks before the strike began, he had indicated his sympathy toward government ownership of the mines. Borah to Heber Blankenhorn, February 18, 1922, Borah Papers, Box 213. Borah telegram to Hoover, June 7, 1922, and Hoover reply, June 9, 1922. While Hoover was discouraging Borah from advocating congressional action, he was at the same time using the excuse of legislative inaction to justify his own approach to the problem. See Hoover to David I. Walsh, June 13, 1922, for a justification of the Secretary's position. Hoover Papers, Commerce Files, Box 1-I/277.

long as Hoover would not admit that soft-coal prices had risen, Borah believed that it was impossible to agree upon a program in the interest of the consumers. Nevertheless, on the basis of the Secretary's promises to give careful attention to the price question, Borah agreed to postpone his threatened investigation until the results of Hoover's approach were clear. The Senator also acted out of deference to Harding, who claimed that a solution was at hand. "In other words," wrote Borah, "I have not felt like I ought possibly embarrass the situation when the Executive felt it was in the course of adjustment." [30]

The Senator's activities attracted the attention of the Committee of 48, a liberal group that since 1919 had dedicated itself to the advancement of progressivism in American politics. The committee, after conducting its own investigation of the coal industry, produced a complete report as well as legislative recommendations calling for a congressional investigation of the coal industry. The Forty-Eighters sent copies of their report to Harding, in hopes that he would act, and to Borah for use in the Senate in case the President ignored the suggestions. When the Senator expressed interest in receiving a draft bill, the committee hastened to provide him with one. The proposal called for separate bituminous and anthracite commissions of nine members each that were to function for a year as fact-finding agencies in the coal industry.[31]

[30] On the Borah-Hoover meeting, see New York *Herald Tribune,* June 10, 1922, Borah Scrapbooks, Reel 4; Baltimore *Sun,* June 10, 1922. For Walsh's reference to Borah's feelings about his major differences with Hoover, see Walsh to Hoover, June 14, 1922, Hoover Papers, Box 1-I/277. Walsh was bitterly unhappy with Hoover's handling of the coal situation and of his "self-opinionated and dictatorial manner" that made it "impossible for others to cooperate with you in getting results for the public welfare." For the quote from Borah see Borah to R. E. Shepherd, July 3, 1922, Borah Papers, Box 213. Ultimately, on July 19, Hoover privately told Harding that the voluntary price restraint "is rapidly breaking down" and that, despite the Secretary's efforts to curtail prices, "the price situation . . . is now rapidly getting out of hand." Hoover to Harding, July 19, 1922, Hoover Papers, Box 1-I/354.
[31] Special News Bulletin, Committee of 48, September 18, 1922, in

In the weeks that immediately followed, however, Borah moved slowly. He was convinced that probably "the Executive Department will not be able to do anything," and yet he refused to push for quick action out of fear that he might embarrass the administration. Although he had a copy of the draft bill by the end of June, he hesitated to introduce it until July 25, almost a month later. And, even when he did present it to the Senate, he emphasized that the measure was "not intended to deal with the present immediate condition with reference to the coal industry." His concern was "with the coal industry in the future." [32] Once he had introduced the bill, he encountered opposition within his Committee on Education and Labor. On July 26, the committee refused to endorse his proposal without the approval of Harding, who urged a delay until the end of the present emergency. Borah resorted simply to "marking time, waiting upon the approval of the President in order to get the approval of the Committee." [33]

Finally, in mid August, he decided to intensify his efforts for government action. Armed with statistics showing that coal prices had doubled despite Hoover's attempts to steady them, Borah challenged the Secretary of Commerce to supply information regarding public protection from such increases. In effect, he directly questioned Hoover's handling of the situation. Borah also clashed with members of the Committee on Education and Labor. When he tried to secure a favorable re-

---

Lynn Haines Papers (Minnesota Historical Society), Box 9; J. A. H. Hopkins to Borah, June 5 and 29, 1922; Borah to Hopkins, June 8, 1922, Borah Papers, Box 213. See also Hopkins to Lynn Haines, June 16, 1922, Haines Papers, Box 9. For more on the Committee of 48, see Chapter 5.

[32] Borah to R. E. Shepherd, July 3, 1922, Borah Papers, Box 213. *Congressional Record,* 67th Cong., 2nd Sess., 1922, LXII, 10609. A month later he again told the Senate that he had introduced the bill "at a time when it was hoped that the Executive would find a solution to the present situation"; hence, he had no intention of interceding in the present emergency. *Ibid.,* p. 11770.

[33] Borah to J. A. H. Hopkins, August 9, 1922. See also Borah to Harding, July 27, 1922, and Harding reply, July 27, 1922, Borah Papers, Box 213.

port for his proposed coal commission bill, four Republicans objected. Angrily, he threatened to resign his chairmanship. At the behest of the four G.O.P. dissenters, he went to the White House to confer with Harding; but, for one reason or another, the President was too busy to see him. Not until a week before Harding's August 18 appearance before Congress, when the President himself requested a commission to investigate the problem, did the committee agree to report Borah's bill favorably.[34]

By August 30, operators and coal miners in both the bituminous and anthracite fields reached agreements, but in each case they requested Harding to appoint a coal investigating commission which would recommend contractual changes based upon its findings. With the administration committed to the strike settlement, the Borah bill thus had little trouble becoming law in mid-September. In its final form, the bill established a seven member fact-finding commission to investigate the coal industry and to suggest further action and legislation. Congress limited the body to a one-year existence.

Borah's victory was, however, a hollow one. With the strike over, public and congressional attention turned away from the coal problem. The administration, which had been dubious about the commission from the start, gave it only limited support. In effect, Borah had lost any opportunity that he might have had to secure meaningful action in the coal industry. When the crisis was at its peak, he had deferred to the administration, rather than possibly embarrass it by relentlessly pressing the issue. As a result, the commission emerged in the

[34] Borah to Hoover, August 16, 1922. See also Heber Blankenhorn to Borah, August 15, 1922, and Borah reply, August 16, 1922, Borah Papers; Borah Scrapbooks, Reel 4. *Congressional Record*, 67th Cong., 2nd Sess., 1922, LXII, 11665. Harding's August 18 call for a coal commission was due to the fact that one of the terms of the August 15 soft-coal settlement called for such a commission. The President was merely responding to the demands of the coal miners and operators, not making concessions to Borah.

wake of the settlement as a harmless, vaguely constituted, and ultimately almost forgotten body.[35]

Upon the appointment of the commission, the Senator insisted "that we ought to bend every energy and make every effort to get real practical results" in the form of legislation from it. During the Senate debates he had stressed several times that the commission must go beyond mere inquiry and crystallize its findings into a recommended program; "if no constructive program is to result, if no statute is to be enacted or no legislation and control to be had, I myself do not care to have any interest in it." But, in its final report, the commission simply recommended that the federal government should in effect limit its powers in the coal industry to investigations. Borah, still seeking "a real constructive bill upon this coal proposition," regretted that the commission had not drafted legislation or guidelines for legislation. Although he understood "that President Harding advised them that was not their business," he believed that "it was their business." Off and on throughout the 1920's, the Senator continued to call for legislation that would remedy the problems in the coal industry. Yet he produced no proposals of his own, and explained in early 1926 that he was having difficulty finding "the constitutional power to do effectively what we want to do." [36]

[35] Zieger, *Republicans and Labor*, pp. 218–24, describes the commission's membership, limitations, and obstacles.

[36] Borah to George Otis Smith, November 14, 1922, Borah Papers, Box 213; *Congressional Record*, 67th Cong., 2nd Sess., 1922, LXII, 11732–33, 12237. Zieger, *Republicans and Labor*, pp. 224–25, discusses the commission's report and describes its recommendations regarding bituminous coal as "vague, platitudinous, and occasionally even meaningless." The commission, for example, recommended against nationalization of the mines, compulsory arbitration, price fixing, complete unionization, and the check-off system which the unions wanted. See Edward Eyre Hunt, et al., *What the Coal Commission Found* (Baltimore, Md., 1925), 403–6. This volume is a summary of the commission's findings, published by members of its staff. On Borah's continued interest in the coal problem, see especially Borah to Paul U. Kellogg, January 26, 1924, Borah Papers, Box 237; to J. A. H. Hopkins, February 11, 1926, Box 265.

Although Borah's activities during the 1922 coal crisis produced no legislative results in that troubled business, his performance evinced sympathy for the miners. In July, Harding, who had first blamed the operators for the strike because of their refusal to negotiate, turned his wrath on the United Mine Workers. The President also issued telegrams, indirectly encouraging the use of strikebreakers, to the twenty-eight governors in coal-producing states. Borah, on the other hand, from the beginning to the end of the strike, made it clear that he held little sympathy for the mine owners who had broken "their solemn contract" and refused to talk with their employees. When he heard that some owners were checking into his political past, he challenged them to communicate with him directly; indeed, he relished the prospects of comparing his activities with the careers of some mine operators. And, when the editor of the United Mine Workers *Journal* sent him statistics on the deplorable wages of bituminous miners, he was "exceedingly pleased to have this information." [37]

Further evidence of Borah's good will toward labor was clear in that part of his bill which asked the proposed commission to consider "the standardized cost of living to the miners" as the "first and irreduceable item of expense" in the production of coal. By implication, according to the Baltimore *Sun*, he hoped "to commit the government to the principle of the living wage." Delaware's wealthy entrepreneur and Senator, Thomas Coleman DuPont, demurred on grounds that such phraseology did not indicate that the miner "should do anything for this 'fair wage per diem'. . . ." The Senate Labor Committee ultimately accepted a compromise position. It instructed the coal commission, as Borah wanted, to consider the advisability of standardizing workers' costs-of-living and reasonable living conditions. But, as DuPont requested, the commission was also to examine the advantages of "standardizing . . . the amount of

[37] Zieger, *Republicans and Labor,* pp. 126–27. Borah to W. H. Coolidge, April 3, 1922; to Senator Howard Sutherland of West Virginia, April 13, 1922; to Ellis Searles, May 4, 1922, Borah Papers, Box 213.

work a man shall perform for a reasonable wage." DuPont, however, was still not satisfied. He wrote Borah that only "in a very
mild way" had the Labor Committee specified that the miner
should work for his wages.[38] Labor was thus fortunate that
Borah, and not a man with DuPont's fundamentally different
scale of priorities, was chairman of the Senate Committee.

Moreover, while DuPont was fretting about what he considered as a too tolerant attitude toward the obligations of employees, Borah again manifested his sympathies for labor by
opposing the sweeping injunction in September against striking
railroad workers. Attorney General Daugherty, who had urged
strong federal action against the strikers since their July 1
walkout, had requested the injunction. Following the issuance
of the order, Borah told Daugherty that it violated constitutional freedoms of speech, press, and peaceful assembly. The
Senator also expressed doubts that the courts had the power to
tie up labor union funds. Speaking on September 28, 1922, before some 5,000 cheering persons who had filled Chicago's Auditorium Theater an hour before he appeared, Borah vigorously
attacked denials of free speech and added: "That applies to
courts hearing injunctions, too." [39] Borah's activities during
these weeks pleased progressives such as those on the Committee
of 48. With obvious satisfaction the Forty-Eighters reported that

[38] Baltimore *Sun,* August 25, 1922; Coleman DuPont to Borah, August
25, 1922, Borah Papers, Box 213; *Congressional Record,* 67th Cong., 2nd
Sess., 1922, LXII, Part II, 11767; Borah to Samuel Gompers, February 18,
1924, and Gompers reply, February 20, 1924, Borah Papers, Box 237.

[39] Daugherty, with Harding's consent, secured the injunction from
Federal Judge James Wilkerson of Chicago. It prohibited union leaders
from "picketing or in any manner by letter, circulars, telephone messages,
word of mouth, or interviews encouraging any person to leave the employ
of a railroad." See Robert H. Zieger, "From Hostility to Moderation:
Railroad Labor Policy in the 1920's," *Labor History,* IX (Winter, 1968),
27–29. For Borah's description of his talk with Daugherty, see Borah to
Ray N. Castle, September 14, 1922, Borah Papers, Box 214. On his
Chicago speech, sponsored by the American League for Freedom, see
Borah Scrapbooks, Reel 4. On the stage were several leading civil liber-
tarians including Clarence Darrow, Jane Addams, Charles E. Merriam, and
Harold Ickes.

"the differences between Senator Borah and the Administration are fundamental. . . . the Senator acts from principle and the desire to see things accomplished; the Administration from a mistaken sense of political expediency." By September of 1922, the committee had turned its attention to Borah as a possible third-party presidential candidate.[40]

Meanwhile, in Idaho, far from the summer heat of Washington, D.C., and the strife-torn eastern coal fields, political events were setting the stage upon which Borah would soon make a dramatic appearance. In August, at the state G.O.P. convention, Republicans adopted a platform which opposed the repassage of a direct primary law, a statute which the Idaho legislature had repealed in 1919.

The direct primary law had long been a political reform for which progressives enthusiastically battled in their efforts to destroy political machines that spoke for special interests. Certainly the issue had ramifications far beyond the boundaries of Idaho. When Hiram Johnson, penning a letter in early 1921, had predicted "black reaction" ahead, he had pointed to "the attack all along the line today upon the Direct primary." Undeniably, to many leading conservative Republicans the direct primary was a central reason for the lack of party unity and the success of G.O.P. insurgents. Chief Justice Taft, for example, viewed general primaries as the means by which "party traders" wrecked the party. National Committeeman Dewey Hilles and New York's Senator James W. Wadsworth, Jr., believed that primary laws made the party "centrifugal." Senators from states with direct primaries were "provincial persons," running on locally oriented platforms, interpreting their election victories as mandates for their views, and looking upon the "party emblem only as a matter of convenience. This condition does not make for party cohesiveness." According to Nicholas Murray Butler, the direct primary "substituted personal politics for the

40 "Which Do You Want," *The Liberal* (September, 1922), p. 1, in Amos Pinchot Papers, Box 11. For a discussion of Borah's subsequent political relations with the Committee of 48, see Chapter 5.

politics of principle." Secretary of War John W. Weeks, himself a victim of a direct primary election, attacked such laws in a Cleveland speech in June, 1922; and Harding, Attorney General Harry Daugherty, Indiana's Senator Harry S. New, and other public officials criticized direct primaries as improper methods by which to nominate candidates. In light of such a wave of opinion, one weekly progressive journal concluded that "opposition to primaries is one of the hobbies of this administration." [41]

Borah was entirely sympathetic to the direct primary. He considered it "the only system by which anything like clean politics can be preserved. . . . The modern convention has become the tool and the plaything of the professional politician and the corrupt interests." Conventions worked to the advantage of industrial and financial interests. The direct primary, on the other hand, brought government closer to the people, allowing them—and not "possible sinister interests"—to select their candidates. "Miserable cowards" in the Idaho legislature had repealed the Idaho primary law without first consulting the people of the state. Borah, after witnessing the "trading and bartering and buying and selling" of many state conventions, refused to "submit to that kind of a proposition." [42]

Angrily, he returned to Idaho convinced that "when a man has the people's salvation at stake a fight is an enjoyable thing. Let us have it." His "spectacular entrance into Idaho" was "the greatest sensation of the [1922] campaign," wrote one observer in *The Nation*. "He stumped the state from one end to the other, defying the Republican machine . . . splitting his party

[41] Hiram Johnson to Raymond Robins, January 9, 1921, Robins Papers, Box 17; Taft to A. I. Vorys, November 13, 1922, Taft Papers, Box 527; Charles D. Hilles to Henry E. Gregory, August 15, 1922, Hilles Papers, Box 203; Nicholas Murray Butler to Hilles, December 28, 1926, *ibid.*, Box 207; "Idaho Primary Fight On," *The Voice of the People*, XI (October 7, 1922), 221, copy in Mercer Green Johnston Papers (Library of Congress), Box 79.

[42] Borah to Byrd Trego, October 6, 1922, Borah Papers, Box 220; to Tom S. Shaw, May 22, 1923, Box 233; to Miss Permeal French, August 8, 1922, Box 220.

wide open, and not giving a care. . . ." Borah opened his tour
of the state by calling for "a political revolution at the ballot
box." "I want the Republican party," he announced, "but I
want it right." After criticizing the convention system and prais-
ing the direct primary, he attacked the state G.O.P. platform as
useless: "Blank paper would have done just as well." He advised the Republican gubernatorial candidate, Charles C.
Moore, to ignore the platform and adopt a real program by
October 20. "The next two years are mine," Borah warned his
party. "Only God Almighty can take them away from me. And
I'll say what I think, do what I believe regardless of the political
effect upon me or anyone else." [43]

Actually, although Borah believed deeply in the principle of
the direct primary, there was also a compelling political reason
for his anger at the state G.O.P. He regarded the party's decision to adhere to the convention system as a plot to unseat him
from the Senate when he faced re-election in 1924. Other progressives shared his suspicions. Indeed, Basil Manly, an important progressive organizer and publicist who directed the People's Legislative Service, was positive that the vulnerability of
liberal candidates such as Borah in state conventions had inspired "the Administration's drive to abolish direct primaries."
Manly pointed specifically to Borah, Hiram Johnson, La Follette, "and several lesser lights" as key examples of progressives
whose political lives depended upon the direct participation
of the voters. When Borah injected himself into the 1922 struggle for the direct primary he thus, in effect, looked to his own
political future.[44]

At Weiser, Idaho, October 13, he suggested publicly that the

[43] Borah to H. A. Lawson, November 15, 1922, Borah Papers, Box 218;
Annie Pike Greenwood, "Bill Borah and Other Home Folks," *The Nation*,
CXVI (February 28, 1923), 236; *The Idaho Daily Statesman*, October 10,
1922.
[44] Basil Manly to La Follette, October 9, 1922, La Follette Family
Papers, Series B, Box 94; news article, September 18, 1922, published by
the Committee of 48's National Bureau of Information and Education,
in Haines Papers, Box 9; Philadelphia *Ledger*, September 27, 1922,
Borah Scrapbooks, Reel 4.

Republicans who comprised the state courthouse faction were determined to defeat him. "If the organization wants to notify the people of this state that in discussing the primary I am fighting for my existence I accept the challenge and defy the whole outfit." There was not "a particle of doubt" in his mind that he needed the direct primary to return to the Senate. Claiming that every one of his votes in the Senate was the product of his own thinking, he declared, "I don't ask to go back to the Senate at the dictation of the organization." His only request was "that the people express their wishes by electing a legislature that will pass a primary law." In the following weeks of the campaign he continued to urge the election of legislators who would restore the direct primary. If the G.O.P. lost its opportunity here, Borah was certain that forces outside the party would take the initiative. By November he was predicting a third-party sweep in 1924 unless the Republicans adopted a "liberal and constructive policy." [45]

Progressives enthusiastically followed the Senator's stumping tour. "Wow! But he does go after them," exulted Ray McKaig, one of the founders of Idaho's third party. "He has smashed the Republican party machine, junked it, and at the present time is one of the biggest boosts for our movement you can think about. . . . Borah Republicans are drifting toward us by squads and companies." After talking to Borah, McKaig felt there was a chance that "we are going to have him with us. . . . You see he is pounding the Republican crowd now; his next step is to pound the Democratic crowd, that only leaves the Borah people one place to go and that is for us." Reformers outside Idaho also looked to the Borah campaign as a portent for the future. One progressive journal predicted that, if Idaho salvaged the direct primary, "the general campaign for the abolition of the primary election system will probably be halted, and . . . primary advocates will organize for a new advance." For this reason the administration reportedly hoped "to find in

[45] *The Idaho Daily Statesman,* October 15 and 25, November 1 and 3, 1922.

the Idaho result in November a means of shearing the Senator's influence in Congress and throughout the country as a leader of protest." [46]

Borah unquestionably perturbed the Republican hierarchy. In Idaho, party leaders in various parts of the state informed the local G.O.P. headquarters that they did not want him to speak in their communities under Republican sponsorship. On October 15, after an emergency meeting of the state's central committee, the party officially declared that "notwithstanding the attitude of Senator Borah," the Republicans would follow their chosen platform. *The Idaho Daily Statesman,* which one leading Idaho Democrat described as the state's "official republican organ," lambasted Borah in a series of editorials. "God knows," the newspaper bitterly observed, that the Republicans received very little from him, other than his efforts to ruin them. Calling for the election of C. C. Moore as governor, the *Daily Statesman* predicted that, despite Borah, the G.O.P. would prevail in Idaho.[47]

In Washington, Chief Justice Taft informed America's ambassador to England that "Borah has gone out to Idaho, has denounced the Republican platform, and has stirred up a mess there." Harding undoubtedly had Borah, among others, in mind when he berated Republicans "who love their individual vote-catching platform and who bear the party banner and rarely if ever respond to the party call of duty." To conservatives, the Senator's Idaho fight seemed part of a larger campaign that threatened to make party labels meaningless. They could hardly have smiled at a cartoon showing a Republican and a Democrat viewing in shock the "Old Party Fences" dangling

[46] Ray McKaig to Henry G. Teigan, October 19, 1922, Henry G. Teigan Papers (Minnesota State Historical Society), Box 3; Greenwood, "Bill Borah and Other Home Folks," p. 237; "Idaho Primary Fight On," *The Voice of the People,* p. 221.

[47] *The Idaho Daily Statesman,* October 11–16, October 26, November 2, 1922. For the description of the newspaper as Idaho's G.O.P. mouthpiece, see John F. Nugent to Thomas J. Walsh, April 24, 1926, Thomas J. Walsh Papers (Library of Congress), Box 376. Nugent was Idaho's Democratic Senator from 1918 until he resigned in 1921.

broken from a limb, while Borah, La Follette, Smith W. Brookhart of Iowa, and Lynn Frazier of North Dakota crouched smirk-
ing behind the tree. There was too disturbing a truth for laughter in the cartoon's caption, "If This Keeps Up People Won't
Know Where Their Fences Are at All." [48]

When the Idaho election results were final, both Borah and
the state Republican hierarchy claimed victory. The party chairman described C. C. Moore's gubernatorial triumph as a direct
slap at Borah bossism: "We see in it that the party cannot and
will not be stampeded to the opposition by one man." Calvin
Cobb, editor of *The Idaho Daily Statesman*, wrote Taft that
"we beat the boots off him [Borah]." On the other hand, there
was ample evidence that the newly elected state legislature favored the direct primary, a goal for which the Senator had
fought. One progressive weekly believed that the fifteen third-
party legislators plus "the Borah Republicans" made the Idaho
senate and house overwhelmingly liberal and would override
"the reactionary governor" in behalf of the direct primary.
Borah himself interpreted the Idaho legislature as ready to "ef-
fectuate what we desire in the way of legislation." He suggested
a program calling for a direct primary, abolition of the state's
cabinet form of government, and election of the Public Utilities
Commission by popular vote.[49]

In February, 1923, while Borah watched anxiously from
Washington, the Idaho legislature passed a primary bill; in the
lower house the vote was an impressive 46 to 19. Immediately
the Senator wired friends to urge Governor Moore, now with
"an opportunity to do a great big thing and unite the Party,"
to sign the bill. On February 22, however, Moore delivered a

[48] Taft to George Harvey, October 17, 1922, Taft Papers, Box 525;
Harding quoted in Sinclair, *The Available Man*, p. 268; cartoon from
New York *Herald Tribune*, reprinted in *The Idaho Daily Statesman*,
October 31, 1922. On the substitution of personalities and small blocs for
political parties, see also editorial, *ibid.*, October 16, 1922.
[49] *The Idaho Daily Statesman*, November 9, 1922; Calvin Cobb to Taft,
February 5, 1923, Taft Papers, Box 533; *The Voice of the People*, XI
(December 23, 1922), in Mercer Green Johnston Papers, Box 79; Borah
to H. A. Lawson, November 15, 1922, Borah Papers, Box 218.

jective was not to establish a third party but to supply broad-based political support for reform candidates whatever their party attachments.[51]

The results of the 1922 elections indicated that such progressive efforts could produce results. In Indiana, Samuel M. Ralston, who had received the CPPA's endorsement, replaced Harry S. New as Senator. In Nebraska, Robert B. Howell, a 1912 progressive who supported the direct primary and received CPPA support, defeated Albert W. "Big Jeff" Jefferis, an anti-labor man. Henrik Shipstead, a Farmer-Laborite from Minnesota, unseated Frank B. Kellogg, an administration standpatter. In North Dakota, Porter J. McCumber, a twenty-three-year man in the Senate, lost to Lynn Frazier, who had the backing of the Nonpartisan League. Smith Wildman Brookhart, a reputed agrarian radical, captured the Iowa Senate seat. In Washington, Clarence C. Dill, a Democrat who received Farmer Labor support, defeated Miles Poindexter, who had fallen from progressive graces. Burton K. Wheeler entered the Senate from Montana. Despite serious opposition from the Republican national hierarchy, the La Follette group swept Wisconsin, returning La Follette to the Senate and placing John J. Blaine in the governorship. Former Bull-Mooser Gifford Pinchot won the Pennsylvania gubernatorial election; and, in Nebraska, Charles Bryan, brother of William Jennings Bryan, became governor at the expense of a conservative candidate.[52]

It was in the context of this progressive upheaval—this "un-

[51] Harry Slattery to Amos Pinchot, November 10, 1922, Pinchot Papers, Box 43; Harry Hunt, "Borah—A Pen Picture," *La Follette's Magazine,* XIV (February, 1922), 23; Norbeck to W. H. King, August 26, 1922, Norbeck Papers (South Dakota); Zieger, *Republicans and Labor,* pp. 173–74, on the CPPA.

[52] Shideler, *Farm Crisis, 1919–1923,* pp. 221–27; and Chester H. Rowell, "Why the Middle West Went Radical," *World's Work,* XLVI (June, 1923), 157–65. Edward Keating, editor of the railway workers journal, *Labor,* recalled that "the elections of 1922 really shook reaction. Most of us who were in the thick of the fight really didn't anticipate such glorious victories." Keating, *The Story of 'Labor': Thirty-Three Years on Rail Worker's Fighting Front* (Washington, D.C., 1953), pp. 114–15.

believable national awakening"—that Borah had urged C. C.
Moore to "kick that [Republican] platform into the dust-heap."
The Senator had, as one reporter wrote, defied "the whole
[G.O.P.] outfit." He had stumped his state in behalf of the
direct primary and had warned that a third party could not help
but benefit from the reactionary positions of the old political
organizations.[53]

On December 1–2, a few weeks after Borah's challenge to
Idaho's Republican leadership and in the wake of the surprising
liberal showing at the polls—"a most significant election indeed," in the Senator's words—he joined hundreds of reformers
from across the country in conferences designed to provide a
plan for cooperation among progressives. The meetings were
the inspiration of the People's Legislative Service, a nonpartisan
group which since late 1920 had functioned as a clearing house
for information relating to progressive legislation. La Follette,
executive chairman for the service, made clear that it was "designed to serve the whole people, not any class or group." Specifically, it supplied information on legislative matters to
reform-minded Senators and Representatives and, through its
small monthly journal, *The People's Business,* furnished public
reports on congressional issues. The director, Basil Manly, had
for several years urged the formation in Congress of a progressive " 'Battalion of Death' " which would protect the public
from partisanship and special privilege. The electoral triumphs
of 1922 seemed to offer a prime opportunity for molding such a
reform "Battalion" and generally uniting progressives throughout the nation. For this purpose the service invited liberals from
Congress and across the country to gather in Washington to
chart future strategy. To *The New Republic,* the meetings were
a major step toward combining the "local progressive insurrec-
tions" of the 1922 elections into a general movement. There
were some conspicuous absentees such as Hiram Johnson who,
despite his lament several weeks earlier about the lack of harmony among progressives, suspected that the conferences were

[53] Quoted in Greenwood, "Bill Borah and Other Home Folks," p. 236.

a selfish effort on the part of La Follette to organize "what Roosevelt used to term the 'lunatic fringe.'" But, all in all, the meetings represented an impressive gathering of people, many of whom had played prominent roles in the progressive movement for some time. Although La Follette was the recognized leader of the sessions, the Baltimore *Sun* said that of the other participants, Borah was "the outstanding figure, the superior of them all." [54]

Initially, Borah had been skeptical of the conferences. He advised Kansas editor William Allen White, who did not want to attend without his "approval and presence," not to go. The Senator was wary of the meetings because he did not agree with La Follette on all things and felt that those who participated would seem to endorse whatever happened. Clearly implying his own misgivings, he doubted that White wanted to place himself in such a position. [55]

Within three days after his admonition to White, however, he decided that the sessions would serve a good purpose. Perhaps La Follette's emphasis on the nonpolitical nature of the meetings reassured him. [56] Since the intent of the conferences was neither to adopt a specific program nor to inspire a political movement, Borah decided to attend. Indeed, since he agreed that there was a need for more unity among progressives in

[54] Borah to Villard, November 17, 1922, Borah Papers, Box 220, on Borah's reaction to the elections; La Follette to Villard, February 12, 1921, Villard Papers, Folder 2158, on the purposes of the service; Belle Case La Follette and Fola M. La Follette, *Robert M. La Follette* (New York, 1953), II, 1026–27, on the organization of the service; Basil Manly to La Follette, August 6, 1920, La Follette Family Papers, Series B, Box 94, on the "battalion of death"; "Progressivism Reborn," *The New Republic*, XXXIII (December 13, 1922), 56–57; Baltimore *Sun*, December 1, 1922; Hiram Johnson to Raymond Robins, November 14, 1922, Robins Papers, Box 18.

[55] William Allen White to Borah, November 27, 1922, and Borah reply, November 28, 1922, Borah Papers, Box 220.

[56] La Follette to Norris, November 18 and 24, 1922, Norris Papers, Tray 81, Box 6. La Follette made it clear that the conferences would be in no way caucuses and that no congressional bloc aimed at serving a particular interest or class would emerge.

Congress, he even chose to deliver a speech at the first assembly.

Behind closed doors on the morning of December 1, thirteen Senators, twenty-two Representatives, Governor Blaine of Wisconsin, and several others listened to La Follette outline the background of the meeting. They nominated Norris as chairman. Borah, arriving half an hour late, addressed the group on the need for more cooperation among progressives in Congress. Everyone supported a resolution calling for future meetings of "progressive-minded Senators and Representatives of all parties" in order to battle special privilege and restore government to the people. They organized themselves into committees to consider legislation involving agriculture, labor, railroads, shipping, natural resources, credits, and taxation. Borah emerged as chairman of the advisory committee to the Committee on Committees, and as a member of the committees on labor and natural resources. The group adjourned in mid-afternoon after also endorsing constitutional amendments calling for abolition of the electoral college, an end to lame-duck sessions of Congress, direct primaries for all elective offices, and effective national and state corrupt-practices acts. In brief, reported the *Sun,* "there is the making of a compact, disciplined legislative force in what has been done today." The next day, at the general conference, several hundred progressives held meetings and concluded with a large banquet.[57]

William Jennings Bryan missed the meetings but was certain that they made it possible to organize Congress along progressive lines; he predicted that a progressive bloc would enjoy "a controlling influence in the next Congress" and hoped that cooperation between liberals in both parties would continue.

[57] Mimeographed report by Basil Manly of the Proceedings of "The Conference of Progressives held in Washington, D.C., December 1 and 2, 1922" in the Gutzon Borglum Papers (Library of Congress), Box 61; signed carbon from George Huddleston listing committee assignments adopted at the December 1 meeting, and letter from Norris to B. Brewer, December 8, 1922, Norris Papers, Tray 81, Box 6; Roy O. Woodruff to Borah, December 6, 1922, Borah Papers, Box 233; Baltimore *Sun,* December 2, 1922.

Peter Norbeck also did not attend, but he observed that the progressives in Washington were "full of confidence." They apparently shared the New York *World's* interpretation that Harding had good reason to worry about Republican insurgency reminiscent of the challenge to Taft in 1910. Moreover, according to the *World,* this movement was "no less formidable because its guiding spirits are Senator Borah and Senator La Follette." [58]

Without doubt, Borah had supplied an important impetus for what *The New Republic* by the end of 1922 hailed as the rebirth of progressivism. "What we should do without you I cannot think," wrote Oswald Garrison Villard to the Senator. There were substantial reasons why conservative Republicans, including major contributors to the G.O.P. campaign fund, classed Borah among those Senators who wore the Republican label while "aiming to destroy the party by boring from within." "A very strong group of Republicans" sounded out the National Committee to see if it would aid them in replacing men such as Borah and La Follette with dedicated party stalwarts. National Committeeman Hilles agreed that it was dangerous to warm such "vipers to our bosom"; if Borah became chairman of the Foreign Relations Committee, La Follette of the Finance Committee, and Hiram Johnson of the Interstate Commerce Committee, "they would hold the pass against a President indefinitely." Taft, who classed Borah among "the blatant demagogues" in the Senate, declared simply that he was not a Republican except when seeking another political term or a committee position. In Harding's estimation, Borah was unstable, disloyal, impractical, and "a spokesman for the persistent opposition to whatever is." [59]

[58] Bryan to La Follette, December 4, 1922, La Follette Family Papers, Series B, Box 93; Norbeck to C. M. Henry, December 2, 1922, Norbeck Papers (Missouri), Folder 2; New York *World,* December 5, 1922, Borah Scrapbooks, Reel 4.

[59] "Progressivism Reborn," *The New Republic,* XXXIII (December 13, 1922), 56–57; Villard to Borah, May 21, 1922, Borah Papers, Box 218; Nicholas Murray Butler to Hilles, April 11, 1922, and Hilles to Butler,

Yet, although Borah enraged Republican standpatters and
gave much-needed encouragement to progressivism, his efforts
in the early Twenties also revealed certain flaws within Borah-
style liberalism. During the coal crisis he had deferred to the
administration at a crucial time, making his challenges to it
muted and oblique. Although his fight for the direct primary
thrilled many progressives, he had aided the state's third party
only incidentally and even inadvertently. As one Minnesota
progressive, Henry G. Teigan, told Idaho's Ray McKaig, "No
doubt, Borah helped you fellows a great deal but I think he
could have put you across had he come out definitely for the
Progressive slate." Since the Senator had at no point endorsed
any candidates of the third party, Teigan, despite his "great
admiration for the fighting qualities of Senator Borah," admitted "a disappointment in his attitude on the recent fight." Although Borah attended the progressive conferences in early
December, he did so with prior reservations, expressions of caution, and intimations of essential differences with La Follette.
"Borah revolves around with the bloc a bit," wrote journalist
William Hard, "but is a comet visiting this system rather than
a planet in it." [60] By 1923 there were thus significant indications
that—while Borah had the potential to inspire progressives and
infuriate Republican regulars—he would do so on his own
terms, according to his own strategy, at his own unpredictable
pace, and well within his own perspectives on reform.

April 13, 1922, Hilles Papers, Box 203; Taft to Horace Taft, March 14,
1925, Taft Papers, Box 575; and to Francis E. Baker, January 22, 1922,
Box 508; Harding quoted in Sinclair, *The Available Man*, pp. 275–76.
On the dispirited condition of the administration Republicans following
the 1922 elections, see, also, Murray, *The Harding Era*, pp. 322–23.

[60] Henry G. Teigan to Ray McKaig, November 13, 1922, Teigan Papers,
Box 3; William Hard to Raymond Robins, December 12, 1922, Robins
Papers, Box 18.

I I I

The Rhetorical Progressive

❧

VIEWING Borah from the Supreme Court in late 1922, William Howard Taft pointed to the Senator's apparent assumption "that when he has made a speech on the subject, the thing is done, the rest is detail." Taft was correct. Although Borah was one of the best-known progressive Senators, his reform zeal was essentially limited to rhetoric. Despite his talk about the "heroic effort," about serving "the general cause," and about starting "the crusade," he was reluctant to go beyond dramatic calls to arms and moral urgings. When it was time to put his commitments into action, he became skeptical. As Gutzon Borglum, the sculptor–political organizer—and Idaho native—said, "Borah's idle voice music has gone farther towards the stars than any other sound waves that have escaped the Senate." He reminded Borglum "of a violinist who is always tuning up beautifully . . . a brilliant bar or two, never concludes, then wraps his golden instrument in silk and puts it silently away." [1]

This discrepancy between rhetoric and action was due partly to Borah's apparent aversion to organizational effort and the details of legislative work. It undoubtedly also suggested a certain amount of political calculation. But, more fundamentally, it pointed to the Jeffersonian nature of his progressivism. In the 1930's, New-Deal liberal Gardner Jackson would angrily

[1] Taft to Horace Taft, December 28, 1922, Taft Papers, Box 530; statement which Borglum wrote apparently shortly after the 1932 election, Borglum Papers, Box 28. For an excellent discussion of Borah's tendency to substitute rhetoric for action, see John M. Cooper, Jr., "William E. Borah, Political Thespian," *Pacific Northwest Quarterly*, 56 (October, 1965), 145–53.

tell the Senator, "Borah, I don't like you. You're not sincere, Borah. You're not a go-through guy." The problem, however, was less one of insincerity than that of an old progressive who had in the prewar days gone as far as his reform vision would allow. While American liberalism moved toward greater emphasis on state intervention and urban politics, Borah maintained his basic distrust of big government and the city.[2] He was thus able to offer only the most fragile kind of bridge over the widening cultural chasm which by the Twenties threatened to divide irrevocably the rural and urban wings of progressivism.

Problems of state intervention and the city had long plagued American liberalism. Although progressives, then more than any previous generation, worked within an urban context and looked to government for support and answers, they vacillated in their enthusiasm. Many leading progressives fled rural backgrounds for the excitement and opportunity of larger towns or cities and played major roles in developing stronger governmental powers built around administrative efficiency and expertise. But village America—with its memory of quiet streets and personal government—was never far removed from many of their minds. Indeed, as they confronted the realities of the city, the nostalgia of boyhood days may ultimately have obscured those elements of boredom and limited choices from which they had earlier sought escape when they departed the countryside.[3]

Although Herbert Croly and other exponents of the "new liberalism" adjusted more easily to urban America and em-

[2] Johnson, *Borah of Idaho,* and McKenna, *Borah,* discuss Borah's rural, Jeffersonian leanings, but see also William E. Leuchtenburg, "William Edgar Borah," *Dictionary of American Biography,* supp. 2 (New York, 1958), esp. pp. 50–51; Edgar Kemler, *The Deflation of American Ideals, An Ethical Guide for New Dealers* (Baltimore, Md., 1941), pp. 104–8; and Graham, *Encore for Reform,* pp. 182–83. Jackson's quote is in David Eugene Conrad, *The Forgotten Farmers: The Story of the Sharecroppers in the New Deal* (Urbana, Ill., 1965), p. 113.

[3] Graham, *Encore for Reform,* pp. 71–72, is especially good on the tension between rural memories and city opportunities in progressive thought.

braced energetic government as the means of bringing direction out of drift, most of the prewar progressive generation undoubtedly was more equivocal. The excitement and challenge of the city could easily give way in their minds to an ominous setting of corruption, treeless streets, and anonymity—or, similarly, an active government as public servant could easily loom as a bureaucratic threat to individual freedom and initiative. Insofar as progressives shaped new bureaucratic techniques, they did so less as consciously developed programs than as groping, inadvertent results of the give and take of social processes. The very rigor with which a Croly struggled to advance his ideas of efficient, strong government suggested the tenacity of the Jeffersonian progressive biases which so exasperated him. Although the efficiency theme was unquestionably a powerful one within progressivism, the main thrust of prewar reform reflected a countervailing and probably even more compelling "evangelical vision of democracy." In this sense, the prewar progressive generation indeed stood at the crossroads, caught between the experience and ideals of traditional, village America and their faith in the promise of the new.[4]

The result was often a curious and volatile mixture of views, not just among progressives but within the individuals themselves. Ray Stannard Baker, for example, debated with himself for years. He rejected poverty and privilege and favored battling with the "interests"; at the same time, under his *nom de plume*

[4] For Croly's battle with the Jeffersonian bias of prewar progressives, see Forcey, *Crossroads of Liberalism*, esp. xxiv, 27–30, 37–40, 145, 207. Robert H. Wiebe's *Search for Order, 1877–1920* (New York, 1967) analyzes the bureaucratic theme in progressivism. As Wiebe clearly shows, spokesmen for emerging new middle-class professionals shaped bureaucratic patterns when they pressed for reforms; but they hardly did so with any grand conception of bureaucracy or understanding of its workings. David Noble's *The Paradox of Progressive Thought* (Minneapolis, Minn., 1958) and *The Progressive Mind* are very good in showing how progressives who seemingly embraced new technological methods—and thus were apparently quite modern—often did so as efforts to salvage old ideals. See also Quandt, *From the Small Town to the Great Community*. Griffen, "The Progressive Ethos," p. 140, stresses the primacy of the "evangelical vision of democracy" in progressive thought.

David Grayson, he voiced his frustrations and fears regarding city life and the organizational revolution which reform seemed to inspire. William Hard, a prominent progressive journalist who for a while in the 1920's wrote a weekly column for *The Nation,* evinced similar contradictions. Although he invoked the tradition of Theodore Roosevelt and although Hiram Johnson found him "radical in sentiment, almost too radical," Hard lined himself up solidly against "governmentalization." In 1924 he placed himself alongside Borah as "progressives of the vintage of the period between 1776 and 1787." This meant, he explained, that he and the Idaho Senator favored liberties, free speech, the right of labor to organize, and constitutional guarantees. "Liberty is what we are for. That's why we're progressive. Because we're progressive, and because we're for liberty, we're against governmentalization. We hate these modern increases in governmental powers . . . we want it [government] small." But Hard realized that not all reformers agreed. "That's why I'm in bad," he wrote. "And Senator Borah would be in bad, too, if he weren't so much cleverer than I." [5]

The problem was that Borah, Baker, Hard, and other progressives of Jeffersonian persuasion steadily found less room in which they could comfortably maneuver. Social and economic wrongs continued to anger them. They still shared the progressive spirit with its hopes of bringing government closer to the people, eliminating waste, thwarting economic monopolies, effecting justice for underprivileged groups, shaping a classless society, and seeing that government was a public servant offer-

[5] Bannister, *Ray Stannard Baker,* esp. pp. x–xi, 67, 90–93, 232–37, 293; on Hard, Johnson to Amy Johnson, August 10, 1918, Johnson Papers, Part IV, Box 1. Johnson liked Hard and described him as "honest . . . independent, and fearless." For Hard on Theodore Roosevelt, see draft of article, "The Spirit of Republicanism," sent to Alf Landon for comments, March 6, 1936, Alfred M. Landon Papers (Kansas State Historical Society), Box "Political, 1936, H-I." Hard defined his and Borah's kind of progressivism in "In Bad All Around," *The Nation,* CXIX (December 3, 1924), 599.

ing services in such forms as rural credits and conservation.[6] Their convictions still led them to seek remedies for the inequities that marked American life. With growing frustration they searched for that progressive middle ground between capital and labor, between laissez faire and "governmentalization," between their faith in old ideals and the demands of urbanism and industrialism. But events were eroding the middle ground from around them. Increasingly, rhetoric became the safest channel through which their reform commitments could find expression. More and more they fell back on moral pleadings, warning of the evil consequences of unsocial acts and trying to arouse and inform the "public" to defend its own interest.

Hard saw correctly that Borah's rhetoric effectively obscured the Senator's basic caution. But Borah's eloquence was often misleading. More than one observer noted that the Senator ultimately disappointed people because he raised their expectations about him so high.

Borah was perceptive enough to see the crux of the progressive dilemma. He declared that "the greatest domestic problem since the Civil War is: What shall the government do and how shall it exercise its purpose?" His own response to this issue was ambiguous. At one moment he demanded more governmental action; in the next, he urged caution and warned of dangers ahead. In October, 1923, for example, he was positive of one thing: "These times call for action, action, action, and sound, but nevertheless, action." Indeed, "if there ever was a time when men in public places were under the necessity of being up and doing, of boldly striking out and taking hold of these great questions, it is now." Within less than a year, however, the Senator in defense of states' rights admonished that "action is not always statesmanship. . . ." He attacked the views that Congress

[6] Graham, *Encore for Reform,* pp. 47–48, notes the dimunition of "room to maneuver" for many progressives. For a discussion of the chief characteristics of the progressive spirit, see George B. Tindall, "Business Progressivism and Southern Politics in the Twenties," *The South Atlantic Quarterly,* LXII (Winter, 1963), 93.

could end "every evil of the body politic," or that commissions could restore virtue. Such beliefs were "the refined and codified creed of official egotism." [7] It was seldom clear, then, exactly what kind of immediate action the Senator wanted. He stressed that "a government which does not look forward will not long have a chance to look backward." Government could not—as it had done in Jefferson's or Lincoln's day—avoid problems involving such things as agriculture and water transportation or the newer demands of electrical power and public utilities. Yet, at the same time, he opposed a child-labor amendment because it would violate the concept of local government and thus wrench America from the sound moorings of the Founding Fathers. [8]

In this same ambivalent manner, he would call vigorously for a national program and then lapse into a vagueness that was hardly conducive to such planning. Now was the time, he believed, for "a brave and determined program," "a thorough and fearless program," and an end to "gum-shoeing for bunches of votes here and there." He regretted the view in Washington that it was "easier to create a bureau and shunt responsibility than to devise a remedy and assume responsibility." Such words sounded forward-looking and critical of past and present mistakes, while intimating courageous and viable solutions. But Borah was disinclined to leave his sweeping phrases and to outline precisely what remedies he had in mind. Instead he urged an end to "shambling party expediency"; once public service was free of political pressures, bothersome questions would appear simple and troubles would diminish by more than half. A Borah-style program meant increased confidence in the Amer-

[7] Typed copy of Borah's Denver, Colorado, speech, June 18, 1927, Borah Papers, Box 285; Borah to A. T. Cole, October 10, 1923, Box 233; copy of Borah's speech, "Integrity of the States," July 5, 1924, Box 246.

[8] See copies of Borah's Manchester, New Hampshire, speech, May 24, 1923, Borah Papers, Box 235; Denver speech, June 18, 1927, Box 285; Detroit speech, September 18, 1928, Box 294. On his opposition to the child-labor amendment, Borah to John H. Wourms, July 15, 1924, Box 237.

ican people, loyalty to the nation's institutions, obedience to law, and a realization "that prosperity and economic strength must come through economy in public expenditure, frugality, industry, self help, and not through the open door of the public Treasury." [9] Beyond such guidelines, however, he was hesitant to move.

Although his repeated demands for action often implied that he was ready for bold innovation, his views of government necessarily blunted his efforts and made him suspicious of any extensive reform proposals. He automatically rejected "the idea that government should be a universal provider and guarantor against all the risks and wants of human existence." As he interpreted it, history revealed that the results of government interference in business were inefficiency, waste, extravagance, and diminished individual initiative. Indeed, "the poorest businessman which this country has yet produced is the government." [10]

Stressing the advantages of local government, Borah continually warned of the dangers of bureaucracy, the "creeping paralysis" of a free people. If there was anything worse, "God in his infinite mercy had not permitted it to curse the human family." He understood, for instance, that a proposed Department of Education in the President's Cabinet was merely to handle facts and statistics; yet he warned that this was "the 'nose of the camel under the tent.' " All bureaucracies started from such harmless origins, but soon "the insatiable maw draws everything that is within possible reach and that which was tepid and tame in the beginning, becomes wide-spread, and autocratic and dominant in the end." A Department of Education would "direct, guide, dictate, and control the whole educational system from the mother's knee to the final departure from campus." Borah even suspected that the real intent behind the federal plan was

[9] See copy of Borah's Akron, Ohio, speech, March 21, 1923, *ibid.*, Box 234, and his Manchester, New Hampshire, speech, May 24, 1923, Box 235.

[10] Borah's speeches at Manchester, New Hampshire, May 24, 1923, Lynchburg, Virginia, March 12, 1926, and Denver, Colorado, June 18, 1927, all concentrated at length on this theme.

to make the national government "omnipotent in educational affairs," an area which particularly needed initiative, individuality, and freedom. Similarly, although the Senator favored conservation, he did not want a Cabinet department dealing with it any more than with education. Why not, he asked, also make a department of athletics, or hygiene, or matrimony? "Why not confess at once that we have become a people utterly without initiative, self-reliance, or self-help and fall down like savages of old before some bureaucratic head and ask for salvation?" Borah would have none of this. To him, the trend toward centralization in Washington was "irresponsible vandalism" and a "vicious program of change for change's sake." [11]

When Borah defended local government and attacked government centralization and bureaucracy, he voiced the feelings of progressives such as William Hard, who had become increasingly disillusioned with liberals who turned to the state for answers. Hard had once believed that such reformers were battling to keep the government from supporting the powerful against the weak; but in 1926 he admonished that they were "trying to strengthen the power of the State to enslave the manager and the capitalist." [12] Such a comment reflected the larger discouragement of many progressives about the fate of their once-prized agencies which had fallen into reactionary hands.

Borah was not surprised, as Hard was, that the regulatory commissions had slipped into the control of reactionaries. He

[11] For Borah's views on the proposed Department of Education, see Borah to Miss Elizabeth Russum, January 2, 1925, Borah Papers, Box 250, and his Lynchburg, Virginia, speech, March 12, 1926; on his opposition to a Department of Conservation, see Borah to O. K. Davis, July 12, 1927, Box 280; on his description of bureaucracy as "God's curse," Borah to William M. Morgan, July 30, 1921, Box 207; on centralization as "vandalism," copy of Borah's Chicago speech, April 4, 1925, Box 259. Governor John J. Blaine of Wisconsin, who became a member of the Senate progressive bloc in the late 1920's, similarly opposed a Department of Education: "I am opposed to all centralization of government, either state or national, on general principles." Blaine to La Follette, Jr., April 28, 1926, La Follette Family Papers, Series C, Box 3.

[12] Hard, "Where Are the Pre-War Radicals," *Survey*, LV (February 1, 1926), 559.

had always been skeptical about the efficacy of such creations. During the Wilson administration he had opposed the establishment of the Federal Trade Commission on grounds that it would become the tool of conservatives who wanted to consolidate their interests. Even though he had anticipated the results, he was nonetheless shocked when they occurred and commented unhappily that he was witnessing "things which I never thought could happen among patriotic people." Corruption was so prevalent that "some of the Members of these Boards and Commissions ought to be hung." [13]

The Senator's views regarding the appropriate role of government underlined the difficult questions that besieged progressives in the 1920's over the proper techniques of achieving reform. Big business and its political allies had not only captured control of the regulatory commissions, but had also expropriated progressive rhetoric and were using it for their own purposes. When public relations agencies stressed that public service, not profits, had become the central concern of private enterprise, some progressives conceded the point. This was especially true of those reformers who looked upon efficiency and technology as prerequisites for social improvement; to them "new era" business practices represented the fulfillment of progressive struggles. William Allen White, who had been a key figure in the Bull Moose movement, found himself giving way to the seductions of "new era" business. The fact was, he explained, that events had moved far beyond the prewar issues concerning democratic control of government and distribution of wealth— "And as times change we change with them and business also has changed. The business that Bryan and Roosevelt railed at in their days is not the business of today." New university-trained "managers" who felt a genuine concern for the public had replaced "the old barons." Indeed, although White admitted that injustices still existed, he concluded by 1927 that the problems of the decade belonged not to politics but to business: "They are essentially engineers' problems."

[13] Borah to Mark Austin, January 28, 1921, Borah Papers, Box 210.

Such opinions led some progressives to look to business prosperity rather than government as the prime agent for achieving
the good society.[14]

The new business "managers" undoubtedly impressed Borah
less than they did White. But just as progressive talk about
efficiency and scientific management lent itself to the business-
dominated culture of the Twenties, so too did Borah's warnings
about federal centralization strengthen the arsenals of organizations and individuals who spurned social justice measures out
of a callous lack of concern for the disadvantaged or powerless
groups. Big government often loomed as a major threat to
powerful local factions who sought primarily to protect their
own advantages. Ironically, it was sometimes reformers seeking
to redistribute some of these advantages who supplied their opponents with powerful arguments. Before World War I, in Wisconsin, for example, the anti-La Follette factions had successfully rebuilt power by using Jeffersonian appeals similar to
those that had helped La Follette initially gain wide support—

[14] On the expropriation of progressive rhetoric, see Paul W. Glad,
"Progressives and the Business Culture of the 1920s," *Journal of American
History*, LIII (June, 1966), 80–81; on business control of one progressive
agency, G. Cullom Davis, "The Transformation of the Federal Trade
Commission," *Mississippi Valley Historical Review*, XLIX (December,
1962), 437–55; on the efficiency movement within progressivism, Samuel
Haber, *Efficiency and Uplift: Scientific Management in the Progressive
Era 1890–1920* (Chicago, 1964), and Jackson K. Putnam, "The Persistence
of Progressivism in the 1920's: The Case of California," *Pacific Historical
Review*, 35 (November, 1966), 398; on White's views of business in the
"new era," the copy of his address "Our Changing Times," delivered before the Kentucky State Bar Association, April 8, 1927, and White to
Victor H. Hanson, November 28, 1927, William Allen White Papers (Library of Congress), Box 105. In fundamental ways, of course, businessmen had shaped progressive legislation in the area of economic regulation.
Robert H. Wiebe, *Businessmen and Reform: A Study of the Progressive
Movement* (Cambridge, Mass., 1962), discusses this important aspect of
progressivism. James Weinstein, *The Corporate Ideal in the Liberal State
1900–1918* (Boston, Mass., 1968), suggests that much of the prewar progressivism lent itself to the control of corporate business leaders. See, also,
Gabriel Kolko, *The Triumph of Conservatism: A Reinterpretation of
American History, 1900–1916* (New York, 1963); to Kolko, business sponsorship of federal regulatory legislation was the essence of progressivism.

appeals which stressed local control, an end to government extravagance, and a return to government by the people. In the Twenties, groups which had no commitments to social justice were able similarly to turn progressive rhetoric back upon itself. *The Week,* "A Republican Paper with established principles" published in Columbus, Ohio, shared the anxieties of Borah, Hard, and other Jeffersonian-minded progressives about the future "of American individualism—self-control and self-direction. . . ." But it used the argument of local government as a defense against reform—a product of "the boo-hoo brothers and the sob-sisters" who waved hankies and sniveled tears in order to pressure "the tender-hearted and the soft-headed among our legislators." Due to the efforts of agitators, Congress, according to *The Week,* was trying to prevent eighteen-year-old girls from washing dishes, to regulate dogfights, and to suppress bad breath. The newspaper, which seldom agreed with Borah, praised his stand for local government.[15]

If the Senator's antagonism toward centralization of authority pleased *The Week,* he similarly evoked applause from a gathering of members of the Association of Stock Exchange Firms in New York's Hotel Astor when he cautioned about the dangers of putting business in a bureaucratic straitjacket. The "vast army of officials" in Washington threatened "the initiative, the self-reliance, the self-helping and the individuality" which had built the nation. Certainly he pleased his listeners by commenting that "a real, genuine bureaucrat is a man or a woman who has utterly failed in private affairs and therefore feels perfectly capable of going to Washington and telling the successful businessmen of the country how to run their business." In light of such assertions, it was understandable why Borah received speaking invitations in the mid-Twenties from such organizations

[15] Herbert F. Margulies sees the Jeffersonian base of progressivism as the central reason for *The Decline of the Progressive Movement in Wisconsin, 1890–1920* (Madison, Wis., 1968). See, esp., pp. vi, 136–50, 191, 285. James Ball Naylor, "Too Much Government," *The Week,* March 19, 1927. Clipping in Calvin Coolidge Papers (Library of Congress), Case File 1832.

as the New York Board of Trade and Transportation, the American Bankers Association of New York City, the New York Chamber of Commerce, the Central Mercantile Association in New York, the Railway Business Association of Philadelphia, and the American Manufacturers Export Association.[16]

Undoubtedly, businessmen had little to fear from the Senator. He was far from being an extremist and often spoke in their behalf, unless the issue involved monopolies. On the surface, it sometimes appeared that he was unsympathetic to business when he voted against such things as the antistrike provisions which some Republicans had unsuccessfully tried to attach to the Esch-Cummins Act of 1920. Because he believed that Congress did not have the "power to pass a law which prevents a man from quitting work," he had sided with labor on that issue. Nonetheless, he also pointed out that "the railroads ought not to be hampered by unnecessary legislation." When his nephew, a New Orleans attorney whose friends were important figures in the railroad business, advised that the roads could solve their own problems, Borah agreed, saying that although some legislation had to exist, "the railroads should be permitted as far as practicable to work out their salvation." [17]

During World War I, Borah had voted against the government take-over of the railways. He had believed that nothing more was necessary than the suspension of anticombination laws. "We should have left them in private hands but given the owners a free hand during the crisis. But they were taken over, a great railroad system was literally wrecked, and now Mr. McAdoo [Wilson's Secretary of the Treasury] has left the bastard

[16] Copy of Borah's speech, April 29, 1927, in Borah Papers, Box 285. See numerous invitations in "New York City Appointments" Folder, Box 253. Borah refused all the invitations along with several others from labor, Jewish, Negro, and law enforcement organizations due to pressing needs in Congress. Nonetheless, such invitations indicated that he was certainly not anathema to business groups.

[17] Borah to W. A. Heiss, January 9, 1920, Borah Papers, Box 198; Wayne G. Borah to Borah, April 10, 1923; Borah reply, April 14, 1923, Box 234.

on the steps of Congress." While McAdoo now made "a hundred thousand dollars a year from the movies," Congress was supposed to resolve the problems which he had left.[18]

Borah disagreed with those people who wanted to retain the roads under government control. If the government continued to operate the rails, the Senator believed that it would mean ruin. Public ownership in the name of the people would be better than "this perfectly vicious system of government control of private property." Although Borah refused to commit himself "against public ownership," there was little indication that he favored it. Despite his anxieties about the disastrous effects in the West of high railroad rates, he did not see what Congress could do about the situation. He explained that, if he knew a solution, he would fight for it. Not having an answer, he merely implored that if someone did know of a particular program, "for heaven's sake, give it to me." By implication, he was rejecting the labor-supported "Plumb Plan" which advocated government purchase of the railroads and subsequent operation by representatives of labor, management, and the government.[19]

Ultimately, on the issue of rail rates, Borah turned not to government ownership but to something far less radical, such as the exemption of coastwise ships from Panama tolls. He would, in other words, encourage lowering of freight rates by increasing competition between water and railroad transportation. He admitted that the Interstate Commerce Commission could control both rate schedules, "but, why should we not have

[18] Borah to Henry Turrish, December 13, 1919, Borah Papers, Box 198. Wilson had appointed McAdoo as director-general of the U.S. Railroad Administration which controlled the government-operated railways.

[19] Borah to W. B. Hussman, February 7, 1920, and to A. Y. Satterfield, July 26, 1921, Borah Papers, Box 204. The American Federation of Labor, despite the opposition of leaders such as Samuel Gompers, endorsed the "Plumb Plan." Although the Esch-Cummins Act returned the railroads to private control, some people continued to urge action along the lines of the Plumb Plan. See Hicks, *Republican Ascendancy,* p. 15, and "A Program for the Coal Mines and the Railroads," *The Nation,* CXV (August 23, 1922), 181.

the benefit of water competition? That is an influence which
cannot be bribed or bought—that is competition." [20] Railroads
were assuredly unhappy about Borah's Panama tolls proposal;
certainly, however, such a strategy was less inimical to their
interests than was government ownership—a remedy which the
Senator never seriously considered.

Although Borah basically opposed government ownership,
his rhetoric sometimes left a different impression. For this
reason, he and Smith Wildman Brookhart, Iowa's junior Senator and heralded farm radical, astonished a group of eastern
progressives with their reluctance to "throw down the gauntlet
to privilege, sound clear a clarion note in favor of government
ownership, and risk all on the issue." [21]

Such surprise at Borah's moderation revealed not only his
capacity to seem more radical than he was but also the wide
divergence within progressivism over the means of reform. Superficially, Borah was in agreement with a man such as Amos
Pinchot, a former Bull Moose Progressive and an active participant in reform circles. Both men opposed monopolies on
the one hand and socialism on the other. Both were committed
to the concept of competition. Pinchot illustrated his position
by distinguishing between Henry Ford, who had used efficiency
alone as a weapon against competitors, and Rockefeller, who
had relied on illegal economic methods. The result, he observed, had been better and cheaper automobiles as opposed to
expensive, low-quality oil products— "And in this there is food
for thought for all who defend monopoly and call competition
old-fashioned." At the same time, Pinchot disclaimed socialism
"which is abolition of competition in the industrial system." [22]

20 Borah to Frederick Sherman, March 20, 1922, Borah Papers, Box
215. Borah introduced a bill along these lines which passed the Senate,
but not the House.

21 Pinchot to Grenville S. MacFarland, March 3, 1923, Pinchot Papers,
Box 45.

22 Typed copy of Amos Pinchot's article, "Three Ways to Make
Millions," undated, Pinchot Papers, Box 49; Pinchot to John Haynes
Holmes, October 18, 1928, Box 51.

Although the Bull Moose apostate and Borah agreed in purpose, they parted company when it came to implementing a program "to break the power of the monopolistic groups, reestablish competitive industrial life and restore in production, distribution, and politics . . . the 'equal chance.' " Borah advocated the vigorous application of the antitrust laws but, to Pinchot, this approach alone was a mere palliative. Effective action, in Pinchot's estimation, would attack monopoly at its origins by providing for government ownership or control of the *sources* of economic power with which privileged groups built monopolies.

The essential difference in the attitudes of the two men was apparent in their approach to disarmament. Borah staunchly campaigned for a program which would reduce world armament projects; his view of international policy on this issue was the counterpart of his domestic views on trusts: namely, to prevent the evils of bigness from threatening society. Pinchot, on the other hand, was skeptical of the ultimate effectiveness of disarmament programs. To end wars (or monopoly) governments had to get to the roots of conflicts (or economic consolidation). "Abolishing war means abolishing the power of the interests that in each country control the destiny of society." These interests built their power "upon the ownership and control of certain entities, of transportation, of the great natural resources that are the sources of energy and raw materials of industry. Those who own and control these things control society." It was thus, according to Pinchot, inadequate to see armies as sources of war or giant trusts as the causes of economic injustices. Such a narrow view would cause people merely "to bite at the stick with which they are struck," rather than to demolish the stick itself.[23]

Pinchot and Borah thus sought essentially the same ends: peace in international affairs and increased domestic competition; but they differed in their insights into problems and over

[23] Pinchot to William Allen White, June 16, 1923, Pinchot Papers, Box 45, and to John H. Findley, November 28, 1921, Box 42.

the means by which they would effect their mutually desired goals. In the 1920's, the gap between the two men was striking and served as yet another example of differing views among progressives over the role of government. Only in the 1930's, when the New Deal expanded governmental powers in ways that both men found unacceptable and even frightening, did the differences between them pale into insignificance. Then, along with many of the old progressives who found much of the New Deal unpalatable, they discovered that their agreements were more fundamental than their disagreements. Ultimately, in 1936 Pinchot would endorse Borah for President, describing him as "a consistent liberal," an honest, level-headed man who opposed a "managed economy." [24] But this occurred only after the events of the Thirties had shifted the context of the progressive debate; in the Twenties, Pinchot could still express surprise at what he deemed Borah's timidity on the question of government ownership.

When Borah talked about possible government ownership, he was registering a threat, not offering a program. For example, when the coal strikes broke out in early 1922, he warned that "if the coal industry is not reorganized in the interest of the public, it will be up to the public to try the experiment of public ownership." The "if" was a big one, for it left the immediate initiative with the coal operators. In an editorial, the Baltimore *Sun* urged the owners to heed Borah's words and correct the situation on their own initiative. However, when *The Outlook* probed the Senator's opinion on the rumors that government seizure of the mines was necessary, he hedged, noting only that his positions were "such that they would likely be construed as a criticism which [would] not be helpful at this time in view of the delicacy of the situation." Over the next few years he did no more than express dissatisfaction with the course of events

[24] Mimeographed copy of radio address, "The New Deal and Senator Borah," delivered by Pinchot in April, 1936, Pinchot Papers, Box 59, and Pinchot to Francis J. Heney, January 11, 1936, Box 58. Pinchot was an organizer in 1936 of the National Committee for Borah.

and—because the lack of fuel jeopardized the health and lives of children—he suggested "speedy, drastic legislation, taking over the mines." Government, he said, had to act in order to protect society. Indeed, "the question is: Are we to freeze to death? Are the industries to come to a stand-still? Are millions to be thrown out of employment? Is this a Government?" Three years later, in November of 1925, Borah was doing no more than saying: "It seems to me we can no longer postpone the problem. Certainly the American people are entitled to be protected from either freezing to death or being robbed in prices." And, in April of 1926, he admitted that he had reached no conclusions on how to settle the coal question. He could only reaffirm that "it is up to the government to do something to relieve the people from the threat of either freezing to death every winter or of being robbed." [25]

Despite Borah's inaction, his rhetoric nonetheless so obscured his intentions and basic caution that Amos Pinchot was astounded in 1928 to hear the Senator disown government ownership. Pinchot asserted that he had "never heard anything more intellectually disarming . . . you and I know—from his own mouth—that he is a firm believer in government ownership and operation." [26] Again, as happened so many times, Borah's eloquence and oratory had sent up smoke signals. Pinchot apparently observed only the smoke, for the fire was a small one indeed.

The underlying fact was that the Senator deeply opposed drastic action. Nationalization, despite his occasional references to it as a possible remedy, was anathema to him. He explained this antipathy to Norman Thomas on grounds that subsequent problems of administration would be subject to political manipulation. "How," he queried, "are you going to have an adminis-

[25] Baltimore *Sun,* April 3, 1922; Borah to *The Outlook,* August 11, 1922, Borah Papers, Box 219; office copy of Borah's press release for August 9, 1922, Box 222; Borah to George S. Viereck, November 9, 1925, Box 251; Borah to Mrs. C. M. Lewis, April 7, 1926, Box 267.

[26] Pinchot to Allen McCurdy, November 2, 1928, Pinchot Papers, Box 51.

tration of this kind of a proposition without its being dominated by politics?" As with the Panama tolls question, his attitudes were clear: competition "cannot be bribed or bought,"
but government ownership and regulatory commissions are
always subject to political influence and corruption. This left
him little room in which to seek remedies to crucial questions.[27]

The most Borah really wanted was a balance among various
groups, whether they were farmers, laborers, or businessmen.
Each of the groups could largely determine its own future by
wrestling with its own problems. "There is no business but
must through organization and ability be prepared to take care
of itself, to prevent unfavorable legislation, and to sterilize competitive selfishness and see that it has a place in the sun." Just
as labor had organized, so too must farmers. Government's role,
of course, should be minimal, limited to keeping the economic
contest clean and seeing that no one group monopolized the
field. The Senator's fervor for breaking monopolies was not
confined to business. He had opposed the Clayton Anti-Trust
Act in 1914 which declared that labor and farm organizations
were not subject to antitrust laws. Likewise, in 1922, he voted
against the Capper-Volstead bill which exempted agricultural
producers and cooperatives from such prosecution. No industries, he believed, should be free from the Sherman Anti-Trust
Act of 1890. "If you eliminate some, you will finally eliminate
all, which will give monopoly free reign in this country. This
would be very much worse for the farmer in the end." While
the Senator believed that there should be laws in behalf of co-

[27] Borah to Norman Thomas, December 12, 1925, Borah Papers, Box
297. In his analysis of Borah and foreign policy, Robert Maddox writes
that Borah worried a great deal about "a 'logic of events.' . . . If the
Senator had a motto, it might well have been 'One Thing Leads to Another.' Any action, however innocuous or well-meaning on its surface,
could set off a train of events totally unforeseen at the outset." Hence the
Senator by nature tended always to move cautiously. Robert J. Maddox,
William E. Borah and American Foreign Policy (Baton Rouge, La., 1969),
p. 8.

operative marketing, he concluded that there was no need to endorse monopoly.[28]

Borah's hesitant approach to the agricultural crisis of the 1920's was not due to a lack of sentiment for the farmer. Indeed, he accepted the Jeffersonian premises of the nobility of the agricultural calling and of the virtues of the tiller of the soil. "Without disparaging others," he wrote, "there is no place where loyalty to American institutions, faith in American ideals, are more universally accepted than among those who live in close touch with mother earth." The farmer "has been a builder of homes, an apostle of orderly and wholesome liberty." [29]

The problem was that, throughout the Twenties, farmers needed more than admiration. A severe economic slump kept them from sharing the benefits of the urban prosperity of that decade. Once the war boom had ended, once Europe's ability to buy American goods diminished, and once European farmers began to produce again, the perennial problem of surpluses that undermined prices returned to plague American agriculture. Accompanying the reduction in foreign markets was a rise in freight rates. Thus while business prospered, farmers watched the price index and the value of land fall. Borah correctly diagnosed the meaning of the farm crisis when he asserted that "the agricultural interests are face to face with the most serious problem which can possibly confront an industry, whether agriculture is going to be permitted to enjoy economic equality with the other industries of the United States." [30]

Despite his sympathy for the aggrieved farmers, he none-

[28] On the need of groups, especially farmers, to protect themselves, see draft of first installment in series of four articles on the farm problem for N. A. Huse in 1923, Borah Papers, Box 235; on the Sherman Anti-Trust Act, Borah to Z. Ballantyne, February 6, 1922, Box 218.

[29] Draft of third installment of articles on farm problem for N. A. Huse, 1923, Borah Papers, Box 235.

[30] On the roots of the farm problem of the Twenties, see John D. Hicks, *Rehearsal for Disaster: The Boom and Collapse of 1919–1920* (Gainesville, Fla., 1961), pp. 64–65, and Shideler, *Farm Crisis, 1919–1923*, pp. 46–47; Borah to George G. Barrett, June 20, 1929, Borah Papers, Box 299.

theless generally opposed any immediate effective relief for them. His suggested remedies were limited to government loans, cooperative marketing, improving European markets, and raising the tariff on farm goods. Since he was convinced that the agrarians' economic troubles were due not "to shiftlessness or laziness or ignorance" but to a lack of organization, he urged them to cooperate in order to market efficiently and effectively. In 1921, to encourage cooperative marketing, he introduced a bill calling for a "central clearing house for the scientific distribution and marketing of agricultural products." The cooperative would receive its impetus from government loans and would operate on two levels: a national coordinating board and thousands of voluntary county associations. The goal was to build and operate elevators, packing and storage houses, and the means of transportation and communication. Once established and self-sustaining, the organization could repay the federal government at a 2 percent interest rate per year. Even though the bill never reached a vote, it indicated the lines along which Borah was thinking: long-range relief with the government's role temporary and strictly on a business relationship. He also emphasized that no farm plan should be compulsory. Cooperatives, for example, would have strictly voluntary membership. As he told a dairymen's association in 1928, the farmer must remain "a free, moral and economic agent." The man who is the object of experimentation must, Borah believed, always have the chance to consent or refuse.[31]

The Senator was well aware that farmers' cooperatives would not automatically supply markets. He believed that "permanent, abiding relief" rested with easing the turmoil which was inducing Europe to close her doors to American trade. Indeed, the farm problem provided him with further opportunities to call for the revision of the Versailles Treaty and settlement of

[31] Draft of first installment of articles for Huse, Borah Papers, Box 235; *Congressional Record*, 67th Cong., Special Sess., 1921, LXI, 525. Copy of the bill, S. 1041, in Borah Papers, Box 212. Borah's speech to Dairyman's Association in Caldwell, Idaho, July 17, 1928, Box 295.

the Russian problem. It was wrong, he said, to talk of America's agricultural overproduction when some children had not seen a drop of milk since 1916.[32] Opening European markets would be a humanitarian accomplishment as well as a practical remedy for the nation's farm crisis. Again, however, his proposals offered no immediate relief to farmers.

Borah feared an emergency "patent medicine scheme" because it might "undermine and destroy the health of the patient." He was particularly concerned lest "the false doctrine of government aid" infect agrarian groups. Once the farmer relied on a "direct feeding from the Treasury," a vicious battle for subsidies and grants would result. Before long, "the weight of officialdom and taxes" would smother agriculture. "God pity the American farmer," he wrote, "if the time has arrived when he is going to depend upon the government for a way out of his difficulties. . . . I never want to see the farmer of America become a governmental peon—and I do not think he will." [33]

A specific type of direct government aid which the Senator detested was price-fixing. The problem, he pointed out, involved who should fix the prices. He doubted that farmers would be willing to let a Washington commission determine what they should receive for their products. Even if they consented to this, there remained the possibility that the commission would fall into the control of other interests. The price-fixing which Borah had witnessed during the war "was practically ruinous in my judgment to all industries which didn't have sufficient influence to control the situation." Hence he was skeptical of the Ladd-Sinclair bill of the early Twenties which planned to revive the U.S. Grain Corporation, allowing it to purchase surpluses and to fix minimum prices on basic farm produce. Borah warned that once government set the price

[32] Borah's speech in Burley, Idaho, July 4, 1923, Borah Papers, Box 234; Borah to J. S. Winslow, February 6, 1923, Box 226; to J. C. Jacobsen, February 23, 1925, Box 248, are several examples.

[33] Borah to W. H. Lyon, October 31, 1927, Borah Papers, Box 274; second installment of Borah's 1923 articles for Huse, Box 235; Borah to W. I. Drummond, July 25, 1929, Box 299.

on something such as wheat, it would inevitably also have to set
prices on other products, including that of labor. This would
result in a vicious circle. Moreover, it would not even aid agriculture; indeed, the "price-fixing proposition would in the end
be the most injurious thing we could do for the farmer." In
Borah's estimation, farmers would have been better off even
during the war if the Grain Corporation had not existed.[34]

The Idahoan's views on price-fixing were in striking opposition to those of such western progressives as La Follette, Norris,
Edwin F. Ladd, and Henrik Shipstead. La Follette contended
that a few interests in almost every line of manufactured commodities already fixed prices. It thus seemed absurd for people
to object to fixing farm prices in order to rescue agriculture
from ruin. Even though such measures often offered a treacherous road to walk, the Wisconsin Senator believed that at times
such means "are the lesser of evils." Shipstead, a Farmer-Laborite from Minnesota, shared Borah's aversions to price-fixing and
bureaucracies; "but when the prairie fire of bureaucracy is
sweeping down to destroy agricultural life, then in desperation
I am willing to set a backfire by establishing another bureaucracy. . . ." As Shipstead saw it, agricultural price-fixing was
simply "a backfire against the bureaucracy that is fast overwhelming us." [35]

George Norris declared that he "would be willing to sacrifice
almost anything" to pass a bill which stabilized farm prices.
"A radical ailment" demanded "a radical cure." Although
Norris hoped to keep government out of business as much as
possible, he believed that America had reached a point "where
it is almost imperative" that government play a major role.

[34] Borah to M. W. Bates, June 1, 1921, Borah Papers, Box 208, for his
opinion of wartime price-fixing; for other examples of his opposition to
fixing prices on agricultural products, see Borah to Alfred H. Weeks,
April 24, 1922, and to Walter N. Kidd, April 14, 1922, Box 212; to
Z. Ballantyne, February 6, 1922, Box 218, and to C. E. Judd, February 24,
1922, Box 215.
[35] La Follette quoted in Baltimore *Sun*, July 28, 1923; Henrik Shipstead, "Price-Fixing for the Farmer," *The Nation*, CXXIII (August 4,
1926), 102.

"The whole world is out of joint. . . . There is but one power large enough to cope with the situation, and that is Government itself. . . ." Norris's response to the farm problem included a government corporation which would buy American farm surpluses and ship them for sale abroad in idle government ships. The export agency would charge only for the expenses of transportation. "The government should go into this business and stay in until the world gets straightened around back into a normal condition. We must steer our Ship of State in accordance with the currents and the winds as they are and not as we might wish them to be." Norris's approach and attitudes toward government's role offered a sharp contrast to Borah's views. Certainly the Nebraskan's proposal to combat high freight rates differed greatly from Borah's suggestion. Norris would force down the rates upon produce which the government export corporation purchased; then he would ship the products in otherwise-idle government vessels. Borah, on the other hand, put his faith in free Panama tolls. Whereas Norris would use the federal government to distribute farm products, and to pare down freight rates, Borah turned to "the utmost natural competition" between water and land transportation as the proper answer to domestic shipment of goods. The Idahoan, unlike Norris, apparently gave no attention to the idea of government involvement in shipping produce abroad.[36]

Actually, on the question of farm relief in general, Borah was never far from the views of the administrations of Harding

[36] The Senate adopted an administration substitute measure providing for increased rural credits instead of the Norris bill. To Norris, it "was one of the cruelest blows that I received"; he was bitter toward those Senators who had "scattered like wild geese," placing party regularity ahead of farm relief and "selling out to the enemy." See Norris to G. H. Payne, November 14, 1921, and to Harry N. Owen, January 14, 1921, Norris Papers, Tray 5, Box 1; and to William T. Chantland, November 26, 1921, Tray 7, Box 6. Peter Norbeck observed "that Norris has been angry at nearly everybody since the failure of his bill. . . ." Norbeck to W. R. Ronald, December 27, 1921, Norbeck Papers (South Dakota). Borah to E. L. Platz, August 22, 1922, Borah Papers, Box 215, on free Panama tolls.

and Coolidge. Harding and his Secretary of Agriculture, Henry C. Wallace, also feared direct governmental action—either in terms of crop disposal or fixing prices—and responded with platitudes and wornout formulas such as farm credits and tariff legislation. Wallace's gradual shift to McNary-Haugenism helped to prepare the way for more intensive legislation, but his death and Coolidge's accession to the White House left official policy in the hands of William Jardine, Wallace's successor, and Secretary of Commerce Herbert Hoover. Jardine, sounding much like Borah, asserted that the farmer "doesn't want to be a ward of the Government." The new Secretary would not, in the words of *The New York Times,* accept "the miraculous power of legislation" to aid farmers who "must work out their own salvation"; government, in other words, must keep out of the farming business. Jardine, as well as Borah, had great hopes for cooperative marketing agencies. Like the Senator, he also favored government—on a strictly business basis—loaning at interest to a central cooperative.[37]

Although Borah had his principles regarding proper farm legislation, he was not politically stupid. He considered himself immune to the appeals of special interest groups but his battles for the general interest could appear quite partisan. When, for example, a flood of letters descended on Borah's office from Idaho Chambers of Commerce, businessmen, and farmers urging him to back the proposal of Idaho's junior Senator, Frank R. Gooding, that government stabilize wheat prices at $1.75 per bushel for three years, Borah's opposition to price-fixing softened. He pledged his aid: "I shall be glad to support the Gooding Bill with reference to fixing a price on wheat." Indeed, he would back "any measure which will insure or guarantee the

[37] See Henry L. Rofinot, "Normalcy and the Farmer: Agricultural Policy Under Harding and Coolidge, 1920–28" (unpublished Ph.D. dissertation, Dept. of History, Columbia University, 1958); Shideler, *Farm Crisis, 1919–1923,* pp. 118–51; Jardine Scrapbooks 3 in Box 7, 4 in Box 8. For examples of Jardine's viewpoint, see copies of his speeches in Champaign, Illinois, January 21, 1926, Box 5, and Osawatomie, Kansas, September 6, 1926, in William M. Jardine Papers (Library of Congress), Box 1.

price of wheat." His position resembled that of La Follette, who could attack the narrow interests of the meat-packing industry and yet support a federal tax on oleomargarine which provided special advantages to Wisconsin dairy interests.[38]

The problem, ultimately, was that since the Senate progressives were generally from agricultural regions, the issue of farm relief threatened to turn their much-acclaimed rejection of interest-based politics into an empty gesture. Shared sympathies for the farmer did not assure agreement among them on the question of aid to agriculture; disagreements in fact weakened their effectiveness as a group and suggested the futility of trying to get reformers from across the country to concur upon programs and tactics.[39]

The labor issue proved as divisive as that of agriculture. And again Borah's views revealed some of the ambivalence and confusion that characterized the response of many progressives. Just as he worried about the disastrous effect of too much governmental interference on the farmer as a free, moral agent, so too did he regret the impact of labor unions on individualism. Although he sympathized during the New Era with the workingman and in significant ways was a defender of the union position, his opinions on labor reflected a longing for simpler days, less urbanized and less industrialized. Since he realized that workers had to cooperate in the face of intolerable conditions, he was quick to champion their rights to organize unions. But, at the same time, he was reluctant to urge a Rural Letter Car-

[38] Borah to George W. Stephen, February 20, 1923; to Perry M. Harding, February 7, 1923; to William Lambie, March 7, 1923; numerous letters to Borah from constituents, Borah Papers, Box 227. The Gooding bill did not reach a vote in that session of Congress. If it had, Borah's pledges would have been tested. Perhaps he might have had second thoughts. This happened later, regarding the McNary-Haugen bill; after promising his support, he changed his mind and voted against it. On La Follette, see John A. Garraty, "Robert M. La Follette: The Promise Unfulfilled," in Garraty (ed.), *Historical Viewpoints Since 1865: Notable Articles from American Heritage,* II (New York, 1970), 168.

[39] See Chapter 8 for further discussion of the divisions among the Senate progressives.

riers' Association to join the American Federation of Labor. "I am a great believer in individuality," he wrote, "both in regard to persons and to organizations, and I sometimes think that by too large organizations, we are handicapped in looking after particular interests." Of course, if the letter carriers wanted to affiliate with anyone, the A.F. of L. would be their best choice. "The whole thing seems to be a question of policy, whether to go alone or with others, and individually, I am so constituted I would be disposed to go alone." [40]

Borah cringed at the idea of a closed shop. During the 1919 steel strike, he criticized U.S. Steel's Judge Elbert H. Gary for refusing to talk with the representatives of union labor. The Senator nonetheless expressed "entire sympathy" with Gary's "view of an open shop and . . . thorough sympathy with the view that every man should be permitted to work and have the full protection of his government whether he is a member of the Union or not." Gary should have met with union representatives; but if they had demanded a closed shop, he in good conscience could have rejected the demand.[41] In taking such a position, Borah seemed oblivious of the fact that the open shop had traditionally been a strong antiunion weapon, a means by which management had kept unions weak and the door through which companies had brought strikebreakers to defeat strikes.

Clearly the Senator shared the mixed emotions of many reformers toward labor. Like many progressives, he often expressed his repugnance for legislation or appeals in behalf of social classes. According to the monthly bulletin of the People's Legislative Service, the most distinguishing characteristic of the progressives on Capitol Hill was that they could "pretty generally be counted upon not to let party, class, corporate or personal obligations dominate their conduct when questions involving human rights and the general welfare come before them." La Follette demonstrated his awareness of the progres-

[40] Borah to Ben L, Thompson, May 6, 1921, Borah Papers, Box 204.
[41] Borah to Thomas C. Stanford, November 10, 1919, Borah Papers, Box 195.

sive hostility toward interest-based politics when he emphasized that the Washington conferences in December, 1922, were *"not proposed to form a Congressional bloc to be representative of any particular interest or class."* Shortly before his death, La Follette reaffirmed his belief that the formation of any political movement had to focus on "the American citizen as the unit" and that organizations such as those of labor should "take no part in a new party movement *as organizations."* Lincoln Steffens, whose muckraking articles had once stirred the reform imagination, perceived the major difficulty inherent in the progressive faith in the general as opposed to the special interest. He concluded that "the people's fight" had not really been fought at all, "especially in America, where there is no people: but only farmers and workers, bankers and—special interests." [42]

Borah, as did so many of the prewar progressives, disagreed. He refused to look upon "laborers as laborers or capitalists as capitalists or any other class as a class." Instead, in typical progressive fashion, he removed himself from the smoke-filled rooms of class interests to the clean air of the public interest: "I recognize our constitutional form of government and everybody regardless of his position or class or place must conform to it so far as my votes are concerned. . . ." He contended that he had "never been a supporter of labor legislation, because it was labor legislation," and for that reason had voted against exempting unions from the Sherman Anti-Trust Act and against the 1916 Adamson Act, establishing an eight-hour day for interstate carrier employees. [43]

Borah opposed conducting a political campaign in association with labor or any one group or class as much as he opposed

[42] Mercer G. Johnston's editorial, "Back Up All Progressives," *The People's Business* (September, 1928), p. 21, La Follette Family Papers, Series C, Box 425; La Follette to George Norris, November 22, 1922, Norris Papers, Tray 81, Box 6; La Follette to William T. Raleigh, April 17, 1925, La Follette Family Papers, Series B, Box 119; Lincoln Steffens to Belle La Follette, June 20, 1925, *ibid.*, Series D, Box 18.

[43] Borah to Thomas C. Stanford, November 10, 1919, Borah Papers, Box 195, and to W. A. Heiss, January 9, 1920, Box 198.

class legislation. During the 1922 coal strike, Oswald Garrison Villard notified Borah that if he could lead the way "a great army of workers" would immediately rally to him. In response to Villard's urgings to "sound the tocsin," the Senator warned that it was always a political handicap "when one is nominated on what is called a labor ticket, or a business man's ticket, or anything of that kind." His attitudes resembled those of other progressives such as Amos Pinchot, George L. Record, the New Jerseyite who had helped to prepare the way for Woodrow Wilson's reform governorship, and Raymond Robins, who had been a familiar face in the Bull Moose party. They too were friendly to labor and courted its support; but, like Borah, they spurned appeals along class lines. Robins, who placed himself in opposition to "the parasites of privilege," eulogized Theodore Roosevelt for supporting "the rights of the whole people against the special interests of any class." Like Borah, Robins believed that workers should receive decent pay and that the sweeping Daugherty injunction of 1922 was unconstitutional; but, similarly, he looked upon the Adamson Act as class discrimination and a step toward "the class cleavage of our country." [44]

When liberals such as Borah, Robins, Pinchot, and Record rejected class legislation, they confronted reformers in the New Era with a predicament. As William Culbertson, a member of the Tariff Commission, correctly observed, reform in the Twenties was "in many of its phases an expression of class conscious farmers and laborers who want more of the income of society turned their way." The concern of special-interest groups such as agarians and workers over "the fundamental question of the

[44] Villard to Borah, August 3, 1922; Borah reply, August 8, 1922, Borah Papers, Box 220. Robins restated his opposition to privilege when he contributed $200 to La Follette's 1922 senatorial campaign; Robins to La Follette, August 28, 1922, La Follette Family Papers, Series B, Box 94. For his views on labor legislation, see Robins to Harding, July 17, 1920, and October 14, 1920, Harding Papers. On the labor views of Pinchot, Record, and other progressives, see Zieger, *Republicans and Labor*, pp. 168–72.

distribution of wealth" supplied a "distinctly economic" impetus to an important segment of political insurgency following World War I.[45] In sum, much of the new energy behind the progressive resurgence in the early Twenties sprang from the very interest-based politics that many prewar progressives found offensive.

Due to Borah's distrust of class thinking and action, his attitudes—as well as those of other progressives who shared his sentiments—were unavoidably paradoxical toward labor. For instance, although he opposed antistrike legislation on grounds that Congress could not prevent a man from quitting work, he also noted that "we can pass laws preventing a man who quits work from interfering with another man who remains or desires to work, or who in any way interferes with the operation of the [rail] road by others. . . ." Not only should there be legislation against such action, but it should be "drastic." Borah failed to spell out, at least in the Twenties, exactly what the implications of antistrike laws should be for the strikers. And, although he believed that workers should receive a living wage, he had no suggestions as to how to transform such feelings into facts. He was never precise about the necessary course of action if employers continued to pay less than subsistence wages. Workers, of course, had the right to quit and to organize; yet they should not keep others from the job, should think always in

[45] Culbertson to William Allen White, December 18, 1922, Culbertson Papers, Box 47. See also Charles Merz, "Progressivism, Old and New," *The Atlantic Monthly*, CXXXII (July, 1923), 102–9. Merz, pp. 106–7, noted that "what stands out in the new Progressivism, in contrast to the trust-busting and direct legislation of the old . . . is a far wider interest in all matters economic. . . ." *The New Republic* expressed this view when it advised progressives to prepare as classes "gradually to take over part of the existing monopoly of economic power." This was the only viable road to reform since "the power of the new plutocracy is not assailable by the route of ordinary political agitation." "The Progressive Direction," XLIII (July 15, 1925), 192–94. Frederick C. Howe, *Confessions of a Reformer*, pp. 317–38, arrived at the same conclusions. On the "new progressivism" in Wisconsin, see Margulies, *Decline of the Progressive Movement in Wisconsin*, esp. pp. 248–49, 280–82.

terms of the public interest, and should shun advocates of violence and disturbers of the general welfare.[46] This still left unanswered questions involving proper sanctions against recalcitrant employers. For them he apparently had only warnings about *possible* government action.

Plainly, when labor questions and crises arose, Borah's reaction was mainly one of logic, rather than a response to felt needs. He was out of his element when the situation involved the complexities of management-labor relations. He had no real understanding of the problems involved. Missing from his personal experiences was that firsthand knowledge of industrial and city working conditions which, among some reformers, provided the impetus for an urban working-class liberalism.[47]

Nevertheless, labor leaders were usually grateful to him because, during labor troubles, he often expressed sympathy and tolerance for the workingman. If his small financial contributions to the causes of striking Pennsylvania and Colorado coal miners in 1928 did not supply any important legislative answers to labor problems, they were at least gestures of goodwill during a decade in which workers received few benefits and only begrudging political attention. It was undoubtedly because of his general posture that ninety-six-year-old Mother Jones, grand old lady of labor's wars, hoped to stay alive to see Borah "in the White House and the Nation safe," and that tough John L. Lewis of the United Mine Workers called the Senator "unquestionably one of the greatest statesman the country has produced." [48]

[46] Borah to W. A. Heiss, January 9, 1920, Borah Papers, Box 198. See copy of Borah speech, undated, sent to Bart Campbell, September 22, 1922, Box 222, for his warnings to workers to beware of labor agitators and class divisions.

[47] See J. Joseph Huthmacher, "Urban Liberalism and the Age of Reform," *Mississippi Valley Historical Review*, XLIX (September, 1962), 231–41, for a discussion of urban lower-class liberalism during the progressive era.

[48] Borah sent $5 for tickets to a benefit football game in Pittsburgh in behalf of striking coal miners and their families; he returned the tickets and asked that they be given to poor people. Borah to Gilchrist

Because of the Idahoan's good relations with labor he represented a potential answer to the split between rural and urban,
western and eastern, divisions within progressivism. This cleavage had long jeopardized unity among reform movements—
William Jennings Bryan's 1896 campaign had failed because
the farm-labor coalition had never materialized; and the progressive movement, from its inception, had confronted the problem. It remained a crucial divisive issue in the 1920's.[49]

Amos Pinchot reflected the eastern prejudice when he
charged that Smith Wildman Brookhart's "pretty shallow opinions" revealed him as "a typical product of the middle west."
On the other hand, Gutzon Borglum expressed western biases.
The sculptor, who served as a chairman of the Nonpartisan
League, asserted that the farmer was "the very backbone of the
nation" and "makes the great political changes of the future."
Whereas Pinchot believed that Brookhart was an unimpressive
Senator, Borglum saw the Iowan as representing "the unknown,
unmeasured frontier that nature has provided since drunken,
power-glutted Rome needed revolt in her far-flung provinces to
keep her clean." "The East has had its innings," Borglum declared happily; "the great West—and that means everything
west of Indiana—is crying out loud for a place in the sun." By
1924, Borglum—who had been trying to keep Republicanism
progressive—turned to Coolidge as the man "to defeat the
Socialistic group in the East and win over the farmers in the

---

and Altmeyer, May 8, 1928. He also donated $10 toward support of un-
employed Colorado coal miners. Borah to Frank L. Palmer, March 19,
1928, Borah Papers, Box 287. Mother Jones to Borah, January 22, 1926,
Box 273; clipping in Borah Scrapbooks, Series II, Reel 5. The secretary of
Pocatello, Idaho's central labor union happily reported "that All the boys
that hang out around Labor Headquarters are Borah good and strong.
. . ." Copy of letter from John A. Anderson to C. C. Cavanah, October 14,
1918, Borah Papers, Box 185.

[49] Lawrence W. Levine writes that "it was this widening cultural
chasm rather than fundamental economic and political differences which
prevented the establishment of a common meeting ground between those
desiring reform, [and] helped to produce the progressive stalemate of the
1920's. . . ." *Defender of the Faith,* pp. 294–95.

West." Watching from the Supreme Court, William Howard
Taft decided that farmers and labor unions lacked a common
bond. "Any association between them in politics can not last."
Senator Irvine Lenroot of Wisconsin doubted, similarly, that
the Farmer-Labor combinations in his own state and the Da-
kotas would survive. That there were tremendous difficulties
in keeping the two groups together was all too apparent to
Henry G. Teigan, secretary to Minnesota's Senator Magnus
Johnson and an active organizer for midwestern progressivism;
Teigan sadly concluded that labor was amenable to a coalition
but agrarians were inclined to remain separate.[50]

The need for a reform alliance between worker and farmer
was obvious. As a contributor to *The Searchlight on Congress*
observed, the future of progressivism depended upon unity
among citizens "of both town and country," or upon a leader
who carried what William Hard described as a "wallop in both
hands": strength with wage-earners and farmers. La Follette
seemed to have such "a wallop," but even his 1924 presidential
platform revealed particular concern for agriculture and signaled out the farmers for special attention.[51]

Borah's sympathies were similarly transparent. Although he,
like La Follette, appeared to offer a bridge between rural and
urban factions, it was only superficially strong. The Senator's

[50] Pinchot to Grenville S. MacFarland, March 19, 1923, Pinchot Papers,
Box 45. For Borglum's views on the farmer, see Borglum to Delmer
Eugene Croft, May 22, 1922, Borglum Papers, Box 60; on Brookhart—
Borglum, "Harding's Challenge to Democracy," *Searchlight on Congress*,
VII (November 30, 1922), 8; on the West—Borglum to J. C. Townley,
April 7, 1922, Borglum Papers, Box 60; on Coolidge—Borglum to Mrs.
Harriman, October 8, 1924, Box 61. Taft to Earl Birkenhead, December
23, 1922, Taft Papers, Box 530; Lenroot to Mrs. Medill McCormick,
August 29, 1923, Irvine Lenroot Papers (Library of Congress), Box 3;
Teigan to Grant Lines, October 16, 1923, Teigan Papers, Box 4.
[51] Charles A. Lyman, "Farmers and the Progressive Movement," *Search-
light on Congress*, VII (June 1, 1923), 9–10; William Hard to La Follette,
June 30, 1920, La Follette Family Papers, Series B, Box 85. On the
agrarian leanings of La Follette's 1924 platform, see Kenneth C. MacKay,
The Progressive Movement of 1924 (New York, 1947), p. 145.

biases were always basically agrarian and western in nature. Along with other Senate progressives such as George Norris, he agonized over the growth of cities and idealized the family farm. "We can not," Borah told his colleagues, "give up the home out yonder on the farm." At stake in "that fatal trek from the open lanes of the country to the congested centers of the city" were questions involving the "home, family, [and] national wealth." With genuine fervor he pointed to the "profound truth" in the motto "The farm, best home of the family, main source of national wealth, foundation of civilized society, natural providence." Cities and industrial strife were not a comfortable environment for a man who detested "crawl[ing] into the big apartment houses from the sidewalks" and who asserted that only his frequent rides in the solitude of Rock Creek Park sustained his Washington existence. "A man who is used to spaces of the West" could never completely adjust to the complexities of an urban, industrial world. "It somehow seems to cramp one's thinking." [52]

At heart Borah always remained a spokesman for the older, village America. He was among those progressives who were uncomfortable about much of "normalcy," who recognized some of the political and economic injustices of that decade, who objected to the plight of agriculture and labor. But he was temperamentally and ideologically equipped to battle only on the fringes of the business culture. Ultimately, just as men such as William Allen White, Smith W. Brookhart, and Raymond Robins, he came to terms with it more often than not. The description that one liberal journalist applied to Hiram Johnson

[52] On Norris's agrarianism and anti-urban feelings, see Norman L. Zucker, *George W. Norris, Gentle Knight of American Democracy* (Urbana, Ill., 1966), pp. 79, 81–82, 92–93. On Borah's, see *Congressional Record*, 71st Cong., 1st Sess. (1929), LXXI, 3651, 3653, and Helen F. McMillin, "Senator William E. Borah, An Interview," *The Granite Monthly* (June, 1923), clipping in Borah Papers, Box 232. "Without Rock Creek Park, Washington to my mind would be uninhabitable," he wrote Rev. James H. Taylor, December 13, 1923, Box 255.

also fit Borah: "radical in his fingers, never in his heart; radical on the circumference of things, never in the centre." [53]

[53] John W. Owens, "Hiram Johnson at Large Again," *The New Republic,* XXVI (May 25, 1921), 379.

Nationalism and Anti-Imperialism: Borah and Foreign Policy

❧

WHEN Borah turned his attention to foreign affairs, his Jeffersonian perspectives were just as apparent as when he discussed the necessities of limited government and civil liberties, the moral virtues of agrarian life, and the dangers of monopolies and cities. "The older I grow," he wrote in late 1922, "the more I become a strong Nationalist." He was certain that international affairs demanded American leadership, but such leadership was to come through "a creed of international honor, morality, decency and justice," not through foreign entanglements or alliances.[1]

Borah's approach to foreign policy was for the most part in step with the other Senate progressives who opposed great power in the central government. Norris, La Follette, Burton K. Wheeler, Hiram Johnson, Shipstead, Brookhart, Blaine, Edwin Ladd, and Gerald Nye of North Dakota were prime examples in the Twenties of progressives who feared an aggressive foreign policy both as a threat to local democracy and as the means by which America would be sucked into European-style militarism and imperialism. Unlike a Theodore Roosevelt—who was concerned primarily with national power and who saw reform as a necessary means to prepare the nation for its international role —the Senate progressives were interested mainly in domestic reform. Ultimately, however, they tended to see a kind of con-

---

[1] Borah to Lyman Abbott, November 25, 1922, Borah Papers, Box 214. On Jefferson's approach to foreign affairs, see, for example, Gilbert Chinard, *Thomas Jefferson, The Apostle of Americanism* (Boston, Mass., 1929), esp. pp. ix–xi, 194–214, 484–88.

spiracy at work by which American industrial combinations
were responsible not only for increasing corruption at home but
also for interventionist policies aimed at protecting American
interests abroad. Once the Senate progressives identified industrial monopoly and gunboat diplomacy with what La Follette
described as "financial imperialism," they emerged as outspoken
critics of American foreign policy.[2]

Among them, Borah was eloquent and powerful. As chairman
of the Senate Foreign Relations Committee from late 1924 to
1933, he was so formidable that no President or Secretary of
State could ignore him on foreign policy matters. His ringing,
patriotic speeches made him one of the most familiar figures in
American diplomatic history. And as one of the most vocal
spokesman for those reformers—largely Jeffersonian and agrarian in persuasion—who were essentially anti-imperialistic, he
added to his stature as a progressive leader.[3]

Although Borah never ceased to celebrate the virtues of the
American republic and its special place in the world, he often
balanced his ardent patriotism with sympathetic insights into
the problems of other countries. In his denunciations of American intervention in Latin America, he was astutely aware of
those nationalistic forces that were steadily remolding inter-

[2] John Milton Cooper, Jr., "Progressivism and American Foreign Policy: A Reconsideration," *Mid-America*, 51 (October, 1969), 260–77, shows
how attitudes toward political power influenced the positions which
progressives took in foreign affairs. Padraic C. Kennedy, "La Follette's
Foreign Policy: From Imperialism to Anti-Imperialism," *Wisconsin Magazine of History*, XLVI (Summer, 1963), 287–93, traces the Senator's growing conviction that the trusts were shaping foreign policy to benefit their
"special interests." For other discussion of the conspiracy idea in the attitudes of some progressives toward foreign policy, see Thomas G. Pater-
son, "California Progressives and Foreign Policy," *California Historical
Society Quarterly*, 47 (December, 1968), 333–34.

[3] There are numerous references to Borah's powerful influence on
American foreign policy. Senator Frank Church relates the story of how
one European agency during the Hoover administration cabled its Washington representative: "Never mind Hoover statement, rush comment
from Borah." In Church's estimation, since 1940 no Senator "has exerted
so much influence over the course of our foreign policy." Church, "Borah
the Statesman," *Idaho Yesterdays*, IX (Summer, 1965), 2–9.

national affairs along lines of rich versus poor nations. Throughout the New Era when he repeatedly urged the recognition of Soviet Russia, he pointed to a potential German-Russian power bloc injurious to world peace. Moreover, he very much recognized the dangers of economic imperialism, even though his own faith in the benefits of America's economic expansion remained vulnerable to the very interventionism he opposed.

Underlying all his observations on foreign policy was, nonetheless, a throbbing Americanism, a patriotic faith that bordered on chauvinism. His emotions bubbled over when he discussed the Founding Fathers or the American Revolution. Enroute to Idaho on the train in 1919, for example, he talked with a young soldier who described how three of his comrades had engaged in fights with Englishmen over the subject of the American rebellion. "I told him," Borah wrote, "if he could get the names of the three boys I would introduce a bill in Congress giving them a medal." [4]

In his opinion, the English had for years made "suckers" out of Americans, and he wished "to God that we might see the end of this truculent subserviency." When one teacher expressed an interest in writing an American-English history, Borah suggested that he write instead only about America. The Senator expressed disgust for historians who stressed Anglo-American unity, who spoke softly about the English injustices toward the colonies, and who contended that American revolutionary leaders had sometimes rashly kindled passions in order to advance personal ambitions. "The mental anemics who indulge in that sickly interpretation of our history" only feebly understood "the vision which guided the Fathers." The revolutionary leaders, too noble to seek the thrones that could have been theirs, had uncompromisingly sought freedom and democracy. Borah feared that in time "some sycophantic intellectual interloper" would defend Benedict Arnold. It was essential to have an American history which repeated again and again the heroic revolutionary struggles, "calling attention perhaps to

[4] Borah to Frank Wyman, March 11, 1919, Borah Papers, Box 214.

the men who tramped the snow at Valley Forge with their bloody feet or Washington kneeling to the God of battle." Borah claimed to have more respect for those people who openly advocated overthrow of the American government than for "those who would subtly undermine the pride and devotion of the American youth" by distorting "the real facts touching our colonial life, revolutionary struggles, and the great events which have led to our present dominance in civilization." "I want," he pleaded, "a truly American history—one which will . . . give us an American mind, an American purpose and American ideals." [5]

Angrily, Borah rebuked "those who grope among the archives of the Revolution to find some excess of statement, something which they call sentimental, by which they mean an American feeling." One reason for his opposition to the Soldier's Bonus bill in the Twenties was because it "reduced the service of the American soldier serving in the cause of human liberty below the level of the unskilled workman earning his daily bread." What America needed, he argued, was a genuine movement to rescue the principles of that nationalism which had built the country and set an example for the world. [6]

Borah's Americanism provided the central thrust to his opinions on foreign policy. He lashed out at "this weakening, simpering, sentimental internationalism which would destroy national character and undermine nationalism." There were those people, he warned, who would turn from the advice of Washington and Jefferson and toward "international domination and control." Quoting from Washington, "the most massive figure in the political history of the world," he called for Americans to adhere to the policies of the Founding Fathers. This meant that the nation must shun all political entanglements with foreign powers. "The United States has never had a policy of isolation.

[5] Borah to P. B. Arnell, April 3, 1922, Borah Papers, Box 214.
[6] Borah statements, undated office copy, Borah Papers, Box 259, on unpatriotic researchers, and undated office copy, Box 234, on the bonus bill; Borah to Arthur Vandenberg, April 20, 1925, Box 256, on the need for nationalistic principles.

We have always, however, enjoyed freedom of action, freedom of policy and I trust God it may be ever thus." [7]

Not all the Senate progressives shared Borah's chauvinistic leanings; indeed, on issues of preparedness or in the use of nationalistic rhetoric, it sometimes seemed that they were deeply divided. Actually, however, the rhetoric surrounding issues such as military preparedness overemphasized differences and obscured agreement among them on certain fundamentals of foreign policy. The western insurgents sometimes parted on specific policies, but it was their shared beliefs that were more important. They generally opposed interventionism; they feared the baneful influence of big business, armament manufacturers, and other special interests in policymaking; they called for an end to secret diplomacy, wartime profits, and annexation of foreign territory; they were suspicious of foreign investors and a military caste; they believed that America must avoid the corrupting influence of the traditional balance-of-power and imperialistic diplomacy; and they advocated that America influence the world through moral suasion alone.[8]

[7] Borah to Millard H. Pryor, May 21, 1925, Borah Papers, Box 255; copy of Borah's Chicago speech, February 22, 1926, Box 272; Borah to Mr. Ashmun, January 27, 1925, Box 252.

[8] For an excellent outline of the views that most of the Senate progressives held, read the speeches of La Follette in Cincinnati and St. Louis on October 11 and 15, 1924. Copies in La Follette Family Papers, Series B, Box 205. On the differences of opinion among them, particularly in regard to the issues of World War I, see Howard W. Allen, "Republican Reformers and Foreign Policy, 1913–1917," *Mid-America*, 44 (October, 1962), 222–29; Warren A. Sutton, "Progressive Republican Senators and the Submarine Crisis, 1915–1916," *ibid.*, 47 (April, 1965), 75–88, and "Republican Progressive Senators and Preparedness, 1915–1916," *ibid.*, 52 (July, 1970), 155–76. Walter I. Trattner, "Progressivism and World War I: A Re-appraisal," *ibid.*, 44 (July, 1962), 131–45, also finds no progressive agreement on the war, but suggests that the pros and cons on the war may actually have had little to do with progressivism itself. Barton J. Bernstein and Franklin A. Leib, "Progressive Republican Senators and American Imperialism, 1898–1916: A Reappraisal," *ibid.*, 50 (July, 1968), esp. 187–205, concede that the insurgents split on important issues, but argue that these disagreements did not reflect opposing views on imperialism. For the most part the Senators agreed that America must not "be a

Although the progressive Senators had supported—or at least acquiesced in—the turn-of-the-century expansionism and Big Stick activities of Theodore Roosevelt, they had generally done so less because of personal commitments than party loyalty, allegiance to Roosevelt, and an indifference to international issues. Following the Republican split during the Taft administration, they voiced a growing anger over America's interference in Latin-American problems and quickly became leading opponents of Taft's "Dollar Diplomacy." Subsequent divisions among them over questions of preparedness and World War I pointed to differences that were more apparent than real. Even the staunchest progressive advocates of preparedness—and Borah was among them—never envisioned the kind of preparations that proved necessary before the war ended. Had they foreseen the extent of such military development, they undoubtedly would have been less enthusiastic in their support of preparedness—indeed, they probably would have opposed such programs.[9]

When Borah warned against the European system of militarism and American interventionism abroad, he spoke with

policeman always on call and certainly not an avaricious guardian pursuing self-aggrandizement."

[9] Bernstein and Leib, "Progressive Republican Senators and American Imperialism," pp. 168–205, analyze the shift of progressives such as La Follette and Borah from support of Philippine expansionism to opposition to Wilsonian interventionism. Padraic C. Kennedy charts the transition in La Follette's thinking in "La Follette's Imperialist Flirtation," *Pacific Historical Review*, XXIX (May, 1960), 131–44, and "La Follette's Foreign Policy: From Imperialism to Anti-Imperialism." See, also, Cooper, "Progressivism and American Foreign Policy," pp. 267–70. Cooper suggests that Borah's support of territorial expansion in the late 1800's provided a possible bridge back into the party following his bolt to the Silver Republicans. Sutton, "Republican Progressive Senators and Preparedness, 1915–1916," shows the different camps into which progressives divided but concludes, p. 176, that "no progressive Republican would have supported the tremendous expansion in the army and navy necessary if America really was to be prepared in case it became involved in World War I."

the support of the other Senate progressives. Constantly he pledged his opposition both to compulsory military training at home and "to any political associations with Europe based on military force." America must assume its world obligation only "as a great moral force, disentangled." His search for a policy that would be noninterventionist, antimilitaristic, subject to public opinion, open to America's moral example, and inherently peaceful, ultimately led him in the 1920's to support the movement to outlaw war. Then, as before and after, he was convinced that "we have a great service to perform, but we must perform it independently." [10]

Borah's fear of threats to the sovereignty of the United States was never more evident than when he vehemently opposed ratification of the Versailles Treaty and its League of Nations. In Borah's eyes the League was more, however, than a terrible "conspiracy to barter the independence of the American Republic." It was also a weapon of imperialism. Although he credited Wilson with "a splendid effort" to offset the spirit of war and vengeance that had dominated the Paris conference, he was convinced that greed and vindictiveness had prevailed, resulting in "a cruel, destructive, brutal document." It had produced "a league to guarantee the integrity of the British empire," rather than an agency to represent the countries of the world. "The League scheme as it was formulated at Versailles was the faith of Prussianism"—a horrendous attempt to place all peoples under the military control of a few countries. La Follette, Norris, Hiram Johnson, and North Dakota's Asle

[10] For a few of many examples of Borah's hostility to militarism, see Borah to John B. Mannerstam, March 7, 1922, Borah Papers, Box 218, and copy of Borah's February 22, 1926, Chicago speech, Box 272; on his opposition to military training at home, Borah to A. L. Lloyd, March 9, 1920, Box 198; on avoiding military alignments with Europe, Borah to Rev. Willsie Martin, February 17, 1921, Box 202; on America's moral role abroad, Borah to Lyman Abbott, November 5, 1922, Box 214, and to Mr. Ashmun, January 27, 1925, Box 252. On Borah and the Outlawry of War movement, see Chapter 6 and the epilogue.

Gronna, along with such liberal journals as *The New Republic* and *The Nation,* expressed similar worries that the League would be the means to guarantee an unjust peace, and to allow the large Allied powers to dominate smaller nations.[11]

During the Twenties, this same antipathy toward meddling in other countries' affairs continued to inspire much of the progressive opposition to American foreign policy, particularly as it applied to Latin America. Borah was one of the most frequent dissenters against a Republicanized version of Wilson's Caribbean policies. He was in touch with a leading citizens' group aimed at halting interference in Latin-American affairs, offered his own vigorous protests in the Senate and in local rallies, and tried to formulate what he felt was a sensible relationship with Latin America. His key theme was that the United States should allow nations to solve their own problems without external meddling. By assailing the Harding administration's position in the Caribbean, he provided a much-needed lift to those critics of American policy who viewed the situation as "relatively hopeless" unless they could get at least "a few in-

[11] Borah to Frank Wyman, July 22, 1919, Borah Papers, Box 196; to Gutzon Borglum, December 22, 1928, Box 299; to Frank Wyman, March 11, 1919, Box 196; to Rev. Doremus Scudder, March 18, 1921, Box 203; and to Frank S. Dunshee, June 22, 1921, Box 211. The Senate fight over the Treaty was not, of course, a progressive–Old Guard battle. The situation was far more complex with some leading conservative Senators joining the irreconcilable group. Ralph Stone, *The Irreconcilables: The Fight Against the League of Nations* (Lexington, Ky., 1969), carefully distinguishes between the various factions among the irreconcilables. For Hiram Johnson's assessment of the Treaty as the product of "the same old game of grab and gouge" and of the League as an instrument by which American troops would be used to "set up the kind of Government we wish in the world, and eliminate, where necessary, the kind of Government the various people wish for themselves," see Johnson to Hiram Jr., May 31, 1919, and December 7, 1918, Johnson Papers, Part IV, Box 1. For discussions of the liberal opposition to the League, see Selig Adler, *The Isolationist Impulse, Its Twentieth Century Reaction* (paperback ed., New York, 1961), pp. 51–52, 55–72; Forcey, *The Crossroads of Liberalism,* pp. 286–91; Arno Mayer, *Politics and Diplomacy of Peace Making, 1918–1919* (New York, 1967), pp. 773, 882–83.

fluential Senators" to take issue with the State Department and the President.[12]

American involvement in Haiti was especially disturbing to Borah. In 1915 marines had intervened there, supposedly to protect law and order. The United States had then brought pressure on behalf of a new Haitian constitution which, unlike its predecessor, allowed foreigners to own and acquire land. Looking askance upon such events, Borah assured the Haiti–Santo Domingo Independence Society that he was devoting all his spare moments to studying the situation. When members of the group stopped in Washington, they found him a sympathetic listener. After Harding had refused to see them and Secretary Hughes had rebuked them for lacking objectivity, they retreated to the friendly confines of Borah's office. The Senator "flatly and categorically" agreed that U.S. marines had no business in the Caribbean.[13] He kept contact with the society regarding the status of loans to Haiti and the Dominican Republic. In Carnegie Hall on May 1, 1922, he spoke under the auspices of the society and denounced America's imperialistic policies in Latin America. Borah himself was excited at the prospects of the Carnegie meeting and, prior to the rally, he urged one correspondent to "pass the word around. This is one feature of the cause in which we are engaged." James Weldon Johnson, vice-chairman of the society, called Borah's Carnegie performance "a tremendous success," signaling "a new advance in the Haitian matter." Ernest Gruening, a member of the ad-

[12] Ernest Angell to Moorfield Storey, December 30, 1921, Moorfield Storey Papers (Library of Congress), Box 4. Henry W. Berger writes, "Borah's Latin American formula was based on laissez-faire: *let them alone.*" "Laissez-Faire for Latin America: Borah Defines the Monroe Doctrine," *Idaho Yesterdays,* IX (Summer, 1965), 17.

[13] Ernest Gruening to Villard, May 5, 1922, Villard Papers, Folder 1424. The society was an American group whose officers and advisory council included such prominent individuals as Moorfield Storey, James Weldon Johnson, Lewis S. Gannett, Felix Adler, Ernest Angell, Judge Ben B. Lindsey, Robert Morss Lovett, Oswald Garrison Villard, and Ernest Gruening.

visory council, was certain that this "most rousing meeting of
the kind in years" had attracted "tremendous publicity and
. . . lifted the question from the realm of obscurity where it
was before." [14]

To Borah, American actions in Haiti and Santo Domingo
were "not a whit better" than the Turkish treatment of Christians in Asia Minor. Indeed, there was even less excuse for what
the United States was doing, since Americans "knew better."
If Americans found it easy to defend their activities in Haiti,
it was only because such maneuvers "seem so intolerable that
people will hardly believe we have been guilty of them." [15]

On June 19, 1922, Borah told the Senate that intervention in
Haiti was absolutely deplorable. His speech offered a sharp
contrast to sensational newspaper accounts currently describing
the voodoo rites and human sacrifices "of the Horror-Ridden
Disciples of Jungle Gods in the Black Republic of Haiti." For
one thing, he denied that the dispatch of the marines in 1915
had been necessary to preserve law and order: "We were there
for a more permanent and abiding reason," including the confiscation of 200,000 acres. "We go to Haiti ostensibly to restore
law and order," he said bitterly. "We immediately begin the
wrecking of their form of government." For 111 years, Haiti had
stood on her own. Now the United States seemed determined
to destroy her. When one Senator attempted to justify American policy by stressing the high illiteracy rate in Haiti, Borah
scoffed. He reminded his colleagues that the United States had
some work of its own to do along these lines and pointed, as an
example, to "one big city [where] 90,000 remained out of school

[14] On Borah's Carnegie Hall speech, see Borah to John D. Moore,
April 24, 1922, Borah Papers, Box 214; James Weldon Johnson to Moorfield Storey, May 2, 1922, Storey Papers, Box 4; Gruening to Oswald Garrison Villard, May 5, 1922, Villard Papers, Folder 1424; *The New York
Times*, May 2, 1922. Regarding his other contacts with the society, see
telegram from Borah to Moorfield Storey, April 8, 1922; telegram from
Judson King to Storey, April 10, 1922; Ernest Angell to Storey, April 10,
1922, Storey Papers, Box 4.
[15] Borah to Wade H. Cooper, May 10, 1922, Borah Papers, Box 218,
and to Gruening, July 3, 1922, Box 216.

last winter because they could not have the clothes necessary to enable them to go to school." He wondered, moreover, how people could learn self-government if they were under a military dictatorship. Although he granted that American troops could not withdraw precipitously, he urged "restoring civil government and giving those people civil government until we can decently get out of that island. . . ." Borah did most of the talking in defense of Senator William H. King's proposed amendment that no funds from the naval appropriation bill go toward sustaining American troops in the Caribbean after December 31, 1922. The amendment failed, but the nine votes for it amounted essentially to a western progressive protest against adventurism.[16]

In the early Twenties, while Borah urged the removal of American troops from Caribbean countries, he also "set the whole world talking disarmament." [17] On December 14, 1920, he introduced a resolution in the Senate asking the President to invite Great Britain and Japan to a conference to discuss the reduction of naval building programs. His resolution was undoubtedly in part a response to the League of Nations' decision a few months earlier to consider the question of arms limitation. Unless the opponents of the League took the initiative, there was a danger that former skeptics might see the organization as an agency for peace, thereby increasing the threat of American entry into it through "the back door." Borah may very well have doubted that a naval conference would convene, or that Great Britain and Japan would ever accept naval reductions. His purpose was surely in part tactical, aimed at presenting an alternative to the League and at exposing British and Japanese

[16] A good example of the sensationalism in the press appeared in the Boston *Herald,* May 14, 1922; under the six-column, four-deck headline, was a story about a girl, rescued by marines, who assisted in human sacrifices upon the Devil Stone. *Congressional Record,* 67th Cong., 2nd Sess., LXII, 1922, 9715–50. Western Senators of progressive persuasion supplied most of the nine votes for the proposal: Borah, Hiram Johnson, Edwin Ladd, La Follette, Norris, and the Montana Democrat, Thomas Walsh.

[17] *Springfield Republican* (Massachusetts), November 19, 1921, Borah Scrapbooks, Reel 4.

opposition to disarmament.[18] But Borah undoubtedly also favored naval reduction as a way of reducing taxes and expenditures.[19]

Harding was unhappy with such attempts in Congress to pressure him, but the truth was that Borah had masterfully struck a major chord of public opinion. His disarmament suggestions appealed strongly to the traditional American distrust of military establishments, the desire for peace, and the perennial concern for lower taxes. In the decade following World War I the word "peace" was prominent in the national rhetoric, and innumerable peace organizations sprang up across the country. Actor-singer Al Jolson reflected the fervor for peace when he proposed to "start the song of peace thinly coated with ragtime, a-echoing through the land." "Take away the gun/ From ev-ry mother's son," Jolson pleaded in his refrain. "We're taught by God above/ To Forgive, forget and love,/ The weary world is waiting for,/ Peace forevermore,/ So take away the gun/ From ev'ry mother's son,/ And put an end to war." [20]

[18] Robert Maddox makes a persuasive case for the tactical objectives of Borah's disarmament proposals. "Borah and the Battleships," *Idaho Yesterdays*, IX (Summer, 1965), 20–27.

[19] Borah also fused his concerns over high taxes and armaments when he opposed cancellation of debts which Europe had accrued in America during the war. He believed that Europe could pay at least the interest rate if it were not channeling its money into armaments and pursuing imperialistic ends. "Every dollar we deduct from this legitimate claim will feed the militaristic maw of that country," he wrote regarding the French debt. Borah to James Davidson, October 1, 1925, Borah Papers, Box 251. It was even more unforgiveable to have such outstanding debts "while in the meantime the business man is harassed and the American farmer is being sold out for taxes." Borah to Charles Edward Ertz, January 17, 1923, Box 227. Borah agreed with William Jennings Bryan, who wrote that "the debt is *worthless* and will never be paid . . . we can use a *worthless* debt to buy a *priceless* peace secured through disarmament with the understanding that upon satisfactory disarmament the interest and all payments will be suspended and the debt cancelled." Borah replied, "If I were a part of the Executive department and dealing with this subject I think I should accept your view." Bryan to Borah, August 5, 1922, and Borah reply, August 8, 1922, Box 214. See also Borah to Bruce Bliven, September 2, 1926, Box 269.

[20] See, for example, Gus Karger to Taft, May 9 and 14, 1921, Taft

The administration may have favored a disarmament policy from the beginning, but it was plainly Borah who had captured the public's imagination. Tremendous popular enthusiasm for the Senator's proposals forced the administration's hand.[21] But, when the administration acted, it did so in a way that was unsatisfactory to him. Secretary of State Hughes, worried about Japanese expansion in the Far East, issued a call to nine nations for a conference to discuss the Far Eastern question as well as disarmament. Immediately Borah demurred. He opposed increasing the number of nations because of the added confusion that would probably result and because it would be difficult to assign blame for any failures in the conference. Moreover, he worried that the discussions about the Far East would divert attention from the central issue of disarmament. The conference would probably fall under "the old system of diplomats, to wit, to settle everything before you talk about disarmament. I am in favor of disarmament and then adjust these questions afterwards in the court of reason and conscience."[22]

The results of the conference, held in Washington from November, 1921, until February, 1922, seemed to fulfill his prophecy. He did accept as an appropriate step toward disarmament the Naval Limitation Treaty, by which the United States and four other major powers accepted a ten-year naval holiday and established a ratio of capital ships. He also voted for the Nine-Power Treaty, which pledged the signatories to respect the

---

Papers, Box 487, on Harding's irritation. Robert H. Ferrell, "The Peace Movement," *Isolation and Security*, ed. Alexander DeConde (Durham, N.C., 1957), pp. 82–83, and Ferrell, *Peace in Their Time: The Origins of the Kellogg-Briand Pact* (New Haven, Conn., 1952), pp. 11–14, discusses the appeal of the peace issue during the 20's. Al Jolson to Harding, December 2, 1921, Harding Papers.

[21] Robert E. Osgood, *Ideals and Self-Interest in America's Foreign Relations* (Chicago, 1953), p. 338, says that public support for Borah's resolution "assumed the proportions of a mammoth revival meeting."

[22] Borah had expressed these fears when he first suggested a naval disarmament conference. See Borah to William Jennings Bryan, December 27, 1920, and, also, Borah to Raymond Robins, July 22, 1921, Borah Papers, Box 202.

Open Door in China and to guarantee that nation's independence. Yet he carefully pointed out that problems regarding China's territorial integrity still remained and that support of the agreement in no way amounted to an endorsement of either the previous exploitation of China or the continued possession of expropriated Chinese territory.[23]

Although Borah gave at least minimal approval to these products of the conference, he looked with shocked indignation upon the Four-Power Treaty. The agreement, which abrogated the Anglo-Japanese Alliance of 1902 (under which England had been a silent partner of Japanese imperialism), bound the United States, Great Britain, France, and Japan to respect each other's rights over Pacific island possessions and to discuss any "aggressive action" in the Pacific. Borah sensed that here, hidden beneath the gloss of the conference's other decisions, was the danger which he had long feared: a quagmire of old-world diplomacy which would suck America into militaristic involvements. Although he had regarded the Anglo-Japanese Alliance as an "extremely unfortunate pact, intended to operate against America," he believed that the four-power accord had created an even more grotesque monster. America had joined the guardians of an unjust status quo in the Far East. "This is dynamite —a little more subtle in structure than the Versailles Treaty, but no less destructive." The Washington meetings had been a repetition of the closed door sessions at Versailles. "They have kept the word of promise to the ear and broken it to the heart." The result, in short, was no victory for disarmament. It was a vital triumph for the old world diplomacy. "It is the old system of alliances. . . . We are going in with the imperialistic nations who have been committing the aggressions in the Far East. . . ."

[23] The United States, Great Britain, Japan, France, and Italy agreed to build no new capital ships and, respectively, to adhere to a tonnage ratio of 5–5–3–1.75–1.75. *Congressional Record*, 67th Cong., 2nd Sess., 1922, LXII, 4497, 4704–6, 4718, 4779, 4784. The Senate passed the Naval Limitation Treaty 74 to 1, and the Nine-Power Treaty, 66 to 0.

On March 24, 1922, Borah cast one of the four Republican votes against the treaty.[24]

He had attacked the four-power pact not only as a threat to America's traditional policy of nonentangling alliances, but also as a disguised form of imperialism. This growing sensitivity to the dangers of imperialism resulted in part from his recognition that nationalism was a growing force in underdeveloped and emerging countries. He was aware of the injustices and long-range dangers that imperialism posed in the midst of rising nationalism, and he was alert to ulterior motives that sometimes underlay attempts to transport American ideals to other countries. He wryly observed, for example, that "whenever a dependent people are discovered to be in the possession of vast natural resources . . . immediately some great nation feels a benevolent desire to go in there and lift them up" and improve their system of government. "I do not believe in that doctrine at all. I think each people have in a measure got to work out their own salvation." [25]

It was from this perspective that Borah interpreted the Monroe Doctrine. That doctrine had been necessary, he believed, because Europe threatened American security, not because the United States hoped "to dominate the Western States or dictate their course." Whenever American policy departed from self-protection and interfered with the sovereignty of the Latin-American countries, it was "obvious and mischievous." America

[24] Borah to the Debate Manager of Reed College, May 5, 1921, Borah Papers, Box 204, on the Anglo-Japanese Alliance; to Arthur H. Vandenberg, to H. A. Lawson, December 19, 1921, and to Mrs. Jennie R. Nichols, March 21, 1922, Box 214, on the Four-Power Treaty. Also voting negatively were La Follette, Hiram Johnson, and Henry Ashurst of Arizona. Maddox, "Borah and the Battleships," p. 27, writes that Borah had learned firsthand some of the dangers in such international conferences. "In the years following, he refused to countenance any program, however innocuous on its surface, which he believed might be similarly perverted by advocates of collective security."

[25] Quoted in "Borah's Attitude," *Searchlight on Congress*, VI (February 28, 1922), 11.

had no right "to invade territory, to tear down governments and to set up other governments." As Borah interpreted it, the Monroe Doctrine meant simply that America favored peace, its own territorial integrity, and "the right of the smallest nation in the family of nations." The existence of American troops in countries such as Nicaragua was contrary to the doctrine, since their presence violated the principle of self-government and protected those men who hoped to exploit another nation's peoples. Attacking "the fetish of force in America," Borah argued that the United States should not "assume the role of censor for Central American revolutions," nor declare war against countries whose political ideals and institutions differed from those of America.[26]

He applied the same standards outside the Western Hemisphere. Convinced that extraterritoriality ran counter to the spirit of the times, he called for the abolition of such claims in China as soon as possible. "The exploitation of China, both in the matter of human life and material interests, should cease." Foreign governments and foreign money had prevented China from establishing a stable order: "Even a giant cannot walk if they succeed in tying his feet and he cannot feed himself very well if they cut off his arms." He was pleased "that nationalism has marched into Shanghai," and he hoped that the United States would not "become a Pharisee among the nations. These backward people may stumble and fall, they may make a thousand mistakes, but their ultimate goal is the same goal toward which our forefathers traveled 150 years ago." [27]

[26] Copy of Borah's article sent to Wm. L. Chenery, *Collier's Weekly*, December 26, 1924, Borah Papers, Box 249—it appeared in the January 31, 1925, issue; copy of Borah's statement for the Baltimore *Sun*, December 14, 1922, Box 234; Borah, "The Fetish of Force," *The Forum*, LXXIV (August, 1925), 240–45. See, also, Berger, "Laissez-Faire for Latin America," pp. 10–17.

[27] Borah's statement, released June 16, 1925, Borah Papers, Box 259; Borah to Thomas F. Millard, July 20, 1925, and to Miss Louise Harrison, October 3, 1925, Box 249; to Rush L. Holland, January 9, 1926, Box 263; Borah's speech, March 25, 1927, to National Good Housekeeping Conference in Washington; Washington *Post*, March 26, 1927, Borah Scrapbooks, Reel 2.

The Senator ridiculed the tendency to see bolshevism whenever people sought to throw off foreign domination and establish their own government. Hence, when newspaper accounts inflated the number of American victims in a Shanghai massacre from three to 125, Borah sardonically noted that "of course, the communists were guilty of both of the massacres, the one which didn't take place as well as the one which did." He was convinced that America exaggerated the effects of communism. "Whenever the nationalistic spirit becomes strong and manifests itself in rebellion, they are called 'reds.'" He viewed the bolshevik regime in Russia as only a momentary manifestation of the Russian people's quest for national identity. Although he disapproved of the Lenin government, he thought it foolish not to recognize the de facto administration of such a vast and highly populated country. That the Russians might establish "a political polity which does not conform with our views is no part of our concern. They have a right to establish the kind of government they want." Speaking before an Idaho audience, he contended that the United States should not tell Russia what kind of government to establish. "If the Russians want a soviet government they have the same right to it as we have to our republic." [28]

Throughout the Twenties, Borah was the leading Senate advocate for Russian recognition, tenaciously filing a resolution for such purposes in the first session of every Congress. His appeals for recognition did not focus only on the principle of self-determination. He was certain that recognition directly affected America's strategic and economic interests. Speaking to

[28] Borah to Charles J. Dow, March 31, 1927, Borah Papers, Box 280; to Cong. R. Walton Moore, November 3, 1926, Box 263; to H. H. Freeheim, January 28, 1921, Box 209; *The Idaho Daily Statesman,* October 13, 1922. Borah believed that Russia was undergoing the growth pains of every country that develops a democratic government. Indeed, he was convinced that America's nonrecognition policy had helped to preserve the bolshevik government. "That which has kept Bolshevism alive . . . has been the policy of the Allies toward Russia since the war," he said on one occasion. Borah to W. W. Trumbull, April 14, 1923, Borah Papers, Box 234.

a Boise audience on October 5, 1922, for example, he warned that failure to recognize Soviet Russia raised the specter of a German-Russian alliance and thereby increased the possibilities of a world war. "Russia and Germany," he predicted, "tonight have the most dangerous alliance in Europe. When there is no recognition of all, those not recognized in an alliance [i.e., the four-power alliance] form an alliance of their own." [29]

Borah thought also that Russian recognition was essential to America's economic development. "It is the greatest under-developed market in the world, and it is ours if we have the courage and vision to seize it." No sane people, in his opinion, should ever allow the question of trade to hinge on their likes and dislikes of government. Since the United States had for years traded with the brutal and autocratic tsarist regime in Russia, or with the Turkish dictatorship, or with Great Britain while the English slaughtered the Irish, he could not understand the hesitancy to strike up commercial relations with the soviet government. If America had more "business sense in international affairs," her Russian policy would be different. In 1925, for example, he observed that the Soviets had recently made a cash purchase in excess of $16 million for wheat and flour in Canada. "Why," he wondered, "should not that trade have come here?" [30]

Borah's talk of finding more foreign markets for American wheat showed that his agrarian background and orientation obviously influenced his position on Russian recognition. Indeed, that same agrarian perspective undoubtedly affected many

[29] Peter G. Filene, *Americans and the Soviet Experiment, 1917–1933* (Cambridge, Mass., 1967), p. 192; *The Idaho Daily Statesman,* October 6, 1922. William A. Williams, *The Tragedy of American Diplomacy* (New York, 1962), pp. 120–21, notes that this "keen analysis of the importance of Russia to America's general security" showed that he "was considerably more astute than the supposed realism of most of the critics who dismissed him as an isolationist."

[30] Borah to Rabbi Ferdinand M. Isserman, December 26, 1930, Borah Papers, Box 321; to Marcus Day, December 10, 1920, Box 204; to Ray E. Harris, January 20, 1925, Box 258; to George Dietrich, November 3, 1924, Box 245; and to C. M. Cutting, October 10, 1925, Box 258.

of his attitudes on foreign affairs, including, for example, his opposition to economic imperialism—which was largely urban in its impetus and its rewards—and to big naval expenditures—which were a boon primarily to eastern shipbuilders.[31] Certainly when he distinguished between political embroilments and economic relations with Europe, he resembled the other major spokesmen of a rural society, from Jefferson to William Jennings Bryan. Time and again he stressed that farmers must find markets for their surpluses; [32] in his view, the politics of the nations involved was irrelevant.

The Senator was firmly convinced that America could adhere to such economic objectives while spurning corrupt political entanglements.[33] When he assumed that "the way to dissipate communism is to bring it in practical touch with capitalism," he reflected his faith in the benign influence of American commerce abroad. As he interpreted human nature, "if a man has a chance to accept a system which accentuates his individual holdings, or possessions, or a system in which he owns nothing, and works for everybody, there is no doubt as to which he will accept." Ironically, then, "the best friends that communism has ever had have been the shortsighted, frightened, white-lipped

[31] See Wayne S. Cole, *Senator Gerald P. Nye and American Foreign Relations* (Minneapolis, Minn., 1962), esp. pp. 3–13, for a discussion of the impact of the "needs, desires, and value systems of major segments of the American agricultural society" on isolationist sentiments.

[32] Certainly this desire to expand commerce helped inspire the Senator's call in 1923 for a world economic conference. See, however, Maddox, *William E. Borah and American Foreign Policy,* pp. 120–35, who views the Senator's proposal for such an international conference as mainly a reflection of his fears that America might join the League, and as an effort to emerge as a constructive statesman. Although his strategy failed to pressure the administration into action, he received much publicity as the "new" Borah.

[33] William Hard noted that Borah "goes off watch as soon as the State Department says that its purpose in Europe is economic only." Since "he seems to divide life into the political compartment and the economic compartment and does not seem to see that there is only a gauze partition between the two," Borah apparently thought "that one can plunge into Europe's economics without getting politically drowned." Hard to Hiram Johnson, November 2, 1923, Johnson Papers, Part III, Box 42.

capitalists with-holding all contact." He had no doubt that, if
the United States helped to establish trade and improve economic conditions, it would help "end hunger, misery and bolshevism." As he told one audience, "Give the people of Russia
the sunlight of prosperity and Bolshevism will disappear." The
restoration of good American relations with Russia would be
both sound business and humane practice. Essentially it would
allow the United States to exercise "the proper influence with
reference to some of the most vital world movements at this
time." He cited his own deep interest "in ridding the world of
bolshevism and that unsoundness and discontent which breeds
bolshevism. But we can only do it by getting in touch with
this great people and exercising our influence along a right
line. . . ." [34]

Such a faith in the potential of American trade as an influence on the internal developments of other countries obviously
carried seeds of that very interventionism he so much opposed.
Indeed, he clearly shared the major assumptions that had provided an important impetus for American expansion since the
Civil War—assumptions that external markets were necessary
to the national economy and that America's quest for such
markets would have a healthy effect on world events.[35] There
were inescapable dilemmas involved in Borah's attempt to
square the concept of self-determination with his hopes of using America's economic enticements to exercise "our influence
along a right line." He was, however, undoubtedly aware of
such dilemmas. And, since he perceived the dangers of an economic imperialism, he alerted himself to any American involvement that came at the expense of another nation's sovereignty.

[34] Borah to Walter Lippmann, July 26, 1929, Borah Papers, Box 304;
to Samuel Gompers, January 31, 1924, Box 245; *The Idaho Daily Statesman*, September 30, 1924; Borah to Ronald Wood, February 13, 1926,
Borah Papers, Box 271; Borah to Will Hays, October 30, 1925, Box 258.
[35] See Walter LaFeber, *The New Empire: An Interpretation of American Expansion, 1860–1898* (Ithaca, N.Y., 1963), regarding the shifting
themes in American expansionism from land hunger to a quest for industrial markets.

Borah's effort to serve as a watchdog on the Potomac to ensure that American influence did not contravene self-determination was a formidable undertaking. But, whatever the difficulties of his task, he brought a number of insights to it. In a world of nationalistic upheavals, he emphasized that Americans must expect change; that such changes, although perhaps alien to American sympathies and traditions, represented an understandable attempt of other peoples to come to grips with their own problems; that such peoples should have the opportunity to work out their own future without external interference; and that a wise American policy should rely upon example, rather than the gunboat.

The Senator, moreover, despite his own beliefs in Anglo-Saxon superiority, rejected arguments that interventionism was necessary to show allegedly inferior peoples how to run their countries. He felt that the Chinese could not at once establish "a democratic form of government in accordance with the standard of the 'best English-speaking people,'" but he asserted that they were moving in the right direction. Under no pretense, then, should the United States or anyone else try to inhibit Chinese development of their own affairs. Nor did he think that Americans needed to train the Haitians in self-government: "I think they are capable now, and so do they." For those such as ex-Kaiser Wilhelm who warned of the peril of the yellow race, Borah countered that "the peril to the white race . . . is not the yellow or the brown race, but the oppressive and imperialistic attitude of the white race towards these races." [36]

Although Borah thus spoke tolerantly of revolutionary world movements and of other nations' attempts to govern themselves, he never stopped thinking of the uniqueness and separateness

[36] See Chapter 9 for a more extensive discussion of Borah's views on race. On letting the Chinese settle their own affairs, see Borah to Bishop Philip M. Rhinelander, March 26, 1927, and to Rev. Harry F. Ward, April 1, 1927, Borah Papers, Box 275; on Haiti, *Congressional Record,* 67th Cong., 2nd Sess., LII, 1922, 9739; on white imperialism, Borah statement, October 19, 1925, Borah Papers, Box 259.

of the United States. He could appreciate the efforts and problems of other countries, but he continued to look upon Benedict Arnold as "the most worthy exemplar I know of for those
who feel America alone is not quite sufficient—that we must be
broader and more pliable—not so pronounced in our Americanism." [37]

It was this attitude that fitted so well with those "narrow
nationalistic tendencies" that one observer found in "most members of the progressive group." [38] There was no one progressive
position on foreign policy, but Borah unquestionably articulated an important aspect of reform thought in regard to America's international posture. *The Searchlight on Congress* was
not alone in pointing to his views on foreign affairs when describing "Borah's progressive character." [39] Moreover, his reputation as a leading commentator on America's foreign policy
fused with his activities as a political guerrilla during the Harding administration to make him even more attractive to reform
groups. By late 1922 a number of progressives were trying to
push Borah to the front of their ranks.

[37] Borah to P. B. Arnell, April 3, 1922, Borah Papers, Box 214.
[38] William S. Culbertson to William Allen White, December 18, 1922,
Culbertson Papers, Box 47. Culbertson, who had recently participated in
the progressive conferences in Washington, was commenting on those
gatherings.
[39] Lynn Haines, "The Official Facts About Senator Lodge," *Searchlight
on Congress,* VII (August 31, 1922), 13. *The Nation,* for example, CXXIV
(January 5, 1927), 4, placed Borah on its "Honor Roll for 1926" because
of "his old-fashioned honesty in denouncing the policy of force by all
the Powers in China and by the United States in Mexico and Nicaragua."

V

The Missing Moses

❧

ALTHOUGH the 1922 elections suggested that progressivism was again becoming a major factor in American politics, the actual strength and future of that resurgence remained open to question. The recent electoral triumphs notwithstanding, George Record concluded in early 1923 that "the Progressive movement in this country is in a most discouraging state." Such a gloomy assessment sprang from Record's concern about leadership and a national program, without which progressives would "continue to wander in the political wilderness for an indefinite time." If no reform-minded leader crystalized public sentiment around a major platform, the 1922 elections would resemble "the Populist eruption of a generation ago," and would be a mere prelude to another era of political reaction. Record was not the only reformer to cast his eyes anxiously about for the leadership so essential to the progressive movement.[1]

The Nation believed that it had found the answer in Borah. As early as the summer of 1922, the journal declared that America was ready for political change and that if Borah would "cut loose from the body of death which is the Republican party and would henceforth lead a new party, people would acclaim him as a Moses. . . ." For a few months, the Idaho Senator seemed

[1] Record to La Follette, March 26, 1923, copy in Pinchot Papers, Box 45. Actually the progressives may very well have read too much into the 1922 elections. Robert Murray, *The Harding Era,* esp. pp. 316, 320-21, 506, doubts that the results indicated either a swing to progressivism or a repudiation of the Harding administration. If the elections could have taken place six months later, after the return of more prosperous times, the results probably would have been quite different.

receptive to such a calling; but, when it was time officially to act, he changed his mind. The liberal Committee of 48 discovered firsthand what an unreliable general Borah could be. After encouraging the Forty-Eighters, promising his personal support on the front lines, allowing them to waste time and much-needed money in preparation for a presidential campaign in his behalf, he deserted them. In doing so, he attested to *The Outlook*'s assertion that he, more than any other Senator, disappointed people because "when his every previous step indicated that he would be there, he was not there." As journalist Claude Bowers recalled, Borah "would gallantly march up to the enemy's guns and seem about to take them by storm, and then, mystifyingly, he would wheel around and march back again." [2]

Borah's vacillations could only confuse progressives who, in the Twenties, needed to determine the best means by which they could channel their commitments into an effective political force. Men such as William Allen White looked to the G.O.P. as the vehicle for reform; others, such as Chicago professor William E. Dodd, put their faith in the Democracy. Amos Pinchot, Oswald Garrison Villard, and the Forty-Eighters were among those who turned to a third party. Through late 1922 and early 1923, Borah's course was not clear. His public and private comments were often contradictory. At one moment his outspoken criticism of the G.O.P. encouraged independent movements; yet at crucial times he helped to cut the ground from beneath a potential third party. On occasion he seemed enthusiastic about the growth and objectives of splinter organizations; at other times, it appeared that he was simply exploiting them. His performance in these critical months revealed some of the difficulties in rejecting interest-based politics in favor of "the cause" or the general good. Borah might have found some assurances

2 "The Duty to Revolt," *The Nation*, CXV (August 9, 1922), 140; Merritt Dixon, "Four Senators," *The Outlook*, CXLVII (December 28, 1927), 531; Claude G. Bowers, *My Life: The Memoirs of Claude Bowers* (New York, 1962), p. 73.

in William Jennings Bryan's view that "that which is right is always expedient"; but, by the end of 1923, the Committee of 48 was unquestionably less convinced that what was expedient for Borah's own political self-interest was necessarily what was best for progressivism.[3]

Since the Senator was basically a proponent of working within Republican ranks,[4] and was also fully aware of the political risks in bolting, he probably intended to use third-party talk as nothing more than a threat by which to bluff G.O.P. regulars into taking a more liberal stance. But, in using independent groups simply as pawns in his political game, he circumscribed their chances of success. *The New Republic* warned him, as well as other Senate progressives, of the dangers in such a strategy. According to that journal, Republican conservatives would never concede enough to transform the party into "an adequate instrument of western progressivism." Since the Old Guard knew that a splinter movement probably would not materialize, they could thus make threats of their own. Hence only a "feeble compromise" would result from efforts to reform Republicanism from within. A third party was "something worth organizing for its own sake. . . . And if it is worth organizing there is no time to be wasted by the progressives in manoeuvring within the Republican party."[5] Borah ultimately

---

[3] Glad, "Progressives and the Business Culture of the 1920's," pp. 81–89, discusses the differences of opinion over political tactics. Bryan's quote is in a handwritten note to La Follette, June 2, 1924, La Follette Family Papers, Series B, Box 97.

[4] Borah believed that Theodore Roosevelt had made a major mistake when he left the party. In bolting, he had destroyed his personal influence within the G.O.P. for future achievements. "There are times," wrote the Senator, "when a complete break with one's party may be justifiable. But my experience and my observation has been that you can fight just as long and more effectively inside your party than you can outside." Borah to O. P. Baldwin, December 29, 1927, Borah Papers, Box 292.

[5] "The Threat of the Third Party," *The New Republic*, XXII (November 15, 1922), 288–89. Beneath the title, the editors quoted from Borah's November 2, 1922, speech in Spokane in which he warned of a "formidable third party movement in 1924" unless the G.O.P. completely changed its program and adopted "a liberal and constructive policy."

decided otherwise; but, before his decision was clear, he gave independents false hopes.

The Nation was among the first to express enthusiasm for him as a third-party leader. Much distressed with the lack of vision and moral stature of the major parties, the journal asserted that "a great responsibility rests upon Senator Borah, to whom Liberals and Radicals and even conservatives are turning as to a savior." A member of *The New Republic*'s editorial board, Professor Robert Morss Lovett of The University of Chicago, considered *The Nation*'s plea for Borah to lead America's liberal forces as "the only suggestion at the present time which has constructive value." Oswald Garrison Villard appealed personally to the Senator: "*please* live up to the responsibility which we have put upon you . . . and sound the tocsin." [6]

On his part, Borah gave every indication that he believed it was time to develop a third party. In early May, 1922, he told Ernest Gruening that, barring a thorough rejuvenation of the two old parties, there would have to be a splinter movement. "He thinks he is the man to lead the fight," wrote Gruening. "There is no question about that. His stature grows every day. . . ." Borah's fiery July 6 speech in the Senate, denouncing various administration programs and proclaiming that the country was in the midst of a political upheaval, convinced *The Literary Digest* that he had personally opened the door for increased discussion of a third party and his possible role in it. In several letters, he opened this door even more. It was "perfectly clear," he wrote, that unless one or both of the old parties underwent a transformation, a new organization would emerge. Neither the G.O.P. nor the Democracy "represents at this time the true interest or the true desires of the people." He compared the 1920's to the 1850's, when the Republicans had

6 "The Duty to Revolt," *The Nation*, CXV (August 9, 1922), 140; Robert Morss Lovett to Villard, August 4, 1922, Villard Papers, Folder 2329; Villard to Borah, August 3, 1922, Borah Papers, Box 220. Lovett's "only hesitation was in view of the fact that, should Senator Borah take this position, he would scarcely possess any political influence during the next two years, when the need of the world is greatest."

first emerged to challenge regular political groups that were no longer responsive to national needs. Perhaps "out of the old Parties will come a new party under the old name. . . . But I am convinced . . . that there must be a new political party." [7]

During the evening of July 21, 1922, Borah talked at length with Villard. The editor came away enthusiastic, convinced that the Senator endorsed a third party as the only hope. "He is ready to cut loose as soon as the sinews of war can be organized, and the plan is laid out." According to Villard, "Borah thinks that if the means were provided we could organize the entire country in thirty days' time." A few weeks later, the Senator informed another third-party advocate that, although he was unsure about whom a new political organization would "put to the front," he wanted "in my way to serve the cause as best I may." [8]

As the December, 1922, Washington progressive conference approached, rumors increased that the Idahoan and La Follette were preparing to launch a third party. However, when regular Republicans such as Edwin C. Stokes, chairman of the G.O.P.'s New Jersey state committee, expressed concern, Borah shrugged off the press reports. It was always his intention, he explained, to work within the Republican party; furthermore, he lacked the inclination and money necessary for a splinter movement. The point which he had been trying to make was simply that *some* party would have to confront the issues of the day. Republicans could perform such a service but if they lacked the "heroic effort" to do so, a new party was inevitable. [9]

Despite Borah's assurances to Stokes concerning his party loyalty, within two weeks he privately indicated his availability

[7] Gruening to Villard, May 5, 1922, Villard Papers, Folder 1424; "Borah and a Third Party," *The Literary Digest,* LXXIV (August 26, 1922), 14; Borah to A. W. Kellogg, June 15, 1922, and to James H. Hawley, August 30, 1922, Borah Papers, Box 220.

[8] Villard quoted in D. Joy Humes, *Oswald Garrison Villard: Liberal of the 1920's* (Syracuse, N.Y., 1960), p. 135; Borah to John L. Beatty, September 21, 1922, Borah Papers, Box 220.

[9] Borah to Edwin C. Stokes, November 17, 1922, Borah Papers, Box 218.

for third-party duties. When Jasper Ewing Brady, editor of a large motion-picture corporation, urged the Senator to bolt and, like "that immortal leader" Theodore Roosevelt, lead a constructive movement, Borah replied that he "would like to act with you and the others along the lines of aggressive action. As to my individual part and what that means I think time will have to develop." Brady wanted the Idahoan to come to New York for "a heart to heart talk" and possibly lunch with some potential supporters. Borah agreed to this, noting that he would "make it a point" to visit Brady and discuss the situation. "If I can be of service in the general cause," the Senator added, "I want to do so." [10]

The Brady venture never materialized but it did illustrate Borah's willingness to encourage third-party talk, his ostensible support and enthusiasm for "the general cause," and his accessibility as a potential leader. Undoubtedly it was for such reasons that the Committee of 48 turned to him as a possible candidate for President on a Liberal party ticket.

The Forty-Eighters had first organized in 1919 in an effort to bring progressives in all states into a national political party, dedicated to government ownership of railroads and natural resources and an end to economic, political, and legal special privileges. They succeeded in attracting support from varied sources, including labor, socialists, and Bull Moose progressives; and they optimistically hoped to provide a third-party ticket in 1920, thereby setting the stage for 1924 when the group might really have a chance for victory. At their Chicago convention in July, 1920, however, troubles arose. Representatives from farm and labor groups were present and, when labor unions angrily split into anti-Gompers and pro-Gompers factions, the Forty-Eighters walked out. Subsequently, the more radical delegates who remained at the meeting formed a Farmer-Labor party committed to a platform along class lines. Disillusioned with the Committee of 48's leadership, important figures

[10] Jasper Ewing Brady to Borah, December 4 and 11, 1922; Borah to Brady, December 6 and 12, 1922, Borah Papers, Box 233.

such as Amos Pinchot and George Record left the organization.[11] Although by 1922 the Forty-Eighters were thus a diminished group, they nonetheless still listed on their letterhead the
names of such prominent reformers as Lynn Haines of *The
Searchlight on Congress;* Frederick C. Howe, who had served
Tom Johnson's progressive crusades in Cleveland; Arthur Garfield Hays, who in 1924 was to be the New York state chairman
for the La Follette ticket; Ray McKaig of Idaho's Nonpartisan
League struggles; and John Haynes Holmes, a New York paci-
fist, intellectual, and religious leader.

J. A. H. Hopkins, a wealthy Bull-Mooser from New Jersey,
was the Forty-Eighters' chairman. He held a prominent position
in a firm of adjusters and insurance brokers and had joined the
Progressive party in 1912, serving as the New Jersey chairman
and national treasurer. In 1913 he had lost a close election
for the New Jersey Senate on the third-party ticket. When
Theodore Roosevelt endorsed Charles Evans Hughes in 1916,
Hopkins turned to Woodrow Wilson and ultimately to the
Forty-Eighters. Under the white-headed but boyish-looking
Hopkins, the committee survived the apostasies of men such as
Pinchot and, as a rump group, continued attempts to form a
new national party. A number of leading progressives continued
to look upon Hopkins as an extremely effective political organizer. Rudolph Spreckels, who had long been an important
figure in California's reform politics, and Gilbert Roe, La Follette's former law partner, were among those who felt "that
Hopkins is about the only fellow who has kept plugging away
in season and out of season, and that he really has a pretty good
Progressive organization in most of the states. . . ."

By early 1923, Hopkins believed that the liberals' grass-roots
efforts indicated that they could field a third party in 1924,
dedicated to ending special privilege, protecting free speech,
press, and assembly, and advocating "the public ownership of

[11] Russel B. Nye, *Midwestern Progressive Politics* (East Lansing, Mich.,
1951), pp. 324–25; Glad, "Progressives and the Business Culture of the
1920s," pp. 82–83.

transportation and public control of natural resources." Initially Hopkins had turned to La Follette as the natural leader of the new party. But, apparently through a series of misunderstandings by which *La Follette's Magazine* failed to print material from the Committee of 48's news-service bulletin, Hopkins shifted his attention to Borah.[12]

Since its inception, the committee had shown a growing interest in the Idaho Senator. In 1920, although a preconvention questionnaire placed him far down the list of preferred candidates, there had been some maneuvering to nominate him for President on the third-party ticket. In subsequent months Hopkins stepped up his efforts to align Borah with the committee until finally, in early 1922, the Senator consented to talk with him "about the whole situation." Borah made it clear, however, that he was still disposed to advance liberal causes without regard to questions of party. Hence he neither closed his door to the Forty-Eighters, nor seemed eager to join them.[13]

[12] On Hopkins, see the information sheet in Mercer Green Johnston Papers, Box 67; for Spreckels's and Roe's view of Hopkins, see Roe to La Follette, April 16, 1925, La Follette Family Papers, Series C, Box 2; on the grass-roots organization of the committee, see Hopkins to Henry Teigan, February 23, 1923, Teigan Papers, Box 3, and Hopkins to Borah, August 11, 1922, Borah Papers, Box 220. For Hopkins's early support for La Follette, see Hopkins to La Follette, May 18, 1921, La Follette Family Papers, Series B, Box 89. The misunderstanding over the use of the committee's news service clearly emerges in Hopkins to La Follette, Jr., August 8, 19, 26, 1921, and to La Follette, September 23, 1921, *ibid.;* to Fred L. Holmes and La Follette, Jr., March 17, 1923, Box 95. Hopkins found himself concluding "that for some reason . . . you do not desire this service," and that "obviously there is a loose screw somewhere." La Follette's refusal to intercede on grounds that he had "neither time nor inclination to take up . . . matters which are not of immediate importance," probably did not help the situation. La Follette to Hopkins, April 5, 1921, Box 114.

[13] The results of the poll, compiled from 1,500 questionnaires that the committee circulated in 1920, placed Borah seventeenth on the list of preferred presidential candidates. Points were awarded on a first-choice, second-choice basis, with La Follette far out front with 310 total points; Borah had four first-place ballots and three second-place votes for a total of only seven points. Under the same arrangement, he placed tenth on the list of vice-presidential favorites with sixteen first-place votes and one

In the following weeks, nevertheless, Borah undoubtedly pleased the committee. His efforts in behalf of the coal bill, proposing a fact-finding commission for the coal industry, certainly increased his standing with the liberals. And they unquestionably enjoyed his criticism of the G.O.P. for responding inadequately to domestic problems, his sniping at Harding's foreign policy, and his assertions that a third party was a growing possibility.

Still, by early 1923 Borah, despite his vociferousness, had not broken from the Republicans, nor did he seem any closer to bolting than in previous months. In this context, his March 23 speech at Akron, Ohio, probably disappointed the third-party people. David Lawrence reported in the Washington *Star* that the Senator's friends had hoped to use the Akron rally as "the big opening gun" in a presidential campaign. In his address, Borah eloquently called for a political alliance which would resolutely meet current problems, bravely march "under the inspiring dawn of a new day," speak in behalf of peace and the Constitution, and oppose intolerance. But he stopped far short of apostasy by emphasizing that, if the old parties acted with courage, they could undercut any potential independent movement. He was, in other words, still leaving the initiative with established parties. His performance, according to Lawrence, created no unhappiness among Republicans; indeed, Borah not only had refused to endorse a third-party organization, but also had stressed that the G.O.P. had an opportunity to become an instrument of progressivism.[14]

The Senator's failure to break with Republicanism obviously disappointed Hopkins, who had gotten the impression that Borah was ready to bolt and participate actively in a liberal

second-place vote for a total of seventeen points. Lynn Frazier won the vice-presidential poll with sixty-two points. Results of poll, June 12, 1920, in Johnston Papers, Box 67. See also clipping from the *Chicago Tribune,* June 15, 1920, Amos Pinchot Papers, Box 40. Borah to Hopkins, January 16, 1922, Borah Papers, Box 218.

[14] Copy of Borah's Akron, Ohio, speech, in Borah Papers, Box 234; Washington *Star,* March 23, 1923.

campaign. A week after the Akron speech, Hopkins decided to inquire into the Idahoan's intentions. His letter strongly intimated that Borah had already given the liberals some definite indications that he would help them. It was time, the Forty-Eighter asserted, for the Senator to declare himself. The state progressive-party conference was fast approaching and the lack of an open statement from Borah reinforced assumptions that he would remain a Republican. "You have assured me that you are thoroughly in harmony with what we are doing, and you will appreciate the importance of putting me in a position of either being able to deny or affirm" such opinions. Hopkins reminded the Senator that—just as Theodore Roosevelt, Woodrow Wilson, Hiram Johnson, and La Follette—he had the rare opportunity "to render a great public service." Roosevelt "through lack of vision and lack of courage" had thrown away his chance; Wilson had been reluctant to champion American liberalism; Johnson had catered to Republican reactionaries; and in 1920 La Follette had rejected the role of leader. "Now, in 1923, only twelve months in advance of the 1924 primaries, we are discussing the same kind of opportunity." The decision this time was Borah's.[15]

An encouraging reply came from the Senator. "With reference to the third party movement and how we can best promote the issues in which I am interested, I am only too anxious to discuss this. . . ." Borah stressed his commitment to vital issues and policies, but added that no one should regard him as a candidate for President on any ticket. This did not mean, however, that he was removing himself from consideration, for he noted that no "man can afford to join a party and then declare himself a candidate for President. . . . he ought to be drafted and there ought not to be any mistake about the drafting." Indeed, in such a situation the prospective nominee had "better be a little deaf than a little over-sensitive with his hearing. . . ." Apparently Borah was at least ready to listen. After complimenting Hopkins's "patriotic motives and the singleness

15 Hopkins to Borah, March 30, 1923, Borah Papers, Box 233.

of purpose with which you would serve the public," he stated that he was "therefore as anxious to see you as you can be to see me. . . . I should be glad to see you Hopkins at any time." [16]

On April 6, after receiving the Senator's letter, Hopkins hurried to Washington. The resulting conversation between the two men in the Senate office building was candid and significant. Borah came directly to the point, asking exactly how he could "be of the greatest service." The Forty-Eighter had no doubts: Borah should be President. Hopkins agreed that "a Presidential candidate should not nominate himself but should be drafted." Hence, he was asking the Senator not to declare himself as a candidate but simply to consent to serve if the liberals drafted him. The strategy would be one of circulating petitions in all states naming Borah for President and asking for pledges.

Borah expressed concern lest there be a misunderstanding. Although he believed that both old parties were beyond salvation, he did not feel that he could in good faith officially leave the G.O.P. without first resigning as Senator. And, if he relinquished his seat, he would forfeit his usefulness there. Although Hopkins believed that Borah was overly conscientious, he reiterated that the liberals were not asking him to make a formal statement at that date but merely wanted him to assure them that he would accept their nomination when they offered it to him. It would otherwise be impossible to organize a campaign after waiting several more months.

The Senator did not want Hopkins to think that he had "any illusions about the Republican party or that my difficulty in answering your question more specifically is due to the fact that I care about them. I don't care a snap for them." He felt that he had demonstrated this in his battles against Idaho's party leadership during the 1922 elections. Not only did Borah want Hopkins to understand that he was "ready to be of service," but he also hoped to make "it distinctly understood that I am

[16] Borah to Hopkins, April 2, 1923, Borah Papers, Box 233.

willing to serve entirely irrespective of whether I am a candidate or not." He believed that the suggested liberal strategy of circulating petitions "would have a good effect." Certainly, it would probably also encourage other candidates, but this did not bother the Senator. Indeed, he wanted "to emphasize again that my interest in the movement is not because I may be the candidate,—although I would like to be President,—but because I want to serve the movement." Even if the liberals selected another nominee, Borah would continue to serve them. He was not even asking for any guaranteed support from Hopkins. The Forty-Eighter might discover that La Follette was interested in the nomination and, without doubt, the Wisconsin Senator "is a splendid fellow; he is sound all the way through." This would not deter Borah; when there was "a demand for a real movement, then I will be ready to serve, and my willingness will not, as I have said before, be affected whether I am nominated or not." If that "fine fighter," La Follette, headed the movement, "well and good!"

Although the Idahoan was apparently eager to serve the cause, the problem of proper strategy still remained. What, Hopkins asked, would Borah say when reporters wanted him to comment on the third party? The Senator answered that he would tell them nice things about Hopkins and his group; that he surely could not know whom the liberals would nominate; that he would not comment on the hypothesis that he might be their candidate, but would only say that "the candidate should be drafted. On the other hand, it seems to me that your answer should be that you are proceeding in a way that it seems to you necessary and that you have drafted me for your candidate." What, Hopkins pressed, if newsmen queried about Borah's position in regard to the liberal program? According to the Senator, this would present no problem for he had examined the Forty-Eighters' goals "very carefully" and could "certainly stand . . . on that platform."

Borah agreed that Hopkins "should certainly" proceed along the lines of political strategy which they had discussed. "I think it will be the means of building up your movement, and I think if we keep in close touch with one another, there will be no difficulty in our agreeing as to what should be done and when we should do it."

One other thing worried Hopkins: what of the tendency of many people to construe the Senator's public statements as implying that he would never leave the G.O.P.? Borah shrugged this off as insignificant, asserting that such impressions were rooted in his decision not to bolt in 1912. The people simply did not know the whole story of that incident. "When Roosevelt asked me to join his Rump Convention, I refused to do so because he came to Chicago perfectly content to take the Republican nomination and . . . to accept its platform." It was only after the Bull Mooser had engaged in "a factional fight with Mr. Taft [that] he started a new party. I told him this to his face and told him that this was not essentially a new movement and that was the reason I would not join it." One thing was certain, Borah pointed out: "1912 is one thing and 1923 another, and I am ready and anxious to be of service in whatever way I can best render it." [17]

After his profitable discussion with Borah, Hopkins immediately started the machinery to draft the Senator. The Committee of 48 printed special stationery with "William E. Borah for President" written across the top, along with the announcement of the National Executive Committee of the Forty-Eighters that Borah was "the Presidential candidate of the Progressive voters of these United States in 1924 on the Platform of the Committee of 48." Campaign headquarters were in New York City. Hopkins circulated letters asking for support in the battle against both parties which were in control of "the financial oligarchy enjoying Special Privilege." Borah, according to the

[17] This account of the Borah-Hopkins meeting of April 6, 1923, is in the Borah Papers, Box 233. Hopkins, on the train to New York after leaving the Senator, wrote down the conversation as he remembered it. He then typed several copies of the discussion, sending one to Borah and asking him to check it for mistakes. Borah made no corrections. See also, Hopkins to Dora Haines, June 4, 1923, Haines Papers, Box 8.

committee, was the answer to the likes of Andrew Mellon and Harry Daugherty. "His only enemies are to be found in the ranks of those sorry sycophants who subsist by the grace of the gluttons of Special Privilege." [18]

On May 8, Hopkins told reporters that his organization was backing Borah for President on a third-party ticket. Replying to the question of whether or not he had the Senator's consent, he observed that it was not necessary to obtain it since "in my opinion our candidates for President should be drafted." Furthermore, when Hopkins had recently talked to Borah, the Idahoan had not put an "embargo on the use of his name." [19]

Hopkins also asked Dora Haines if *The Searchlight on Congress* would prepare a copy of Borah's voting record for circulation. Since finances were a problem, however, the chairman wondered if Mrs. Haines would supply, "just out of your goodheartedness," a summary of the highlights of Borah's Senate record. Hopkins gave assurances that this was no fleeting cause for, after "going into the subject very carefully," he and the committee knew "just what we are doing." Lynn and Dora Haines agreed to construct a synopsis of Borah's activities for $100; such a task usually cost $500 but they would regard the discount as their personal contribution to the liberals. "You certainly have shouldered a big responsibility," Mrs. Haines added, but "your stand I think clarifies the political situation a good deal." Hopkins appreciated the offer; yet, even by June 4, finances were so limited that he could do no more than stress the probability that he would request a copy of Borah's record after some of the campaign funds arrived.[20]

Money was a problem for Hopkins, but so too was Borah, who refused to do anything which might make the Forty-Eighters' efforts easier. Only a few days after his April 6 talk with the

[18] Hopkins to Borah, April 12, 1923, and copy of the Committee of 48's "Borah for President" letter, undated, Borah Papers, Box 233.

[19] *The New York Times*, May 9, 1923.

[20] Hopkins to Mrs. Dora B. Haines, May 10, 1923; Dora Haines to Hopkins, May 16, 1923, Lynn Haines Papers, Box 9; Hopkins to Dora Haines, June 4, 1923, *ibid.*, Box 8.

liberal chairman, the Senator's enthusiasm waned. He expressed appreciation for the work of the committee, but emphasized that he was in no way "a candidate for President and do not want to be so considered." He could not affiliate with any party other than the G.O.P. unless he first resigned from the Senate. Any public-spirited movement or organization with high standards would certainly receive his best wishes but "in so expressing myself I am not bidding for office." He did not lack White House ambitions, but "my course these days is not the Presidential course. And I do not want my friends to be embarrassed." [21]

Hopkins, in light of his conversation with the Senator, did not believe that Borah's position was a departure from their original understanding. He completely understood "you again emphasizing the fact that you are not putting yourself forward as a Presidential candidate"; this was in harmony with their agreement. "We have proceeded after the matter discussed with you in Washington the other day and I have already made great progress. . . ." [22]

Nevertheless, in subsequent weeks, Hopkins began to have his doubts about the Senator. It was time, he advised Borah, to act as "you know so well how to do," placing himself at last on the "fighting ground" of "Abolition of Special Privilege, the taking over of the railroads, the revision of our Taxation and the solving of the Banking problem." When no such attack came from the Senator, Hopkins revealed his growing suspicions by asking Borah to confirm in writing his belief in the liberal platform. He realized that Borah had made his position clear during the April 6 conversation and he also appreciated Borah's later assurance that he had not changed his mind. Yet, if the Idahoan would put his commitment to the liberal cause on paper, he thereby "could render a service to many of our friends who are seriously desirous of knowing just where you stand in relation to these matters. . . ." The committee was working ac-

[21] Borah to Hopkins, April 14, 1923, Borah Papers, Box 233.
[22] Hopkins to Borah, April 17, 1923, Borah Papers, Box 233.

cording to plan and Hopkins knew "that we may depend upon you to do nothing that will embarrass us or put any obstacle in the way of our carrying out what I am convinced will prove to be a service of inestimable value to the American people." Obviously, Hopkins was skeptical about the Senator's verbal assurances and wanted something more tangible. But Borah cagily avoided committing himself in a letter. At one point, the Forty-Eighter tried to elicit a comment by informing the Senator that an old friend had charged Borah with deserting principle in 1920 and endorsing the Republican platform in hopes of getting the nomination. The friend also wondered how Borah hoped to campaign on a platform of government ownership while he sanctioned the appointment of such a spokesman of privilege as Pierce Butler to the Supreme Court. Hopkins, claiming that he wanted to rebut this man, asked if Borah would provide him with the ammunition. The Senator refused to take the bait. Any individual who would make such comments was simply "either grossly ignorant . . . or a cowardly liar. In either event . . . I haven't any time to spend with him whatever." [23]

By June, the liberal chairman clearly had his problems. He implored the Idahoan to make a statement. People who were interested in the Borah petition wanted some assurances. Although Hopkins told skeptics that the Senator was dedicated to the reorganization of American politics, some proof from Borah was necessary. The Senator need not frame his speeches as a candidate, but should at least focus on issues so as not to disappoint his progressive supporters. The Forty-Eighter even briefly suggested some of the solutions which Borah could pose to "the most vital problems": government ownership of railroads, a living wage for labor, government banking through government facilities, election reforms, taxing land at its true value, and placing community ahead of class interests. It was important, Hopkins explained, "that we should talk the same

[23] Hopkins to Borah, April 26 and 30, May 7 and 16, 1923; Borah reply, May 17, 1923, Borah Papers, Box 233.

language in reference to these fundamental questions. . . ." [24]

Hopkins's efforts to secure a formal announcement from Borah were essential because the Senator's position on domestic issues was not clear. Amos Pinchot, for example, admitted that he liked the Idahoan, but wanted "to know what he stands for and what . . . he would do if he were elected." Writing Pinchot for support, Hopkins could merely assert that he had personally received "an unequivocal statement" from Borah that he would stand on every word of the liberal platform.[25]

Doggedly, the Forty-Eighter persisted in his attempt to advance Borah's cause within the progressive party. When the Senator told Chicago newspaper reporters that he would not head a third party and doubted that La Follette would either, Hopkins followed the suggested pattern of his April 6 conference with Borah by informing the press that such stories were amusing; "I thought everybody knew that he had not left the Republican party." It was true, the chairman elaborated, that Borah's friends were circulating petitions to draft him. The liberals wanted a fighter of privilege and "if Senator Borah qualifies for this position and wins the support of the delegates we shall be entirely satisfied." [26]

Still unable to secure a written statement from Borah, Hopkins finally asked Dora Haines if she would talk to the Senator, "draw him out in the form of an interview, and then send it to us so that we can use it for our press service in your name. . . ." Lynn Haines was dubious about such an approach and advised that, since Hopkins intended to make public use of the information, he should talk to Borah himself. "His attitude should come directly through you." Via the telephone, however, Hop-

[24] Hopkins to Borah, June 11, 1923, Borah Papers, Box 233.

[25] Pinchot to A. L. Hood, May 14, 1923, Pinchot Papers, Box 45; Hopkins to Amos Pinchot, June 14, 1923, Box 44.

[26] News Article 37A of the Committee of 48's National Bureau of Information and Education, Special News Bulletin, undated, Pinchot Papers, Box 11; *Chicago Herald and Examiner*, June 12, 1923, Borah Scrapbooks, Reel 4.

kins ultimately prevailed and Haines sent Charles A. Lyman
to talk with the Senator. The interview, undoubtedly to Hopkins's distress, was unrewarding. The *Searchlight* arranged the
meeting with Borah, who was supposedly fully aware that the
purpose was to obtain for publication his opinions on public
questions. Lyman, while waiting in the Senator's outer office,
jotted down for possible discussion queries concerning the tariff,
taxation, transportation, agricultural relief, militarism, money
and banking, profiteering, relations of labor and capital, constitutional reforms, the world court, and the necessity for providing national publicity on important national issues. Borah
subsequently caught Lyman off guard in the opening minutes
of the interview when he asked for a list of questions "so that I
can give a little time to their consideration." The reporter, who
had originally intended to use his hastily scribbled topics for
his own reference, ended up giving them to Borah and leaving
without any statement from him. Borah explained that he
would himself prepare something for the magazine before he
left for the West.[27] This he apparently failed to do, since the
Searchlight printed no such story.

By the fall of 1923, the Borah boom was obviously coming to
naught. The Senator himself told Hopkins on October 18 that
Henry Ford would probably be the third party nominee. As a
Chicago planning conference for the independent movement
approached, the liberal chairman asked what messages he could
deliver and when Borah would "be in a position to publicly
cooperate with us in the organization of our new party convention in 1924?" Certainly, Hopkins averred, "no progressive
can afford to give the Republican Party any further comfort
and encouragement." [28]

Borah, however, had lost interest in the Forty-Eighters. This

[27] Hopkins to Dora Haines, June 4, 1923, and Lynn Haines to Hopkins,
June 7, 1923, Box 8; Hopkins to Lynn Haines, June 19, 1923; Dora Haines
to Hopkins, August 24, 1923; Charles A. Lyman to Dora Haines, August
24, 1923, Haines Papers, Box 9.
[28] Borah to Frank E. Johnesse, October 19, 1923, and Hopkins to Borah
October 31, 1923, Borah Papers, Box 233.

was due perhaps in part to Hopkins's failure to get the machinery of an overwhelming draft movement in motion, but probably more significantly because of an unexpected change in the political scene. On August 2, President Harding died suddenly in San Francisco. A few days earlier, William Howard Taft had expressed hopes that Harding would survive because he was "the only possible solution of the next Presidential campaign." By controlling the Republican convention, Harding could eliminate candidates such as La Follette, Hiram Johnson, and Borah; it was "of the utmost importance" that this should happen.[29]

When Harding died, Ernest Gruening of *The Nation* saw a marvelous opportunity for Borah. America's thoughts, he informed the Senator, "are turning to you." Whereas the brief rise in progressivism following the 1922 elections had "flattened out" and had thereby increased the prospects of Harding's renomination, "the situation is again acutely alive." The G.O.P. nomination was no certainty now. Coolidge would try to capture it but would, in the process, evoke dissension among other standpatters. Secretary of War John W. Weeks and Senator Henry Cabot Lodge, for example, had little love for the Vermonter, and Charles Evans Hughes was probably grooming for his own future. That "strategic moment" had arrived "for a definite move toward real political progress, toward the realization of the finest and realist [*sic*] Americanism. . . . You, Senator, are the man to lead it." A third party was out of the question since it would require too much money and organization. The appropriate strategy would be to capture the Republican convention and since Borah's statesmanship over the past few years had been "conspicuous above that of any other figure in our national life," he was "the one logical man" to assume command.[30]

Borah assured Gruening that he was ready for the occasion. It was indeed time "to make a most determined effort . . . to liberalize the political program of the future." It would take a

[29] Taft to Clarence H. Kelsey, July 31, 1923, Taft Papers, Box 541.
[30] Ernest Gruening to Borah, August 6, 1923, Borah Papers, Box 233.

determined fight and would require organization on a wide
basis. Certainly the mood of the country was ready and "the
machinery of the situation is also susceptible to control. . . . I
want to do my part in every way that I can and do it effectively.
I am ready to go into it for all there is in it," at least in terms of
establishing principles. Borah preferred to postpone mention of
his leadership until later when he and Gruening could converse.
"But in the meantime I hope you will have an opportunity to
see many who think like we do. I would like to see the crusade
started as early as possible." [31]

The Senator had definitely lost whatever lingering interest
he had in Hopkins and the liberal party. The Forty-Eighter
mourned that he had received little encouragement from Borah
during the autumn months in regard to the committee's legislative proposals. Furthermore, the increasing reports that the
Idahoan was supporting Coolidge on several issues bothered
Hopkins. Borah, evincing little sympathy for the chairman,
bluntly and coldly denied that he had a place in any third-party
movement or aspirations for a splinter nomination.[32]

It was probably a discouraged Hopkins who now turned to
George Norris, declaring that "nothing would give me greater
pleasure than to see you or Sen. La Follette step to the front"
of the liberal movement. Although "there has been a good deal
of talk, as you know, of Senator Borah and Mr. [Henry] Ford,"
the Forty-Eighter hoped that Norris and La Follette would
consider a possible role.[33]

While the liberals looked elsewhere for a third-party candidate, Borah altered his perspectives on the new administration.
Coolidge's domestic program—with its emphasis on reducing

[31] Borah to Gruening, August 22, 1923, Borah Papers, Box 233.

[32] Hopkins to Borah, December 10, 1923; Borah reply, December 11,
1923, Borah Papers, Box 238.

[33] Hopkins to George Norris, December 12, 1923. Although Norris expressed sympathy for the liberal effort, he refused to put his faith in a
third party. Indeed, he felt that a splinter movement might "do more
harm than good. It would have a tendency to increase the already out-
rageously partisan spirits." Norris to Hopkins, January 6, 1924, Norris
Papers, Tray 81, Box 6.

spending and taxes—quickly won the Senator's support. Moreover, Coolidge's apparent malleability and the attention which he immediately showered on Borah convinced the Senator that he might be able to exert considerable influence over the President and prod him along progressive paths.

The flurry of White House attention which encouraged Borah's optimistic definition of his future role also fit well with Coolidge's own political strategy. The President apparently agreed with Will Hays, Harding's Postmaster General until 1922, that Borah's support was essential to the Vermonter's hopes for a 1924 election victory. Certainly Coolidge had scarcely entered office before he began making plans to capture the G.O.P. nomination and, to cut the ground from beneath potential liberal opposition, he needed to make friendly gestures to the progressive Republicans. He thus made special efforts to ingratiate himself to Borah, summoning him back from Idaho to discuss agricultural conditions and sending him numerous White House invitations. By December, Borah concluded that Coolidge was "a man of ability and courage" whose statements, particularly in regard to agricultural reform, were encouraging. He may have suspected that the President, as William Howard Taft learned firsthand, had no intention of dealing seriously with these "wild wheat market reformers" and their "impossible schemes." But Borah himself looked with considerable distress at some of the more drastic farm relief proposals; although he sought relief legislation he wanted it within proper lines—the architecture of which generally resembled the President's plans.[34]

In late 1923 and early 1924, Borah's admiration for Coolidge

[34] Robert J. Maddox, "Keeping Cool with Coolidge," *Journal of American History*, LIII (March, 1967), 772–80, discusses Coolidge's courtship of liberal Republicans, especially Borah and Raymond Robins. On the Coolidge-Borah relations, see Borah to Mrs. A. Wagner, September 18, 1923, and to N. R. Selover, September 20, 1923, Borah Papers, Box 228; Borah to George Sievers, Box 212; Borah statement to press, Box 235; "Wright" telegram to Boise *Capital News*, October 30, 1923, Box 232; Frederick William Wile Scrapbooks, September 25, 1923, 17; international newsreel photo, September 28, 1923, Borah Scrapbooks, Reel 4. For Will

went beyond the President's response to the farm problem. Indeed, he became a conspicuous advocate for the administration, backing the veto of the Soldier's Bonus bill and endorsing the general principles behind the Mellon tax reduction plan; such steps, he felt, would initiate a reduction in the "mad saturnalia" of government spending. Indeed, the Senator's performance made him, in the eyes of Chicago lawyer Silas H. Strawn, "the most able and consistent supporter of the Administration during the last session." Apparently Borah sincerely believed that Coolidge was the antidote to the ills of the G.O.P., for he converted Raymond Robins "to a fair consideration" of the new President "and his claims." [35]

Borah's expectations soon disintegrated, however. When Coolidge failed to request the resignation of Attorney General Daugherty, a growing symbol of reaction in the Cabinet, the Senator's estimation of the administration turned sour. By March 1, 1924, he had "never been so discouraged and demoralized by a situation as I am now. The whole thing seems rotten to the core." [36]

The Senator was low in spirits, but one thing seemed certain: judging from his relations with the Committee of 48 in 1923, he was not of the stuff from which martyrs emerge. He had rejected the chance to convert a martyr's crown "into battle

---

Hays's views on the necessity of Borah's support, see Raymond Robins to Salmon O. Levinson, November 30, 1923, Salmon O. Levinson Papers (University of Chicago Library), Box 76. On Coolidge's early efforts to secure the nomination, see Taft to Charles D. Hilles, September 8, 1923, Taft Papers, Box 543, and to Horace Taft, September 29, 1923, Box 544. Borah to J. Wesley Miller, December 6, 1923, Borah Papers, Box 243, contains the Senator's compliments on Coolidge's ability. Taft assessed the President's attitude toward the more radical advocates of farm relief after a discussion with the President. Taft to Horace Taft, September 29, 1923, Taft Papers, Box 244.

[35] *The New York Herald,* January 6, 1924, Borah Scrapbooks, Reel 4; Silas H. Strawn to Kellogg, June 13, 1924, Frank B. Kellogg Papers (Minnesota State Historical Society), Box 8; Robins to Borah, September 18, 1924, Borah Papers, Box 243.

[36] Borah to John W. Hart, March 1, 1924, Borah Papers, Box 238.

headgear that would inspire a fighting host as did the Helmet of Navarre." He was not yet ready for Armageddon, to assume the leadership of a third party and "be the prophet of its faith and the captain of its host." [37]

[37] Editorial clipping from *The* [Long Beach, Calif.] *Daily Telegram,* July 2, 1923, Borah Scrapbooks, Reel 4.

Political Proteus: Borah and the 1924 Election

🌑

IT became even clearer during the 1924 campaign that Borah
was remarkably adept in the art of political self-preservation.
He emerged from a treacherous political thicket with a staggering re-election victory and the potential for even greater national influence. Indeed, his performance confirmed Raymond
Robins's description of him as "one of the niftiest little waiters
and side-steppers that ever came down the political pike." [1] On
one hand he successfully met the challenge of Republican leaders in Idaho who were hostile to his re-election. On the other, he
adroitly handled the added problems that La Follette's presidential candidacy thrust upon him in Idaho where his relationship with the state's Progressive party—more powerful than the
Democrats and a strong threat to the G.O.P. itself—became
quite delicate. At the same time, he cautiously built his political strength outside Idaho, especially by keeping in the good
graces of the budding Outlawry of War movement which actively courted him.

Progressives, Republicans, and champions of the Outlawry of
War program sought throughout the campaign to force a commitment from him, but Borah ingeniously kept himself in all
camps while raising no flag except his own. Through tactics of
evasion, delay, and noncommitment, he avoided alienating any
group and increased his prestige without anyone knowing in
which direction he would move. Albert Beveridge, former progressive Senator from Indiana, believed that one thing was

[1] Raymond Robins to Salmon O. Levinson, December 10, 1924, Salmon
O. Levinson Papers (University of Chicago Library), Box 76.

clear: "you, dear Borah, will now be in a position of such strategic importance that it will be definitive." [2]

One of the crucial challenges that Borah confronted during the campaign involved his relations with the Idaho Republican machine. His fight with state G.O.P. leaders during the 1922 election in regard to the direct primary issue had definitely placed him and his friends in an embarrassing position with the party regulars. By mid-1923, events gave credence to rumors that the statehouse, anti-Borah faction hoped to unseat him. In June, when Harding stopped in the state on his fatal trip west, Idaho Republicans used the President's visit as an opportunity to develop the opposition against Borah's return to the Senate the following year. With the Senator standing immediately behind Harding at the Pocatello train station, Governor C. C. Moore turned his introductory comments into attacks on Russian recognition, which Borah favored, and praise for the Fordney-McCumber tariff, which Borah had voted against. By 1924, state regulars were intent upon finding an opposition candidate.[3]

Finally, however, the statehouse group and the Borah forces established a tenuous truce from which each hoped to gain. The Senator had to win his nomination at the party's nominating convention in August. G.O.P. regulars, on the other hand, were well aware that Borah's tremendous popular support made him a formidable opponent. As Frank Gooding, former state governor and Idaho's junior Senator, appraised the situation: "To h——, I am not a friend of Borah's, but if you

[2] Albert Beveridge to Borah, November 13, 1924, Borah Papers, Box 243.

[3] Clipping from Boston *Globe*, June 29, 1923, in Calvin Coolidge Papers (Library of Congress), Case File 130; Ezra R. Whitla to Borah, January 18, 1924, Borah Papers, Box 243. State regulars were seldom happy with the Senator. As one observer reported in 1936, "the talk was all for Borah but 75% of the leading Republicans hate his 'insides' because he has never helped the party in Idaho and if he could be eliminated from State politics it would be satisfactory to a large number who want to run for his place in the Senate." Ben H. Matkins to Alf M. Landon, February 29, 1936, Landon Papers, Box "Political, 1936, C&C."

want to defeat the Republican party, the most successful way
to do it is to pursue your present course," namely, trying to find
another Republican nominee. There was no alternative, Gooding said, except "to nominate Borah and elect the Republican
ticket." [4]

John Thomas, former state party chairman, played a key
role in outlining the terms of the political truce. He proposed a
harmony plan for the party's March convention in Lewiston,
Idaho, which would choose delegates to the state and national
nominating conventions. According to his strategy, there would
be no contest between Governor Moore's state machine and
Borah over delegates to these meetings; the delegates in turn
were to understand that they should name both Moore and
Borah to the Idaho group which would attend the national
G.O.P. gathering in Cleveland. Furthermore, the direct primary should not become an issue. Thomas communicated his
plans to Borah, Senator Gooding, Governor Moore, and
friends of these men.[5]

Borah agreed to the "harmony program" after he had met at
his Boise residence with some of his supporters. At these meetings, the majority opinion favored a truce, rather than an all-out
fight against the state leaders. The Senator did not intend to
fight Moore's nomination, but he warned that the Governor
should also avoid harassing him. Otherwise, Moore would force
the Senator to return the blows "as a matter of self respect."
Borah was also prepared to avoid the direct primary issue, so
long as no one tried to force him to compromise on principles.
He agreed, further, that the national convention should be for
Coolidge and that there could be unanimity in regard to the
selection of state delegates to the state and national conventions.
But he also served warning that, "unless there is harmony all
along the line and fair treatment of my friends, there will be no

[4] Quoted in letters from E. H. Dewey to Borah, November 19, 1923,
Borah Papers, Box 233.
[5] See, for example, C. C. Cavanah to Borah, December 24, 1923, Borah
Papers, Box 243.

harmony at all." As Borah saw it, the object behind the truce was to effect party unity; such a goal rested ultimately upon "good faith" among all members.[6]

On March 25, 1924, at the Lewiston meeting, the peace program survived its first test. The general tranquility on the convention floor, however, belied backstage differences. Evening and early morning caucuses, not without steamroller tactics, disposed of outward frictions, but it was "a hard-boiled peace." The organization leaders were careful to see that Borah—who was not present—got just enough to placate him, and no more. Allowing no chance for error, the machine carefully watched the "Borah-firsters" in order to prevent departures from the "me-too" sentiment. The Borah group, lacking the strength to name the entire delegation to Cleveland, used "every tactical advantage" to ensure that the delegates were at least friendly to the Senator. They had hoped to gain a strong convention endorsement of him and his policies, but the party avoided any statement which would imply approval of Borah's 1922 election conduct. "The last stand of the Boise Borah faction" failed when it could not capture control of the resolutions committee.[7]

The Borahites did take advantage of one incident in an effort to convince the national party leaders that the Senator was more loyal to the G.O.P. than were the state's regulars. This occurred during confusion over the instruction of the national delegation for Coolidge. Although Senator Frank Gooding's followers backed the endorsement of the President, they did not want to instruct the delegates for him. A strong "Borah-firster," John Hart, heard about this and saw an opportunity to embarrass the state machine. He immediately threatened to insist on instructions. The convention, not wanting a fight on such an issue, yielded. Hart then wired Coolidge that the Idaho delegation was his and wrote to the President's secretary, C. Bascom

[6] Charles F. Koelsch to Borah, March 27, 1924; Borah to C. C. Cavanah, December 28, 1923, and to M. A. Kiger, January 19, 1924, Borah Papers, Box 243.

[7] Clippings from the Spokane *Spokesman-Review*, March 26, 1924; *The Idaho Daily Statesman*, March 24–25, 1924.

Slemp, informing him that Senator Gooding's group had opposed instructions while Borah's friends had fought for Coolidge. When Borah heard of Hart's maneuver "to gain a little
political advantage," he heartily commended him: "I never
thought you [had] lost your cunning." [8]

In general, the Borah faction had fared very well at Lewiston.
Undoubtedly the state clique's adherence to the harmony plan
had demonstrated a healthy respect for the Senator's political
power. As one of Borah's followers informed him, "The machine is just as bitter against you as ever, but they are afraid of
your shadow." The machine had not tried to force embarrassing concessions from Borah although it had been able to dictate,
to a large extent, the convention's proceedings. Members of the
Borah group warned, however, that they must be stronger at the
Idaho Falls nominating assembly that August. The party still
remained "in bad hands" and needed a thorough cleaning job.
The Senator agreed that "the old gang" should not be in control at Idaho Falls; it had to learn that it could "not continue
to rule with the old iron hand." [9] Apparently, principles were
to come ahead of harmony when the state G.O.P. reconvened
in August.

In Washington, Calvin Coolidge was just as concerned with
the appearance of party unity and with gaining Borah's support
as were the Idaho Republican leaders. Certainly the situation
had improved since September, 1923, when William Howard
Taft had doubted that the G.O.P. would win the next election
and had worried about the movements within the party to capture the nomination from Coolidge. No available man of the
conservative group had challenged the Vermonter; the President had successfully parried the challenge of Gifford Pinchot,
progressive governor of Pennsylvania, during the 1923 coal

[8] John Hart to Borah, March 30, 1924; Borah reply, April 3, 1924,
Borah Papers, Box 244.
[9] Charles F. Koelsch to Borah, March 27, 1924; C. E. Arney to Borah,
March 26, 1924; Ben E. Bush to Borah, March 27, 1924, Borah Papers,
Box 243; C. N. King to Borah, April 10, 1924, and Borah to King, April
24, 1924, Box 242.

strike which had been replete with political implications; [10] Arthur Capper, leader of the Senate farm bloc, had said that he was for Coolidge, and the National Committee had fallen overwhelmingly behind the President's nomination. Indeed, by December of 1923, Coolidge was confident that he could win at Cleveland in June.[11] Beyond the nomination, however, remained the election in which western votes could be crucial. The administration thus turned to Borah for aid on several occasions before, during, and after the convention.

The Senator was, however, reluctant to endorse Coolidge. He was convinced that the Vermonter would get the nomination, but he was not ecstatic about it. He thanked Gutzon Borglum for the suggestion that Borah throw his own hat into the political ring and admitted that he was "very restless and unhappy . . . over the political situation these days. The condition at Washington is suffocating, the atmosphere is tainted with political corruption." [12]

A major reason for Borah's growing disillusionment with Coolidge was the President's failure to dismiss Attorney General Harry M. Daugherty and Secretary of the Navy Edwin N. Denby, both of whom had been closely associated with the oil scandals of the Harding administration. The Vermonter, a master of inaction, characteristically deferred making a decision in hopes that the problem would eventually solve itself. Borah feared that, insofar as Coolidge failed to take the initiative, he jeopardized the Republican party. "Drastic, uncompromising

[10] Taft to Dewey Hilles, September 8, 1923, Taft Papers, Box 543. Dewey Hilles to Taft, October 16, 1923, *ibid.*, Box 545, noted the lack of an Old-Guard challenge to Coolidge. On the Pinchot boomlet, see Robert H. Zieger, "Pinchot and Coolidge: The Politics of the 1923 Anthracite Crisis," *Journal of American History*, LII (December, 1965), 566–81, and Taft to Horace Taft, September 29, 1923, and to J. B. Woodward, September 29, 1923, Taft Papers, Box 544.

[11] Taft to Mrs. Frederick J. Manning, December 9, 1923, and to Horace Taft, December 14, 1923, Taft Papers, Box 548. Taft had heard from Hilles, a member of the committee, that Coolidge had tremendous committee support, except for four or five Hiram Johnson men.

[12] Gutzon Borglum to Borah, January 27, 1924, and Borah's reply, January 29, 1924, Borglum Papers, Box 61.

and remorseless" action was essential in order to save "the moral fibre of the country." The Senator granted that a political re-alignment might be necessary and he "certainly would be a party" in any movement to effect such a change. "No half-way or dilatory methods will suffice to meet the situation." Yet the Senator did not want to be rash or impetuous. For the moment he was willing to give Coolidge every chance to make good.[13]

Some Senators undoubtedly felt that Borah was giving the President benefits far in excess of doubt, particularly when he opposed the Senate resolution asking Coolidge to dismiss Denby. To the Idahoan, it was a constitutional problem. He argued that the Senate would establish a precedent if it told the Execu-tive "whom he should dismiss from office." The only constitu-tional method was impeachment of Denby. Indeed, Borah urged such a step against the Secretary of the Navy in light of the momentous charges against him. Impeachment proceedings, of course, could not begin until the House pressed charges. Borah realized this but still saw no reason for the Senate to pass its resolution. In his estimation, the responsibility for Denby rested entirely upon Coolidge, not the Senate. Except for the usual standpatters, most Senators disagreed with the Idahoan and, by a 47 to 34 vote, sent the resolution to the White House.[14] Coo-lidge ignored the request but, a few weeks later, Denby volun-tarily resigned. When the President accepted the resignation, however, he explained that Denby had acted from a sense of public duty, and that the Secretary's honesty and integrity were not in question.

Daugherty still remained in the Cabinet. As long as this was so, Borah could not continue to have it both ways—to urge im-mediate action and to extend the administration's period of grace. In mid-February, the Senator discussed the situation with both Coolidge and Daugherty at the White House. Apparently Borah agreed to withhold comments in the Senate on the prob-lem until Coolidge had conferred with G.O.P. leaders. On Feb-

[13] Borah to John W. Miller, February 8, 1924, Borah Papers, Box 244.
[14] *Congressional Record,* 68th Cong., 1st Sess., 1924, LXV, 2072–80.

ruary 20, Henry Cabot Lodge and George Wharton Pepper spent more than an hour telling the President about the increasing sentiment in favor of Daugherty's retirement. Three days later, since Coolidge had still taken no action, Borah told the Senate that the Attorney General must resign. According to the Idahoan, public confidence in the Justice Department was waning at the very time when legal hearings were due concerning the oil lease cases, the Veteran's Bureau, and alien property disposal. He still left the initiative with the President but noted that the Senate had the weapon of impeachment. His main point was clear: "Mr. Daugherty cannot remain in the Cabinet an hour unless the President desires that he remain there." [15]

Within twenty-four hours, Coolidge called Borah to the White House, agreed with his speech, and said that it had prepared the way out of the predicament. But when the Senator again demanded Daugherty's resignation, Coolidge refused to commit himself. Borah came away "fighting mad," convinced that he could not cooperate with the administration until Daugherty was out of the Cabinet. "I have just left Borah," Raymond Robins wrote, "and he thinks that if Coolidge does not act within the next 48 hours that he (Borah) has been triffled [sic] with. This is based upon his talk with the President. . . ." [16]

This trend of events disturbed Robins. He and Salmon O. Levinson, a wealthy Chicago attorney, had for several years hoped that the Senator would pilot through Congress their program to outlaw war. Outlawry—"the Greatest Cause known to mankind," as Robins described it—was a peace plan whereby nations would renounce war, making it a crime; countries would agree to turn over to an international court those of its citizens who urged war. Since 1921 Levinson had worked to bring Borah

[15] *The Idaho Daily Statesman,* February 19, 21, 24, 1924; *Congressional Record,* 68th Cong., 1st Sess., 1924, LXV, 2892–93.
[16] Raymond Robins to Levinson, February 25, 1924, Levinson Papers, Box 76.

into the Outlawry crusade. The Senator's enthusiasm had fluctuated enough already to frustrate Robins and Levinson but they continued to solicit his support. They particularly hoped that Coolidge would seek Borah's political backing because, to the extent that the Idahoan could influence the President, Outlawry might benefit. "We must," Robins told Levinson in early 1923, "use all our intelligence and our art to win some advantage for our cause in the ebb and flow of the next campaign." The problem for the Outlawry people was that of making the administration realize that "only Borah, Levinson, Robins et al. can save the ticket" when La Follette "waves the tomahawk and starts on the warpath. We get more valuable each day—I think." Hopefully, then, Coolidge would see the value in endorsing the Great Cause.[17]

By February 12, 1924, Robins believed that the supporters of Outlawry held the initiative. Since members of the Republican National Committee had been "more willing to talk Borah and our plans" than previously, it seemed that the Senator was "at the apex of his power." [18]

The difficulty was, however, that Borah was not as zealous as Robins and Levinson in his commitment to Outlawry. Whereas they were fulltime disciples of the Great Cause, he refused to see it as the only, or even the most important, issue. As Robins sadly had to admit, the Senator was more concerned about recognition of Russia, the dismissal of Daugherty, and reforming the Republican party.[19]

[17] Robins to Levinson, January 1, 1925, July 16, 1923, December 15, 1923, Levinson Papers, Box 76. It was time, Robins wrote, to "bring up the reserves now on Coolidge," making him realize the necessity of having "Borah and myself and our crowd for him to the hilt." Robins to Levinson, January 28, 1924, *ibid.* For analyses of the Outlawry movement and Borah's relationship to it, see John E. Stoner, *S. O. Levinson and the Pact of Paris* (Chicago, 1943); John C. Vinson, *William E. Borah and the Outlawry of War* (Athens, Ga., 1957); Ferrell, *Peace in Their Time;* and Maddox, *William E. Borah and American Foreign Policy,* pp. 135–82.

[18] Robins to Levinson, February 12, 1924, Levinson Papers, Box 76.

[19] See, for example, Robins to Levinson, January 12 and 25, 1924, Levinson Papers, Box 76. Maddox, "William E. Borah and the Crusade

This became clear in early March when Coolidge, manifesting his desire for Borah's support, asked the Senator to breakfast. The invitation followed an hour-long discussion between Robins and the President, during which Robins stressed the terms on which he and Borah could back the administration. Coolidge, seemingly eager to get the Idahoan's endorsement, assured Robins "that Daugherty *goes* but *how soon* he did not say." Borah, however, in his subsequent breakfast talk with the President, refused to accept such a vague position. Although Coolidge indicated that he was behind the Outlawry program and urged the Senator to make a speech on that issue, Borah demanded Daugherty's dismissal as the precondition to any political backing.[20]

During the next few days, Borah was greatly discouraged. "He feels that he has been bunked by the Silent Lad." Robins tried to convince him that the President's inaction regarding the Attorney General did not justify Borah's indifference to Outlawry. To the Senator, however, Daugherty symbolized the old corruption from which he hoped to disassociate the G.O.P. "Borah does not want any part in salvaging Coolidge if he does not act by tomorrow NOON." By this time Robins himself was chafing under the "platitudinous bunk" from the White House, and he joined the Senator to commiserate over the political situation. That evening, the Colonel felt like he should "get drunk, or go to a fire or start a riot—or most any old thing." After leaving for Florida, Robins wrote Borah, telling him that his course in the Senate was the "wise" one. "I find serious thought of you as the one possible savior of the Republican Party in the fall election. Coolidge is either dead or can be resurrected by your aid only."[21]

---

to Outlaw War," *The Historian*, XXIX (February, 1967), 211n., writes "His letters clearly show that the Senator was far more interested in party reform than in Outlawry."

[20] Robins to Levinson, March 4 and 5, 1924, Levinson Papers, Box 76.

[21] Borah admitted his discouragement to John W. Hart, March 1, 1924, Borah Papers, Box 238; Robins to Levinson, March 9, 1924, Levinson Papers, Box 76; Robins to Borah, March 18, 1924, Borah Papers, Box 245.

For a few weeks, Levinson struggled on alone, trying to convince the administration of the political advantages inherent in the Outlawry program and a cooperative Borah. In late March, he journeyed to Washington. After learning from Borah that the Senator had turned his back on a White House speaking request, Levinson conversed with C. Bascom Slemp, Coolidge's secretary. While Slemp took notes, Levinson underlined the importance of Daugherty's dismissal. After a few minutes, Slemp talked with Coolidge and then reported to Levinson that the situation would soon improve to Levinson's satisfaction. Immediately the Chicago attorney visited Borah again. The Senator, however, was by now alert to possible deception and insisted that action and not more promises was necessary to convince him of the administration's good faith. Despite Borah's suspicions, by the next morning Daugherty—undoubtedly due to rising public pressure upon the President—had resigned. Levinson exulted; circumstances now seemed ready for Borah's much-postponed Outlawry speech in the Senate.[22]

But again the Senator hesitated, this time using the excuse that other matters needed prompt attention. He would postpone the big Outlawry effort until he could do it justice. "If only Borah would shoot!" moaned Robins. "He is losing one of the great opportunities of life and the political issue of this generation is in danger of slipping from his grasp. . . ."[23] Even if the Idahoan would not give his Outlawry speech, Levinson and Robins hoped that he would at least cooperate with Coolidge in the approaching campaign and, by doing so, gain an advantage for the Great Cause.

Meanwhile the administration, interested primarily in giving the President a western and progressive stamp of approval, attempted to draw Borah into an active role in the approaching national convention by offering him the temporary chairman-

[22] Levinson to Robins, March 31, 1924, Levinson Papers, Box 76.
[23] Borah to Charles Clayton Morrison, April 26, 1924, Borah Papers, Box 242; Robins to Levinson, May 17, 1924, Levinson Papers, Box 76.

ship. The Senator rejected the position. When Dewey Hilles, chairman of the Republican National Finance Committee, heard about the refusal, he urged further efforts to bring Borah "into the picture." If the Idahoan would nominate Coolidge, for example, it would be unnecessary "to invade the West for a man to make a seconding speech." Slemp, the President's secretary, ultimately visited Borah's apartment where he proposed that Borah serve as Coolidge's running mate. When the Senator spurned the offer, Slemp asked that he deliver the nominating speech. Again Borah's response was emphatically negative.[24]

Indeed, Robins found Borah "determined not to play with the Coolidge forces. He has a deep personal resentment against them," including the President.[25] Rather than intimating even possible aid for the administration, Borah instead directed his attention toward vindicating Montana's Senator Burton K. Wheeler from charges of fraud.

The Wheeler case had become a progressive *cause célèbre*. It grew out of an indictment against the Montana Democrat for allegedly accepting a retainer from an oil man, in return for securing oil and gas permits from the Secretary of the Interior. To progressives, the entire episode was part of an insidious effort to take revenge upon Wheeler for his key role in the Senate investigations of Daugherty and corruption in government.[26]

Borah looked upon the affair with anger. As the appointed chairman of the Senate committee to examine the charges against Wheeler, he claimed objectivity; yet he confided to Robins that the whole case was a "frameup." Robins compared the Idahoan's attitude to that of the Bull-Moosers just before

---

[24] C. Bascom Slemp to Borah, April 19, 1924, Borah Papers, Box 243; Charles D. Hilles to Slemp, May 5, 1924, Coolidge Papers, Case File 608; Hilles to Frank W. Stearns, May 3, 1924, Hilles Papers, Box 206; Robins to Levinson, May 9, 1924, Levinson Papers, Box 76.

[25] Robins to Levinson, May 10, 1924, Levinson Papers, Box 76.

[26] Burton K. Wheeler, *Yankee from the West* (New York, 1962), pp. 213–43, has a general chronology of Wheeler's efforts to expose Daugherty and of his own defense against the charges of fraud and conspiracy.

the 1912 bolt. For the moment, "this Wheeler Investigation has become the most important thing to him personally"; indeed, the Senator's partisanship for Wheeler seemed to feed upon his resentment against Republican officialdom.[27]

Borah's dissatisfaction with the G.O.P. hierarchy boiled over during an interview with a witness whom the Senate had subpoenaed from Montana to testify in the case. Wheeler had charged the witness and George Lockwood of the Republican National Committee with trying to frame him. During the hour-long private meeting in Borah's office, the discussion became quite heated. At one point the witness suggested that Borah had prejudiced the case in favor of Wheeler. The Senator responded with a bitter critique of Republican leadership. Fuming that he was "ashamed of the Republican National Committee," he threatened to denounce it upon the conclusion of the investigation. "If the Republican party can't do any better than throw bricks at the Democrats in the Senate, it has no right to existence." It was this very kind of nonsense that might lead to a third-party victory in November. Indeed, Borah was not sure whether to remain with the G.O.P. or join a splinter movement. In his opinion, the Republicans had one major assignment: "that is clean out the crooks they have in office and fumigate the offices after they leave." Was the Senator referring to such cabinet officials as Hubert Work, Andrew Mellon, and Hoover? "I mean all of them," Borah shot back. "If the men in office were not vulnerable they would not be attacked." [28]

As the Wheeler case dragged on, Raymond Robins groaned that Borah's "isolation is for the moment complete." The Outlawry of War movement was "at zero in the political situation" and "Hamlet" was in good part responsible. Levinson, however, would not give up. He refused, for example, to accept Borah's rejection of the vice-presidential offer as conclusive. He worried

27 Robins to Levinson, May 9 and 10, 1924, Levinson Papers, Box 76.
28 Typed copy of the interview, held on April 18, 1924, in Hoover Papers, Commerce Dept. File, Box 1-I/272.

instead that other people might take the Senator at his word, look for another candidate, "and thus cut off this avenue." [29]

Yet it was Borah himself who continued to close "this avenue." Following the Senate's 56 to 5 vote to accept the Borah committee's report wholly exonerating Wheeler from all charges, Robins found him "flushed with his victory . . . on the Wheeler vindication and inclined to be very bitter toward the National Committee." He was more obdurate than ever in declining to work with what he called the "Coolidge gang." [30] Actually, as early as April 21, Borah had decided not even to attend the Cleveland convention. He wrote to his sister confidentially that, barring the unexpected, he would not go. Since Coolidge could control the nomination, Borah could do nothing except tire himself. By the end of May, he was convinced

[29] Robins to Levinson, May 10, 1924, and Levinson to Robins, May 10, 1924, Levinson Papers, Box 76.

[30] Robins to Levinson, May 25, 1924, Levinson Papers, Box 76. The Wheeler case was not completely settled until spring, 1925. In Great Falls, Montana, a jury acquitted him of the original charges of fraud; and in Washington, D.C., a judge threw out an indictment charging Wheeler with conspiracy to block the first indictment. In 1924, Borah volunteered to be an assistant counsel in Wheeler's defense. When the Great Falls trial occurred, however, he declined to participate for two reasons: he would be in the position of defending his own judgment in his own report based on the Senate hearings; and, since Wheeler seemed certain to win his case, it would be tactically inadvisable for Borah to go to Montana—it "would be advertising to the country a desperate case when there is no desperate case." Borah to Wheeler, August 25, 1924, Borah Papers, Box 247; to La Follette, April 10, 1925, Box 259. See, also, Wheeler, *Yankee from the West*, pp. 238–42. La Follette, Norris, James Reed, and Thomas Walsh also offered to defend him. La Follette and Walsh were especially anxious to bring Borah into the courtroom to defend Wheeler. See handwritten letter from La Follette to Wheeler, March 30, 1925, La Follette Family Papers, Series B, Box 119. In the Mercer Green Johnston Papers, Box 79, there is a folder on the Wheeler Defense Committee, a voluntary group that solicited contributions to defray Wheeler's expenses. The committee included such reformers as Josephus Daniels, Norman Hapgood, William Allen White, Broadus Mitchell, Villard, Harold Ickes, William Kent, Father John Ryan, Sidney Hillman, Norman Thomas, Roger Baldwin, J. A. H. Hopkins, John Haynes Holmes, Louis Post, and Herbert Croly.

that Republicans faced a rubber-stamp gathering. He complained of fatigue and of politics "so chaotic, so sordid, and so discouraging" that a man remained "in the game" only because "it seems cowardly to get out of a thing that is so bad." [31]

Obviously Borah had grown increasingly antagonistic toward the administration, but there was another reason behind his decision to avoid the convention. He admitted that there were arguments why he should be present; but there was "another more controlling one" why he should not.[32]

This "controlling" explanation undoubtedly concerned the Idaho Progressives. Borah had little to gain at Cleveland and much to lose. Since he could have no real voice at the convention, his presence would serve only to endorse the Coolidge candidacy and platform, something he was not ready to do. Furthermore, the Senator had learned that Ray McKaig, the leading Idaho Progressive, was worried that he would nominate Coolidge. Although McKaig wanted his third-party group to support Borah's re-election to the Senate, there was a danger that the state Progressives would refuse to vote for a man who adhered too closely to the G.O.P. McKaig hoped that Borah would "not embarrass any of us fellows in the third party movement in this state by taking too prominent a part in the National Convention at Cleveland." The Senator replied that he would not disappoint them at all. In this case, the maxim " 'Stand still and see the salvation of the Lord' " was sound advice.[33]

The administration, however, would not accept the policy of standing still. It continued its attempt to pull Borah into the Republican vanguard by again offering him the vice-presidential spot on the ticket. The Senator's value as a western drawing

[31] Borah to Mrs. Mattie Rinard, April 21, 1924, Borah Papers, Box 243; to E. H. Dewey, May 20, 1924, Box 237; to H. A. Lawson, May 31, 1924, Box 244.

[32] Borah to John W. Hart, June 6, 1924, Borah Papers, Box 244.

[33] L. W. Thrailkill to Borah, May 17, 1924; Ray McKaig to Borah, May 12, 1924; Borah to Ray McKaig, May 19, 1924; and to L. W. Thrailkill, May 21, 1924, Borah Papers, Box 243.

card was obvious. As Frederick Wile observed in his news column, "by every means at the President's command the Coolidge steam roller at Cleveland is to be lubricated with western grease." With the growing boom for Robert M. La Follette signaling that farmers were still unhappy, the G.O.P. was determined to capture votes in disaffected rural areas. Furthermore, Borah as vice-president would perhaps be more manageable and also give the administration a certain progressive aura. The Senator himself was well aware of the handicaps that such an office would force upon him. "I have no desire to sit mute and be a figure head [*sic*] for four long years; in fact, I would die of nervous prostration." He believed, moreover, that he had finally reached a position in the Senate "where I can be of real force in affairs." He lacked "any suicidal bent, politically or otherwise." [34]

But the Republican hierarchy, just as Levinson, refused to take him at his word. Around one o'clock on the morning of June 12, word emerged from the fourth floor of the Hotel Cleveland that the Coolidge managers had named the Idaho Senator as their candidate for second place on the ticket. Immediately a reporter for the *Cleveland Plain Dealer* routed Borah out of his Washington bed only to learn that the Idahoan definitely did not want the job. [35]

Borah then telephoned Albert Beveridge, a member of the Indiana delegation, and instructed him to withdraw his name if anyone presented it. He also sent Beveridge a telegram of declination to read to the convention if it insisted on nominating him. Telegrams stating unequivocally "that I cannot and will not accept" went to Slemp, Senator James Wadsworth of New York, Secretary of War John W. Weeks, and Frank Mondell, the permanent chairman. "Don't let this happen," he ordered John Hart of the Idaho delegation. There was still con-

[34] Washington *Star,* June 3, 1924, Wile Scrapbooks, 19; Borah to A. T. Cole, October 10, 1923, Borah Papers, Box 233; to James F. McCarthy, June 13, 1924; and to Wayne B. Wheeler, May 31, 1924, Box 244.
[35] *Cleveland Plain Dealer,* June 12, 1924, Borah Scrapbooks, Reel 4.

fusion. The Baltimore *Sun* featured a front-page picture and story of Borah's acceptance of the vice-presidential offer. Such headlines frightened conservatives such as William Howard Taft, who doubted that the Senator "would be a safe man." The Chief Justice need not have worried, for Borah remained adamantly opposed to the proposition. When Beveridge wired of rumors that Secretary Weeks was insisting that the Senator would accept, Borah warned that "Secretary Weeks has no such assurance and you rely upon what I have telegraphed." [36]

Still the administration forces persisted. Shortly before noon on June 12, Coolidge's secretary, Edward T. Clark, found Borah horseback riding in Rock Creek Park and whisked him to the White House. After talking to Coolidge for about thirty minutes, the Senator wired Beveridge that he had "just conferred with the President and there is absolutely no change in my position." The Indiana delegate must not accept any contrary statement.[37]

After much confusion the Borah "candidacy" finally ended. His near-candidacy had plainly resulted from a reluctance to believe him. Most significantly, however, it was also the product of the birth pains of the new Republican leadership. Indeed, it almost signaled a party miscarriage. The "Coolidge gang" represented a new look, different from that of the Old Guard of 1920. The performances of many Old Guard Republicans during the fights over such things as the bonus and postal-salary-raise vetoes had displeased Coolidge. Hence, in delegating assignments for the Cleveland convention, the President ignored such traditional Senate leaders as Henry Cabot Lodge, James Watson of Indiana, Medill McCormick of Illinois, George H. Moses and Frank Brandegee of Connecticut, Utah's Reed Smoot, and Charles Curtis of Kansas. The steady loss of influ-

[36] Series of telegrams dated June 12, 1924, Borah Papers, Box 244; Baltimore *Sun*, June 12, 1924; Taft to Horace Taft, June 12, 1924, Taft Papers, Box 560; Beveridge to Borah, June 12, 1924; and Borah reply, June 12, 1924, Borah Papers, Box 244.

[37] Borah Scrapbooks, Reel 2; Borah to Beveridge, June 12, 1924, Borah Papers, Box 244.

ence angered the old leadership. They held "indignant pow-
wows" about it and quietly bore the cloakroom taunts of Democrats. At Cleveland, Coolidge turned party control over to
William M. Butler, wealthy textile industrialist from Massachusetts. While Old Guardsmen complained about being mere
figureheads, Butler's room was the real scene of activity. John
T. Adams, whom Butler was replacing as national party chairman, found that his room was outside the center of action and
mainly a place to which ticket-hunters came. Lodge received a
backhanded slap when he got an offer to serve as *vice*-chairman
of the Massachusetts delegation, a position which he under-
standably declined.[38]

The anger of the Old Guard leaders mounted as Butler's
domination grew at Cleveland. Their sullen opposition broke
into open rebellion over the vice-presidential question. The
Coolidge-Butler group, hoping to control the convention from
first to last, paid the "inevitable penalty of being overslick."
Butler, usually with Frank W. Stearns, the President's confidential adviser, sat in his sixth-floor suite and refused to support
the boomlets for Frank Lowden of Illinois or Herbert Hoover.
On the fourth floor, in Secretary Weeks's room, Senators such
as Pennsylvania's George Wharton Pepper and David A. Reed,
and New York's James Wadsworth sat with Theodore Roosevelt, Jr., Ohio Congressman Nicholas Longworth, Postmaster
General Harry S. New, Speaker of the House Frederick H. Gillett, Secretary of the Treasury Andrew Mellon, Dewey Hilles
of the National Committee, and C. Bascom Slemp discussing
the vice-presidential candidates. Butler kept rejecting the suggestions which he received from them but offered no advice of
his own. The group in Weeks's room struggled through one

[38] Philadelphia *Public Ledger,* June 6, 1924, Borah Scrapbooks, Reel 4.
William Allen White, *A Puritan in Babylon* (New York, 1938), p. 296,
tells how Coolidge turned direct—no longer indirect—control over to
business; he put "much of the control of the Republican party directly
into business without mediation of the political machine." Also, Donald
R. McCoy, *Calvin Coolidge* (New York, 1967), p. 243. On Lodge, *The
New York Times,* June 10, 1924.

night until New departed for bed at 4 A.M., commenting disgustedly that "the kind of man you are looking for as Vice-President was crucified nineteen hundred years ago." Finally, by midnight of the following day, the men around Weeks swung their support to Senator Charles Curtis from Kansas. At this point Butler suddenly decided to exercise his influence. When Weeks's group told Butler about their decision, the chairman said impassively that he had just communicated with Coolidge and that "We must nominate Borah for Vice-President." There was silence. Weeks fumed when Butler asked for opinions; and, when Butler inquired as to what Secretary Mellon thought of the Idaho Senator, Mellon retorted, "I never think of him until somebody mentions his name." [39]

Despite some dissatisfaction, however, the Weeks faction dropped the Curtis boom and assumed that the issue was settled. Borah shattered this assumption with his telephone and telegram rejections to the convention. The Senator also inadvertently undermined the position of Butler who, after postponing his grand entry onto the convention stage, made a fool of himself by muffing his lines. According to Borah, the Coolidge-Butler axis was "not willing to believe me when I said 'No.' . . . They simply didn't credit my sincerity. . . ." Perhaps, he mused, the enthusiasm about placing him "into a state of 'mummification' " revealed that someone was tiring of his voice and his vote.[40]

[39] Borah Scrapbooks, Reel 4; Frank Kent in the Baltimore *Sun*, June 13, 1924; Nicholas Murray Butler, *Across the Busy Years*, I (New York, 1935), pp. 280–82. Butler was a participant in these proceedings. James Sheffield, whom Coolidge ultimately named as ambassador to Mexico, was also in the room when "the noble Butler" sprang his announcement about the Idahoan. "Among the twenty or more men gathered not a single voice was raised in favor of Borah, and many of the men had served with him in the Congress for many years." Sheffield to Dewey Hilles, Hilles Papers, January 4, 1935, Box 219.

[40] Borah to Edward E. Whiting, June 25, 1924, Borah Papers, Box 231, and Borah to J. H. Eble, June 16, 1924, Box 244. Upon hearing that the Spokane, Washington, Chamber of Commerce had been ready to blow the city whistles if he got the nomination, Borah jokingly commented on

Whatever the reasons for Butler's miscalculation, when he botched the Borah announcement the Old Guard leaders reasserted themselves. They had no confidence in an incoming national chairman who, through "sheer political stupidity and complete managerial fumble-bumble," had allowed the vice-presidential problem to become an embarrassing source of party confusion. By ignoring them and by flaunting his power, he had taken the well-oiled party machine off the smooth road and "out for a cross-country jaunt, jumping ditches and banging into rock piles." Butler's one-man management sputtered to an end, and the Old Guard controlled the duration of the convention.[41] Charles G. Dawes, an Illinois man who supposedly would attract western farm votes, received the vice-presidential nomination.

Although there was general Republican harmony over the chosen standard-bearers, the convention had exposed cracks in the elephant's hide. As Henry W. Taft, brother of the Chief Justice and a participant at the convention, observed, "We seemed to be in a state of transition. There were many men and many minds, but little centralized authority. One could not but observe the curious change by which men such as Lodge were retired to the sidelines." There was eagerness among some Republicans about "sitting on" the Old Guard Senators. William Howard Taft, for example, believed it was time to "create a new crop of influential Republicans. The only hope of the party is in Coolidge, and it is time that Lodge and Brandegee and Curtis and Watson were swept up and out." [42]

This "state of transition" within the G.O.P. would have subsequent ramifications. A lack of substantial Republican leader-

such willingness "to celebrate my disappearance from active political life." Arthur Shaw to Borah, June 23, 1924, and Borah reply, June 27, 1924, Box 243.

[41] Baltimore *Sun*, June 13, 1924; "The Federal Machine Okays Coolidge," *Searchlight on Congress*, IX (June and July, 1924), 5–6.

[42] Henry W. Taft to William Howard Taft, June 14, 1924; Isaac M. Ullman to Taft, June 16, 1924; Taft to Elihu Root, June 9, 1924, Taft Papers, Box 560.

ship had already allowed the western insurgents to enhance their position in the Senate. At the convention the party captains had hardly strengthened their hand. The new organization leaders, trying to shunt the Old Guard aside, had bungled the job and sent some Republicans "away with a bilious taste." G.O.P. regulars needed unity. Without it, even though Coolidge might win the November battles, the party elephant could be impressive in size but hamstrung and vulnerable to insurgency. As events shortly proved, the very lack of party command, so evident during the collision over a vice-presidential choice, would be partially responsible for the momentary success of the "Borah bloc" the following year.[43]

With the Cleveland convention over, the question of Borah's relationship to the Republican ticket was still unanswered. He had refused the offer to run with Coolidge. At this point he was neither definitely in nor out of the party camp. His decision before November could be crucial. As columnist Edward Whiting observed, Borah's "course in the immediate future is of national importance." The Senator was "the oratorical giant of his party. No other Republican has an equal forcefulness of utterance. No other Republican can campaign so effectively." Undoubtedly, the G.O.P. management would try to utilize "this exceptional ability" before November. But, in mid-1924, no one knew what Borah's course would be—"except Mr. Borah." [44]

The emergence in June of the La Follette national ticket and Borah's own political situation in Idaho, where the third-party vote was important, made his future role more difficult. His decisions in the next months would affect his own chances for re-election and, assuming he returned to the Senate, his position in that body after the election. Nor could he completely ignore the Outlawry of War people. Raymond Robins, for example, undoubtedly had influence in many circles and could be a boon

[43] "The Federal Machine Okays Coolidge," *Searchlight on Congress*, p. 6. See following chapter for a discussion of the "Borah bloc."
[44] *The Boston Herald*, June 18, 1924.

to Borah's own political future and certainly to his often-stated hopes of reforming the G.O.P.[45] And, since Robins and Levinson were convinced that the Republican party held the only hope for Outlawry, they continued to pressure the Senator to take the stump for Coolidge.

Progressives—national and state—also counted on Borah's support. Gutzon Borglum believed that Borah, like Norris, Howell, and other independents, would "inevitably fall into line" behind La Follette. Hopkins of the Committee of 48 assumed that the Idahoan intended to support the third-party ticket. He recalled his conversation with Borah in April, 1923, at which time the Senator had said that he was not so much interested in being a candidate as in serving the movement. The Forty-Eighter reminded Borah that when they had discussed the possibilities of La Follette's presidential candidacy, "you told me how highly you regarded him and said that he would be all right, and that if it turned out that he came to the front, well and good." Hopkins hoped that Borah was now ready to declare publicly for La Follette. Gilson Gardner of the Scripps-Howard newspapers also remembered Borah's earlier enthusiasm for the Wisconsin progressive. "You know I am for Bob," the Idahoan had said. Gardner doubted that Borah had changed his mind; surely he would not choose to be window dressing for the "reactionary riffraff lined up with Coolidge." [46]

Yet, as the summer passed, Borah refused to take sides. In Idaho, he denied rumors that he was endorsing a Progressive, H. F. Samuels, for governor; the press, he conjectured mysteriously, was merely "interpreting the trend." He carefully avoided making any public comment on the national campaign until the candidates had spoken, on grounds that the platforms of the major parties did not impress him. Before he committed

[45] See Maddox, *William E. Borah and American Foreign Policy*, p. 142, for comments regarding Robins's usefulness to Borah.

[46] Borglum to Robert M. La Follette, July 4, 1924, Borglum Papers, Box 61; J. A. H. Hopkins to Borah, September 10, 1924; and Gilson Gardner to Borah, September 11, 1924, Borah Papers, Box 243.

himself, he wanted to see how the nominees themselves defined the issues.[47]

Borah's most immediate concern was his own nomination at the state conventions in late August. This would entail another test of "the harmony program" which had prevailed in the G.O.P. gathering at Lewiston in March. There was also the question of whether the Idaho Progressives would choose him or turn to an opposition candidate for the Senate. And, in Idaho, the Progressive party was nothing at which to snivel. Indeed, in 1922 it had become the second most powerful political faction in the state, surpassing the Democrats and moving within 10,000 votes of the Republicans.[48]

Whether Borah actually needed the Progressive nomination or not,[49] he desperately wanted it. His thoughts were not only on winning re-election in November, but also on the additional leverage an impressive victory might give him when he returned to Washington. In short, his reputation was on the line. Borah's concern with such matters was clear in a handwritten memorandum to Raymond Robins expressing the Senator's wish that the Democrats would not challenge him. He urged Robins "to feel out [the] situation with leading Democrats." Borah was proposing no deals, "but if matters should so develop that I would have no opposition at home it would . . . give me prestige in the Senate." If the Democrats would leave him unopposed, "I would feel it most helpful—not so much as to the election as to influence it would contribute for my work in the future. *You understand.*" The Senator held similar views re-

[47] Raymond Robins telegram to Borah, July 20, 1924; Borah telegram reply, July 21, 1924, Borah Papers, Box 243; Borah to John W. Owens of the Baltimore *Sun,* July 19, 1924, Box 231.

[48] The letterhead of the Idaho Progressive Party State Central Committee read, "Watch Us Grow." In 1920, Progressive voters numbered 28,752; the Democrats, 38,509; and the Republicans, 75,748. In 1922, Progressive votes reached 40,516; the Democrats, 36,810; and the Republicans, 50,538.

[49] Orde Pinckney quotes from the unpublished manuscript of a leading Idaho political observer that "Borah had an almost pathological fear of defeat." "Lion Triumphant," *Idaho Yesterdays,* III (Summer, 1959), 14.

garding any Progressive opposition; but by June the situation was such that he was pessimistic about getting the third-party endorsement.[50]

Borah's hopes within the third party depended on the extent to which his supporters, under the leadership of Ray McKaig, could overcome the increasingly vocal anti-Borah elements. McKaig, a member of the Committee of 48 and a founder of the Idaho Progressive party, used his impressive credentials within the state to press vigorously for the Senator's nomination.

Among Idaho Progressives, Borah became a major issue. On August 5, a former secretary of the party stood on the capitol steps and told several hundred listeners that Borah was more concerned with the G.O.P. than with progressivism. The Senator, "by a circuitous route," would take the Progressives into his own party. A few days later, a group of Progressive leaders threatened to force the resignation of McKaig, as salaried manager of the party, because of his alleged efforts to throw Progressive votes to the Republican Senator. "The only way we can exist as a party," one of the men explained, "is to place a complete ticket in the field and not endorse the candidates of the two old-line parties." At a heated county meeting of Progressive precinct committeemen at Twin Falls, a majority aimed a direct blow at McKaig and Borah by agreeing to oppose any affiliations with, or endorsements of, any regular party candidate. In Caldwell, Idaho, a Progressive assembly broke into debate over a resolution backing Borah's return to the Senate. One individual wondered if the Progressives were cogs in Borah's machine or if he belonged to the Progressive party. No one seemed to know. Although the chairman pointed out that La Follette wanted a showdown between progressivism and conservatism—not along party lines—the Borah resolution went back into committee without recommendation. The same day,

[50] Borah to Robins, undated, although penciled editorial remarks place it in August, 1924, Robins Papers, Box 19. Despite Borah's hopes, the Democrats nominated an opposition candidate. Ray McKaig to Borah, November 17, 1930, and December 26, 1930, Borah Papers, Box 325, recalled the Senator's pessimism about Progressive support.

several speakers at a Boise gathering attacked the Senator and accused McKaig of showing more interest in Borah than in La Follette. During these weeks a much-harassed McKaig constantly had to defend Borah from charges of lacking progressive convictions.[51]

At the state convention, the McKaig forces nonetheless prevailed. When the moment of decision arrived, the anti-Borah sentiment gave way and the Progressives overwhelmingly nominated the Senator. After the chairman had declared that Borah would not decline the nomination, a unanimous ballot carried with a burst of cheers. A resolution hailed the Senator's "consistent course at all times" and called for voters to elect men "who will stand with him in the battle for human rights as against the so-called vested rights of property." As McKaig later reminded Borah, such a quick and overwhelming nomination "put you in a very strategic position" and proved "to the world that you wore no man's collar."[52] This was precisely the impression that the Senator hoped to convey outside Idaho.

There remained, however, the task of winning the Republican nomination. Within the state G.O.P.—just as among Progressives—political lines formed around the Senator. In Boise, on the evening of August 15, the statehouse group held a caucus to promote party harmony. To counter this, "the friends of Senator Borah" called a rival meeting for the same time. "The harmonizers" met, adopting a set of resolutions urging party peace and endorsing Borah, Coolidge, and Governor Moore. They then sent three representatives to the "Borah first" people to urge unity. The Borah group spurned the truce offer, saying that harmony could not come at the expense of principles.[53]

Although Borah also stood on the side of principle, he was not seeking a fight. Several months earlier, he had said privately that the state machine must not control the Idaho Falls nomi-

[51] *The Idaho Daily Statesman,* August 5, 15, 17, 20, 1924; McKaig to Borah, December 26, 1930, Borah Papers, Box 325.
[52] *The Idaho Daily Statesman,* August 27, 1924; McKaig to Borah, November 17, 1930, Borah Papers, Box 325.
[53] *The Idaho Daily Statesman,* August 16, 1924.

nating convention. But by August, he was less interested in a confrontation. Instead, he decided to avoid a head-on collision with Republican regulars by missing the convention altogether. He explained to one friend that he would certainly attend if he could defeat the statehouse clique in a platform fight. Since a victory over the party machine seemed impossible, however, his appearance at the convention would do more harm than good. He would either have to engage in a futile fight that would split the party, or appear to surrender his own views. By staying away, he could protect both G.O.P. unity and his own principles.[54]

His decision to avoid the Idaho Falls assembly was politically wise. At that meeting his future rested—not with the Idaho populace as he would have preferred—but with the railroad, beet sugar, wool, and mining interests in the state. His vote against the 1922 tariff had certainly diminished his political capital with the wool groups. In August, 1924, he wanted to do nothing else which might hurt his chances for re-election.[55] Since he apparently lacked the strength to control the convention, he could either engage in useless and politically dangerous fighting, or he could leave well enough alone, abide by the earlier harmony agreement, and stay away.

Choosing the course of expediency was understandable, but Borah tried to inflate it into an act of courage: "I intend to preserve my principles and views if I never see the inside of the Senate Chamber again." He failed to say, though, in what way he jeopardized his Senate seat by dodging showdowns on the platform and, particularly, on the explosive direct primary issue. A decision to battle the machine would have involved the greater risk. He said that he would remain absent from the convention so that he would not have to sacrifice his principles; hence he stayed away and sacrificed them anyway. The "grand,

54 Borah to Shad L. Hogdin, August 22, 1924, and to John W. Hart, August 24, 1924, Borah Papers, Box 243.

55 See, for example, Edward G. Lowry's column, "Mr. Borah's Plight," in the Philadelphia *Public Ledger*, September 27, 1922, Borah Scrapbooks, Reel 4.

harmonious session" which nominated Borah in absentia also adopted a platform which praised Coolidge, and said nothing about the direct primary or legislative reforms.[56]

The Senator engaged in wishful thinking when he asserted that the eulogistic nominating speeches in his behalf "must have had a nerve wracking effect in certain quarters." Ironically, it was not the pro-Borah speeches that worried the statehouse people as much as the man who leaped to his feet, shouting the only "no" against the motion to choose the Senator by unanimous vote. The incident was innocuous enough, since the delegate was merely trying to refute charges in his home district that he lacked the "guts" to oppose Borah at the convention. Nonetheless, the convention leaders feared that his dissenting vote would force a roll call, in which case disgruntled anti-Borah delegates might have endangered the harmony agreement. The machine representatives, who had "leaned over backward in their efforts to make peace with the 'super-Borah' men," hurriedly talked to the man and persuaded him not to block the motion for unanimity. Strangely enough, "the so-called opponents of Senator Borah, in control of the convention," had rescued him from possible embarrassment.[57]

Principles aside, the harmony program had prevailed. The state machine went unchallenged, Borah got his renomination, and the Idaho G.O.P. presented an image of unity to the voters. However much the Senator may have been anathema to the courthouse group, he was certainly an important drawing card on the party ticket. Certainly, if it was politically expedient for him to avoid a showdown, it was equally beneficial for the Idaho regulars to put him on the ballot.

Borah had his nomination from both parties, but the problem of the campaign still confronted him. On the national level, the administration continued to seek his support. Chairman

[56] Borah to John W. Hart, August 24, 1924, Borah Papers, Box 243; *The Idaho Daily Statesman*, August 28, 1924.

[57] Borah to Irvin E. Rockwell, August 29, 1924, Borah Papers, Box 243; *The Idaho Daily Statesman*, August 28, 1924.

Butler hoped, in early September, to persuade him to speak in Wisconsin for the Republicans. David A. Reed, standpatter from Pennsylvania, asked the Idahoan to come to Pittsburgh and wrest the labor vote from the Progressives. Steadfastly, Borah eschewed such commitments on the grounds that the national committee had earlier indicated that he should concentrate his efforts in the northwest.[58]

The Outlawry of War advocates also implored Borah to aid the administration. Raymond Robins had for a while wanted nothing to do with "$oolidge and $awes," the spokesmen of Wall Street privilege. But when the Republican hierarchy praised the Colonel as "the best person to help keep the Progressives from going astray after La Follette," he again saw an opportunity for Outlawry and changed his mind. Robins's conditions were clear: the Idaho G.O.P. convention must nominate Borah, and Coolidge must endorse Outlawry. Chairman Butler was amenable to both propositions. He agreed to do what he could to help Borah get the Idaho endorsement, if such aid proved necessary, and to speak with the President about the Great Cause. Coolidge subsequently, in his speech accepting the nomination, approved of "covenants for the purpose of outlawing aggressive war by any practical means"; although his use of the word "aggressive" demonstrated his lack of knowledge of the Great Cause, the Outlawry people accepted it as a White House commitment. When the Idaho Republicans nominated Borah, Robins believed that "Butler had delivered absolutely on both his promises, and is now entitled to a good faith support by all of us." Future strategy was clear: "we must . . . get our Hamlet into action, even if we both must go to Idaho and personally conduct our Prima Donna on the Grand Circuit." Both Butler and the chairman of the G.O.P. national speaker's bureau believed that it was indeed time to get Borah

[58] Max Pam to William Howard Taft, September 6, 1924, Taft Papers, Box 565; David A. Reed to Borah, October 2, 1924, and October 6, 1924; Borah reply, October 6, 1924, Borah Papers, Box 238.

to "swing around the circle" for the administration. Robins and Levinson hoped, of course, that Borah could thus put "the OUT-LAWRY idea across in this national campaign." [59]

"Delivering Borah," however, was a discouraging assignment. Robins tried several tactics. He warned the Senator that the course of the campaign was favoring the Democrat, John W. Davis, whose election would "be the death knell of the Out-lawry of War program" and a revival of the League of Nations concept. He remembered, moreover, that it was Borah who had "first won me to consideration of him [Coolidge] and his claims. Baffled as I was for quite a while—I am now convinced in his favor." The Colonel, before taking the stump himself from Wisconsin to Oregon, wrote that "it would give me a special personal assurance if I knew that you were fighting the common enemy and leading the Issues that you have made to victory." Levinson tried to convince the Senator that he had a great opportunity "to be the real adviser and power behind the throne." If Borah would make an enthusiastic party speech, future power within the G.O.P. would be within his grasp. Remember, Levinson admonished him, "if Davis wins, we lose everything." [60]

Yet Borah continued what Robins called his "hesitation waltz." He explained that he could not leave Idaho, abandoning his own affairs to campaign on a national level. There was a chance that he might leave the state for a ten-day stumping tour and then return; but, for the moment, "I am doing the best I can to serve the cause . . . that is, serve it ultimately." [61]

Frustrated, Robins decided that the Senator had missed his chance. "Borah will be a Republican pariah—under suspicion by all the groups in American politics from now on." If the campaign left liberals without any real leadership it was be-

[59] Robins to Borah, June 17, 1924, Borah Papers, Box 245; Robins to Levinson, August 6 and 30, 1924, Levinson Papers, Box 76. See also, Stoner, *S. O. Levinson and the Pact of Paris*, p. 134.

[60] Robins to Borah, September 18 and 28, 1924; Levinson to Borah, September 19, 1924, Borah Papers, Box 238.

[61] Robins to Levinson, September 27, 1924, Levinson Papers, Box 76; Borah to Levinson, September 30, 1924, Borah Papers, Box 238.

cause "our Hamlet allowed the drift of petty personal selfishness to land us." As for Outlawry, Coolidge might lose interest "by reason of Borah's selfish folly." It was ironic, Robins wrote, that "we will be more or less dammed [sic] as the most intimate friends of Hamlet, for we have delivered in so far as he is concerned—just exactly nothing." Because of the Colonel's many assurances to G.O.P. leaders about the Senator's willingness to help, there was the possibility that they might now view Robins as deceitful or ignorant. "Borah has left us high and dry in a political land of sand and sickness and sorrow." [62]

By October, it indeed seemed that the administration was less in need of Borah's support. Coolidge's popularity was increasing across the nation, including the west where La Follette's strength supposedly rested. One observer commented that while the G.O.P. itself was secondary with the electorate, "the real platform, the real slogan, and the real strength of the Republican party is Coolidge." The President seemed "reliable, honest, earnest and modest," and his economy program was having great influence. In Minnesota, for example, farmers, convinced that frugality was a virtue, called him the "penny pinching President." From Kansas came word that western crops were so good "that they wouldn't let a Democratic orator even light for gas," and that William Allen White, influential editor of the *Emporia Gazette,* was supporting Coolidge. Elihu Root, former Cabinet member and Republican Senator, predicted that La Follette—"a pretty weak imitation of Roosevelt, with a little French Revolution thrown in"—would lose handily because the western reform Senators, with "a mighty keen eye for their own safety," would not support him." [63]

Root's prognostications appeared increasingly accurate as the campaign continued. Robert M. La Follette, Jr., stated confidentially that, even though his father was allaying possible Pro-

[62] Robins to Levinson, October 20, 1924, Levinson Papers, Box 76.
[63] Max Pam to Taft, September 6, 1924, Taft Papers, Box 565; original of letter from William Allen White to George Harvey, August 2, 1924, in Coolidge Papers, Case File 32; Elihu Root to Taft, September 16, 1924, Taft Papers, Box 565.

gressive opposition to Borah in Idaho, Borah probably would give no support in return. Even Hiram Johnson, who was to charge Borah with only "half-delivering," straddled the political fence. In July he endorsed La Follette and later he fought the move in California to exclude La Follette and Wheeler from the ballot. Yet he refused to take the stump for the Progressive ticket and, as the election drew closer, his silence moved *The New Republic* to question his future as a liberal Senator. In early November a California supporter of La Follette pointed out with disdain that Johnson was maintaining "a somber and discreet silence." Gus Karger, touring the west for the Cincinnati *Times-Star,* observed that Norbeck and William H. McMaster were supporting Coolidge in South Dakota, and that Nebraska's Robert Howell, "a pretty wild-eyed person," was not deserting the party and would help to keep Norris in control. Norris privately asserted that he would withdraw as the Republican nominee for the Senate and campaign for La Follette if the Progressive had a chance to win. Since the Nebraskan could not foresee the slightest chance of a La Follette victory, however, he resigned himself to doing nothing more than speaking kindly of the third ticket and avoiding opposition to it. Indeed, of the Senate's liberal Republicans only Brookhart, Ladd, and Frazier actively supported La Follette.[64]

Undoubtedly just as disconcerting to the La Follette people was the tendency of former participants in the 1912 Bull Moose party to reject the 1924 Progressive ticket. For a variety of reasons the bulk of the remaining leadership of the 1912 movement shied away from La Follette. Some could not forget the feud which had long separated him from Roosevelt, while

[64] La Follette, Jr., to J. A. H. Hopkins, September 13, 1924, La Follette Family Papers, Series B, Box 119, on Borah; *The New Republic,* XL (October 15, 1924), 153, and letter to the editor from John Harrowby, *The Nation,* CXIX (October 22, 1924), 446, on Johnson; Gus Karger to Taft, July 26 and August 15, 1924, Taft Papers, Box 563; Norris to C. W. McConaughy, July 24, 1924, Norris Papers, Tray 81, Box 6. MacKay, *The Progressive Movement of 1924,* pp. 195–96, discusses Borah's and Norris's failure to support actively La Follette's candidacy.

others looked aghast upon the labor and farm groups who rallied to La Follette as harbingers of class conflict and radicalism. For many of the former Bull Moosers the price which they had paid for political apostasy in 1912 was not worth paying again.[65]

By early October, the momentum of the Coolidge movement seemed uncheckable. William Howard Taft visited the President "and found him very cheerful. I think he is quite confident of election." The course of the campaign seemed to confirm the July observation of Henry W. Taft "that progressivism has waned as a slogan." [66]

This trend of events undoubtedly pressured Borah for he, just as the other Senators, had "a mighty keen eye" for his own security. The administration wanted his support. The Outlawry people were urging him to advance his own political fortunes and the Great Cause by stumping for Coolidge; and national sentiment—including the West—seemed increasingly favorable to the President. Thus far in the campaign, Borah had remained on the fence, giving several nonpartisan speeches which emphasized the need for lowering taxes, giving more attention to the farm problem, and recognizing Russia. As Gus Karger reported, the Senator was "talking a little for himself" in Idaho "but apparently not strenuous in his support of Coolidge." To *The Idaho Daily Statesman,* Borah was not even in the campaign; instead of speaking for his party he was pleading for the recognition of Russia, a country which could not "even run a sewer" and where "atheistic bandits" ruled Christians.[67]

Finally, on October 7 at Idaho Falls, Borah attempted to placate the G.O.P. without alienating his Progressive supporters. His speech, necessarily vague and contradictory, was a masterful effort in which he touched all his political bases. The setting for

[65] Alan R. Havig, "A Disputed Legacy: Roosevelt Progressives and the La Follette Campaign of 1924," *Mid-America,* 53 (January, 1971), 44–64.

[66] Taft to Robert Taft, October 12, 1924, Taft Papers, Box 566, and Henry W. Taft to Taft, July 7, 1924, Box 562.

[67] *The Idaho Daily Statesman,* September 1, 13, 29, 30, October 1, 2, 5, and 6, 1924; Gus Karger to Taft, September 23, 1924, Taft Papers, Box 565.

the Idaho Falls announcement had all of the trappings for a great occasion. An informal prespeech reception ran into the dinner hour. People began to jam the theater hours before the Senator spoke, then crowded into the aisles and into the lobby. An unhappy throng, almost as many as were inside, massed outside the auditorium. Republican dignitaries from throughout the state were present in force. Prior to the Senator's introduction, a quartet harmonized "Keep Cool with Coolidge" and a troop of Boy Scouts sang a hearty "How Do You Do Mr. Borah, How Do You Do." [68]

When Borah took the platform, he rebuked his party, and then partly rationalized its sins away; he lavished high praise upon Coolidge, but stopped short of giving him an explicit endorsement; he thanked the Progressives for their nomination, and then stressed the virtues of Republicanism; he complimented La Follette and then took issue with his position regarding the Supreme Court. Borah's stated purpose was to rise above partisan politics and to discuss what was best for the general interest. Although he appreciated the confidence that Idaho Progressives had in him, he emphasized that he would fight for progressive principles within the Republican party—"Republicanism is government free from monopolistic control and equally free from domination and political entanglements abroad." Although he called La Follette a friend "for whose sincerity of purpose, ability and honesty, I have the greatest admiration," he was more complimentary to Coolidge. Borah reminded the audience that the President had taken office when bureaucracy was threatening to destroy America. Coolidge had challenged the bureaucrats and called for economy in government. It had taken courage to veto popular bills in an effort to halt unnecessary and unjust demands on the American public. When Borah turned his attention to the G.O.P., he at first attacked the venality within it, but then added that even "the

[68] *The* [Idaho Falls] *Times-Register*, October 10, 1924. Copy in Borah Papers, Box 243.

Savior could not choose even twelve men all of who could prove true against corruption." [69]

The reaction to the Senator's performance was mixed and the interpretations varied. Part of the confusion was because Borah had departed from his prepared text and ad libbed his comments regarding Coolidge and La Follette. The resulting controversy over exactly what he had said reflected the attention that the speech received and the concern over exactly what his position was in regard to the national campaign. An Associated Press story quoted him as saying that Coolidge was "the greatest man in the political history of the United States." The Senator explained that this "was somewhat of an exaggeration," although he had "most heartily and sincerely commended Mr. Coolidge." [70]

One puzzled constituent aptly summed up the overall impression: "I, a very humble citizen, and a great admirer of Sen [sic] Borah am very much undecided as to where he stands today." While the *Lexington* [Kentucky] *Daily Leader* believed that the Senator had earnestly declared for Coolidge, another newspaper reported that his speech as a whole was kinder to La Follette and the third party. *The New Orleans Item* asserted that Borah had in effect delivered Idaho's four electoral votes to Coolidge; yet *The New York Times* noted that even the Democratic candidate, John W. Davis, had not produced "a more biting indictment" of the G.O.P. Someone recalled that William Jennings Bryan, like Borah, had recently described Coolidge as "a

[69] There are several versions of Borah's speech. He handed out advance copies to the press but departed from the prepared text on several occasions. A court reporter, however, took down the speech as the Senator delivered it, and *The Idaho Daily Statesman*, October 8, 1924, printed the transcript. A typed copy of the address is in the Borah Papers, Box 244, but it is presumably the advance copy. Whatever the case, Borah said that although the stenographic report was not "wholly accurate . . . it is reasonably and substantially so. More of verbal inaccuracies than of substance." Borah telegram to George A. Seipel, Associated Press correspondent, October 10, 1924, Borah Papers, Box 243.

[70] Borah to George A. Seipel, Borah Papers, Box 243; James H. Powers to Borah, October 8, 1924; Borah reply, October 12, 1924, Box 231.

fine man, a man who is personally and politically clean"—
Bryan's only objection to Coolidge was that he was reactionary.
The Manchester [New Hampshire] *Union* wrote that Borah's
public declaration to remain within the G.O.P. had come at a
time when some Republicans were deserting it and was thus
extremely valuable to his party; yet the *Chicago Herald-Examiner* said that the speech, "one of the most severe excoriations of
the Republican management," had stirred consternation within
the party's national headquarters. *The Chicago Evening Post*
and columnist Charles Michelson were both convinced that
Borah's decision not to follow Iowa's Brookhart out of the party
had relieved many Republican minds; *The New York Times,*
on the other hand, averred that the Republicans already had
too many who kept the party label but seldom hesitated to bolt
party traces in Congress. The Republicans needed party discipline and solidarity more than anything else; in this respect,
according to the *Times,* the Idahoan had been of little real
help. "He is not delivering as he promised the Coolidge people," wrote Hiram Johnson, "but he half delivers." Nonetheless
Borah's actions seemed to confirm Johnson's suspicions that he
had "sold himself out for the smoothing of his political path in
Idaho." [71]

Despite some confusion as to the precise nature of Borah's
speech, the Republican hierarchy was pleased. Shortly afterwards, the party headquarters asked for facts regarding the Senator's public record so that publicity people could distribute it
as campaign literature in Idaho. "It seems," wrote Borah's secretary, "they have discovered that they have a candidate for Senator. . . ." From C. Bascom Slemp came a telegram of "heartiest
thanks for very forceful speech in behalf of President." Republicans subsequently published parts of the October 7 message in
a small circular which contrasted Borah's compliments of Coo-

[71] Harry C. Prior to Borah, undated, but written in response to the
Idaho Falls speech, Borah Papers, Box 244; Borah Scrapbooks, Reel 4;
Johnson to Harold Ickes, October 8, 1924; and to Frank P. Doherty, Oc-
tober 15, 1924, Johnson Papers, Part III, Box 7.

lidge with his criticism of La Follette's court plan. In Chicago, Salmon Levinson was happy again and praised Borah for his "beautiful statement." [72]

Circumstances forced the Senator even farther into the G.O.P. camp. When the state supreme court ruled that a candidate's name could appear only once on the ballot, he chose the Republican ticket. Most Idaho Progressives probably expected the Senator—if he had to make such a choice—to decide to run as a Republican. But this decision plus his October 7 speech gave them a double jolt. They understood his difficult position and were willing to hear neutral statements from him, but some believed that he had left the impression that he was backing Coolidge and Dawes. One Progressive, already unhappy about the Idaho Falls speech, called Borah's resignation from the third-party ticket "a slap in the face . . . it begins to look as though you are trying to double cross your best friends. . . ." Some demanded clarification of the Senator's position and one, who had spoken in Borah's behalf at the third-party convention, bluntly inquired as to what he was "willing to do for us." [73]

With the Progressives demanding clarification, and with the administration hoping to hear more from him "any time," he chose to retreat from the campaign altogether. He thus started

[72] Cora Rubin to Borah, October 18, 1924, Borah Papers, Box 244; Slemp telegram to Borah, October 9, 1924, Box 238; copy of "Read What U.S. Senator W. E. Borah said about President Coolidge and Senator La Follette at Idaho Falls, October 7, 1924," Box 244; Levinson to Borah, October 9, 1924, Box 242. On the day that Borah delivered his Idaho Falls speech, Levinson talked with William Butler, the national party chairman, and then sent a letter to Robins: "B. [Butler] is most anxious you see Borah and get him out *now*." Levinson to Robins, October 7, 1924, Robins Papers, Box 20.

[73] Borah to F. A. Jeter, Idaho Secretary of State, October 11, 1924; Charles J. Daufau to Borah, October 25, 1924; W. H. Rogers to Borah, October 24, 1924, Borah Papers, Box 244. See also A. H. Wilkie to Borah, October 11 and 22, 1924; J. C. Steuart, of the Progressive State Central Committee, to Borah, October 24, 1924; V. W. Young, Secretary of Oneida County's branch of the third party, to Borah, October 24, 1924; William J. Maudry, Oneida County's Progressive chairman to Borah, October 24, 1924; George C. Barrett, Progressive candidate for state senator, to Borah, October 23, 1924, *ibid.*

and concluded his national campaign role on the same day. Already worried that his Idaho Falls speech had reduced his Progressive support, he found a way out of an increasingly delicate situation. That exit came in mid-October in the form of the Senate investigation of campaign expenditures. As chairman of the Senate committee to conduct the probe, Borah left Idaho and headed East. For justifiable reasons he could now refrain from making political statements that would only add to his troubles. Hopefully, moreover, since the committee was a product of a motion that La Follette had made in the Senate, Borah's duties in its behalf might placate state Progressives. Again, as in the Idaho Falls Republican convention, principle and moral calling conveniently intervened, rescuing him from the scene of battle: "As much as I should like to remain in Idaho, I think you will agree with me that I cannot shirk this duty." [74]

Serving on the committee in Chicago and then in Washington, Borah received praise from *The New Republic* for "the personal sacrifice involved in halting his own campaign in Idaho" to conduct the investigation. At the same time, he was able to avoid the dilemmas of the state and national campaigns. When he received urgent notice from Republicans that Idaho Progressives and Democrats were fusing behind La Follette, he asked innocently, "What do you suggest I do?" When his Democratic opponent—who was in the race despite Borah's earlier hopes of being unchallenged—wanted a public debate, the Senator had a good excuse for being hundreds of miles away.[75]

[74] C. Bascom Slemp to Borah, October 9, 1924, Borah Papers, Box 243, for continuing G.O.P. pressure. Borah indicated after the election that he had assumed that the Idaho Falls speech would cost him Progressive votes. See Borah to E. F. Winn, November 15, 1924, *ibid.* For the quote on not shirking duties, see Borah to Victor Smith, October 10, 1924, Box 238.

[75] *The New Republic,* XL (October 22, 1924), 187; telegram exchange, H. A. Lawson to Borah, October 24, 1924; Borah reply, October 25, 1924, Borah Papers, Box 244; *The Idaho Daily Statesman,* October 23, 1924.

A silent Borah thus allowed Ray McKaig, La Follette's national headquarters, and other groups to speak for him. McKaig busily assured third-party voters that the Senator was neglecting his own campaign to conduct—at La Follette's request—a worthwhile investigation. If Borah were in Idaho, McKaig was able to say, he would refute the false statements of the opposition. "But as he is absent on official duty he must depend upon the loyalty and understanding of his friends to take care of his interests." Some two months earlier, La Follette had urged state Progressives to back the Idahoan. In mid-October, the national Progressive headquarters restated this position, pointing out that Borah's Senate record was "such that no Progressive should fail to vote for him." [76]

Letting others campaign for him, Borah was able to avoid the messy entanglements of state election politics. He made no public comments, for example, on the gubernatorial race. Privately, however, he seemed to be in both the Republican and Progressive camps. On one occasion he confided that if Progressive candidate H. F. Samuels won, it would be not "upon his own strength but upon the failure of *our* fellows to meet the situation." Yet a few weeks later, when he sent $250 to the Progressives to help defray their campaign deficit, he congratulated Samuels for "a splendid fight"; promising to send "some additional help shortly," he added: "all this matter, Samuels, is purely personal upon my part and personal toward you." [77]

[76] Copy of letter from McKaig to W. H. Rogers, October 28, 1924, Borah Papers, Box 244; copy of telegram from Robert M. La Follette to H. F. Samuels, August 11, 1924, Box 237; copy of letter from John M. Nelson, national manager of the La Follette-Wheeler progressive headquarters, to H. F. Samuels, October 18, 1924, Box 244. Borah also received endorsements from labor, prohibition, and farm groups. On labor's support, see various letters in Box 243; on the dry organizations, see Wayne B. Wheeler, general counsel of the Anti-Saloon League of America, to Cora Rubin, Borah's secretary, October 14, 1924, Box 244; on agriculture, R. A. Cowles, Secretary of the American Council of Agriculture, September 30, 1924, to Borah, Box 243.

[77] Borah to Alfred J. Dunn, September 22, 1924, Borah Papers, Box 244; and to H. F. Samuels, November 5, 1924, Box 243. My emphasis.

The Senator's campaign strategy—in Harold Ickes's words, "the twistings of Borah"—worked superbly. By keeping quiet and, except for his ambiguous October 7 speech, remaining aloof from local and national political struggles, he swamped his Democratic rival four to one. His plurality exceeded the total votes that either Coolidge or La Follette received. The "ability, perhaps you would call it the cunning, with which Borah can be on both sides and get away with it," consistently provoked Hiram Johnson, who was torn between envy and disgust. "I think it is the most remarkable exhibition we have ever seen in our politics." Ickes concurred: "he is always looking out for number one." [78]

Most important for the future was the fact that his "Borahesque" performance had strengthened his national position. Already there was speculation that he would be more influential in the Senate than ever before. As William Howard Taft pointed out, although Borah was among those Senators who had "an umbilical cord between themselves and La Follette," he had kept his voice—and his influence—within the G.O.P.[79]

[78] Ickes to Hiram Johnson, October 16, 1924, Johnson Papers, Part III, Box 45; Johnson to Ickes, June 10, 1924, and Ickes to Johnson, July 17, 1925, Ickes Papers, Box 2. Ray McKaig jubilantly wrote that "Borah got our unanimous endorsement and his majority was more than the republican governor had for his entire vote. Just think of that." McKaig to Henry Teigan, December 3, 1924, Teigan Papers, Box 5. Borah received 99,797 votes, Democrat Frank Martin, 25,199. The Idaho presidential vote was Coolidge, 69,711; La Follette, 53,891; John W. Davis, 23,856. The gubernatorial results were C. C. Moore, 65,508; H. F. Samuels, 58,167; Democrat A. L. Freehafer, 25,081. Clipping from *Idaho Evening Capital News*, November 25, 1924, Borah Papers, Box 244. See, also, "Abstract of Votes of the State of Idaho," La Follette Family Papers, Series B, Box 99.
[79] On the "Borahesque" performance, William Howard Taft to Calvin Cobb, November 12, 1924; on Borah's continuing influence within the G.O.P., Taft to Robert Taft, November 9, 1924, Taft Papers, Box 568. For some predictions of Borah's growing power in the Senate, see Mark Sullivan's November 8, 1924, column, editorials in the Brooklyn *Daily Eagle*, November 11, 1924, and *The Manchester* [New Hampshire] *Union*, November 8, 1924, Borah Scrapbooks, Reel 4.

And he had done this at a time when progressive forces nationally had fallen into considerable disarray. Few of La Follette's supporters had expected a victory but they had anticipated a clear indication of national reform sentiment. Instead, La Follette had lost ground during the campaign and the electorate had rallied overwhelmingly behind the status quo, leaving "Coolidge Conservatism Triumphant," and *The New Republic* unable to find any encouragement in La Follette's showing for third-party strategies in the future. The liberal journal wondered if even the minority of reformers in the country would eventually fade away. Herbert Croly disconsolately speculated that progressive efforts in the future might be limited to mere harassment aimed at convincing the conservative majority that it should act responsibly.[80] The breaking up of the Conference for Progressive Political Action a few weeks after the election signaled further difficulties within the progressive movement. By the mid-Twenties progressivism was thus fragmented, leaderless, and far removed from the optimism that had followed the 1922 election.

But for Borah—who had confronted a treacherous political campaign—it had not been a bad year at all. Not everyone agreed with Albert Beveridge that Borah's future activities would be definitive, but few could deny that they would be important. Even though Raymond Robins believed that the Senator was "rotten in his team play," both he and Levinson continued to think that Borah held the key to the future of the Outlawry of War movement. Similarly, to reformers who anticipated freeing the Republican party from "bad hands," Borah held a pivotal position. Walter Lippmann assessed his role in sweeping terms: "on you more than any other man depends the future of liberalism in America." Lippmann's praise may have

[80] *The New Republic*, XL (November 12, 1924), 257; "Coolidge Conservatism Triumphant," *ibid.*, 261–62; "The Possible Consolation" (November 19, 1924), 285; Herbert Croly, "The Outlook for Progressivism in Politics," XLI (December 10, 1924), 60–64.

been effusive, but unquestionably Borah's finest moments as
a progressive insurgent were yet to come.[81]

[81] Robins to Levinson, November 13, 1924, and January 1, 1925, Levinson Papers, Box 76. Levinson thanked Borah for having "given us the
momentum, the backing, the lime-light, the moral power that no one else
could." He suggested that they meet soon with Robins to discuss Outlawry
and Borah's political future. Levinson to Borah, November 5, 1924, Borah
Papers, Box 242. For an example of a reform-minded Republican looking
to Borah to help clean up the party, see copy of letter from C. A. Sorenson
to Frank A. Harrison, December 2, 1924, Norris Papers, Tray 81, Box 6.
Walter Lippmann to Borah, November 5, 1924, Borah Papers, Box 243.

VII

Out of the Coolidge Wagon

❀

FOR those political pundits who believed that Coolidge had turned the "Idaho lion" into a thoroughly domesticated White House cat, Borah soon offered some startling surprises. In a series of dramatic confrontations with the administration, the Senator spectacularly demonstrated his abilities as a political insurgent and enjoyed his finest hours as a progressive Republican.

While party regulars moaned about Borah-led "Half-Breeds" who threatened prosperity, the Idaho Senator threw down a series of challenges to the administration. He opposed penalizing La Follette and his supporters for political heresy in 1924, and played a crucial role in the Senate's humiliation of Coolidge during the explosive fight over the confirmation of Charles Beecher Warren as Attorney General. For a while in mid-1925, there was much speculation about a "Borah bloc" that could determine the administration's success or failure. Although the bloc's supposed threat to the Coolidge program soon dissolved, its very appearance illustrated Borah's importance to progressivism within the Republican party. Borah, moreover, was increasingly confident that the nation was ready for a genuinely liberal movement. Ultimately, in 1926, he launched a personal campaign to reshape the G.O.P. before the next presidential election. He hoped to make Republicanism more susceptible to reform and western influences, less interventionist in foreign affairs—and more open to his own political aspirations. One cartoonist portrayed the situation by showing the Coolidge Conestoga safely across the 1924 campaign river but now entering the "political badlands" where cowboy Borah slyly plotted in the bushes with senatorial Indians. The elephant riding shotgun asked, "Now where's that half-breed of ours gone?" "Search me," replied driver Calvin Coolidge, "he was in the wagon until we got safely across the river." [1]

Even though Borah left the administration's "wagon" quite soon after the 1924 election, there was a brief period when his actions seemed to confirm *The Washington Post*'s optimistic prediction of harmony between him and the White House. Indeed, the Senator supported the President on an issue which Coolidge interpreted as a critical test of party loyalty: the postal pay-raise veto. Coolidge deemed congressional approval of his veto as vital to the administration's future. "I cannot," he wrote Wisconsin's Irvine Lenroot, "put too much emphasis upon the need of having a comfortable margin against this bill. Unless the veto is sustained, I shall be in despair about any attempt to maintain a party organization." When Lenroot replied that he could not be in Washington because of his wife's serious illness, Coolidge groaned that "if this veto is not sustained it means the breakup of the Party." Senator James Wadsworth of New York was convinced that the President was making "this bill a test of friendship and Republicanism." [2]

The worried Coolidge found a much needed ally in Borah. The Senator gained valuable time for the administration when he blocked Senator Walter Edge's motion for a consent agreement on the bill and, in February, he supplied an essential vote in favor of the veto. During the final balloting, which gave the President a narrow victory of one vote, some of the usual G.O.P. regulars such as Wadsworth, Charles Curtis, William B. McKinley, James E. Watson, Simeon Fess, and Frederick Hale deserted Coolidge. Mark Sullivan consequently observed that in

[1] New York *Herald Tribune,* March 18, 1925.

[2] *The Washington Post,* February 12, 1925; Coolidge to Lenroot, December 24, 1924; Lenroot to Coolidge, undated reply to Coolidge's December 24 letter; Coolidge to Lenroot, January 3, 1925, Lenroot Papers, Box 2; Wadsworth to Nathan L. Miller, January 3, 1925, Wadsworth Papers, Box 19. See also memo of Charles D. Hilles's conference with Coolidge, December 20, 1924, Taft Papers, Box 571.

regard to the President's economic policies, "Borah is more regular than some of the other Senators whose regularity is their stock in trade." [3]

The point was, however, that Borah's position on the President's veto was no real test of his allegiance to the administration. Almost a year earlier, when the postal pay-raise bill had first reached a vote, he had been one of three Senators to oppose it. He regarded the proposal as an unnecessary addition to the general tax load and believed that those people benefiting from postal service should share the burden of additional expenses through increased rates.[4] It was thus not the President's bidding, but Borah's opposition to government spending which prompted his support of the veto.

While Borah sympathized with Coolidge's desire to cut government expenses, he refused to accept the decision to punish Senators Lynn Frazier, Smith W. Brookhart, and Edwin F. Ladd for supporting La Follette in the previous campaign. The weight of party opinion was that the G.O.P. could not ignore such political apostasy. Chief Justice Taft, for one, wanted to throw the La Follette people out of the party and hoped that "a man like Borah, who isn't a real Republican," would not undermine the determination to do so. The basic questions were, as journalist Edward Whiting wrote: "Can a man be a Republican by saying he is? Or can a man be proved not a Republican by saying he is not? And what ultimately becomes of party government, in either case?" [5]

The Republicans chose to read La Follette, Frazier, Brook-

[3] *The Boston Herald,* December 10, 1924, Borah Scrapbooks, Reel 4, regarding Edge's motion; Sullivan's comment in New York *Herald Tribune,* June 21, 1925. Knud Wefald, progressive Congressman from Minnesota, called the Senate vote "the crucial test of the strength of Calvin Coolidge as relates to his domineering of Congress." Wefald's weekly newsletter, January 17, 1925, Knud Wefald Papers (Minnesota State Historical Society), Box 19.
[4] Borah to A. B. Sampson, June 14, 1924, Borah Papers, Box 244; *The Boston Herald,* December 10, 1924, Borah Scrapbooks, Reel 4.
[5] Taft to Robert Taft, November 16, 1924, Taft Papers, Box 568; *The Boston Herald,* March 9, 1925.

hart, and Ladd out of the party. On November 28, 1924, a
G.O.P. senatorial caucus adopted a resolution ostracizing them
from future party meetings. Unaware that the regulars were
planning such punitive steps, Borah, Norris, Frazier, Brookhart,
Johnson, and La Follette had not attended the caucus. Ladd
said that he had received assurances that the conference would
take no such action. An angry Norris described the resolution as
"a nice little case of vaudeville—both foolish and silly"; he supposed that the caucus also ousted from the party all Republicans who voted for La Follette. Borah, who for years had not
attended a caucus, expressed disapproval at the outcome but
reserved comment for the floor of the Senate.[6]

Several hours after hearing about the party decision, Borah
talked with Coolidge. Frederick Wile believed that "it would
make prime reading to know exactly what the most independent spirit in Congress said . . . about the biggest bomb-
shell sprung in Washington for many a moon." Such party action could provide the impetus for the Senator to place "his
broad Idaho back" against the administration.[7] Certainly, insofar as Coolidge stressed party loyalty, he would not endear
Borah. The Senator's speeches and writings were replete with
urgings and promises to vote according to conscience, not party
demands. It would thus be difficult for him to accept penalizing
men who had declined to adhere to a party platform, particularly one for which Borah himself had little enthusiasm.

Coolidge was determined, however, to score a victory against
party heresy. In his inaugural address on March 4, 1925, he
stated that "if there is to be responsible party government, the
party label must be something more than a mere device for securing office." An elected Republican must "exhibit sufficient
loyalty" to the party and its platform principles; otherwise "the
election is a mockery." A majority party owed the public "such

[6] Clipping from *The North Dakota Nonpartisan*, December 3, 1924,
Borah Papers, Box 259.
[7] Wile Scrapbooks, November 29, 1924, 19.

unity of action as will make the party majority an effective instrument of government. . . ." [8]

On March 7, when regular Republicans tried to follow the President's lead by demoting Ladd, Frazier, and Brookhart to the bottom of standing committees, they confronted an irate Borah and Norris. Borah, who was the first to object, scoffed at what the Republican caucus had decided several weeks earlier; to him, the important point was that "these men indicated their desire to be assigned as Republicans." If the "narrow partisanship" of the caucus prevailed, it would be a direct and regrettable blow to "the Republicanism of hundreds of thousands of voters." Indiana's Senator Watson retorted that a Brookhart-style Republicanism would have put La Follette, not Coolidge, in the White House. Nonetheless, Borah and Norris successfully blocked the motion for unanimous consent on the committee assignments and postponed the issue over the weekend.[9]

In the subsequent debate on Monday, Borah asserted that the issue was sectional in nature: "I know that their demotion is a demotion of the West. I know it is diminishing the power of the West in this Chamber. I know it is a distinct political action against our part of the country." The crucial point was that "these men truly and faithfully represent their constituencies, and . . . those constituencies claim they are Republican constituencies. . . . I know how sorely their Republicanism has been tested. Do not test it any further." Moreover, as long as the G.O.P. failed to fulfill its promise of agricultural relief, it would produce even more discontented western Republicans. Borah charged that some people were simply seeking an excuse by which to purge the party of alleged radicals; in doing so, they courted political disaster by ignoring the fact that voters disagreed on what comprised Republicanism. Following Borah's theme, Senators Norbeck and Frazier also emphasized that punishing La Follette and his followers would be a blow to the

[8] Text of Coolidge's speech in New York *Sun*, March 4, 1925.
[9] *Congressional Record*, 69th Cong., Spec. Sess., 1925, LXVII, 14–17.

northwest. Their efforts failed. By a 65 to 11 count, the Senate accepted the proposed committee assignments.[10] The administration's success was momentary, however, for in a few days the westerners took revenge.

The dispute over the fate of the La Follette bloc was but a prelude to the explosion that subsequently occurred over Coolidge's nomination of Charles Beecher Warren as Attorney General. This clash between President and Congress rocked the American political scene. It filled newspaper front pages and editorials for two weeks and, before it ended, even the stock market dipped alarmingly. Borah played a crucial role in the conflict and, by the time it was over, he had emerged as the newly recognized leader of the Senate progressive bloc.

The Warren affair began when Coolidge moved Harlan Fiske Stone from the Justice Department to the Supreme Court and appointed Warren as the new Attorney General. Not since Andrew Johnson's administration had the Senate refused to confirm a Cabinet selection. Initially there was little doubt about Warren's chances. Opposition, however, began to form on grounds that Warren had allegedly violated antitrust laws when he was president and counsel of the Michigan Sugar Company.

Despite murmurs of discontent, on February 24 the Senate Judiciary Committee voted 9 to 4 in favor of confirmation. Borah was the only Republican to vote in the negative. At this point, Coolidge confidently wired his appointee, "I feel certain of favorable action." Although the President expected no real problems, he and "the close little Coolidge circle" were reportedly piqued at Borah's antagonism toward Warren. "For eighteen months Mr. Coolidge has been assiduously cultivating, not to say courting Senator Borah," wrote Frank Kent in the Baltimore *Sun*. The President had invited Borah to the White House for conferences and breakfasts many times; the Senator and his wife were among the first guests on the executive yacht; and in 1924 Coolidge had turned to Borah as his vice-presiden-

[10] *Ibid.*, 42–67.

tial choice. Yet apparently the White House had earned little more for its efforts than the Senator's opposition to Warren. Borah was prepared to fight on this issue. He regretted having let the earlier Daugherty appointment pass in the face of charges resembling those which Warren now faced. "I felt then and I have felt a thousand times afterwards I did not do my duty. I determined I would not escape responsibility again." [11]

Hints of trouble for the administration came on March 7 when Borah, Norris, Frazier, Ladd, and other western insurgents joined the Democrats in a 38 to 39 vote to block a closed session on Warren's confirmation. The ensuing debate lasted three days. Borah said nothing but was reportedly still smoldering about the demotion of La Follette and his followers from their committee positions. On March 10, as debate moved into its third day, Borah personally convinced Peter Norbeck to vote against Warren. Before noon, Norbeck had been aligned with the President; but, after talking with Borah, he changed his mind. The South Dakotan then discussed the situation with his newly elected colleague, William H. McMaster, who also switched to the opposition.[12]

While the Senate moved toward a showdown, a tired Vice-President Dawes consulted with the majority and minority leaders, learned that six more speakers were scheduled before a roll call, and departed for a nap in his Willard Hotel suite. While the unsuspecting Dawes slumbered, five of the six scheduled Senators decided not to join the debate and the Senate held a sudden vote. When the Vice-President received word of the new course of events, he frantically rushed to the Capitol in a taxi only to arrive too late to save Warren from a 40 to 40

[11] New York *World*, February 25, 1925. Norris also opposed Warren but was not present at the meeting. Coolidge to Charles B. Warren, March 2, 1925, Coolidge Papers, Case File 10A; Baltimore *Sun*, February 20, 1925; Borah to W. H. Taylor, March 21, 1925, Borah Papers, Box 259.

[12] *Congressional Record*, 69th Cong., Spec. Sess., 1925, LXVII, 17. (Senator Reed's subsequent motion for an open session passed, 46 to 39, *ibid.*, p. 18.) *The Boston Herald*, March 12, 1925.

vote.[13] Before Dawes arrived, North Carolina's Lee Overman switched his position on the second ballot to defeat Warren, 41 to 39. For the first time since 1868 the Senate had rejected a President's Cabinet choice.

Such "sensational news from Washington" received headlines as the "worst setback" in Coolidge's career. "It is a directly personal rebuff" to Coolidge, reported Frederick Wile. "Is there to be a 'Borah bloc'?" It seemed that "a hydraheaded nightmare in the Senate, with names like Borah, Couzens, Johnson, McMaster, Norbeck and Norris as its outstanding terrors" was replacing the earlier La Follette "nightmare that kept the GOP writhing in maddening dreams." Previously, Borah had been "a vigorous beginner, but an early quitter"; now, however, he seemed ready to offer bold leadership. Charles Michelson, columnist for the New York *World,* agreed that "when Vice President Dawes pulled the biggest boner since Merkle failed to touch second, he may have started a series of events" in which Borah would play a vital part. The incident had provided the impetus for "an insurgent group, beside which the little La Follette clique of the last session is a feeble memory." Whereas La Follette's group included only three or four Senators, the new rebels were more numerous and looked to Borah, who "wields an influence in the Senate superior to that of any other member, regardless of party." Washington's *Evening Star* editorialized that "temporarily at least, and on the surface, Mr. Borah seems to have succeeded Mr. La Follette in the leadership of the progressive bloc in the Senate. . . ." And, since the Idahoan was no radical, his opposition "is not to be considered lightly. The administration must reckon with the Senator from Idaho. It would seem the part of folly to do otherwise." [14]

Borah was undoubtedly not the sole cause of Coolidge's re-

[13] Bascom N. Timmons, *Portrait of an American: Charles G. Dawes* (New York, 1953), p. 246. *Congressional Record,* 69th Cong., Spec. Sess., 1925, LXVII, 101.
[14] *The Boston Herald,* March 11, 1925; Wile Scrapbooks, March 11, 1925, 20; New York *World,* March 14, 1925; Washington *Evening Star,* March 12, 1925.

buff. Yet if he, "the senator whom no tether can hitch and no yoke constrain, had for once made a team play," the result would have been different. The President had needed one more vote. Borah had not only refused to give his but had also cost the administration the support of Norbeck and McMaster, both of whom Coolidge had earlier assumed would back Warren.[15]

Coolidge, despite his setback of March 10, refused to give ground. He decided to resubmit Warren's name, explaining that the appointee deserved "the benefit of another nomination." Warren "was a man of high character, eminence at the bar, and great ability." Although some Senators wanted a saint, the President regretted that he had "to appoint human beings to office." Honest and conscientious servants were essential but, if some Senators continued to set impossible standards, "I shall not be able to make any appointments." It was essential for the Executive to have men in his Cabinet in whom he had genuine confidence. Hence, unless Senators "find a real blemish on a man, I do not think they ought to make partisan politics out of appointments to the Cabinet." Coolidge's gauntlet was down; opposition to the appointment had become mere "partisan politics." Such comments to the press affirmed Frederick Wile's prediction that "Warren is to serve as the case for testing whether Calvin Coolidge or the 'Borah bloc' is to prevail in the Sixty-ninth Senate of the United States." [16] Undoubtedly the President's characterization of the opposition as partisan was not the way to win Borah's support.

Again Warren's name went to the Judiciary Committee but, unlike the first time, it received an adverse report by a 9 to 7 vote. As the meeting of the committee got underway, a White House car appeared at the Capitol and took Borah to the executive offices. Coolidge kept his Cabinet waiting for twenty minutes while he cajoled the Senator to switch his position. When

[15] See *The Boston Herald,* March 11–12, 1925; New York *World,* March 14, 1925.

[16] Howard H. Quint and Robert H. Ferrell (eds.), *The Talkative President: The Off-the-Record Press Conferences of Calvin Coolidge* (Amherst, Mass., 1964), pp. 93–95; Wile Scrapbooks, March 13, 1925, 20.

Borah emerged from the White House he admitted that the Warren matter had been the subject of discussion but refused to make a public statement. In response to a query whether the President had persuaded him, he answered simply, "You know me." By proxy he cast his committee vote against the nominee, joining with Norris to register the only Republican nays.[17]

Clearly the Warren issue had become a matter of principle to Coolidge. An administration defeat at the outset could herald future party chaos. Desperately the President tried to rally support. He called Senators to the White House and sent telegrams trying to get Frank Gooding and Richard Ernst back to Washington in time for the vote. Senators Walter Edge, Lawrence C. Phipps, and Frank L. Greene were aboard ship enroute to Europe but paired in favor of Warren. At one point, the administration tried to entice Peter Norbeck's support by telephoning him about a patronage matter. Although Coolidge's secretary later denied it, Norbeck knew "the game well enough to know that there might have been a little significance in that call." Regardless of the administration's motives, Norbeck "rather resented" the call "coming at the time it did." [18]

Friends of Coolidge contended that he must win the second Warren vote. The issue went beyond the nomination to the question of party control. The President's new Congress was ostensibly five votes stronger than the previous one. If he could not dominate a Senate in which his party had the majority, a session of trouble for him lay ahead. At the very time that administration sympathizers stressed the importance of a Coolidge victory, the New York *Sun* carried headlines that "The Borah Bloc Is Real Ruler of New Senate." This "liberal bloc, the insurgent bloc or the Borah bloc" controlled the Senate balance of power in the way that the La Follette group had done in the past. Comprising the new group were Republicans who had not deserted their party in 1924, who were not interested in bolting

17 New York *Sun*, March 13, 1925.
18 *The Boston Herald*, March 13 and 16, 1925; Norbeck to John Hirning, March 19, 1925, Norbeck Papers (South Dakota).

from the G.O.P., and who still held high party positions in the Senate. The first vote on Warren had allowed the new faction to flex its muscles, but there were other indications of its strength and activity. For one thing, on March 12 for the first time in years Borah attended a senatorial Republican meeting which unanimously agreed that conference actions would be advisory, not binding. A Senator could thus feel free to vote according to conscience, not party dictation. Moreover, the participants at the March 12 meeting decided not to deprive the La Follette bolters of their patronage. "It was the opinion among Republicans," *The Washington Post* learned, that the conference's decision "was a distinct concession to the new group of insurgents led by Senators Borah and Norris, each of whom holds an important chairmanship in the party organization." [19]

A Coolidge supporter sent the *Sun*'s article about the "Borah bloc" to the President and attacked Borah and Norris as "radicals of the most dangerous sort, Norris a bare-face Bolshevik, and Borah a cleverly camoflouged [sic] friend of Soviet Russia, and Germany. . . . I call Norris, Benedict Arnold, and Borah, Charles Lee. . . ." Several other constituents wrote to Coolidge in reference to the sorry spectacle of Borah leading the insurgents.[20]

On March 16, the day of the second Warren vote, "typhoon weather," with "the ship of State in the vortex," hit the usually drowsy Senate. By 9 A.M. the Senate galleries were jammed and people hoping to witness the debate crowded the stairways. Elevator service completely stopped. The wife of Vice-President Dawes joined with some of her friends and brought sandwich

[19] Baltimore *Sun*, March 14, 1925; New York *Sun*, March 14, 1925. Hiram Johnson apparently took the initiative in getting the Republican conference to agree that its decisions should not be binding on individual Senators. "This was agreed to, and thereupon I related to Borah the agreement, in which he acquiesced, and the day following, he and I both attended the conference of Republicans." Johnson to Charles K. McClatchy, March 18, 1925, Johnson Papers, Part III, Box 7. *Washington Post*, March 13, 1925.

[20] See Coolidge Papers, Case File 10A–15.

lunches to the gallery. Indeed, one correspondent observed, "Never did a coliseum audience assemble . . . with greater interest than did the fashionable Washington come to the Senate Chamber today."

On the Senate floor, the participants prepared for a clash similar to that earlier "conflict on the council meadows at Runnymede." As young pages rushed about, "a suppressed excitement was in the air. Vice-President Dawes had a hell 'n Maria look." Borah conferred softly with Maryland Democrat William C. Bruce. James Wadsworth and George Wharton Pepper talked urgently, and other Senators gathered in small groups. West Virginia's Guy D. Goff, "a stout man, in the sixties, with bulging cheeks of carmine and a voice rattling thunder," opened the debate by speaking in behalf of the administration, defending Warren's reputation and reading letters from Coolidge and Charles Evans Hughes to prove his point. Democrat James Reed of Missouri answered that the only trust to which Warren was faithful was the Sugar Trust. Later, in a "badly delivered" address, Frederick H. Gillett, ex-speaker of the House, charged that "a combination of Democrats and radicals" formed the opposition to Warren.

As Gillett sat down, "the name of Borah could be heard from every gallery as the people bent forward." The Idahoan was on his feet claiming that he had not originally intended to speak but could no longer remain quiet. Despite his pretenses, the Senator's address was not spontaneous. "It showed the closest preparation," according to one observer; certainly it was not by accident that Borah was able to quote extensively from speeches of Daniel Webster. Talking with "dignity, persuasiveness, balance, logic, and substance," he pointed to the "one feature of the subject" which was important for all time. This involved the duties of the Senate regarding its constitutional power to advise and consent. This power was not perfunctory. A Senator, as much as the President, had the duty to see that government remained strong and clean. When the Executive asked for advice, a Senator out of duty to his constituents must answer with honesty. The Warren case was not, Borah argued, "a mere party matter." As for Gillett's charges about the opposition containing radicals, he could only reply that "I think it has come to the time when a radical is a man who believes in the Constitution of the United States." He denied that he was challenging the President's authority and sincerity or that he was a spokesman for any faction. "I am trying to meet my constitutional obligations as a Senator."

At the finish of Borah's thirty-minute speech, news reporter James O'Donnell Bennett's "eyes were so full of tears [that] I could not see to take notes for several seconds and my heart was going like a triphammer." It was a performance "that made you proud to be an American" and it stimulated "a whisper which . . . ran from lip to lip. It was 'is this the next President of the United States.' " Charles Michelson agreed that Borah's was "the big speech of the day." It was, according to Frederick W. Clampett of the *San Francisco Examiner,* "the one event of the debate. It so surpassed all others that they were not in the same class." Frederick Wile believed that, following Borah's merciless grilling, Senator Gillett was "in somewhat the prostrate condition occupied by one of the flapjacks Mr. Coolidge serves at White House breakfasts."

As the time for the vote approached, the Republican whip, Senator Charles Curtis, appeared pale and tired. Reed Smoot of Utah, who two days earlier had left the chamber because of illness, struggled to his seat to support the administration. For the opposition, La Follette, who had rushed from Florida where he had been recuperating from sickness, entered "with the stride of a tired man" to vote against Warren. By a 46 to 39 count, the Senate again delivered Coolidge a blow which no President since Andrew Johnson had suffered.[21]

21 Excellent descriptions of the Senate battle over the second Warren vote appear in Frederick Clampett's "The Senate in a Storm" in the *San Francisco Examiner,* clipping in the Borah Papers, Box 255, and in James O'Donnell Bennett's account in the *Chicago Tribune,* March 17–18, 1925. See also Charles Michelson's column in the New York *World,* March 17, 1925, and Frederick Wile's comments of March 18, 1925, Wile Scrapbooks,

Foolishly, Coolidge continued to press the issue, threatening to give Warren a recess appointment, losing his poise when he was discussing the situation in a press conference, and reappointing Warren, who then declined. The result of his "terrible miscalculation" seemed clear. The President had further ruptured his party and had discovered that he apparently could not control the Senate. A disappointed William Howard Taft brooded that Coolidge had "made a mess of the Warren case." Dewey Hilles reported that the incident "had a very sobering effect" on the Republican National Committee. "Our people are apprehensive lest we are to have four or five more years of chaos in Washington." Progressives, on the other hand, applauded. If Coolidge had won, Lynn Haines averred, "the result would have been complete and perhaps final surrender of Senatorial rights and duties to the desires and exigencies of party politics." Basil Manly of the People's Legislative Service, who had initially resigned himself to the pessimistic view that the administration was at the peak of its strength and would easily obtain Warren's confirmation, rejoiced at the "body blow" inflicted on Coolidge. Oswald Garrison Villard believed that the Senate had emerged with honor. "To see Borah, Johnson, Norris, MacMaster [sic] . . . and Norbeck refusing to obey the crack of the President's whip is to make one wish to throw up one's hat and give three hearty cheers." [22]

There was no jubilation on Wall Street or elsewhere in the

20. For Borah's speech, *Congressional Record*, 69th Cong., Spec. Sess., 1925, LXVII, 256–59. See, also, Felix A. Nigro, "The Warren Case," *The Western Political Quarterly*, XI (December, 1958), 835–56. Warren was the sixth Cabinet nomination which the Senate rejected; once it had rebuffed Andrew Jackson, three times John Tyler, and once Andrew Johnson.

22 On Coolidge's press conference, see Quint and Ferrell, *The Talkative President*, pp. 95–96, and Charles D. Hilles to Taft, March 24, 1925, Taft Papers, Box 576, and on the G.O.P. split and Coolidge's problems with the Senate, see *The New York Times*, March 18, 1925, and Baltimore *Sun*, March 22, 1925. Taft to Charles D. Hilles, March 25, 1925,

business world. On the day of the second Warren vote, the stock market, already shaky due to a decline in wheat prices, slumped. Almost 100 shares dropped to their lowest figure to that date in 1925. Except for one day in February, the March 16 decline was the worst setback on Wall Street since Coolidge's election. *The New York Post* wailed that "a bloc-locked Congress" threatened prosperity. Industry and business had supposed that after La Follette's defeat in 1924 "the wolves were gone, but they heard the hunting song of the pack on the March winds blowing out of Washington." The major cause of the chilled industrial optimism was that group of Senators—with Borah and Norris at the front—who had "rubbed the peace paint from their faces and revealed themselves as Half-Breeds." These "half-breeds" were "the fly in the ointment of prosperity." Senator Norbeck, after several visits at the White House, wrote that Coolidge also viewed the Warren defeat as harmful to business. Certainly "the business men are sure for the President and the Supreme Court, and against Congress." [23]

Horace Taft, "a good deal troubled about the fight in the Senate," fretted about the future. "It looks as though the whole Progressive faction, including those demoted and those left, like Borah, in magnificent isolation, will form a faction like that of the Irish in Gladstone's time, bent simply on making mischief. . . ." While Taft saw Borah as a fighting Irishman,

---

and Hilles to Taft, March 18, 1925, Taft Papers, Box 575; Basil Manly to La Follette, March 5 and 11, 1925, La Follette Family Papers, Series B, Box 102. Lynn Haines, "Vital American History in the Making," *Searchlight on Congress*, X (March, 1925), 5; Oswald Garrison Villard, "In Defense of the Senate," *The Nation*, CXX (March 25, 1925), 315. "There was a real fight here over Warren," wrote Hiram Johnson. "It is a fundamental fight. . . . The letters in evidence plainly prove [Warren] was the mere messenger boy and slave of the great sugar magnate. . . . I am glad he was rejected." Johnson to Charles K. McClatchy, March 17, 1925, Johnson Papers, Part III, Box 7.
[23] New York *Herald Tribune*, March 17, 1925; New York *Evening Post*, March 9, 1925; Norbeck to C. M. Henry, April 4, 1925, Norbeck Papers (South Dakota).

The Rocky Mountain News suspected "the fine Italian hand of Borah" in the messy Warren incident.[24]

"It is the truth . . . that but for Borah there would have been no fight" over Warren, asserted Frank Kent of the Baltimore *Sun.* "Borah was the backbone of the whole thing. Without him the fight would not have been made and without him it could not have been won." Until he decided to dispute the nomination, the Democrats had viewed any opposition on their part as completely futile. But when Borah threw his influence and prestige against the White House, "the Democrats jumped joyfully in." Clinton W. Gilbert agreed that "Mr. Borah alone . . . caused that rejection." The half-dozen Republicans who were loosely attached to the party "would have behaved like tame cats if there had not been a man about whom they could rally when they tended to differ with their party." Borah, unlike Norris or La Follette, offered the necessary "touch of respectability to irregularity." When the Idahoan made his stand, the others took courage. The Democrats noted the G.O.P. split and "very slowly committed themselves." Without the Republican nucleus, the Democracy would have kept quiet. Borah supplied the nucleus which in turn rallied the Democrats. "Thus for the first time in his legislative career Mr. Borah finds himself with a band of followers. I doubt if he sought them. They gravitated to him. It is a political phenomenon worth recording." [25]

Borah posed problems for the administration. The "Borah bloc"—Norris, McMaster, Norbeck, James H. Couzens of Michigan, Robert Howell of Nebraska, and Hiram Johnson—had replaced the La Follette bloc as the balance of power. Previously the La Follette men had aligned with the Democrats to produce a bare majority; now such a combination lacked five votes to control. "The only other foot-loose, free lance, inde-

[24] Horace Taft to Taft, March 17, 1925, Taft Papers, Box 575; *Rocky Mountain News* editorial quoted in the New York *Herald Tribune,* March 17, 1925.

[25] Baltimore *Sun,* March 20, 1925; New York *Evening Post,* March 25, 1925.

pendent, devil-may-care Senate group is composed of Borah and the handful of so-called Republicans who more or less habitually follow him." With the "Borah bloc" allied with the Democrats and the "La Folletistas," the administration was in the minority. For this reason, said "T.R.B." in *The New Republic*, "the real leader of the Senate in the next session is Borah." One newspaper declared that "whatever history the United States Senate makes within the next two years will be written largely in terms of one man": Borah. When the Senate adjourned in late March, the *Oregon Journal* declared that "nine-tenths of the Republican side of it remains in Washington"; Borah, without whom the G.O.P. could face only defeat, was still in the city. *The Independent* called the Senator "the man second in power in our Government" and "the man who has taken La Follette's place as the hope of the West." Without doubt, according to Edward Whiting in *The Boston Herald*, only he "could at all qualify by a combination of brains and repute" as leader of the Senate liberals. North Dakota's Senator Ladd apparently agreed. In the middle of the Warren episode he wrote, "To my mind, the ablest man in the Senate, the most courageous and with sound judgment for the Progressive group is . . . Senator Borah." In May and June *The New Republic* featured three articles on "This Man Borah," portraying him as "a fearless and a persistent fighter . . . at all times with a passion for realities, a zest for righteousness, and a record for having done as much to restore Americanism in the humane and liberal meaning of that word as any living man." [26]

The deaths of La Follette and Ladd in June seemed further

[26] Baltimore *Sun*, March 22, 1925; "T.R.B." 's "Washington Notes," *The New Republic*, XLII (March 25, 1925), 126–27, and (April 1, 1925), 157–58; *San Francisco Daily News*, March 31, 1925, and *Oregon Journal*, March 29, 1925, Borah Scrapbooks, Reel 5; "Borah's Keynotes," *The Independent*, CXIV (April 18, 1925), 429; *The Boston Herald*, March 31, 1925; portion of letter from Edwin Ladd to Rev. E. E. Saunders, March 14, 1925, which Saunders quoted to Borah, June 29, 1926, Borah Papers, Box 270; Charles Merz, "This Man Borah," *The New Republic*, XLIII (May 27, 1925), 9–13; "The Idaho Majority of One," *ibid.* (June 3, 1925), 66–70; "Borah's One-Man Party," *ibid.* (June 10, 1925), 66–70.

to emphasize Borah's position as new leader of the Senate progressives. Frank Kent, who wrote the "T.R.B." column for *The New Republic,* wrote that while Hiram Johnson and George Norris could not rally the insurgents, "there is still Borah. As a matter of fact Borah is the real hope—the one best bet." Besides the Senator's influence at the White House, he "has a sound progressive heart. His friends here have a feeling, which I fully share, that the La Follette death will force him forward as the real Progressive leader. . . ." And, if Borah assumed the responsibility, his leadership would be more effective than that of anyone else. "Inherently and heartily progressive," he would not foresake his calling and abdicate the political field to the financial interests. He would, Kent was certain, realize the need for an active Senate faction and would lead the fight with a Senate group as large as La Follette's had been. The journalist could "not conceive of Senator Borah's doing anything else. I cannot conceive him content tamely to accept the big business program prepared by Mr. Coolidge. . . . he would have to make himself over. There is no danger of his doing it." [27]

Mark Sullivan, an early muckraker and a Bull-Mooser, concurred that Borah had a tremendous opportunity to make progressivism respectable. According to Sullivan, La Follette had actually been a handicap to the Idahoan. La Follette's radicalism had restricted the activities of Borah, "a very moderate Progressive" who would "now be the accepted leader of the progressive thought in the country." [28]

Borah himself believed that the death of La Follette—and a month later that of William Jennings Bryan—opened the door for genuine progressivism. Frank Knox, a prominent New Hampshire Republican and newspaper editor, recalled how Borah had suggested to him "that possibly the removal of La

[27] *The New Republic,* XLIII (July 8, 1925), 178–79.
[28] New York *Herald Tribune,* June 22, 1925. See also, Wile Scrapbooks, June 19, 1925, 20; New York *World,* June 20, 1925; New York *Sun,* June 23, 1925; Baltimore *Sun,* June 24, 1925, for more comments on Borah's enhanced position.

Follette and Bryan from the stage may pave the way to the organization of a real liberal movement in America." The Senator
wrote Knox that "there is an opportunity for tremendously big
things. I am not speaking now particularly about official big
things, but the bringing about of a support of some great policies." Talking with Frederick Wile, Borah predicted a shift
from " 'radicalism' " to a "distinctly liberal movement in politics." The people wanted government to attack the problems of
transportation, coal, and agricultural legislation, and the settlement of the international debt question. In the progressive
heartland, the west and northwest, farmers had "a claim on the
Republican party that must not be ignored." For too long,
Borah told Wile, government had snubbed agriculture in deference to industry and finance. The people were not radical, but
they opposed programs of favoritism and neglect. It was time
for liberalism, for "giving the people a clean and economical
Government and of legislation upon these public questions in
the interest of the whole people. It is only after 'liberalism' is
rejected and discarded that 'radicalism' has a hearing." [29]

In September, he gave the press corps enough information to
reaffirm Frank Kent's faith "that there is something inherent
and instinctive in his makeup that will prevent his 'going
along' with this smug little group . . . known as the Coolidge
Circle." For one thing, the Senator clearly indicated that he
opposed the administration's approach to tax reform via the
reduction of surtaxes. He was also prepared to fight the World
Court proposal, another major tenet on the Coolidge docket.
Kent happily reported "that the main opposition to the administration program, not on one thing but on everything, is really
going to centre around Mr. Borah." By the end of November,
the liberal journalist Norman Hapgood declared that he could

[29] Frank Knox to Borah, September 17, 1925, and Borah to Frank Knox,
September 19, 1925, Borah Papers, Box 255. Borah quoted in Wile's arti-
cle, "La Follette Radicalism Doomed, Borah Declares," June 28, 1925,
Wile Scrapbook 20.

"not remember the time when one personality was so far ahead of all others in Congress in the attention paid to his views." [30]

The administration's tax program, which the La Follette group had stalled in 1924, supplied an early test for the "Borah bloc." When Congress convened in December, 1925, Borah loomed as "the key man"; if he opposed the tax measures, a Senate majority would supposedly rally behind him. The attention that Coolidge continued to direct toward the Idahoan reportedly demonstrated the President's awareness that Borah directly influenced the votes of at least five other Senators. Time and again the White House limousine took the Idahoan to the Executive's office. There were rumors that if the administration failed to gain Borah's support, its program would "be shot full of holes and the hearts of our men of high finance who pay the maximum surtax well-nigh broken." "T.R.B." echoed this view, asserting that the tax fight "revolves around Borah and anyone capable of analyzing the Senate is compelled to admit it." [31]

But Frank Kent and others who saw Borah as the determinant in the tax struggle were wrong. When Congress reassembled it proved quickly that the strength of the "Borah bloc" as the balance of power had been an ephemeral thing. The administration, despite the protests of the Idahoan, Norris, and other "half-breeds," won a smashing victory for "the millionaire tax bill," as Senator Howell labeled it. The votes of the "bloc" hardly represented the balance of power when Howell's amendment to salvage parts of the surtaxes failed, 15 to 70, and when the Norris motion to raise the surtaxes met a 29 to 54 fate. Even the attempt to open tax returns to investigation and examination as public records fell short by seventeen votes. Certainly the fight did not revolve around Borah, as some Washington observers had predicted. On numerous occasions the Senator and his "bloc" opposed the administration's financial program.

[30] The New Republic, XLIV (September 30, 1925), 152–53; Washington Herald, November 28, 1925, Borah Scrapbooks, Reel 5.

[31] Baltimore Sun, November 18, 1925; The New Republic, XLV (December 2, 1925), 46.

At one point Borah ridiculed the argument of Oscar Underwood that surtaxes represented government confiscation of "some of the great wealth of the nation." Why, he wondered, did the confiscation argument become important only after incomes had reached $100,000? In his opinion a progressive tax structure which took only a certain per cent of a man's income —and did so according to his ability to pay—fell far short of confiscation. The Idaho Senator's words had little impact on his colleagues. Nor did his defense of the inheritance tax, which the Senate ultimately repealed 49 to 26.[32]

Some important truths emerged during these futile struggles of the "Borah bloc." For one thing, its potential as the balance of power depended upon Democratic opposition to the administration. During the tax fight, the Democrats had almost unanimously joined the G.O.P. to achieve a bipartisan victory. With the absence of party lines, "the little band of Progressives" had nowhere in which it could effectively throw its weight. La Follette, Jr., commented bitterly that "the patent collapse of the Democratic party" had reduced progressive efforts to a mere "matter of protest and of putting all hands on record." He worried that it was responsible for the apparent loss of zeal among Senate liberals who, although they had not given ground, lacked "punch in their fighting." [33]

Moreover, it was increasingly evident that the Senate battle over the Warren appointment had been a poor test upon which to predict the administration's future strength. During the Warren fight, which had stimulated discussion of the power of the "half-breeds," the insurgents had enjoyed the advantage of Republican inertia. Important Republicans such as Wadsworth, Watson, Smoot, and Curtis had remained quiet simply because their sympathies were not with Warren. Coolidge had unwisely

[32] *Congressional Record,* 69th Cong., 1st Sess., 1926, LXVII, 3211, 3219, 3221, 3273–74, 3526, 3687–88, 3696.

[33] "T.R.B." in *The New Republic,* XLV (February 3, 1926), 296–97; XLVI (March 10, 1926), 71, and (March 24, 1926), 142; La Follette, Jr., to Phillip La Follette, February 18, 1926, La Follette Family Papers, Series A, Box 34, and to Frederick C. Howe, April 9, 1926, Series C, Box 4.

decided to fight for a cause which could not enlist the enthusiasm and convictions of G.O.P. regulars. William Howard Taft
had advised him not to make an issue of Warren, whose reputation was unlikely to attract strong support. When the Senate
refused its confirmation, Peter Norbeck noticed that even "the
Standpat Senators" welcomed it. Since Warren's questionable
background made him "a pretty big load to carry," Republican
regulars believed that his defeat would save the President from
future embarrassments.[34]

As the issue shifted from Warren to the administration's tax
program, however, the Republicans tightened their ranks. New
York's James Wadsworth had said nothing in Coolidge's behalf
during the Warren episode; yet he moved from the Foreign Relations Committee to the Finance Committee in order to pilot
the tax bill to the Senate floor. By 1926, the solid front of the
administration Republicans and the dissolution of Democratic
opposition quickly rendered the "Borah bloc" ineffective. "Of
course," wrote La Follette, "the progressives can do nothing but
protest unless the Democrats are willing to offer some resistance
to the Coolidge program." [35]

Borah suddenly seemed less the arbiter of the administration's
success than a mere devil's advocate.[36] This became even more
evident when, despite his protests, the Senate by a 76 to 17

[34] Baltimore *Sun,* March 18, 1925; Norbeck to John Hirning, March 19,
1925, and to John H. Kelly, March 31, 1925, Norbeck Papers (South
Dakota). Arthur Capper of Kansas voted for Warren, but said nothing
in his behalf and doubted the wisdom behind Coolidge's strategy. Capper
to William Allen White, March 14, 1925, White Papers, Box 82.

[35] Wadsworth to William J. Wells, July 14, 1926, Wadsworth Papers,
Box 19; La Follette, Jr., to W. T. Rawleigh, La Follette Family Papers,
Series C, Box 5. According to "T.R.B.," Coolidge could claim success on
Capitol Hill because of Democratic "pusillanimity and stupidity. . . .
The fact is that the Democratic surrender at this session is complete." *The
New Republic,* XLVI (March 10, 1926), 71. The following January he
described "the damned fool Democrats" as Coolidge's "real friends." *Ibid.,*
XLIX (January 26, 1927), 275.

[36] "President's Policies Making Progress," *The World's Work,* LI (February, 1926), 345.

vote accepted a resolution that would attach the United States to the World Court. To Borah, this was a revival of the League of Nations issue; he inveighed against the Court as the arm of "a supergovernment" league which was largely under the domination of Great Britain. Although in the Foreign Relations Committee he was able to help saddle the resolution with crippling reservations,[37] he opposed accepting it even in its emasculated form. Angrily, he responded to the Senate's vote. "They have determined," he warned, "to put this country into Europe." He recognized that the adopted resolution was so replete with reservations as to render the Court "utterly worthless." Nonetheless, while the Senate was "willing to destroy the Court," it was "not willing to separate the institution, whatever it may be called, from the League." He pledged to devote "every inch of energy and ability I have to this cause from now on. I do not want to neglect other things and shall not if my health is spared, but in the cause I must fight." On Washington's birthday, he participated in an anti-Court extravaganza in Chicago. "As America's new Paul Revere," he led a mammoth automobile caravan, received extensive newsreel coverage, spoke over the radio, and then addressed a packed Coliseum.[38]

[37] McKenna, *Borah*, p. 226. These reservations in effect demanded that the forty-eight member nations of the League Court grant America special privileges. Specifically, the Court could not render an advisory opinion involving the interests of the United States without first obtaining American consent. The United States also claimed what amounted to a veto power over any case to which America was a party. All member nations had to agree to these terms. Such reservations were hardly acceptable to other World Court members. See Adler, *The Isolationist Impulse*, pp. 186–93.

[38] Borah to C. C. Cavanah, January 29, 1926, Borah Papers, Box 263. Borah said that he did not oppose the concept of an international court. But he wanted an independent judicial tribunal, not a political or military arm of the League of Nations. His kind of court would rest upon a thorough code of international law which outlawed war; it would not make its own laws. "What would any one think in this country of authorizing a court, say the Supreme Court of the United States, to make its own laws and establish its own legal principles regardless of the constitution

The Court, however, was essentially a dead issue. Although
the resolution had passed the Senate, there was little likelihood
that other nations would accept the Senate reservations which
awarded special privileges to America. In his 1926 Armistice
Day speech, Coolidge shelved the entire question by saying that
he would not ask the Senate to modify its position and that
there was no prospect of American adherence to the Court
on different terms.

Although Coolidge dropped the Court issue, Borah was still
dissatisfied with the state of the Republican party. In July, 1926,
he announced his intentions to stump the country "to acquaint
the public with what is going on in politics and government."
He believed that the G.O.P. had fallen under the control of
moneyed interests and had wandered from traditional foreign
policies. The most important assignment was thus to educate
the people about facts and problems. If proper interest developed in these issues, the necessary political organization with
which to effect a progressive program would follow. The immediate requirement was to throw open the Republican doors
so that the fresh breezes of an informed electorate could blow
down the suffocating cobwebs of industrial and financial combinations. He hoped to supply the impetus for such party reform
before the 1928 election.[39]

and the statutes." Borah to Humphrey Sullivan, August 7, 1925, Box 252.
Any international court acceptable to him would resemble the American
Supreme Court in its handling of controversies between the states. See
for example, Borah to Rev. J. A. Glendinning, November 14, 1925; to
J. B. Murray, January 19, 1925; and to Frank Martin, May 22, 1923, *ibid.*,
Box 228. As prestigious a jurist as Harvard's Roscoe Pound sympathized
with Borah's fear of America becoming "part of a machine for preserva-
tion of a pax Gallica which in the end can only result in more war."
Pound to Borah, January 24, 1925, Box 252. To supporters of the Court,
however, Borah's plan was a ruse: to wait for an acceptable code of international law to develop before establishing a court was, in effect, to give
up on ever having a court. On his Chicago appearance, see telegram from
William Hale Thompson to Borah, February 20, 1926, Borah Papers, Box
263, and Borah Scrapbooks, Reel 5.

[39] Borah to John C. Eakin, July 12, 1926, Borah Papers, Box 270; A. H.
Ulm, "Mr. Borah Goes to the Country," *The New York Times Magazine,*

To national committeeman Dewey Hilles, Borah's motives were "transparent." *The New York Times* had no doubt that the Senator was at last making himself available for the 1928 nomination. "There is a consensus of opinion here," said Hiram Johnson, "that Borah is an avowed candidate now, and I think he really is. . . ." Although Borah openly admitted that he wanted to be President, he scoffed at his chances by saying that "those in control" would have no part of him.[40]

Privately, however, he gave indications that his thoughts were indeed on the White House. In early 1926, he wrote "in strictest confidence" about his political future to a long-time Idaho friend. He admitted that his "considerable popular support" probably would not influence the convention to endorse him. Nonetheless, a realistic understanding of the odds against him did not preclude future changes "which might bring on in this country a political revolution in the near future." Certainly the unprecedented and "astounding" amount of mail that Borah was receiving made him pause: "I do not myself know just what it means." Undoubtedly the possibilities of changes in the political currents warranted postponing any conclusions until more time had elapsed.[41]

By June Borah was apparently optimistic. After talking with him, Raymond Robins reported that the Senator had opened the door for a political movement in his behalf, "but he does not want a platform as yet nor does he want to be in the open as a candidate. He wants to fight with an America First warcry, law enforcement [prohibition], anti-international bankers and anti-cancellation [of European debts] program."[42]

There were signs by mid-1926 that the Senator's future as a

August 15, 1926, pp. 1, 20; *The New York Times*, June 12, 1926; *The Idaho Daily Statesman*, July 7, 1926; "Borah Starts Stumping Tour to Reform Republican Party," Wile Scrapbooks, July 18, 1926, 21.

[40] Charles D. Hilles to Taft, June 28, 1926, Taft Papers, Box 602; *The New York Times*, June 12, 1926; Hiram Johnson to Harold Ickes, July 6, 1926, Ickes Papers, Box 2; Ulm, "Mr. Borah Goes to the Country," p. 1.

[41] Borah to James H. Hawley, March 23, 1926, Borah Papers, Box 270.

[42] Robins to Levinson, June 30, 1926, Levinson Papers, Box 77.

presidential aspirant was not hopeless. According to veteran journalist Mark Sullivan, "Borah today . . . has a monopoly of what in the past generation was divided among four men— Roosevelt, Wilson, Bryan and La Follette." Sullivan did not mean that the Idahoan combined their ideas or consolidated their followers. "The sense in which Borah is their heir is that he is the one political leader who speaks out strongly, who takes a position of spokesmanship for ideas, of leadership." His prestige did not rest so much on what he said as on "the fact that he speaks out strongly about something. As the politicians put it, the public mood is getting hungry for a voice, and Borah supplies it." [43]

Moreover, the Republican party lacked strong leadership and real organization and thus appeared vulnerable to reform. No machine controlled it with an iron grip. Coolidge lacked the temperament to shape a formidable hierarchy within G.O.P. ranks. To Chief Justice Taft, the political situation was "a complete jungle"; the party was "all broken up" with nobody perceptive enough to guess what would happen. "The direct primary has shot us all to pieces," moaned Nicholas Murray Butler, who was convinced that the party had become an undisciplined assemblage of men.[44]

If the Republican leadership appeared shaky, it also seemed that public opinion was turning against the administration regulars. In the 1926 primaries, the Coolidge forces lost Senators William B. McKinley of Illinois, George Wharton Pepper of Pennsylvania, Robert N. Stanfield of Oregon, and Wisconsin's Irvine Lenroot. The loss of Lenroot especially hurt the administration since he had been the White House's official leader in

[43] *New York Tribune*, July 21, 1926. Hiram Johnson believed that Borah's stature had fallen among his colleagues, but averred that "he still has the greatest forum of any man in the congress." Johnson to Sons, November 27, 1926, Johnson Papers, Part IV, Box 3.

[44] Taft to Mrs. Charles Taft, July 8, 1926, Taft Papers, Box 603; Nicholas Murray Butler to Hilles, December 28, 1926, Hilles Papers, Box 207. On Coolidge's leadership, see McCoy, *Calvin Coolidge,* pp. 193–98.

the fight to ratify the World Court resolution. Coolidge had even spoken in his behalf in Wisconsin.[45]

The trend of events undoubtedly bolstered Borah's guarded optimism that the nation stood ready for political change. He was certain by mid-1926 that the public was hungry for issues and that the insincerity of political conventions and platforms was driving people away from parties and toward individuals. Although he granted that this was not an ideal permanent condition, he believed that for the present it was necessary. Until the character and intelligence of political parties again demanded respect, the voters would focus on men and ideas.[46] For Borah, whose political ambitions depended upon an upsurge of public sentiment and who viewed himself as a man of principle, the political climate indeed seemed promising.

During the summer of 1926, he took his message to the country. Although sixty-one years old, he was at the prime of his career—vigorous, exceptionally fit, his shaggy head greying at the temples, his countenance ruggedly handsome, his reputation well established as a powerful orator. With twenty years of sena-

[45] Wile Scrapbooks, June 10 and September 28, 1926, 21. "The result of the Illinois primary is given large political significance by everyone here," wrote La Follette. "Many Senators interpret it as an indication that Coolidge is losing his grip." La Follette, Jr., to W. T. Rawleigh, April 22, 1926, La Follette Family Papers, Series C, Box 5. This trend continued through the November elections. In Massachusetts, William M. Butler, despite Coolidge's endorsement and dramatic entry into the state to cast his vote, lost by a considerable margin—"a tremendous slap in the [President's] face," according to Hiram Johnson. New York's James Wadsworth, who ran on his support of the administration, also failed to gain reelection. "The old standpatters," wrote Johnson, "are morose, sullen, disgruntled, and vengeful; the insurgents exceedingly cheerful and gleeful. . . . All over the United States, there was a cracking of the Coolidge myth and a recession of the Republican wave." Johnson to Sons, November 6, 1926, Johnson Papers, Part IV, Box 3. See also, Johnson to Sons, November 13, 1926, *ibid.*, and McCoy, *Calvin Coolidge*, pp. 311–13. La Follette also "was much encouraged by the trend of the November elections." La Follette to W. T. Rawleigh, February 12, 1927, La Follete Family Papers, Series C, Box 6.

[46] Borah to Frank Knox, May 28, 1926, Borah Papers, Box 269.

torial service behind him, he no longer needed introductions. Indeed, by this time he could command the public's attention better than any other politician. Humorist Will Rogers quipped that when Borah left the Senate, the gallery seats would become firewood.[47]

Constantly on the move throughout July and August, Borah spoke in Augusta, Georgia; held conferences with Robert La Follette, Jr., and others in Chicago; addressed audiences in Wichita, Denver, and numerous Idaho communities; traveled through Washington, Oregon, and California; returned to Washington, D.C., for a few days, and then headed west again to speak in Kansas City. He discussed such subjects as the World Court, farm relief, prohibition, war debts, and the need for reducing bureaucracy.[48]

While the Senator was barnstorming the country, events occurred in Latin America which soon provided him with another issue. By January of 1927 a map of the Western Hemisphere had suddenly gone up in President Coolidge's usually unadorned office and people were asking, "What is Nicaragua?" [49] From Taft's administration until 1925 American marines had been in Nicaragua to keep order. Coolidge had removed the few remaining troops but, the following year when violence again erupted, he returned the marines in numbers greater than before the withdrawal. The United States threw its support behind the conservative government of President Adolpho Díaz, and against the liberal rebels of Juan B. Sacasa. To complicate matters, Mexico's President Plutarco Elías Calles recognized and backed the Sacasa group.

Borah initially defended the decision to return the marines. He had looked upon the earlier existence of American troops in Nicaragua as an "intolerable and indefensible" violation of

[47] *The New York Times,* January 7, 1923.

[48] Borah Scrapbooks, Reel 5; Cora Rubin to Robert M. Clarke, August 19, 1926, Borah Papers, Box 265; *The Idaho Daily Statesman,* July 7 and 14, 1926; August 1, 4–6, 9, 14, 16, 18, 20, 1926; October 3 and 20, 1926.

[49] Wile Scrapbooks, January 12, 1927, 25.

the internal affairs of another nation; Nicaraguans, he had said in 1922, were subjects "under the domination of certain special American interests." In 1925, when he had attacked "the fetish of force in America," he had pointed specifically to the "unnecessary and therefore immoral" invasions of Nicaragua as a prime example of America's unjustifiable use of its great power. But, in late 1926, he felt the situation was different. This time it seemed to be a case of self-defense. As he understood the problem, American citizens had requested protection for their lives and property. Such protection did not amount to American intervention. The United States was not, he presumed, "going to assume the role of censor for Central American revolutions," nor was it declaring war against countries whose political ideas and institutions were contrary to those of America. The government must, he warned, do nothing beyond what was absolutely necessary to protect American citizens and property; the marines should withdraw as soon as these citizens were "reasonably safe." Borah cautioned the administration, however, to beware of a possible trick on the part of Nicaragua's Díaz to pull the United States into a war with Mexico.[50]

The Senator was obviously concerned lest the Nicaraguan crisis become the pretext for American intervention against Mexico's President Calles. In Mexico, the revolutionary atmosphere had expanded beyond the political liberalism of the 1910 upheaval and had become charged with a growing desire for social reform. The eminent domain clauses of Venustiano Carranza's 1917 constitution had grown in significance with the emergence of Calles, who was genuinely committed to the principles of the revolution. As American oil companies felt the pressures of increased restrictions, they demanded American military action to halt Mexican "bolshevism." [51]

[50] Borah statement for the Baltimore *Sun*, December 14, 1922, Borah Papers, Box 234; Borah, "The Fetish of Force," *The Forum*, LXXIV (August, 1925), 240–45; Borah statements to the press, December 24 and 29, 1926, Borah Papers, Box 285.

[51] For a discussion of Mexico and Nicaragua as "barometers of inter-American pressures," see L. Ethan Ellis, *Frank B. Kellogg and American*

Borah emphatically opposed trouble with the Calles government. "The truth is," he told the press, "that effort is being
made to get this country into a shameless, cowardly, little war
with Mexico." He insisted that America had no obligation in
Nicaragua to defend Díaz against the Mexican-backed Sacasa.
"If Díaz could induce us to begin that war with Mexico in defense of his country, he would be serving wittingly or unwittingly, the scheme of those who would like to see us in trouble
with Mexico." Suspicious of the State Department's activities
in Latin America, he began a private inquiry into the situation. The public needed accurate information and he feared
that the proposed senatorial investigation of the problem
would be useless except as a postmortem.[52]

On January 7, 1927, after a White House conference, Borah
emerged with Secretary Kellogg and formally announced his
opposition to the administration's support of Díaz. He considered U.S. interference in Central-American controversies as rep-
rehensible; but it was even worse, he continued, to intervene
on the side of Díaz, the unconstitutional leader who owed his
authority entirely to the "sheer force of foreign arms." According to the Senator, Juan Sacasa held the legal title to power in
Nicaragua.[53]

Five days later, Secretary Kellogg added to the tension in
Washington by telling the Senate that Russian interests in Mexico were partly responsible for Nicaraguan resistance to the
United States. It was in this context that Borah allied with the
Democrats and worked closely with Arkansas' Joseph Robinson
to secure quick passage of a Senate resolution recommending
arbitration with Mexico, lest events tumble into war. The 79

Foreign Relations, 1925–29 (New Brunswick, N.J., 1961), pp. 58–59. See,
also, Hicks, *Republican Ascendancy,* pp. 154–56.

[52] Borah press statement, December 24, 1926, Borah Papers, Box 285;
clippings from the Chicago *Herald-Examiner* and the Chicago *Daily Tribune,* December 27, 1926, Box 280.

[53] *The Washington Herald,* January 8, 1927, carried large front-page
banner headlines that Borah had broken with the administration over
Nicaragua. Borah Scrapbooks, Reel 2.

to o vote on January 25 for the resolution reminded Salmon
Levinson of "the score of a football game between Harvard and
Brooksville High School. . . . It is a tremendous victory for
Borah who, in a dignified, statesmanlike, and masterful way led
the fight and carried the banner through to victory." Coolidge
was less impressed; he ignored the resolution and the possibilities of arbitration faded.[54]

While State Department officials such as Assistant Secretary
William Castle fretted that "Borah is not helping to make things
any happier," the Senator continued to pressure the administration. By the end of February, 1927, he was deeply enmeshed
in the Latin-American controversies. His efforts prompted letters of appreciation and encouragement from such people as
Bartelome Martinez, ex-President of Nicaragua; from Arturo
Alessandri, ex-President of Chile, thanking him for his "brilliant defense in favor of sovereignty of all the nations of the
earth, equal before the law"; from "Various Admirers" in Ha-
vana for his "valiant phases in defense of justice and respect
toward the Latin American Republics," and from the Secre-
taries of the Congress of Costa Rica.[55]

With such support, and undoubtedly sharing the growing
fears of fellow progressives about the emerging diplomatic crisis,
Borah plunged ahead, introducing a resolution calling for the
Senate Foreign Relations Committee to investigate relations between the Central-American countries, Mexico, and the United
States. When the Senate blocked the consideration of his proposal, he communicated directly with Mexico's President Calles
in order to secure information about American oil interests.
Earlier he had requested such information from the State Department, but the data that he received was supposed to remain

[54] Borah to William Allen White, January 27, 1927, Borah Papers,
Box 280; Levinson to Raymond Robins, January 26, 1927, Levinson
Papers, Box 77; Ellis, *Frank B. Kellogg and American Foreign Relations*,
p. 40.
[55] Castle to Jose Camprubi, January 14, 1927, William R. Castle, Jr.,
Papers (Hoover Presidential Library); letters from various Latin-American
groups to Borah in Borah Papers, Box 282.

confidential. Since he was certain that the facts he wanted were not of confidential nature, he contacted Calles himself, asking if the American government was aiding oil companies whose titles were invalid.[56]

Several weeks later he defended his telegram to Calles. In the middle of a speech on American foreign policy that he delivered in New Haven, Connecticut, a heckler from the gallery charged him with having violated the Logan Act, which forbade unauthorized negotiations with foreign governments over questions at issue with the United States. "As chairman of the Senate Foreign Relations Committee," he answered, "I have a right to get my information from any source I wish. This I propose to do, and I know of no power that can stop me. We have not yet got Mussolini in the United States." In his address, he called for an end to unjust statements about Mexico and, with a stirring burst of eloquence, he said: "God has made us neighbors, let justice make us friends." [57]

During these early months of 1927, Borah was at his best. By April, Congress had disbanded but the Senator remained in Washington as the "Watchdog on the Potomac," the "Horatius at the bridge, working alone to counteract the White House Spokesman" by holding daily news conferences in his office. He bluntly told the director of the Association of Producers of

[56] Borah described his point of view and actions in a special interview with David Lawrence, New York *Sun*, March 3, 1927. For examples of progressive concern about America's Latin-American policy, see Basil Manly's editorial, "Delirious Diplomacy," *The People's Business* (February, 1927), La Follette Family Papers, Series C, Box 428; *The Nation*, especially CXXIV (January 26, 1927) and (February 2, 1927), which carried editorials, cartoons, excerpts from foreign newspapers on "What the World Thinks of America," and essays by William Hard, Lewis Gannett, and Frank Kent; and *The New Republic*, especially XLIX (January 12, 1927). In late 1928, Gerald Nye pointed to the consistent opposition of the Senate progressives to the American intervention in Nicaragua. Nye's October 15, 1928, radio address in St. Paul, Minnesota, endorsing Shipstead for re-election, Gerald P. Nye Papers (Hoover Presidential Library), Box 31.

[57] *The New York Times*, March 21, 1927; an extract of Borah's New Haven speech appeared in *The Nation*, CXXIV (April 13, 1927), 392–94.

Petroleum in Mexico that powerful interests hoped "to see Mexico Cubanized." Although he agreed that the legitimate rights of American oil companies deserved protection, he "utterly disagree[d] with the policy which would seek that protection by a break with Mexico." He scoffed at the government's penchant to see bolshevism wherever people sought to throw off foreign domination and establish their own rule. In an article that he wrote for exclusive publication in South and Central America, he charged that Díaz had captured the Nicaraguan presidency through intrigue and was retaining power "through the courtesy of the United States marines." American recognition of Díaz encouraged revolution and challenged the concept of free government. With admitted distress, he accused his country of having succumbed to the "fascination of dominance" that occurred when a strong nation approached a weak one. In Cleveland on May 9, with his hair in disarray and his cheeks flushed from the vigor of his oratory, he again attacked the doctrine of force in foreign affairs.[58]

The Coolidge administration probably wanted to avoid further conflict in Latin America, but Borah surely was at least partly responsible for the fact that American policy remained favorable to moderation throughout the early months of 1927. By mid-year, caution replaced the impetuosity of the administration's approach, particularly in regard to Mexico. The important appointments of Dwight W. Morrow as new ambassador to Mexico and of Henry L. Stimson as Coolidge's personal representative to Nicaragua reflected a shift in the administration's attitude. The subsequent efforts of both men proved the advantages of a policy of moderation, prudence, and patience—a

[58] Raymond Clapper, "Borah—Watchdog on the Potomac," *The Nation*, CXXIV (April 13, 1927), 394–95; Borah to Guy Stevens, March 5, 1927, Borah Papers, Box 280; Borah article, "Nicaraguan Adjustment," written for J. H. Furay, United Press Associations, for *La Prensa*. In his letter to Furay, May 18, 1927, Box 274, Borah noted that his understanding was "that these articles are to be published only in South and Central America. I say this for the reason that they are written with that idea in mind." *The Cleveland Press* and *Cleveland Plain Dealer*, May 10, 1927, Borah Scrapbooks, Reel 5.

policy for which Borah had been striving. His endeavors to shape this new approach—at least in the negative sense of his helping to counter the earlier, more rash response—marked a significant chapter in the twentieth-century struggle of the Senate to influence foreign policy.[59]

But, although postponements in the Nicaraguan settlement and the dispatch of more troops there occurred, Borah slowly turned his attention from Latin America and toward internal matters. Briefly, at the end of August while he was taking a short vacation in Idaho, he became involved in the Sacco-Vanzetti case. In a speech at an Idaho picnic celebration, he referred to the fact that two men had faced death for seven years while discussions continued about their guilt or innocence. It reminded him of days when men were thrown into jail and forgotten. Speedy dispensation of justice was essential, he asserted, for any free government. Certainly Americans would consider it barbarous if any other nation took seven years to administer justice.[60]

[59] Ellis, *Frank B. Kellogg and American Foreign Relations,* is excellent on the administration's responses to Mexico and Nicaragua. The early months of 1927 were indeed tense. Oswald Garrison Villard, after talking in mid-January with Borah and six other progressive Senators, described the situation as "very grave." Villard to Paul Kellogg, January 17, 1927, Villard Papers, Folder 2013. Almost two months later, Robert La Follette, Jr., was "very apprehensive" and felt "very helpless about the situation." La Follette to Villard, March 9, 1927, *ibid.,* Folder 2159. Williams, *The Tragedy of American Diplomacy,* p. 120, and McKenna, *Borah,* p. 167, attribute Borah with a substantial role in the appointment of Morrow. Maddox, *William E. Borah and American Foreign Policy,* p. 176n., however, shows that "actually, the Senator was finessed by Coolidge on this matter and did little more than agree to Morrow's selection." Initially, Borah distrusted Morrow because of his connections with J. P. Morgan's firm. Raymond Robins helped to convince the Senator that Morrow's nomination was a good one. See Raymond Robins statement, February 1, 1931, in the Hermann Hagedorn Papers (Library of Congress), Box 1. I. F. Stone has compared Senator J. William Fulbright's attack on President Lyndon Johnson's Dominican intervention to Borah's challenge to Coolidge's interference in Nicaragua in 1927. *The New York Review of Books,* January 26, 1967, p. 10.

[60] *Kellogg* [Idaho] *Evening News,* August 20, 1927, Borah Scrapbooks, Reel 5. The Sacco-Vanzetti case was one of the most sensational murder

At the request of the Citizens National Committee, which was battling to save Sacco and Vanzetti from execution, Borah wired Coolidge and the Attorney General to ask if the Justice Department would open its files to investigation. He also indicated a willingness to examine the record and—if he was convinced that the two men were indeed innocent—to argue the case before the Supreme Court. Although his proffered services "injected new life into a desperate situation" at the headquarters of the Citizens National Committee, it all came to nothing. The execution of the accused men on August 23 ended the struggle to save their lives. During the last critical days of the controversy, Borah made several things clear: he adamantly opposed any execution for reason of political views; and he just as vehemently opposed letting world opinion influence American actions. He told Jane Addams, who had asked him to intervene in behalf of the accused, that the fight had to rest on the innocence of the men or on unjust legal proceedings—not on international relations. "It would be a national humiliation and a shameless cowardly compromise of national courage to pay the slightest attention to foreign protests or mob protests at home." Indeed, he considered "this foreign interference . . . an impudent and willful challenge to our sense of decency and dignity and ought to be dealt with accordingly." [61]

trials in American history. In 1920 the State of Massachusetts convicted and sentenced to death Nicola Sacco and Bartolomeo Vanzetti for the murder of a paymaster at South Braintree, Massachusetts. The belief grew, however, that the trial judge and jury had really convicted the two men because of their foreign backgrounds, their philosophical radicalism, and their evasion of military service in World War I.

[61] Box 284 in the Borah Papers has a number of letters and telegrams relating to the Sacco-Vanzetti case. See, especially, Borah to Jane Addams, August 18, 1927, and to F. G. Bobette, September 2, 1927. His telegram to Jane Addams indicating his anger at any thoughts of bowing to foreign opinion elicited contrasting responses. Ralph M. Easley of the National Civic Federation found it a "ringing patriotic" message—an "intellectual bomb" that bomb-throwing anarchists deserved to hear. (Easley to Borah, August 19, 1927.) On the other hand, in England, Harold J. Laski wrote that Borah's "incredible remark" had disturbed thinking people. "As one Frenchman said to me, 'if we have to mobilise five thousand troops to

It was to national politics, however, that he directed his main interests. Coolidge's announcement in August, 1927, that he chose not to run again for office undoubtedly surprised the Senator, but it also pleased him. Previously, when Borah had said that Coolidge could have another term if he wanted it, he had stated a fact, not a preference. When he heard of the President's latest decision, he stated with obvious satisfaction that the Republicans could now work for the national good without the stigma of playing politics. Coolidge—"out of the race and free from the imputation of playing for advantage"—could provide vital leadership for deeds that would ordinarily become "the playthings of personal politics." Borah hoped that the party would devote the next six months to serving public needs and shaping policies, not to fighting over individual candidates.[62]

Despite his plea for the Republicans to keep their attention on legislation and away from politics, Borah personally took an active interest in the political future. With Coolidge moving himself from the stage, conditions seemed more favorable to the type of party that Borah wanted. The days ahead offered "some fine possibilities," he wrote William Allen White. He added hastily that he "was not referring to any personal ambition but to the general situation." [63]

Conveniently, though, "the general situation" and Borah's own fortunes were entwined. He could work to his own advantage while helping to reform his party. This was clearly evident when he offered to pay Ray McKaig $1,000 to expand in western states his presidential campaigning for Borah. The Senator informed Idaho Republicans that such efforts would help the

---

protect American lives and property, we are at least entitled to consideration.' " Harold J. Laski to Oliver Wendell Holmes, Jr., September 2, 1927, in Mark DeWolfe Howe (ed.), *Holmes-Laski Letters* (Cambridge, Mass., 1953), 976–77.

62 Borah to George A. Schreiner, July 12, 1927, Borah Papers, Box 274; Borah telegrams to *The New York Times* and the New York *Herald Tribune*, August 2, 1927, Box 282.

63 Borah to William Allen White, September 7, 1927, Borah Papers, Box 277.

party more than himself. As he explained it, the third party was dissolving in the west and drifting toward the major parties. His possible candidacy would "have a very strong tendency" to attract these drifters into the G.O.P. Since the stated strategy was to aid Republicanism rather than himself, he believed that those friends who really supported his nomination should not have to pay for this campaign. Although he was privately confident that the Republican hierarchy was "interested in this matter" and would help to subsidize the project, he offered personally to assume the financial burden for "reorganizing and regenerating the party" in the west.[64]

At the very time that he was attempting to Republicanize the west, he turned his attention to westernizing the Republicans. Seeking to strengthen the western reform influence within the party, he abandoned his traditional lone-wolf role and sought to organize the insurgent Senators. The "Borah bloc" of the Warren fight had never approached formal organization. Essentially it had been nothing more than the joint response of western insurgents with somewhat similar views to specific political events. By the autumn of 1927, however, Borah was intent on making it a more cohesive and formidable group on Capitol Hill.

[64] McKaig had already sought progressive endorsements of Borah in Idaho and Utah. He planned to do the same in California, Oregon, Washington, and Nevada, and estimated that such work would require two months, a $300-per-month salary, and $7 per day in expense money. See E. H. Dewey to Borah, September 16, 1927, and Borah reply, October 4 and 6, 1927, Borah Papers, Box 275.

VIII

Progressivism against Itself: Borah and the Senate Western Bloc

🏵

IN early December, 1927—after several weeks of meetings in which Borah was a key participant—nine smiling western Senators posed for newsreel cameramen and photographers to advertise a newly formed progressive bloc. With Borah were George Norris and Robert Howell of Nebraska, Gerald Nye and Lynn Frazier of North Dakota, Robert La Follette, Jr., and John J. Blaine of Wisconsin, Smith Brookhart of Iowa, and Henrik Shipstead of Minnesota. Although their primary purpose was to increase the west's influence in national affairs, they hoped, as Mark Sullivan observed, "to stand before the country on the broad set of principles, some of which Roosevelt was identified with, and others of which were associated with La Follette." Due to the prominence of the bloc's members, among whom Borah was the best known, it represented "in many respects the most important development of the year in Congressional affairs." [1]

The gathering of Senate progressives on their office steps for the picture-taking festivities gave the impression of unity, but the bloc was far from harmonious. It sought to make the Republican party more aware of western economic and political interests; yet, from its inception, the western group was divided

[1] *The New York Times,* December 4, and for a picture of the group, December 5, 1927; New York *Herald Tribune,* October 18 and November 13, 1927. According to the Washington *Star,* October 13, 1927, "Should the insurgents be able to organize on the scale they have outlined, they will have a larger welded group than ever before in the Senate and they would constitute a force with which the Old Guard leaders would have to reckon."

within its own ranks over problems that were of special concern to the west itself. Its members disagreed over McNary-Haugenism—the most significant farm relief plan of the decade —over the issue of prohibition, and over the question of which candidate they would back for the 1928 Republican nomination. Indeed, far from being a study in unity, the bloc was so racked by internal discords and suspicions that it failed to attract the support of other agrarian Senators such as Norbeck and McMaster of South Dakota. Borah, who initially helped to organize the group, became a center of contention within it and ultimately abandoned it.

Disagreements within the bloc manifested the lack of unanimity within the west itself, but they also contributed to the weakness of progressivism in the 1920's. While some individuals looked to labor as "the nucleus" of reform, or to the city "as the basic unit" in progressivism, the Senators attempted to build upon a base that was primarily agrarian and rural. Amos Pinchot viewed the bloc as better than nothing but felt that its perspective was wrong; it demanded "that the West be allowed to stick its snout in the hog trough in common with the Eastern hogs" when, in fact, there should be no trough at all.[2] At the very time when progressivism was suffering the crippling effects of this widening cultural chasm between eastern and western reformers, it was further handicapped by the internal cleavage among agrarian insurgents themselves. The differences among members within the Senate bloc prevented them from effectively championing progressivism within their own region, let alone nationally.

Despite the bloc's general ineffectiveness, it was nevertheless the product of a real need for positive, united political action if the western progressives expected a significant voice in na-

[2] On labor and reform, Albert Coyle (editor of the *Brotherhood of Locomotive Engineers Journal* and an organizer of the CPPA) to Oswald Garrison Villard, November 10, 1924, Villard Papers, Folder 741; on the city and reform, Basil Manly to Fiorello La Guardia, September 14, 1925, La Guardia Papers, Box 2521; Amos Pinchot to Smith Wildman Brookhart, November 14, 1927, Pinchot Papers, Box 50.

tional affairs. The slight Republican majority in the Senate—
49 to 47, with Farmer-Laborite Shipstead included in the
G.O.P.—seemed to provide the insurgent group with political
leverage. Following the 1926 elections, Hiram Johnson had
noted that "the recalcitrants, among whom I am numbered, are
in a position at any time to raise Cain." It was with precisely
this purpose in mind that La Follette had attempted in early
1927 "to outline a constructive position for our group," but
Congress adjourned before he accomplished much. In September Senator Nye talked of organizing a progressive bloc before
Congress reconvened. He wished that "our own group" were
less individualistic, but he remained optimistic about the proposed bloc's ability to control the balance of power in the
coming months. Villard of *The Nation* encouraged him: "If
the group only stands together it can put the fear of God in
the hearts of the leaders in both camps and really accomplish
something." [3]

Although Nye had spoken about organizing the progressive
faction, it was Borah who took the initiative. He maintained
that the west had stampeded for too long "into the Eastern
corral at the crack of somebody's whip." Since the "favors of
politics follow the exhibition of power," the west had to demonstrate its strength. In early October he met in his office with
Nye and Brookhart, where they laid plans for larger meetings
before and after Congress reconvened in December. On October 10, Norris conferred with Borah and Nye. The next day in
Norris's office, Borah, Norris, Nye, Brookhart, and Frazier discussed such topics as farm relief, the "power trust," the pro-
motion of an inland waterway project, and tax legislation. In
future sessions they hoped to gain the services of McMaster,
Norbeck, La Follette, Blaine, Charles McNary, and Frederick
Steiwer of Oregon, James Couzens of Michigan, Robert Howell,

[3] Hiram Johnson to Sons, November 6, 1926, Johnson Papers, Part IV,
Box 3; La Follette, Jr., to W. T. Rawleigh, February 12, 1927, La Follette
Family Papers, Series C, Box 6; Nye to Villard, September 13, 1927, and
Villard reply, September 16, 1927, Villard Papers, Folder 2873.

Hiram Johnson, and perhaps other western Senators. Borah, serving as the group's spokesman after the meeting, issued a public statement explaining that the group hoped to obtain unity of purpose and action on political and legislative questions that pertained to the west. The bloc assumed that since the Republican party was a national organization, G.O.P. policies should not come from the east alone. Commenting on the approaching election year, Borah stated that the agrarians had taken no action regarding a possible Republican presidential nominee; but individually, they would gladly support Norris.[4]

The most immediate concern, of course, was simply to mold the bloc into an influential senatorial body. In order to achieve this goal, the western leaders were well aware that they would have to confront forthrightly and successfully the problem of farm relief. As Borah said, "There is little hope for farm legislation at the next session, unless there is some unity of purpose among the Western people and others interested in agriculture."[5] It was, however, this issue, so crucial to thousands of farmers in western states, that quickly split the tiny bloc and revealed Borah's weakness as a regional leader. Almost as soon as the agrarian group had formed, it divided over the McNary-Haugen farm relief plan.

Since its introduction in Congress in early 1924, the McNary-Haugen proposal had become a major rallying point for many advocates of farm legislation.[6] Farmers increasingly believed

[4] Borah to Roscoe Balch, October 8, 1927, Borah Papers, Box 283; *The Washington Post* and *The New York Times,* October 11, 1927; copy of Borah's statement in Borah Papers, Box 285; Baltimore *Sun* and *The Washington Post,* October 12, 1927. See also, Basil Manly, "The Power of the Progressives," *The People's Business,* II (October, 1927), 1, in La Follette Family Papers, Series C, Box 425.

[5] *The New York Times,* October 15, 1927.

[6] The scheme would place agriculture on par with industry by using the tariff, a parity price system, and an equalization fee. A tariff wall would separate the American market from that of Europe. On the American side, the government would set prices on certain basic farm products on the basis of parity—that ratio at which each product had stood in relation to other commodities in the years 1905–1914, a period which had been generally good for agriculture. The result would be higher farm

that the fate of this bill would determine the future of agriculture itself within the American economy. As a symbol during the Coolidge administration, McNary-Haugenism became for agrarians what free silver had been for the Populists. The question, it seemed to many farmers, was whether the nation would continue to industrialize at agriculture's expense.[7]

Initially, in the spring of 1924, Borah had indicated that he was "thoroughly in favor" of the McNary-Haugen plan. He had "sincerely" hoped that it would become a law and had done "everything" he could for it, which included telling Coolidge that the proposal deserved at least a chance to prove itself. In March of that year, he had voted against the Norbeck-Burtness measure, which called for agricultural diversification in wheat regions, on grounds that it would "prevent the successful consideration of a more important measure such as the McNary Bill." Although the McNary-Haugen plan did not reach a Senate vote in 1924, he maintained that he would have fought for it.[8]

---

prices on the domestic market. A government corporation would buy the surpluses and sell them abroad at the going market price. The government would receive reimbursements for its losses through an equalization fee, a tax, that each farmer who sold a product that came under the bill's protection would pay whenever he sold a bushel of that particular commodity. Gilbert C. Fite, *George N. Peek and the Fight for Farm Parity* (Norman, Okla., 1954), discusses at length the origins and development of the McNary-Haugen plan. See especially pp. 38–202. Theodore Saloutos and John D. Hicks, *Agricultural Discontent in the Middle West, 1900–1939* (Madison, Wis., 1951), also is excellent on the subject.

[7] Fite, *George N. Peek and the Fight for Farm Parity*, p. 123; Shideler, *Farm Crisis, 1919–1923*, p. 275; John D. Black, "The McNary-Haugen Movement," *The American Economic Review*, XVIII (September, 1928), 405. See also, Mark Sullivan, "The Waning Influence of the Farmer," *The World's Work*, LI (April, 1926), 660.

[8] On his early support for McNary-Haugenism see, for example, Borah to William Lambie, April 4, 1924; to Carroll S. Jones, April 18, 1924; to Thomas J. Jones, May 10, 1924; to C. Bascom Slemp, May 10, 1924, Borah Papers, Box 236. For his opposition to the Norbeck bill, Borah to William Michaelis, March 10, 1924; to F. H. Sherwood, March 5, 1924, Box 240. In helping to defeat the Norbeck bill, Borah departed from the other

By 1926, however, Borah had changed his mind about Mc-Nary-Haugenism. Perhaps it was a more careful study of the bill that reversed his earlier enthusiasm and convinced him that the proposed compulsory equalization fee was unconstitutional. He told the Senate that the plan was an insidious governmental attempt to confiscate private property via the commerce clause of the Constitution. No one, he warned, could take one farmer's property for the benefit of others: "His property is private property used in private enterprise and not dedicated to public use, and therefore is beyond the control of the Government in that respect." Borah would only accept a scheme that was voluntary. When Norris contended that a voluntary act would fail and that farmers who refused to share in the costs would still reap the benefits, Borah countered that this was a moot point; the farmers, he said, would cooperate.[9]

Disagreement over McNary-Haugenism plagued the newly organized progressive bloc from its beginnings. Obviously, the problem of agricultural depression presented the western Senators with a crucial test. Their ability to agree on a program and to present a united front would have great bearing on their future effectiveness as a group. But Borah, the "Chief Insurgent" in the group and its recognized spokesman,[10] con-

western progressives who, almost to a man, decided to support the plan and also to fight for more legislation. Fite, *George N. Peek and the Fight for Farm Parity*, pp. 88–89; *Congressional Record*, 68th Cong., 1st Sess., 1924, LXV, 4073–84. Borah to C. A. Cowles, September 26, 1924, Box 243, regarding how he would have voted on the McNary-Haugen proposal.

[9] *Congressional Record*, 69th Cong., 1st Sess., 1926, LXVII, 11441–45. Norris believed that eliminating the compulsory fee would be equivalent to removing a man's heart and then expecting him to be as active as ever. See Norris to M. F. Harrington, October 28, 1927, Norris Papers, Tray 5, Box 1.

[10] *The New York Times*, October 24, 1927; *The Washington Post*, October 11, 1927. The Baltimore *Sun*, October 13, 1927, editorialized about "Borah's insurgents." "From a legislative point of view," wrote Lewis Gannett in *The Nation*, CXXV (November 2, 1927), 470, "the most interesting thing about this Progressive revival is that Senator Borah is leading it." "T.R.B." reported that, "by common consent, Senator Borah has recently

tinued to oppose the McNary-Haugen plan, while the other members generally favored it.

Borah was convinced that the western bloc could find a middle ground on farm legislation. First off, he discounted the importance of McNary-Haugenism among most farmers, other than wheat growers. Following the October 11 meeting in which the Senators organized their progressive group, rumors circulated on Capitol Hill that several of the agrarians would abandon the equalization fee in order to keep Borah with them. Immediately, however, Norris denied such stories and asserted that "the so-called Progressive group" had not considered such action. Norris, Frazier, and Nye emphasized that they still favored the fee. The western coalition seemed hopelessly split, with only Brookhart apparently willing to abandon the compulsory tax in order to placate Borah.[11]

While disagreements over the McNary-Haugen scheme quickly threatened to disrupt the bloc, the political implications of the bill similarly portended troubles for it. Insofar as the Senators endorsed Norris for President, they faced conflict with the supporters of Frank O. Lowden, former governor of Illinois and a strong advocate of McNary-Haugenism. When Coolidge, who vetoed the farm bill in February of 1927, decided in August to refuse another term, some leading agricultural groups started a boom for Lowden.[12]

On October 23, Nebraska's Governor Adam McMullen, an important figure in farm-relief politics and a supporter of both McNary-Haugenism and Lowden, threw a verbal bomb into the middle of the struggling progressive group. In a public state-

---

become the spokesman of the Progressives, as the small band of western Republican senators unaffiliated with the administration call themselves." *The New Republic*, LII (November 2, 1927), 284–85.

[11] *The New York Times*, October 15, 1927, for Borah's assessment of the support for McNary-Haugenism; Norris to M. F. Harrington, October 28, 1927, Norris Papers, Tray 5, Box 1; *The Washington Post*, October 22, 1927; Baltimore *Sun*, October 21–22, 1927.

[12] See, for example, Fite, *George N. Peek and the Fight for Farm Parity*, p. 187.

ment he accused Borah of trying to corner western delegates in order to block genuine agricultural relief. McMullen claimed that the Idahoan hoped to undermine the presidential chances of Lowden, or a similar candidate who would be loyal to the agrarian cause. To those Senators who allowed their names to appear in connection with Borah's "widely propagandized move," McMullen served warning. Although they had previously demonstrated their desire for effective farm legislation, they must break relations with Borah or be vulnerable to charges of sacrificing rural needs on the altar of politics.[13]

The following day, the western conferees in Washington discussed McMullen's challenge. Borah subsequently wired the Governor: Did he prefer Lowden to Norris? Did he oppose a Nebraska delegation instructed for Norris? The Governor, suddenly on the defensive, replied that he liked Norris and would not block a delegation for him. The critical point, according to McMullen, was that Lowden had a better chance to receive the Republican nomination. McMullen charged Borah with dividing western ranks and thereby aiding the eastern Republicans who hoped "to continue their reactionary and industrially-minded control of government." He asked Borah, who had endorsed Norris, if he would also support Norris's efforts for McNary-Haugenism. Borah continued the public exchange of widely publicized telegrams by countering that his opposition to the equalization fee in no way interfered with his endorsement of Norris. Angrily, McMullen answered that Borah and the "eternal horse play around agriculture" were "scattering our forces." Since the Senator could suggest nothing more equitable than the equalization fee, he should agree to "stand together and secure the best proposal at hand."[14]

The Borah-McMullen clash attracted much attention. Clearly it revealed Borah's precarious position among those agrarian

[13] *The Washington Post,* October 24, 1927.
[14] Telegram exchange, Borah to Adam McMullen, October 24 and 26, 1927, and McMullen to Borah, October 26 and November 1, 1927, Borah Papers, Box 283. These telegrams were published in many newspapers.

reformers who were devoted to McNary-Haugenism. As the Senate bloc's leading spokesman, Borah also became its most conspicuous target. Hence, while the western progressives strove to be catalysts of sectional unity, their "Chief Insurgent" became an object of suspicion in the west itself. From Iowa, heartland of McNary-Haugenism, came charges that "this Borah leadership is merely part of a program for an eastern farm bill and an acquiescent west. This is what Borah represents in politics." In St. Louis, 400 leaders of the Corn Belt and Southern Conference on Farm Problems called for passage of the Mc-Nary-Haugen bill and harshly criticized the Senator. The convention adopted a resolution accusing Borah of seven years "of indifference and obstruction . . . on the question of agricultural policy." Suspicious and resentful, the St. Louis gathering evaluated "his apparent assumption of the right to speak for a group of progressive Republican senators on farm legislation as well as on presidential politics. In view of his record, certainly no true friend of agriculture will be misled by him." When Borah heard of the resolution, he vowed that "if they push their candidate into the field far enough so I can see the white of his eyes I'll have something to say. I hope no friend of agriculture will be misled." [15]

In Des Moines, a few days later, the Corn Belt Committee of farm organizations hoped indeed "that neither farmers nor members of Congress will be misled by his [Borah's] eleventh hour assumption of authority in the great struggle for agricultural justice." The committee resolved that the Idahoan was "a pretended friend of agriculture" and a "carping critic to whom the industrial east has pointed with pride." Convinced "that Senator Borah has no right to speak for agriculture,

[15] Des Moines *Register,* November 5, 1927. One cartoonist portrayed Borah as "The Kidnapper," racing away with a baby carriage but not knowing that in the background a gloating farmer still clutched the "Farm Relief" baby. *Ibid.,* November 12, 1927. On the St. Louis meeting, *The Washington Post,* November 3, 1927. See, also, *The New York Times* editorial, "Expatriating Mr. Borah," November 4, 1927.

either in the corn belt or in the west," the farm group "deeply resent[ed] his professed interest in these premises." [16]

William Hirth, chairman of the Corn Belt Committee and influential editor of the *Missouri Farmer,* warned Norris to beware of Borah, who might be using Norris's popularity as a vehicle "to forward schemes and ambitions best known to himself." In Hirth's estimation, Borah's opposition to the McNary-Haugen bill was dividing agrarian forces at a critical time. Certainly the Idahoan's fight against McNary-Haugenism had been "as deadly as that of any other Senator . . . because when Borah speaks the whole World is led to believe that he is fresh from a conference with the gods." [17]

Such public and private criticism of Borah cast shadows over the future of the little bloc of progressive Senators. The agrarian coalition, hoping to present a united western front on Capitol Hill, threatened to become only another cause of western disunity. This was due in part to Borah's opposition to McNary-Haugenism, but it also closely stemmed from the group's preference for Norris as the Republican presidential nominee. Increasingly, the bloc resembled an anti-Lowden movement. Borah, Norris, and Brookhart were openly hostile to the former governor, largely due to charges that in 1920 Lowden had tried "to buy the Presidency" with massive campaign expenditures. Indeed, Borah had been an instigator of the Senate investigation which revealed that Lowden's campaign (along with that of General Leonard Wood) was heavily indebted to big business. Norris, placing Lowden in "the other faction" in the G.O.P., asserted that "he does not represent, in the broad sense of the term, what I want to see in a President of the United States." Although Frazier and Nye believed that Lowden was correct on the farm problem, they felt that he contributed little

[16] Des Moines *Register,* November 15, 1927. The *Register* ran a large banner headline on its front page saying: "Corn Belt Men Spurn Borah."

[17] William Hirth to Norris, November 5, 1927, Norris Papers, Tray 5, Box 1.

else to the west's progressive arsenal against the industrial, conservative east.[18]

The Lowden forces charged the Senate bloc with attempting "to sidetrack" the west. "If a program could be announced that would effectively block the west in the coming campaign it is this program of pushing Norris," lamented the Des Moines *Register*. Since the 1928 political conventions would be "a test of the farm west," the *Register* believed it was essential that the west back a candidate with a real chance of winning, and not "commit hari kari in the most absurd fashion" by merely endorsing a voice of protest such as Norris. Other Iowa newspapers accused "Borah, Brookhart, Frazier, Nye, et al," with "selling out the Iowa farmer who believes that the former Illinois governor would serve them best"; the Senators were "likely to 'gum the cards' for the forces of the man who has a fighting chance for the nomination." [19]

The Senate bloc thus added to those very divisions in western politics that it had hoped to end. Moreover, as one South Dakota editor noted, "continued horse-play" over the question of nominees might "develop the opinion that farm relief is merely a matter of politics, not of necessity. . . ." Regardless of whether Norris or Lowden was preferable, this was "not the proper time to fight about it. A split in the ranks of those fighting for agricultural relief would be disastrous." In some agricultural areas there was fear that disagreements among westerners played into the hands of those easterners who hoped to create the impression that the farm cause was collapsing. A Des Moines editor, for example, was convinced that *The New York Times* relished "the exchange of shells between Borah and Governor McMullen," because it heralded a "hurtful division in the farm camp." "The west, once more divided,"

[18] See, for example, Washington *Evening Star*, October 25, 1927, and *The Washington Post*, October 25, and November 1, 1927; Norris to William Hirth, November 8, 1927, Norris Papers, Tray 5, Box 1.

[19] Des Moines *Register*, October 14, and 17–19, 1927; Davenport, Iowa, *Times*, quoted in Sioux City, Iowa, *Journal*, October 21, 1927; Atlantic, Iowa, *News-Telegraph*, quoted in *ibid.*, October 22, 1927.

lamented one newspaper, "faces the united east in a battle for its place under the sun. We can hardly hope to get far under those conditions." [20]

On October 24, in this context of western factionalism and contention, members of the Senate group agreed with South Dakota's McMaster that it was imperative for the bloc to represent a broad cause, not individuals. McMaster, whose support the western coalition had been vigorously seeking, attended the meeting only after much urging and a personal invitation. Once there, he convinced Borah, Norris, Brookhart, Frazier, and Nye that no information regarding definite plans or presidential candidates should reach the public until all of the progressive Senators had arrived in Washington and participated in the decisionmaking. McMaster had been skeptical about the bloc before he attended the session but, now convinced that the group had placed itself in a position of potential influence, he planned to attend subsequent meetings.[21]

No sooner had the bloc brightened its future with the addition of McMaster to its ranks, than it suffered a setback, perhaps as embarrassing as the Borah-McMullen exchange had been. Before McMaster could describe the agreements of the October 24 conference to Norbeck, his senatorial colleague who had not yet left South Dakota for Washington, Norbeck stated publicly that he was endorsing Lowden. *The Independent* found this turn of events amusing. The "Senate wrecking crew," which had recently lifted the name "Western confer-

[20] Sioux Falls, S.D., *Daily Argus-Leader,* October 27, 1927; Des Moines *Register,* November 2, 1927; Madrid, Iowa, *Register-News,* quoted in Sioux City, *Journal,* November 10, 1927. See, also, the *Register*'s editorial "Divide and Conquer," October 21, 1927. *Wallace's Farmer* contended that information regarding the Norris boom was coming chiefly from Senator Borah, "who has never taken any special interest in farm legislation. Most of the publicity on the subject is being put out by newspapers that are opposing the farm measures and that are looking eagerly for some signs of a split in farm organizations." This editorial, "Norris and Borah," was reprinted in the Des Moines *Register,* November 15, 1927.

[21] William H. McMaster to Peter Norbeck, October 24, 1927, Norbeck Papers (South Dakota).

ence"—a title "which most people associate[d] with the ath-
letic league of Stagg and Zuppke"—had confused its signals.
After a "Washington huddle the new Western conference team
put across one undisputed first down when it named Mr. Norris
as candidate for president." Most spectators thought the game
was over until "Senator Peter Norbeck, South Dakota broken-
field runner, tried a new shift play and carried the ball across
the wrong goal line." His statement for Lowden turned the
team's first game "into a dismal rout." [22]

According to McMaster, Norbeck's declaration "had a chill-
ing effect" on the progressive bloc, which hurriedly convened in
Norris's office. Amid rumors that McMaster now also planned
to endorse Lowden, the bloc decided that events were forcing
them into open opposition to the former governor. On November 2, Borah, Norris, Nye, Frazier, and Brookhart held a
lengthy meeting to outline an anti-Lowden strategy. Most am-
bitious among their considerations was a plan to establish a
small radio station that would allow them to broadcast to the
west "educational" messages regarding the bloc's legislative and
political efforts. The Senators listened to Raymond Baker, a
man hostile to Lowden and the owner of a powerful broadcasting plant in Muscatine, Iowa, describe how the progressives
might transmit from Washington, D.C., to the west. Baker
would help finance the construction and operation of a small,
ten to fifty kilowatts, station in Washington. He would seek
other financial aid from farm groups sympathetic to the insurgents. Once the Washington station was in operation, Baker's
Muscatine plant would pick up and relay its messages over
longer distances. In conjunction with this broadcasting strategy,
the bloc agreed that Nye and Frazier should attack Lowden in
a telegram to the State Farmers Union convention which was
assembling at Jamestown, North Dakota. There was discussion

of sending Borah to South Dakota to stump against Lowden in the primary election campaign.[23]

Prior to its meeting, the bloc had tried unsuccessfully to reach McMaster. By now, however, McMaster had additional doubts about the group. Wavering toward Lowden, he believed that some of the progressives merely hoped to advance their own political fortunes. He decided that rather than openly endorse Lowden, he instead would try to influence the agrarian group to abandon its plans to campaign against him in the South Dakota primary. "If the Progressives stay out of South Dakota," he wrote Norbeck, "and the old-guard put up a man against Lowden, it ought to be easy to win for Lowden." "Using a little diplomacy," McMaster believed that he had convinced Borah—"the man that we want to keep out of the state" —not to interfere in the primary. Norbeck doubted that Borah, who was "an enigma" on the farm question and did "not know a thing about the subject," would come to South Dakota anyhow; he agreed, nonetheless, that "we don't want him here." [24]

Both McMaster and Norbeck were skeptical of the motives of members within the "western conference." Norbeck believed that "the self-appointed political leaders of the Northwest on the Agricultural question" were simply "playing Politics." They were "going in the guise of Progressives playing a political game against the farmer of the Northwest." Events would force them to confront the farm issue forthrightly, "or get out of the way for somebody who will. The sooner they start a

[23] McMaster to Norbeck, November 8, 1927, Norbeck Papers, and, also, *The Washington Post,* November 1, 1927, and Des Moines *Register,* November 1, 1927, on the impact of Norbeck's statement. *The New York Times* and *The Washington Post,* November 3, 1927, cover the bloc's radio and campaign plans. Baker was in Washington to complain to the radio commission about the awarding of a Sioux City, Iowa, station the same frequency as Baker's KTNT at Muscatine. Brookhart, Nye, and McMaster accompanied him, informing the commission that the Sioux City station—which represented the views of the "Reactionary School"—was aimed at stifling KTNT which represented the progressive position.

[24] McMaster to Norbeck, November 4 and 10, 1927, and Norbeck to McMaster, November 2 and 15, 1927, Norbeck Papers.

fight with us the better our position will be." According to McMaster, Nye was as interested in publicizing himself as he was in championing Norris. Borah's objectives also seemed clear. The Idaho Senator "wants to be President. He wants to kill off Lowden and in a measure support Norris, knowing that Norris has no chance and that if things should break right in the Convention that he (Borah) would inherit Norris' strength. . . ." [25]

Other observers shared McMaster's impressions of Borah's motives. Lewis S. Gannett, associate editor of *The Nation*, believed it possible that the Idahoan's own political hopes "may have something to do with his zeal for Norris." Elsewhere, a cartoon, "Off on a Bum Steer," showed a mother and her squalling "agriculture" baby watching Norris and Brookhart carry an empty "farm aid" pail across a pasture toward some distant "moos." They found not a cow, but the bull Borah, smiling slyly, with strips of the tattered McNary-Haugen bill on his horns.[26] Suspicions thus plagued the tiny progressive bloc and threatened to jeopardize its growth and effectiveness. The agriculture problem and politics imperiled its future as a vehicle for western unity. Certainly the turmoil that ripped it and the controversy that surrounded it diminished the western challenge to the eastern wing of the G.O.P.

There was, moreover, evidence that Borah was indeed considering his own political fortunes as well as those of the western bloc. Writing to an Idaho supporter, he denied rumors that he was not and would not be a presidential candidate. He admitted that public enthusiasm for him had not crystalized into delegates and that he was thus not building his hopes. Still, he emphasized that he had made no statement removing himself as a potential candidate. Before making any such decision, he promised to inform his friends. In November, Hiram Johnson,

[25] Norbeck to McMaster, November 7 and 15, 1927, and McMaster to Norbeck, November 4, 1927, Norbeck Papers.

[26] Lewis S. Gannett, "Norris for President," *The Nation*, CXXV (November 2, 1927), 470; New York *Herald Tribune*, October 31, 1927.

who had spurned the progressive bloc from its inception because, as he said later, he preferred his independence and was not about to follow Borah, learned that "the most intimate and confidential friend of Senator Borah" had given some provocative information to members of the old La Follette organization in California. Borah's friend—presumably Ray McKaig—had reported that the Senator was publicly for Norris, that hopefully Norris would pick up some delegates, that Borah would also gain delegate strength, and that at the convention there would be a stampede to the Idahoan.[27]

Politics may thus have played a major part in Borah's decision to concentrate on the prohibition issue, even though it most certainly would widen the fissures within the progressive bloc. On October 26, Raymond Robins found him anxious "to throw down the gauntlet to the wet Republicans of the country." According to Robins, Borah was "pleased with the present political outlook, and more than ever sure of the wisdom of his plan of campaign." By engaging the wets in a battle over the enforcement of the Eighteenth Amendment, the Senator "feels that he is on the ground where he loves to stand." Salmon Levinson could "just see the old boy beaming with joy at his comfortable position. He is with a perfectly safe crowd [drys] that he likes and he can shoot all kinds of political machine guns ad lib." Significantly, the Senator's November 18 speech to several thousand members of the National Grange, one of the nation's foremost farm organizations, completely ignored the question of agricultural relief and focused on enforcing prohibition.[28]

If the prohibition question was, as Ray McKaig advised him, "going to be the one big wild fight that we have had in presi-

[27] Borah to C. W. King, October 28, 1927, Borah Papers, Box 275; Johnson to Harold Ickes, November 5, 1927, Ickes Papers, Box 3. For Johnson's preference for independence and aversion to any Borah-led group, see Johnson to Ickes, March, 1931, *ibid.*

[28] Robins to Levinson, October 26, 1927, and Levinson reply, October 28, 1927, Levinson Papers, Box 77; *The Washington Post*, November 19, 1927.

dential elections for twenty years," Borah was placing himself in good political position. McKaig, whose stumping efforts for Borah in California were encouraging, urged the Senator to announce his candidacy and turn "loose that bunch of wild Grangers on the wet and dry battlefield." One San Francisco resident, who believed that Borah could carry the Bear state with one radio speech, told McKaig: "I know a cat with nine lives when I see it and that dry cat is coming back to California bigger than ever." Borah was "not wholly dissatisfied with the situation by any means" but, for the moment, chose to await more political developments.[29] Nonetheless, he had for some time been tenderly caressing the "dry cat" and in late 1927 he devoted a growing amount of attention to it.

Insofar as he insisted on the prominence of the prohibition issue, he could only damage the Senate western bloc. Blaine and La Follette, Jr., both of whom joined the western group in late November, opposed the Volstead Act in its present form and favored the sale of light beer (2.75 alcoholic content). Norris hoped to diminish the importance of the dry question. It was, in his opinion, "not the only pebble on the beach" and was less vital than having "public officials fundamentally correct" on "what is right and fair for the people of our country." In early October, Norris averred that the wet-dry controversy probably

[29] McKaig to Borah, December 28, 1927, and Borah reply, January 4, 1928, Borah Papers, Box 286. McKaig to E. H. Dewey, December 13, 1927, reported that many leading progressive spokesmen in California were pleased to learn of Borah's political aspirations. "Telling them frankly that Borah would be a candidate has put new life in them. I got the leaders to promise that they would register as Republicans and urge the half million voters of the old La Follette following to do the same." Ray McKaig to E. H. Dewey, December 13, 1927. Dewey sent the letter to Borah on December 16, Borah Papers, Box 286. Furthermore, for several months a San Diego lawyer, Marcus W. Robbins, had been circulating postcard copies of "The Borah Pledge" across the nation. Signers of the pledge were supposed to dedicate themselves to using "all honorable means" to promote Borah for the Presidency. Wile Scrapbooks, August 26, 1927, 25. A copy of the pledge is in the Borah Papers, Box 275. Small car-window stickers with a picture of the Idahoan and captioned "Senator W. E. Borah for President, 1928," were also available. *Ibid.*

would not become an important problem in the coming campaign. Borah, on the other hand, turned to the enforcement of prohibition as *the* crucial issue. At the end of November when Norris, Brookhart, Nye, Frazier, Blaine, Shipstead, and La Follette gathered for a western conference, Borah was conspicuously absent. The western bloc, so recently the object of his endeavors, was fading quickly from his sight.[30]

By early December, the bloc was in shambles. Borah, once the "leading spirit" in the group, had apparently lost interest in it. The other members were divided among themselves. On December 1, the New York *Sun* announced that the "Progressives Cannot Agree on Big Issues." That day, the bloc, after a number of conferences which Borah did not attend, failed to agree on a legislative program. La Follette struggled in vain throughout the morning to unify the group but succeeded only in emphasizing the "determination on the part of each [member] to stand by his own convictions no matter what the progressive bloc proposed." [31]

The list of demands that the progressives ultimately presented on December 2 to the G.O.P. majority leader, Charles Curtis, contained only five signatures. La Follette, Blaine, Nye, Frazier, and Shipstead requested that the Republicans back adequate farm relief legislation (along the lines of McNary-Haugenism), a bill to limit jurisdiction of federal courts regarding labor injunctions, and a resolution to investigate American policy in South and Central America. "I am sorry that we could not get more than five signers to the letter to Curtis and also that the program was cut down to three propositions,"

[30] *The New York Times,* January 22 and 24, 1928, on La Follette and Blaine; Norris to Charles W. Bryan, October 30, 1927, Norris Papers, Tray 5, Box 1, and Baltimore *Sun,* October 9, 1927, on Norris; *The Washington Post,* December 1, 1927. Des Moines *Register,* December 6, 1927, in an editorial "Borah Absent," observed that he was "playing his old familiar game." Between sessions he talked insurgency, but "the time for organizing the senate now having come, the insurgents called a conference of their group"—only to have Borah not attend.

[31] The New York *Sun,* December 1, 1927. See, also, *The Washington Post,* December 1, 1927.

wrote a disconsolate La Follette who had been "devoting all [his] time . . . in an effort to get the progressives to take a militant position. . . ." Borah, Norris, and Brookhart—all members of the progressive bloc when it first took shape—did not sign, reportedly because they disagreed with the tactics of La Follette's move and felt that emphasis should be on obtaining favorable committee assignments rather than on specific measures. Other progressive hopefuls such as McMaster, Norbeck, and Nebraska's Howell similarly kept their names off the letter. All signs indicated that "the threatened war between regular Republicans and Progressives would collapse. . . ." [32]

The dreams that inspired the formation of the progressive bloc had come to nothing. By the end of 1927 it was more shadow than substance. An unsympathetic western newspaper asserted that it had staged "a poor performance," which had turned into "a hilarious political burlesque, with the actors throwing pies at each other. Verily, the bloc has a crack in it, and it will take more than King Borah's men and trumpeters to nail it up." [33]

Perhaps the most impressive of the western bloc's achievements was the convening of its members on the steps of the Senate Office Building for photographs on that early December day in 1927. On that occasion, the group at least presented a picture of unity. Unfortunately for the bloc, however, the re-

[32] La Follette, Jr., to William T. Evjue, December 5, 1927, La Follette Family Papers, Series C, Box 5; New York *Herald Tribune*, December 3, 1927. In his original draft letter of November 29, 1927, La Follette also urged senatorial action on Norris's proposed amendment to abolish lame-duck Congresses, on the development of Boulder Canyon Dam, on flood control, on negotiating a St. Lawrence waterway project, and on "the prudent investment theory in valuation of railroads." Copy in La Follette Family Papers, Series C, Box 5. La Follette to Phil La Follette, December 3, 1927, Series A, Box 35, asserted that he had hoped the progressives would use "their alleged balance of power for the advancement of legislation, rather than a scramble for committee assignments." Raymond Clapper reported that it was this view which separated those who signed the letter to Curtis from those who did not. Clipping of Clapper's article, December 3, 1927, in Nye Papers, Box 56.
[33] *Fargo Forum* (N.D.), November 9, 1927.

sulting photographs represented only pose, not performance. Indeed, by December the agrarian coalition was actually making its curtain call, rather than opening the first act of a new progressive drama on Capitol Hill. And Borah, once the star of the troupe, had resumed his more accustomed monologues.

The Politics of Law and Order

🏵

"WE are going to hold a great national referendum in 1928" concerning law and order—"obedience to the law as the people have written the law"—Borah told a banquet gathering in early 1927. The Senator's decision to make support of the Constitution the major issue of the next election brought him up against two crucial constitutional dilemmas of the Twenties: prohibition and race. His attempts to cope with these problems revealed much about him and an important aspect of the progressives' social vision. Many progressives, including Borah and his Senate colleagues, wanted an America that was white and dry. To achieve this they resorted to that very bending of principles which they so abhorred. When Borah vigorously supported prohibition while rationalizing away the failures of states to enforce the rights of Negroes, he illuminated some of the contradictions among progressives, many of whom worried a great deal about the baneful effects of alcohol but all too often ignored questions of racial injustice. The inconsistency of Borah's constitutional arguments, and the apparent political opportunism that at least partially inspired them, ultimately rendered hollow his struggles to reshape the Republican party, making it the party of morality, law and order, and constitutional principles. Moreover, he made increasingly evident those cultural divisions that in the 1920's were sundering the earlier progressive consensus, separating Borah-style progressives—with their attachments to an ethnically homogeneous, rural-oriented society—from urban-based liberals.[1]

---

[1] The speech, which Borah delivered at the New Willard Hotel in Washington, D.C., on January 7, 1927, was reprinted in the *Congressional Record*, 69th Cong., 2nd Sess., 1927, LXVIII, 1302–4. The Citizens

When Borah summoned his party to the defense of constitutional government, he drew upon his prestige as "the greatest constitutional authority in Congress" and upon a deep interest in the law.[2] He prided himself on his devotion to the Constitution and on his knowledge of constitutional questions. James M. Cox, who had lived in the same apartment building with Borah from 1909 to 1913 and had spent many evenings talking with him, believed that the Idahoan's "great ambition was to be elevated to the bench." Borah himself admitted that he had turned to politics because Boise was too small to allow him to advance further his aspirations in the legal profession. But, even in politics, the law remained his first love and the source of his greatest interest.[3]

Committee of One Thousand, a dry organization, issued this speech in a small pamphlet entitled "The Real Referendum." Borah's picture appeared on the cover. Copy in Borah Papers, Box 279. This same group also printed a pamphlet, "Uphold the Constitution," which contained Borah's April 14, 1926, Senate speech on the Eighteenth Amendment. Copy in Lynn Haines Papers, Box 1. On the progressive link with prohibition see James H. Timberlake, *Prohibition and the Progressive Movement, 1900–1920* (Cambridge, Mass., 1963), and Norman Clark, "The 'Hell-Soaked Institution' and the Washington Prohibition Initiative of 1914," *Pacific Northwest Quarterly*, 56 (January, 1965), pp. 14–16. On race, see Dewey W. Grantham, Jr., "The Progressive Movement and the Negro," *South Atlantic Quarterly*, LIV (October, 1955), 461–77, and George M. Fredrickson, *The Black Image in the White Mind: The Debate on Afro-American Character and Destiny, 1817–1914* (New York, 1971), chap. 10.

[2] Oswald Garrison Villard, "Presidential Possibilities, William E. Borah," *The Nation*, CXXVI (March 14, 1928), 290. One contemporary asserted that Borah was "the accepted successor" to the long line of "leading expounders of the constitution in the Senate," which included such men as New York's William M. Evarts and Elihu Root and Wisconsin's John C. Spooner. Henry L. Stoddard, *As I Knew Them, Presidents and Politics from Grant to Coolidge* (New York, 1927), p. 527. Certainly Borah enjoyed bolstering his arguments with references to constitutional precedents and Supreme Court decisions. Before the 1920's, his concern for the Constitution had also found expression in his significant contributions in the Senate to the passage of the Sixteenth and Seventeenth Amendments. Johnson's *Borah of Idaho* and McKenna's *Borah* describe his important role in the struggle for these two amendments.

[3] An excellent example of Borah's confidence in his own knowledge of the Constitution occurred in 1938 when Borah, citing portions from one

The issue of enforcement of the Eighteenth Amendment afforded Borah an opportunity to expound on the Constitution, and he made the most of it. He viewed the Constitution as an almost sacred document, a "sublime guarantee of personal rights and privileges" and the product of "the all but divine wisdom of its framers." One Washington observer commented that "the Constitution is the Idahoan's Bible. When he discusses it, Borah ceases to be a politician and becomes an evangelist." [4]

The Senator idolized Lincoln, in part because Lincoln had supported the Constitution and the law despite his aversion to slavery and the fugitive slave statute. The same breed of cowards who had attacked Lincoln were still active in the 1920's, Borah warned; working under the guise of patriotism and decency, they refused to follow the law when it failed to "conform to their individual appetites or because it would possibly lose a few votes in an election." [5]

Supreme Court case after another, helped southern Democrats block anti-lynch legislation. When Senator Sherman Minton of Indiana confronted the Idahoan with the question of the police powers of the federal government, Borah declared flatly that "police power is exclusively a state power." He abruptly dismissed Minton's contention that the authority to regulate interstate commerce gave the federal government implied police powers. The Supreme Court, he argued, had "never held in any instance that the Congress has any police power as such." When Minton pressed the issue, Borah simply refused to repeat what he had just said; the Idahoan was apparently confident that he had conclusively settled the issue. *Congressional Record*, 75th Cong., 3rd Sess., 1938, LXXXIII, 1490–97. Ironically, Minton later became an Associate Justice on the U.S. Supreme Court. A year before Borah died, James M. Cox had an occasion to tell him that, if Cox would have won the 1920 election, he would have made Borah a Supreme Court Justice. "The man's eyes filled with tears as he expressed his gratitude." Cox, *Journey Through My Years* (New York, 1946), pp. 99–100. Helen F. McMillin, "Senator William E. Borah, An Interview," *The Granite Monthly* (June, 1923). Clipping in Borah Papers, Box 232. Borah granted this interview when he was in Manchester, New Hampshire, on May 24, 1923.

[4] Borah to Louis A. Cuvillier, June 10, 1926, Borah Papers, Box 271; Wile Scrapbooks, January 24, 1927, Scrapbook 25.

[5] *Congressional Record*, 69th Cong., 1st Sess., 1926, LXVII, 7438–45; Borah to H. L. Hoard, November 9, 1927, Borah Papers, Box 282.

Borah equated many opponents of prohibition with the adversaries of Lincoln. Both groups, he believed, intended to subvert the Constitution and the principles of law and order. The main targets of his anger were wets who advocated that each state should define what was "intoxicating." On April 14, 1926, before crowded galleries, Borah touched off heated Senate debate with a slashing assault upon such proposals. Challenging these suggestions as threats to constitutional government, he urged loyal citizens to support the Eighteenth Amendment as part of the law of the land.[6]

Ostensibly, Borah's argument was simply one of obedience to the Constitution; in fact, however, his commitment to prohibition went beyond concern for law enforcement. On May 30, 1926, speaking in Baltimore at the Presbyterian General Assembly, the Senator revealed his sentiments. Sounding much like an Anti-Saloon League propagandist, he probed beneath the question of adherence to the law. The liquor traffic, he said, was "a curse of the human family. Whether sold in the open saloon or the brothel, its natural haunt, or secretly purveyed in defiance of the law, the wicked stuff works its demoralization and ruin to individuals, communities and states." Liquor, he maintained, was the source of crime, poverty, and death. In an increasingly mechanized society, it was especially dangerous because it fogged the worker's brain, making him less alert and more subject to danger. "When safety is involved," the Senator expounded, "we are all drys."[7]

Borah's Baltimore performance, *The New York Times* asserted on its front page the next day, "brought him forward as a leading, if not the leading, dry champion." With this speech, he had become the political captain of the antisaloon people, since no equally prominent national politician had "so squarely and unqualifiedly" spoken on behalf of the principle of prohibition. On June 12 the Senator's picture appeared on

[6] *Congressional Record*, 69th Cong., 1st Sess., 1926, LXVII, 7438–45.
[7] Text of Borah's speech in Borah Papers, Box 272.

the cover of *The Independent* over the caption "A Leader of the Drys." [8]

Seven weeks after his Baltimore address, the Senator gave another rousing defense of the Eighteenth Amendment in Augusta, Georgia. He attacked the proposed referendums in which states such as New York would establish their own definitions of illegal liquor. To Borah, this was nothing short of nullification, a "slinking, silent, cowardly sapping of the very foundation of all order, all dignity, all government." Such ideas were "whelps from the same kennel" as bolshevism and fascism. Until the people removed the Eighteenth Amendment from the Constitution, they must adhere to it.[9]

Although Borah had seemingly demonstrated great courage in Georgia by vigorously attacking the doctrine of nullification, he had confined all his remarks to the dry amendment. The Augusta *Chronicle* drew no connections between the Senator's remarks and Negro voting rights. Indeed, the *Chronicle* proclaimed that Borah was "firing a shot" to defend America from the nullificationists of "the East where there is a vast population of foreign born and where politics are dominated by machines." The Senator's speech seemed not to threaten Dixie, but to make possible the long-awaited alliance "between the dry West and the dry South, the agricultural West and the agricultural South in allegiance against the East of political corruption, of machine politics. . . ." [10]

The Independent remarked caustically that Borah had delighted the drys in Georgia, "that shining home of one hundred per cent constitutionalism, where negroes vote in the same ratio that turtles fly." While the Idahoan was enlarging the

[8] *The New York Times,* May 31, 1926; *The Independent,* CXVI (June 12, 1926). In 1933, Hiram Johnson described Borah as "by far the strongest of the drys in the Senate." Johnson to Sons, February 19, 1933, Johnson Papers, Part IV, Box 4.

[9] Typed copy of Borah's speech delivered at Augusta, Georgia, July 18, 1926, Borah Papers, Box 271.

[10] Clippings from the *Augusta Chronicle,* July 18–19, 1926, Borah Scrapbooks, Reel 5.

"cult of the Constitution," the south was defying some of its mandates. *The New Republic,* agreeing that "the geographical scene of his assault upon nullification was not the happiest," noted that many decades of southern violation of other constitutional amendments had "never called from Senator Borah himself the resounding epithets he used last week. It makes a difference, evidently, how near to your heart is the amendment which is to be nullified." [11]

A number of people found the Senator's position on liquor inconsistent with his attitude toward the rights of Negroes. A New York state legislator asked Borah why he did not do something about the Fourteenth and Fifteenth Amendments. "We all know that their provisions are ignored in the Southern states," he contended. "You, as one of the leaders of the United States Senate could accomplish a lot—if you wanted to. But you don't even TRY to do anything." The New Yorker suspected that perhaps Borah believed the Eighteenth Amendment was more important than the others. [12]

Such remarks irritated Borah. He replied that, regarding obedience to the Constitution, he was consistent and held precisely the same feelings about each of its provisions. After "an extended study" of the south's political and economic treatment of Negroes, he was convinced that no southern law contradicted the federal charter. The educational voting tests in Dixie were "just and wise laws" which embodied Lincoln's principles and were in the interest of the Negro and the south. In Borah's opinion, the Fifteenth Amendment should have dealt with intelligence, not color; Reconstruction politics, however, had not permitted such sagacity. He had no doubts whatsoever that southerners were "in good faith seeking to solve the negro problem, and seeking to solve it . . . in harmony with the Constitution of the United States." The difference between the south and the wets was, he explained, a matter of intent.

[11] "Borah Blows Again," *The Independent,* CXVII (July 31, 1926), 114; *The New Republic,* XLVII (July 28, 1926), 265.
[12] Phelps Phelps to Borah, June 6, 1926, Borah Papers, Box 266.

Whereas the south was "trying in good faith and sincerity to work out its problem in harmony with the Fifteenth Amendment," opponents of the Eighteenth were "openly and flagrantly proposing nullification." [13]

Frank Kent and Mark Sullivan, the well-known Washington correspondents, agreed that Borah's position was correct. The south, they believed, was not violating the Fourteenth and Fifteenth Amendments. If Negroes failed to vote in elections, it was not because of unconstitutional barriers. Suffrage restrictions bore no discriminatory passages; whites had to pass the same tests as did colored registrants. Thus, if Negroes did not get to vote, it was due to their own inadequacies, not to inequitable laws which were contrary to the Constitution. Kent predicted that if the prohibition debate continued to resemble the old slave controversy, Borah would be "the Webster of his day." [14]

Walter Lippmann was more skeptical than the Senator and his defenders. He agreed with Borah that determination to obey the law was the crucial factor. But Lippmann then accused the south of deliberately "nullifying the whole *intent* of the Fifteenth Amendment." He doubted that Borah really believed that the south's educational qualifications were in harmony with the Constitution; certainly, the Idahoan knew that the white man escaped the unreasonable and excessive enforcement of the tests which Negroes confronted. Borah was, in Lippmann's estimation, "inviting New York to be as ingenious as the South and to obtain legal nullification by some ingenious subterfuge just as the South has done." [15]

The Senator remained unwilling to concede any truth in Lippmann's contentions. But, as a man who prided himself on his principles, he had at least to go through the motions of inquiry. Hence he sent telegrams and letters to such men as

[13] Borah to Walter Lippmann, July 23, 1926, Borah Papers, Box 263, and to Henry L. Holstein, August 15, 1926, Box 269.

[14] Clipping of Sullivan's article in the New York *Herald Tribune,* July 11, 1926, Borah Scrapbooks, Reel 5. Sullivan quoted Kent at length.

[15] Walter Lippmann to Borah, August 3, 1926, Borah Papers, Box 271.

Thomas J. Hamilton, editor of the Augusta *Chronicle,* asking whether any laws in their states nullified the Constitution. He was pleased when he received a copy of an article, printed in the *Political Science Quarterly* some twenty years earlier, concluding that the south was not circumventing the Fifteenth Amendment. "This is precisely what I was most anxious to have—a thorough and candid analysis of the situation," he wrote.[16]

Borah obviously believed what he wanted to hear. Despite his aura of objectivity and his seemingly passionate dedication to the Constitution, his penchant to rationalize the problem of Negro rights in the south betrayed a double standard. He was certainly aware of the status of the black man in Dixie. On several occasions he had gone south; and his brother Charles was a lawyer in New Orleans who spoke in terms of "a good, clean White Republican party" in Louisiana. During a Senate exchange in mid-1926, when Borah asked Senator William C. Bruce of Maryland whether or not the south was violating the Constitution, Bruce replied that there was no "use of asking me to say something that everybody knows." Southerners, Bruce continued, faced a "choice between constitutional abstractions and civilization and they selected civilization." Borah granted that Negro enfranchisement, when it came, was a mistake. But he flatly rejected what Bruce asserted was common knowledge: that the south was acting purposely outside the Constitution.[17]

It was thus not coincidental that southern newspapers were generally very cordial to the Idahoan and on occasion averred, as did *The Fayetteville* [North Carolina] *Observer* that "the South, and for that matter, the whole country, would welcome

[16] Borah to William H. Fleming and Thomas J. Hamilton, July 21, 1926, Borah Papers, Box 263; to Hunter Wykes, October 20, 1927, and Fleming, October 24, 1927, Box 284; to Byron Paine, October 26, 1927, Box 280; to Francis G. Caffey, September 9, 1926, Box 269. Caffey's article, "Suffrage Limitations at the South," appeared in the *Political Science Quarterly,* XX (March, 1905), 53–67.

[17] See Charles F. Borah to Borah, October 3, 1927, Borah Papers, Box 277, and June 28, 1928, Box 293; *Congressional Record,* 69th Cong., 1st Sess., 1926, LXVII, 7441.

more public men of the type and courage of Senator Borah."
Senator Carter Glass of Virginia said, "without hesitation . . .
of all the public men of the adversary political party, Borah has
a better understanding of southern problems and is more sympathetic with the difficulties in that section . . . than any
other." [18]

Borah's dual standard on prohibition and Negro rights derived in part from his opinions on race. His attitudes toward
Negroes and new immigrant groups reflected the nativist thinking which had influenced much of progressive thought. Not all
progressives were nativists, of course, but probably a majority
of them believed that the new immigrants embodied many of
the evils which were undermining traditional American values
and democratic principles. They worried about antidemocratic
tendencies in new immigrants who seemed to pose threats of
economic serfdom, class differences, and a frightening illiteracy
rate. Also disturbing was the interest-based politics of the new-
comers; by trading votes for favors the immigrants not only sustained corrupt big-city political machines but also flagrantly
displayed that immoral self-interest which progressives incessantly inveighed against as the enemy of the general welfare.
And, in the minds of those progressives with rural perspectives,
the new immigrants and the city undoubtedly seemed to feed
upon each other, creating that urban leviathan which jeopardized the national heritage.[19]

Borah fretted about the effects of the new immigration on
American life. He favored "a drastic immigration law, one
which will prevent the country from being overrun with for-

[18] *The Fayetteville Observer,* January 30, 1928, Borah Scrapbooks, Reel
5; copy of letter from Glass to E. E. George, November 24, 1928, Borah
Papers, Box 294.
[19] Thomas B. Hartshorne, *The Distorted Image: Changing Conceptions
of the American Character Since Turner* (Cleveland, Ohio, 1968), pp. 43–
49, points out links between progressivism and nativism. Norman L.
Zucker, *George W. Norris, Gentle Knight of American Democracy* (Urbana, Ill., 1966), p. 28, suggests a connection between Norris's nativism
and his agrarian suspicion of cities.

eigners." He was not a racist in the sense of believing that other races were permanently or inherently inferior to Anglo-Saxons. Indeed, when noting that even Anglo-Saxons had not adjusted to self-government in regions such as the Phillipines, he stressed the impact of traditions, geography, and climate on the development of racial characteristics. For the present, however, he clearly had no doubts that Anglo-Saxons were best equipped to sustain a republican form of government. He thus expressed "entire sympathy" with the suggestion that legislation must prevent "the uneducated hordes of any foreign government" such as Armenia, Greece, or Italy from entering the country. He praised the Japanese but stressed that they were "a different people. They have a great civilization, but it is a different civilization." He favored "a rigid exclusion act" against Orientals "in the interest of our institutions, of the happiness of our people, of the stability of our government, and the permanency of our civilization." The Japanese should realize, he wrote, that immigration restriction was a necessity, "not a brand of inferiority upon Japan at all, and for her to say so is an absurdity. . . ." [20]

In 1924, when Congress effected a "Nordic Victory" with new immigration quotas, Borah joined the majority. He voted for the amendment to exclude Japanese immigration; against the attempt to raise the quota based on 1910 statistics from 2 to 3 percent; for the motion to base the quota on the 1890 census—which was largely free from the new immigration from

[20] See, for example, Borah to Mrs. Ed Lantzer, March 28, 1924, Borah Papers, Box 238, for his general views on immigration restriction; on the "uneducated hordes" from southeastern Europe, see Brotherhood of Railroad Signalmen of America, Local No. 111, to Borah, February 2, 1923, and Borah reply, February 20, 1923, Box 230; on the Japanese, Borah to Professor James W. Garner, April 21, 1924, Box 231, and to Miss Dorothy Garrison, December 19, 1921, Box 215. Maddox, *William E. Borah and American Foreign Policy*, pp. 7–8, discusses Borah's kind of racism which closely resembled that of Theodore Roosevelt. On Roosevelt, see Howard K. Beale, *Theodore Roosevelt and the Rise of America to World Power* (paperback ed., New York, 1962), pp. 43–47.

southern and eastern Europe—instead of the 1910 count, and in favor of the final restriction bill.[21]

He viewed even this act as inadequate, however, and urged that the quota system extend also to the independent countries of North, Central, and South America. When he introduced on several occasions a bill to amend the 1924 legislation, he explained that it was "a mistake to limit certain other countries to the quota and leave Mexican immigrants out. We certainly do not want them as citizens." He admitted that many good people lived in Mexico, but added that "they do not seem to come here. And, besides, their ideals and ideas are quite different from ours." Countenancing the argument that they did not assimilate quickly and lowered the nation's moral tone, he was "greatly pleased" to accept for use in committee hearings information which attested to the mental and physical inferiority of Mexicans.[22]

On immigration restriction, Borah and the other Senate progressives presented a united front. Their views were clear: Peter Norbeck, for example, felt that "the purety [sic] of the race overshadows all other questions in importance"; Hiram Johnson echoed such faith in the dominant white race, "the race that believes in Christianity and has given us civilization"; George Norris, believing the government had been "too lenient" on the immigration question, advocated "more stringent laws to bar the undesirable foreigner"; Borah sympathized with a proposal to suspend immigration for five years, then to have

[21] *Congressional Record,* 68th Cong., 1st Sess., 1924, LXV, 6460, 6538–39, 6546–47, 6649. The Los Angeles *Times*'s headline of April 13, 1924, declared that "Nordic Victory Is Seen in Drastic Restrictions." Quoted in John Higham, *Strangers in the Land: Patterns in American Nativism, 1860–1925* (paperback ed., New York, 1963), p. 300.

[22] Borah to W. G. Swendsen, January 9, 1928, Borah Papers, Box 288; to Carl W. Berryman, December 23, 1928, Box 296; to M. L. Pearson, December 23, 1927, Box 288. "I do not see," Borah wrote, "if we make an exception with reference to the Mexicans, why we should be bothered in regard to immigration otherwise. I do not look upon the Mexican as by any means the best accession to our social or economic life." Borah to W. R. Armstrong, October 7, 1929, Box 302.

"a general naturalization day for those who are fit to become citizens," and deportation for those who were not fit.[23]

To Fiorello La Guardia, who usually applauded the western progressives, such attitudes were incomprehensible. The fiery Congressman from New York City, who himself was a member of a marginal ethnic group, had no sympathy for people who wanted to ensure that "proper" racial types entered America. He sardonically observed, for example, that although his dog came from "a distinguished family tree" the animal was still "only a son of a bitch." But to Borah and his western colleagues the race question demanded a more reverent approach. La Guardia and the agrarian liberals thus collaborated in struggles for political and economic justice but, when the problem was racial equity, cooperation gave way to suspicion and division—the price of cultural conflict in the Twenties.[24]

The racial views that informed the thinking of many progressives on immigration restriction also influenced their feelings about the Negro. Senator Thomas Walsh of Montana, who had led the fight to expose the Teapot Dome scandal, admitted that he would "make very little showing to the colored man." Although Walsh claimed that he always favored justice for Negroes, he opposed proposals such as the Dyer antilynching bill in 1922. William Jennings Bryan, who defended white supremacy as "a doctrine absolutely essential to the welfare of the south," looked upon the Dyer bill as a "grave mistake." Peter Norbeck wanted "to send all the negroes back to Africa. . . ." Hiram Johnson thought "that perhaps our idea of the fatherhood of God and the brotherhood of man as applied to our

[23] Norbeck to W. C. Gemmill, May 20, 1924, Norbeck Papers (Missouri), Folder 4; Hiram Johnson to Amy Johnson, March 30, 1918, Johnson Papers, Part IV, Box 1; Norris to Ray Mitchell, May 24, 1924, Norris Papers, Tray 2, Box 1; United Brotherhood of Carpenters and Joiners of America, Local 1258, Pocatello, Idaho, to Borah, January 28, 1923, and Borah's reply, February 3, 1923, Borah Papers, Box 230.

[24] For La Guardia's opposition to the quota system—"the creation of a narrow mind, nurtured by a hating heart"—and a comparison of his and the western progressives' views on racial equity, see Mann, *La Guardia, A Fighter Against His Times*, pp. 187–89.

citizens of African descent may be a little wrong." He described
Negroes as "a shiftless and stupid set," and referred to the king
of the Sandwich Islands as "a big, buck nigger." The 1924
Progressive platform of La Follette and Wheeler remained
quiet on the subject of the Ku Klux Klan despite appeals from
the National Association for the Advancement of Colored People. The NAACP regarded such evasion as "inexcusable" and
concluded that La Follette had "no convictions as to the rights
of Black Folk." Although La Follette ultimately sought to rec-
tify this by criticizing the Klan in public statements, he apparently made no real effort to enlist Negro support, although
some progressives such as Oswald Garrison Villard urged him
to do so.[25]

Walter F. White of the NAACP could never understand "the
extraordinary attitudes of several Western senators who were
regarded as liberals on economic questions but who have been
among the most injurious to the Negroes' cause." He singled
out Borah as being the most conspicuous among this group.[26]

Borah openly admitted his belief that Negro enfranchise-

[25] Senator Thomas J. Walsh to J. T. Carroll, November 13, 1924,
Thomas J. Walsh Papers (Library of Congress), Box 374; Bryan, quoted
in Levine, *Defender of the Faith*, p. 257 (according to Levine, although
Bryan had little to do with the Ku Klux Klan, "his attitude toward the
Southern Negro . . . was worthy of any Klan member"); Norbeck to
W. C. Gemmill, May 20, 1924, Norbeck Papers (Missouri), Folder 4; John-
son to Hiram, Jr., May 12, 1918, to Mrs. Amy Johnson, August 31, 1918,
Part IV, Box 1, and to Sons, November 27, 1926, Part IV, Box 3; *The
Crisis*, XXVIII (August, 1924), 154; MacKay, *The Progressive Movement
of 1924*, p. 218. Zucker, *George W. Norris*, pp. 28–29, indicates that Nor-
ris's attitudes on the Negro resembled those of his western colleagues. For
a roll-call analysis which concludes that on the question of Negro rights
Senate progressives "did not qualify, it would seem, as 'advanced progressives,'" see Howard W. Allen, Aage R. Clausen, and Jerome Clubb,
"Political Reform and Negro Rights in the Senate, 1909–1915," *Journal
of Southern History*, XXXVII (May, 1971), 191–212.

[26] Walter F. White, *A Man Called White* (New York, 1943), pp. 170–
71. See also Mann, *La Guardia, A Fighter Against His Times*, p. 226. For
discussions about those progressives—generally among the urban, settlement worker groups—who were more sympathetic to the Negroes, see
Allen F. Davis, *Spearheads for Reform: The Social Settlements and the
Progressive Movement, 1890–1914* (New York, 1967), pp. 94–102, and

ment after the Civil War "was a stupendous error." It was "to take a people out of two thousand years of slavery and make them citizens over night and clothe them with all the responsibility of citizenship in a representative Republic." Such a policy was unfair to Negroes because no race had ever been able to assume the obligations of citizenship that quickly. Responsibilities which Anglo-Saxons had taken "a thousand years to understand and appreciate" had gone to Negroes as a sudden gift, rather than as a privilege earned "in the school of experience." Borah could "perfectly understand how the people of the South, and for that matter, the people elsewhere, should advocate a change in our Constitution and how they could openly and candidly go about to make this a white man's government." [27]

He cited the Negro problem as a key reason why he opposed the national woman suffrage amendment. "I have been an advocate of woman suffrage for twenty years," he wrote, but "the race question makes it impossible to apply the same principle that we apply to the intelligent women in Idaho." The alternatives seemed clear to him: "Either the negro women will vote in the South and together with the negro men control the situation . . . or they will be disenfranchised by fraud and deception. I do not propose to be a party to either proposition." He did not want "to fasten upon the South four million more ignorant negro voters." Nor did he want to write a law that would be a "cowardly lie," giving Negroes a paper rather than a real vote. Instead, he felt it would be "more wholesome and more in accordance with tolerance and justice" to leave the problem with local governments.[28]

The Senator questioned the desirability of the Fifteenth

Gilbert Osofsky, *Harlem: The Making of a Ghetto* (New York, 1966), pp. 53–67.

[27] Borah to J. S. White, May 19, 1921, Borah Papers, Box 206; and to W. E. B. DuBois, July 16, 1926, Box 263.

[28] Borah to E. H. Dewey, January 29, 1918, Borah Papers, Box 186; to John W. Hart, March 25, 1918, Box 187; to F. G. Mallet, October 19, 1918, and to S. D. Taylor, May 27, 1918, Box 192.

Amendment but, since it was part of the Constitution, he would not advocate that anyone disobey it. Indeed, he rebuked lily-white Republicans in North Carolina for urging Negro disfranchisement. "Are we going to leave the Constitution unchanged . . . and seek to build up a political party whose fundamental principles are thwarting the enforcement of those constitutional guarantees and denying to one class of our people rights which we take an oath to give them?" This, according to Borah, was "cowardly, lawless and immoral"; it would be "government founded upon perjury and Constitutional immorality." Moreover, there was the question of political expediency. If the Republican party opposed Negro voting in the south, it would be open to reprisals from northern Negroes: "That which we step on in North Carolina will sting us in Illinois." [29]

If proper and successful G.O.P. strategy had to oppose Negro disfranchisement, party commitment could, however, put the emphasis elsewhere. When Borah discussed the Negro problem, he urged nothing more than trust and confidence in the south's good intentions. He did not claim that the south had "established absolute equity between the two races"; yet he was certain that the "proud and brave people" of Dixie were finding constitutional solutions to a difficult problem. Northerners, who certainly could not deny playing politics with Negroes and exercising intolerance against them, needed to show less distrust and more confidence in the south. Cooperation between the two sections, not legislation such as antilynching and force bills that reflected suspicion of the south's intentions, was the proper approach to securing justice for Negroes.[30]

When Borah turned to the issue of prohibition on the other hand, he urged more than a policy of faith and forbearance. In behalf of dry principles, Republicans should order an advance, raising "that old banner of constitutional integrity," not "a white flag" in deference to the liquor interests. The Idahoan's own predilections allowed him to make other distinc-

[29] Borah to J. S. White, May 19, 1921, Borah Papers, Box 206.
[30] Borah to DuBois, July 16, 1926, Borah Papers, Box 263.

tions. While he asserted that the defects of the Fourteenth and Fifteenth Amendments were inherent in the "Amendments themselves and not in their enforcement," he refused to admit the possible relevance of the same point to the dry question. This was exactly the criticism that men such as Walter Lippmann leveled at the Eighteenth Amendment, but Borah rejected such reasoning ex cathedra.[31]

There was also the matter of the proper role of the federal government. When Borah spoke about prohibition, he stressed that the federal government, not the states, was the custodian of constitutional integrity. The Civil War had made this clear. The national government's "peculiar, exclusive and supreme duty" was to enforce the Constitution; if corresponding laws were nonexistent or insufficient, it was the duty of Congress "to find more effective means by which to make the Constitution effective." He was willing to admit that the Fifteenth Amendment was inadequate because it lacked the equivalent of a Volstead Act and left enforcement to the states. But, after making such an admission, Borah was not the man to try to correct the inadequacies—not, at least, when the matter concerned the voting rights of Negroes. He could declare emphatically that it was despicable and treasonable to leave the interpretation of prohibition to the states; there was little indication in his past record, however, that he would have supported a national law to enforce the Fifteenth Amendment. Indeed, when the issue involved Negro rights, he was most comfortable in his familiar role of warning about threats to states' rights.[32]

In 1922, for example, Borah played a key role in blocking a federal antilynching law on grounds that it was an unconstitutional redistribution of governmental powers. The NAACP importuned the Senator to change his position, or at least to stop fighting the proposal and let the courts decide on its con-

[31] See Borah's prohibition debate with Nicholas Murray Butler, April 8, 1927, copy of Borah's argument in Borah Papers, Box 278; Borah to George Holden Tinkham, July 24, 1928, Box 272.

[32] *Congressional Record*, 69th Cong., 1st Sess., 1926, LXVII, 7439; *The New York Times*, November 13, 1927.

stitutionality. Moorfield Storey, the NAACP president, urged Borah not to be so confident that only he had the correct constitutional view. After all, Storey pointed out, many members of Congress, leading lawyers, and other prominent men including Charles W. Eliot, president of Harvard, believed that the bill was constitutional.[33]

Such comments only bridled the Idahoan, who retorted that he found nothing more offensive than to have people tell him that he could not inquire into the constitutionality of a measure. At one point, Borah, looking "from under his shaggy eyebrows, but with that expression characteristic of him, which makes you uncertain as to whether he is in earnest or laughing at you," had suggested to James Weldon Johnson, secretary of the NAACP, that a constitutional amendment would be better than the proposed bill. The Senator had even indicated willingness to draft the resolution, but Johnson emphasized that the amendment would never secure enough state support for adoption. In September, when the bill fell victim to a Senate filibuster, Johnson received "a glance from Senator Borah. This time I felt sure he was laughing at me, and somewhat maliciously." [34]

Borah's fight against the antilynching bill in 1922 was not an

[33] James Weldon Johnson "recognized that Senator Borah was the most commanding figure in the Senate" and thus hoped that he would champion the legislation. Johnson, *Along This Way* (New York, 1943), p. 368. *The Crisis,* official organ of the NAACP, asserted that Borah's support of the bill would guarantee its success. "The Status of the Dyer Bill," *The Crisis,* XXIX (May, 1922), 25; NAACP, Springfield, Massachusetts, Branch, to Borah, May 5, 1922, Borah Papers, Box 212; NAACP, New York City Branch, to Borah, June 1, 1922, Box 212; Moorfield Storey to Borah, May 31, 1922, and Borah to Storey, June 21, 1922, Box 212; Borah to Editor of the Boston *Transcript,* June 8, 1922, Box 212.

[34] Johnson, *Along This Way,* pp. 367–71. James A. Cobb, an attorney who served on the Washington, D.C., board of directors of the NAACP, described some of Borah's objections to the antilynch bill as "nothing more than a smoke screen." To Arthur B. Spingarn, one of the founders of the NAACP, Borah was trying "to drag a herring across the trail." Cobb to Spingarn, June 14, 1922, and Spingarn reply, June 15, 1922, Arthur B. Spingarn Papers (Library of Congress), Box 2.

isolated example of his position on issues dealing with the Negroes' cause. As Walter White of the NAACP said, the Idahoan "persistently and consistently used his oratory and reputation as an authority on constitutional law to oppose federal anti-lynching laws and other legislation of that character." [35]

While Borah used the states' rights argument to block federal laws against lynching, he made adjustments in his logic when it came to prohibition. Reaffirming his dedication to local government, he argued that the Eighteenth Amendment was essential in order to protect dry from wet states. "No state can be dry," he reasoned, "while the Interstate Commerce clause of the Constitution remains, unless there is a prohibition which covers all states." Otherwise, some liquor passing from one wet state to another invariably would become "lost" enroute in a dry area.[36]

If the Senator's personal sentiments and prejudices allowed him to make such distinctions on questions of prohibition and the Negro, so too did his political aspirations. He was, of course, well aware that his positions on these issues would be crucial in determining his future as a presidential aspirant. On June 30, 1926, he commented to Raymond Robins that Negroes did

[35] White, *A Man Called White*, p. 171. During the Hoover administration when the NAACP objected to the appointment of John J. Parker to the U.S. Supreme Court on grounds that he was a racist, White testified before a Senate subcommittee of the Judiciary Committee. Borah, who had shared North Carolina Senator Lee S. Overman's anger "at the temerity of a Negro organization presuming to voice an opinion" regarding a judicial nomination, tried to place White "on the defensive by asking involved questions about legal decisions. . . ." White, who was not a lawyer, felt that it would be foolish to try to answer Borah's queries. White, pp. 104–6. On January 20, 1938, South Carolina's Senator James Byrnes pointed to "a concurrent resolution adopted by the General Assembly of South Carolina thanking the Honorable William E. Borah . . . for his valuable, able, and patriotic fight against the passage of the so-called antilynching bill now pending in the . . . Senate." *Congressional Record*, 75th Cong., 3rd Sess., 1938, LXXXIII, 813.

[36] See Borah's April 8, 1927, debate with Nicholas Murray Butler, Borah Papers, Box 278. Significantly, Borah was one of a Senate subcommittee of three that helped to frame the Eighteenth Amendment. Borah to Editor, *The Boston Herald*, June 20, 1931, Borah Papers, Box 325.

not like him because of his opposition in the Senate to anti-lynching legislation. But, instead of expressing regret, Borah was apparently pleased to confide that his chances of carrying the southern states had consequently improved. As Robins saw it, the Senator seemed addicted to "a wil [sic]-of-the-wisp in this attitude of tenderness toward the south on the negro question." Borah had continued by speaking "at length" about an influential Georgian who had written him optimistically concerning the Senator's chances in that state. There was thus justification for the NAACP's belief that political expediency influenced the Idahoan and that his opposition to antilynch legislation reflected in part his hopes of building his White House ambitions upon a southern base. Robins was skeptical about such strategy and believed that Borah needed "some vital northern or national issue." Otherwise, the Senator might win the south but lose the north and west.[37]

It was perhaps because Borah realized the need for such a national issue that he found the dry cause especially attractive. His ardor for prohibition had become increasingly warm and evident in 1926—a year in which the wet-dry controversy seemed to be the only public question of note and when the Senator chose to announce that he was going to stump the country in a solo effort to reform the Republican party before the next election. For a man hoping to effect, and to benefit from, changes in the political environment, the need for a popular national issue was obvious.[38]

[37] Raymond Robins to Salmon O. Levinson, June 30, 1926, Levinson Papers, Box 77; Robert Lewis Zangrando, "The Efforts of the National Association for the Advancement of Colored People to Secure Passage of a Federal Anti-Lynching Law, 1920–1940" (unpublished Ph.D. dissertation, University of Pennsylvania, 1963), pp. 451–52.

[38] Wile Scrapbooks, November 2, 1926, Scrapbook 25. Wile observed that only prohibition was diverting public attention from such things as the Hall-Mills murder case, Rudolph Valentino, and college football. News columnist Charles Michelson believed that, through prohibition, Borah could become the "best advertised man in the United States." The Senator might use the issue to rally the drys and to break the solid south. The situation was the most interesting "since Roosevelt split the party."

His choice of issues was a natural one considering the moralistic underpinnings of his progressivism. He claimed an interest in prohibition only as a constitutional matter, yet he did not hesitate to say that "the liquor question presents a great moral problem. . . . I do not underestimate nor do I wish to be understood as minimizing the hurtful results of drink." He noted some of its effects on the community: "the pauperism, the insanity, the suicides, the broken families, the cries flowing in one constant steady stream from drink. . . . It is an unmitigated curse." Language simply could not "exaggerate or overstate its demoralizing and decimating effect upon the individual, upon the state and the nation." [39]

Repeatedly, in speeches and debates, the Senator urged the Republican party to champion law enforcement in the 1928 campaign. *The Independent,* reading "the Borahmeter," sarcastically observed that even though he was turning to the prohibition issue in an effort to rally his "skeleton army," his chances for the nomination were "smaller than a flea's tooth." Nonetheless, by the end of November, 1927, he considered having his three major speeches on prohibition printed and widely distributed in a pamphlet. H. L. Mencken concluded that "Senator Borah, after having long been a professional Liberal, is now a professional Prohibitionist." [40]

In the following months, Borah steadily revealed the nature

New York *World,* June 3, 1926, Borah Scrapbooks, Reel 5; *The New York Times,* June 12, 1926.

[39] Typewritten copy of Borah's article for *Collier's* and Borah's letter to the managing editor, Charles Colebaugh, April 15, 1929, Borah Papers, Box 299. The article appeared under the title "Speak Up or Dry Up" in the May 31 issue. Later Borah asked, "We do not want to go back to the saloon, do we? And every proposal which I have seen as a substitute, or alternative, for the Eighteenth Amendment would lead . . . inevitably to the front door of the saloon." Borah to H. G. Fitz, March 21, 1931, Box 327.

[40] "The Borahmeter Registers Squalls," *The Independent,* CXIX (November 19, 1927), 506; Raymond Robins to Levinson, November 16, 1927, Levinson Papers, Box 77; Mencken, December 5, 1927, as quoted in Malcolm Moos, *H. L. Mencken on Politics* (New York, 1956), p. 164.

of his commitment to law enforcement. When he sent questionnaires to prospective Republican candidates, all four of his
queries dealt with the Eighteenth Amendment. The law enforcement plank that he placed into the Republican platform
singled out only the Eighteenth Amendment for special mention. And during the campaign, he turned to prohibition as a
subject about which he felt "more deeply than any other." [41]

The flaw in Borah's constitutionalism had become clear. It
made a difference, however much he tried to deny it, whether
prohibition or the voting rights of Negroes was at stake. Negro
groups such as the NAACP consequently remained skeptical of
him and later concluded "that the record of Borah makes it
impossible for Negro Republicans to lend him any aid whatsoever." It seemed that he lacked "any conception of the hopes,
ambitions and rights of Negro Americans." Senatorial colleagues such as Peter Norbeck and Hiram Johnson were also
suspicious of Borah's constitutionalism, if for different reasons.
Johnson observed bitterly that the Idahoan "has always found
some 'constitutional' objection where he wished to align himself with privilege." Norbeck noted that Borah was "often
clever" in finding a plausible explanation by which he could
justify his actions. If, for example, the Idahoan did not like
something, he usually found a constitutional argument against
it.[42]

Interpreting the Constitution so as to bolster his position

[41] See Borah to Herbert Hoover, February 9, 1928, Borah Papers, Box
294. He asked if the individual favored a plank that pledged the party to
enforcement of the Eighteenth Amendment, what the person would do
to enforce prohibition if he got into the White House, what his views
were on the New York referendum proposal, and if he favored repeal of
the amendment. Borah's speech in Richmond, Virginia, October 15, 1928,
copy in Carter Glass Papers (University of Virginia Library), Box 423.
[42] Editorial, "The Problem of Borah," *The Crisis*, XLIII (March,
1936), 80; editorial summary and article by Louis L. Redding, "Borah—
What Does He Stand For?" *ibid.*, 70–71, 82; Johnson to Harold Ickes,
September 29, 1928, Ickes Papers, Box 3; Norbeck to A. A. Chamberlain,
December 29, 1929, and to Guy F. Barnes, March 30, 1931, Norbeck
Papers (South Dakota).

was, of course, not unique with Borah. Many leading Americans, including Jefferson, Calhoun, Lincoln, and Theodore Roosevelt, had done the same thing. But, just as Jefferson's constitutional adjustments in regard to his purchase of the Louisiana territory revealed much about his attitudes concerning the future of the American nation, Borah's construction of the Constitution regarding prohibition and Negro rights disclosed a great deal about the variety of progressivism for which he spoke.

X

Fighting for Traditional Values: The 1928 Election

🏵

BY the 1928 election, the progressive movement stood in shambles, the victim not only of postwar reaction and "New Era" prosperity but also of cultural conflicts relating to values, morals, traditions, and personal liberties. Prohibition and immigration restriction were key examples of issues that cut along ethnic and religious lines, creating tensions in the ranks of American reform and shattering the earlier progressive ethos as effectively as they reduced Wilson's prewar Democratic coalition to the feuding, impotent factions of 1924. Throughout the postwar decade such conflicts had time and again divided progressives against each other and within themselves.[1]

The 1928 presidential campaign clearly illustrated the extent to which the widening cultural chasm precluded the rebuilding of a major progressive consensus. The contest between New York's Alfred E. Smith and Herbert Hoover was fought out in large part between the forces of urban and rural America—a lineup that cut across reform groups and evoked more passion and intensity than did the progressive splits during the previous election. Elizabeth H. Tilton, who had long struggled for a variety of social reforms, voiced anxieties surrounding the campaign when she aligned herself with Hoover and "My America against Tammany's. Prairie, Plantation and Everlasting Hills against the sidewalks of New York!" Mrs. Tilton was

[1] Buenker, "The Progressive Era: A Search for a Synthesis," pp. 189–92, and Levine, *Defender of the Faith*, pp. 179–81, point out the divisive effect of cultural conflicts on progressivism. For the rural-urban split within the Democratic party, see David Burner, *The Politics of Provincialism: The Democratic Party in Transition, 1918–1932* (New York, 1967).

being characteristically effusive, but she nonetheless placed her finger on the underlying concern which drove many progressives into Hoover's camp. Certainly there was a direct correspondence between her words and the fact that the presidential campaign of 1928 was the only one in which Borah ever threw himself with genuine zeal and energy. Although the Senator had previously not been an enthusiast of Hoover, he came to look upon him as a genuine progressive alternative to Smith.[2]

Those ideas and assumptions that had marked Borah's progressivism—and that of the western liberal Senators generally—came into clear focus during the election. As the year unfolded, his western, rural vision and the heritage of progressive morality that characterized his thinking were much in evidence. His objectives were still to make the Republican party a vehicle of liberalism, to increase the voice of western progressivism within the party, and to protect the social experiment of prohibition and the moral values that it represented. In his eyes the candidacy of Al Smith—an eastern, urban, machine-oriented Democrat—drew even more plainly the lines of battle between the party of Lincoln and the party of corrupt politicians who threatened old values and traditions. Intensely committed, he sallied forth to meet the challenge of Tammany Hall and the evils that it symbolized. At the Republican convention and during the campaign the Senator disappointed some reformers who earlier had looked favorably upon him. Yet, he sincerely believed that he was aiding, not deserting, the progressive cause.

[2] Elizabeth Tilton quoted in Clarke A. Chambers, *Seedtime of Reform: American Social Service and Social Action, 1918–1933* (Minneapolis, Minn., 1963), p. 142. Paul A. Carter, "The Campaign of 1928 Re-Examined: A Study of Political Folklore," *Wisconsin Magazine of History,* XLVI (Summer, 1963), esp. pp. 269–71, stresses that the campaign was not between liberals and conservatives or wets and drys but between town and country. Don S. Kirschner, *City and Country: Rural Responses to Urbanization in the 1920s* (Westport, Conn., 1970), pp. 50–53, describes the rural image of Smith and says that "it should not be surprising either that the accumulated wrath of the rural Midwest was vented in 1928 against Al Smith . . . a man who represented every evil that ruralites despised. . . ."

A strong touch of irony pervaded his efforts. His attempt to remove the oil scandal stains from his party received more ridicule than support. His great emphasis on the Republican platform in 1928 contrasted sharply with his views in 1922 when he had scornfully said, "I don't care two cents about a platform. Who remembers the platform on which Harding was elected?" Insofar as he hoped that his services as "premier campaign orator of the Hoover forces" would increase his voice in the G.O.P., he faced disappointment. Hoover as President was to show little enthusiasm for his suggestions or for those of the other western progressives. Moreover, serious flaws weakened the strategy by which Borah hoped to strengthen the Republican party. In trying both to increase western influence within the G.O.P. and to break the Democratic south, he turned his back on the real political force of the future: urban America, which was finding its home in Al Smith's Democracy. Ultimately the emerging urban masses would shift the main source of reform itself onto grounds which to Borah and perhaps most of the prewar progressives were uncomfortable and even alien.[3]

In early 1928, the Senator was still hopeful about his own political chances as a presidential aspirant. He had no intention of announcing his candidacy and running for the Presidency because it would be "a hazardous political enterprise," too expensive and time-consuming. There remained the possibility, of course, that a convention deadlock might change the situation in his favor. Hence he noted that "in the language of the Arkansas poet, I am going to simply saw wood." When he heard reports that twelve North Dakota delegates would back Frank Lowden on the first ballot "as a camouflage" and would then turn to him, he commented that "the situation with reference to the Presidency is becoming more interesting and more com-

[3] *The Idaho Daily Statesman,* October 10, 1922; Baltimore *Sun,* November 1, 1928, on Borah's role in the 1928 campaign. Graham, *Encore for Reform,* shows clearly that the dominant view of old progressives in the Thirties was adverse to the New Deal.

plicated. . . . The present outlook is that no man will go to Kansas City with sufficiency to nominate." Another favorable sign in Borah's opinion was the apparent tendency of the public to concentrate on issues.[4]

His repeated statements urging candidates and party platforms to confront issues forthrightly thus served a dual purpose of guiding the direction of political discussion and also of bolstering his own presidential stock. As one columnist observed, the prohibition questionnaire that Borah sent to Republican candidates definitely stamped Borah's name in the public's mind. "The mention of the names of all the avowed and presumptive candidates suggests to the general run of citizens not even the slightest idea of an issue of national significance." On the other hand, "mention of the name of Borah registers at once in every man's mind and every woman's mind an issue and an idea: Prohibition. An amazing situation indeed!"[5]

There was a chance that the launching of Borah's "Redemption Fund" would have a comparable effect. Early in March, 1928, the Senator startled Republican leaders by suggesting that the party return the $160,000 donation that Harry F. Sinclair in 1923 had contributed to their organization. Since the subsequent Senate committee investigations had exposed Sinclair's role in the Teapot Dome scandal, the Idahoan contended that the party shared responsibility for the corrupt deed unless it repudiated the transaction and refunded the money. "We can not in self-respect or in justice to the voters in the party keep it." He was convinced that Republicans would contribute a dollar or more apiece "to clear their party of this humiliating stigma."[6] The Senator's decision was not merely a product of political expediency. He undoubtedly was deeply sincere. More

[4] Borah to W. Scott Hall, February 21, 1928, and to Ray McKaig, March 6, 1928, Borah Papers, Box 286. See also, McKaig to Borah, March 2, 1928.

[5] "Whiting's Boston Letter," in the Springfield *Daily Republican*, February 16, 1928, Borah Scrapbooks, Reel 5.

[6] Borah to William M. Butler, March 5, 1928, Borah Papers, Box 703.

than anything, his crusade to rescue his party's name displayed the moral nature of his progressivism. It nonetheless also contained possibilities for his own political future. Surely the issue of clean government, as well as that of prohibition, could summon the name of Borah to the public's mind.

The Republican hierarchy was hardly ecstatic about his plan. He had obviously placed the G.O.P. in a dilemma. If it did not return Sinclair's money, it would be vulnerable to charges of venality. But, if it refunded the donation, it would stand as "a culprit compelled to make belated and reluctant restitution." Hence, when one Republican regular heard untrue rumors that Borah was ill, he stated caustically, "I do hope it is nothing trivial." National Chairman Butler refused to take immediate action, explaining that not all the facts about the Sinclair transaction were yet clear. Borah, who had little sympathy with such reasoning, was even more dissatisfied when he learned that leading aspirants for the Republican nomination refused even to comment on his suggestion.[7]

When the National Committee continued to hesitate, the Senator announced that he was beginning an independent campaign to raise the money. He appealed "to Republicans over the country to come forward and lift this obligation of shame." From his own pocket he contributed $100 to the "Redemption Fund." "I shall not be satisfied nor silent," he avowed, "until the last damned dirty dollar is taken out of the coffers of the party of Lincoln and Grant and McKinley and Roosevelt." "You," William Allen White excitedly told him, "could do the party no greater service than to purge it now. It will be hard, but it is the only salvation." The immediate response to Borah's calls was encouraging. Into his office from across the country poured contributions. Although Salmon O. Levinson and New Mexico's Bronson Cutting contributed $1,000 apiece, most of the gifts were small. "A young Republican" in Philadelphia sent a dime, all he could spare for the moment but hoping to "be of assistance in the drive to pay back Sinclair." One check,

[7] Baltimore *Sun*, March 13, 1928.

totaling a dollar, went to "Senator W. E. Borah, Evangelist-Experimenter." [8]

Few people criticized the Senator's motives, but the press generally agreed that his "hat-passing is a pound of mis-placed cure." Even if the party paid back Sinclair, "the smell of oil will still cling to the records. . . ." Moreover, it seemed strange to take a collection in behalf of a millionaire who was hiring attorneys in a frantic effort to circumvent federal laws. According to one magazine, the conscience fund was the most useless of Borah's "many futile paper chases for the purpose of slaying phantom foxes." The G.O.P. could not buy its honor. Even his progressive colleagues in the Senate were for the most part skeptical of the idea. Gerald Nye told a Baltimore audience that the fund drive was "the most foolish step Senator Borah ever took." Nye admired his good intentions but felt that "he is unfair to the people. . . . it is the poor devil who can't afford it, who will put in his $1, $5, or $10 contributions." [9] A less gracious critic reported that "Borah's proposal . . . gets a big laugh in any crowd where it is discussed. . . . He has communed with himself so damned long that he interprets his reactions as rheumatic pains extending throughout the nation." One individual composed a poem on Republican corruption in

[8] Baltimore *Sun*, March 16, 1928; "Redemption Fund" list, Borah Papers, Box 704; Borah to Irvin E. Rockwell, March 31, 1928, William Allen White to Borah, March 13, 1928, and numerous other letters, Box 703.

[9] "Mr. Borah Passes the Hat," *The Independent*, CXX (March 31, 1928), 291; "Whitewash," *The World's Work*, LVI (May, 1928), 10; on Nye, *The Washington Post*, March 19, 1928. Bronson Cutting, who entered the Senate in late 1927, wrote that "a good many of the senators, especially in the radical wing, such as Nye and Brookhart, are very much opposed to Borah's move. Senator Couzens summed up their attitude in saying 'What good would it do to give a thief back his money?' " Cutting was more sympathetic. He described Borah's gesture as "the only serious attempt that is being made by anyone" to deal with a major phase of political corruption. His only regret was that Borah had trusted "his personal magnetism alone," and had thus not established the necessary organization to make such a collection of money. "For my part," Cutting said, "I should hate to have it fail." Cutting to R. Fulton Cutting, March 21, 1928, Bronson M. Cutting Papers (Library of Congress), Box 7.

the Twenties and included a verse saying, "Borah went forth for a conscience fund/ To pay back all boodle from the time it begund.[sic]/ His plea for righteousness brought a raucous laugh,/And he only collected a dollar and a half." [10]

Actually, the collection swelled quickly to almost $7,500 before inertia set in. Contributions arrived steadily during the first two weeks, but after that they almost completely stopped. The "Borah Purification Fund" had crashed, according to one cartoonist, because of fog, wind, and lack of gas.[11]

As the conscience fund campaign began to sputter, Borah attempted to thwart the political aspirations of Herbert Hoover. Earlier, in October of 1927, Raymond Robins had discussed the election with Borah and got the impression that he was "least friendly to Hoover—possibly because the Hoover boom is growing very substantially." Nor did Hoover's evasive reply in February to the Senator's dry questionnaire satisfy Borah. Although Hoover stated his opposition to repealing the Eighteenth Amendment and endorsed vigorous enforcement of the law, he ignored those queries concerning his position on the New York referendum and on the inclusion of a dry plank in the Republican platform.[12]

Hence, in late March, Borah suddenly injected himself into the Ohio presidential primary where Hoover was running against Senator Frank B. Willis, a staunch prohibitionist who had replied unequivocally to the Idahoan's dry questionnaire. Speaking over the radio, Borah told Ohio listeners that the party must pledge itself to strong enforcement of the Eighteenth Amendment. His disavowal of any intentions to influence the Ohio primary was, however, unconvincing. Earlier, he had re-

[10] *The Washington Post,* March 19, 1928; W. H. Daugherty to Irvine Lenroot, April 12, 1928, Lenroot Papers, Box 7; Kent E. Keller to Thomas Walsh, June 11, 1928, Walsh Papers, Box 180.

[11] Baltimore *Sun,* April 5, 1928; Borah Scrapbooks, Reel 2. By fall, Borah gave up on raising the $160,000 and began returning the contributions.

[12] Raymond Robins to Levinson, October 26, 1927, Levinson Papers, Box 77; Hoover to Borah, February 23, 1928, Hoover Campaign Correspondence, 1928, Hoover Papers, Box 1-H/57.

fused to speak in the state lest people construe his efforts as taking sides in the election. His subsequent change of heart and his emphasis on prohibition seemed a definite rebuff to Hoover, since Willis wanted to inflate the dry issue into a crucial difference between himself and the Secretary. Regardless of Borah's pretense of neutrality in his radio address, he in effect placed "in bold relief" the reminder that Willis was committed to a dry plank while Hoover had spoken only in more general terms of his sympathy for prohibition.[13]

Borah may have hoped that Willis, a native Ohioan, would take the impetus out of Hoover's drive toward the nomination. Any such expectations, however, were short-lived. On March 30, prior to speaking before a political rally, Willis staggered in the anteroom. While the Buckeye Glee Club, unaware of the grim events offstage, joined in a campaign chorus (ironically called "Farewell"), Willis called feebly for his wife and died a few minutes later of a cerebral hemorrhage. Hoover, now alone in the primary, added Ohio to his growing list of victories.[14]

Thereafter, Borah himself looked with growing favor upon the Secretary of Commerce. The strength of Hoover's nomination machinery was too obvious to ignore. Furthermore, as Borah's own chances for the nomination steadily declined, Hoover's attitude on the prohibition issue offered a sharp contrast to the views of the other Republican contenders. Frank Lowden refused to answer the Idahoan's dry questionnaire. Indiana's James Watson, who had also announced his candidacy, threatened to blow Borah "out of the water" if he quizzed him. According to rumor, Watson's defiance was the result of a 1924 conversation with Borah. At that time, the Indiana Senator had solicited advice regarding a prohibition plank and Borah had reportedly told him that it would be unwise to rouse sleeping dogs. Watson's belligerence, along with Willis's death and Lowden's silence, convinced some observers that Borah's

---

[13] *The Washington Post*, March 29, 1928.
[14] Baltimore *Sun*, March 31, 1928.

offers to elevate the dry issue had "died a natural death." In
this context, Borah began to look with higher regard upon
Hoover, who had at least generally endorsed prohibition. Moreover, by this time, it appeared that Governor Smith would be
the Democratic candidate. The specter of Smith, a New York
City wet and Tammany machine politician, greatly worried
Borah.[15]

By early June, George Norris feared that Borah would probably back Hoover and was thus lost to the progressive cause for
the 1928 campaign. The Idahoan and Hoover huddled in almost daily conferences to discuss a possible Republican platform and, to the dismay of the eastern Old Guard, the Secretary
was amenable to Borah's suggestions regarding such items as
prohibition, denunciation of oil corruption, tariff studies to aid
the farmer and the American market, Outlawry of War, and
farm relief. As a result of these meetings, when the Senator
arrived in Kansas City to serve on the Republican resolutions
committee, he spoke with greater authority. Certainly in part
due to Hoover's sanctions, Borah played a major role in con-
structing the party platform. He personally wrote the planks
dealing with prohibition, campaign funds, Outlawry of War,
and much of the labor and agricultural pledges. If Borah himself could not get the nomination he would at least attempt to
formulate his party's program.[16]

The farm plank, which Borah helped to draft, touched off the

[15] Baltimore *Sun*, April 9, 1928. According to Hoover, "Senator Borah
entertained a deep dislike for the Governor whom he stigmatized as the
representative of the bar rooms nominated by Tammany Hall. The Senator also entertained a great dislike for the other gentlemen being mentioned at that time, such as Senator Watson, General Dawes, and Governor Lowden. In casting around for a place to support which would
embarrass those gentlemen, and not from affection towards myself, he
indicated to my friends that he hoped that I would allow my name to be
presented to the country." Hoover's typed manuscript about Borah, June
4, 1933, Hoover Papers, Box 1-K/14.

[16] Baltimore *Sun*, June 10, 1928, on Norris's worries; "Herbert's God-
father," *Collier's*, LXXXII (August 4, 1928), 32; *New York Journal of
Commerce*, June 9, 1928, Borah Scrapbooks, Reel 6; Borah to H. G. Peckham, June 29, 1928, Borah Papers, Box 286; Baltimore *Sun*, June 9, 1928.

most explosive controversy at the convention. Three weeks before the party gathered at Kansas City, Coolidge vetoed the McNary-Haugen bill for the second time. Subsequently, when the Republicans moved into farm country to nominate their candidate, they found the surroundings charged with tension. Not since 1896 had agriculture assumed such political importance. Nebraska's Governor McMullen called upon 100,000 farmers to march on Kansas City to demonstrate their grievances. Angry farm groups prepared to block the candidacy of Hoover, who sympathized with Coolidge's agricultural policies. A Des Moines meeting of the Corn Belt Federation, "speaking for more than a million farmers," adopted a unanimous resolution in opposition to the Secretary. Senators Norris, Norbeck, and Nye also expressed dissatisfaction with Hoover because of his agricultural views. When the convention opened, a local band and 500 marchers wearing overalls and straw hats chanted outside the auditorium, "We Don't Want Hoover." [17]

On the convention's third day, Borah "galloped up the ladder and turned on the hose" to squelch the flames of agricultural discontent. He acted when Lowden's supporters presented a minority platform devoting about one-fourth of its space to the farm relief issue and specifically endorsing the McNary-Haugen bill. The majority platform, in contrast, awarded much less space to the farm problem and called simply for protecting the home market (Borah's contribution) and for more orderly marketing of farm products. Senator La Follette introduced the minority suggestions and several other McNary-Haugenites delivered fiery supporting speeches. Borah dissented vigorously. Speaking for thirty minutes to the 14,000 people in the convention hall, he attacked the McNary-Haugen bill as uncon-

[17] "Political Dynamite in a Coolidge Veto," *Literary Digest*, XCVII (June 9, 1928), 5; Gilbert C. Fite, "The Agricultural Issue in the Presidential Campaign of 1928," *Mississippi Valley Historical Review*, XXXVII (March, 1951), 635–56; Farm-Labor Press Service release, June 11, 1928, Teigan Papers, Box 7; Baltimore *Sun*, June 10, 1928; Norbeck to L. E. Camfield, April 18, 1928, Norbeck Papers (South Dakota); *The New York Times*, June 11, 1928.

stitutional. In conclusion he praised Coolidge's veto as "the greatest benefit and the greatest favor which has been rendered to the American farmer." The time would come, he prophesied, when agrarians would hail the courage and statesmanship of the President who saved them from bureaucratic serfdom. As Borah sat down, the convention applauded wildly and rejected with a roar the minority platform 806 to 278. One reporter believed that Borah's "eloquent and devastating" assault on McNary-Haugenism had helped to secure at least a million votes for the G.O.P. Certainly the repudiation of the minority platform "marked the death knell of the most disrupting force in the Republican party." [18] Following the defeat of the minority platform, Lowden withdrew as a candidate on grounds that the party was not ready to cope with the farm problem. The path was clear for Hoover's nomination.

The following day, when the convention selected its vice-presidential candidate, Borah again asserted his influence. He threw his weight unequivocally to a westerner, Charles Curtis of Kansas, and even threatened to carry the fight to the floor of the convention. The eastern wing of the party hierarchy preferred Massachusetts' former governor, Channing Cox, or the present governor, Alvan T. Fuller. But, largely due to Borah's determination to fight all the way to the convention floor, the eastern faction gave way. On the afternoon of June 15, the Idahoan was again before the delegates, this time to nominate Curtis, who joined Hoover on the ticket.[19]

Borah's conduct at Kansas City surprised some observers who had expected "the Borah-Norris-La Follette Republicans" to harass the regulars unmercifully. "Instead of being the flaming mouthpiece of the minority, protesting against the wickedness

[18] Newspaper account quoted in Johnson, *Borah of Idaho*, p. 421; Borah to H. G. Peckham, June 29, 1928, Borah Papers, Box 286; *Official Report of the Proceedings of the Nineteenth Republican Convention* (New York, 1928), pp. 133–57, 166–74; C. A. Herter, "Looking Back on Kansas City," *The Independent*, CXX (June 30, 1928), 615.

[19] *Christian Science Monitor*, June 16, 1928, Borah Scrapbooks, Reel 6; *The New York Times*, June 16, 1928.

and injustice of the steam-roller methods of the organization, Borah this time was not only with the majority, but one of its directing heads." The Senator had written "the really vital planks of the platform" and was mainly responsible for the nomination of Curtis, "an amiable old party hack." According to Oswald Garrison Villard, Borah "pleased nobody when he stooped to nominating Charles Curtis." Some columnists believed that at Kansas City Borah had lost the earlier zeal that had inspired his "Redemption Fund." He had made no attempt to force a denunciation of Sinclair into the platform and had issued no stirring appeal to the convention about the issue; indeed, "he had apparently forgotten there was such a person as Sinclair in the world." H. L. Mencken, with characteristic sarcasm, noted "how far his [Borah's] horror of corruption fell short of actually embarrassing such hacks as Smoot, Watson, and Moses. . . ." In Mencken's estimation, he had been one of the convention's clowns, rather than "the frank and candid man he could be if he would." George Norris bitterly reminded one of the Idahoan's supporters that Borah "never once raised his voice . . . to have any plank included which would condemn the Power Trust, whose sins were smelling to high heaven." Another disappointed individual recalled Borah's earlier declaration that he would fight for a progressive candidate and platform. "In the end, we found him pulling shoulder to shoulder with Vare and Hays and Slemp and Smoot to put over Hoover and Curtis and the same old platitudinous twaddle." *The Nation*'s only consoling reply to the Senator's critic was that at least Borah had not received money for his actions.[20]

Borah was at a loss to understand why his efforts at Kansas City distressed liberals such as Villard. For one thing, the Senator's convention talks with Hoover had "greatly encouraged"

[20] "T.R.B." in *The New Republic*, LIV (May 16, 1928), 379; LV (July 4, 1928), 173; LVIII (February 20, 1929), 16; Oswald Garrison Villard, "The Elephant Performs at Kansas City," *The Nation*, CXXVI (June 27, 1928), 712; H. L. Mencken, "Clown Show," *ibid.*, 713; Norris to H. C. McNew, June 19, 1928, Norris Papers, Tray 8, Box 3; Frederick Babcock to Editor, June 15, 1928, *The Nation*, CXXVII (July 11, 1928), 42.

him. Raymond Robins had no doubts about Borah's "delight in the platform and the nomination. He really prefers Hoover to anyone other than himself." The Senator surely believed that he had secured important concessions from the Old Guard at the convention. The enhanced position of the west within the party was strikingly apparent. Never before had both candidates on a ticket come from states west of the Mississippi. In regard to the farm relief issue, the party had routed the McNary-Haugen forces and their bureaucratic panaceas. The G.O.P. had also, at Borah's insistence, dedicated itself on paper to the principle and enforcement of the Eighteenth Amendment. As columnist Edward Whiting wrote, "Until Mr. Borah grabbed the reins, the issue of prohibition had no status in the national councils . . . of the party. It has such a status now solely by virtue of this one man's insistence that it should." The Republican commitment on law enforcement was unequivocal enough to inspire one prohibition group to announce that King Alcohol, who "had ruled the political roost with clammy claw and cloven hoof," met "his waterloo when he hit the Kansas line on the shores of the crystal Kaw." [21]

The Democratic nomination of Al Smith gave Borah further assurances that his position was correct. "He wants Smith beaten and beaten decisively," Raymond Robins remarked after spending more than an hour with the Senator. "He really has the spirit for this fight apparently. He wants me to get in and drill." [22]

As the campaign grew in intensity, Borah's private and public statements underscored the nature of his progressivism while also illuminating the throbbing cultural battle that marked the election. As *The New Republic* had perceptively noticed several years earlier, "the impending conflict" would be between rural and urban cultures, between "differences in ideas and

[21] Borah to Ernest Gruening, June 20, 1928, Borah Papers, Box 292; Robins to Levinson, June 24, 1928, Levinson Papers, Box 77; Borah Scrapbooks, Reel 5; National United Committee for Law Enforcement bulletin, June 19, 1928, Norris Papers, Tray 1, Box 5.

[22] Robins to Levinson, June 24, 1928, Levinson Papers, Box 77.

ways of life." The urban immigrants and their immediate
progeny presented a growing challenge to "the small-town
native-born Protestant American" who had formulated traditional American views. When "this urban hyphenated democracy" attempted to place Al Smith in the White House, the
result would inevitably "be one of the bitterest contests which
have ever occurred in American national politics." *The New
Republic* had also seen the possibility of "Senator Borah as the
standard-bearer of a dry agrarian progressive faction," with its
roots in "the grievances of an economic class which inhabits a
single large contiguous area," pitted against "a wet candidate,
who would represent in addition to anti-prohibitionism the
urban, labor, white-collar polyglot democracy of the Northeast
and Middle West." [23]

In 1928, Borah was not the candidate of any party, but he
was a conspicuous figure in a campaign that closely resembled
the rural-urban scenario that *The New Republic* had envisioned. A large number of progressives joined with Borah in
the battle to vanquish the urban hosts of Al Smith. Even some
liberal Democrats such as William E. Dodd and Josephus
Daniels were among those progressives who rejected the governor because of his urban connections; while Dodd had little
use for Hoover, he utterly deplored Smith's limited knowledge
"of the old America." William Allen White opposed Smith
largely because he came from a city "maggot-eaten with saloons"
and was "urbanite with an urbanity unrestrained . . . city
born, city bred, 'city broke,' city minded and city hearted." [24]

[23] "The Impending Conflict," *The New Republic,* XLV (December 2,
1925), 30–31, and XLVII (June 9, 1926), 71. See, also, "Politics and Prohibition," XLV (January 6, 1926), 178–79. Andrew Sinclair, *Era of Excess,
A Social History of the Prohibition Movement* (paperback ed., New York,
1964), pp. 285–306, discusses the 1928 election ("Last Victory") in terms
similar to that which *The New Republic* anticipated.
[24] On confusion among progressives and the disintegration of the progressive movement, and for the quotes from Dodd, Daniels and White, see
Glad, "Progressives and the Business Culture of the 1920s," pp. 86–89;
Carter, "The Campaign of 1928 Re-Examined," pp. 270–71, is very good
on White's reaction to Smith as an "urbanite."

Many social workers who generally were more sympathetic than White to the city also found they could not support Smith, primarily because of his opposition to prohibition. Only seventeen of the sixty-six respondents to a letter from Lillian Wald and John L. Elliot regarding their political preferences endorsed Smith; forty-five (including such prominent leaders as Jane Addams and Mary McDowell) declared for Hoover. For those social workers who had long attacked the saloon as a cause of poverty, violence, graft, and family quarrels, it was difficult to spurn Hoover who had promised to enforce the Eighteenth Amendment—a law for which Smith had demonstrated open contempt. Hoover, moreover, had a progressive reputation of his own. At the end of the war he had received high praise from journals such as *The New Republic.* And to some progressives—especially those concerned with efficient administration—the Secretary continued to fit within the reform tradition because of "his scientific methods in government." Also his campaign speeches articulated a number of programs that many reformers had long held dear: the possibilities of abolishing poverty in the nation, of jobs for all men, of shorter work days, of increased educational opportunities, and of limiting the use of injunctions in labor disputes and relying more on collective bargaining.[25]

Smith himself made the choice easier for those progressives who opted for Hoover. Although the New Yorker had a rather impressive reform record as governor, a number of contemporaries noted his fundamental conservatism. Perhaps more importantly, he unwisely flaunted his urban biases before rural America rather than attempting to reconcile the two cultures.[26]

Some progressives nonetheless found Smith more appealing

[25] On the social workers, prohibition, and the election, Chambers, *Seedtime of Reform,* pp. 138–43; Burner, *The Politics of Provincialism,* pp. 193–95, discusses Hoover's progressive appeal in 1928; for pro-Hoover letters in *The New Republic,* see LI (September 26, 1928), 155 (October 3, 1928), 178 (October 17, 1928), 250–51, which comments on his "scientific" approach, and (November 7, 1928), 330.

[26] Burner, *The Politics of Provincialism,* pp. 179–216.

than Hoover. *The New Republic* hesitated at first but ultimately threw its support behind the governor on grounds that the only chance to find a much-needed alternative to Republican rule was "to seize upon promising progressive seedlings in the Democratic party and try to fertilize them." *The Nation* appealed to its readers not to vote for Hoover but instead to choose between socialist Norman Thomas, the journal's sentimental choice, and Smith, who was clearly preferable to the Republican nominee. Although the People's Legislative Service declared that "neither Smith nor Hoover is a real champion of a living Progressive issue," it decided that Smith's campaign had earned the reform vote. A Progressive League for Alfred E. Smith took shape under the direction of labor attorney Frank P. Walsh (a founder of the Committee of 48), California's veteran reformer Rudolph Spreckels, liberal journalist Norman Hapgood, Rabbi Stephen S. Wise, and Mrs. Louis Brandeis. *The New Republic*'s straw poll in October showed that liberal intellectuals—such as Morris Cohen, John Dewey, Felix Frankfurter, Paul U. Kellogg, Heywood Broun, Charles Merz, and Clarence Darrow—were generally pro-Smith, although some, including Paul Douglas, W. E. B. Du Bois, Freda Kirchwey, and Art Young supported Thomas.[27]

The Senate progressives, on the other hand, were generally united against Smith. Only Norris and, to a much lesser extent, Blaine endorsed Smith. La Follette and Shipstead refused to commit themselves; even though they were thoroughly dissatisfied with Hoover, their suspicions of Smith were enough to keep them from supporting him. Illness conveniently forced Norbeck back to South Dakota for a rest during the campaign;

[27] "Why Progressives Should Vote for Smith," *The New Republic*, LVI (September 5, 1928), 58–60, and "Agitation Through Action" (September 12, 1928), 84–86; "Should Liberals Vote for Smith," *The Nation*, CXXVII (September 26, 1928), 284–85; and "The Dirtiest Political Campaign" (October 31, 1928), 440; Mercer G. Johnston, "Governor Smith Qualifies," *The People's Business* (October, 1928), I, in La Follette Family Papers, Series C, Box 425; "How They Will Vote," *The New Republic*, LVI (October 17, 1928), 245–46.

but, despite his preconvention attacks on Hoover, he stated publicly that he was not about "to bolt the Republican party this year. There is no place to go." Brookhart, Frazier, Howell, Nye, and Hiram Johnson joined Borah in announcing outright for Hoover. Although Johnson in one speech described Hoover as "one of the world's greatest leaders," the California Senator attempted to distinguish between his and Borah's support for the Republican candidate. According to Johnson, he was speaking for himself while Borah was following the commands of the national committee. "I shall not go outside of the state during the campaign, and in the state, while announcing myself for Mr. Hoover, and urging his election, I shall not stultify myself in any fashion. I am too old to be a Borah now." [28]

Johnson's comments told far more about him than Borah, however. No mere party loyalty or willingness to follow the dictates of the G.O.P. committee induced Borah to enter the national campaign with unprecedented vigor. He sincerely viewed "the success of Tammany in national politics as nothing less than a national disaster." A main theme of the speeches that he delivered during his exhausting stumping tour for Hoover in the fall centered on prohibition and the iniquitous city machine. Certainly what Montana's Senator Walsh described as "Borah's recent conversion to Hoover" sprang in large part from his own personal involvement in the cultural

[28] For La Follette's rejection of both candidates and pledge to fight only in support of progressive Congressmen, *The New York Times*, October 27, 1928; Johnson's quote on Hoover, *ibid.*, October 26, 1928, and comments on Borah, Johnson to Ickes, September 28, 1928, Ickes Papers, Box 3; on Norbeck, Gilbert C. Fite, *Peter Norbeck: Prairie Statesman* (Columbia, Mo., 1948), p. 134. Fite suspects that Smith's opposition to prohibition was a key determinant in Norbeck's refusal to support him. Although Blaine gave at least one speech aligning himself with Smith, and although Smith thanked him for his "attitude in the recent campaign," one critic charged him with playing "a weasel's game." Copy of Blaine's October 20, 1928, speech in Madison, and Smith to Blaine, December 1, 1928, John J. Blaine Papers (Wisconsin State Historical Society), Box 61. The criticism is in "The Progressives of the Senate," *The American Mercury*, XVI (April, 1928), 385.

struggle between city and country. He sharply disagreed with the views of Norris, himself a dry, that prohibition was a "sham battle" in the election which obscured more pressing economic issues; unlike the Nebraska Senator, he was not about to assume that Smith would, if elected, work out a satisfactory solution for law enforcement. Indeed, Borah's feelings about the campaign were so keen that on one occasion he startled Hoover by breaking into "a tirade against Norris," who had endorsed Smith.[29]

To those progressives who were less sensitive than Borah to the cultural conflict, it was difficult to understand why he could so actively champion Hoover when in 1919 he had strongly attacked Hoover's qualifications and performance as U.S. Food Administrator. At that time, Borah had accused him of malfeasance, extravagance, "perverted views of decency," and collusion with food-packers in the extortion of profits from farmers. Hoover had complained to Wilson that the "general mud bath" to which Borah and others were subjecting him was impeding his efforts to settle crucial food problems with the Allied governments. Now, in 1928, "Borah's Right-About Face" left Oswald Garrison Villard "shocked and pained and hurt." Villard had been among those who had looked to him "as a great national leader of the Progressive forces of the country." It was "nauseating" to see the man who had sharply criticized Hoover in public and private now saying that Hoover should lead the country. For this reason *The Nation* declared that Borah, "the sorriest figure in this campaign," could "no longer be carried on the roster of independents and Progressives."[30]

[29] Borah to Bronson Cutting, August 20, 1928, Borah Papers, Box 704; Tom Walsh to James H. Hawley, October 8, 1928, Walsh Papers, Box 377; *The New York Times*, October 25, 1928, for Norris's comments on Smith and prohibition and, for Norris's analysis of prohibition as "a sham battle," Norris to Clinton N. Howard, July 12, 1928, Norris Papers, Tray 8, Box 5; Herbert Hoover, *The Memoirs of Herbert Hoover* (New York, 1952), II, p. 174.

[30] Hoover to Woodrow Wilson, January 23, 1919, Hoover Papers, U.S. Food Administration Correspondence Files; on "Borah's Right-About

Ironically, Borah undoubtedly believed that he *was* battling for progressivism. When Ray McKaig warned him that Idaho progressives were becoming uneasy over Hoover's opposition to public ownership of water power, Borah replied, "You know precisely how I feel upon these matters but let us go through with the fight for *in the sum total it will be infinitely better for us all.*" He saw the Republicans "fighting the most persistently corrupt political machine in the whole history of our country (Tammany)." [31]

Time and again in his stump speeches for Hoover, the Senator inveighed against the evils of Tammany Hall graft and venality. He contrasted the machine-dominated Democracy with the G.O.P., "the great party of Lincoln, made up of millions of clean men and women," that would "continue to fight for the policies and the principles which have made this country great and powerful." He attacked Tammany for living "in close partnership with the saloon for 149 years" and for battling "against the control of the liquor traffic from the beginning of its history. . . ." He warned that Al Smith intended "to destroy the Eighteenth Amendment," the vehicle with which a great people were conducting a commendable social experiment. The prohibition issue, Borah told his audience, "involves not only the economic life but a moral life." For years men and women struggled to end "the great evil of the liquor traffic. . . . they fought on and on, believing, as they did, that they were fighting for the American home, and . . . for American civilization." Now, however, Governor Smith was out to

---

Face," Farmer-Labor Press Service release, October 1, 1928, Teigan Papers, Box 7; "Borah and Hoover," *The Nation,* CXXVII (November 7, 1928), 471, and (October 3, 1928), 307.

[31] Ray McKaig to Borah, October 25, 1928; Borah reply, October 26, 1928, Borah Papers, Box 294 (emphasis added); Borah to Bronson Cutting, August 20, 1929, Box 704. Borah regretted only that the Republicans had not rid themselves of the stigma of the Sinclair contribution. This meant that while the party fought Tammany, it did so "handicapped by a shameless period of corruption and by a refusal to purge the party at a time when it could be done."

destroy this experiment. It was Smith's Tammany group, moreover, that had opposed immigration restriction. "When the immigration law was before Congress, every member of Tammany there except one voted against it," Borah reminded his listeners. Tammany would allow "the poorly paid races of Southwestern Europe to enter this country. I can't conceive of anything more detrimental." [32]

Borah's exhausting ten-day swing for Hoover through Virginia, North Carolina, Kentucky, Tennessee, Texas, and Missouri was entirely his own idea. "I had to fight really to get to go as no one seemed to think anything could be accomplished. But I finally announced I was going." He looked back upon the stumping tour as "one of the finest campaign experiences in my whole life," and as "an experience which I shall never forget." The "gracious and warmhearted reception" that he received confirmed his belief that "they are a wonderful people and they have a wonderful country." [33]

The Democrats anxiously sent Virginia's Carter Glass in Borah's footsteps to counteract the Idahoan's influence on southern voters. Writing to Glass, North Carolina Senator Lee Overman reported that "the political situation in this section is extremely serious. . . . Borah spoke here last night and we need you to follow him up." Jesse Jones, wealthy Texas banker, volunteered to pay broadcasting expenses so that as much of Glass's speech as possible, "including that about Borah," would reach Texas. Despite such efforts, each of the southern and border states in which Borah spoke voted Republican. Obviously the Idahoan had not singlehandedly brought the states into the G.O.P., but he had certainly done the Republican

[32] Copies of Borah's Minneapolis speech, October 1, 1928, Borah Papers, Box 294, and his Richmond speech, October 15, 1928, Carter Glass Papers, Box 423; for his comments on immigration restriction, Kansas City *Star*, September 27, 1928, Borah Scrapbooks, Reel 6, and Baltimore *Sun*, November 1, 1928.

[33] Borah to Evan Evans, November 19, 1928, Borah Papers, Box 294; to J. G. Eimers, November 26, 1928, Box 291; to Alfred J. Dunn, November 21, 1928, Box 294; to Mrs. Mattie Rinard, November 28, 1928, Box 293.

cause no harm. His messages on prohibition, immigration, and
the evils of the New York political machine were not such as to
alienate many southerners. Judge William S. Kenyon, formerly
Borah's progressive colleague from Iowa in the Senate, saluted
him "as the conquerer of Texas. . . . You reversed a great
historic miracle and made water Republicans out of wine
Democrats." [34]

Borah considered the overwhelming decisiveness of Hoover's
November victory as "a blessing to the country." He had campaigned strenuously because he believed "sincerely that great
issues were involved." Confidently he predicted "that Mr.
Hoover will give us a great administration." Writing to National Committeeman Hilles, he asserted that "we have an
opportunity to put the Republican party in a position where
it can remain in power without much trouble for the next
twenty years." This future included the likelihood of building
a Republican south. [35]

The Senator undoubtedly hoped that the Republicans would
now be responsive to his kind of liberalism. Probably he believed that his work in the campaign had strengthened his
position in the party. News columnist David Lawrence was
certain that Borah was the new Republican leader. After being "off the reservation," the Senator had solidly fought for
Hoover and had in effect committed the new administration
to an extra session on farm relief and to a progressive approach

[34] Millard E. Tydings (Chairman of Speakers Bureau Democratic Headquarters) to Glass, October 18 and 27, 1928; Sam Rayburn to Glass, October 18, 1928; Jed C. Smith, National Committeeman from Texas, to Glass,
October 17, 1928; Lee Overman to Glass, October 17, 1928; Breckinridge
Long to Glass, October 30, 1928, Glass Papers, Box 253; William S. Kenyon to Borah, November 12, 1928, Borah Papers, Box 294. When Borah
left the south he correctly predicted to a newspaper reporter that the Republicans "would carry North Carolina, Florida, Kentucky, and Tennessee,
and that we have a fine chance in Texas and Virginia." Borah to J. H.
Peterson, November 9, 1928, Box 294. He had spoken in each of these
states, except Florida.
[35] Borah to Dwight Morrow, November 17, 1928, Borah Papers, Box
288; to Shad L. Hogdin, November 17, 1928, Box 283; to Charles D.
Hilles, November 7, 1928, Box 284.

to major policies. Hoover himself expressed appreciation for "the enormous effect" of his support. Hilles credited Borah with rendering "a service of incalculable value to the party and the country," while former party chairman Will Hays asserted melodramatically that "his speeches probably exerted a greater influence upon the electorate than was ever before exercised by a human voice in a political campaign." Insofar as Borah sought to influence his party's course, such compliments were certainly encouraging. "What a brave old lion you are!" exulted William Allen White. "How splendidly you waged the battle. You knew what the issue was when no one else did." [36]

Not all progressives agreed with White. To George Norris, for example, prohibition had not been a fundamental issue; more urgent was the Power Trust's exploitation of natural resources. Norris feared that Hoover's victory had dealt progressivism a harsh blow, "if indeed it is not absolutely defeated." *The Nation,* similarly discounting the importance of prohibition and Tammany, looked instead to "greater economic security for the worker . . . old age pensions, insurance against sickness, accident, and unemployment . . . [and] greater industrial democracy and greater economic justice." [37]

Borah and the other Senate progressives who endorsed Hoover were certainly in favor of greater economic justice, but to them it could never come at the expense of traditional values. And such values were, they firmly believed, very much

[36] Washington *Star,* January 5, 1929; Herbert Hoover to Borah, November 5, 1928; Charles D. Hilles to Borah, November 6, 1928; Will Hays to Borah, November 15, 1928, Borah Scrapbooks, Reel 6; William Allen White to Borah, November 9, 1928, Borah Papers, Box 294. The Hoover forces were genuinely pleased with Borah's performance. Walter H. Newton, director of the party's Speaker's Bureau, reported that the effectiveness of Borah's "tremendous" October 2 speech in Minneapolis "simply cannot be estimated." Newton telegram to Hoover, October 2, 1928. See, also, other telegrams in Hoover Papers, Campaign Correspondence, 1928, Box 1-H/57.

[37] Norris to W. T. Rawleigh, November 9, 1928, Norris Papers, Tray 1, Box 6; "The Real Issues of the Campaign," *The Nation,* CXXVII (October 24, 1928), 414.

at issue in 1928. The "Washington Correspondent" in *The American Mercury*, on the other hand, refused to find any honor in their position. With the exception of Norris, the Senate progressives were a "small forlorn and measly gang of false leaders. . . . They pather, trim and hedge." Their weaknesses had never been so apparent as during the recent campaign when "they all ran out—Norris excepted." In the Senate they lacked militancy, wailing and shaking heads but invariably "voting right." In sum, as progressives they were frauds. La Follette lacked his father's fighting zeal. Blaine was an opportunist with the views and abilities of a village lawyer. Nye was no threat to the Old Guard who found him pleasantly agreeable. Frazier had integrity but was easily confused; "a blast of hot air from a guileful opponent gets him all tangled up. . . ." Brookhart was gullible, "scatter-brained," and a man who loved public attention. Shipstead was notable as "a gas-bag without the gas"; he accomplished little beyond "colossal bombast" and boring speeches. "But the biggest sham of them all is the principle-peddler from Idaho, the Great God Borah," who had undermined progressivism more than all of the other progressive Senators together. "The list of his welchings is as long as his years of service in the Senate." To this reporter, Borah sadly represented "what Liberalism has come to in America." [38]

[38] "The Progressives of the Senate," pp. 385–93. A few weeks earlier, "T.R.B." had written a less vitriolic but highly critical assessment of the Senate progressives: "Sometimes it almost makes you weep to see the opportunities lost." The editors felt his portrait of the insurgents was "not inaccurate." *The New Republic*, LVIII (February 20, 1929), 2, 15–16. Ironically, the Senators' evaluations of each other were not much less scathing than those in *The American Mercury*. Norbeck asserted that Brookhart was simple-minded; "he is the most easily fooled man in Washington but does not realize it afterwards." (Norbeck to James Quigg, April 22, 1924, Norbeck Papers [South Dakota], and to G. J. Moen, April 20, 1929, Norbeck Papers [Missouri], Folder 6). Hiram Johnson noted Borah's "egregious vanity and overwhelming conceit," and described Brookhart as "a great, big simpleton." (Johnson to Ickes, July 2, 1925, Ickes Papers, Box 2, and to Hiram Jr., March 29, 1926, Johnson Papers, Part IV, Box 3.) Borah charged Johnson with "trimming" (Lincoln Colcord to Villard,

Despite such criticism, Borah ended the year in good spirits, convinced that he had fought on the side of principle and had served progressivism well. All was not perfect, but he was sufficiently satisfied to write that "the New Year of 1929 begins in the most exhilarating period of the world's history." [39] The appearance of *The American Mercury*'s critique of the progressive Senators probably did not greatly disturb him. After all, that journal belonged to the crowd of H. L. Mencken—an iconoclast and an urbanite who enjoyed lampooning prohibition and baiting the "yokels" of agrarian America.

December 16, 1919, Villard Papers, Folder 655), while Norris believed that the Californian "did not measure up to what his prior record indicated it would be" (Norris to Rev. B. F. Eberhart, March 8, 1924, Norris Papers, Tray 2, Box 1). La Follette, Jr., was convinced on one occasion that Norris "for personal reasons" was avoiding a necessary legislative battle (La Follette to Phil and Isen La Follette, January 25, 1927, La Follette Family Papers, Series A, Box 35).

[39] Borah telegram to New York *World,* December 28, 1928, Borah Papers, Box 299.

Epilogue

❦

WHEN *The Nation* decided in October, 1928, to remove Borah's name from its progressive roster, it was obviously an indication of dissatisfaction with the Senator; but it was also an act of frustration in a world that seemed to have rejected progressivism. Shortly before, William Allen White had raised a question reminiscent of *The Survey*'s famous query several years earlier: "Why is it that the people are deaf to the cause of reform? . . . I don't know. I'm all unsettled and confused." Most of the prewar reformers shared White's confusion and—although their explanations of the problem differed—they agreed generally with Harold Ickes that "this isn't the day for our kind of politics." [1]

Events and decisions of the postwar decade had completed the dissolution of the progressive consensus. The deaths of familiar leaders such as Roosevelt, Wilson, Bryan, and La Follette created problems of command. The Red Scare and the general affluence of the "New Era" exacted a heavy toll on reform enthusiasm. Some progressives retreated at least temporarily to private life; Frederick Howe, for example, wearied of working with political movements, defined liberalism as "open-mindedness," and turned momentarily to cultivating the inner spirit. The 1922 election failed to initiate the anticipated major reform upheaval. La Follette's 1924 movement was more a display of weakness than strength, and even it had quickly

---

[1] *The Nation*, CXXVII (October 3, 1928), 307; White's letter to Basil Manly, quoted in *The People's Business* (June, 1927), 1, La Follette Family Papers, Series C, Box 425; Ickes to Hiram Johnson, September 3, 1927, Ickes Papers, Box 3.

dissolved. Coolidge's appointment of Warren, his interventions in Latin America, and his inability and unwillingness to direct his party and Congress undoubtedly confounded those reformers who initially attempted to place him in the progressive tradition. The Senate progressive bloc, despite its publicity, proved ineffective due to the lack of Democratic support and its own suspicions and divisions. The 1928 election hopelessly dispersed liberal forces. By the late Twenties some reformers found solace only in making themselves better individuals or looking to the future when, as Basil Manly envisioned it, "a new liberal, progressive organization" with a long-range program and "a magnetic leader" would once again unite the nation around progressive ideals.[2] Ironically, however, when that new reform coalition and charismatic leader emerged during the crises of the Thirties, many progressives discovered that this was not what they had expected at all. In an important sense they had looked "backward into the future," projecting memories surrounding the prewar reform movement onto the horizon and using past experience as a blueprint for the coming age.

It may have been for precisely this reason that Senator Borah had loomed so large in their discussions, hopes, and ultimately their disappointments. Oswald Garrison Villard, Basil Manly, Frank Kent, and Hiram Johnson were just a few of the progressives who felt that the Senator's refusal to assume responsible leadership had greatly handicapped the reform movements of the 1920's. Significantly, their frustrations and criticism of him focused on his unpredictability and timidity—his "hesitation waltz," as Raymond Robins described it [3]—rather than on the content of his progressivism, on his reform perspectives, on his vision of the good America, or on his ideas and ideals. It was, after all, none other than Hiram Johnson who dubbed

[2] See Manly's analysis of progressive problems and needs in *The People's Business* (June, 1927). Frederick Howe describes his retreat from external to personal reform in *The Confessions of a Reformer,* esp. pp. 339–43.

[3] Robins to Levinson, September 27, 1924, Levinson Papers, Box 76.

him "our spearless leader." And Johnson was no more willing than Borah to "cut loose" from the bedrock principles of the older, village America and the principles of Jeffersonian liberalism.

Many of Borah's weaknesses as a progressive leader in the Twenties were endemic to the prewar progressivism. Indeed, his appeal to liberals in the "New Era" rested substantially on his ability to invoke the turn-of-the-century reform tradition. As Walter Lippmann realized, the Senator was representative of "grass roots progressivism." In the words of another columnist, Borah belonged "in spirit to those days before 1912 when the people are supposed to rise every morning with a new determination to improve the world." [4]

Borah represented only a short step in American reform beyond the great spokesman for rural America, William Jennings Bryan. Even their backgrounds were strikingly similar. They had spent their boyhoods a few miles apart in Illinois and, although as youths they never met, their fathers had been friends and often discussed the scriptures. Borah and Bryan reflected the impact of the cultural patterns of the Middle Border. Both rose to fame in part because of their oratorical abilities. Both spurned tobacco and liquor and supported prohibition. Both aspired to the White House, although Bryan was by far the more diligent campaigner and came much closer to succeeding. Each remained within his party, trying to influence the direction in which it moved, attempting to purify it and make it more responsive to the people. Both evinced the attitudes and commitments of village America. And both men were intense moralists with tendencies toward self-righteousness. "Borah," as one newspaper described him, "has that vital spiritual quality that kept William Jennings Bryan in his unrivaled place of moral leadership from 1896 until he died." [5] But if Borah re-

[4] Walter Lippmann, "Borah Versus President," New York *Herald Tribune*, April 18, 1936, Borah Scrapbooks, Reel 3; clipping from Chicago *Journal*, February 7, 1929, Borah Papers, Box 304.

[5] *The Christian Herald*, July 2, 1928, Borah Scrapbooks, Reel 6.

sembled Bryan, so too did the Senate progressives in general, none of whom represented a very long step away from the Great Commoner.

Nor did Borah's individualistic tendencies place him outside the progressive orbit. Later, Alfred Landon of Kansas would classify him as a prima donna because of his aversion to the details of organization, both in Idaho and Capitol Hill. Landon nonetheless carefully pointed out that in this respect the Idahoan was like Hiram Johnson and Woodrow Wilson. They "had the greatest opportunity that ever came to three men since the invention of the printing press. And they couldn't work it out, because they couldn't work with anyone else." [6]

Ironically, the very lone-wolf qualities that helped limit Borah's effectiveness as a leader were high among the attributes that earned him so much respect. Undoubtedly many liberals in the discouraging years after World War I found him appealing because, as Raymond Clapper observed toward the close of Borah's life, "he, perhaps more than any other great public figure of our own times, was entirely his own man." [7] There was an undeniable attractiveness in a man who sought to follow his own conscience, who spurned social climbing, and who refused to become an organization man.

In fundamental ways—in his actions, bearing, and appearance—the Senator symbolized that rugged individualism which many Americans valued so highly and which had supplied a potent theme within prewar progressivism. To George Norris, the very essence of progressivism was this ability to be true to one's self. Shrugging aside the lack of agreement among Senate liberals, Norris wrote that "one of the very foundations for which the Progressive cause stands is that every man, whether he be an official or a private citizen, should vote his conscientious convictions and should not be controlled or influ-

[6] Landon to Raymond Clapper, March 29, 1940, Landon Papers, Box "Political, 1940, Washington D.C."

[7] Unpublished column, dated February 2, 1939, but held for release, Raymond Clapper Papers (Library of Congress), Box 107.

enced by any machine, organization or political boss." When
Gerald Nye discussed the contribution of the Senate progressives to American politics, he stressed the "service of independence" which they provided. Hiram Johnson wished for more
unity among progressives, yet at the same time he "expected
in the few years remaining to continue to be a block [*sic*] of
one, and to walk alone in my own path. . . . I am going
ahead in my own fashion and do as I damn please." One of
Johnson's explanations for his independent course was that he
"couldn't follow the recognized leader of Progressives, the
great Senator from Idaho"; but this alone hardly accounted for
Johnson's general inclination to work alone. Peter Norbeck,
who applauded the Senate progressives for being more intelligent and fair than any other group in Congress, believed nonetheless that the essential differences between party regulars and
the progressives was that "the progressives will not work together, they are jealous of each other." Pointing to the divisions
among them, Norbeck noted, "They are so individualistic you
know." [8]

There were thus good reasons why Landon could write about
prima donnas in the progressive movement and why Frank
Kent could say, "There are too many stars in the Progressive
troupe. . . . Each plays his own game." [9] But, to a Borah or a
Norris or a Hiram Johnson, to have had it any other way
would have been at the expense of progressivism itself. Insofar
as Borah's individualism limited his potential as a reform
leader, it was symptomatic of problems within Senate progressive leadership in general.

[8] Norris to Henry Field, April 16, 1932, Norris Papers, Tray 5, Box 3;
Nye's October 15, 1928, radio speech endorsing Henrik Shipstead for re-
election, Gerald P. Nye Papers (Herbert Hoover Presidential Library),
Box 31; Johnson to Harold Ickes, March, 1931, Ickes Papers, Box 3; and
to Bronson Cutting, October 18, 1932, Cutting Papers, Box 10; Norbeck
to W. H. King, April 16, 1921, and to Kent E. Keller, December 20, 1929,
Norbeck Papers (South Dakota).

[9] Landon to Raymond Clapper, March 29, 1940, Landon Papers, Box
"Political, 1940, Washington D.C."; Frank Kent, "The Reconstruction of
Herbert Hoover," *Scribner's Magazine*, XCI (May, 1932), 259.

Perhaps more than other Senate progressives, however, Borah turned a tendency into a way of life. He so isolated himself and was such a political maverick that potential disciples were unsure what to expect. He was, in Raymond Robins's words, "so uncertain a quantity." Although the Senator was affable, warm, and kind, he was also aloof, detached, and distant. William Allen White recalled that Borah, during his brief stay at the University of Kansas, "just didn't jell as a collegiate character"; instead, he resembled "a big Newfoundland dog among smaller and more agile pups, who is good-natured so long as he is not disturbed." [10]

In the Senate, Hiram Johnson initially "felt closer to him than to any other man" in that body. Johnson at first saw him a great deal, liked him very much, felt they had lots in common, and respected his "real 'guts,'" his eloquence, and his "exceptional ability." But the Californian also found him "a very, very strange character . . . so temperamental, that he generally goes alone." Indeed, "he plays an absolutely lone hand . . . does not mix socially at all, and mixes even little in the Senate during its sessions." By 1921, four years after Johnson entered the Senate, he was "endeavoring to maintain our intimacy" but found Borah "as responsive as cold marble, and it has been hard work constantly to be the one to make the advances." [11]

Borah's aloofness need not in itself have detracted greatly from his potential as a progressive spokesman. The strength of his commitments to principle, his power of persuasion, his positions on important questions could—and did—evoke much enthusiasm among reformers. But when he wavered in his com-

[10] Robins to Levinson, December 11, 1925, Levinson Papers, Box 76; White quoted in Johnson, *Borah of Idaho*, p. 18. For examples of men who admired Borah greatly but despaired over his leadership abilities, see William E. Sweet (ex-governor of Colorado) to Villard, February 22, 1930, Villard Papers, Folder 3766, and Henry J. Allen (ex-governor of Kansas) to Frank Gannett, January 9, 1936, Henry J. Allen Papers (Library of Congress), Box C-3.

[11] Johnson to Sons, September 8, 1921, Johnson Papers, Part IV, Box 2.

mitments, and when he continually substituted rhetoric for
action, the political results were devastating.

His reluctance to "cut loose" inspired descriptions of him
as a halfback who gained much ground in midfield but lacked
punch at the goal line, as a slugger who hit more home runs
than anyone else on Capitol Hill but never got beyond first
base, as a man who spoke for righteousness, voted with the boys
and burst into tears, and as the human equivalent of the MGM
lion—only the growl was there. Senator Norbeck, who initially
applauded Borah's courage, finally threw up his hands in dismay: "Nobody knows what he is going to do." [12]

Despite Borah's limitations as a progressive leader, he was a
pivotal figure during the Twenties. Herbert Hoover, although
still bitter over Borah's political conduct during his administration, conceded in 1933 that "when his voice was raised
against injustice, it was one of the most powerful voices of
our period." The Senator eloquently drew upon an inveterate
liberal heritage that stressed individualism in opposition to
all concentration of power and special privilege. In a time of
growing complexity, he articulated old principles based on
simple morality and justice. In a period of growing organizational threats to the ordinary citizen, he talked of his desire
"to encourage young men who say, 'I've got no means, I've got
no organization. What can I ever hope to do in public life that
will amount to something?' " Borah hoped with genuine sincerity "to show them what certain builders and shapers of
government and molders of opinion accomplished through the
sheer power of agitation. I want to show them the power of a

[12] Richard L. Neuberger to John P. Robertson, November 12, 1935,
Norris Papers, Tray 97, Box 4; Wile Scrapbooks, July 7, 1926, 21; Hamilton Owen of the Baltimore *Sun,* quoted in Gerald Johnson, "Gentleman
from Idaho," *The New Republic,* CXLIV (June 12, 1961), 18; the southern liberal Charles Ervin on the similarity between Borah and the MGM
lion in Graham, *Encore for Reform,* p. 182; Norbeck to Kent Keller,
March 9, 1922, Norbeck Papers (Missouri), Folder 2, and to Keller, December 20, 1929 (South Dakota).

man with an idea." And he offered as proof the example of himself—Borah of Idaho, "the Crusoe of the Senate." [13]

Even after *The Nation* had rejected his progressive credentials in 1928, he quickly re-emerged as one of the most publicized Senate insurgents, inflicting upon "the Hoover administration more damage than any individual not paid for it." In 1931, at a large gathering of progressives reminiscent of the conferences in December, 1922, he was again a prominent figure. Indeed, he carried his progressive reputation with him throughout the Thirties, fighting corruption, centralized power, foreign entanglements, and crusading for a Republican party of "the people" rather than "the interests." [14]

He sensed that all was not well. For one thing, there was the New Deal, substantial parts of which he opposed because its increases in federal power and bureaucracy seemed to jeopardize the concept of separation of powers and local government.

[13] Hoover's June 4, 1933, manuscript on Borah, Hoover Papers, Box 1-K/14; Borah quoted in James O'Donnell Bennett, "Presidential Possibilities: Borah," *Liberty*, March 3, 1928, p. 34, in Borah Scrapbooks, Reel 2; clipping from R. M. Washburn's column, December 31, 1925, Borah Papers, Box 269, for the description of him as "Crusoe." Walter Lippmann, New York *Herald Tribune*, April 18, 1936, Borah Scrapbooks, Reel 3, is especially good on Borah's link with the American liberal tradition.

[14] Frank Kent, "The Next President," *Scribner's Magazine*, XCII (November, 1932), 259. For Hoover's description of Borah's "capacity for political mischief-making," see Hoover's June 4, 1933, manuscript on Borah, Hoover Papers, Box 1-K/14. Hoover wrote, for example: "His mind was confused as to the confidential character of many discussions, and leaks at his press conferences as to the policies of the Administration which he gleaned from these frank discussions were often most embarrassing." By late 1930 Hoover apparently believed that Borah bore a grudge against him and was plotting with other progressives to launch a third party. See Jordan A. Schwarz, *The Interregnum of Despair: Hoover, Congress, and the Depression* (Urbana, Ill., 1970), p. 51. On the Progressive Conference of 1931, see copy of the "Proceedings" in Norris Papers, Ac. 6900, Tag No. 49, Box 20, and numerous clippings in Tray 8, Box 4. For a "confidential" list of those attending the conference, see memo from "M.O." to Edward Costigan, July 24, 1931, Edward P. Costigan Papers (University of Colorado Library), Box 33. Borah served as chairman of the Committee on Agriculture and addressed the conference on March 11, charging Hoover with failing to come to grips with the farm problem.

For another, the "fatal trek" to the cities continued at a growing rate, rapidly transforming the face of the continent. Also,
the Kellogg Peace Pact, which he had defended in 1929 as the
grand culmination of the Outlawry of War effort,[15] appeared
increasingly impotent in the face of aggressive nationalism.

In 1936, Borah, now in his seventies and obviously worried
about the course of events, made his only formal bid for the
Republican presidential nomination. Hiram Johnson believed
that his lack of success left him "very bitter and really quite
stunned." Although Johnson was often indignant with him, he
confessed feeling pity "for him in his old age, with his old fight
and eloquence lacking, just wandering around imagining that
all that was necessary for his success was to say he was a candidate," and conducting his campaign "in an archaic fashion of
a half a century ago." To Johnson, Borah's efforts were both
futile and tragic: "He has seen himself always as such a great
figure; his vanity has been so nourished by abnormal publicity;
his threats in the past have apparently been so effective, that
he cannot understand that he has now even little or no nuisance
value." In 1937, a bewildered Borah referred to the years since
1912 as "the Gethsemane through which humanity has passed.
They have been mad, confusing, discouraging years." [16]

Borah bridged reform eras, but emotionally and intellectually he belonged with the older prewar America. As New Deal

[15] Charles G. Dawes wrote that "Borah has won his fight and to him
should go credit, both for his masterful leadership and conduct of debate
on the floor and for the last addendum which turned the scale." *Notes
as Vice President, 1928–1929* (Boston, 1935), p. 236. Maddox, *William E.
Borah and American Foreign Policy,* doubts that Borah ever had much
faith in Outlawry itself but used it skillfully to block other proposals that
might entangle America in European affairs. See esp. pp. 135–36, 179–82.
The problem was, though, that with Outlawry unsheathed in 1929, Borah
had to look elsewhere for alternatives to American embroilments abroad
as the international crises of the Thirties threatened to involve the nation
in war.

[16] Johnson to Hiram, Jr., May 9 and 15, 1936, Johnson Papers, Part IV,
Box 4; reprint of Borah's September 16, 1937, address on "Constitutional
Government," p. 12, Borah Papers, Box 12.

enthusiast Edgar Kemler observed, he "was overtaken by obsolescence at an early age," belonging to the moralistic prewar progressives, standing with "cogs blunted and . . . pipes rusted," clinging to "their vestigial reputations." To later reformers such as Kemler, with different perspectives and dreams, the Borahs, the "annual contests with the saloon," the steadfast faith in old values and certainties, the easy distinctions between "the people" and "the interests," and the evangelical reform fervor of prewar progressivism seemed naive and fatuous.[17] It was easy to forget that the Idaho Senator had once loomed as a "Moses" to reformers and as the man who held the key to the future of American liberalism.

Following World War I massive changes—industrial, technological, urban, population, and moral—had jarred the nation with tremendous force. In view of such rapid shocks, Rexford Tugwell described the Twenties as the longest decade in history, and in 1933 one of Coolidge's ex-secretaries commented that Coolidge's administration was as far away as McKinley's. Yet Borah, still attached to the visions and ideas of an earlier period, was able to write confidently in late 1927: "I cannot think of any views which I now have that I did not have before the war." [18]

Events simply swept by him. In 1936, *Time* magazine, calling him "the most famed Senator of this century," concluded that "for a generation Borah was the great Moral Force of the Senate, the one member who could arise and deal with Right

[17] Edgar Kemler, *The Deflation of American Ideals, An Ethical Guide for New Dealers* (Baltimore, Md., 1941), pp. 73, 104–8. Even before World War I, of course, a number of intellectuals had turned from the innocence of the prewar progressivism. See Henry May, *The End of American Innocence* (New York, 1959), and Christopher Lasch, *The New Radicalism in America, 1889–1963* (paperback ed.: New York, 1967), esp. pp. 251–54.

[18] Tugwell's comment on the Twenties in Graham, *Encore for Reform*, p. 186; Edward T. Clark to William E. Brigham, February 17, 1933, Edward T. Clark Papers (Library of Congress), Box 2; Borah to Rev. Charles Clayton Morrison, October 12, 1927, Borah Papers, Box 275.

and Wrong in an electric way. Now the conscience of the country has been placed in other pockets." [19]

In the early evening of a bitterly cold January 15, 1940, Borah left his office on Capitol Hill for the last time. Under trees laden with ice, he trudged through the snow in Plaza Park, his shoulders somewhat bent, his long, greying hair hanging shaggily over his collar. The next morning he collapsed in his apartment from a brain hemorrhage. "Of course," Hiram Johnson wrote his son three days later, "the absorbing news here is Borah. He is dying. It may be that this is his last afternoon." It was. Before the day ended, Borah was dead. Shortly thereafter, long-time Washington news columnist Raymond Clapper viewed the Republican party with despair and asserted that "there are no fighters on the progressive side—no men like T.R. . . . Borah was the last." [20]

[19] "Long Ago and Far Away," *Time*, XXVII (March 30, 1936), 21–22.
[20] "Man in a Toga," *Time*, XXXV (January 29, 1940), 18–19; Johnson to Hiram, Jr., January 19, 1940, Johnson Papers, Part IV, Box 4; Raymond Clapper to E. H. Taylor, March 20, 1940, copy in Landon Papers, Box "Political, 1940, Washington D.C."

BIBLIOGRAPHICAL
ESSAY

🏵

Manuscript Collections

This list is provided for reference convenience. The manuscripts are discussed in the bibliographical essay.

Allen, Henry J., Papers, Library of Congress.
Beveridge, Albert J., Papers, Library of Congress.
Blaine, John J., Papers, Wisconsin State Historical Society.
Borah, William E., Papers and Scrapbooks, Library of Congress.
Borglum, Gutzon, Papers, Library of Congress.
Capper, Arthur, Papers, Kansas State Historical Society.
Castle, William R., Jr., Papers, Herbert Hoover Presidential Library.
Clapper, Raymond, Papers, Library of Congress.
Clark, Edward T., Papers, Library of Congress.
Coolidge, Calvin, Papers, Library of Congress.
Costigan, Edward P., Papers, University of Colorado Library.
Couzens, James, Papers, Library of Congress.
Culbertson, William S., Papers, Library of Congress.
Cutting, Bronson M., Papers, Library of Congress.
Garfield, James R., Papers, Library of Congress.
Glass, Carter, Papers, University of Virginia Library.
Hadley, Herbert, Papers, Western Manuscripts Division, University of Missouri.
Hagedorn, Hermann, Papers, Library of Congress.
Haines, Lynn, Papers, Minnesota State Historical Society.
Harding, Warren G., Papers, Ohio State Historical Society.
Hilles, Charles D., Papers, Yale University Library.
Hirth, William, Papers, Western Manuscripts Division, University of Missouri.
Hoover, Herbert, Papers, Herbert Hoover Presidential Library.
Ickes, Harold, Papers, Library of Congress.

Jardine, William M., Papers, Library of Congress.
Johnson, Hiram, Papers, Bancroft Library, University of California.
Johnston, Mercer Green, Papers, Library of Congress.
Kellogg, Frank B., Papers, Minnesota State Historical Society.
Kent, Frank, Papers, Maryland State Historical Society.
King, Judson, Papers, Library of Congress.
La Follette (Robert M.) Family Papers, Library of Congress.
La Guardia, Fiorello, Papers, Municipal Archives, New York City.
Landon, Alfred M., Papers, Kansas State Historical Society.
Lenroot, Irvine, Papers, Library of Congress.
Levinson, Salmon O., Papers, University of Chicago Library.
McNary, Charles L., Papers, Library of Congress.
Norbeck, Peter, Papers, University of South Dakota Library and
    Western Manuscripts Division, University of Missouri.
Norris, George W., Papers, Library of Congress.
Nye, Gerald P., Papers, Herbert Hoover Presidential Library.
Peek, George N., Papers, Western Manuscripts Division, University
    of Missouri.
Pepper, George Wharton, Papers, Charles Patterson Van Pelt Li-
    brary, University of Pennsylvania.
Pinchot, Amos, Papers, Library of Congress.
Robins, Raymond, Papers, Wisconsin State Historical Society.
Root, Elihu, Papers, Library of Congress.
Shipstead, Henrik, Papers, Minnesota State Historical Society.
Spingarn, Arthur B., Papers, Library of Congress.
Storey, Moorfield, Papers, Library of Congress.
Strauss, Oscar, Papers, Library of Congress.
Taft, William Howard, Papers, Library of Congress.
Teigan, Henry G., Papers, Minnesota State Historical Society.
Villard, Oswald Garrison, Papers, Houghton Library, Harvard
    University.
Wadsworth, James W., Papers, Library of Congress.
Walsh, Thomas J., Papers, Library of Congress.
White, William Allen, Papers, Library of Congress.
Wile, Frederick W., Scrapbooks, Library of Congress.

Primary Sources

Manuscripts provided the bulk of the material for this study. The William E. Borah Papers (Library of Congress) are massive, comprising more than 700 file boxes for his senatorial career. Despite its size, the collection is of varied quality. Borah almost never discussed his feelings about his senatorial colleagues or the workings of Senate politics. He had no person to whom he poured out his inner feelings on paper. Most of the letters are brief replies to constituents, and tend to be repetitious. Yet occasionally there are very useful bits of information. The Borah–J. A. H. Hopkins exchanges in 1922–23 and Borah's letters to Ray McKaig and to James H. Hawley in 1926–27 are good examples of correspondence that provide insights into his political views and strategies. Of considerable aid are the Borah Scrapbooks (LC), on microfilm, which contain an abundance of clippings—both friendly and unfriendly to him.

Several collections are invaluable for any study of Borah in the Twenties. The Salmon O. Levinson Papers (University of Chicago Library) contain two boxes of correspondence with Raymond Robins, most of it during the years between 1923 and 1927. Robins had frequent visits with the Senator and reported these conversations to Levinson in long, immensely informative letters. The major theme in these communications is Outlawry of War, but there is also a good deal on Borah's political maneuverings and attitudes. Hiram Johnson's Papers (Bancroft Library, University of California, Berkeley) are also extremely valuable particularly for the years from 1918 to 1924. Johnson wrote lengthy "diary" letters to his sons describing Senate activities and characterizing a number of Senators. During Johnson's first years in Washington, he wrote often (some letters run more than fifteen pages) about national politics. There are many revealing references to Borah. Since Johnson tended to be increasingly jealous of the Idahoan, the letters must be read with caution; nonetheless, they provide excellent assessments of Borah and corroborate in a number of ways the views that other leading progressives developed toward him. As Johnson became more involved in the Senate, his diary letters became less frequent and are not as useful from the mid-Twenties on; still, these letters—plus others in his general correspondence files—make the Johnson collection of major importance to historians of recent American political history.

In Herbert Hoover's Papers (Hoover Presidential Library, West Branch, Iowa) there is some enlightening material, especially Hoover's intriguing thirteen-page evaluation of Borah, dated June 4, 1933. This document is far more useful regarding Borah than are the Hoover *Memoirs*. Although the Raymond Robins Papers (Wisconsin State Historical Society) are somewhat disappointing, particularly in view of the immensely informative letters from him in the Levinson collection, there are several good items relating to the Senator.

Manuscripts which are excellent on progressivism in the Twenties are those of Amos Pinchot (LC), Oswald Garrison Villard (Houghton Library, Harvard University), and the Robert M. La Follette Family (LC). All of these collections contain numerous communications from other outstanding reformers, and include many references to Borah. The recently opened La Follette papers are voluminous, and well indexed. They contain exceptionally good material on such groups as the Committee of 48 and the People's Legislative Service (including many copies of *The People's Business*), as well as many illuminating letters from leading progressives. The James R. Garfield Papers (LC) also provide perspective on progressivism, although there is little information specifically about Borah. Also useful are the collections of Mercer Green Johnston (LC)—which has folders concerning the Wheeler Defense Committee and the Committee of 48 and contains several copies of the *Voice of the People,* a reform journal—and of Fiorello La Guardia (Municipal Archives, New York City), which contains a number of informative exchanges relating to problems confronting reformers in the Twenties. Particularly helpful for western progressivism are the papers of Gutzon Borglum (LC), Lynn Haines (Minnesota State Historical Society) (which have some significant letters regarding Borah and the Committee of 48), Henry G. Teigan (Minnesota State Historical Society), William S. Culbertson (LC), and William Allen White (LC). The Henry J. Allen Papers (LC) contain material on the Kansas Court of Industrial Relations and movements of some former Bull Moose Progressives in 1919-20;

there are also some communications regarding Borah's 1936 presidential bid, and several letters between Allen and Joseph Bristow which provide superb examples of the agonies of several old progressives during the New Deal.

The papers of Senators vary greatly. Especially good are those of Hiram Johnson and Peter Norbeck. Norbeck's collection (University of South Dakota Library) has indispensable information on the efforts of the western Senate bloc in 1927 and has numerous perceptive appraisals of Senators, including Borah. There are also ten folders of copies of Norbeck's correspondence in the Western Manuscripts Division, University of Missouri Library. The large George W. Norris collection (LC) is quite valuable. Norris, much more than Borah, wrote informative letters on the state of Senate affairs and on his own feelings. The Bronson M. Cutting Papers (LC) include several items concerning Borah and Senate progressivism. Gerald P. Nye's Papers (Herbert Hoover Presidential Library) are thin on correspondence, but contain some useful letters regarding his commitment to progressive ideas and La Follette in 1924, several folders on his Senate seating contest (1925–26), and clippings on the 1927 progressive bloc. The collections of Irvine Lenroot (LC) and James W. Wadsworth, Jr. (LC) are helpful on several key issues of the New Era and have several informative letters on Republican politics. Carter Glass's Papers (University of Virginia Library) are good regarding the Democratic reaction to Borah's stump for Hoover through the south in 1928. The George Wharton Pepper Papers (Charles Patterson Van Pelt Library, University of Pennsylvania) are quite good on labor but contain little on Borah. Very disappointing are the collections of James Couzens (LC), mostly letters from his financial secretary about private business matters; Henrik Shipstead (Minnesota State Historical Society), of little use at all; John J. Blaine (Wisconsin State Historical Society), mostly concerned with patronage matters; Thomas J. Walsh (LC), a large collection but not very enlightening on Senate politics; Charles L. McNary, quite thin on the New Era; Arthur Capper (Kansas State Historical Society), with only the most routine kind of correspondence; and Edward P. Costigan (University of Colorado Library), with few personal letters relating to Senate activities.

On politics in general the William Howard Taft Papers (LC) are superior. Taft's own observations, plus the letters he received from people such as Charles Dewey Hilles on the Republican National Committee, are extremely helpful although they diminish in value in the late 1920's. Taft referred quite often to Borah. The Hilles Papers (Sterling Library, Yale University) are also good on Republican national politics and include a number of letters regarding Borah. The collection of Alfred M. Landon (Kansas State Historical Society) includes a number of illuminating references to Borah from the mid-30's until the Idahoan's death. There is scattered information on Borah in the collections of Calvin Coolidge (LC) and Warren G. Harding (Ohio State Historical Society); for politics in general the Harding papers are the more revealing. The Harold Ickes Papers (LC) provide insights into New Era politics and include several folders of letters from Hiram Johnson; neither was fond of Borah and both made numerous evaluations of him.

Several newspaper columnists supply information about Borah. The Raymond Clapper Papers (LC) contain several quite useful items and the Frederick William Wile Scrapbooks (LC) assemble the articles that Wile wrote, many of which are good on Borah. The Frank Kent Papers (Maryland State Historical Society) are very disappointing.

Other manuscripts consulted include those of Edward T. Clarke (LC), Coolidge's secretary, which have a few political items; Herbert Hadley (Western Manuscripts Division, University of Missouri), an early associate of Borah but who was concerned mainly with state matters in the Twenties; Hermann Hagedorn (LC), with information on Borah's position regarding Coolidge's appointment of Dwight Morrow to Mexico in 1927; William Hirth (Western Manuscripts Division, University of Missouri), which, considering the several good letters in the George Norris Papers regarding Borah, is disappointing in general on the New Era; William M. Jardine (LC), mostly newspaper clippings and copies of speeches which have nothing on Borah but do present the Coolidge administration's agricultural policies; Frank B. Kellogg (Minnesota State Historical Society), disappointing during Kellogg's tenure both as Senator and as Secretary of State; Judson King (LC), helpful on civil liberties in the early 20's; Elihu Root (LC), which has some correspondence on New Era politics and a few references to Borah; Arthur P. Spingarn (LC), which includes several illuminating remarks relating to Borah's position on civil rights; Moorfield

Storey (LC), useful on Borah and the opposition to American intervention in Haiti and Santo Domingo; Oscar Straus (LC), with some interesting items on progressivism but almost nothing on Borah; and William R. Castle, Jr. (Herbert Hoover Presidential Library), with correspondence relating to diplomatic problems in the Twenties and some unfavorable references to Borah's attack on Coolidge's Latin-American involvements.

Several journals were of special importance for this study. On progressivism in the Twenties, *The Nation* and *The New Republic* are essential. Also of considerable value is *The Searchlight on Congress* (called *The Spotlight* from July 1, 1923–November, 1923), a monthly edited by Lynn Haines of the Committee of 48 and including much information on congressional activities. Haines cheered the efforts of the Senate insurgents. *Survey* has a number of articles concerning reform, especially the much-cited "Where Are the Pre-War Radicals" (February 1, 1926). *The Independent,* which in mid-1922 officially aligned itself with the Republican party, has numerous discussions of politics and Borah. *The Literary Digest* is especially good for its gathering of quotes from other sources. *The Outlook* and *The World's Work* are other standard journals of the period.

Among newspapers, *The New York Times,* because of its elaborate index and broad coverage, is of inestimable value. The Baltimore *Sun* is particularly good on politics in the New Era, largely because of the Washington reporting of John W. Owens and the columns of Frank Kent and H. L. Mencken. Columnists who were especially informative in the New Era were Clinton W. Gilbert (*New York Post*), Mark Sullivan (New York *Herald Tribune*), Charles Michelson (New York *World*), Norman Hapgood (Washington *Herald*), James O'Donnell Bennett (Chicago *Tribune*), and Edward Whiting (Boston *Herald*). *The Idaho Daily Statesman* is invaluable on Idaho politics. A number of other newspapers proved useful on specific topics, such as the Senate rejection of Charles Beecher Warren and the attempts to form the Senate progressive bloc in 1927; these included *The Washington Post,* the Washington *Star,* and the New York *Sun.*

Secondary Materials

William E. Leuchtenburg's essay on Borah in *Dictionary of American Biography*, supplement 2 (New York, 1958), pp. 49–53, is a superb biographical sketch of the Senator. Two full-scale biographies of Borah are Claudius Johnson, *Borah of Idaho* (New York, 1936; reprinted with a new introduction, "Borah of Idaho: His Last Years and a Re-Evaluation," by University of Washington Press Americana Library, 1967), and Marian McKenna, *Borah* (Ann Arbor, Mich., 1961). Both are based largely on the Borah Papers and supply much information about the Senator's activities. Neither, however, draws upon numerous other manuscript collections and neither takes the particular focus of this study. On Johnson's book, see the interesting review by Oswald Garrison Villard, "Borah, the Great Mystery Man," *The Nation*, CXLII (June 3, 1936), 718–19. See, also, Johnson, "Borah's Bequest to Democracy," *Idaho Yesterdays*, I (Winter, 1958), 11–20.

More recent interpretations are John M. Cooper, Jr.,'s provocative "William E. Borah, Political Thespian," *Pacific Northwest Quarterly*, LVI (October, 1965), 145–53. I think that Cooper is largely correct in his assessment of the Senator, but see the comments by Claudius Johnson and Merle W. Wells, pp. 153–57. Also provocative—and I believe on target—is Robert J. Maddox, *William E. Borah and American Foreign Policy* (Baton Rouge, La., 1969). Informative on Borah's approach to politics is Orde Pinckney, "Lion Triumphant," *Idaho Yesterdays*, III (Summer, 1959), 12–15, 18–24. On Borah and the politics of the New Deal, see Pinckney, "William E. Borah and the Republican Party, 1932–1940" (unpublished Ph.D. dissertation, University of California, Berkeley, 1957).

On progressivism in general, one of the finest recent interpretations is Otis L. Graham, Jr., *An Encore for Reform: The Old Progressives and the New Deal* (New York, 1967). Although Graham does not discuss the New Era, his analysis of progressivism is mandatory for any student of the subject. My research and conclusions would seem generally to support his point of view. For a different interpretation which argues that progressives in the Twenties provided a strong link between prewar reforms and the New Deal, see Robert S. Maxwell, "The Progressive Bridge: Reform Sentiment in the United States Between the New Freedom and the New Deal," *Indiana Magazine of History*, 63 (June, 1967), 83–102. John Buenker, "The Progressive Era: A Search for a Synthesis," *Mid-America*, 51 (July, 1969), 175–93, is a very fine essay and is especially useful in suggesting how cultural questions increasingly disrupted the coalition process which had produced the early progressive legislative achievements. Equally important is Clyde Griffen's analysis of "The Progressive Ethos," in Stanley Coben and Lorman Ratner, *The Development of an American Culture* (Englewood Cliffs, N.J., 1970), 120–49, both for its summary of key components of the progressive consensus and for suggestions as to why the progressive vision had become less compelling by the Twenties. An outstanding analysis of the nature of progressivism (and a highly perceptive interpretation of the collapse of the progressive consensus) is Richard M. Abrams's "The Failure of Progressivism," in Abrams and Lawrence W. Levine, eds., *The Shaping of Twentieth Century America* (2nd ed., Boston, Mass., 1971).

Other recent studies which illustrate well that internal tensions within progressivism ultimately limited the extent of reform commitments and divided reformers include David Noble, *The Progressive Mind, 1890–1917* (Chicago, 1970), Robert C. Bannister, Jr., *Ray Stannard Baker, The Mind and Thought of a Progressive* (New Haven, Conn., 1966), Herbert F. Margulies, *The Decline of the Progressive Movement in Wisconsin, 1890–1920* (Madison, Wis., 1968), R. Jackson Wilson, *In Quest of Community, 1860–1920* (New York, 1968), esp. chaps. 4 and 5, and Jack Tager, *The Intellectual as Urban Reformer: Brand Whitlock and the Progressive Movement* (Cleveland, Ohio, 1968). Robert H. Wiebe, *The Search for Order* (New York, 1967), is a major work, full of insights into the nature of progressivism and also useful in explaining in what sense "the illusion of fulfillment" had by the Twenties blunted the struggles of even the urban-oriented progressives who had sketched out the bureaucratic organizational techniques characteristic of modern industrial society. Also very helpful for an understanding of the plight of progressivism by the New Era is Herbert F. Margulies's historiographical essay, "Recent Opinion on the Decline of the Progressive Movement," *Mid-America*, 45 (October, 1963), 250–68.

Significant treatments of progressivism in the Twenties include Richard Hofstadter's seminal *Age of Reform* (New York, 1955), chapter 7, which sees reform in the New Era largely as a farce; William E. Leuchtenburg's discussion of "tired radicals" in *The Perils of Prosperity, 1914–32* (Chicago, 1958); Eric Goldman's analysis of New Era progressivism as "a beaten army, muscles aching, its ranks seriously depleted," in *Rendezvous with Destiny* (New York, 1952); Arthur S. Link's "What Happened to the Progressive Movement in the 1920's," *American Historical Review*, LXIV (July, 1959), 833–51, which is more favorable to the progressive contributions in the 20's; Paul W. Glad, "Progressives and the Business Culture of the 1920s," *Journal of American History*, LIII (June, 1966), 75–89, which emphasizes several key reform dilemmas in the New Era; Clarke A. Chambers, *Seedtime of Reform; American Social Service and Social Action, 1918–1933* (Minneapolis, Minn., 1963), which finds active reformism among the social-worker elements in the Twenties; George B. Tindall, "Business Progressivism: Southern Politics in the Twenties," *The South Atlantic Quarterly*, LXII (Winter, 1963), 92–106, important beyond its subject; Stuart Morris, "The Wisconsin Idea and Business Progressivism," *Journal of American Studies*, 4 (July, 1970), 39–60, which shows how the prewar progressive search for efficiency-minded leadership—merging university training with government service— had shifted by the Twenties to a "business progressivism"—merging university training with business management and encouraging faith in the abilities of "business intelligence" to effect national progress; Jackson K. Putnam, "The Persistence of Progressivism in the 1920's: The Case of California," *Pacific Historical Review*, 35 (November, 1966), 395–411, which shows how some progressives successfully adapted reform policies to fit New Era business virtues of economy and efficiency; and Kenneth Campbell MacKay, *The Progressive Movement of 1924* (New York, 1947). James Shideler, "The Neo-Progressives: Reform Politics in the United States, 1920–1925" (unpublished Ph.D. dissertation, University of California, Berkeley, 1945), is an insightful and helpful chronical of progressivism on the national level. Shideler had access only to the manuscripts of the

People's Legislative Service, but he utilized to the fullest extent journals, newspapers, and the *Congressional Record* to illustrate the rural-urban split as the main problem for reformers in the 1920's.

Excellent for an understanding of the vantage point of western progressivism are Paul W. Glad, *The Trumpet Soundeth; William Jennings Bryan and His Democracy, 1896–1912* (Lincoln, Neb., 1960), and Lawrence W. Levine, *Defender of the Faith, William Jennings Bryan: The Last Decade 1915–1925* (New York, 1965), which impressively captures the agony of the cultural conflict that sundered progressivism in the New Era. For perceptive analyses of a different vantage point—that of the eastern, urban liberal who belonged to an ethnic minority group—see Arthur Mann, *La Guardia: A Fighter Against His Times, 1882–1933* (New York, 1959) and Howard Zinn, *La Guardia in Congress* (Ithaca, N.Y., 1959), both very good on progressivism in the Twenties.

Although dealing with neither the progressive movement nor the Twenties, Paul Kleppner's *The Cross of Culture: A Social Analysis of Midwestern Politics 1850 1900* (New York, 1970), and Frederick Luebke's *Immigrants and Politics, The Germans of Nebraska, 1880–1900* (Lincoln, Neb., 1969) clearly show some of the pitfalls in talking loosely at any time about a cultural conflict between urban and rural America. Both studies point out, for example, that religious backgrounds and perspectives have been crucial determinants of party allegiance and have cut across geographical and occupational lines. Nonetheless, Don S. Kirschner's *City and Country: Rural Responses to Urbanization in the 1920's* (Westport, Conn., 1970) is a superb example of how a framework of rural-urban conflict can provide useful insights. Using legislative roll-call analysis, he finds that in Illinois and Iowa sharp economic and cultural battles divided rural and urban forces. According to Kirschner, there was an overwhelming consensus among rural legislators on cultural issues. Granting that the small minority of dissenters from the rural pattern may have reflected ethnic differences, it is the rural consensus that stands out even if it was because (as Luebke emphasizes in his review in *The Journal of American History*, LVII [December, 1970], 748) "persons with pietistic attitudes were relatively more numerous in the country." Other studies which draw insights from within the context of a rural-urban cultural struggle during the Twenties are David Burner's *The Politics of Provincialism: The Democratic Party in Transition, 1918–1932,* which shows how the battle between "rural traditions and urban encroachments" ruptured the Democratic party following World War I; Paul Carter's *The Twenties in America* (New York, 1968), chapter 3; and Loren Baritz, "The Culture of the Twenties," in Coben and Ratner (eds.), *The Development of an American Culture.*

Monographs on topics relating to progressivism in the New Era which are particularly valuable are Robert H. Zieger, *Republicans and Labor, 1919–1929* (Lexington, Ky., 1969), a model study; Gilbert C. Fite, *George N. Peek and the Fight for Farm Parity* (Norman, Okla., 1954), and James H. Shideler, *Farm Crisis, 1919–1923* (Berkeley, Calif., 1957), both outstanding on the farm problem; Andrew Sinclair, *Prohibition: The Era of Excess* (Boston, Mass., 1962) and James H. Timberlake, *Prohibition and the Progressive Movement, 1900–1920* (Cambridge, Mass., 1963), both perceptive on their subject; Alpheus T. Mason, *William Howard Taft: Chief Justice* (New York, 1964), good on the Court; Donald Johnson, *The Challenge to American Freedoms* (Lexington, Ky., 1963), informative on civil liberties; and John Higham, *Strangers in the Land: Patterns of Nativism, 1860–1925* (New Brunswick, N.J., 1955), and Paul L. Murphy, "Sources and Nature of Intolerance in the 1920's," *Journal of American History,* LI (June, 1964), 60–76, both excellent.

On foreign policy and progressivism, see the contrasting studies of William E. Leuchtenburg, "Progressivism and Imperialism: The Progressive Movement and American Foreign Policy, 1898–1916," *Mississippi Valley Historical Review,* XXXIX (December, 1952), 483–504, and John M. Cooper, Jr., "Progressivism and American Foreign Policy: A Reconsideration," *Mid-America,* 51 (October, 1969), 260–77. Focusing on the "Progressive Republican Senators and American Imperialism, 1898–1916: A Reappraisal," *Mid-America,* 50 (July, 1968), 163–205, Barton J. Bernstein and Franklin A. Leib also take issue with Leuchtenburg. *Mid-America* has become a key source of information regarding the relationship between progressivism and American foreign policy. Besides the articles above, see those by Howard W. Allen, Warren A. Sutton, and Walter I. Trattner, all cited in Chapter 4. Similarly, the cited articles by Padraic Kennedy are indispensable. Wayne S. Cole,

Senator Gerald P. Nye and American Foreign Relations (Minneapolis, Minn., 1962), is particularly suggestive on the agrarian perspective on foreign policy. Jerry Israel, *Progressivism and the Open Door; America and China, 1905–1921* (Pittsburgh, Pa., 1971), pp. xi–xxiv, has a useful summary of scholarly writings on progressivism and expansionism.

The most recent and important evaluation of Borah and foreign relations is that by Robert Maddox. But see also Henry W. Berger, "Laissez Faire for Latin America, Borah Defines the Monroe Doctrine," *Idaho Yesterdays*, IX (Summer, 1965), 10–17, good on the Senator's anti-imperialism, and Charles W. Toth, "Isolationism and the Emergence of Borah: An Appeal to American Tradition," *The Western Political Quarterly*, XIV (June, 1961), 555–68, a perceptive analysis of Borah's views on foreign policy which holds that "Borah came close, indeed, to hitting the mood of the hour in his generation"; John E. Stoner, *S. O. Levinson and the Pact of Paris* (Chicago, 1943), and John Chalmers Vinson, *William E. Borah and the Outlawry of War* (Athens, Ga., 1957), both very useful on Borah's relationship to the Outlawry movement. John Braeman, "Seven Progressives," *Business History Review*, XXXV (Winter, 1961), 581–92, includes a discussion of Borah and draws a line between the "traditionalist" and "modernist" views that split progressives in their approaches both to foreign affairs and the problem of large domestic corporations.

INDEX

❧

Abrams, Richard M.: on progressivism, x; quoted on progressives and the "general interest," 13n
Adams, John T., 157
Adamson Act, 87, 88
Addams, Jane: efforts to save Sacco and Vanzetti, 216; endorses Hoover, 274
Agriculture: problems in 1920's, 79; policies of Harding and Coolidge administrations, 83-84, 137; importance to 1924 Progressive platform, 92; issue in 1928, 268-70. *See also* Farm relief; McNary-Haugenism
Aldrich, Nelson, 35
Alessandri, Arturo, 211
Allen, Howard W.: quoted on Senate progressives and race, 250n
American Civil Liberties Union, 28, 29
American expansionism, 114
American Mercury: critical of Senate progressives, 3, 282, 283
Arnold, Benedict: Borah on, 116
Ashurst, Henry, 109n
Association of Producers of Petroleum in Mexico, 212
Augusta *Chronicle:* praises Borah, 242

Baker, Newton D.: optimism in 1918, 24
Baker, Ray Stannard: on the "progressive movement," x; aversion to cities and organizational revolution, 63-64
Baker, Raymond, 230
Baltimore *Sun:* on Borah and labor, 40; evaluates 1922 progressive

conferences, 58; on Borah's vice-presidential "candidacy," 156
Bennett, James O'Donnell, 193
Berger, Henry W.: quoted on Borah's Latin American policies, 103n
Bernstein, Barton J.: quoted on Senate progressives and foreign policy, 99-100n
Beveridge, Albert J.: on Borah's importance, 140-41; mentioned, 155, 156, 179
Blaine, John J.: elected governor, 55; attends 1922 progressive conferences, 58; anti-imperialism of, 95; opposes Volstead Act, 234; and progressive bloc, 218, 220, 235; in 1928 election, 275, 276n; criticized as false progressive, 282
Bolshevism, 11, 213
Bonus bill, 98, 138
Borah, Charles (brother of William E.), 245
Borah, William E.: early years, 8, 286; ambitions to be on Supreme Court, 239, 239-40n; evaluated as insurgent during Harding administration, 24-25, 60; efforts to reform Supreme Court, 25, 30-34; opposes Taft's appointment as Chief Justice, 30; supports emergency tariff bill of 1921, 36; opposes Fordney-McCumber tariff, 36-37; relationship to farm bloc, 35-36; becomes chairman of Senate Committee on Education and Labor, 40; threatens to resign Senate Committee on Education and Labor, 44; response to 1922 coal crisis and strike, 25, 40-46,

Hoover, Herbert (*continued*) opposition, 291n; criticized as U.S. Food Administrator, 277; mentioned, 84

Hopkins, J. A. H.: background of, 123; as progressive organizer, 123; misunderstanding with La Follette, 124 and n; growing interest in Borah, 124; efforts to lure Borah into third party, 126-34; conference with Borah, 127-29; frustrations with Borah, 130-34, 136; turns to Norris and La Follette, 136; recalls Borah's praise for La Follette, 161; opposes special privilege, 131, 132

Howe, Frederick H.: quoted on war's impact on attitudes toward government, 12; advocates working with special interests, 13-14; turns inward, 284; mentioned, x, 123

Howell, Robert: elected to Senate, 55; and 1924 election, 170; included in "Borah bloc," 196; supports tax reform, 200; and progressive bloc, 218, 220, 236; supports Hoover, 276; mentioned, 161

Hughes, Charles Evans, 103, 107, 123, 135, 192

Ickes, Harold: evaluations of Borah, 4, 16, 17, 178; on decline of progressivism, 284

Idaho Progressive party: strength of, 140, 162; importance to Borah in 1924, 154, 160; disagreements over Borah, 163-64; nominates Borah, 164; growing dissatisfaction with Borah, 175; enthusiasm with Borah, 60

Illinois primary, 207n

Immigration restriction: reflects cultural conflict, 8, 249, 260; progressive support for, 246-49;

Borah criticizes Tammany Hall opposition to, 279

Independent, The: on Borah's influence, 197; on Borah as antisaloon champion, 241-42; on Borah's constitutional double standard, 242-43; on Borah's presidential strategy, 257; critical of Senate progressives, 230

Inland waterway project, 220

Iowa: as heartland of McNary-Haugenism, 226

Jackson, Gardner: expresses dislike for Borah, 61-62

Janick, Herbert: quoted on progressives and urban conditions, 7-8n

Japan, 107, 108

Jardine, William, 84

Jefferis, Albert W., 55

Jefferson, Thomas: as progressive influence, 61-64; mentioned, 113, 259

Johnson, Andrew, 186, 193

Johnson, Gerald: quoted on Borah's moral certainty, 16n

Johnson, Hiram: reflects cultural conflict, 22; moderation of, 93-94, 286; individualism of, 232-33, 287, 288; self-righteousness of, 15; racial views of, 248, 249-50; and Harding administration, 25-26; opposes Taft's appointment, 30, 31; Taft criticizes, 34; misses Newberry vote, 39 and n; and direct primary, 48, 50; absent from 1922 progressive conferences, 56-57; as anti-imperialist, 95; opposes League of Nations, 101-2 and 102n; opposes Four-Power Treaty, 109n; suspicious of La Follette, 56-57; on fence in 1924, 170; included with "Borah bloc," 188, 196; on Warren fight, 195n; on the 1926 elections, 207n; on Senate progressives and balance of

power, 220; progressive bloc seeks support of, 221; avoids progressive bloc, 232-33; supports Hoover, 276; criticizes Brookhart, 282n; Borah criticizes, 282n; Norris criticizes, 283n; weakness as insurgent, 198; on William Hard, 24 and n; evaluates Borah's influence, 27, 206n; on Borah and the press, 19, 20; assesses Borah as politician, 17, 174, 178; on Borah's constitutionalism, 258; dubs Borah "spearless leader," 285-86; criticizes Borah's vanity, 282n; on Borah's individualism, 290; refuses to follow Borah, 288; criticizes Borah's conduct in 1928 election, 276; on Borah's presidential ambitions, 205, 232-33; evaluates Borah's 1936 candidacy, 292; on Borah's last hours, 294; mentioned, 59, 126, 135, 184, 191n
Johnson, James Weldon: applauds Borah's speech on Haiti, 103; describes Borah's opposition to antilynching bills, 254; recognizes Borah's influence, 254n
Johnson, Magnus, 92
Johnson, Tom, 123
Jolson, Al, 106
Jones, Jesse, 279
Jones, Mother: praises Borah, 90

Kansas: support for Coolidge in 1924, 169
Karger, Gus, 170
Kazin, Alfred: quoted on individualism and early twentieth-century cultural revolt, 10n
Keating, Edward: quoted on 1922 elections, 55n
Kenyon, William S.: opposes Newberry, 38; praises Borah, 280; mentioned, 40
Kellogg, Frank B., 55, 210
Kellogg, Paul U., 275
Kellogg Peace Pact, 292

Kemler, Edgar, 293
Kent, Frank: on Coolidge's relations with Borah, 186; on Borah's role in Warren fight, 196; sees Borah as key to administration's future, 199; on individualism of progressive Senators, 288; on Negro voting rights, 244. *See also* "T. R. B."
King, William H., 105
Kirchwey, Freda, 275
Kirschner, Don S.: quoted on rural image of Al Smith, 261n
Knox, Frank, 198-99
Ku Klux Klan, 250

Labor: Borah's views on, 25, 46-47, 64, 72, 85-91; progressive ambivalence on, 86-90; importance to progressivism, 219; enthusiasm for Borah, 90, 91n
Ladd, Edwin: as anti-imperialist, 95; supports La Follette, 170; GOP penalizes, 183-86; opposes Warren, 187; evaluates Borah as progressive leader, 197; death of, 197; mentioned, 82
La Follette, Robert M., Jr.: on Borah's lack of support for La Follette, Sr., 169-70; criticizes Democratic party, 201, 202 and n; apprehensive over Latin American crisis, 214n; on significance of 1926 elections, 207n; attempts to unify Senate progressives, 220, 235-36, 236n; opposes Volstead Act, 234; introduces minority farm plank, 269; position in 1928 election, 275; criticized as false progressive, 282; criticizes Norris, 283n; mentioned, 208, 218
La Follette, Robert M., Sr.: self-righteousness of, 15; opposes interest-based politics, 56, 85, 86-87; and cultural conflict, 92; as western spokesman, 197; views Borah as progressive, 20; opposes Taft's appointment, 30; criticizes judi-

GOLDEN BOY

GOLDEN BOY

Memories of a Hong Kong Childhood

MARTIN BOOTH

Thomas Dunne Books
St. Martin's Press ♠ New York

THOMAS DUNNE BOOKS.
An imprint of St. Martin's Press.

www.stmartins.com

ISBN 0-312-34817-7
EAN 978-0-312-34817-5

First published in Great Britain by Doubleday
a division of Transworld Publishers

10 9 8 7 6 5 4 3 2

for Helen, Alex and Emma, with love
and
in memory of my mother, Joyce, a true
China Hand

The colophon – – used in this book is of a dragon riding the waves. It dates to the pre-Christian Han dynasty and is thought to suggest that the legends of dragons were based upon saltwater crocodiles then extant in South China but now long extinct.

Gweilo – Chinese slang for a European male – translates literally as *ghost* (or *pale*) *fellow*, but implies a ghost or devil. Once a derogatory or vulgar term, referring to a European's pale skin, it is now a generic expression devoid of denigration. The feminine is *gweipor*.

CONTENTS

AUTHOR'S NOTE

It had never been my intention to write an autobiography. To do so smacked of arrogance: it was not as if I were a rock star, an explorer, a footballer or a member of the miscreant aristocracy. It is true that I have had an interesting and remarkably lucky life, but that is far from unique and I never thought to document it. I have never kept a diary, except when travelling, but I do have a very retentive memory, all the more so for its being permanently exercised by my being a writer.

Then, in October 2002, I was diagnosed with the nastiest type of brain tumour around. A craniotomy did little but confirm I was suffering from a curiously named cancer known as a *glioblastoma multiforma grade IV*. It was incurable, essentially inoperable and immune to chemotherapy. Whilst I was convalescing, with a metal plate and half a dozen screws in my head, and most of the cancer still *in situ*, my two children – both in their twenties – asked me to tell them about my early life.

Having tried, without even a smidgen of success, to persuade my father to do the same for me, and tell me about our forebears – he went to his grave in adamant silence on the matter and I had

never thought to ask my mother, who had died suddenly and at a comparatively young age seven years earlier – I decided I would tackle the task of writing about my childhood, which was spent in Hong Kong.

Once I had set out upon the task, the past began to unfold – perhaps it is better to say unravel – before me. I did have some assistance in the form of a scrapbook and several photograph albums my mother had compiled, yet these did not so much prompt as confirm certain memories, flesh out anecdotes that have spun in my mind for years, rekindle lost names and put faces to them.

If the truth be told, I have never really left Hong Kong, its streets and hillsides, wooded valleys, myriad islands and deserted shores with which I was closely acquainted as a curious, sometimes devious, not unadventurous and streetwise seven-year-old. My life there has been forever repeating itself in the recesses of my mind, like films in wartime cartoon cinemas, showing over and over again as if on an endless loop.

This is hardly surprising. Hong Kong was my home, was where I spent my formative years, is where my roots are, is where I grew up.

Martin Booth
Devon, 2003

1

PORT OUT

FIFTY FEET BELOW, MY GRANDPARENTS STOOD SIDE BY SIDE. IT WAS A warm spring day, yet my paternal grandfather, Grampy, wore a grey trilby with a black band and an overcoat buttoned to his neck. From far off, he looked like a retired Chicago mobster. His wife wore a broad-brimmed Edwardian hat decorated with faded feathers and wax flowers, which, even at that distance, gave the impression of being on the verge of melting. Her mound of white hair being insufficiently dense to retain her hat pin, every time she craned her neck to look up at me, the hat slid off backwards and Grampy deftly caught it.

It was late on the afternoon of Friday, 2 May 1952, and I was seven.

A deck steward in a white uniform approached. He carried a silver salver bearing rolls of coloured paper streamers.

'Where're you going to, sunshine?' he asked me as he handed me three rolls.

'Hong Kong,' I replied. 'My father's been posted,' I added, although I had not the faintest idea what this meant. As far as I knew, one only posted letters.

'You'll need to grow your hair, then,' he announced, making a show of studying the nape of my neck. 'Far too short . . .'

I asked why.

'Well,' he went on, 'in China men wear their hair in pigtails. You're not going to be able to put a plait in that.' Then he winked at me and moved on down the deck.

Aghast at the thought my hair would be put in a braid, I asked my mother if this was true but her response was obscured by the thunderous blare of the ship's horn, high up on the funnel, announcing our imminent departure.

Further along the rail, my father threw a streamer over the ship's side. I followed suit, hurling mine with all my might into the sky. It arched through the air and, striking the corrugated iron roof of a dockside warehouse, bounced then rolled down to lodge in the drain. It was then I realized one was supposed to keep hold of one end of the ribbon. I threw another streamer. My grandfather caught it and held it firmly until, eventually, it tautened and tore as the ship edged away from the quayside. It was over three years before I saw him again.

The vessel upon which we were embarked was the SS *Corfu*. According to my father, she (not *it*, he impressed upon me) was a twenty-two-year-old liner operated by the Peninsula & Oriental Steam Navigation Company and accommodated 400 passengers.

At first, the ship's movement was infinitesimal; yet, quite suddenly it seemed, my grandparents were minute figures on a dockside far away, indistinguishable from others in the waving crowds. Once well clear of the dock, I watched the land pivot round as the bow gradually turned to face the open sea, the deck beneath my feet beginning to vibrate gently as the engines gathered speed.

My father disappeared to his cabin, but my mother and I stood at the ship's rail for over an hour. The wind ruffled her short

blond hair and tugged at her dress as we passed the Isle of Wight to head down the English Channel. Above us, the funnel pumped out a plume of smoke and the windows of the bridge glistened with the late sunlight reflecting off the sea. Every now and then, a passenger or crew member passed us by but otherwise we were alone with the lifeboats. My mother held my hand, not once letting it go. It was not that she was afraid I might fall overboard but that she wanted to share her exhilaration, too wide for words. As we sailed down Southampton Water, one might have expected her to cry, yet she did not. This was an adventure and one did not cry on adventures. She had told me as much the night before as I lay in the bed in her mother's terraced house in Wykeham Road, Portsmouth, in which she had slept throughout her childhood.

At last, with England a small but thin line on the darkening horizon, she said, 'Let's go and sort out our cabin.'

Ahead was an ocean of sea water and endless possibilities.

My mother and I shared a twin-berth, second-class cabin whilst my father 'bunked up', as he put it, with another male passenger, a forestry officer travelling solo to Colombo. Although attached to the Royal Navy, my father was no more than an Admiralty civil servant, having left school at sixteen to become a clerk in the chandlery offices of Portsmouth Royal Naval dockyard. He never wore a uniform with a rank on it, yet this did not prevent him from assuming naval ways and speech. He drank pink gin, called sausages 'bangers', ate curry puffs and kedgeree, never let a knocked glass chime (for fear it sounded a sailor's knell), referred to his superior as 'the Old Man' and used nautical expressions whenever possible.

The cabin I shared with my mother was fairly basic: two bunks, one above the other, a wardrobe and a small chest of drawers, a steel washbasin the top of which folded down to make a vanity table, two collapsible stools and a chair. I was allotted the top

bunk. The ablutions (or, as my father would have it in navy-speak, 'the heads') were communal and a little way down the corridor. The cabin walls were cream-painted iron bulkheads lined with rivets, the ceiling the same but traversed by girders and ventilation pipes. Under an oblong of patterned carpet, the floor was made of iron painted dark green. The furniture was fashioned out of heavily varnished mahogany.

That I was surrounded by metal did not concern me. I somehow accepted that, as houses were made of bricks, plaster and wallpaper, so a ship would be made of iron plates and paint. What was strange was the fact that everything continually quivered, never changing its frequency. It was like living in the entrails of a vast, benign beast, the corridors its bowels, the pipes its arteries and the various cabins its organs or dead-end intestines. What was more, everything smelt of paint, diesel, tar, brass polish and warm lubricating oil.

We unpacked our cases and the steward took them to stow away for the duration of the voyage, then my mother ran me a bath of what I quickly realized, from the taste and sting in my eyes, was hot sea water. On returning to the cabin, I found a silver tray on the table bearing a plate of thin-cut sandwiches, a freshly sliced pear and a glass of milk.

'Supper,' my mother announced. She lifted one end of a sandwich and exclaimed, 'Roast chicken!'

This was opulence indeed. In England, still held in the grip of post-war austerity, chicken was an oft-dreamt-of, but rarely experienced, luxury. So was a pear.

As night settled upon the sea, I climbed the three-step ladder into my bunk, pulled the blanket up to my neck and lay on my side. Next to my pillow was a porthole, closed tight by heavy brass clamps. Pressing my forehead to it, I looked down. The sea was speeding by, the white tops of the wake catching the light from

other portholes and the promenade deck above. Now well down the French coast, the *Corfu* rolled gently in the Atlantic swell.

My mother leant up and kissed me. 'We're on our way now,' she whispered with hardly suppressed excitement. 'Aren't we the lucky ones?'

The voyage to Hong Kong took a month, with seven ports of call *en route*. My father, assiduously studying our course on a daily progress map pinned to a notice board in the lounge and maintained by the officer of the watch – whom he accosted whenever he could for a mariners' chat – announced what we might see each day. His first prediction was that we should see Gibraltar 'off the port beam', but it was hidden in sea mist. This upset him greatly. To see Gibraltar was, he considered, a rite of passage.

'You've not lived until you've seen Gib.,' he informed me with an eye as misty as the distance.

'Why not?' I replied. 'It's just a big rock.'

'Just a rock! Did you hear the boy, Joyce? Just a rock . . . What did they teach him in that bloody school?'

'To read and write,' my mother answered. 'Well.'

My father, not to be wrong-footed, went on, 'The Romans used to think that if you sailed too far out from Gib., you fell off the edge of the world.'

'But you don't,' I rejoined. 'It's round. You just come back again.'

This piece of puerile logic was met with a brief snort of contempt.

We arrived at our first port of call, Algiers, three days out of

Southampton. The city consisted of low buildings encircling a bay into which several moles and pontoons projected. Only a very few minarets poked upwards into the sky, contrary to my expectations, my father having lectured me on Muslims and mosques. There was little shipping in the harbour and almost every vehicle was either of pre-war vintage or ex-military, both Allied and German. All the cars, without exception, were black French Citroëns. The air, warm and dry, tasted of the desert, which I knew from geography lessons covered north Africa.

As soon as the ship was berthed, our steward entered our cabin and, closing the porthole, warned us to keep it shut whenever we were in port in order to deter pole-fishers.

'What's a pole-fisher?' I enquired.

'Pole-fisher's a thief,' he explained in his cockney accent. ''e 'as a long flex'ble pole with an 'ook on it. 'e shoves it through the por'hole an' sees what 'e can catch. But,' he added sternly, 'if you see the pole wigglin' about in the cabin, don't make a grab for it, even,' he glanced at my bunk, 'if 'e's 'ooked yer teddy bear. See, 'e'll've set razor blades in the pole. You grab it an' – zip! – 'e pulls the pole an' you ain't got no fingers.'

I immediately put the bear in the wardrobe, hid it behind my mother's frocks and closed the door.

My mother was eager to go ashore. This was the first time she had set foot outside Britain. I was just as eager to follow. My father, conversely, was not at all enthusiastic. A friend of his had been stabbed to death in Algiers during the war and he considered the place unsafe. That this friend had been in military intelligence, that Algiers had been under the influence of Vichy France and that the war against Hitler had been in full flood at the time did not seem to occur to him. However, my mother prevailed and we set off to see the sights in a small, decrepit bus with some other passengers from the ship. Our ride culminated in the Casbah, the

sixteenth-century fortified part of the old Ottoman city. Here, we got out of the bus and, after my father had exhorted us to stay close together and be alert, wandered through the narrow thoroughfares of the *suq*.

Every street and alley was an animated illustration from my grandfather's morocco-bound copy of *The Thousand and One Nights*. Men wearing turbans and baggy trousers passed by, leading donkeys. Some of the women wore burkas, their eyes bright in the darkness of the slits. Dogs scratched themselves indifferently or lay asleep in the shade. Stalls erected under arcaded buildings sold vegetables I had never seen before, quaintly shaped copper jugs, vicious-looking daggers (the better for stabbing British spies with), leather ware and sand-coloured pottery. In coffee shops, men sat around tables drinking from small cups or smoking hookahs, the scent of their tobacco alien when compared to my father's Sobranie Black Russian or my mother's State Express 555 cigarettes. Away from the smokers, I found the air heavy with smells reminiscent of my grandmothers' spice cabinets, of minced pies and apple tart – and the odour of donkeys, camels and human sweat. My mother purchased some fresh dates from a stall and set about eating them, much to my father's alarm.

'How can you tell where they've been?' he remonstrated with her.

'They've been up a date palm,' my mother replied.

'And they picked themselves, I suppose?'

'No,' she responded, in the same tone of voice as she might have used to a dog sniffing at the Sunday dinner table. 'I expect they were plucked by a scrofulous urchin and thrown down to his tubercular aunt who wrapped them in her phlegm-stiffened handkerchief.'

'Well, if you want to poison yourself, at least don't give one to Martin. The last thing he'll want is dysentery.'

'But I want one,' I butted in.

I had no idea what I was being forbidden, but I was determined not to miss out on it or the promise of dysentery. Surreptitiously my mother slipped me a date. Its taste and texture reminded me of solidified honey.

Once through the *suq*, we climbed up to a battlement where I sat on a large cannon. From this vantage point, I could see camels down below, their wooden-framed cargo saddles being laden with sacks. My mother asked me what I thought of the city and was later to write to relatives that I compared Algiers favourably to the outer-London suburb of Woking.

As we retraced our steps through the *suq* to catch the bus, we were beset by a hoard of children, many of them about my age, dressed in flowing rags and the fragrances of warm humanity. They called vociferously for *buksheesh*, their hands outstretched, their eyes devious and pleading. One or two of the more courageous plucked at my father's tropical-weight linen jacket. He raised his hand as if to strike them and they adroitly retreated.

'What do they want?' I asked my mother, somewhat shocked that my father had thought to hit someone else's child. Smacking me was one thing, but clipping the ear of a stranger was an altogether different matter.

'They want money,' my mother answered. 'They're beggars. Ignore them.'

This seemed callous but I did as I was told.

My mother's first encounter with a camel was more costly. She had an inbuilt attraction to anything of fur or feather. Only a month before sailing, she had narrowly missed having her neck broken by a peeved circus elephant which, bored with being offered currant buns, swung its trunk full force at her. She had just dropped one of the currant buns and, with the timing of

Laurel and Hardy, had bent down to retrieve it. The wind of the passing trunk had ruffled her perm.

The camel was sitting on the ground, fully laden, chewing the cud. I wondered if it was dreaming of a wide desert of rolling dunes and a far-off oasis of palms, for its eyes were shut. My mother approached, hand outstretched, to stroke its muzzle, much as she might have caressed the velvet nose of a placid horse. In an instant, the beast was wide awake and getting to its feet with the alacrity of a sprinter leaving the starting blocks. Its neck arched forward, it sneezed and then it spat. A shower of bactrian spittle lodged in my mother's hair. In the sharp north African sunlight, she looked as if she had been sprinkled with glutinous tinsel. She stepped back sharply, discretion the better part of affection. The camel, thinking it had her on the run, lunged after her but its front feet were hobbled. The camel herder hurried over and struck the beast on its rump with a stout stick, shouting a spate of invective at it in Arabic, for the camel's benefit, and then in pidgin French for ours. The camel lay down again. The camel's owner looked balefully expectant so my father parted with all his loose change, no doubt hoping this would be sufficient for us not to be knifed in revenge on our way back through the *suq*.

When we stepped into the square where we had left the bus, it had gone. Panic entered my father's eyes. He had been to the movies. He knew the cash value of a blond white woman of shapely form and a matching potential catamite. His friend had bled to death in a gutter hereabouts. At this point, my mother disappeared down an alley of tightly packed stalls selling lengths of multicoloured cloth.

'Joyce!' my father called after her. 'Joyce!' His voice rose half an octave with anger, frustration and fear. 'Joyce! You don't know what you're doing. This isn't Piccadilly . . .'

Yet, in less than a minute, my mother returned, unscathed by blade or bullet. Following her was an elderly bearded Arab in a flowing blue-and-gold striped robe leading a morose-looking donkey in the shafts of an ancient trap. My mother was ever a resourceful woman.

My parents, Joyce and Ken, were in many ways an incompatible pair from the very start. My mother was a very pretty strawberry blonde, petite and lithe; my father slim and handsomely dark in an almost Latin-American way. They looked the ideal couple, yet they were not. My mother was full of fun, with a quick wit, an abounding sense of humour, an easy ability to make friends from all walks of life and an intense intellectual curiosity. She was also as determined and tenacious as a bull terrier.

By contrast, my father was a stick-in-the-mud with little real sense of humour and an all-abiding pedantry. Furthermore, he had a chip on his shoulder which insidiously grew throughout his life. He came to hold all relationships at arm's length, considering himself a cut above most of his contemporaries.

My parents' coming together was perhaps unavoidable: born within five weeks of each other, they lived out their childhoods virtually next door to each other in Portsmouth. The marriage, however, greatly discommoded my paternal grandmother who thought my mother and her parents to be socially inferior. Her husband, Grampy, had been a commissioned officer, but his son had married the daughter of a non-commissioned officer from the lower deck. What was worse, my mother was a Modern Woman, had a job as a General Post Office telephonist and smoked cigarettes. In my grandmother's eyes, she was an upstart

and could not be more common unless she worked behind the counter in Woolworths.

During the Second World War, my father spent a good deal of his time overseas in south and west Africa and the Middle East. When the hostilities ended, he was employed at the Admiralty in London, his office overlooking Horse Guards' Parade. Although he made himself out to be an important man, he was in fact little more than a superior clerk. Indeed, my mother had had an almost equivalent wartime job provisioning submarines for the Battle of the Atlantic.

After the war, our lives had seemed settled enough. We lived in a semi-detached house at the end of a cul-de-sac in Brentwood, Essex. My mother was a housewife in the outer suburbs of London, my father a daily commuter into London.

Then, one day, my father came home to announce that he had been posted to Hong Kong, to serve upon a Royal Fleet Auxiliary naval supply ship plying between the British crown colony and the Japanese military dockyard of Sasebo. The Korean War was in full flood and he was, he claimed, to be a part of it.

A debate followed as to what was to be done with me. My father was all for sending me to boarding school in England: I could spend my holidays with his parents. He and my mother, he pointed out, would only be gone three years. The quality of schooling in Hong Kong was an unknown and he would not have me educated in a school for children of military personnel.

'In with Army children?' he declared. 'Out of the question! A rabble of East End brats with snot-besmirched faces and grimy fingernails, the spawn of bloody corporals and squaddies—'

'I'm sure there are local schools,' my mother said, with no foundation whatsoever for her optimism.

'Full of Chinese,' my father announced from an equally strong foundation of ignorance.

'Well, I'm not leaving him here,' my mother pronounced obdurately. 'He'll wind up like some poor child in a Kipling story. Parents in the Orient, boy in—'

'Don't be ridiculous, Joyce! If he's in England, he'll be safe. The Far East isn't Farnham. There are tropical diseases, civil unrest, an inclement climate, native—'

'It's a British colony, Ken. I'm sure they have hospitals and a police force.'

'All the same, we leave him here. In the long run, it's for the best.' My father's mind was made up. He had clearly worked it all out.

'No, we bloody don't,' my mother exploded. 'I didn't go through nine months of pregnancy and twelve hours of labour – while you were swanning around in the Mediterranean – to leave the product behind. I had a child – a son – to raise him, foster him, shape him, not foist him off on a gaggle of minor public school masters, half of them as interested in the contents of his under-pants as his mind.'

'Don't be so bloody stupid, Joyce. The masters at Hilsea . . .'

Hilsea College, an insignificant private boys' school in Portsmouth, was my father's Alma Mater, from which he had attained little but a basic matriculation and a few certificates for proficiency in Music.

'Hilsea!' my mother echoed in a voice verging on the falsetto. 'You can have another think coming! Martin's going to be with us. It's a family posting. We're a family. Fix it!'

I overheard this conversation through a closed door and missed bits of it but the gist was clear and the outcome decided. I was going too.

Life aboard ship quickly settled into a routine. It seemed to me that, for many passengers, the voyage was an extended and free holiday, away from the austerity of Britain. Mornings were spent reading in deckchairs, writing letters in the lounge or smoking room, both of which were forbidden to unaccompanied children, or walking briskly in circles round the promenade deck. Some joined in physical exercise classes on the boat deck. At mid-morning, a steward served beef tea in small china cups. According to my mother, it was supposed to give the white man salt and strength. After luncheon, most passengers either took to their cabins or lay supine in deckchairs. A few participated in deck sports, most of which seemed to involve quoits of tough rope that one threw over a net, shuttled across the deck or tossed from hand to hand frisbee-style. One passenger spent much of his time driving golf balls over the side, from what seemed to be an inexhaustible supply.

As far as I was concerned, the voyage was also a prolonged vacation although, early on, a blot appeared on this landscape of bliss.

Passengers under the age of twelve were expected to attend school lessons every morning in the ship's nursery, a room decorated with poorly executed versions of Disney and nursery tale characters, furnished with chairs and desks of Lilliputian dimensions and overseen by a crabby-faced woman in a nanny's uniform. The content of the instruction offered bore no relation to any syllabus and my mother, after visiting me shoe-horned into a desk, excused me from all future attendance. Thereafter, she taught me geography and history herself for an hour a day at a table in the lounge, her lessons anticipating the next port of call. My father attempted twice to teach me the basics of geometry but his patience expired before half time and he gave up in exasperation.

The days at sea were euphoric, reading Enid Blyton and Arthur Ransome in a deckchair, playing with the children of similarly educationally enlightened parents and painting watercolours of imaginary volcanic desert islands. A sub-tropical sun beat down from a cloudless sky, its heat deceptively cooled by a stiff sea breeze. I quickly acquired a tan with the aid of a noxious-smelling liquid my mother basted me with at every opportunity.

To amuse the younger passengers, 'diversions' were arranged. The chief engineer conducted a trip to the engine room, a cathedral-sized cavern filled with mechanical noise, spinning fly-wheels and governors, polished copper and brass pipes and brackets, heaving piston rods, levers, taps and the vast propeller shafts which incessantly turned whilst being lubricated by a muscular man with a towelling rag tied round his neck, stripped to the waist and glistening with sweat. The air stank with the all-pervading odour of diesel and lubricating oil, which convinced me that whilst a life at sea might have suited my grandfathers, it was definitely not for me.

Another excursion took us to the bridge, where we feigned interest in engine room telegraphs, radar screens, compasses and assorted nautical navigational aids. We were shown a blip on a green radar screen then given binoculars, identifying it as another P&O vessel heading west. On passing it at a mile, I was chosen to greet it with a blast on the ship's horn, to which it responded. We were also permitted to steer the ship, keeping her on her bearing with the aid of a large gimbal-mounted compass and the officer of the watch whose hand did not once leave the wheel. This feat accomplished, we were each presented with a certificate to say we had taken the helm of the P&O liner *Corfu* off the north African coast on such-and-such a date.

One morning I awoke to find the ship still and alongside a quay seething with activity. A quaint-looking railway engine passed by,

its flat trucks laden with baggage. Men in white turbans mingled round the entrance to a warehouse, chivvied into order by a portly man in a bedraggled suit and red fez. Shouting stevedores pushing hand carts steered around each other with considerable alacrity.

'Port Said,' my mother announced, entering the cabin. 'Egypt,' she added, standing under the ceiling blower and towelling her hair. 'This is where the pharaohs lived. Remember our history lesson?' I nodded. 'Well,' she said finally, 'this is where it all happened.'

After breakfast, four or five elderly Arabs appeared squatting on the promenade deck, each with a lidded basket before him. None of them, it occurred to me, looked as if he might be even distantly related to monarchy. Their loose-fitting robes and turbans were grimy. They were barefoot, the underneath of their feet soiled, cracked and as thick as the soles of military boots. Their toenails were horny and ridged like a tortoise's shell. As I walked past the first, he reached out, his fingers ruffling the hair behind my ear from which he produced a day-old yellow chick, showing it to me with a grin framed by yellow-stained teeth. The little bird cheeped dejectedly and the man dropped it into his basket. As he performed this magic, he muttered, 'Gully-gully-gully,' in a cracked, guttural voice.

'They're called gully-gully men,' my mother explained unnecessarily and she put a coin into the man's open hand. His fingers were calloused, his long, curved fingernails striated like an ancient nag's hoof. He touched his forehead, secreted the coin in the folds of his clothing and produced a hen's egg from inside my other ear. I felt his talon of a fingernail scrape against my ear hole.

My father decreed we could quite safely go ashore. He had been here during the war, had lost no friends to enemy agents or native collaborators and purportedly knew his way around. A decaying

landau with faded cream leather seats, pulled by a gaunt pony with a hang-dog look, took us into the centre of town. Once there, we entered a museum of ancient Egyptian antiquities filled with glass display cases containing faded turquoise faience *ushabtis*, scarab beetle amulets, wooden and sandstone carved figurines, framed strips of linen and parchment upon which had been written dynastic poetry in hieroglyphs, bead necklaces, pottery oil lamps and bronze jewellery. The difference between this museum and those I had visited in England, however, was that everything here was for sale. Captivated by the *ushabtis*, I attempted to persuade my mother to buy me one, even desperately arguing that it might help me with my history lessons, but the price was too high and this was not, she told me in hushed tones, an emporium in which one haggled the price down.

'What does haggled mean?' I asked. My mother's reply was a severe keep-your-mouth-shut look. I complied.

Further along the same street we came upon a low, colonnaded building which seemed to be attracting passengers from the *Corfu* as a picnic did ants. The interior was dark and cool, large wooden and rattan-bladed ceiling fans spinning overhead, blue sparks dancing in their electric motors. This was the Simon Artz department store, almost as famous in Egypt as the Sphinx or the pyramids, alabaster replicas of both of which it sold in a variety of sizes. In addition, one could buy copies of ancient Greek amphorae; grotesque leather poufs decorated with hieroglyphs, high priests and heavy brass studs; camel saddles (labelled as being *genooine Bedooine*); beaten copper water jugs; wooden boxes inlaid with brass, lapis lazuli or ivory; carved camels, red felt fezes; brass salvers, alabaster ash trays and a working model of a water-raising system called a *shadouf* which I coveted but was forbidden to purchase by my father in case it harboured woodworm. That said, he purchased an alabaster ash tray. Without his knowing, my

mother bought me a small wooden camel supposedly devoid of insect infestation.

Wherever we went, my father was addressed as *effendi*, my mother as *Mrs Simpson*. This I found puzzling in the extreme.

'*Effendi* is like saying Sir or Mister,' my mother said when I questioned her.

'But our name's not Simpson,' I went on.

'That's Mrs Simpson, the Duchess of Windsor.'

'Are you related to the Duchess of Windsor?' I enquired wondrously.

'No!' my mother replied tersely. 'She's a tart.'

The look on my mother's face precluded any further discussion of the duchess or her pastries.

We took lunch in a small hotel overlooking the sea, which my father had frequented during the war. The meal consisted of cubes of nondescript gristle immolated on metal skewers and served on a bed of gummy rice mottled with dark brown objects that might have been unhusked grains, mouse droppings or steamed weevils. My mother ate one piece. I masticated another for the better part of ten minutes before swallowing it with difficulty. My father liberally soused his in Tabasco and ate the full portion. His face went red, his brow broke out in a sweat and he drank a number of glasses of pilsner. This, he declared, was an ideal prophylactic for malaria. (Nevertheless, he periodically suffered from a recurrence of the disease, regardless of this occasional medication, until he was in his late thirties.)

As he ate, my father embarked upon a tale of his wartime exploits.

'I was having dinner in this very room in 1942 – er 3 . . . It doesn't matter – when an Arab approached my table. "*Effendi*," he said, "I have some very fine dirty French postcards." He started to open his jacket.'

My father started to open his as if he, too, had something to offer.

'Ken . . .' my mother remonstrated in vain.

'"I have fifty, *effendi*. Just one hundred piastres."'

My father gave me a salacious wink. His eyes were somewhat glazed as if, in his mind, he was back in early-forties Egypt.

'That's enough, Ken,' my mother muttered sternly.

'I bought them,' my father continued unabashed, his voice now quite loud, having gradually increased in volume through the telling. 'And do you know what they were? Fifty grubby identical photos of the bloody Eiffel Tower.' He laughed loudly – a sort of braying sound – and drained his glass of pilsner.

That evening, the *Corfu* left the dock to join a line of vessels waiting to sail in convoy through the Suez Canal; the following morning, she started down it. Along the west bank ran a road and a railway line. It seemed bizarre to be travelling on a ship through a desert landscape dotted with low, square houses and palm trees. Moving at only six or seven knots, it was not long before a train overtook the ship, cars and trucks continually passing it on the road. The only form of transport the ship overhauled were donkeys and camels plodding methodically in the merciless, shadowless landscape.

By late morning, the dry heat was oppressive. My mother insisted I wore a white straw sun hat at all times. As it resembled a cross between a Mexican sombrero and a surrealist's lampshade, I resisted, yet to no avail. Instead, I contrived to forget it whenever possible, eventually managing to engineer for the detestable thing to blow over the side, only to discover the ship's shop had a seemingly inexhaustible supply of them. At least, I placated myself, it was preferable to the absurdly embarrassing knotted cotton handkerchief my father sported, which made him look like a retired London bus driver on the beach at Margate on a Whitsun

bank holiday. It gave him little solar protection. The following day, his face was as pink as a prawn. The day after that, it started to peel so that he looked as if he was sloughing his skin.

'It's your own silly fault, Ken,' my mother chastised him as she rubbed calamine lotion on to his forehead, nose and cheeks. The lotion, being coloured faintly pink and drying to the texture of whitewash, did little to alleviate his general over-cooked appearance. 'I mean, what did you do when you were stationed out here?'

'Work,' he replied sullenly. 'I didn't have time to sunbathe. There was a war on.'

Despite the blowers being on full blast and the porthole wide open, our cabin on the port side (facing the supposedly cooler east bank) still reverberated with heat like the sides of a blast furnace. Luncheon consisted of a green salad in a bowl immersed in a tray of ice. Even the sliced roast beef was served on plates set in beds of ice. Ice-cream, provided in greased paper cups with a wooden spoon like a miniature canoe paddle, melted in minutes into a thick, warm, vanilla drink.

My mother spent the afternoon wallowing in the ship's minuscule swimming pool or lounging in a deckchair, 'doing a reptile', as she referred to it. She wore tight, brief shorts and a blouse with flounced sleeves: it was to become her informal norm for the rest of her life in the tropics. Meanwhile, my father pretended he was the officer of the watch. He busied himself with his binoculars, watching out for shipping coming the opposite way through the canal and dhows that looked as if they had recently set sail out of the pages of the child's illustrated edition of the Old Testament which Granny had given me the previous Christmas. She was a Salvationist.

Gradually, the *Corfu* edged by the town of Ismailia and entered the Bitter Lakes. The desert receded and the air cooled slightly.

Around dusk, the lights of Port Suez twinkled in the hot night air and, shortly afterwards, we entered the Red Sea which, to my disappointment the following morning, was not in the least red.

More on-board diversions were planned to stave off boredom. There was a gala and tombola night for the adults and a casino evening. Every day, a sweepstake was held to guess how far the ship had sailed in the previous twenty-four hours. My father addressed this with mathematical precision, filling several sheets of the ship's notepaper with calculations every day. He did not win once. My mother, by pure guesswork and common nous, won three times, my father taking her success with such bad grace that, at the third win, he sulked and retired to his cabin claiming an upset stomach. We did not set eyes on him again until the following day when he complained my mother had not visited him in his sick bed.

'No, Ken,' she replied, 'I did not. A sick tummy I can fix with chlorodyne but a sick mind's beyond my reach.'

This did not improve matters and my father continued to brood for another day, his mood only being broken by an invitation from the captain to drinks that evening with a number of other male passengers in or connected with the Royal Navy. Women were excluded. He returned from this party with his plumage puffed up and his head held high.

A fancy-dress tea party was thrown for the children. I was dressed by my mother as a pirate in a crêpe paper cummerbund, one of her head scarves and an eye-patch borrowed from the ship's doctor and painted black with a mixture of indian ink and mascara. A cardboard sword was tucked in the cummerbund and I carried an empty whisky bottle. I took home no prizes. First place was awarded to a tubby boy of twelve whose parents had seized their opportunity in Simon Artz. He wore a pair of round sunglasses, a real cummerbund, baggy pantaloons, Egyptian felt

slippers and a fez. A long ivory cigarette holder completed his ensemble. He was King Farouk.

The ocean provided its own diversions. Dolphins cavorted ahead of the bow wave and we were permitted, under the supervision of a parent and a deck officer, to go for'ard to the fc'sle (as my father would have it) and look down on them. They were sleek and grey, the colour of torpedoes. On occasion, they swam on their sides, the better to look up at us with an almost human eye. Flying fish scudded over the waves, their fins outspread like grotesque, ribbed wings. Occasionally the wind took them and they glided up on to the deck to be spirited away by the Lascars, low-caste Indians who cleaned, painted and polished the ship, who ate them. Off the Horn of Africa, a vast pod of at least fifty whales was sighted, blowing and diving, the huge flukes of their tails rising into the air only to slide under the surface once more.

Every evening, I lay in my bunk watching the sea speed by and reading or pondering what lay ahead of me. At least I knew the pigtail was unlikely, for my mother had insisted I had a haircut from the ship's barber soon after departing Algiers. But for the rest, I could only let my imagination wander. My father refused point blank to discuss anything about his job, claiming it was top secret. I considered the chances of him being a spy and asked my mother one night as I got ready for bed if this was his role in the Navy.

'A spy!' she retorted. 'In the Navy? What gave you that idea?'

'Daddy said his job was secret.'

'Your father could no more be a spy than I could be a spanner,' she replied, always keen to find an alliterative metaphor. 'He's a Deputy Naval Stores Officer. A naval grocer! It's his job to see ships get fresh supplies of lettuces and eggs. Secret!' She laughed. 'I'm sure the Commies're not interested in how many tins of sardines HMS *Ark Royal* is carrying.'

At seven o'clock — or nineteen hundred hours, as my father preferred — my mother, having seen me into my bunk, would join my father on deck for cocktails and dinner. Although, once in the tropics, the formal evening dress code for the dining room was waived unless there was a dinner dance or the like being held, my father insisted on wearing a lounge suit when all that was demanded was a tie. This greatly embarrassed my mother and, one afternoon between Aden and Bombay, it created an argument conducted *sotto voce* in my cabin. I only heard a part of it, eavesdropping at the door.

'. . . but it's unnecessary, Ken,' I heard my mother say insistently. 'You stand out like . . . like . . . like a daffodil in a daisy field.'

'Just because the mercury touches eighty, Joyce, it doesn't mean we have to abandon all our bloody standards.'

There was a pause.

'You know what they call you, don't you?' She did not wait for a response. 'Commodore Blimp.'

'I don't give a bloody damn,' my father answered, yet I could tell his anger had been goaded.

'And that knotted hankie. I mean! That's setting a standard? You'll be rolling your trouser legs up next. You could at least buy a panama in the shop.'

'I'll wear what I bloody like, when I bloody like, where I bloody like. It's a free bloody country, thanks to the likes of me.'

'Here we go,' I heard my mother say with an air of well-tried boredom. 'Tell me, Ken, I forget: which submarine did you serve on? Which Atlantic convoy did you escort? Which landing craft did you command on D-Day?' She fell silent for a moment. 'None. And whose father was imprisoned for three years in Germany after his ship went down under him at the Battle of Jutland? Mine. And whose mother snubs mine because her

husband was only a Chief Petty Officer? And you talk of standards. Double standards in your case, Ken. Double standards.'

There followed a brief scuffling at the end of which there was a loud bang as my father slammed his hand on the wardrobe door. I later saw the dent his signet ring had made in the veneer.

'Don't you ever speak like that to me again, Joyce, or . . .'

'Or? Or what, Ken? A divorce? My! That would look good on your record sheet, wouldn't it? A real blot rather than a splat of ink. Set tongues wagging in the wardroom. And what about Martin?'

'What about him?' my father answered.

It was then I decided to make myself scarce and scurried away down the corridor. An hour later, my father appeared on the deck wearing a straw panama hat with a dark blue band.

Shortly before eight o'clock every evening, and the sounding of the chimes for dinner, my mother would return to the cabin with two silver-plated bowls. One contained salted potato crisps, the other small, pickled gherkins speared by variously coloured satinized aluminium cocktail sticks shaped like arrows and bearing the ship's name. I had never come across either delicacy in England and saw them as harbingers of a new and wondrously strange life to come.

My mother detested Bombay. The streets were dirty, the beggars persistent and frequently mutilated, either by accident, design or disease. Like the beggars, the buildings were in various states of decrepitude. Even the monkeys in the public gardens were a ragged, flea-ridden lot. The liberty with which cattle wandered about, dunging where they chose, also disturbed her, not because

they left steaming piles behind them but because no-one bothered to clean it up.

'It would not have happened before independence,' my father declared in hushed tones, perhaps in case the Algerian assassin had a cousin who had migrated eastwards. 'Standards were maintained.'

I asked what cows were doing wandering in the city and sitting in the middle of the road. In my experience, they lived in fields, slept in barns and ate grass.

'They're considered holy,' my mother said. 'People here worship them.'

This struck me as too bizarre to be true. She had to be pulling my leg. Yet, with each port of call, I was realizing the world was not as I had previously anticipated it.

'What about the elephants?' I enquired, having seen several walking sedately down a wide street, their mahouts balanced cross-legged on their necks and armed with a vicious-looking iron spike with which they intermittently jabbed their mount behind its ears. 'They mess in the road, too.'

'That, too, is disgusting, but in India,' she went on, 'elephants are beasts of burden. Like Nanny's milkman's horse.'

By my mother's reasoning mind, this somehow allowed the elephants their defecatory habits and expunged them of all lavatorial responsibility.

'Doesn't anyone grow roses in India?' I asked.

'What?' my father, who had not been following the conversation, responded sharply.

'Nanny puts the milkman's horse dung on her roses.'

My parents exchanged glances and we crossed the road. A passing car ran through a particularly fresh and fluid cow pat which spattered my father's shoes and indelibly stained his socks.

Later, I was shown – from a discreet distance – the Parsee

death tower. My father explained to me that the Parsees did not bury their dead but left them for the vultures to eat. No sooner had I been told this than a flurry of plump crows took to the wing from the tower, several of them trailing ribbons of flesh from their beaks. They flew into a nearby park to squabble over their bounty, tugging it between them. One of them tossed a finger into the air for another to catch and fly off with, cawing jubilantly. Meanwhile, the vultures with their vulgar naked necks and hooked beaks perched in the flame-of-the-forest trees laden with scarlet blossoms, preening themselves and letting go pressurized streams of excrement on to the flowerbeds and monkeys below.

Yet the memory of Bombay that was to linger was that of a scrawny cat on the dock. It came each of the two evenings the *Corfu* was berthed alongside. Slinking out of the shadows, it moved with its belly flat to the ground like a leopard stalking a gazelle. Its ribs and shoulder blades protruded through its skin and it had a bloody, torn ear. I tossed it a gherkin which it ignored but it relished the potato crisps. The night before we were due to sail, I spent a long while trying to persuade my mother we should give it a good home but she resolutely refused to cave in. Finally, she allowed me one concession. In the warm dusk air, she led me down the gangway and along the quay where I placed two cocktail sausages and a pile of crisps on the quayside, to keep the cat going at least until its ear healed. I was then given my bath and climbed into my bunk just in time to watch through the porthole as an urchin detached himself from the shadows of the warehouse, ran to the food, crammed it into his mouth and fled.

In contrast, Colombo was paradisiacal. We arrived in the early afternoon, tieing up to a mooring about a mile out. In the distance were beaches of coral sand fringed with palms. No sooner were the ship's engines shut down than a plethora of small naked boys no older than I was appeared in the sea off the starboard side.

Bronzed and lithe, they must have swum out from the shore, for they had no boat. Like marine nymphs they cavorted in the sea, oblivious to the dangers of jelly fish or sharks. Shouting up to the passengers, they invited us to throw money down to them. As each coin struck the surface, it quickly sank. The boys, thrusting their bare brown bottoms into the air like ducks did their tails, dived after them. They missed not a coin but, as they were stark naked, I could not understand where they stored their booty.

'They put the coins in their mouths,' my mother said.

'What if they swallow them?' I asked, aghast at the thought.

'They don't,' my father said perfunctorily. 'If they do, they get beaten.'

After half an hour, a canoe arrived on the scene sculled by a wizened old Fagin and a girl of about twelve. The passengers, sensing the show was over, drifted away. The boys clambered into the boat, arched themselves forward and either spat out or retched up – I was not sure which – a substantial amount of small change. The old man rowed back to shore, the boys following him like brown porpoises.

That evening, we went ashore in a motorboat to a wooden jetty.

'Who are we going to see?' I enquired as the wavelets lapped against the side of the boat.

'Uncle Bud and Auntie Cis,' my father replied.

'But I don't have any uncles and aunts,' I remonstrated.

'Out here you call a man "uncle" if he is older and wiser than you,' my mother informed me. 'It's a term of respect.'

This seemed to me to be as bizarre as worshipping cows but I decided to keep that opinion to myself.

We were met by my newfound 'uncle' and 'aunt' who were, in fact, my father's cousin Cis and her husband, Bud. They piled us into a vast black Humber saloon and drove us to their home at Mount Lavinia, on the coast south of Colombo. It was, I realized

as we made our way along a tree-lined road in the tropical twilight, swerving to avoid potholes, the first time I had set foot in a foreign land at night.

Our destination was a rambling bungalow with a wide veranda on three sides. The pillars supporting the roof were ornately carved with glaring, snarling demons. Upon the veranda stood rattan furniture and a number of collapsible roorkee chairs. Oil lamps hung from hooks or stood on the table. Drinks were served by an almost black-skinned, barefoot man in a patterned sarong. The whites of his eyes shone in the lamplight. My parents drank gin and tonic but I was given a tall glass filled with an opaque liquid in which were suspended small white flecks. I tentatively sipped it. It was exquisite, cooling and strangely sweet. I asked Uncle Bud what it was.

'Coconut juice,' he replied.

'Where do you buy it?' I enquired, hoping I might successfully implore my mother to purchase a supply.

'We don't,' Uncle Bud answered. A ripple of night breeze teasing the lanterns was followed by a dense thud in the darkness. 'There's your answer.'

Uncle Bud called the manservant who led me into the night to pick up a coconut the size of my head.

'Now you know why we don't park the cars under palm trees,' Uncle Bud declared. 'When I first came out, I did so. Once. Didn't think. Had to get a new bonnet shipped out from the UK. Terrible cost . . .'

When we had eaten, I sat on one of the roorkee chairs and looked out into the night. Bats the size of English thrushes wove their shadowy flight through the darkness, issuing barely audible squeaks. Atlas moths as large as my outspread hand, with antennae like feathers and translucent windows in their fore-wings, fluttered round the lamps. Tiny grasshopper-like insects no

bigger than a grain of rice scorched themselves to death on the hot lamp glass while beetles the size of my first thumb joint flew into the circles of lamplight with a whirling clockwork sound but were wise to the heat and avoided it.

The most fascinating creatures to be drawn to the lamplight were the geckoes. No more than a finger long, these tiny lizards gathered round the ring of light to pick off any insect they felt they could handle. They stalked their prey, made a headlong dash at the last moment and delicately chewed on their quarry, a bulbous tongue folding wings and legs into their maws. When they swallowed, one could see the insect they had eaten in their stomachs, sometimes twitching to escape. Fascinated by them, I caught one in my cupped hands. It quickly escaped, however, shedding its tail which, for a minute or so, thrashed to and fro on the floorboards between my feet.

Sitting there, the adults talking in the background, I gradually became aware of someone standing just over my shoulder and turned. Beside my chair stood a beautiful Singhalese girl of about my age. Her eyes were as wide and as black as a starless night, her hair long and cascading like threads of jet upon her shoulders.

'Hello,' I said. 'I'm Martin.'

Her response was to put her hands together as if in prayer and bow to me. This formality over, she sat on the floor by my side and remained there unspeaking until we left for the ship. I tried several times to take her hand for I was utterly smitten by her, but she demurely shunned any physical contact with me.

Returning to the *Corfu* in the motorboat, I watched the shore recede with a curiously heavy heart. The quayside lights rippled on the sea with a clarity that I had never before seen. It was as if the balmy tropical air transformed it into something magical and I was leaving behind a singular, mystical place I knew I would never find again.

Two days out of Colombo, we sailed past the Great Nicobar
Island, changed course, skirted the northern tip of Sumatra and
headed east across the Strait of Malacca, bound for Penang. A
small British colony founded in 1786, it consisted of an island
bearing the main settlement of Georgetown and a parcel of the
Malayan mainland opposite. Once again, we went ashore to walk
along an esplanade, drink a lemonade that was ubiquitous east of
Gibraltar and look at a number of sedately squat nineteenth-
century colonial buildings, one with a tower, the only building
above three storeys in the town. Sated with colonial architecture,
my parents then decided we should take the funicular railway to
the summit of Flagstaff Hill from which, my father declared, one
was afforded a panoramic view of Georgetown. Quite why one
should particularly seek out this vista escaped me but my father
had his binoculars round his neck so perhaps he intended to
ensure that the Imperial Japanese Navy was not poised for a sneak
attack, as – he informed us several times – it had been in 1941.

The funicular consisted of a single carriage resembling the
hybrid of a horse-box and a guard's tender with open windows.
Moving at not much more than a walking pace, it took twenty
minutes to arrive at its destination, passing over viaducts and
through dense expanses of jungle.

Halfway up the mountain, the carriage slowed. As it did so, a
troop of several dozen macaques materialized out of the luxuriant
undergrowth and invaded it. The first we knew of this simian
assault was the patter of their hands and feet on the roof: then they
swung in through the windows into the carriage. Pandemonium
broke loose. The monkeys grabbed what they could with the
well-rehearsed proficiency of an experienced pirate boarding

party. One seized on my father's binoculars and, finding them attached to him by a strap, proceeded to chew through the leather. My father batted it away with the back of his hand only to have a second monkey take its place. Another, to my considerable gratitude, grabbed my sombrero lampshade hat and made off with it into the tropical undergrowth.

'Let him have it!' my mother wailed. 'Let him have it!'

I willingly complied.

'Don't resist! Don't let them bite!' one of the other passengers from the *Corfu* yelled whilst at the same time lashing out with a black furled umbrella at a large male, and swearing in what I took to be a local language.

'They'll be rabid!' shouted the umbrella lunger's wife, a plump, middle-aged woman in a sun dress. She turned to my mother. 'I lost my firstborn to rabies at a tin mine up-country from Ipoh.'

My mother hugged me to her bosom in much the same fashion as a female monkey balancing on the window frame clutched its own infant. As she did so, nimble fingers skilfully plucked a handkerchief from her blouse pocket not two inches from my eye and I found myself face-to-face with a big-eared monkey. It bared two rows of yellowed teeth at me and promptly vanished.

Meanwhile, my father was engaged in his own tussle, retaining his binoculars only because, being wartime Royal Navy issue, they were too heavy for the monkey to carry off. Another man was not so lucky and watched as a monkey snatched his Kodak camera and started to rip open the bellows. Throughout this attack, the monkeys uttered not a sound. It was as if they were working with military precision to a set plan requiring no orders.

In less than a minute, the raiding party of hirsute imps retreated into the jungle to be followed by a hail of pebbles hurled inaccurately and far too late by the funicular brakeman. Once in

the cover, they chattered and screamed and howled. Victory was theirs and they knew it.

On our way back down the mountain, I caught a brief glimpse of my detested sun hat hanging from a thorny creeper, shredded. There were, I subsequently discovered with ill-disguised glee, none left in the ship's shop.

Whereas the monkeys' ambush had been pure pantomime, our next excursion ashore lacked any potential to degenerate into farce.

In Singapore, our next port of call, we were greeted by a friend of my father's who whisked us off in a large black Cadillac, through Singapore to the causeway crossing to Johor Baharu, where we had to halt at a military checkpoint. Once through it and across the causeway, our host drove at breakneck speed. It was then I noticed, with a certain quiver of excitement, that there was a sub-machine-gun propped against the front seat between the driver and my father, with a number of spare magazines on the top of the dashboard. Tucked into the crease of the seat was an automatic pistol. At intervals along the road were stationed Bren gun carriers or armoured scout cars with soldiers sitting in them.

After half an hour of driving through serried rows of what I knew from my mother's shipboard lessons were rubber trees, we turned off down a gravelled drive at the gates to which were posted several British soldiers in a sandbagged emplacement. They wore steel helmets covered in camouflage netting stuck through with leafy twigs, the muzzle of a heavy machine-gun protruding through a gap in the sandbags. To one side, a soldier in his shirt-sleeves was boiling a dixie of water over a tiny solid-fuel stove.

I asked why there were so many soldiers. I thought it impolite to enquire why we had a veritable arsenal in the car.

'It's the Emergency,' our host told me.

'What's the Emergency?' I replied.

'It's a war between the British and the Malayan Communist Party,' came the reply.

I wanted to ask why but my father cast me a keep-your-mouth-shut look so I kept quiet.

We had arrived at an extensive bungalow raised on brick piles under a wide tiled roof and surrounded by trim gardens of huge, fan-like travellers' palms, elephant-eared banana trees and what I later discovered were cycads, a plant dating back to the times of the dinosaurs. Thorny bougainvillaea bushes grew supported on bamboo trestles. By the veranda was a virtually leafless tree in full blossom, the exquisite perfume unlike anything I had ever come across. When I asked what it was, my father abruptly told me not to interrupt and our host informed me it was called a frangipani.

The entire garden was surrounded by intermeshing coils of barbed wire. We had a hurried lunch, after which I was permitted to play in the garden – so long as two Chinese men oversaw me – and an equally hurried tea and then we were driven once more at speed back to Singapore and the *Corfu*.

'Why did we have guns in the car?' I asked my mother that night as she brought me my gherkins and crisps.

'We could have been ambushed by terrorists,' she answered matter-of-factly.

At that moment it dawned on me that what I had previously taken to be a safe existence was quite possibly going to be anything but from then on.

The following night, my parents attended a formal end-of-voyage dinner, my mother dressed in a long evening gown, my father in a tuxedo. They cut a dashing couple. If there had been an adults' fancy dress party, he could have gone as a thirties matinée idol or a jazz band leader.

The next day, the steward returned our suitcases from the store

and we spent the day packing. I realized all I had to show for my voyage halfway around the world was a collection of multi-coloured cocktail sticks, the small wooden camel and a coconut. My mother persuaded me to abandon the latter which I did with reluctance, but not until the cabin steward had drained the juice from it which I sipped slowly, as if it were ambrosia.

The morning of 2 June dawned overcast. I woke to find the *Corfu* barely vibrating, the sea outside my porthole hardly moving by. I dressed quickly and went up on deck to find my mother standing at the rail. A hundred yards off, a red and white launch bobbed on a low swell, the word *Pilot* emblazoned on its hull. As we watched, it edged alongside the *Corfu's* hull, a rope ladder was flung over the side from one of the gangway ports and a man in a white uniform clambered up it. A short time later, the *Corfu* picked up a little speed and sailed slowly into a channel only two or three hundred yards wide. On the starboard side were scrub-covered mountains descending to a treacherous rock-strewn shore against which a light swell broke. To port were more steep hillsides covered in grass and intersected by several bays containing sandy beaches. The shoreline otherwise consisted of more sharp rocks. On a stubby headland was a small village and some low houses set apart in trees beside, to my astonishment, a golf course. The summits of the mountains were lost in a thick fog. The air was warm and humid.

'That's Hong Kong,' my mother remarked. 'Our home for the next three years.'

My father joined us wearing starched white shorts and a white shirt with long white socks and brown brogues. It was tropical kit

for a naval officer save that his shoulders were not adorned by 'scrambled egg', as my father termed gold braid.

'And who are we today, Ken?' my mother enquired amiably.

Ignoring her, my father raised his binoculars to his face and scanned the shore for dangerous rocks and underwater sand bars.

'Which one?' I asked.

'Which one what?' my father replied, lowering his binoculars and peeved by my mother's gentle sarcasm.

'Which one?' I repeated. 'Mummy says this is Hong Kong where we're going to live for three years. Which of the houses is ours?'

'You blithering idiot!' my father responded, yet he typically made no attempt to elucidate.

'No,' my mother said tenderly, 'we aren't living in one of those exact houses. We don't know where our quarters are yet. Just wait and see.'

The *Corfu* steamed slowly to port round a headland lined with warehouses, a shipyard and a large factory complex with the word *Taikoo* painted on its roof.

'What does *Taikoo* mean?' I enquired.

'I have absolutely no earthly idea,' my mother replied. 'Not the foggiest.'

I crossed to the starboard rail. A peninsula of land culminating in some docks, a large cube of a grey stone building and a railway station with an ornate clock tower jutted out towards the ship. Behind them was a city of low buildings. In the distance was an undulating range of mountains, free of mist. One of the summits was, in profile, vaguely like the lions around the base of Nelson's Column in Trafalgar Square. Rejoining my mother at the port rail, I discovered the *Corfu* was moving slowly past a city which extended up the slopes of the mountains close behind. In

the centre were two tall buildings and a Royal Naval dockyard, the basin and quays lined with grey-painted warships.

'That's HMS *Tamar*,' my father said.

'Which one?' I asked.

'What do you mean?' my father snapped back.

'Which ship is HMS *Tamar*?'

'None of them. That's the name of the dockyard,' he answered tersely. 'That ship there,' he pointed to a grey vessel devoid of armaments, 'is a Royal Fleet Auxiliary. An RFA.' He lowered his voice in case there were any shiv-carrying Communist Chinese spies loitering near us. 'I'll be on one of them. She's called RFA *Fort Charlotte*.'

Aided by nudging tugs, the *Corfu* very gradually eased round to moor alongside a substantial jetty on the western side of the peninsula. Immigration and health officials came on board and we were obliged to congregate in a passenger lounge to go through the disembarkation formalities. These completed, my father met a naval officer dressed as he was in a tropical white uniform but with his rank in black and gold braid epaulettes on his shoulders. He also wore a peaked cap with a white cover on it and the naval anchor and crown badge. Our cabin baggage was collected from our cabins by two naval ratings. Both were Chinese. Neither, to my relief, had his hair in a pigtail: similarly, none of the Chinese stevedores or the men pulling rickshaws along the jetty, laden with baggage, had theirs plaited either.

At exactly noon, as signified by the dull boom of a cannon somewhere across the harbour, we walked down the gangway and into a large, dark blue saloon car with the letters *RN* painted on the side in white.

We had arrived.

2

THE FRAGRANT HARBOUR

THE DRIVE TO OUR LODGINGS, THE SOMEWHAT OSTENTATIOUSLY named Grand Hotel, took but minutes. My room was on the third floor next to my parents'. It had a narrow balcony on to which I stepped the moment the door was opened, to look down upon a street lined with wrist watch, jewellery, camera, curio and tailors' shops. Directly below me was a rickshaw stand, the coolies who pulled them squatting or lying between the shafts of their scarlet-painted vehicles. Those not asleep smoked short pipes, the sweetly pungent, cloying fumes rising up to tease my nostrils.

Before I could begin to unpack my suitcase, my mother entered. She ran a damp flannel over my face and a wet comb through my hair, then hustled me down to the hotel lobby and out into the dark blue saloon once again.

'BB,' my mother whispered as I got into the car. It was her code for *Best Behaviour*.

'Where are we going?' I murmured.

'Lunch,' my father replied sternly. 'And mind your Ps and Qs.'

The saloon drove through a gateway guarded by two army sentries and pulled up in front of a large, long Nissen hut with

very un-military gingham curtains hanging in the windows. Along the walls were prim flowerbeds of low, pendulous scarlet and orange blossomed bushes being watered by a barefoot Chinese man in a conical rattan hat with two watering cans suspended from a bamboo pole balanced over his left shoulder. His hair was not tied in a cue either.

Inside the building was a large dining room with a bar at one end. The tables and chairs were made of rattan, the cushions, tablecloths and napkins matching the curtains. We were joined by the officer who had met us on the *Corfu*. He handed his peaked cap to a Chinese waiter and we sat at a table. Another waiter dressed in loose black trousers, a white jacket fastened with cloth buttons and black felt slippers took our order for drinks. I requested the usual east-of-Gibraltar lemonade, but this was countermanded by the officer who ordered me a brown-coloured drink in a green fluted bottle with a waxed paper straw in it. The glass was running with condensation.

'What is it, sir?' I enquired, heedful of the Ps and Qs – whatever they were – and my father's previous instruction that I was henceforth to address all men as *sir* unless I knew them very well indeed. Or else . . . That veiled threat implied a succession of brief consecutive meetings between the sole of his slipper or the back of my mother's silver hairbrush and my nether regions.

'It's called Coca Cola. If you don't like it,' the officer replied, 'you don't have to drink it and I'll get you that lemonade.'

He was not to know it but that first day in Hong Kong, he started me on a lifelong addiction as effectively as if he had been peddling dope.

The same thing happened when we came to order our meal. To be on the safe side, I asked for an egg and cress salad. What appeared before me was a salad with, arranged around it, some bizarre, pink, curled objects with long feelers, a battery of legs and

black shoe-button eyes. Each of these weird creatures was about four inches long.

'Prawns,' the officer said, leaning across the table to me in a conspiratorial fashion. 'Have you ever eaten crab?'

I nodded, a little overwhelmed at his paying me so much attention, not to mention his forthcoming and amicable manner: to him I was not a child so much as an adult-in-training. My father certainly never treated me in such a fashion.

'These are first cousins to the crab,' the officer went on. 'Much nicer and without the stringy bits and chips of shell.' He picked one up and deftly stripped off its carapace with his thumbnail, dipping it in a ramekin of mayonnaise and holding it out to me. I bit it in half and another addiction was given its first rush. He then showed me how to shell one, rinsed his fingers in a bowl of warm water with a segment of lime floating in it and turned his attention back towards my parents.

At the end of the meal, which was punctuated by steam locomotives periodically hauling trains along a railway track not thirty feet from the Nissen hut, the officer shook my hand.

'A word of advice, my lad,' he said. 'So long as you are in Hong Kong, whenever someone offers you something to eat, accept it. That's being polite. If you don't find it to your fancy, don't have any more. But,' he looked me straight in the eye, 'always try it. No matter what. Besides,' he went on, 'Hong Kong is the best place in the world to eat. Promise?'

My mother listened to this counsel with an ill-suppressed look of maternal anxiety but she did not protest: assuming the officer to be superior to my father, she was perhaps afraid to speak out for fear of disregarding naval protocol. I never knew the officer's name, nor ever saw him again, but I was never to break my promise.

As dusk fell, the street below my balcony at the Grand Hotel

underwent a remarkable transformation. Drab hoardings and shop signs erupted in numerous shades of neon colour. Peering over the balcony was like looking down on a fairground: even the lights of the circus or the seaside funfair in Southsea could not compare. There, the lighting had been provided by ordinary light bulbs. These were fashioned out of thin neon tubes shaped into Chinese characters, English letters, watches, diamonds, suit jackets, cameras and even animals. Just down the road was a restaurant bearing a red and yellow dragon ten feet high. The illuminated words were strange, too: Rolex, Chan, Leica, Fung, Choi, Tuk . . .

That evening, my parents were invited to a welcoming cocktail party and I was left in the care of the hotel child-minding service, which consisted of a middle-aged Chinese woman with her black oiled hair severely scraped into a tight bun. I was introduced to her by my mother.

'This is Ah Choo,' she said.

I collapsed into paroxysms of laughter which were promptly silenced by a stern maternal grimace.

'Ah Choo is the hotel baby amah,' my mother went on.

'What's an amah?' I enquired to defuse the situation, ignoring the deprecatory implication that I was a baby.

'A female servant,' my mother replied, 'and you'll do exactly as she tells you. Exactly!' She turned to the amah standing in the door. 'Ah Choo, this is my son, Martin.'

'Huwwo, Mahtung,' the amah replied, then, looking at my mother, said, 'You can go, missee, I look-see Mahtung. He good boy for me.'

'Behave yourself,' my father said pointedly as my parents bade me goodnight. 'If I hear from Ah Choo that you've been monkeying about . . .' He left the rest unsaid. I caught a brief vision of a leather slipper.

The first thing Ah Choo attempted to do after my parents had departed was undress me. I had not been undressed before by anyone in my life save my mother and grandmothers and I wasn't going to let this diminutive, alien stranger called Sneeze be the first.

As soon as she unfastened one button and turned to the next, I did the first up again. Finally, unable to undo more than three shirt buttons at a time, she gave up, informing me, 'You bafu w'eddy.' Going out of the room, she left me to disrobe and wash myself.

I gave her a few minutes, wet the bar of foul-scented hotel soap, pulled the bath plug and glanced outside the bathroom. I had expected to find her in my bedroom. She was not there. The door to the corridor was open. Leaving the room, I headed nimbly along it and down the stairs, into the lobby and out on to the street. I knew this excursion came under the 'monkeying about' heading yet I could not resist it. The street called to me as a gold nugget must beckon to a prospector. Until then, my life had been bounded by my parents' small suburban garden, a nearby playing field, an ancient tractor and, more recently, a ship's rail. Now, it was colourfully lit, boundless, unknown, exciting and throbbing with adventurous potential.

No-one paid me any attention. The hotel doorman completely ignored me. Reasoning that I would not get lost if, at every corner, I turned left and would therefore end up where I started, I turned left.

Buzzing with the frisson of an explorer stepping into un-mapped territory, I made off down the street. The first shop I stopped at was a jeweller's. In the brightly illuminated window, gold bracelets, necklaces and chains glistened enticingly. Strings of pearls glowed with a matt marbled lustre. A black velvet-lined tray of diamonds sparkled like eyes in a jungle night. Inside the

shop stood a sailor, his arm round the waist of a young Chinese woman wearing a very tight dress that shimmered under the shop lights. The sides of the garment were slit from the bottom hem to the top of her thigh. When she moved, almost her entire leg was visible. I had never seen anything like it – the dress or the female limb.

The sailor's uniform was very different from a British naval rating's. It was all white with thin blue edging and insignia, topped off with a pill-box-shaped hat that made me think of Popeye. His sleeves were rolled up tightly to his armpits showing the tattoo of an anchor, a palm tree and the words *San Diego*. As my grandfather had several faded tattoos, these did not surprise me. What did take me aback was that, as I watched him, he slid his hand in one of the slits in the dress and squeezed the young woman's buttocks. She made no sign of complaint and I wondered if this was how one greeted all Chinese women.

I was still contemplating the social manners of the Orient when the shop door opened and the pair came out, the young woman admiring a gold bangle on her wrist.

'Hey, kid!' the sailor addressed me. 'How yah doin'?'

Not quite understanding him, I answered defensively, 'I'm not doing anything, sir.'

'Why you out late time?' the young woman asked. She stroked my hair. Her fingernails were long and painted vermilion. So were her toenails, visible through the ends of her high-heeled sandals.

'Where d'yah live, kid?' asked the sailor. I pointed down the street. 'Well, y' come along now, y' hear? Ain't right for yah to be out so late.'

They took a hand each and walked me back to the Grand Hotel, passing me into the custody of the desk clerk who was given an earful of invective by the young woman. A brief but

heated argument ensued at the end of which the hotel doorman arrived. An uncharacteristically burly Chinese, the sailor took a swing at him. It did not meet its intended target. More invective followed before the sailor, holding the young woman's hand, grinned at me and said, 'Stay lucky, kid!' and with that they were gone.

Back in my room, Ah Choo had run another bath. I closed the door, undressed, washed and put on my pyjamas. I had just pulled up the bottoms and was tying a bow in the cord when Ah Choo came in without so much as a brief knock, bending down to gather up my clothing. I seized the moment to test my rudimentary understanding of local etiquette and squeezed one of her buttocks. It was soft and pliable like a semi-deflated balloon.

She stood bolt upright as if a lightning shaft had run along her spine.

Turning sharply to face me, she exclaimed, 'You v'wy lautee boy, Mahtung!' Yet, behind her castigation and indignation there lingered a smile.

She put me to bed, switched on a pedestal fan, lowered the slatted blinds and left. I slid out of bed and went on to the balcony. The rickshaw coolies were sharing a saucepan of rice on top of which was a complete boiled fish – head, fins and all. I watched as they dissected it with their chopsticks, spitting the bones on to the street. Opposite my balcony was a tenement building which housed a workshop over a tailor's establishment. Under the blaze of strip lights, a dozen men deftly cut and sewed suits. Next door, four Chinese men shuffled what looked to me to be cream-coloured dominoes. They rattled loudly on the metal table top as they were mixed up, sounding with a report as they were slammed down. From a window higher than mine, a small boy was peering out through metal bars. I waved to him but he did not respond: instead, he disappeared and I heard him calling out. A

shirt on a hanger hung from the bars of another window. In yet another was a dark blue glazed pot holding a single, red lily. The illuminated windows reminded me of an advent calendar except that this was secular and alive.

I climbed into bed. My cotton pyjamas were sticking to me with the heat so I removed them and fell asleep to the staccato rattle of the game tiles, the passing traffic, the occasional raised voice or laugh from the rickshaw coolies and the drone of the fan.

The next morning, I woke with a nagging headache. So did my parents.

Sitting at breakfast in the hotel dining room, my mother remarked, 'I only had two G 'n' Ts last night. I hope we're not all coming down with something.'

'You didn't sleep well, Joyce,' my father observed. 'Tossing and turning . . .'

'Well,' she answered, 'what with the whine of the fan, the clatter of that infernal mahjong game opposite and the stench of the rickshaw coolies' pipes, is it any wonder? I really don't think, Ken,' she went on, 'we can go on staying here.'

I was not a little dismayed at this turn of events. I wanted to explore more of the streets. Furthermore, Ah Choo had not ratted on me. I wondered why until it dawned on me that to do so would have been to bring her job into jeopardy.

'I like it here,' I chipped in. Then, hoping to justify my statement, added, 'I like the smell of the coolies' pipes.'

For a long moment, my parents looked at each other.

'That does it!' my father agreed. 'We move as soon as we can. Another week here and we'll all be ruddy opium addicts.'

3

SEI HOI JAU DIM

THE NEXT SEVEN DAYS WERE FILLED WITH ACTIVITY. MY FATHER prepared to join his ship at the Sasebo naval base in Japan. I was enrolled in Kowloon Junior School, and kitted out with several pairs of khaki shorts and white short-sleeved shirts, on to the pockets of which were attached a chocolate-brown and yellow school badge, held in place by press studs. My mother frantically wrote letters to inform her many correspondents of our change of address.

During this time, we stayed with a colleague of my father's in a spacious bungalow at Mount Nicholson halfway up a mountain on Hong Kong Island, which I was told was known as Hong Kong-side, the peninsula upon which we were to live being referred to as Kowloon-side. Indeed, many places were suffixed with -side: I'm going shopping was I go shop-side, beach-side (swimming), office-side (work), school-side (school) and so on.

A car collected us from the Grand Hotel and drove us over the harbour by way of a vehicular ferry. *En route*, we saw the *Corfu* departing on its return journey to Southampton.

'Just think,' my mother said, 'in a month that'll be back in England.'

I could not tell if she was wistfully yearning for England's shores or horrified at the thought of returning to austere, drab British towns filled with dowdy-looking people, strikes, grey skies and snow.

The air was much cooler at the bungalow. The only sounds were birdsong and, in the evenings, the metallic click of the geckoes encircling the ceiling lights to pick off mosquitoes, gnats and small moths. The proliferation of mosquitoes demanded we sleep under mosquito nets: the bungalow was above the Wong Nei Chong valley, an infamously malarial area in the early days of the colony. One could pick up the high-pitched whine of these minuscule insect fighter bombers approaching only to hear it abruptly halt when they hit the netting. This would then agitate as a gecko ran down the muslin to consume the insect, returning to the top of the net to await the next one. My mother wondered aloud that if evolution moved any faster, geckoes would soon learn to weave webs as spiders did.

The lantana bushes on the edge of the lawn were in full multicoloured blossom and frequently visited by black-and-emerald-green butterflies the size of sparrows. The verdant undergrowth of the hillsides coming right down to the edge of the bungalow garden and a border of azaleas and bougainvillaea bushes did more than encourage merely insects into the house. On our third morning, the houseboy entered my bedroom and woke me with a gentle shake.

'Young master,' he addressed me in hushed tones, 'you come. Slowly, slowly. No makee noise.'

With that, he took me by the hand and headed for the french windows to my bedroom. Cautiously, he led me out on to the

veranda where everyone else in the house – servants and residents – were gathered in a silent group.

'No talkee,' he whispered. 'No makee quick.'

To lend weight to his instructions, the man who lived in the bungalow with his wife and a son six years my senior, muttered, 'Don't make a sound or move a muscle, old boy.'

In the sitting room, the gardener and another Chinese man seemed to be rearranging the furniture. Suddenly, one of them darted behind a rattan settee and scrabbled about unseen on the parquet flooring. When he stood up, all the Chinese muttered *Ayarh!* in unison.

In his hand, held by its neck between a long thumb nail and index finger, was a cobra over four feet long, its hood expanding and contracting against the man's palm. He carried it out on to the lawn and killed it by cracking it once, like a whip. The tenant of the bungalow gave the gardener and his companion a purple dollar bill each before the former walked off with the reptile's carcass.

'That'll make a nice purse,' my mother remarked.

'I doubt they'll take the snake to a tanner,' came the answer. 'They'll cook it. The Chinese'll eat anything that can move under its own locomotion.'

Remembering my promise, I decided to assiduously avoid the gardener until after the next main meal.

Five days after arriving in Hong Kong, we booked into two adjacent rooms with a connecting door on the third floor of the Fourseas Hotel at 75 Waterloo Road, Kowloon.

Built on one of the main thoroughfares running down the

Kowloon peninsula, it was a modern, E-shaped three-storeyed block with a flat, tiled roof, modest gardens and a short, sloping, crescent-shaped driveway leading to a covered entrance. Beneath the front lawn and giving directly on to the pavement was the hotel garage. My parents' room had a balcony: mine did not. On either side of the hotel were low-rise apartment buildings whilst opposite, across the wide road, was the steep bare dome of a hillside rising about a hundred feet from the street. It contained a deep fissure I was sure, in my romantic imagination, was an old volcanic vent just waiting to erupt.

'This is definitely a leg-up,' my mother declared as, for the third time in a week, she unpacked our cases.

'How long will we be staying here?' I asked, having grown used to a peripatetic existence.

'At least until Christmas,' she replied. 'Now,' she continued, 'if you ever get lost, this hotel is called *sei hoi jau dim* in Cantonese. It means *four seas hotel*. You say that to a taxi driver and he'll bring you home safe and sound and the receptionist will pay him. Repeat it.'

These were my first words in Cantonese and I was not slow in realizing that as many Chinese did not speak English, if I wanted to explore as I had on my first night, I would need a command of their language. In next to no time, I possessed a substantial vocabulary ranging from a polite *Nei wui mui gong ying mun?* (Do you speak English?) to such commonly used colloquialisms as *Diu nei lo mo* which, I discovered, implied anything from You don't say! to Well, I never did! to Bugger me! to Don't bullshit me, you sonofabitch! And worse. Much worse . . .

Early the following Monday, my father reported to Kai Tak airport to depart for Japan. My mother was very anxious, not because my father was in effect heading for a theatre of war – Korea – but because he was flying out of Hong Kong. According

to my father, who was never loath to dramatize if it boosted his ego, the wind direction was crucial to a successful landing or take-off. If at all possible, he declared, aircraft took off towards the south-east, the runway aiming for the sea. However, rarely, aircraft had to take off facing inland. This meant that as soon as it was clear of the ground the aircraft had to veer sharp left to avoid crashing into the Kowloon hills. These rose to nearly 1,900 feet at a distance from the end of the runway of not much more than two miles. Pilots regarded it as one of the most dangerous and demanding airports in the world.

Standing at the steps of an RAF twin-engined MacDonald Douglas 'Dakota' DC3, my parents atypically hugged each other for several minutes. My father then bent down, gave me a cursory embrace and shook my hand.

'While I'm away,' he ordered, 'look after your mother. You're the man of the family now.'

It was a pure Hollywood moment, my father handsome enough to have been played by James Stewart, his wife petite and blond enough for the part to have gone to Doris Day. I suppose I would have been played by Mickey Rooney: it would have been my luck.

'Yes,' I replied noncommittally but, as usual with my father, I had been instructed to do something without any guidance as to how to do it. Was I, for example, to see my mother across the road, ensure she washed behind her ears, went punctually to bed and so on? I was about to enquire but my father was already at the aircraft door and stooping to step aboard. A moment of fear swept through me. I had been given a serious task, yet how could I, in my ignorance, hope to do it efficiently? There was, I saw, only one outcome – a slippering for failure. Even before the DC3 took off, I was already dreading my father's return.

The engines started with billows of black smoke and the plane moved away. My mother crossed her fingers. The gesture failed.

The Dakota turned right and taxied to the very south-eastern extremity of the runway. It was to be a take-off into the mountains.

At this point, my mother noticed a main road crossed the runway at about three-quarters of its length, the traffic controlled by a set of lights. This added hazard unsettled her further. I saw her watching avidly to ensure the traffic lights were working and the drivers obeying them.

The Dakota rumbled forwards. As it passed by us, its tail wheel lifted off the runway, the plane taking to the air at the road crossing. Its ascent seemed excruciatingly slow. For a moment, I was quite certain it was heading straight for the mountains and followed its progress with terror mingled with fascination.

'I can't watch,' my mother declared and she studied her shoes. Her hands shook.

At what seemed the last minute, the DC3 banked so sharply to the left I could see both wings as if I were looking down on top of it. It flew along the face of the hills, climbing slowly, levelled out and began its gradual ascent until it disappeared in the haze of the day, the sound of its engines suddenly dying.

'What's happened?' my mother asked, almost in tears and still not daring to look.

'Nothing,' I said, exercising my licence as head of the family for the first time. 'It's flown so far away so we can't see or hear it.'

A Royal Navy saloon car took us back to the Fourseas Hotel.

'When does Daddy come back?' I enquired.

'In about twelve weeks,' my mother replied. 'On his ship,' she added with evident relief.

'What happens if I don't look after you very well?' I said anxiously.

'Don't you worry,' my mother answered, sensing my concern and putting her arm around me. 'You'll do just fine.'

A telegram arrived that evening from my father. Opening it, my mother visibly relaxed. It had been an uneventful flight. She poured herself a gin and tonic.

The Thursday after my father's departure, I started school.

Kowloon Junior, as it was known, bore as much resemblance to my previous school as a cat did to a caterpillar.

Since beginning my education at the age of five, I had attended a small dame school in Brentwood, Essex. Owned and operated by a kindly, elderly spinster called Miss Hutt, Rose Valley School provided a very sound basic schooling from the huge, dark front room of a mid-Victorian terraced house. A noxious lavatory, the floorboards irredeemably stained by years of small boys with a poor aim, was in the basement and the rear garden had been flattened, surrounded by a picket fence and covered with cinders to make a playground of sorts. Beyond the fence were vegetable allotments in which the citizens of Brentwood attempted to supplement their rations. Every lunchtime, the pupils – there were about a dozen of us aged from five to twelve – were marched in single file to Brentwood High Street where we were fed in a café with oil-cloth-covered tables. The monotony of the menu never varied – scrag end of beef or mutton stew with boiled potatoes, mashed swedes and cabbage, helped down with a glass of milk. Dessert was invariably a bowl of semi-liquid, lumpy custard. Sometimes this was supplemented by an apple or, on one occasion, a banana the skin of which was turning black.

By contrast, my new school was a long, two-storeyed building with veranda corridors, bright, airy classrooms with ceiling fans and individual desks: at Rose Valley, we had hunched round two old dining tables. Everyone wore a uniform which somehow gave the place an added appeal. Outside, the playground was beaten earth with patches of grass surrounded by a six-foot chain-link fence on the other side of which was a steep drop to the dusty

football field of another school. In one place, the fence stopped at a vertical earth bank into which the boys had cut mountain road-ways for Dinky cars.

The school was less than a mile from the Fourseas and so I walked there most days, my mother at first seeing me across Waterloo Road. If it was raining, I was sent in a scarlet-painted rickshaw with a green pram-like hood and two huge spoked wheels with solid rubber tyres.

Riding in a rickshaw was a strange sensation. The coolie lowered the shafts to the ground, one stepped between them on to a footboard in front of a padded seat covered in a loose white cloth and sat down. At this stage, the whole contraption was sloping forwards and downwards. I had to hold on to the sides to stop sliding off – the cloth didn't help. The coolie then picked up the shafts, his elbows bent at right angles. This meant the rickshaw suddenly tipped backwards and the passenger fell to the rear of the seat.

The coolie set off at a walk, building to a steady trot. His bent arms acted like leaf-springs on a vehicle, reducing the shock of the road bumps for his body.

The coolies were usually bare to the waist, except in winter, and one could see their muscles flexing across their shoulders, the tendons tightening and relaxing under their skin. Most of them were sallow, with sunken chests, gaunt faces and drawn skin on their necks: and when they sweated, they exuded a faint, strangely sweet body odour. They all looked old enough to be Confucian sages, but they were almost all certainly no older than their late twenties. A rickshaw coolie's lifespan seldom reached thirty-five. It was not long before I realized virtually every one of them was an opium addict.

They wore small, domed rattan hats with numbers painted in scarlet on them: it was from these I learnt to count and read

numbers in Cantonese – *yat, yee, sam, sei, ng, lok* – and the coolies were called by their number. Of the half dozen who lingered near the hotel, I always chose number 3, hailing him by shouting, 'Ah Sam!' I never knew his real name.

What really fascinated me about him were his legs. First, he was barefoot, the slap of his soles on the road as distinct as the sound of a shod horse. In the hot weather, this was accompanied by the suck of warm tar as he took the next step. Every varicose vein stood out, the sinews like cables, his calf muscles huge and powerful. One day, I witnessed an altercation between Ah Sam and a taxi driver. With one kick, the coolie stove in the taxi door, deforming the panelling and frame to such an extent the door would not close.

In a letter to her mother, my mother wrote, *Ken gone to Japan. Lonely*. She was also anxious, even though she knew my father was not going into the actual line of fire. To counteract her solitude, if not her apprehension, she turned to me and I found myself exploring Kowloon with her.

We started after school one afternoon by going to the Peninsula Hotel for tea. Known locally as the Pen, the hotel was considered one of the best in the world. We sat in the grandiloquent entrance lobby, surrounded by gilded pillars and serenaded by a string quartet. Silver pots of Indian, Earl Grey or jasmine tea, cradling over methylated spirit lamps, were served with wafer-thin sandwiches and delicate little cakes. The bread and butter came with four different jams. My mother was in seventh heaven. To her, this was a film star's existence. When the bill was discreetly presented, she blanched.

'Martin, go outside and wait round the back of the hotel. I'll be out in a moment,' she said abruptly.

'Where are you going?' I enquired.

'For a pee,' she replied.

I did as I was told. Five minutes later, my mother appeared, walking briskly along the street. Taking hold of my hand as if I were a baton in a relay race, she headed for the nearest bus stop.

Yet my mother was a woman of honour. Returning the following afternoon, she made straight for the head waiter's desk. Holding out the previous day's bill and payment, she blushingly explained the situation. He consulted the *maître d'hôtel*. I am sure my mother was anticipating the view from the nearest police lock-up. The *maître d'hôtel*, a Frenchman, stepped over and said, 'Madame, these accidents may happen.' He closed her fingers over the bill and money in her hand. 'Please, be our guest for tea for yourself and your son this afternoon.'

And we gained more than four free teas from this escapade.

Leaving the Pen, my mother made her way down Hankow Road, one of a grid of back streets, window-shopping the jewellers' shops. She paused outside the Hing Loon Curio and Jewellery Company. In the window was something that caught her eye and we entered. Thereupon began a friendship that was to last decades.

The interior of the shop was like a treasure cave. Heavy Chinese furniture stood piled piece on piece to the ceiling, layers of cardboard protecting them from marking each other. Glass cabinets contained cloisonné trinkets, ebony carvings, ivory figures and beads, trays of gold rings set with multicoloured stones, displays of unmounted gems, gold chains, pendants and brooches. One display case was filled with netsuke, another with jade miniatures and Chinese snuff bottles, Siamese silver and enamel fingernail covers and models of junks.

The proprietor, Mr Chan, approached my mother, smiling. 'You like a drink? Very hot today. You like a Coke, Green Spot, San Mig.?'

My mother, not knowing one from the other and feeling

it impolite not to accept such a kind invitation, went for a San Mig. At this, Mr Chan poured her an ice-cold beer. I, being adventurous, asked for a Green Spot and was passed a bottle of sickly orange juice.

Whilst well intentioned, the drink was of course a means of keeping a would-be customer in the shop. For twenty minutes, we sat on leather-topped stools in front of a glass-topped counter. My mother bought a curio or two to send 'home', which meant Britain. When she was done, Mr Chan asked me, 'What year you born?'

'Nineteen forty-four,' I replied.

'What mumf?'

'September.'

'You *mahlo*.'

From a jam-packed cabinet behind him, he produced a small, crudely carved ivory monkey.

'For you,' he said, handing it to me. 'I see you again.'

Mr Chan was to be my mother's jeweller for the rest of his life and his two sons thereafter until the end of her life. She never bought a single item of jewellery from any other Hong Kong shop, declaring to all who would listen that Mr Chan was the only man of his trade who had not once attempted to swizzle her. For years, she directed friends, acquaintances, visitors and even tourist strangers who accosted her for directions in the street to his shop – 'Just mention my name – Joyce Booth – and you'll not be done,' she would tell them.

It was not long before my mother acquired a social life. The wives of my father's colleagues began to invite her out during the day, and to dinner or cocktail parties in the evenings. When this social whirl began in earnest, she delegated the job of seeing me safely to and from school to one of the hotel room boys. Tall for a Chinese, he was handsome, in his late twenties and spoke English

without the usual Cantonese accent or pronunciation. His full name was Leung Chi-ching, but we called him Ching. In a very short time, I came to love this man as if he were a favourite uncle. Every morning, he guided me across the traffic on Waterloo Road, Chinese-style. This meant crossing to the central white line and lingering there as vehicles zipped by on either side, waiting for a gap in the traffic to complete the journey to the far pavement. He insisted on carrying my rattan school case – an oblong sort of picnic hamper-cum-briefcase known as a Hong Kong basket – containing my books and some sandwiches wrapped in translucent greaseproof paper. Some of my fellow pupils were taken to school by an amah; some came by car. I stood out, accompanied by this imposing but obviously gentle man who acted like a bodyguard.

One day, I asked Ching where he lived. He was reluctant to inform me. However, he embarked upon his life story, which he told me over the next few days, walking back slowly from school with the warm, late-afternoon sun in our faces, little eddies of wind lifting miniature dust tornadoes off the road surface.

His father had been a wealthy landlord in Kwangtung province, not far from Canton. I asked how he came to speak such good English if he had lived in China. He replied that his father had been rich enough to send him to a Christian missionary school.

'It was a very good school. The brothers were trained teachers, men of learning. I was taught by them, not only English but mathematics, geography, history. One, a Chinese brother, also taught Cantonese and Mandarin. Then, one day when I was eight years old, there was much fighting. People were shot in the street and the paddyfields. It was Japanese fighting Chinese. Then, when I was seventeen years old, there was more fighting. This time, it was Communist Chinese fighting Kuomintang Chinese.'

'What are Kuo—' I began.

'Nationalist Chinese,' Ching explained. 'The army of Generalissimo Chiang Kai-shek.'

'What happened?' I asked.

'They lost,' Ching said candidly. 'Then the Communist soldiers came, and the officers, and they took away my father's land and our house. Our belongings were taken, our farm animals killed. My father had a motor car. They burnt it. We had horses to ride. They shot them.'

'Were the horses ill?' I enquired. I knew sick horses were shot: I had stayed for a holiday on a farm in Devon the year before when a dray horse broke its leg and was put down.

'No.' Ching shook his head. 'They just shot them.'

It seemed incomprehensible that anyone would deliberately set fire to a car and barbaric that they should shoot a perfectly healthy horse.

'What happened to you?'

'We were told to go, so we went. If we had not they would have killed us. They killed our friends who refused to go. I came to Hong Kong.'

'If your father is so rich,' I ventured as we waited to cross at a busy junction, 'why do you work as a hotel room boy?'

'I have no money,' Ching answered. There was no regret in his voice. 'All I have are my clothes. When the Communists drove us away, we could only take what we could carry.' We crossed the road and started walking slowly along the pavement towards the hotel. 'There are many, many people like me in Hong Kong.' Ahead of us, the Fourseas Hotel transport, a cream-painted, American shooting brake with varnished wooden bars on the side, drove out of the hotel garage and across both lanes. 'You see Mickey, the hotel driver?' Ching asked. 'He is one who escaped from the Communists. At least half the room boys have

escaped from China. Some with their families, some, like me, alone.'

I felt a terrible sadness for Ching and took hold of his hand.

'You've got me and my mum,' I said comfortingly.

I never discovered where Ching laid his head, but I found where others did. A week or so later, my mother was invited out to a dinner party on Hong Kong-side.

It was already dark before she left in the Studebaker shooting brake for the Star Ferry to cross the harbour to Hong Kong island. I waited a respectable time, got dressed and walked out of the hotel tradesmen's door, a steel gate that gave on to a street called Emma Avenue. I turned left and headed for Soares Avenue, a fairly busy thoroughfare used by traffic taking a short cut to the next main road, Argyle Street.

At the time I was not to know it, but these streets were to be my patch, my playground, and I was to become as well-known in them as any of the shopkeepers.

The streets were warm, the air heavy with the unfamiliar scents of exotic food cooking in the tenements. Traffic fumes fought to suppress these smells but failed. Above the sound of passing cars was a trill of argumentative birdsong from the trees. Finches in bamboo cages, hung outside the tenement windows for an evening airing, joining in the conference with their free-living brethren.

Walking along the streets was mildly hazardous. First, one was periodically peppered with bird seed and desiccated droppings as a finch had a scratch-about in the bottom of its cage three floors above. Second, one was dripped on from laundry hanging out to dry over the street on bamboo poles. Third, and less benign, was the fact that one could be hit by a chicken bone or other detritus from a completed meal. This I found curiously incongruous. The Chinese were a fastidious race and yet here they were throwing

their garbage out of the window and into the street. Without looking first. From some way up. When I passed my thoughts on to Ching, he explained that it was habit: in China, one threw waste food into the street and the local pigs or dogs ate it. That there were no pigs wandering the streets of Kowloon seemed immaterial to the residents. At least there were pi-dogs – stray mongrels – although none of them looked porcinely overfed.

In Soares Avenue, there was a line of shops. I crossed the road and started to inspect them. They did not have front windows, being more like square caves giving directly on to the pavement. One sold everyday kitchen utensils, but even some of these were alien to me. Shallow, cast-iron cooking pots, which I subsequently learnt were called woks, hung from hooks overhead, a shelf bore what I was to discover were rice steamers and there were sets of woven baskets, one inside the other. Packets of chopsticks, rice bowls, serving dishes, quaint porcelain spoons tied together with string, minute bowls, soy sauce dispensers, teapots decorated with red and gold dragons and handle-less tea cups and bowls with lids stood or lay in profusion on a table board balanced on trestles. Near by were displayed wooden cutting blocks bound by steel hoops, meat choppers and knives of medieval ferocity.

Moving on, I came to a fruit seller whose stock, spread out under bright lights, was even more unusual. He sold oranges, lemons, bananas and apples, but the remainder of his offerings might well have been picked on another planet – waxy-looking star-shaped fruit reminiscent in texture of my grandmother's hat flowers only not as dusty; huge grapefruit-like fruits, split open to show pale citrus-like segments within; knobbly custard apples; deep sea-green watermelons bigger than footballs; spiky ovals I discovered to be durians; and what appeared to me to be short lengths of leafless tree branch.

The shopkeeper, seeing me standing admiring his stock, came

round the front and spoke to me, picking up the grapefruit-like pomelo and holding it out. By now, I had picked up more than a smattering of Cantonese and said, '*M'ho cheen.*' To emphasize my impecuniosity, I patted my pockets. He laughed, stroked my blond hair, took out a sharp knife, sliced open the pomelo and offered me a segment. It was time to keep my promise.

I accepted it, said, '*Dor jei,*' and put it in my mouth. It was sweet and tart at the same time, the cells of the segment erupting upon my tongue. '*Ho!*' I said and I meant it. It was very good.

The fruit seller smiled and picked up one of the lengths of branch. It was pale silvery-green and about an inch thick. He shaved the bark from all of its length but a few inches at one end, with which he handed it to me like a truncheon. I had no idea what to do with it. Seeing this he prepared another length, bit some off the end and chewed it. I followed suit. It was sugar cane, saturated with syrupy sap. When he had sucked the stringy cane dry, he spat it out on the pavement. I copied him. Then a fish head hit me on the shoulder. I was, I considered, now at one with the streets, duly initiated and baptized.

I made friends at school but rarely visited my friends' homes or spent time with them away from the classroom or playground. My life was centred on the Fourseas and the adjacent streets and alleyways.

In one fetid passageway, I came across a family of four who lived in a large crate that had been used to ship a Heidelberg printing press from Germany. They had improved their abode by nailing a sheet of tin to it to protect against the elements, putting a plank across the entrance to stop any rubbish drifting in and

standing the crate on four short blocks to keep it clear of the ground and rainwater that cascaded down the alley. Inside, some planks had been erected to pass as shelving. Otherwise it was still a packing crate. My Cantonese was insufficient for me to converse with the family, but they smiled at me when I passed and greeted them. When the hotel started to redecorate some of the public rooms, replacing the venetian blinds with curtains, the manager agreed to give me one. I gave the blind to the family to hang over the crate entrance. They were delighted with it but, a week or so later, they had vanished. It was not just that the family had gone. So had the crate. Their departure left a hole in my life, even though I had only known them for a fortnight. I never saw them again.

My primary circle of acquaintances consisted of the shopkeepers to whom I was introduced by the fruit seller. His name, I came to discover, was Mr Tsang. It was from him that I picked up a knowledge of pidgin Cantonese – it was commonly referred to as kitchen Cantonese, because it was what the European lady of the house spoke with her domestic servants. In exchange, Mr Tsang learnt pidgin English from me.

Next door but two or three to Mr Tsang was a tiny shop squeezed into the sloping space under a staircase. It consisted of a single display counter with a pigeon-hole arrangement of shelves behind it made out of fruit boxes courtesy of Mr Tsang. Owned and operated by an elderly man and his teenage son, it sold plastic biros, ten-cent notebooks, rubbers, plastic rulers, toy guns that spat sparks, tin rocket ships with the same sparkling mechanism in them, playing cards, glass marbles, combs, nail clippers and files . . . It was Soares Avenue's equivalent of a department store. It also sold something that at first bemused me. Packed into small cardboard boxes and surrounded by fine sawdust were what appeared to be clay marbles. I picked one up and put it between

my thumb and forefinger as if to flick it marble fashion. The store owner quickly cupped my hand in both of his and shook his head vigorously. Then, taking the clay ball, he waited for a break in the traffic and tossed it into the road. It exploded loudly with a drift of clay dust. He gave me another and gestured for me to throw it into the road. I did so. It too went off with a loud report. A flock of birds rose from one of the trees and a passing rickshaw coolie volubly cursed me. I returned in minutes with a dollar and bought a boxful. They were confiscated the following morning by the teacher on playground duty, who informed me they were called cherry bombs, they were illegal and if I ever brought one into school again I would be expelled. A letter was sent home to my mother and I was roundly chastised and stripped of that week's pocket money. Yet, at the same time, I felt with that innate seventh sense of childhood that my mother did not entirely disapprove. From that moment, I knew she was not unduly averse to my wandering the streets and I began ranging more widely.

Five hundred yards down Waterloo Road from the Fourseas was a railway bridge beyond which were the streets of Mong Kok. This was almost another land, the railway a national border. The streets contained few shops. Instead, there was a large hospital and a good number of factory units that turned out belt lengths, sandal parts, brightly fluorescent coloured plastic twine, plastic flowers and metal-framed hand trolleys. Other workshops manufactured metal buckles, cheap tin padlocks, trouser waist catches, metal buttons and washers. Most of these items were pressed out of sheets of metal. The air reverberated with the hiss of hydraulics, the ring of hammering and the whine of the cutting or sharpening of metal. Brilliant oxy-acetylene torches lit up the interiors and the sparks of welding guns spattered on to the pavements. On one occasion, I found a fifty cent coin on the pavement outside one of these metal workshops and, no-one

looking, pocketed it. Later, Mr Tsang refused it in payment for a pomelo and showed me why. When he dropped it on the pavement it made a dull clunk: the coin was made of aluminium. There were, additionally, several car repair shops, their concrete floors thick with black oily grime, the pavements scattered with discarded ball-bearings and wadges of multicoloured cotton waste. I was addicted to the smell of these garages, of warm oil, rubber, leather and newly sprayed paint: it was like none other I had ever encountered.

As the weeks passed, I grew bolder and – more confident in facing traffic – I traversed Nathan Road, the main artery running up the spine of Kowloon, to enter the district of Yau Ma Tei, an area that was more residential than Mong Kok. Many of the three- or four-storey buildings were old, with arcades, their balconies lined with green-glazed railings patterned to look like bamboo. The roofs of some were covered in green-glazed tiles and curved upwards at the eaves. A few bore ceramic ridge tiles of dragons and lions in faded blue, red or gold. I felt an added excitement coming upon old rusty signs at the entrance to some side streets declaring *Out of Bounds to Troops*. It was as if I was the first explorer of my race to tread these urban jungle paths. Even soldiers had not come this way before.

The shops here were more traditional than those in Soares Avenue. A bakery sold soft bread buns with red writing stamped on them. Dried fish shops displayed desiccated shrimps, squid, cuttlefish, scallops, mussels, sharks' fins (hanging from the ceiling like triangles of light grey leather) and other unidentifiable seafood. Butchers offered raw meat hanging from hooks under 100-watt bulbs beneath red plastic shades. Poultry shops sold chickens, ducks, quail, exquisitely plumaged pheasants and geese but, whereas the butchers' fare was slaughtered, the live poultry was crammed into bamboo cages. No self-esteeming Chinese

housewife bought fowl that was not still breathing and it was commonplace to see someone walking down a street with two trussed hens clucking with avian irritation.

One afternoon I wandered into a back-street butchery thinking that I might watch the meat being portioned. Unlike British butchers who carefully shaped specific cuts, Chinese butchers merely chopped the carcass up with razor-sharp cleavers. Turning a corner in the shop, out of sight of the street, I was suddenly confronted by the corpse of a black chow dog hanging by a hook that had been thrust through the tendons of a hind leg. Its black tongue hung down from its mouth. There was a massive wound on the back of its head.

No sooner had I seen it than the butcher arrived, grabbed me by the neck and, swearing volubly, turfed me out into the street. Subsequent questioning of Ching ascertained that the Chinese ate dogs – black ones, preferably – and they killed them by pole-axing them. However, he added, dog-eating was illegal in Hong Kong because the *gweilos* liked dogs as pets and that was why I had been given the bum's rush out of the shop.

Rice vendors were also prevalent in Yau Ma Tei, displaying different types of rice in open sacks or, if they were of especial quality, in dark polished barrels with brass hoops. The variety and price were displayed on a tablet of dark wood with the information painted on them in red calligraphy. To me, one rice grain looked much like the next but there were several dozen strains, types and grades available. The tops of the unopened rice sacks were invariably the resting place of sleeping cats which doubtless earned their place keeping vermin down in the early hours.

I was fascinated by the egg shops too, where fresh duck and chicken eggs were on offer alongside dried egg yolks and 100- (or 1000-) year-old eggs. These preserved duck eggs were prepared by

soaking them in strong tea then rolling them in a coating of wood ash, salt and lime. They were then stored in a huge earthenware jar and surrounded by fine soil rich in humus. In this state, they were left for just over three months during which time the yolk hardened and turned grey-green, the white of the egg turning into a semi-transparent black jelly that looked like onyx. Another preserved egg was made by coating it with red earth and ash, salt and lime bound together with tea and rolled in rice husks. They were then stored in an airtight jar sealed with candle or beeswax. When consumed, they were not cooked and were usually taken raw as an hors-d'oeuvre.

Several streets were lined by food stalls known as *dai pai dongs* from which exotic and enticing aromas wafted. One evening, much to the consternation of the stallholder-cum-chef who was cooking over a charcoal brazier, I hoisted myself on to a stool, passing cars inches from my back and, ordering by pointing, asked for one of the preserved eggs. It was served sliced on a plate with a small bowl of pickled sweet vegetables and a dipping bowl of Chinese vinegar, rice wine, soy sauce and thinly sliced ginger. I picked up the chopsticks. A crowd gathered. The spectacle of a blond European boy sitting at a *dai pai dong* alone of an evening was more than most could resist. The traffic slowed. Then stopped. A jam began to form.

Tentatively, not because I was suspicious of the egg but because I was aware that I was the centre of attention and not yet fully proficient at using chopsticks, I picked up a piece of yolk, dipped it in the sauce and ate it, following it down with a nibble of ginger. The taste was unique, savoury and rich and not at all egg-like. I ate a piece of pickled cabbage. The stallholder put a bowl of steaming green tea before me. I held it up as if giving a toast. The crowd applauded, laughed and gradually dispersed, not a few of them touching my head in passing. I then tackled the problem

of eating egg jelly with chopsticks. When I was done, the stall-holder refused payment. I tried to press him. He refused again. I then saw why. I had brought him good luck. He had not a vacant stool.

My excursions into what my mother referred to her friends as Darkest Kowloon were, during term time, limited to the late afternoon and early evening. This was an exciting time of metamorphosis. Pawnshops vied for electric space with restaurants and shops. The *dai pai dongs* commenced a vibrant trade, steam or charcoal smoke redolent with the odours of frying rising from them to glimmer in the neon above. Stalls appeared selling clothes – anything from children's vests to ladies' frilly knickers, all piled haphazardly under canvas awnings – or shoes, kitchenware or bolts of cloth, or offering services such as grinding knives or cutting keys. The streets, busy in the day with people going about their work, now filled with shoppers or those merely out for a stroll. Men walked by promenading their birds in cages. In a few places, people gathered to read the daily papers pasted to a wall or congregated at a street library where they could read books for a minimal charge but not take them away.

Just off Nathan Road, there stood a large temple dedicated to the deity Tin Hau, also known as the Queen of Heaven and the protectress of seafarers. Next to it in the same complex of build-ings were smaller temples to To Tai, the earth god, Shing Wong, the city god, and She Tan, a local god without, it seemed, a celestial portfolio.

Tin Hau was a major goddess of the first league: this I learnt from a book in the minute hotel library – contained within one glass-fronted case in the first-floor residents' lounge – called *Chinese Creeds and Customs*. I frequently consulted it.

According to legend, Tin Hau was born in Fukien province in the eleventh century. One day, her father and brothers went

out to sea to fish. She fell asleep and dreamt their junk was foundering in a typhoon so she flew to their aid on the clouds and rescued them from drowning. It is also said she could predict rough weather and was deified on her death at the age of twenty.

In keeping with her position in the heavenly pantheon, her temple was ornate. The roof ridge was lined with glazed china figurines and all the interior woodwork painted deep red. A little way in front of the altar stood four very tall effigies. They represented the goddess's bookkeeper who tallied up mankind's sins and virtues, the keeper of her seal and two generals of yore called Favourable Wind Ear and Thousand Li Eye who could help to foretell the weather for those going to sea. Elsewhere in the temple were the goddess of mercy, a small altar to Shing Wong whose role it was to intercede with Tin Hau on behalf of the dead, a green-glazed china horse god, a tiger, several deities of prosperity, a god of beauty, a heavenly dog and the effigy of Tong Sam Chong, of whom I had heard at school. He was a Buddhist monk who had brought the Buddhist scriptures from India to China in a sort of Chinese odyssey which had become a famous fairy tale.

Tin Hau's idol sat on her altar wearing a Ming dynasty headdress hung with pearls. The effigy's face was expressionless, painted a garish flesh pink, the same colour as prosthetic limbs, her own appendages out of sight under a red cloak embroidered with gold dragons. Before her were brass candlesticks, offerings of oranges, small china effigies and a brass bowl of sand for worshippers to stand their joss-sticks in. Every so often, a drum or bell sounded, the former so resounding it caused sound waves that were visible in the joss-stick smoke.

In the evenings, the area in front of the temple attracted me as a magnet does iron filings. Crowds flocked there to consult

fortune-tellers, necromancers and phrenologists who had their charts of the human head spread out on the ground.

The fortune-tellers would invite their customers to cast small elliptical pieces of wood or shake numbered bamboo splints out of a bamboo cup, which they would then interpret according to the way they fell or the number written on them. One had a tortoise with a highly polished shell which seemed to possess the powers of divination. In their midst, an old man, a four-inch-long wisp of grey hair sprouting from a mole on his cheek, sat at a small lectern writing letters for illiterate coolies at five cents a time. A black silk skullcap that had seen better days, topped off with a red soapstone finial, lent him the air of an imperial scholar down on his luck.

They all fascinated me in their way but one of them held my attention every time. He was employed in the most bizarre occupation I had ever seen. Seated on a stool, his client – man or woman – perched on another before him. He plucked their eyebrows with tweezers, then either pulled out or clipped their nasal and ear hair. The high point of his service came when he produced a tiny steel spatula and assiduously scraped out his customer's ear wax which he put in a tiny bottle. What he did with this disgusting gunge was left to my vivid imagination.

On the western edge of Yau Ma Tei was the sea and a typhoon shelter, a large artificial basin surrounded by a sea wall of massive boulders, behind which fishing junks and other small craft took shelter during storms. It was also where fishermen landed their catch. Some Saturday mornings, I would go to the shelter to watch the night's haul landed – green and blue-backed crabs and azure lobsters, sea bass with electric-blue scales and black lines, gold and black mottled grouper, thin, silver needlefish, octopi that slid their tentacles across the quayside, squid, sea cucumbers, long-spined sea urchins, eels, rays and sharks ranging in length from a few feet to such as it took four men to lift them, their eyes sunken and

their mouths bloody. Nothing, it seemed to me, had been thrown back: everything was up for sale as edible and women jostled to buy the entire catch. Even the seaweed snagged in the nets sold for ten cents a bundle.

On one occasion, I squatted down to look closely at a large shark when it spasmed, opened its mouth wide and slammed it shut within inches of my hand. Before I could leap away, a fisherman grabbed me by the armpits and hauled me rapidly backwards.

'He lo dead!' he warned me. 'Sometime liff long time lo wartar.'

He picked up an iron bar, smote the shark on its head, rammed the bar in its mouth, twisted it to and fro and, breaking off some of the shark's teeth, scooped them up and gave them to me. They had a sharp, serrated edge. When the bar struck the fish, it sounded like someone hitting a semi-inflated football with a cricket bat.

Three types of vessels predominated in the typhoon shelter. The smallest and most numerous were sampans, ranging from little more than skiffs to boats about fifteen feet long. Constructed of wood, they were propelled by a single stern oar, although some had a short mast with a square-rigged sail. Most had arched canvas awnings that ran their length, beneath which lived a complete family. There was even a place for a charcoal cooking stove. The majority of sampan dwellers were fishing folk who cast gill nets or fished with sleek, long-necked cormorants.

I was intrigued by cormorant fishing, a typically devious and clever method the Chinese had developed. The cormorants were black sea birds about the size of small geese. When a sampan reached a shoal of fish, the fisherman would let the bird go. It would dive into the sea, catch a fish and swallow it. However, the fish could not reach the bird's stomach because of a ring affixed

round its neck. Once the fish was caught, the cormorant returned to the sampan and, unable fully to swallow its prey, spat it out; with its wings clipped, the cormorant could not fly off. When it had caught a few fish, the fisherman would remove the ring, let the bird have a fish as a reward, re-affix the ring and wait for another shoal to pass.

At night, the sampan fishermen caught their quarry with the aid of a bright hurricane lantern. This was hung over the stern, the fish being attracted to it only to be taken in dip nets.

The next boats up in size were the walla-wallas. These were motorboats that operated round the harbour as water taxis. They acquired their name from the puttering sound their exhaust pipes made when a wave momentarily covered them, although I was given an alternative explanation of the name by one of my mother's friends who claimed they were named after the town of Walla Walla in the USA. Curious about this, I looked the place up in an atlas. It seemed improbable to me: the town, little more than a pinprick on the map, was in the state of Washington, at least 170 miles from the Pacific coast.

Third, and most impressive of all, were the huge ocean-going and long-distance coastal fishing or trading junks. Three-masters, they lay alongside the typhoon shelter quay like the remnants of the lost age of sail, prehistoric maritime monsters inexorably creeping towards extinction. Made of seasoned teak, some over eighty feet long and twenty wide, they were not only boats but family enterprises. Infants to grandparents lived upon them, as did cages of chickens and ducks, dogs, cats and even baskets with pigs in them. The poultry and pigs spent much of their lives suspended in mid-air over the stern, their droppings falling to the sea, not the deck.

Not infrequently, I was invited aboard one of these wooden leviathans. My blond hair, considered by the Chinese to be the

colour of gold and therefore likely to impart wealth or good fortune, was my passport to many a nook and cranny of Chinese life. It was also the reason why, whilst walking down the street, a passer-by would often briefly stroke my head. I was a walking talking talisman.

At the stern of the junk were the living quarters for the captain or owner and his family, low-ceilinged compartments that smelt of snug humanity, soap, sandalwood incense and paraffin. Weighted oil lamps hung from hinged brass mountings; two boarded-off *kangs* – traditional Chinese beds – were made up with thinly padded quilts and hard head rests the size of building bricks but made of lacquered papier mâché and painted with flowers or dragons. In one bulkhead, a cubby-hole contained maps, brass and steel dividers, a navigator's ruler and a sextant. Upon a bulkhead was a small shrine to Tin Hau, the effigy seated demurely behind a tiny offertory bowl of rice wine, four kumquats arranged as a pyramid and a smouldering joss-stick.

Below the main deck was the hold which, according to the usual cargo, smelt of fish or a mixture of cloth, rice and, for a reason I never understood, dry earth. In the fo'c's'le were the crew's quarters: up to thirty men crewed the biggest junks. Every junk occupant was deeply tanned, almost the colour of the vessel's hull, and as sinewy as a rickshaw coolie but with a healthy glow to their skin. The junk children were lithe and sharp-eyed, like maritime gypsies. Even the dogs seemed to have a spring to their step, unlike those on the dock that just slept curled up in a convenient patch of shade. Other than to trade or buy supplies, the junk folk seldom stepped ashore and considered themselves a cut above land-dwellers.

Perhaps because she was lonely, perhaps because she missed our cat Gunner (so-called because he had been born in a cannon on HMS *Victory*) who had been left behind in England with my grandparents, or perhaps simply because her love of animals was getting the better of her, my mother decided she wanted a pet. As we lived in a hotel, a cat or a dog would be impractical and were, in any case, prohibited by the management. This did not, however, deter her.

'What animal would you like?' she asked me.

'A monkey,' I replied. It would, I considered, be like owning a little caveman whom I could teach to be civilized or, like those in Penang, criminal. The possibilities for entertainment were boundless.

'One monkey in this family's quite enough,' she retorted. 'What else?'

'A snake.'

'No!'

'Why not? They're not all poisonous.'

My mother thought and said, 'Because it would be stolen and eaten.'

It seemed a good enough reason.

'A pangolin, then,' I suggested.

I had seen one in a market a few days before, curled in a defensive ball with its scales capable of protecting it against every enemy save the butcher's knife. I had wanted to buy it then, to save it from pride of place on a menu, but the asking price was fifty-five dollars and I only had three.

'No.'

Lee Chun Kee and Company at 646, Nathan Road offered, according to their business card, to 'procure strange animals from all countries', a claim I found highly suspect. What if, I wondered aloud, I had the money and wanted a hippopotamus?

An elephant? A tapir? A platypus? Best of all, a panda . . . ?

'They could probably get you one of those,' my mother remarked. 'I don't think you could keep it on the balcony, though. And every day you'd have to get several hundredweight of bamboo shoots for it to eat.'

The walls of the shop were lined with cages containing a multitude of song birds, most of them species of finch. Other cages were occupied by guinea pigs, terrapins, rabbits, white sulphur-crested cockatoos, kittens with their eyes barely open, macaws, love-birds, mynahs, mongrel puppies with eager tails, budgerigars and canaries. My mother drooled longingly over the kittens and puppies with all the emotion of a child peering in the window of a well-stocked confectioner's shop. At last, we were approached by a man we assumed was Mr Lee. He smiled ingratiatingly, display-ing a solid gold canine tooth.

'You wan' baby dog, missee?' he enquired, swiftly opening a cage door and depositing a puppy in my mother's arms, from where it immediately proceeded to furiously lick her face. I could almost see her heart melting.

'Fifty dollar,' Mr Lee said, 'but for you, firs' customer today, speshul p'ice forty-fi'e dollar.'

As it was mid-afternoon, I found his salesman's pitch to be dubious in the extreme, but said nothing. Reluctantly, my mother returned the dog and, after much soul-searching, she purchased a budgerigar, a bamboo cage, a porcelain water bowl, a tin seed bowl, a mirror, a bell and two pieces of cuttlefish. These accoutre-ments cost over three times as much as the bird despite my mother beating Mr Lee down by fifteen dollars.

'What shall we call him?' my mother suggested as we retraced our steps through the back streets. 'How about *Sai Juk*?'

As this translated as Little Bird, I was not impressed. My mother's desire, which lasted the rest of her life, to give everything

— dogs, cats, cars — a Cantonese name did not always show imagination or an extensive vocabulary.

In the end, we settled for Joey. He was happy in his cage, trilling to the wild birds outside, kissing his image in the mirror, ringing his bell, hopping from perch to perch and nibbling at his cuttlefish to keep his beak sharp. This, my mother deemed, was insufficient exercise, so every afternoon she switched off the fan, closed all the windows, locked the doors and gave Joey the freedom of her hotel room. With a flutter of wings, he darted about the room depositing birdshit wherever he went. This continued for two months until the day my mother omitted to close the fanlight window. Joey hopped out of his cage, chirped once and was out the window like a ballistic missile. My mother was devastated and we returned to Mr Lee bereft of a budgie but the proud owners of a miniature aviary with all mod. cons. except running water.

Despite being fully equipped, my mother decided not to get another bird because, she declared, 'You can't cuddle a bird or talk to it like you can a cat or dog. And it's cruel to keep them in cages.'

So she bought a terrapin, a glass tank to keep it in and a stone for it to sit on out of the water.

About two inches in diameter, its carapace was grey on top with a yellowish-green underside. Its head was yellow and black striped with bright red flashes by the ears. My mother, being new to terrapin ownership, asked Mr Lee what it ate.

'He eat w'ice, missee.'

'Rice?'

'Yes, missee. Plenty w'ice. An' dis one.' He reached under the counter to bring out a container of writhing bloodworms.

My mother recoiled but it was too late. She had paid for the terrapin.

On the walk back, we determined to call it Timmy, my mother not knowing the Cantonese for terrapin.

'It's a shame we couldn't have a puppy,' she mused. 'I don't like to dwell on their fate . . .'

'They'll be all right,' I said to placate her. 'The Chinese only eat black dogs.'

My mother stared at me. 'How do you know that?'

'I just heard it. One of the room boys . . .' I replied innocently. 'Besides, it's against the law in Hong Kong to eat dogs.'

My mother looked relieved. I did not admit to having seen the black chow.

Timmy and his tank were delivered an hour later. Convinced that terrapins did not exist on a diet of rice and bloodworms, my mother telephoned the University of Hong Kong Biology Department to get the truth, which was that red-eared terrapins were carnivorous and ate fish. They could also grow to twelve inches in length. Our tank was about fifteen inches by ten. My mother hung up with a thoughtful look on her face. Luckily for us, but unluckily for Timmy, he was dead in three months despite a diet of fresh boiled fish which stank out my mother's room, even when the tank was placed on the balcony so, as my mother put it, he could feel the warmth of the sun on his back. Her reptilian consideration may have been what put paid to him. In the wild, terrapins avoided the sun and took to deep water. Timmy's tank water was barely an inch deep and contained pieces of uneaten fish and terrapin droppings.

Timmy's death did not, however, occur before my father's first return from Japan and his presence, when discovered, caused ructions.

On the second morning of his shore leave, my father stepped out on to the balcony of my mother's room to be confronted by Timmy the terrapin.

'Martin!'

I came running.

'What, for Pete's sake, is this ruddy thing?' He pointed at the noxious tank in which Timmy was perching on his rock.

'It's Timmy,' I replied.

'I didn't ask what its bloody name was. Get rid of it.'

'He's Mum's,' I said defensively.

'What?' my father replied.

'He's Mum's,' I repeated. 'She bought him in a pet shop in Nathan Road.'

At that moment, my mother entered the room.

'Joyce, what is this benighted thing?'

'That's Timmy.'

'Dad doesn't want to know his name,' I said.

'Timmy the terrapin.'

'Get rid of it. It smells to high heaven.'

'That's only because his tank needs cleaning. I'm doing it later. He doesn't smell at all.'

She reached into the tank, picked Timmy up and held him level to her face. His head came out from under his shell, his legs treading air.

'Get rid of it,' my father again commanded.

My mother looked from him to the terrapin, as if she were a young girl deciding which suitor to date.

'He means no harm,' she remarked and tickled his throat with her fingernail. 'Do you, Timmy?'

'I'm going back on board,' my father declared, bringing the argument to an abrupt conclusion. 'You've got the ship-to-shore number.'

With that, he left, not to return until nightfall.

'We could sell Timmy back to the pet shop,' I suggested.

'I don't think we would make much of a profit on a

second-hand terrapin,' my mother said. 'Besides, he isn't going anywhere and your father sails back to Japan in a week.' She paused. 'Maybe I should've listened to you and bought a snake. On the other hand, one poisonous viper in this family is, I think, sufficient. Don't you?'

Despite the escape of Joey and the demise of Timmy, fortuitously before my father's next return, my mother had still not learnt her lesson. On another trip to Mr Lee, she purchased a cute lop-eared rabbit, naming it *To Jai* which, entirely predictably, meant Rabbit. It too succumbed in a matter of months. By then, my mother had made a number of new friends amongst the members of the United Services Recreation Club and no longer felt lonely. The cavalcade of pets mercifully ceased.

I had only been at school a matter of weeks when the summer holidays began, which posed my mother a problem. She was loathe to take me everywhere with her but, on the other hand, she was just as loathe to leave me to my own devices. Consequently, a compromise was reached. I was given a crossing-the-road examination and restricted to the areas bounded by Nathan Road in Mong Kok to the west, Prince Edward Road to the north and the far side of the hill opposite the hotel to the south. To the east, where there was no obvious boundary, I was told to use my discretion. From my mother's viewpoint, there was little risk involved – except from the traffic – for Hong Kong was famously street-safe. Muggings were unheard of, child molesters non-existent and street violence usually restricted to a territorial fight amongst hawkers and stallholders. The nearest a European was likely to come to crime was when he had his pocket picked.

In exchange for this liberty, I was to accompany my mother at any time she requested without 'whining, whingeing, binding or generally being a little bugger'. I consented with alacrity. The restriction cut off Yau Ma Tei but I felt I had seen all there was on offer there: and there were *dai pai dongs* in Mong Kok.

A day or two into the holidays, my mother tested my submissiveness. She was going to Tsim Sha Tsui that afternoon and I was going with her.

'Are we going to tea at the Pen?' I asked hopefully as we waited for a number 7 bus at the stop opposite the hotel.

'No,' she replied. 'Somewhere far better.'

The Pen, I considered, would take a bit of bettering.

The bus pulled up, the gate of silver-painted bars slid open and we boarded. The conductor rang the bell twice by pulling on a cord running the length of the roof and we set off. We disembarked in Tsim Sha Tsui, an area at the tip of the Kowloon peninsula filled with watch and camera shops, restaurants and tailors who would make a three-piece suit in twelve hours. This was where the tourists from the big liners or staying in the better hotels unwittingly mingled with touts, pickpockets and other ne'er-do-wells.

When we alighted, it was to head through the streets behind the Pen and into a small baker's shop with a display bow window such as one might have found on any Edwardian street that had survived the Second World War. The window glass was flawed, the frame darkly varnished. Above was the establishment's name – *Tkachenko's*. Inside were a number of rattan chairs and tables, also darkly stained. Along one wall ran a glass-fronted cool cabinet which contained a cornucopia of cakes and pastries the likes – and sumptuousness – of which I had never seen: gateaux covered in flaked dark chocolate, puff pastry slices filled with fresh cream and cherries, white chocolate-coated éclairs with

segments of glacé fruit and angelica embedded in them and tortes containing fresh fruit slices.

My mother and I sat opposite each other at a table. The rattan scratched the backs of my legs. She ordered a pot of Assam tea, a tumbler of cold milk and four cakes.

'What is this place?' I asked in tones of wonderment.

'A long time ago,' my mother began obtusely, 'there was an uprising in Russia called the Bolshevik Revolution. Many people were killed. Others lost their homes and businesses and had to flee.'

'Like Ching?' I suggested. My mother glanced at me, surprised I knew of his past.

'Yes, much like that,' she confirmed. 'Some fled to France, a few to London even, but most came east, through Siberia to Manchuria and on to Shanghai, always being forced to move along by war. Finally, they settled here in Hong Kong. And where they went, they took their skills with them. And the Russians are famous for their cakes and pastries.'

An elderly European woman, her grey hair in a dishevelled and disintegrating bun at the back of her neck, approached our table with a tray.

'Herrre iss your orderrr, madame,' she announced in a thick accent, sliding the tray between us.

The milk was fresh, chilled and tasted quite unlike that served in the Fourseas. The cakes were summed up by my mother, her upper lip moustachioed with cream.

'If God was a baker,' she said, 'this is what he'd bake.'

When the bill came, she ordered a box of cakes to go and paid with ease.

As we walked to the bus terminus at the Star Ferry, I felt some-how uneasy. It was not that I had over-indulged at Tkachenko's but more a feeling of unaccountable foreboding, as if something

was not quite right, not just with me but with the whole world. The air seemed heavy, more humid than usual. Blustery breezes blew along the street, peppering my legs with fine gravel. An old man who usually made lucky grasshoppers out of woven bamboo strips by the fire station had packed up his pitch and gone. Glancing down Salisbury Road towards Signal Hill, I could see the observatory tower on its hill. From the signal mast hung a black symbol like an inverted T. In the harbour, the sea was choppy. The sampans and walla-wallas were conspicuous by their absence and the ferries were having difficulty coming alongside their pier.

In fifteen minutes, we were back in the Fourseas. Even in that short time, the sky had darkened. When we arrived, the room boys were busy in the first-floor lounge, fitting strips of towelling into the french window frames whilst the gardener was occupied removing the pots of flowers from the lounge balcony and the sides of the driveway.

'There's a typhoon coming,' my mother told me.

'What's a typhoon?' I asked.

'The word is English but it comes from the Cantonese, *tai fung*, which means a big wind. It's the Chinese equivalent of a hurricane.'

Throughout the evening, the wind increased. When I went to bed, it whistled through the window frame. Ching came in just before I fell asleep and stopped it with lengths of rag. At intervals during the night, I woke to the sound of the wind but fell asleep again. Just before dawn, the pelt of rain on the windows finally woke me. I got out of bed and raised the venetian blinds. The street lights were still on, the thirty-foot-high concrete lampposts swaying like saplings. The rain came by in sheets. Under an overhang in the wall separating the Fourseas from the next building was gathered a crush of small birds, different breeds all

huddled together. The bushes lining the hotel drive thrashed and shed leaves as if an invisible hand was stripping them. Across Waterloo Road, a waterfall was roaring down the fissure in the hillside, gushing on to the road in a torrent of orange, muddy water. No traffic drove by, no pedestrians were about. I wondered where Ah Sam and the other rickshaw coolies might be sheltering.

By noon the rain had abated somewhat, so I sneaked out of the hotel rear gate and made my way to Soares Avenue. The streets were strewn with paper, twigs, leaves and a sheet of galvanized steel. The shops were all boarded up. Pressed against them were the rickshaws in a line, their awnings raised, the shafts of one fitted under the rear of the next. The coolies were hunched up inside, with the tarpaulin covering that protected the passengers' legs pulled tight. Only the drift of smoke eking out from under the tarpaulins alerted me to their presence. By mid-afternoon, the sun began to break through, the wind dropped and life slowly returned to normal. The flowerpots reappeared, the waterfall ceased and the buses started running. So did the rickshaws.

'It didn't last long,' I observed to my mother.

'That wasn't a direct hit,' she replied laconically. 'The centre passed over seventy miles away. All we had was a tropical storm. You don't want to see a direct hit.'

But I did.

The residents of the Fourseas were a mixed bunch. There was a small contingent of British forces wives with their children, whose spouses were either involved in the Korean War or waiting to be allocated permanent quarters. There was a fluid population of troops temporarily billeted in the hotel whilst in transit to the war.

On the rear top storey of one of the wings, four rooms were occupied on a rotational basis by a dozen Chinese whores who worked a twenty-four-hour shift pattern. The rest of their floor was taken up by itinerant American or Canadian salesmen who visited Hong Kong from time to time to buy cheap goods to ship home.

It was not unusual to see boxes of samples in the corridor outside the salesmen's rooms. When they had decided what to buy, they gave the remaining samples to me and another boy of my age whose father, like mine, was in Japan. I quickly became the proud owner of three torches that changed colour, a pair of magnificent six-guns and an eight-bladed penknife with a multi-tude of hidden tools. It was only a matter of time before I took to trading my surplus and was involved in selling torches, cap guns, penknives, manicure sets, nail clippers, pocket staplers, plastic hair clips set with paste diamonds and Zippo-style cigarette lighters to the shopkeepers of Soares Avenue at well under the wholesale price. This led one day to my having a stand-up row with a real wholesaler, from which I was rescued by Ching, who pointed out to the man that Hong Kong survived on free enter-prise and always would.

The expatriate wives were not always a docile clientele. Under my mother's leadership, they forced the hotel manager, a tall, inoffensive and highly educated Chinese man called Mr Peng, to instigate a special children's menu, and to place a large Kelvinator refrigerator in the third-floor lobby for their use: my mother kept New Zealand butter, jam and Tkachenko's cakes in it. She also tried to have the whores evicted, but in vain. They paid well over the going room rate, the troops in transit keeping them busy twenty hours a day at what I came to know as *bouncey-bouncey* or *jig-a-jig*, although I did not know exactly what this entailed. Mr Peng no doubt received a percentage not to report their presence

to the hotel owner, a stern, grim-faced Chinese who appeared monthly with his accountant and hovered behind the reception desk as the books were checked in the back office. Even if he had known of the whores, it was unlikely they would have been removed: an occupied room was an occupied room. So long as they turned a buck, the owner was satisfied and probably regarded them as an asset, for they kept the troops in the hotel buying beers and eating food there rather than wandering off to bars on Hong Kong-side. In short, they were an in-house attraction.

This disparate community was catered for by the room boys. By and large, they were happy young men despite the fact that many, like Ching, were refugees from Communism and had had to abandon their families back in China. They were efficient, thorough and paid a pittance. Yet they were grateful for a job. Thousands had none and they each knew only a tweak of fate's tail lay between them and sleeping on the pavement. Or pulling a rickshaw.

My mother befriended them all. Perhaps because she was an expatriate like them, perhaps because she had lost her father and her widowed mother lived 7,000 miles away, she identified with them and, over the years, as they improved their lot, she remained in touch with them, attending their weddings, becoming god-mother to their first born, giving them advice and loaning them money.

One member of the hotel staff was my especial friend and not infrequent enemy. My mother called him Half-pint (abbreviated to Halfie) because he was short and wore a white uniform with a pillbox hat that made him look like a bottle of milk. His real name was Ah Kee and he was the bellboy. I learnt much from Halfie: how to roll tight, aerodynamic (and therefore accurate and painful) rubber-band-propelled pellets and fold paper planes out

of PanAm timetables, flying them off the hotel roof to see if we could get one over the hill opposite. We never did succeed.

Halfie also played on my *gweilo* gullibility. One day, he persuaded me to eat a chilli from one of the ornamental bushes growing in the hotel grounds. I thought he had eaten one first but, by sleight of hand, he had avoided it and secreted it in his pocket. I spent three hours eating sugar lumps, drinking cold water, chewing on ice cubes and, ultimately, retching my stomach inside out. For a week, we were sworn enemies. Mr Peng was of a mind to sack him but my mother interceded on his behalf. A week later we were friends again, our camaraderie cemented by our jointly dropping a dead Atlas moth covered with stinging ants into the jacket pocket of a passing coolie then following him to see how far he went before the ants started in on him. As they abandoned the moth for living flesh, he began to prance and cavort along the street, a man with St Vitus's dance and no way to relieve himself of it.

The third-floor captain was Ah Kwan. My grandfather would have described him as a leery fellow. He spoke English and Cantonese fluently and was the *de facto* manager of the whores' rooms. He also collected their rent, paying it into the front desk after doubtlessly taking a cut. Although married with several children, Ah Kwan had a favourite trick. He would think himself up an erection, placing his penis along the inside of his thigh in his trouser leg. Then, seated on his stool behind the floor captain's desk, he would invite the hotel children to try to squeeze it to judge how firm it was. It was some time before any of us realized exactly what it was he kept in his trousers. We did not report him to our parents. It seemed a harmless activity, did not occur frequently and, besides, we liked him. He was funny.

Every fortnight or so throughout the second half of 1952, drafts of Australian servicemen passed through the Fourseas *en route* for

Korea. They arrived by sea or military transport aircraft and marched from Kai Tak airport to the hotel, carrying their kitbags over their shoulders. Once there, they were 'processed' by officers seated in the lounge. I hung around the door and fell into conversation with them. They were mostly in their late teens or early twenties, wore the ubiquitous Aussie cocked hat and had a kangaroo on their brass badges. Some gave me pennies with kangaroos on them. One gave me his hat badge and address in Japan. A few years older than most of his comrades, his name was Frank Martin and he was a Flight Sergeant in the Royal Australian Air Force. I wrote to him every month: he replied with stamps for my stamp collection until, late in 1953, an official communication arrived. My mother opened the envelope while I was at school. On my return that afternoon, she took me aside.

'Your Aussie friend who writes to you . . .' she began. 'He's been lost in action.'

She handed me the letter. It was succinct in the extreme and gave no details other than to assure me he had been courageous and honourable. It was signed by his unit officer.

I thought for a minute and said, 'What does that mean?'

'It means he's dead,' my mother explained solemnly.

I did not cry. It somehow seemed like an inevitability. You went to war, you died.

American troops passing through the Fourseas were mostly non-commissioned and junior commissioned officers. They were aloof, handing out packets of Wrigley's PK chewing gum with almost divine largesse. I was never a chewing-gum person. It seemed pointless to me to chew on a sweet then spit it out to stick to the side of the waste-paper bin or lavatory pan in which if it did not hit the water first go, any number of flushings would not shift it.

Regardless of nationality or rank, they all visited the third-floor in-house entertainment area.

The system ran like this: one innocent would be given a 'ride for *kumshaw'*. In other words, a free ten-minute tumble. This was a loss-leader and the whores took it in turns to provide it. Once the word got round, those seeking servicing waited in the hotel bar to be ushered discreetly upstairs to their fifteen minutes of carnal release. I, of course, had no idea what went on in the rooms but I was aware that it was secret, private and out of bounds. Ah Kwan had said as much and that was good enough for me.

The bar, where I chatted to and drank Coke with the soldiers and, on occasion, flyers while they waited, was a vaguely art-deco counter in the reception lobby to the left of the main entrance. The back wall – and the ceiling above – consisted of lime-green plastic panels with strip lights behind them. To the right was the entrance to the hotel dining room. Grandly named *Grill*, it had clearly been designed by the architect with a penchant for art deco and lime-green, back-lit plastic. Next to that were the main stairs: there was no lift. On the other side of these was the reception desk and back office with a reception lounge area.

It was not long before I knew every corner of the Fourseas. The minuscule gardens drew little interest other than to provide a place to play and a supply of tart kumquats which I occasionally ate. The fire escape staircases to the rear of every floor were a mild distraction but only for their contents.

Had there been a fire, we would all have been burnt to death, for the staircases were piled high with stores. Catering-size tins of fruit, tomatoes and peas, drums of cooking oil, packs of Heinz sauces, boxes of jars of jams and marmalades, cans of Brasso, Mansion House floor polish and shoe blacking were balanced on the steps, five or more high. The passing space beside them was at best one thin person wide. What's more, the hotel gardener had made the tiny landing at the top of one flight of steps his own. Every night, he went on to the hotel roof, washed himself at

the tap from which he watered the rows of plants he nurtured there, then spread out a quilt on the landing and laid his head on a large tin of fruit which he tucked into his neck shot-putt fashion.

He was fiercely territorial about the top of his staircase. The same applied to the kumquat bushes and a stand of paw-paw trees in front of the hotel. If he caught me or one of the other child residents even approaching them, he came at us with a vicious-looking curved pruning knife, moving with the mobility of a mongoose. He did not shout but grunted unintelligibly at us in a bestial language all his own. Had he caught us, we were certain he would have maimed or killed us. His face like that of a skull, the skin drawn tightly over the bones and his eyes sunken, he had the temper of a demon. There were effigies of him in temples, guardians of the underworld.

Some way down Waterloo Road from the hotel, a dirt track ran up behind the hill opposite. It was rutted from rain water and unsuitable for motorized vehicles. Despite this fact, people always seemed to be going up and down it, laden with bundles. Coolies with heavy loads suspended from their poles were frequent pedestrians. Rickshaws went up empty but returned loaded with packages. Curious, I followed the track one sweltering day in August.

For a few hundred yards, it rose steeply before coming out on a mildly sloping plateau upon which there was an area of about fifteen acres crammed with shanties. Most were made of wood with tin roofs constructed of flattened oil drums and any other metal to be had, whilst a few had scraps of tarpaulin patch-

worked over them in lieu of metal. Doors fitted loosely and windows were shuttered without glass. A thin pall of smoke hung over them.

At first, I thought they were residential shacks for there were dogs wandering about, laundry drying on poles, women attending to domestic chores with babies strapped to their backs and infants staggering here and there with no seats to their pants as was the Chinese way. However, I soon found out at least half the shacks were thriving industrial units. Men and women toiled over paraffin or charcoal stoves. In one shack, a man was cooking up what smelt like Brylcreem hair tonic. In another, a woman was stooped over a vat of bubbling sugar making boiled sweets. A third was steaming the flesh off fish to shape into fishballs. I saw two men roasting a whole pig over a pit of charcoal, turning it on a spit and cooking it in its own fat, which fell spitting into the fire, bursting into puffs of flame like tiny meteors hitting the surface of a burning star. By the time I arrived on the scene, the pig was almost done, its whole carcass, including the head and feet, golden brown and shining.

I sauntered on through what I now realized was officially called a squatter area. These people were on the bottom rung of Hong Kong's social ladder, only the street sleepers below them. All of them refugees, they were setting out to rebuild their lives and here was where they were starting.

My presence caused no little curiosity. Men laughed a greeting, women smiled and the boiled-sweet maker offered me one of her wares. I took it. It was flavoured with cinnamon and was a cough sweet. The infants generally took one look at me and fled, screaming. To them I really was a *gweilo*.

The shanties had no sewage. That flowed away down the hill in a network of shallow ditches to soak into a stinking gully. The only water supply was provided by a standpipe down near the

school on Waterloo Road and had to be fetched in a bucket. That one tap had to cater for several thousand people.

I continued through the squatter area and up on to the ridge of the hill. The ground was dry and covered in loose volcanic gravel which glittered like discarded gemstones. It sloped steeply like a dome down towards Waterloo Road, with very little plant life other than a few nondescript bushes. I kept well back from the edge of the slope. One slip would certainly have been fatal.

On the far side of the plateau, as far away as it could have been from the squatter area, was a small cemetery. The graves were unlike those in a Christian graveyard, being low, oblong stone plinths with a headstone at each end bearing inscriptions that were in neither English nor Chinese. They were old and looked untended. Desiccated grass grew between them. I was pondering these when a strange pattern materialized in the soil beside one of them. I knelt to discover, half buried, the skeleton of a snake about three feet long.

It was exquisitely beautiful, delicate and graceful. With my penknife, I carefully excavated it but as soon as I tried to lift the bones, they broke. All I was able to retrieve was the skull and mandible but these, cosseted in my cupped hands, shattered into white dust before I had gone twenty steps.

When I returned to the Fourseas, I asked Ching about the graveyard.

'The graves are those of people of Islam,' he informed me. 'They did not worship God or Buddha, but Allah. Many of them were Indian soldiers in the British Army a long time ago when the soldiers camped on the hills of Kowloon. Some were merchants. It is a very unlucky place,' he continued. 'You see how the squatters do not build near there? There are many restless ghosts.'

Over the summer, I frequently went up the hill, sitting on a huge boulder that must have been its summit. From there, I could

see most of Kowloon, the Kowloon hills, Kowloon Bay, the island of Hong Kong and the western harbour. It was a breathtaking panorama and always set me humming one of my mother's favourite songs, 'I'm sitting on top of the world'.

Early one afternoon as I was sitting on the boulder, I heard a faint droning coming from the direction of Lei Yue Mun, the narrow strait of water the *Corfu* had sailed through to enter Hong Kong harbour. As the sound grew in volume, I could make out a dot in the sky. It became bigger and descended until its shape was obvious: it was a Short Sunderland flying boat like the ones I had watched with Grampy, taking off from Poole harbour not thirty miles from my grandparents' homes.

Very slowly indeed it lost altitude, its four engines by now thundering. Had it not been for the noise that echoed off the mountains, it could have been taken for a huge lumbering sea bird. Its flight almost horizontal, it dropped slowly but surely to the water, a huge spray suddenly clouding out behind it as it touched down. At last, it settled on the sea, a hatch opening near the nose. A crew member moored the aircraft to a buoy even as the propellers were still turning under their own momentum. In a minute or so, a motor launch pulled alongside and the passengers started to disembark. It was, I thought, strange to think that just five days before, it had been in England.

For a moment, I felt homesick for England. I wanted to be back in my grandfather's garden shed with him, surrounded by worm-eaten, Gallipoli souvenir Turkish rifles, a huge pedal car my father had owned as a boy, biscuit tins of straightened nails and rusty, obsolete tools. I wanted to go with Nanny to the fish 'n' chip shop in Powerscourt Road and order a plaice and six penn'orth. It soon passed. Here the sun shone, you could buy cherry bombs and go to Tkachenko's: no-one made cakes like that in Portsmouth.

Dissatisfied with the rudimentary hotel laundry service, which really only catered for bed linen, my mother decided to employ a wash amah. This entailed a new experience for her: interviewing for a servant.

'I want you to be with me, Martin,' she declared. If she used my Christian name in such a way I knew something serious was going on. Just before the first applicant arrived, my mother grinned nervously and said, 'Isn't this funny? Nanny used to be in service. She was a maid in a big country estate in Sussex. Now here's me, a proper madam of the house—'

There was a knock on the door and a middle-aged Chinese woman entered. Her black hair was scraped into a bun and she wore a white tunic jacket and baggy black trousers – the same uniform as the hotel room boys and amahs. On her feet were black slippers.

'Me name Ah Choy,' she said softly. 'I good wash-sew amah for you, missee.' She saw me standing by the window. 'You young master?' My mother introduced me. 'Ve'y han'sum boy,' Ah Choy replied, no doubt perceiving my blond hair and anticipating many brief daily encounters with good fortune. 'Good, st'ong boy. Be plentee luckee.' At that point she produced some sheets of paper bearing references from previous employers dating back to the late 1930s with a gap from 1941 to '45.

'Where did you go in the war?' my mother enquired.

'I go quick-quick China-side,' she replied. 'Master go soljer p'ison Kowloon-side. Missee and young missee go war p'ison Hong Kong-side. Japan man no good for Chinese peopul.'

She got the job, my mother paying her $100 (about £6) a month.

A gentle soul, Ah Choy arrived at nine in the morning,

collected the laundry and took it on to the hotel roof where the wash amahs of other long-term residents congregated around the tap. They chattered like hens as they worked, squatting at basins with their sleeves and trouser legs rolled up and their shoes off. When the laundry was done, they hung it to dry from lines strung across the roof. At midday, they vanished in the direction of Soares Avenue, returning at two o'clock to collect the laundry. This was bundled up and taken away, I never knew where to but it returned three hours later ironed, starched, as pristine as the day it was made. Missing buttons had been replaced and rents sewn. A pair of shorts I had torn in the school playground returned invisibly mended. My mother couldn't believe it.

Ah Choy was one of a group known as *saw hei* amahs: *saw hei* meant *combed* and referred to the way they kept their hair in taut buns. Originally from Kwangtung province, they were members of a sorority of single Chinese women who had sworn to each other strictly to maintain a vow of celibacy. Traditionally, they were silk factory workers from the Three Districts of the Pearl River delta but, in the thirties, they had been displaced by the advancing Japanese forces during the Sino-Japanese War, most fleeing for British Hong Kong, where they became servants, particularly to Western families.

During the Japanese occupation of Hong Kong, many *saw hei* amahs remained in the colony, at very great risk to themselves. It was not unknown for them to smuggle food into their former employers in prisoner-of-war camps, sometimes tossing it over the wire by night. Others fled into China, crossed north of the Japanese lines and somehow eked out an existence. When Japan capitulated in 1945, they returned to Hong Kong, sought out their former employers and took up where they had left off.

It was not long before Ah Choy started to assign herself other duties than washing and sewing. She insisted on seeing me over

the road to school, even though Ching had long since given up the task as I was now considered traffic-wise. At the end of the day, or if I returned home at lunchtime, she would waylay me halfway to school in order to carry my Hong Kong basket for me. I found this agonizingly embarrassing. Should I not feel well, she would come into my room and curl up on the floor by my bed. If I woke in the night, she would too, to fetch me a glass of milk from the Kelvinator or call my mother. Many years later, my mother told me how Ah Choy had once walked in on her and my father as they were making love in the middle of the night. Not fazed in the least, she walked straight to the bed, shook my mother's shoulder and said, 'Come quick, missee. Young master . . .' She then did a passable imitation of vomiting and rushed back to my room.

I came to love Ah Choy and even permitted her to undress and wash me. She was kind, tolerant and loyal. Yet, in three months, she was gone, employed by someone with an apartment and servants' quarters. We could hardly blame her.

There followed a succession of interviews, culminating in the appointment of Ah Fong. She was the antithesis of Ah Choy. A young, smiling woman, she wore her hair in a perm and lacked the devotion to service of her celibate compatriots. She could be brusque and determined to brook no nonsense from me. I consequently led her a merry chase, especially at her evening call of 'Barfu, Martung!'

It was a matter of principle.

Beneath the main hotel staircase was a snug hideaway in which Halfie and the luggage porter huddled whilst waiting for their

services to be called upon. In this little den was a telephone, a shoeshine box, a shelf of telephone directories, three stools and an electric ring on which they boiled tea for themselves and the office staff.

Returning from school one September afternoon not long after the beginning of the new academic year, I walked up the hotel drive to see Halfie twirling something round his head on the end of a six-foot length of cotton. When he stopped swinging it round, it flew of its own volition.

'I wan' one,' I said.

Halfie tantalizingly hid the object in his pocket and, pointing to the lobby clock, answered, 'You wan', you get. Light-time, I show you.'

At six thirty that evening, I met him and the porter in their den and followed them out into Waterloo Road. We stood under one of the neon street lights and waited. Twilight fell. We were joined by several more people. Beneath the other street lights, small groups of three or four were gathering. I was about to ask what we were waiting for when the street lights came on. In a few minutes, once they had reached full brilliance, something hard hit me on the head. Before I could react, Halfie ran his fingers through my hair and showed me a beetle nestling in his palm.

The insect was the size and shape of a large plum stone, its glossy carapace smooth and a dark green which was almost black. A bright yellow stripe lined the edges. Its underside was deep yellow, its two hindmost legs at least as long as its body and jointed in the mid-point.

'What is it?' I enquired.

'Wartar bee-chew,' Halfie answered.

Suddenly, more began to fall around us. They were attracted to the street light, flew into the bulb, knocked themselves senseless

and fell to the pavement. Halfie and the porter collected the dazed
water beetles and put them in a saucepan. As soon as they gained
consciousness, they took to the wing inside it, banging against the
lid and sides. In thirty minutes, we must have collected a hundred.

'What do we do now?' I asked.

'Tomowwow,' Halfie answered.

The following morning, as I left for school, Halfie presented
me with my beetle-on-a-line. He had tied a length of cotton to the
insect's two hind legs and showed me how to swing it round.

'No too fas',' he warned. 'You do too fas', leg b'okun.'

I gently swung the beetle round my head. It took to the wing
and flew above me like a miniaturized motor-powered kite. All
the way to school, I was accompanied by its whirring flight as it
kept ahead of me. It was a wonder to behold. Inevitably, however,
it was confiscated and given its liberty the moment I entered the
school premises. My liberty that lunchtime was sequestered and I
was given a hundred lines to write on the topic of cruelty to
animals.

As soon as I reached the Fourseas that afternoon, I went
straight to the niche under the stairs. Halfie and the porter were
hunched over a pan on the electric ring.

'Bee-chew gone,' I said, miming its supposed escape. I was
loathe to lose face by admitting what had actually happened.

'Lo ploblum,' said Halfie. 'Can get wung more light-time.'

He opened the lid on the pan. Inside, the remainder of the
water beetles were gently simmering. 'You wan?'

This was, I considered, the severest test of my promise to the
naval officer so far. Halfie removed a beetle from the pan with a
spoon, blew on it to cool it then split the carapace open with his
thumbnail, flicking the wing casing, wings and legs into a rice
bowl already containing other beetle parts.

'You eat . . .' Halfie made a kissing-cum-sucking noise '. . . lo go

down.' He pointed to his throat then mimed spitting the bits into the bowl.

I put the beetle in my mouth and chewed it thoroughly, swallowing the mushy liquid of its innards mixed with my own saliva. It tasted slightly muddy, yet the overriding flavour was like the smell of stagnant freshwater ponds mixed with smoked fish. I spat the bits out, ate another just to show willing, accepted a toothpick holder and a bowl of jasmine tea, the contents of which were more than welcome. Every tooth in my head had a bit of bee-chew wedged against it. Expecting to be violently sick at any moment, I went to my room and sat on the bed to await the advent of regurgitated beetle and tea but it never came so, half an hour later, I went down to the hotel bar and ordered a cold Coke. In the cubby-hole, all the beetles had been consumed.

4

THREE LIVES ON THE EDGE

IN THE FOURSEAS, WITH ITS PREDOMINANTLY NOMADIC POPULATION, only the staff, the whores, one other expatriate woman and her son, a European man who lived in a single room at the back of the hotel and my mother and I were more or less permanent over the winter of 1952.

My father came back from Japan on the *Fort Charlotte* for Christmas, bearing gifts. I received a battery-powered wooden motor boat and a superb model of a Chinese junk with hand-sewn sails and windlasses that worked. The hotel did its best to become seasonally cheerful, with decorations in all the public rooms, gifts of bottles of VSOP brandy in each occupied room (including mine) and Christmas dinner of an American turkey and Australian roast potatoes, brussels sprouts and carrots. The Christmas pudding was brought in fiercely burning but was inedible: it turned out the cook had set it alight with paraffin instead of brandy. One kindly old Chinese, who did not speak English and was the night watchman and odd-job man, went around wishing everyone a 'Happee Kiss-Mee'.

My father's return was not the happy occasion it should have

been. After delivering his largesse, for which he demanded expressions of deep gratitude, he soon slipped into his old short-tempered ways which he had presumably had to keep in check whilst he was on board ship. He was enough of a sailor to know that one pain in the arse in a wardroom was enough to unsettle an entire ship's crew.

The day before the ship sailed back to Japan, we were invited aboard the *Fort Charlotte* for lunch. I was shown my father's cabin, the wood- and brass-work polished, his clothes neat in the drawers, his bunk immaculately made. Lunch was taken in the wardroom with the Chief Engineer and the Captain, both of whom wore uniforms with gold braid. The meal was beef curry and rice to which were added 'bits' consisting of crisp-fried onion, croutons, diced cucumber and pineapple, grated coconut, currants, chopped tomatoes, mango chutney, hot lime pickle, poppadoms, chipattis and flaky Bombay duck which, I was surprised to discover, was not duck at all but dried fish. When it was over, we were given a tour of the ship which did not impress me. I had seen bridges and engine rooms before.

Leaving the wheelhouse, my father muttered, 'Show some interest. The Old Man doesn't have to show you round.'

I had an answer to that but wisely kept it to myself.

Returning to Kowloon across the harbour on a naval launch, my father set upon me.

'You are a rude little ingrate,' he said irately.

'What now, Ken?' my mother wanted to know.

'Martin,' my father answered. 'Taken all over the bloody show. Might just as well've left him behind.'

'Well, Ken,' my mother replied, 'he did see it all on the *Corfu*. Let's face it, unless you're a marine engineer, one ship's boiler looks very much like the next.'

'Neither the *Corfu* nor the *Fort Charlotte* have boilers,' my

father retorted irritably. 'Not in the accepted sense. They're diesel driven. That's what I mean. The two of you. Blind as bats to life's opportunities. As inquisitive as a building brick. Curious as a dead cat.'

For the remainder of the day, my father sulked. That evening, I asked my mother – foolishly in my father's hearing – why the other men on the ship wore gold braid but my father did not.

'Go to your room!' he shouted at me. 'Put your pyjamas on.'

'I was only being curious,' I defended myself.

'Get out!'

I went.

Ten minutes later, he entered my room. I was bent over a chair and hit twice across the buttocks with the flat of my mother's silver hairbrush.

'That's for your bloody insolence,' my father said spitefully as I wiped my tears away and rubbed my running nose against my pyjama sleeve.

I had hit a raw nerve.

One afternoon early in January, my mother took me to Tsim Sha Tsui. She was going to Hing Loon to collect a ruby and gold pendant she had ordered and I was to have a new pair of shoes. It was a cold day, the wind had an edge to it and I wore a thick pullover.

As usual, we boarded the number 7 bus across the road from the Fourseas and set off. As it slowed for the last stop before turning left down Nathan Road, a face surrounded by rats' tails of dishevelled, filthy grey hair appeared at the window next to me.

I instantly recognized it. It was that of an old European woman

who lived in a cockloft – a sort of semi-permanent shanty – on the flat roof of a tenement block in Liberty Avenue. I had often seen her wandering the back streets of Mong Kok, scavenging from restaurants, buying (or stealing) fruit from stalls and eating at the cheapest *dai pai dongs* where she swore volubly in fluent Cantonese at the coolies beside whom she sat. Most shop and stallholders kept an eye open for her, shooing her away with a broom or stick as if she were an alley-cat or pi-dog. I saw one or two Buddhists who were honour-bound to give alms to the poor taking pity on her but almost everybody else was hostile.

She ran along the side of the bus as it slowed, banging her hands on the panelling. I broke into a sweat. This old woman knew me, in a manner of speaking. Whenever she saw me in the street, she would run towards me, an animated pile of old rags that stank of urine, sweat, rice wine, tobacco, opium and garlic. And, on occasion, shit. I avoided her and fled but, with an alacrity one would not credit her with, she would stagger after me, shouting, 'Alexei! Alexei!'

The bus stopped, she boarded it and headed straight for me and my mother. On the way down the aisle, the conductor accosted her for her fare. She snarled at him, muttered incomprehensibly and elbowed him into an empty seat.

As the bus set off, the woman stood next to my mother, swaying to the motion of the bus and alcohol.

'Gif me one thousan' dollaire!' she demanded, holding out a filthy hand.

My mother looked over my head and out the window.

'Ignore her, dear,' she instructed me, *sotto voce*.

I was only too glad to obey. Any second now the old crone was going to recognize me.

'Gif me fife hundred dollaire,' she insisted, holding her hand out close to my mother's chin. Her nails were split, the skin of her

hand ingrained with dirt. Her face was made up but badly, the lipstick smeared around her mouth, rouge heavy on her cheeks, the remainder pancaked with powder in which was etched a map of sweat, the contours highlighted by grime. Over her shoulder hung an expensive leather bag in good condition, almost certainly a recently filched acquisition. On her feet were a pair of common Chinese felt slippers.

My mother ignored her.

The bus stopped.

'Gif me two hundred dollaire!' the old woman insisted, her voice growing louder.

'Would you mind going away?' my mother said through gritted teeth. We were becoming the object of much curiosity from the Chinese passengers and she was getting embarrassed.

'Gif me one hundred dollaire!' the crone insisted, her voice louder still and even more insistent.

My mother opened her handbag on her lap, unclipped her purse and removed some dollar bills. The old woman snatched at them and, as she did so, dropped something wrapped in pink lavatory tissue into the handbag. At the next bus stop, she got off and swiftly disappeared, pushing her way through the pedestrians, moving with the gait of a practised drunk. We carried on to Tsim Sha Tsui and went into Tkachenko's. When it came time to settle the bill, my mother opened her purse. In with the coins was the tissue paper. She took it out, felt it, unwrapped it, studied the contents for several minutes, replaced it in her purse and paid the bill.

When we entered his emporium, Mr Chan was sitting behind his counter reading the newspaper. He stood up, welcomed my mother, poured us each a Coke and produced the ruby pendant set in rose gold my mother had commissioned from him. He tutted disapprovingly at it. Rose gold had a high copper content. The

Chinese preferred 24 carat, 99.99 fine gold which was brassy and looked almost fake.

As he put the pendant and matching chain into a small brocade bag, my mother took the pink tissue out of her purse and placed it on the counter.

'What is this, Mr Chan?' she asked, adding, 'It's probably paste.'

He unwrapped the tissue and tipped a colourless stone on to the counter, rolling it about on the glass top with his finger. He then picked it up with a pair of tweezers, held it against a bare light bulb in a desk lamp and placed it in a velvet-lined tray.

'Is a good quality diamung,' he said. 'Little bit damage, no too much. Can recut, make maybe t'ree, four nice stone. For ring maybe for you?'

'How big is it?' my mother wanted to know.

'Maybe two-half carat,' Mr Chan replied.

For a moment, my mother was silent before asking, 'How much is it worth?'

'Is damage,' Mr Chan repeated, 'but maybe fife t'ousan'd dollar.'

My mother stared at him. At the current exchange rate, the sum approximated to £312.

For the next fortnight, my mother caught the same bus at the same time every day in the hope of coming across the woman again and either returning the stone to her or giving her the *fife hundred dollaire* she had demanded. It was the highest sum to which my mother could go. She never saw the woman again. The diamond was duly re-cut and my mother had the resulting three stones set in a ring as Mr Chan had suggested.

I, of course, could have told my mother exactly where to find the old woman, but I did not for fear that, had she discovered some of the more insalubrious haunts I frequented, my freedom to roam would have been severely curtailed.

The Chinese in the streets called the old crone the Queen of Kowloon. Bit by bit, I came to know her story, or what it was perceived to be. The truth would be somewhere near it.

She was a White Russian, the wife of a high-ranking army officer who was also possibly of minor nobility. When the Bolshevik Uprising occurred, he was killed and she headed east with the White Russian diaspora. After some time, she reached Shanghai, settling there and making her living as a courtesan and piano teacher. She became the mistress of a Chinese gangster or warlord – the story varied on this point and may have been a romantic fictional episode – and lived very comfortably for a while. Then war intervened again and she moved on, drifting ashore in Hong Kong in the mid-thirties. In those days, she lived comfortably if frugally in a tenement apartment where, once again, she gave piano lessons. However, it was not long before she took to the bottle and pipe which were the start of her decline into beggary.

Her looks now gone, she no longer had any steady source of income. Or had she?

From time to time, she appeared at pawn shops in Mong Kok and Yau Ma Tei with pieces of jewellery, valuable gems and the occasional gold coin, most of them of tsarist origin. Her tenement was burgled several times and thoroughly turned over, as once was she, but the thieves found nothing despite knocking down internal walls. Clearly, her stash was hidden elsewhere, so the thieves began to tail her but she was as sly as a leopard. Years of living on the edge had honed her senses to feline acuity. All that anyone could deduce was that, at irregular intervals, she disappeared for hours at a time into the foothills behind Kowloon.

What had happened to her during the Japanese occupation of Hong Kong was unknown. Those who stayed behind and suffered the atrocities never saw her. Some thought she ran for

neutral Macau, others that she had a Japanese 'protector' although that was unlikely as, by 1941, she could no longer have been a beautiful woman. Some thought she ran a bordello for Japanese officers but that was improbable as they had rounded up any women as and when they wanted on the street.

In later years, as her mind began to slip and opium fumes befuddled it, she claimed to be Princess Anastasia, who had survived the assassination of the Russian Royal Family, but no-one believed her. She still came up with jewellery but at less frequent intervals and the local Chinese just tolerated her rantings in the street, her foul mouth and her stench.

One day, a month or two after my mother's reluctant audience with the Queen, I was trapped by her in a dead-end alley. She advanced on me slowly, her every step measured as if she were tiptoeing from stone to stone across a river. All the while, she was muttering incomprehensibly. Finally, not two yards away, and certainly close enough for me to be swathed in her odour in the windless alley, she stopped and studied me closely.

'Why do you run, Alexei?' she asked in English.

'My name's not Alexei,' I replied.

She smiled at me. Her teeth were grey. For a moment, a shard of the beauty she must once have been shone through her decrepitude.

'One day, you will be the Tsar,' she prophesied.

I looked round her to see if I might make my escape. She glanced over her shoulder.

'Are they coming?'

Terrified, I shook my head.

'If they come,' she went on, wagging her index finger at me in an admonishing manner, 'you will tell me. Yes?'

I nodded, having no idea who might be coming – thieves, the police, a man from the Lai Chi Kok mental asylum . . .

'I liff herre.' She pointed vaguely to the sky and, stepping forward, stroked my hair before I could do anything about it. She then moved past me, her rags brushing against my face. I sprinted for the Fourseas and, to my mother's consternation, for it was the middle of the afternoon, immediately ran myself a bath and shampooed my hair twice. It was one thing to have the Chinese touch my golden hair for luck. They were clean. She was a different matter altogether.

A week or so later, I joined a gang of Chinese boys pelting her with gravel from the railway line. I felt no pity for her. She had defiled me.

In 1952, The Bank of China building on Hong Kong island was the tallest in the world between Cairo and San Francisco. As for the remainder of Hong Kong, most buildings were over fifty years old. The streets of Kowloon could have changed little in that time, the arcades bustling with shoppers then as they had at the time of the Q'ing empire when men really did wear their hair in waist-length cues and pirates were executed by the sword on the beach in Kowloon Bay.

True, Hong Kong was just beginning its metamorphosis into one of the financial powerhouses of Asia, but it was still essentially a very Chinese city with bicycles and a non-interventionist British administration.

Men in pigtails may have vanished but little else had changed. Rickshaws were commonplace. Coolies carried extraordinarily heavy loads on bamboo poles over their shoulders. Conical rattan hats were widely used whilst the Hakka women wore hats with black cloth fringes like curtains hanging from the rim. People ran

like hell across the street through fast-moving traffic to shake off the demons they believed were perpetually following them: sometimes, someone walking along the pavement would suddenly dart into an alley, slip into a shop or board a departing bus at the last minute, in the hope of giving the slip to these malevolent supernatural entities. For the same reason, many Chinese assiduously avoided having their photo taken for fear the demons would see the picture and be able to track them down. Unlicensed street hawkers sold sweetmeats, sugar cane, melon seeds and *wah mui*. These were plums soaked for several days in sea water then dried in the sun. When one sucked them, they puckered the inside of one's cheek, the salt and the fruit sugars mingling together. Others carried braziers on poles, selling roasted peanuts or chestnuts, slices of hot roast pork with the crackled skin still on the meat, cut from a whole pig such as I had seen cooking in the Ho Man Tin squatter area.

These were everyday sights in the streets around the Fourseas. What were much less frequent were itinerant street entertainers. Few had survived the war years and the advent of Radio Hong Kong, but one who did was the plink-plonk man: and I was there for his final act.

My mother based his moniker upon the rosewood xylophone he played. His pitch was in Emma Avenue, directly behind the Fourseas, where he occasionally appeared to place his instrument on the pavement under the shade of the trees, squatting on his haunches behind it. After striking a few of the keys as if tuning up, but in fact to alert those in the buildings around to his arrival, he invariably launched into a Chinese classical arrangement of 'Tipperary'. Once this was over, he opened a wooden box he carried over his shoulder from which pranced a small monkey dressed in the clothing of a Ming dynasty mandarin. To prevent any escape, the monkey was tethered to the box by a long leather leash.

The plink-plonk man's second tune was usually a rendition of the Japanese song known in English as 'Rose, Rose, I love you' followed by 'Marching through Georgia' in an arrangement possibly conceived for a Cantonese opera. He finished with an embellished version of 'Swing Low, Sweet Chariot'.

As he played, his monkey cavorted about in a haphazard jig that bore no rhythmical relationship whatsoever to the music, while people threw down ten-cent coins from windows and balconies. At the end of each tune, the plink-plonk man pitched a hard olive on to the balconies or through the windows of those who had tossed down money and at the end of the whole performance, musician and monkey collected up the coins.

All went well until one day when, halfway through 'Marching through Georgia', the monkey finally managed to bite through its leash. I was on the opposite side of the road and watched the whole drama unfold.

In a flash, the monkey was up the nearest tree. The music stopped abruptly and the plink-plonk man stood up to survey the situation. The monkey was out of reach, the tree too stout to bend and the remnant of the leash too short to be grabbed.

At first, the musician tried to sweet-talk the monkey down, holding up a piece of a bun. The monkey just peered down through the branches. Not to be hoodwinked by this, it then slowly, strip-tease fashion, divested itself of its ludicrous costume, letting each piece drift to the ground where the musician collected them up, folding them as he might those of a child. His attention taken by this task, the plink-plonk man's eye was briefly off the monkey which, holding on to its little cock, gave it a few masturbatory tugs before proceeding to urinate upon its erstwhile master.

It was a moment or two before the musician realized what was happening. He unwisely looked up to be hit in the face by the full stream. This not surprisingly drove him into an irate frenzy,

cursing the monkey at the top of his voice, throwing the clothing at it and then pelting the monkey with unripe olives, some of which it caught and returned with considerable accuracy, the hard fruit bouncing off the musician's head.

Tiring of this game, the monkey headed off down the street, swinging Tarzan-like from tree to tree, always keeping just out of reach of the musician who ran below, jumping up to attempt to grab the dangling leash.

It was pure pantomime and, by now, had gathered a crowd far greater than any the plink-plonk man could ever have hoped to collect through his music. He ran along behind the escaping monkey, his face wet with urine, his fists clenched, pleading, cussing, cajoling and threatening the creature by turns. His swelling audience, meanwhile, hooted with laughter, shouted spurious advice and encouragement to the escapee.

At the junction of Emma Avenue and Soares Avenue, a network of electricity wires spanned out from a junction box. The monkey, blithely swinging through the foliage, was unaware of the danger. The plink-plonk man saw it and tried in desperation to turn the monkey back. Enjoying its liberty, it ignored him. There was a violent blue flash accompanied by an equally brief high-pitched squeak. The lights in the shops flickered. A few bulbs exploded. The monkey was instantly immolated. All that was left was a charred corpse stretched between two wires, a drift of smoke and the acrid smell of burnt hair.

The plink-plonk man sat on the curb, his feet in the gutter, and broke into tears. The crowd, now subdued, dispersed.

I never saw him again.

The single European man who lived in the cheapest room in the Fourseas was universally known as Nagasaki Jim.

My mother emphatically warned me against him. So did Ching, Ah Kwan, Halfie and all the other hotel staff with whom I was friends. Even the manager, Mr Peng, who was usually aloof unless remonstrating with me for misbehaving, told me to avoid him.

He was British, in his mid to late thirties, of average height with ginger-ish hair cut short and badly. His face and arms were freckled and he had watery blue eyes. Like the Queen of Kowloon, he also reeked of tobacco, alcohol and, not infrequently, opium. His clothes were always just the clean side of filthy although he laundered them himself once a week on the roof. He did not eat at the hotel but went every evening to a *dai pai dong* — always the same one   in Mong Kok.

I knew this because I followed him there on several occasions, keeping to the shadows, stalking him as one might a wild beast.

Indeed, he was like one. He could fly into a fit of anger at the drop of a chopstick, rushing at the object of his ire, his arms flailing. He seldom swore or shouted but breathed heavily. If he caught someone when in one of his rages, as I saw him do with one of the room boys, he would beat them about the head with clenched fists or slap them hard in the face. His assault over, he would speak rapidly and incomprehensibly in a high-pitched, faltering voice. Only later did I come to understand from my mother that Nagasaki Jim spoke Japanese in his raging.

He did not spend his whole time in the Fourseas but, when he was there, he tended to keep to himself in his room, looking out of his door every so often to peer down the corridor. His actions were tentative, guarded, like a hermit crab periodically glancing out of its shell to check there were no predators about. Where he went apart from the Mong Kok *dai pai dong* and the shops in Soares

Avenue, I never discovered. His life was a mystery, closed behind his hotel-room door.

Over time, I gleaned the story of his past, as exotic and romantic and brutal as any of those of the other Europeans or White Russians who had run ashore in Hong Kong.

Nagasaki Jim was said to be the heir to a famous British biscuit manufacturer but the family had disinherited him save for a small monthly stipend. He had joined the British Army at the outbreak of war and, by 1940, was stationed in Hong Kong with the rank of Captain. When the Japanese overran the colony on Christmas Day 1941, Nagasaki Jim was taken prisoner and incarcerated in the Sham Shui Po prisoner-of-war camp.

Life in the camp was harsh in the extreme. Food was insufficient and barely edible. Diphtheria, dysentery and cholera were endemic and medical supplies exceedingly scarce. Escape was virtually impossible: of the few who managed to get away, most were rounded up, hideously tortured then shot or bayoneted to death on the seashore, in full view of the mustered lines of their comrades.

In September 1942, the Japanese prepared to take a draft of 1,800 Allied prisoners to Japan to use as slave labour in their war effort. The men, along with 2,000 Japanese soldiers returning on leave, were loaded aboard a cargo vessel, the *Lisbon Maru*. The prisoners were accommodated in the locked-down holds, the Japanese soldiers making do with the main deck spaces.

Early on the morning of 1 October, an American submarine called the USS *Grouper* came across the ship off the Chusan Islands. Seeing all the Japanese troops on board, it was assumed to be a troopship. The submarine torpedoed and sank it. The Japanese battened down the hatches. Hundreds of PoWs drowned in the holds. Some succeeded in getting out but were machine-

gunned in the water by Japanese gunboats. In all, 846 perished. Nagasaki Jim was not amongst them.

Along with other survivors, he was trans-shipped to Japan and put to work. Conditions in the mines and factories were worse than they had been in Sham Shui Po but he still survived and was somehow to end up near Nagasaki when the Americans dropped the second atom bomb on the city on 9 August 1945. It was said Nagasaki Jim was near the city and not only saw the bomb fall but witnessed its horrific aftermath. This experience, I was told, turned his head.

When prisoners-of-war in Japan were repatriated, he wound up in Hong Kong and, upon his discharge from the Army, did not return to Britain. Quite why was unknown.

Of course, I knew little of this at the age of eight and yet I was well aware that Nagasaki Jim had more than a few loose screws: as my mother put it, he only had one chopstick. I was street-wise, too. What with Princess Anastasia and various deranged beggars who wandered the streets – not to mention the crazy hotel gardener with his pruning knife – I knew there were boundaries in life and roughly where they lay. Yet if, playing in the hotel corridors, one of us strayed in the direction of Nagasaki Jim's abode, one of the hotel staff would run towards us and admonish us.

'You lo go dis place. Dis Nagasaki Jim place.' A finger would sternly shake in our faces. 'You lo go! You savee? Lo go!'

One day in the spring of 1953, I was playing cowboys and indians with friends along the corridors of the Fourseas. Or cops 'n' robbers. Whichever. The salient point was that I was carrying a cap gun six-shooter and strayed towards Nagasaki Jim's place, intending to dodge down the stores-packed staircase to the floor below and come up on my enemies from behind. There were no hotel staff about: they were attending the monthly staff meeting with Mr Peng in the dining room.

Just as I drew level with Nagasaki Jim's door, it opened. I was not a yard away from it.

'Hello,' he said pleasantly. It was the first time he had ever spoken to me.

'Hello,' I replied cautiously. If needs be, I was ready to run.

'What's your name?' he went on and, not awaiting an answer, added, 'That's a nice gun you've got. Would you like to see my gun?'

Were I a year older, the innuendo and ambiguity of this question would not have been lost on me, but I was eight and a half and a bit.

'Yes,' I said.

He disappeared into his room. There was the sound of a scuffling about in drawers.

'Come in,' he called amicably.

'I'll wait here,' I answered. My seventh puerile sense was tingling like a high-tension cable.

Nagasaki Jim came to the door and knelt down, his face level with my own.

'Here you are,' he announced and, from behind his back, he produced a British Army .38 service revolver. The gunmetal shone with a parade-ground lustre. The wooden butt was as polished as my grandmother's dining-room table.

All my fears of Nagasaki Jim evaporated at the sight of this wondrous object. It was the first time I had ever been close to a firearm with the exception of the rusting Turkish rifles in my grandfather's garden shed, a heavy brass First World War Verey pistol he let me play with and the guns in the car in Singapore.

'Would you like to hold it?'

He held the revolver out to me by the barrel, took my six-shooter and put it on the floor between us.

The .38 was much heavier than I had expected. I could not hold

it up to aim, even with both hands. The metal was warm and smooth and smelt of gun lubricating oil. Whilst my hands were occupied with the revolver, Nagasaki Jim leant forward and, hooking his index finger under the leg of my shorts, said, 'Show me your winkle and I'll buy you a gun like mine.'

Letting the revolver go, I was off like a startled hare. Naïve I may have been, stupid I was not. As my mother would have put it, I was not as green as I was cabbage-looking.

With the fluidity of a rat, Nagasaki Jim was up and after me. He threw my six-shooter at me but it missed and hit the wall ahead of me, smashing into pieces. I kept going, to be saved by two hotel guests turning a corner into the corridor. Nagasaki Jim retreated into his room like an earthworm down its burrow.

I did not report this incident to my mother for the same reason that I had kept tight-lipped concerning the whereabouts of the Queen of Kowloon. However, I did tell Ah Kwan. That night, he and three other room boys let themselves into Nagasaki Jim's room on a pass key and lay in wait for him. When he returned from the *dai pai dong*, they gave him a sound working over.

Two months later, under threat of eviction for non-payment of rent, Nagasaki Jim hanged himself.

5

FIRECRACKERS, FUNERALS
AND FLAMES

IN 1953, CHINESE NEW YEAR FELL OVER THE END OF JANUARY AND THE beginning of February. Dependent upon the lunar calendar, the date varied from year to year. All that could be counted upon were the keen northerlies which blew down across China from the steppes of Siberia, the skies blue and more or less cloudless, and the astonishing spectacle of the festival. Friends advised my mother to leave the Fourseas for the duration of the main festivities, and we were invited to the bungalow at Mount Nicholson, but my mother declined. She wanted to be in the thick of it.

Over the weeks leading up to the festival, firecrackers had been on sale in practically every shop. Even the fruit shop owner sold them. Mostly, they came in square cardboard boxes the size of a paperback book, sealed with a label printed with images of laughing children letting them off and crude drawings of demons or dragons. In the boxes, the fuses were plaited together so the individual firecrackers had to be shaken loose from what was otherwise a short string of them. Always coloured red, they varied in size from those not much fatter than a thick pencil lead and

about an inch long – and named by us tom thumbers – to others three inches in length and thicker than a cigarette.

I bought a box of fifty cigarette-sized crackers for a dollar and, with several of the other expatriate children who lived in the hotel at the time, went up on to the hill to let them off. We put them in holes in the ground or under rocks, lighting them with a small joss-stick. When they exploded, they made the holes bigger and one rock as big as a football split open. We had also taken an empty Coke bottle with us as a finale. I held the firecracker in the mouth, lit the fuse, dropped it in the bottle and ran. The others stood at a safe distance. There was a muffled sort of *thoomp!* behind me, quickly followed by a searing pain in my upper leg. I looked down. Blood was beginning to ooze out of a cut in my thigh as neat as a surgeon's incision. I staggered back down the hill, my sock becoming glutinous with the stream of blood running down my leg. I was scared but, within a few moments of reaching the hotel lobby, the porter had staunched the flow. My mother arrived, decided I did not need stitches and bandaged me up. In an hour, I was being taught by Halfie how to let off a tom thumber whilst holding it.

Although tiny, these firecrackers packed a punch sufficient to blow a five-inch-wide, two-inch-deep crater in the earth of a pot of the chrysanthemums that decorated the hotel front lawn. It was easy once you realized that the gunpowder was concentrated in the middle of the firecrackers. If you held one by the base, gripping it between two fingernails, you could light it and let it explode with no danger – so long as you kept your eyes closed. The first I held as it went off left a tingling feeling in my fingers. The second hurt but machismo demanded I did not show it and lose face. Thereafter, we embarked upon tom thumb fights, hurling them at each other. No-one was hurt. It was good seasonal fun.

The first day of the fortnight-long, but not continuous, festival

was quiet. All the shops in Soares Avenue were shut. The hotel room boys who were my friends gave me *lai see* and I returned the compliment, having been tipped off to do so. *Lai see* was a small red paper packet containing a small amount of money. It was not so much a gift as an omen of good luck and prosperity for the year ahead. I was warned by Ching not to swear, not to mention death, illness, bad luck or anything of that ilk, even in passing. Our amah refused to take anything but Chinese New Year's Day off, despite my mother's protestations; yet she did accept a thirteenth month's salary as was common practice.

On the second day, the celebrations started in earnest.

Across the road from the rear of the Fourseas was a pro-Communist secondary school which occupied a triangular plot between Emma, Julia and Soares Avenues. Every morning, the pupils gathered in the school yard behind twelve-foot-high stone walls like those of a prison and sang patriotic songs about labouring in the fields, striding ahead for liberty, equality and fraternity under the red flag and in the footsteps of Mao Tse-tung. The accompaniment was provided by a phonograph with a set of well-worn records.

Shortly after dawn, the school staff had hung strings of firecrackers over the walls. In all, there must have been two hundred of them, the walls looking as if they had suddenly been festooned with vermilion ribbons. And these firecrackers were by no means the little bangers such as might have graced a British Bonfire Night party. These were the size of a grown man's index finger, the fuses woven together around a core of hessian twine. What was more, they were grouped in threes down the twine. The aim was not to provide a display but to create as much noise as possible to drive off devils, demons and the pantheon of other supernatural ne'er-do-wells which every Chinese believed occupied every spiritually inhabitable niche.

I went into the street to watch. One of the teachers appeared at the corner with Soares Avenue, another at the corner with Julia Avenue. Both held large joss-sticks, the smoke drifting away on a keen breeze: it was cold enough to wear a padded jacket. There was no-one else in the street. A whistle was blown in the school yard. The teachers ignited the end of the first string of fire-crackers, moving immediately on to the next. After a brief fizzle, the explosions began in the first string, then the second, then the third . . . In a matter of seconds, my head was filled with the report of the explosions. They echoed off the walls of the buildings as they might have off the sides of a canyon. The air went blue with smoke, and the acrid smell of gunpowder was suddenly inescapable and almost choking. A dense blizzard of paper blew along the street, thicker than snow. The explosions continued uninterrupted for at least twenty minutes.

I re-entered the hotel with a blinding headache but a feeling of elation. This had been an exhibition of raw power, the elimination of demons, the establishment of good fortune and the cleansing of the underworld.

Over the next few days, Kowloon sounded as if it were a war zone. In some places the streets were inches deep in fragments of acrid-smelling paper. The traffic stopped to allow fifty-foot strings of firecrackers to explode down the front of the taller buildings. Some of these, every two or three feet, contained an extra large firecracker the size of a tin can which went off with an ear-splitting detonation. Gradually, the firecrackers died down and a semblance of peace returned. On either side of many shops and doorways, new red scrolls with black writing upon them were pasted over the previous year's, presaging good fortune.

When I visited the temple to Kwun Yum (or Kwan Yin), the goddess of mercy, it was doing brisk business. The temple was always in semi-darkness, even on the sunniest day. At the rear of

the altar, mysterious in the half-light of guttering red-wax candle flames and a few bare, low-wattage light bulbs, the deity's effigy sat demurely, with attendant gods to either side, leering through the twilight. The altar was hung with an embroidered cloth in imperial yellow, red and gold. From the tarnished brass incense burner rose a column of smoke.

In front of the altar was a throng, mostly of women and children, making offerings, praying or casting fortune-telling sticks. Amongst the offerings being made, mostly of fruit and food, was money. I was amazed to see otherwise poor-looking women dropping fistfuls of banknotes into a brass cauldron of hot embers. In a flare of flame, they were incinerated to a drift of ash rising on the hazy heat of the fire below. It was not until a partially scorched note escaped the fire that I came to see the currency. It was not dollars issued by the Hongkong and Shanghai Bank but Hell's Banknotes in vast denominations – $100,000, $1,000,000, $10,000,000. This was celestial, not terrestrial, cash.

As all this went on, a low-toned bell sounded, striking once every time a worshipper made a donation of real money to the idol. The temple staff hurried between the devotees, removing the burnt-out joss-stick and candle splints, pushing aside the last round of offerings, the food by now inedible as a result of the cascade of ash falling from the incense coils. One man re-placed candles on the altar, two others trimmed wicks and cursorily removed ash from the effigy with a duster made of ginger cockerel's feathers fixed to a long bamboo cane.

Pushing through the crowd of worshippers, I purchased a fifty-cent pack of joss-sticks from an elderly man by the door, lit them all from a candle and stuck them in the urn full of sand provided. It was not that I was a devotee of Kwun Yum but that I was bent on doing what everyone else present was – hedging their

bets for the coming twelvemonth by getting on the good side of the gods.

The general stores in Soares Avenue opened on a self-agreed rota throughout the first five days of the festivities. There was a purpose to this: not only did they open for the convenience of their customers but also to collect debts and settle tabs unaddressed before the new moon. By the time the new year started in earnest, all outstanding debts should have been paid. The day before the holiday commenced, Ching and I went into one of the shops to buy a packet of *wah mui*. The shopkeeper and his family were standing before a shrine positioned in a scarlet-painted box at the rear of their shop. I watched for a while in silence.

'What are they doing?' I whispered to Ching.

'This is the shrine of the kitchen god,' he explained.

The family kow-towed several times to the shrine then the shopkeeper's wife smeared the god's face with something in a bowl.

'What is that?' I murmured.

'Sweet food,' Ching replied. 'Soon, the kitchen god will go to heaven and tell the Jade Emperor if this has been a good family for a year. To make sure he says good words, they give him rice and honey. Make him talk sweet.'

This done, the shopkeeper tore out from the shrine the picture of the god, printed on red paper and faded over the year. He then took it outside on to the pavement and set light to it.

'Now the god goes to heaven,' Ching said.

This act smacked to me of writing a wish list to Father Christmas, whose non-existence I no longer questioned, and sending it up the chimney, but I kept my thoughts to myself. When the ashes had drifted down the street to mingle with the firecracker confetti, a new picture was pasted into the shrine and the shopkeeper stepped back behind his counter.

The lighting of firecrackers was not restricted to Chinese New Year. Whenever a new shop or business opened, the front of the building was decorated with bamboo scaffolding covered in paper flowers and characters propitiating good fortune. Long strings of firecrackers suspended from roof to pavement would be lit, the street soon filling with choking smoke and the continuous cacophony of explosions. If the building was over five storeys high, they could last an hour.

At only one event were firecrackers not let off – funerals.

When I saw my first Chinese funeral procession, I thought the circus had come to town. The initial indications of the approaching funeral procession were the muted sounds of inharmonious music. I went out on to the communal balcony of the hotel to watch.

Soon, a small truck appeared further down Waterloo Road. A large bamboo frame had been fixed to the front of the truck and adorned with paper flowers, gold and scarlet bunting and, I presumed, the name of the departed in huge characters. In the centre of this was a large monochrome photograph of the deceased. This vehicle was followed by a two-hundred-yard procession containing delivery tricycles similarly decorated. Interspersed between these were men carrying tall poles topped by Chinese fringed umbrellas, a large paper orb with a ladder rising through it and a number of other incomprehensible ceremonial items. At the rear of this came the coffin. I had expected a hearse but it was in fact carried in a sort of palanquin between eight perspiring coolies. The sides were decorated with white and yellow flowers. The coffin itself was highly polished and of a curious shape, in section rather like a four-leafed clover. To the rear of the coffin walked the relatives of the deceased, the foremost being a small boy of about my age wearing a white cloak. Every so often, he wiped his eyes and nose on the sleeve of his coat.

'Who is he?' I asked a room boy standing beside me.

'He dead man son. Now he Number One man for him family. Big job for him.'

The other primary mourners also wore white cloaks whilst everyone else was soberly dressed, with the men sporting black arm bands. It was all most dignified – except for the music.

Just behind the leading truck walked a small classical Chinese band of about eight musicians. They wore white bandsmen's uniforms with peaked caps and looked like a rather run-down English seaside town band. The music they played was doleful, the woodwind instruments high-pitched and keening, the small gong cracked and discordant. Not far behind them came a band equipped with Western brass instruments. They played 'When the Saints Go Marching In' – badly. Three other bands in the procession played 'Doin' What Comes Naturally' (from *Annie, Get Your Gun*, a recent cinema hit), 'Greensleeves' and finally, on the correct instruments, Chinese classical music once again. Each band played in apparent ignorance of the others so the whole musical contribution to the event was a raucous medley of disconnected tunes from three cultures.

My mother, who watched this procession with me, remarked that she preferred firecrackers to the assassination of music but she had by then forgotten the five-day migraine that marked Chinese New Year.

My father returned for good from Japan in the early summer of 1953. The Korean War was winding down, truce talks had been held and his job at the Sasebo naval base near Nagasaki was becoming redundant.

Immediately after my father's return, moves were put underway for us to leave the Fourseas. It was deemed an unsuitable billet for a family. There was, however, a shortage of quarters due to the pull-back from Japan, so we were tabled to move temporarily into a flat on the top floor of a building in Boundary Street, pending a more suitable quarter falling vacant.

Although less than a mile or two from the Fourseas, I was, at first, reluctant to go. I had many friends and acquaintances amongst the hotel room boys and in the streets of Mong Kok, with which I was as familiar as a rickshaw coolie or a pedlar. It would seem strange living in a self-contained home once again, without them around.

As the name implied, Boundary Street marked the periphery between British Kowloon and the hinterland of the New Territories, ceded to the British for ninety-nine years from 1898. As our flat was on the northern side of the street, this worried me. We were being housed in a no man's land that was only provisionally British. For several weeks, I had nightmares of being overrun in my sleep by Communist Chinese troops, bayoneted in my bed or sent to a slave labour camp, nevermore to see my mother.

In spite of my misgivings, I was beginning to feel excited by the impending move. It meant new horizons, new challenges and, more importantly, a new area to explore. Yet, two weeks before the move, the most dramatic event of the months I lived in the Fourseas occurred on Ho Man Tin hill.

Late one afternoon, I was walking back from school alone when I saw a thin wisp of smoke rising from over the hill. I gave it no thought and trudged on down Waterloo Road. As I reached the hotel, I saw the wisp was now a column. People were running down the track by the school and spilling out on to the main road, blocking the traffic. In a few minutes, the smoke was denser,

rising faster with sparks glimmering in it, despite the sunlight. Then I heard the far-off bells of fire engines.

I ran into the hotel garage, dumped my Hong Kong basket and headed for the hill. Hordes of squatters were pouring off it, every one carrying something. Even toddlers, one hand held by their mother, clumsily dragged a cooking pot or enamel basin. Adults laden with bedding – men with complete beds – struggled down the track, slipping on the loose gravel. Laden rickshaws wove between them. The exodus was orderly but noisy. Everyone was shouting.

The police and the fire brigade turned up simultaneously. In minutes, hoses were snaking up the track and the police had instigated a cordon to prevent squatters returning to the fire to rescue more belongings. This, however, was soon considered futile so they took to directing the flow of people and getting the traffic moving again.

I hurried to the bottom of the track. The smoke was by now hundreds of feet high but, the squatter area being over a ridge, I could not see the seat of the blaze. Consequently, I joined the throng of people returning to save their belongings.

Cresting the ridge, I was so shocked by the scene before me I just stood still in stunned wonderment. In my naïvety, I had assumed a squatter shack had caught fire and those running away with their belongings were simply being cautious. What lay before me was an inferno. At least half the squatters' shacks had been reduced to piles of smouldering ashes with, here and there, uprights burning brightly. The conflagration was moving through the area like a forest fire through a plantation of pines. The noise was terrifying, with tin sheeting cracking as it warped, explosions caused by tinned food and the incessant hiss and spit of burning wood accompanied by the crash of shacks caving in. A strong wind blew towards the fire, sucking in paper and scraps of cloth,

feeding it with oxygen and peppering my legs with fine gravel. As the fire progressed, it instantly ignited whole shacks at a time. One moment, a flimsy building looked intact, the next it was alight. Before my eyes a shanty exploded as if an artillery shell had hit it. A fountain of flame rose from it only to die in the rising smoke.

Ahead of the fire, people were running in and out of their shacks, piling their belongings on the ground, on handcarts, on their children. I circumnavigated the blaze, upon which the fire brigade were preparing to play their hoses, and started to gather up armfuls of clothing from a pile, folding them in on themselves to make a tight bundle. A young Chinese man ran out of a shack to accost me, stopped and went back in. I tumbled the rest of the pile into a sheet, tying the corners together, using them to pad out some rice bowls and other crockery. The young man appeared and added a framed sepia photo to the bundle. It showed a family group seated on upright chairs. In the centre sat an ancient woman with a baby on her knee, her feet tiny where they pro-jected from under an old-fashioned long gown.

I waited. The fire was moving nearer, and quickly. I could feel its intensity on my bare arms and legs. My eyes began to weep from the heat and smoke.

'*Wei!*' I shouted. '*Ché! Ché! Fide! Fide!*' (Hey! Go! Go! Quick! Quick!)

My pronunciation and the grammatical accuracy of this dog-Cantonese were doubtless atrocious but more than sufficient. The man came out of the shack followed by a woman carrying a babe-in-arms. He was laden down with a very battered suitcase and a wooden box. I gathered up the pile of linen and crockery and, hugging it to my chest, started down the track. I could not see my feet and frequently stumbled. Once, I fell, but my burden broke my fall. In a crowd of others, I reached the police line and was allowed through by an English inspector.

'Got a squatter hut, have we?' he enquired with a wry smile.

'I'm just helping,' I answered.

He looked at me for a moment and said, 'Where do you live, son?'

'Down the road, sir,' I replied, jutting my chin in the direction of the Fourseas and hoping my politeness would deflect the ticking off likely to be coming next.

'Well done, son,' he said and he patted my head. 'Go up that road over there.' He indicated Soares Avenue which, closed to traffic, was now a sort of squatter holding pen.

Once there, the young man gave his name to an official and we were guided into Emma Avenue where the pavements were filling up with groups of squatters. They sat chattering and tidying their belongings. To my astonishment, no-one was looking miserable or crying or showing any real sign of distress.

There was a touch on my head. It was the young man.

'You luckee boy for me,' he said in pidgin English. 'T'ankee you plentee plentee.'

'Martin,' another voice remonstrated, 'you're filthy.'

My mother stood before me, arms akimbo. I put the pile of clothes and bedding down at my feet and studied myself. My legs and arms were covered in ash: no doubt my face and hair were, too.

'What have you been doing?'

'Dis you littul boy?' the young man asked my mother. 'He plentee good littul boy. Plentee good for me. You no beatee, missee. No beatee.'

At this point, it came to my mother what I had done. She hugged me, ash and all. The young man touched my hair again, either for luck or in gratitude. His wife did likewise. I was sent in for a bath and my mother offered her assistance to a Red Cross worker.

Lying in the warm water smelling of my mother's perfumed salts, I realized just how fragile life was, that everything one counted upon could come crashing down in less than the time it took for a double maths class. I also learnt that whilst it was one thing to live in a large box, a shack, a cockloft or between the shafts of a rickshaw, it was quite another to lose everything.

6

DENS, DUCKS AND DIVES

133 BOUNDARY STREET HAD BEEN BUILT IN THE 1920S AS A BIJOU residence on the edge of the countryside. By the time we moved in, it had gone down in the world. The exterior stonework was blotched with dead lichen and algae, the kitchen was dark and dank, the servants' quarters smelt of mould and the flat roof leaked into the bathroom. The city had reached out to it and the countryside was no more, although the barren foothills of the Kowloon hills did come down to within a hundred yards of the garden of the ground-floor flat.

Moving to a flat necessitated my mother employing more servants. As it was usual to employ a husband and wife wherever possible, the wash amah who had replaced Ah Fong was let go. She was genuinely sad at leaving us but my mother secured her a good job with an Army major and his wife who preferred to do her own cooking so only required an amah. That they had a blond-haired daughter no doubt helped to sweeten the bitterness of parting.

After an in-depth culinary interview, my mother took on Wong and his wife, Ah Shun. With them came their four-year-old son,

Chan-tuk, to whom my mother took an instant liking and nick-named Tuppence.

So far as we knew, Wong — whose references gave his name as Hwong Cheng-kwee — was a Shanghainese who, like so many others, was a refugee from Communism. He and Ah Shun had several other children whom they lodged in the New Territories or had had to leave with relatives in China. A tall, round-faced man, Wong had apparently worked in a top-class hotel in Shanghai as a pastry chef. At least, that was what one of his well-thumbed references stated. My mother gave him a month's probation. This ended after a day when he made his first sponge cake. It did not so much sit on the plate as float over it. We had never tasted anything like it. He had a permanent job from my mother's first mouthful. Ah Shun became the wash and sew-sew amah and the two of them shared the chores of keeping house.

To say that Wong was a one-in-a-thousand cook-houseboy was not to be guilty of hyperbole. He was utterly superb, with the attentiveness of a high-class butler, the culinary skills if not of Escoffier then certainly of his *sous chef*, the attention to detail of a water-colourist and the mien of a true gentleman's gentleman. He and Ah Shun wore the customary *sam fu* white jacket and black, loose-fitting trousers with felt slippers, in which they glided across parquet floors they had so highly polished you could see the reflection of the windows in them. They also served at table, which at first I found most peculiar. I had been served in restaurants, on the *Corfu* and the like, but in our own home . . . It was like being a member of the aristocracy.

There were some teething problems. Ah Shun starched my father's white shorts which he wore to the office. The hems chafed his legs raw. Thereafter, she artfully starched only the crease. When the monthly provisions bill came, my mother found Wong had used six dozen eggs, which accounted for the levitatory

sponges. My mother asked him to cut down: then she saw he had used nine bottles of Heinz Salad Cream. As Wong did all the basic shopping, only discussing the matter of provisions or menus with my mother if she were holding a drinks or dinner party, this wanton purchase of salad cream seemed not only extravagant but suspicious. Wong was called into my mother's presence. It was not long before I was summoned too.

'What is this?' my mother muttered, glowering at me as she held out the invoice.

I was inclined to tell her it was the bill, but kept my peace.

'This!' she repeated, indicating an item on the bill. 'And this. And this. Wong tells me this is your doing.'

I had no idea why she was cross but I admitted I ate salad cream.

'Eat it!' my mother replied. 'Wong tells me you put it on your bloody breakfast!'

Every morning, I ate breakfast alone, after my father had departed for work in HMS *Tamar* and whilst my mother was still preening herself for a hard day at the canasta table. Wong always provided a fried egg on crisp fried bread, a fried tomato and stiff rashers of brittle, grilled bacon. I ate the bacon first with my fingers then waded into the remainder which I smothered with salad cream. How I first discovered this curious amalgam of tastes I do not know, but I loved it. Indeed, I could go through a bottle in three days, especially if I asked Wong for salad cream instead of Marmite and lettuce sandwiches to take to school. My father being at the office, I was not punished for my abnormal gourmandizing but that avenue of pleasure was promptly closed.

Wong was paid $300 (approximately £19) a month plus an allowance of $75 for food. He lived with Ah Shun and Tuppence in the servants' quarters beyond the kitchen: a closed-in balcony and laundry sink, two small bedrooms equipped with cast-iron

bunks and a shower room with a squat-down toilet which my father referred to (in what he claimed to be submariners' slang) as *the shit-shave-shower-shampoo-and-shoeshine*. Wong and his family used our kitchen to prepare their food but they ate it squatting on the balcony until my mother found out. Thereafter, they ate at the kitchen table.

My mother found having servants somewhat disquieting and, if anything, ambiguous. She was a humanist at heart who believed no man should lord it over another. Yet here she was with two people who were there at her beck and call. Indeed, there were to be many times when my parents returned from a party in the early hours to find Wong staggering into the lounge, bleary-eyed and dopey with sleep, to see if they wanted a nightcap or a sandwich. She suffixed every request with *please* and *thank you* and made sure I did, too. It was impressed upon me that I should never make unreasonable demands of Wong or Ah Shun and I was never to say *Fide! Fide!* or *Chop! Chop!* (Quick! Quick!) at him. (I did once, out of pique, and he clipped my ear, whereby a mutual respect was born.)

Although not much more than a mile from the Fourseas, the environs of the flat were very different. Close by was La Salle College, a major Roman Catholic school primarily for Chinese. To the north-west was the one-time garden suburb of Kowloon Tong, to the north were the barren lower slopes of the nine Kowloon hills. Indeed, the name Kowloon derived from the Cantonese *gau lung*, meaning *nine dragons*. To the south was a residential area and the wooded grounds of the Kowloon hospital. Only the foothills offered the slightest opportunity for exploration and that was soon exhausted, my only find being that of a white plaster-of-paris death mask in a cave and a large chunk of mauve transparent volcanic rock. My mother and I hoped it was beryllium, a piece of which had been found in Hong Kong the

month before, making its finder rich. She took it to the geology department of the University. It wasn't beryllium but silicate – glass.

Not a mile to the east, however, was the most romantic and allegedly dangerous place in the colony. It was called Kowloon Walled City.

The name was a misnomer. It was not and never had been a city. It covered not much more than 25,000 square yards and, although it had been surrounded by a crenulated wall, the defences had been demolished by British prisoners-of-war under Japanese command and used as hardcore for an airport runway extension and sea wall.

According to a history of Hong Kong owned by my mother, it had originally been established in the eighteenth century as a far-flung outpost of the Chinese empire; its subsequent history was convoluted and its sovereignty confused. After the British gained control of Hong Kong and, later, Kowloon at the end of the Opium and *Arrow* Wars in the early 1840s, the Chinese imperial government insisted on maintaining a local presence so the British turned a blind eye towards Kowloon Walled City. Behind its walls, a nominal Chinese garrison was maintained which primarily kept a watch on the foreign invaders and en-forced Chinese law in the area not under colonial control. Pirates being a problem in the region, the mandarin stationed in the settlement was kept busy suppressing and executing them. When the New Territories were ceded to the British, Kowloon Walled City was to find itself twenty-five miles from the border with China, completely surrounded by British territory. The cessation treaty was also ambiguous. Kowloon Walled City was now, in effect, cut off and ruled and possessed by neither – or both – countries.

It remained a backwater for fifty years, visited at the turn of the

twentieth century by Europeans in Hong Kong for vicarious excitement, a fragment of the 'real' China on their doorsteps. Ruled by a mandarin from his *yamen* in the centre, it was quaint and exotic. The salacious aspect of the place lay in the fact that British law did not necessarily apply there, depending upon the interpretation of the treaty. Few Hong Kong policemen patrolled it and no government official collected taxes. The power supply was illegally tapped from the main grid and the water supply from the main. Kowloon Walled City was in effect a minute city state all on its own, arguably the smallest ever to have existed.

When China fell to the Communists in 1949, many criminal refugees fled to Hong Kong, some of them gravitating to the walled city area where they quickly established fresh enterprises. When the buildings were full, they built more, many little better than substantial squatter shacks. A disastrous fire in 1951 destroyed half the city but gave the new arrivals the opportunity to clear and build: it was said they set the fire in the first place. Thereafter, Kowloon Walled City remained an enclave governed by no-one. It was to Hong Kong what the Casbah was to Algiers, with one exception: it was more or less closed to outsiders. Trippers avoided it. It was said that any European who entered it was never seen again unless floating out of it down the *nullah* that served as a sewer. If ever the police entered the area, they went in armed patrols of three.

We had not been in Boundary Street a day when my mother took me aside.

'Martin,' she started, signifying her seriousness, 'I know you like to roam and explore, and round here that's all right. But,' she continued, unfolding a map of Kowloon, 'you do *not* go even near here.'

She pointed to the map. Kowloon Walled City was left as a blank uneven-sided square.

'What is it?' I enquired.

'Ask no questions and be told no lies,' my mother replied evasively, 'and *don't* go to find out.'

To utter such a dictum to a street-wise eight-year-old was tantamount to buying him an entrance ticket.

The following afternoon, homework hurriedly completed, I had a quick glance at the map and headed east down Boundary Street. In ten minutes, I was on the outskirts of Kowloon Walled City.

Nothing indicated to me why this place should be forbidden. A number of new six-storey buildings were being erected, with several already occupied or nearing completion; and a lot of shanties and older two-storey buildings were leaning precariously. It looked like a squatter area but with permanent structures in the middle in ill repair. A *hutong* lay before me, winding into the buildings and shacks. There being, I reasoned, no way my mother was ever going to find out, I set off down the alleyway, easing my way past a man pushing a bicycle, the pannier laden with cardboard boxes. He paid me not the slightest attention.

Through the open doors I spied scenes of industrial domesticity. To one side would be a *kang* or metal-framed bed, piled with neatly folded bedding; to the other several people seated at a table sewing, assembling torches, placing coloured pencils in boxes or painting lacquer boxes. Behind other doors were businesses, pure and simple. In one a baker was placing trays of buns in a wood-fired oven; in another, two men were involved in making noodles, swinging sheets of thin dough in the air around a wooden rolling-pin, the interior of their shack ghost-white under a layer of flour dust.

Wherever I went, the air was redolent with the smells of wood smoke, joss-sticks, boiling rice and human excrement. The effluent from this community, I soon discovered, flowed down

open gullies at the side of the *hutongs* to disappear through holes in the ground lined by stone slabs.

Arriving at one of the older stone buildings, I was about to peer in through an open door when a Chinese man rushed out and slammed it shut. Stripped to the waist, he bore a coloured tattoo of a dragon on his back. He glowered at me.

'W'at you wan'?' he asked.

'Nothing,' I said, fighting to stop myself sounding guilty, although of what I did not know. Then, hoping it might soften him a bit, I added, '*Ngo giu jo* Mah Tin.' I held my hand out. '*Nei giu mut ye meng?*'

He was much taken aback by my introducing myself – especially in Cantonese – and it was at least thirty pensive seconds before he took my hand and firmly shook it. During that time, he eyed me up and down, much as a butcher might a bull being led to slaughter.

'Mah Tin,' he said at last. '*Ngo giu jo* Ho. Why you come?'

'Just looking,' I answered, shrugging and adding in pidgin English, 'Come look-see.'

'You no look-see,' he answered sternly. 'No good look-see for *gweilo* boy.'

I smiled, nodded my understanding, said, '*Choi kin,*' (goodbye) and turned to go.

'You look-see,' he declared, changing his mind. He opened the door, indicating I follow him.

What until now had seemed a harmless saunter through just another warren of passageways immediately took on a sinister aspect. No-one knew I was here. What, I considered, if this old stone building with its substantial door was the headquarters of the evil Fu Manchu? I had recently read Sax Rohmer. If I stepped over the high lintel, I could vanish. For ever. On the other hand, not to accept Ho's invitation would result in a massive loss of face.

I would never be able to come here again: and I had seen nothing yet. And so, I threw caution to the wind and followed him into the building.

The entire ground floor consisted of one vast room, heavy beams holding up the ceiling and second floor. It was furnished with upright rosewood chairs, the wood even darker with age, low tables and several ornately framed mirrors, the silvering missing in places. Halfway down the room stood a wooden screen, the top half pierced by intricate fretwork, the rest a painting depicting sheer-sided hills and lakes. I sensed I was being observed through it but, as I walked by the end, there was no-one there. The wooden floor was devoid of any covering. There was an air of much-faded gentility about the place.

To the rear was a staircase beneath which a door opened and an old hunched woman entered, walking with the aid of a stick. She took one look at me and grinned toothlessly, hobbled to my side and, inevitably, stroked my hair. This put me at ease. First, Fu Manchu was hardly likely to employ crones (unless, god forbid, this was his mother) and second, my golden hair was a passport to my security. No-one would risk harming such a harbinger of good fortune.

'You come.' Ho beckoned me up the stairs.

I followed him into a room along three sides of which were placed wooden *kangs*. Upon one of these lay a supine man asleep upon a woven bamboo mat, his head on a hard Chinese headrest, his legs drawn up, his hands twitching like a dog's paws in a dream of chasing rabbits.

'*Nga pin*,' Ho announced and beckoned me further towards the fourth wall, the whole length of which was shuttered. I refrained from asking him what *nga pin* was for fear of seeming ignorant. Again, the last thing I wanted to do was lose face with him. He unlatched one of the shutters and we stepped out

on to the balcony, which sloped forwards alarmingly towards a crumbling balustrade.

From here, I was afforded a panoramic view of the walled city. The shacks were so tightly packed, it was well nigh impossible to see where the *hutongs* ran between them. Yet the real surprise was the few larger buildings tucked between them. One stood in a wide rectangular courtyard with a number of outbuildings close by; from another rose a faint cloud of bluish smoke which meant it had to be a temple. Three or four were in a row suggesting that, in olden days, they had stood upon a street. In the distance was Kowloon Bay, a cargo ship riding at a quarantine buoy. Over to my left was the bulk of Fei Ngo Shan, the most easterly of the Kowloon hills, the slopes sharp and clear in the late sun. To the south-west, indistinct in the haze, was Hong Kong Island.

Ho took me back inside. We passed the sleeping man, who was beginning to wake, and descended the stairs which creaked loudly. Once outside, Ho bade me farewell and went back into the house, closing the door. I set off along the way I had come, considering to myself that I had taken a terrible risk. Other than a shop, I had never accepted an invitation into a building. Reaching the edge of the squatter shacks, and stepping out on to a road with traffic going by, I resolved not to be so foolhardy again. Yet, where Kowloon Walled City was concerned, I knew I had to return to investigate the temple and the building in the courtyard.

When I returned to our apartment, I went into the kitchen where Wong was preparing supper and asked him what *nga pin* meant. He stopped stirring a pan for a moment, looked quizzically at me and replied, 'Opium.'

On his return to Hong Kong, my father had taken delivery of a Ford Consul saloon which he promptly had resprayed two-tone grey with white walled tyres: my mother, with her penchant for Chinese names, called it *Ch'ing Yan*, which translated as *Lover*. *Ch'ing Yan* opened up a wide horizon for all three of us. It also gave my father a pastime. Never a man for a hobby, the car became the centre of his leisure activities. Having never owned a car before, he mollycoddled it as much as he might have done a mistress. The interior was kept pristine: no food or drink might be consumed therein. He checked the oil and tyres at least weekly and spent hours polishing the bodywork, dusting the interior and hoovering the carpets and seats. No-one was allowed to help in this endeavour. He rejected all the approaches of the itinerant car washers-and-waxers who did the rounds of residential areas every Saturday afternoon. When he saw Wong knocking dead leaves off the bonnet with a feather duster, he hurtled downstairs to stop him: the ends of the feathers, he explained, might be scratching the paint.

The first Sunday after the delivery of the car, my father announced we were going for a drive around the New Territories. And so, after a hearty breakfast which Wong insisted on cooking although it was his day off, we departed.

My father had decided to take a circular route without deviation, digression or diversion. My mother had been hoping we might have a look at a few places on the way, but my father was adamant and my mother did not drive. I really did not care. For the first time, I was going to find out what lay the other side of the Kowloon hills.

We crossed them by way of a pass on the Tai Po road next to a deep blue reservoir and descended to Sha Tin, a small fishing village on the shores of a large inlet. The tide was out, leaving mudflats upon which sampans lay settled on their hulls. Across on

the other shore, on the northern slopes of the Kowloon hills, was a rock outcrop that, if the imagination was stretched, looked in silhouette like a woman with a baby in a carrier on her back.

'Amah Rock,' my mother declared, reading from a notebook she was compiling in the hope that, one day, she might write a Hong Kong guide and history. She went on to relate a story about a fisherman lost at sea, his loyal wife who waited on the outcrop for his junk to return and the gods who changed her into stone so she could wait for ever. The story I had heard was that the stone was a childless baby amah who had stolen her mistress's baby and been frozen in stone by punishing gods, but I said nothing.

We drove along the shore until my mother's eye alighted on a small isolated building ahead between the road and the sea wall, surrounded by paper bark trees. It had an awning and a few car parking spaces, but little else.

'Pull in, Ken,' she said as imperiously as she dared. 'I fancy a coffee.'

'You've only just had breakfast, Joyce,' he replied peevishly, edging his pride and joy into a parking space. He checked there were no boughs likely to become detached from the tree overhead in the next hour and led us inside.

The Sha Tin Dairy Farm Restaurant (aka The Shatin Road-house) was a small American-style diner with considerable pretensions. The menu was designed to be mailed to friends and it referred to itself as *the magic kiosk by the side of the magic Tidal Cove*, which bore reference to the fact that the Sha Tin inlet had four tides a day. At the top of the menu, in small print, were the words *Please let us service your car while you eat*. ('Fat chance!' my father remarked on reading it.) We sat at a table overlooking the inlet. The mountains were just beginning to shimmer in the day's heat. On the other side of the inlet, a cluster of ancient houses stood between woods and the water's edge. A junk sailed sedately

but slowly by, heading for the open sea. My father studied them all with his binoculars.

'The rice grown in Sha Tin was so good it was reserved for the emperor alone,' my mother remarked, reading from her notes.

I studied the menu. All the main dishes – even salads – were served with rice or toast. My parents ordered a coffee each and I requested a Chocolate Soldier, a sickly sweet bottle of thick, cold cocoa made with cow and soya milk. All three were automatically accompanied by toast.

As my parents drank their coffee, I read the blurb on the menu which outlined the attractions of the roadhouse: *This is the only place you can watch and feel a roaring train while you eat . . . Occasionally you'll be thrilled by the shooting vampires smacking out of the Blue . . . Your junior folks may enjoy fishing, fording, boating, ferrying, crabbing, clamming or simply playing around in the shallow mangroves. This is the place you'll enjoy most! Please come again and save a trip to Miami or Geneva!* I gazed out at the mudflats and tried to envisage my car-proud father's response to a request to go crabbing in the mangroves (whatever they were: all I could see was an expanse of mud). I saw no vampires.

Leaving Sha Tin, the road more or less followed the coast and the railway, grass-covered hills rising on the left with heavily wooded valleys. The next town was another fishing community called Tai Po. My father, having lost time over the enforced coffee stop, drove straight through it. My mother attempted to take some photos from the moving car but had to give up.

Just beyond the town, the road divided. Left went through the Lam Tsuen valley to the market town of Yuen Long, right took a longer route to the same destination. My father signalled left. My mother wanted the scenic route. We drove three hundred yards towards the Lam Tsuen valley, my father swore a lot, reversed into a farm track, muddied one wheel arch, got out, wiped the

mud off with a rag and a bottle of water provided for just such an emergency and took the other road. We scowlingly bypassed Fanling and Sheung Shui, not stopping save for petrol. Then we entered old China.

The land became a patchwork of rice paddies separated by low dykes, the rice beginning to sprout above the water, bright green and pristine. The villages and farmhouses were ancient and could have changed little in two centuries. Farmers walked slowly along the side of the road wearing wide-brimmed conical hats, their trousers rolled up to the knee, leading docile-looking buffaloes. Man and beast had mud caked on their legs. Hakka women with coolie poles over their shoulders carried heavy loads of fodder or bundles of *pak choi*. It was my favourite Chinese vegetable, delicious when steamed and served at most *dai pai dongs*. Dogs ambled along just off the tarmac, moving from the shade of one eucalyptus or paper bark tree to the next.

Every now and then, my mother demanded my father stop for her to take a photo. Inevitably, every time she requested a halt, it was twenty yards before we came to a standstill so my father had to back up. Before long he was seething. When my mother suggested turning into a side road into the countryside, he lost it completely.

'Joyce!' he said through gritted teeth. 'We've come to drive round the New Territories. Not into them. I am *not* driving into the blithering hills. For all I know, we could wind up in Communist China.'

'That's not likely,' I injudiciously piped up. 'If we take a road on the left we'll stay in Hong Kong. China's to the right. Anyway, you can't drive into China because there's a border and a river to cross and the river's only got one bridge for the train and the police and the army—'

'Shut up!' my father exploded.

Several hundred yards further on, his patience was again tested by a duck farmer moving his gaggle of about two hundred birds from one pond to another, driving them ahead of him by means of two long, thin and very flexible bamboo poles. The ducks and a few geese waddled down the middle of the road. My father tentatively beeped his horn. The duck farmer turned. My father signalled curtly with his hand for the man to get a move on. At this, he turned and walked towards the car. My father unwisely wound his window down.

'*Mat yeh?*' the farmer said, somewhat belligerently. This trans-lated roughly as: What d'you want? The added sub-text was: Damn your eyes, foreign devil.

My father, who spoke barely a word of Cantonese, looked blank.

'*Mat ych?*' the farmer repeated, more antagonistically.

My father, still with a vacant look on his face, then suggested, 'Martin, you're always playing in the street. What's he saying?'

'I don't know,' I lied.

At this juncture, the farmer shrugged and turned. The ducks had meantime broken ranks and were all over the road and grass verge. The farmer picked up his herding poles. Taking his time, he rounded them up and continued to make his steady way ahead of us. We edged forward in a grinding first gear accompanied by my father's grinding teeth.

At the next left junction, we turned up a narrow road towards a steep hill, the road eventually petering out in a grassy bank. We stopped and got out. My mother took photos of the view, my father stood wondering how he was going to do a three-point turn. Whilst he pondered, my mother and I set off up a path.

In a short distance, we came to a semi-circular stone platform with a horseshoe-shaped wall about two feet high running round half its circumference. In the wall was a tiny stone door upon

which some characters had been written in red paint. In front of the door were two rice bowls containing a sludge of dead leaves and rainwater and a stone weighing down a wad of faded Hell's Banknotes.

'What is this?' I asked.

'It's a grave,' my mother answered. 'Behind that door is the coffin.'

I looked at it with a feeling of suppressed terror. I had visited my maternal grandfather's grave in a municipal cemetery in Portsmouth but had never really come to terms with his body lying six feet under an oblong of stone chippings. Here, there was a man reclining in death just behind a door.

Higher up the slope we came upon a narrow terrace cut into the hillside. It was overgrown with grass and held a row of very large urns with lids like inverted plates. The view was spectacular, a vista of wetlands over which soared flights of ducks and, beyond, the sea.

My mother busying herself with her camera, I decided to look in one of the urns. It seemed strange that they had been left there, in the middle of nowhere, on a bleak and windswept mountainside. I took hold of one of the lids and lifted it clear. Inside, neatly packed away so that it might all fit in, was a human skeleton, the skull on top. The bones were brown and looked as if they had been lightly varnished. I quickly replaced the lid.

'It's called a *kam taap*,' my mother said, not taking her eye from the viewfinder. 'I've been told that when a Chinese dies, they bury the body for seven years then they exhume it, clean the bones and put them in an ossuary – that's one of those urns.'

We walked down to the car. My father had turned it round and was buffing off scuff marks – caused by his reversing into a bush – on the rear bumper with a soft cloth.

'The view's wonderful,' my mother said sweetly as we joined him.

'You're a bloody nuisance, Joyce,' my father snarled.

We drove down to the main road and along it as fast as the surface and law would allow and my father's temper could contain. It was not until my mother saw a sign off to the right reading *Kadoorie Beach* that she spoke.

'Go down there, Ken,' she commanded in a voice that would brook no opposition.

My father did as he was asked and we drove down a narrow lane overhung by Chinese pine trees, the wispy, delicate variety one saw in classical paintings. The lane culminated in a small car park and a sandy beach gently lapped by the sea. Removing her shoes, my mother tripped off down to the water's edge. Beyond her, indistinct under the early-afternoon sky, was the island of Lan Tau, its peaks rising into a sub-tropical sky almost devoid of colour in the hot sun. A request that I might be allowed to join her was bluntly rebuffed by my father, so I sat in the car for fifteen minutes with my mouth shut.

When my mother returned to the car, my father said, 'Make sure there's no sand on your feet. I don't want to be hoovering the bloody carpets for weeks.'

'I do wish you'd shut up, Ken. It's only a bloody car,' she answered and, without removing the sand from her soles or putting her shoes back on, she got in the front and slammed the door.

In a mile or so, we came upon another sign by the road. It pointed to The Dragon Inn. My father, unbidden, turned and parked. Inside the inn, a cross between an English country pub, a Chinese tea house and a French café, we were served a plate of hot buttered toast, which my mother and I now considered must be obligatory once one crossed the Kowloon hills. My

mother ordered tea, I asked for a Coke and my father requested a San Miguel beer. Then he had another. At the third, my mother reminded him he was driving. He ordered a fourth to make his point. She commented that the car was brand new, the first he had ever owned, and would it not be a pity if it got dented.

'Already bloody ruined by that benighted bush,' my father grumbled, but he did not order a fifth beer.

The bill settled, we went to look at a tortoise the size of a half barrel that was said to have been hatched in the Ming dynasty. A notice stated rather obviously: *A Tortoise Several Hundred Years Old*; it occurred to me that it would have to be in a country where eggs could be a century old. The poor creature lived in a concrete-walled enclosure about four times its size, with a trough of stale water and a pile of bedraggled greens. At least it had a roof to protect it from the searing heat of the sun.

Disturbed by these conditions, I suggested to my mother that we either set up a tortoise protection society or come back that night and kidnap it. Her reply was that the car boot could not take the weight, with which I had sadly to concur. However, I was permitted to sit on it to have my photo taken.

At about five o'clock, we arrived back at Boundary Street. My mother strode directly into my parents' bedroom and locked the door. I heard her running herself a bath. My father spent an hour rubbing imaginary scratches off the rear panelling of the Ford Consul. I went to my room and kept a low profile.

Over the coming weeks, I paid repeated clandestine visits to Kowloon Walled City. I did not, however, become acquainted

with many people. Whereas the stall-and shopkeepers of Soares Avenue and Mong Kok were open and welcoming, those of the walled city were polite but reticent.

Whenever I arrived, Ho appeared before I had gone twenty yards, trotting towards me and smiling expansively. It was as if some unseen sentry had been watching out for me, relaying news of my impending arrival. For as long as I was in the enclave, he would accompany me, talking all the time, improving his English and my Cantonese. Sometimes, we took a bowl of soup together in a shack done out as an eating-place, with tables and chairs and an elderly waiter who limped. On many occasions, I offered to pay but Ho invariably pushed my money aside. On the other hand, he never paid either.

Apart from inviting me into the opium den and to drink tea or broth with him, Ho took me nowhere else. I had hoped he would show me the temple but any attempt to steer the conversation or our feet in its direction were futile.

After a while, Ho told me he was going 'long time Macau-side' and introduced me to his *ho pang yau* (his good friend).

This man was in his mid-twenties, not tall but immensely handsome, lacking the prominent cheekbones, Adam's apple and slightly flared nostrils of the average Cantonese male. He could, I thought, easily have been a film star. Muscular in a trim way, his hands were small but very strong. To my surprise, he spoke good pidgin English.

'My name is Lau,' he introduced himself when we first met. 'I am Ho's friend.'

'I am Martin,' I replied.

'*Mah Tin*,' he repeated. 'In Cantonese, this mean *horse, electric*. You are electric horse.' He grinned at his interpretation and mimicked riding a lively steed. 'Like at Laichikok fun garden.' It was a reasonable translation of *fairground*.

We shook hands and drank tea to cement our new-found friendship.

'When you come Kowloon Walled City-side,' he went on, slurping at his bowl of tea, 'I be here for you. If I not here, you no come. You unner-stand? If you are good boy, I will show you this place.'

I agreed to these terms. After all, to have a personal guide to this maze of shanties and ancient buildings was more than I could have hoped for.

Our tea finished, I said goodbye to Ho and set off with Lau. He walked with a measured, easy pace. Everyone greeted him and stepped aside to let him pass in the narrow alleys. In his turn, he invariably made way for heavily laden coolies and young women. The former breathlessly grunted their thanks whilst the latter giggled.

'I will show you some thing,' Lau said as we made our way past the building with the balustrade. 'From long time before. When China have emperor.'

We reached a place where the *hutong* widened. Lying beside the wall of a larger than average shanty were two massive cannons.

'This,' Lau began, 'Chinese gun one time on city wall. Fight English like you.' He grinned. 'But no more fight. Now live no trouble, make money.'

Carrying on, we arrived at the temple and entered. At first, my eyes adjusting to the gloom, it looked no different from any other – dim lighting, incense smoke, the occasional wavering candle . . . Yet, as my eyes accepted the twilight, I saw that this one was grander than any I had previously seen. First, it had three larger-than-life-size effigies completely covered in gold except for the carving of their tightly curled, black painted hair: yet even that had a gold finial on top. All three were seated in front of intricately embroidered gold tapestries. The altar table was huge,

made of black wood and finely carved with gold-painted designs of leaves, dragons and curlicues. Upon it were not only the customary offerings but also exquisitely painted porcelain vases and two gold-leaf-coated lanterns. To one side, an old man was carefully applying gold leaf to one of the idols with a damp sponge. Second, the temple was spotlessly clean: usually they were dusty places, the floor scattered with the ashes of Hell's Banknotes or the fine powder of burnt joss-sticks. Third, there was a sleeping dog chained to the wall on the left which got to its feet and snarled menacingly at me.

'You like?' Lau enquired.

'Like plenty,' I replied, took a joss-stick and, lighting it, bowed to the effigies with it held between my supplicating hands before sticking it in the sand of the incense bowl.

Lau watched me, bemused.

'You no . . .' he looked for the word in English and failed to find it '. . . *Gai duk toh?*' He made the sign of the Cross on the palm of his hand.

'Yes,' I answered. 'Church of England.'

'Why you . . . ?' He pointed to the altar and made a cursory bow.

'Respect,' I said, but Lau just smiled in his incomprehension.

We walked on. Suddenly, Lau stopped and said, 'You no like ovver *gweilo* boy.' For the first time, he touched my hair. 'Now I show you good place.'

Our destination was the balustraded building I had visited on my first excursion into the Walled City. We entered it, passed through the downstairs room, still devoid of occupants although I could hear the noise of snoring emanating from upstairs, went behind the screen, out through a door into what might once have been a flagstoned courtyard and down some steps to a semi-cellar about thirty feet square. At the bottom of the steps was an old

wooden door secured by a large padlock. Lau produced the key and we entered.

There was a small table in the centre of the room, the walls of which were lined by benches similar to those used for gym lessons in the KJS school hall. Upon the walls hung various pennants and banners in red with serrated black borders and black writing upon them. Opposite the door was an altar bearing a small idol of a male god with a fierce-looking face, one candle alight before it.

'God Kwan Ti,' Lau explained. 'This my god.'

Yet it was something other than the banners and Kwan Ti that caught my eye. Hung between the banners were macabre, sadistically ferocious-looking weapons. One was a chain with a ball set with spikes at one end; another chain culminated in a spear-point blade. Balancing in a wooden rack were a number of metal six-pointed stars of varying diameters. From their shine, the points were clearly well sharpened.

'What is this place?' I enquired.

Lau made no attempt to explain but said, '*Gweilo* no come here. You *vew'y* lucky boy I show you.'

Taking the chain with the point on it, he gave it a quick flick. The blade flashed through the air, faster than the eye could follow, and embedded itself in the rear of the door. It took both Lau's hands to dislodge it. Once the blade was free and hanging back on the wall, he took down one of the smallest stars. With a brief twist of his wrist, it spun through the air and also lodged itself in the door timbers.

'More good gun,' Lau said. 'No boom boom.' He ushered me out. 'You no tell you see here,' he added as he locked the door. 'You tell, plenty trouble for me. Plenty more for you.' He made the sign of a knife slicing across his throat. 'You, me,' he said pointing from me to himself.

I nodded and we went back the way we had come. As we

moved through the big room in the building, a boy of about my age descended the stairs carrying a tray upon which there was a small lamp, several minute bowls, a number of metal needles and the most bizarre pipe. My grandfather always smoked a simple-looking Dunhill with a wooden bowl; my father, on occasion, smoked a swan-necked Meerschaum. This was very different. A good fifteen inches long, the stem was made of bamboo, the mouthpiece of milky-coloured jade or soapstone. The bowl was a curious device for it had nowhere that I could see in which to put the tobacco: indeed, it appeared to be a virtually sealed container. All there was in it was a tiny hole in the top.

'*Nga pin?*' I asked tentatively.

Lau stared at me.

'How you know *nga pin?*'

'I know,' I shrugged, still not knowing exactly what it was.

He took me by the hand and led me up the stairs.

'No talk,' he whispered.

As my head rose above the first-floor level, I saw half a dozen men lying on the *kangs*. All but one were asleep on their sides, their hands tucked between their drawn-up legs or under their necks. One snored, another intermittently moaned softly, the only other sound was their breathing. The air had a strange and familiar perfume to it and it was at least a minute before I recognized it as the scent of the rickshaw coolies' pipes on my first night in Hong Kong.

The man who was awake had by his head one of the little lamps, the flame contained within a thick glass funnel. The boy moved past us, giving me a quick and puzzled glance. He went to the man and impaled a small bead of something on one of the needles, starting to revolve it in the lamp flame: then, very adroitly, he placed it over the tiny hole in the pipe bowl, passing it to the man who lay on his side and sucked evenly on the pipe.

After doing this three times, the man lay down and closed his eyes. The boy removed the pipe and blew out the lamp.

'We go,' Lau murmured.

Once we were outside, I asked, 'What was that man doing?'

'He smoke opium,' Lau answered. 'Get dream, go good time-side.'

'Can I smoke *nga pin*?' I suggested.

'No,' Lau said emphatically. 'No good for *gweilo*. Only for Chinese people.'

As I went to leave the walled city, Lau escorted me. Passing a very big shack indeed, I glimpsed a large pig through the wide door. Its feet were tied together. A man in a pair of bloodied shorts stepped up to it, grabbed one ear and yanked it back. The pig squealed, an eerie, unearthly sound. The butcher ran a sharp knife under its neck and slit its throat, stepping smartly backwards. The pig fell on its side, thrashing about and gurgling obscenely. Blood sprayed from its neck.

Lau put his hand on my shoulder in an affable manner and said, 'You talk you see, maybe you like this.'

He pointed to the pig, its lifeblood soaking in the earth floor of the shack. And I knew he meant it.

The row of old buildings stood to the eastern end of the walled city. One day, as Lau and I were walking through the *hutongs*, the heavens opened. We ran for cover under one of the balconies. Standing on what must once have been the arcaded raised side of a street, I somehow sensed in a daydream the ghosts of history walking by: a mandarin in his fine brocades, a peacock feather in the jade finial of his hat, his retinue behind him; a Chinese soldier with an axe-bladed pikestaff; a British naval officer in a cocked hat accompanied by a platoon of marine ratings, bayonets drawn.

The rain fell in torrential sheets, curtains of water moving inexorably across the shacks.

'What you think?' Lau asked.

'I think long time before Kowloon Walled City,' I answered, his question snapping me back to the present. 'See people walk here.'

'You see ghost,' Lau replied matter-of-factly. 'Plenty ghost Kowloon Walled City-side.'

I accepted this without question. England had hardly any ghosts but China was steeped in them. Wherever one went, it seemed, there were ghosts, demons, devils, spirits and gods to ward them off.

'I show you *ve'y* old place,' Lau said. 'All same like China long time before.'

He turned, walked ten paces along under the balcony, from which rainwater was pouring down, and knocked on a narrow double door. Once again, my heart fluttered and thoughts of evil men with wicked intentions momentarily filled my mind, but I had now been into two buildings – the *nga pin* house and the half-underground house – and had come through each time unscathed.

'You come,' Lau beckoned.

I stepped over the characteristic high lintel to find myself in a small entrance hall. To one side, seated at a tiny desk, was an old woman. Lau greeted her and they spoke in quiet voices until Lau stepped aside to reveal my presence. The moment she saw me, the woman cackled asthmatically and entered into a conversation with Lau that was filled with much suppressed hilarity and sidelong glances at me.

Feeling I was being made the butt of their humour, and not quite knowing how to react, I looked down. It was then I saw the old woman's feet projecting out from under the desk. They were minute, encased in scuffed brocade slippers no bigger than a baby's knitted bootees. The toe end was squared off like the ballet dancing pumps girls wore at school.

'Lotus foot,' Lau said, following my line of sight. 'Long time before, China-side, men say tiny foot on lady ve'y . . .' he paused, searching for a word '. . . booty full. Like lotus flower.'

I nodded sagely but could not see how, with the wildest imagination, a foot could resemble a flower.

After the obligatory caress of my golden hair by the old woman, Lau led me down a corridor of dark wooden panelling, passing a number of narrow doors split like those of a stable. At intervals, dim bulbs provided the minimum of light. Towards the end of the passageway, Lau stopped at a door and knocked. The top half opened and a pretty Chinese woman looked out. She wore an imperial yellow silk cheongsam, her hair piled up and held in place by a soapstone pin. As they spoke in subdued voices, she did not take her eyes off me for an instant. Needless to say, she still reached out to touch my head.

There was the sound of a pulling bolt and the bottom half of the door also opened to reveal a panelled cubicle lit by a red lamp in front of a tiny shrine. The only furniture was a wide *kang* raised higher than normal from the floor and a Chinese-style chair. Upon the *kang* were a tangle of quilts and a Chinese paperback book on the cover of which were portrayed a man and a woman kissing. On a shelf below the shrine was a row of Chinese scent bottles.

'You go in,' Lau instructed. 'Sit down.'

I perched on the rim of the *kang*. The young woman sat next to me, talking to Lau through the door but all the while watching me. The air – and the young woman – smelt of orange blossom slightly tainted with sweat.

'You know this place?' Lau enquired at length.

'No know,' I admitted.

'This old place,' Lau continued. 'Maybe more one hundred year. Long time before place for rich man come jig-a-jig. Fam'us

place. Man come long way from Canton jig-a-jig here. Fam'us girl stay here long time before.' To lend meaning to his words, he put his thumb between his index and middle finger and wiggled it. The young woman giggled. I was lost as to the meaning.

'You lo know jig-a-jig?' Lau asked.

I shook my head.

'Lo ploblum,' he replied dismissively. 'Come! We go now.'

He said goodbye to the young woman. I added my own *choi kin*. She burst into a peal of giggles, put her hand demurely to her mouth to stifle them and closed the doors on us.

Whenever I visited Kowloon Walled City, Lau was always there, ready to guide me around, drink tea with me and talk. When, after a few months, the place started to lose its appeal and I stopped visiting, I never saw him again.

It was some years before I realized that he and Ho had been Triad members – Chinese *mafiosi* – infamous for their utter ruthlessness, whose secret fraternity ran the opium dens and brothels, and held Kowloon Walled City in its thrall. The semi-subterranean room had been their meeting place.

My growing penchant for reading gave me a new reason to seek permission to range farther afield than I had previously. Both my parents agreed that I should be permitted to go to Tsim Sha Tsui where, in the next street to Mr Chan's jewellery and curio company, there stood the Swindon Bookshop. The only stipulation placed upon this extension of my legitimate borders was that I did not, under any circumstance, take the Star Ferry to Hong Kong island.

Tsim Sha Tsui was a completely different world from Mong

Kok. The latter was the world of *dai pai dongs* and whole roast pigs whilst the former was camera-toting, rubber-necking tourist country, banker and briefcased businessman territory.

I had been there on a number of occasions with my mother. Indeed, my first night in Hong Kong had been spent there, for the Grand Hotel was in the heart of the district. However, apart from Tkachenko's, Hing Loon and the bookshop, I hardly knew it and savoured discovering it on my own.

Using Hing Loon as an informal Coke-provisioning station, I wandered the streets. Here, the shopkeepers stayed behind closed doors. If they were jewellers, their doors were sometimes guarded by bearded, be-turbaned Sikhs in old British military uniforms and carrying blunderbusses or shotguns. The only vendors to appear on the pavement were Indian tailors vying for custom. The Chinese tailors viewed this flagrant touting with distaste. They were never so pushy and their workmanship was far superior.

Apart from the tailors' window displays of lengths of cloth and suits hanging off mannequins, every shop window was a glittering tableau of expensive watches, men's and women's jewellery, pens, cameras, lenses and binoculars.

I knew I could not just walk into one of these shops so I worked the obvious ploy, waiting until a tourist couple entered and tagging along camouflaged as their child. It worked time and again and I got to study – close up – such marvels as Audemars Piguet, Longines and Vacheron et Constantin gold watches, emeralds as green as still water and as big as peas, and Rolleiflex and Leica cameras with a shutter movement so silent you could not hear it. All of these I gazed at with the avidity of a magpie. At times, the palms of my hands actually itched with temptation and desire.

Yet the crimes of Tsim Sha Tsui were not conducted by me but by the wily shopkeepers and even more artful pickpockets.

One of the shopkeepers' scams was brilliant in its simplicity and succeeded because of the arrogance and gullibility of, particularly, American tourists. Be they civilians or sailors on shore leave all were open to it, from well-heeled world cruisers and senior United States Navy officers down to ratings and stewards off the liners. The first time I saw it happen was in a watch shop. I was lingering by the counter when I overheard a conversation that went something like this:

'OK, buddy, I'll take this one.' (*Tourist*)

'V'wy good choice. Suit you good.' (*Shopkeeper*)

'How much is it?'

'Fi'e hund'ed dollar.'

A few minutes of haggling followed, culminating in an agreed price of $450, the shopkeeper declaiming with a disarming smile, 'You too cleffer for me. Beat me down too much. Now my p'ofit only small.'

At this point, it must be appreciated that all the prices were shown in Hong Kong dollars and the price label on the item marked up by at least 100 per cent over the wholesale buy-in cost.

Then came the question bolstered by a belief in the universal power of the US greenback.

'Say, buddy, is that American or Hong Kong dollars?' *Hong Kong* was always spoken with a slight air of condescension.

The shopkeeper, after a brief pause as well timed as the best comic actor's, would always reply, 'Ame'ican dollars.'

Out would come the wallet of American Express traveller's cheques, the customer grinning broadly at his bargaining skill.

In 1953, when I first saw this trick pulled, the foreign exchange rate was approximately HK$6: US$1. Even my elementary school arithmetic, at which I was a resoundingly poor pupil, told me the customer had paid HK$2700, over five times the original, and already much inflated, asking price.

I could never feel any sympathy for these dupes. In my puerile opinion, they asked for it. Besides, I was a *gweilo* on the shop-keepers' side. With the victims of Tsim Sha Tsui's other tourist crime, who could be of any nationality, I felt considerable empathy but, whereas I could have exposed the exchange rate scam, I could do nothing about their plight.

The pickpockets of Tsim Sha Tsui must have been the slickest in the world. They mostly operated in pairs, keeping in the crowds. Once a worthwhile target had been spotted, they would move in, one bumping hard into the victim, knocking them slightly off balance. The other, with lightning speed, would slip their hand into bag or pocket, grab a wallet, purse or billfold and immediately pass it to the barger who would disappear in the crowd. This was a failsafe. If the victim found they had been pickpocketed, had a suspicion who had done it and accosted him, he could plead innocence. The proof – the wallet or purse – would already be three streets away and moving fast towards a fence who dealt in traveller's cheques.

Another form of theft was considerably less clandestine. A number of urchins would accost a target under the pretence of begging. Once the target's attention was distracted, one of the urchins would produce a pair of very sharp tailor's scissors, slide a blade under the victim's leather watch strap and cut it free, catching it and disappearing in the crowd. If the target was aware of what had happened, they could not give chase for the obstruction of the throng.

Only one class of person was completely pickpocket proof: the US Navy ratings who carried their wallets folded over the front of the very tight waistbands of their uniform trousers. They were in full view of any pickpocket but not one could pull a wallet clear without the owner knowing.

Although these kinds of street theft must have ruined many

a holiday, I could not bring myself to condemn them. The perpetrators were often boys even younger than myself, street urchins, the children of squatter shack dwellers and pavement sleepers. They were doing the best they could to stay alive and I could not help wondering whether some of their fathers had owned cars and horses in China and were now reduced to sweeping out offices or serving in restaurants. Or worse.

Despite their criminality, I felt at one with them. They were expatriates who had made their home here. So was I. There were even moments when I wondered how I might join them in their illegality, but I realized I would not have had the stomach for it. And that was the difference between a *gweilo* and a Chinese: we were bound by the rules that ruled the rulers and they were not.

One sweltering day, the humidity over 90 per cent, my mother and I went shopping, our mission to buy a wedding anniversary gift for my paternal grandparents.

Under normal circumstances, I would have strenuously attempted to avoid this outing. Traipsing in my mother's wake round shops containing little of interest to me, in streets I had explored and which were now fairly sterile to me, was not my idea of an ideal morning. However, I wanted to take part in the choice of a gift for Grampy.

With a military methodology, my mother went up and down the streets, traversing Tsim Sha Tsui in a mental grid, but she could find nothing suitable. It was either tourist tat or too fragile to post, or too expensive and therefore likely to cost my grandparents inordinately high customs duties. Finally, having exhausted most of Tsim Sha Tsui – and me – we had a Coke each at a

pavement stall and headed up Nathan Road at a brisk pace. My shirt clung to my back: through my mother's sweat-soaked blouse I could see her bra strap and felt very embarrassed that it was so prominent. None of the Chinese women seemed to be even lightly perspiring.

My mother's intention was, if she could find nothing in an area catering mostly for European taste, she would have a go in that providing for the Chinese. Turning into Shanghai Street, we started to patrol the shops selling crockery. It was utilitarian stuff but one variety caught my mother's attention. Known as rice-patterned ware, neither of us could understand how it was mass-produced. Each dish, bowl or cup was made of white porcelain with a patterned blue border and base, between which the porcelain was speckled with what looked like rice grains fired in the matrix. If the bowl was held to the light, each grain appeared translucent.

'This is it,' my mother declared as she held up a large serving bowl to the light. 'Bugger the fragility! This is the one, don't you think?'

I agreed. My grandmother would regard it as a nice bowl to put on the dresser but my grandfather would see it for what it was – an exotic piece sent from a far-off land with all my love brimming out of it. It cost only a few dollars.

'It's a bit on the cheap side,' she commented as the shopkeeper wrapped the bowl in wood straw and newspaper.

'It's the thought that counts,' I remarked.

She smiled and sauntered round the shop, picking up a piece here and a piece there. I sat on a stool and sweated. The shopkeeper did not offer me a drink for he no longer had reason to keep us in the place. We had parted with our money and the cost of a Green Spot would simply erode his profit margin.

Finally, my mother returned to the counter, said, 'Sod it!'

and ordered a six-setting complete dinner service of the same sort, asking for it all to be delivered to the Boundary Street address.

The shopkeeper beamed, shouted for an assistant, relieved my mother of $110 (about £6) and gave us each a chilled bottle of Watson's lemonade.

'I don't think,' my mother said as we walked at a leisurely speed towards Nathan Road, 'that we need to mention this to your father.'

'Why not?' I asked. 'How can you hide ninety plates and bowls and things?'

My mother took my hand and jauntily swung it back and forth as we walked on.

'I'm a wife,' she answered obtusely.

The arcaded pavement ahead was obstructed by a row of barrels being off-loaded from a green lorry with a canvas awning. As we entered the restricted space, we were ambushed by a young Chinese woman. She wore the clothes of a coolie – a stiff black cotton jacket and matching baggy trousers. She was barefoot, her hair awry and her face, as my mother would put it, in need of a kiss from Mr Flannel. In her arms she carried a baby about a month old. There was no way we could avoid her without turning heel.

'Missee! Missee!' she said as she approached us.

My mother opened her handbag, snapped the catch on her purse and took out a violet-coloured dollar bill. To my mother's surprise, the young woman refused it.

'No *kumshaw*, missee. No *kumshaw*!'

The woman held the baby out. It gurgled with infantile pleasure and kicked the air. Its legs were podgy. I could see it was a girl.

'You tek, missee, pleas'.'

My mother stopped dead in her tracks. The look on her face was one of sheer bemusement.

'Missee! You tek. You tek.'

She reached forward with the baby, trying to convince my mother to accept it in her arms.

'You tek, pleas'.'

The woman was pleading now. The pain in her soul tainted each of the only four English words she knew, had learnt especially for just such a confrontation.

'Pleas', missee. Pleas', missee.'

I looked at my mother. Tears ran down her cheeks. She made no effort to wipe them and they dripped on to her already sweat-dampened blouse. She shook her head.

The Chinese woman made one last attempt, as if she was a stallholder pressing my mother to buy something she did not need.

'*M'ho*,' my mother murmured.

At that, the woman turned and disappeared down a narrow and fetid *hutong* from which blew the stench of open drains.

We walked on in silence until we reached a rickshaw rank. My mother hailed one and we travelled home together. Once in the apartment, my mother poured herself a gin and tonic and sat heavily in a chair.

'What did that woman want?' I enquired.

'She wanted to give me her baby.'

'Why?' I replied, taken aback at this information.

'Who knows,' said my mother with a sigh. 'Perhaps she can't afford to feed it. Perhaps the father told her to get rid of it. It was a girl . . .'

'So what?' I came back.

'In China, boy children are precious. They are even sometimes called little emperors. Girls are not.'

I could see no difference between a girl baby and a boy baby, other than the obvious anatomical one, and said so.

She took a big swig of her gin and tonic. 'To the Chinese, nothing is more important than keeping the family name going. So sons are important and daughters, who will marry and take another name, aren't.'

'But what will happen to the baby girl?' I half-wondered aloud.

My mother was silent for at least a minute before speaking.

'She will die. Either her parents will smother her or they'll take her into the Kowloon foothills and leave her to die of exposure.'

'But that's murder!' I exclaimed.

'Yes,' my mother agreed dully, 'and this is China.'

'Can't we go back again?' I began. 'I don't mind if . . .'

The appeal of an adopted Chinese sister was suddenly growing on me. And it was now of paramount importance to me that we did something.

'No,' my mother said, 'I'm afraid it doesn't work like that . . .'

She patted the cushion on the settee beside her. I sat down and she put her arm around me.

'It is terrible, but it has been going on for centuries in China. There's nothing we can do about it. You cannot change a culture overnight.'

'What about calling the police . . . ?' I suggested.

My mother sadly shook her head and said, 'She's long gone now.'

That night, lying in bed with the lights of Boundary Street barred by the venetian blinds on the ceiling, I wondered if the baby was already dead. I wanted to cry – and felt I should – but found I could not. I had already accepted the inevitable cruelty of life in the Orient. It was, I considered as I drifted warily to sleep, no surprise China was so full of ghosts.

By early May 1953, Hong Kong was gripped by Coronation fever. A vast *pi lau*, a sort of Chinese triumphal arch, was erected across Nathan Road near the Alhambra cinema. Made entirely of bamboo poles lashed together by bamboo twine, it looked like the scaffolding on a building site, within which it was intended to construct a pagoda-cum-watchtower. By the week before the Coronation, it was festooned with gold and scarlet decorations, a row of lanterns, a picture of the new Queen and the letters *EIIR*. These also appeared on virtually every lamppost on every major thoroughfare. Shops displayed framed pictures of the Queen, sometimes next to ones of Chiang Kai-shek. It was a brave shop-keeper who displayed the Queen next to Chairman Mao. Even if he had Communist sympathies, which some had, discretion was deemed the better part of colonial valour and he joined in with the festivities.

On Coronation Day itself, there was a huge parade on Hong Kong-side. Keeping to Queen's Road, it wound its way through the city for six miles, the pavements jammed with tens of thousands of spectators. The queues for the Star Ferry on Kowloon-side stretched for well over a mile but we avoided these by crossing the harbour on a Royal Navy launch from which we were ushered into a dockyard office building overlooking Queen's Road and allotted seats at a window.

The parade was interminable. Soldiers, sailors, airmen, marching military bands, St John Ambulance volunteers, Boy Scouts, *kai fong* associations, nurses from the Bowen Road and Mount Kellett military hospitals, police and fire brigade marched by in dizzying, monotonous ranks, flags flying, pennants whipping the warm air. The tedium was only relieved by a drive

past of tanks, howitzers, scout cars and other military para-
phernalia. Several times, I tried to make my escape to explore the
dockyard but had my collar felt by my father and was forced back
into my seat.

It was just as well. After the pageant of imperial militarism, and
a break of a quarter of an hour during which I managed to get my
father to buy me a Coke, came the Chinese half of the parade.

At the head were two stilt-walkers and a classical marching
orchestra – and it did not play 'When the Saints Go Marching
In' but stirring melodies and lilting airs. Other Chinese bands
followed, instilling in me that day a lifelong love of Chinese
classical music. Between each of them were several flatbed trucks
decked out as floats with tableaux being enacted on them by
children dressed as characters out of Chinese mythology. They
wore pancake make-up, as detailed and as stark as a Chinese
opera singer's. My mother commented several times on how uncomfortable it must have been for them under the hot sun.

The highlight of the whole parade, however, were the lion and
dragon dances.

Their approach could be guessed at by the increasing agitation
of the crowds on the pavement opposite us. They began to grow
restless, craning their necks and pointing. Finally, to the clashing
of cymbals and striking of hand gongs, the lion appeared. It
consisted of a brightly coloured stylized head on a bamboo frame,
with fur-lined jaws and bulbous eyes. As big as a barrel, it
was held aloft by a dancer who swung it to and fro, ducked
it down and lunged forward with it, shook it from side to side
and generally acted in a ferocious fashion. Behind him was
the lion's body, a covering of less decorated cloth under which
another dancer jostled and jived. The movements of the head
were dictated by the cymbals and gongs. It was, for all intents and
purposes, a sort of legendary Oriental pantomime horse.

Stilt-walkers and jugglers followed the lion, there was a gap and then the dragon arrived on the scene.

It was magnificent. Its head was at least nine feet high, excluding the horns on top. Its mouth – red-mawed and lined with white teeth – was big enough for me to have sat in. The mouth was operated by a man walking in front of the dragon with a pole connected to the dragon's lower lip, whilst the remainder of the head was held high by one man. As with the lion, he swung it to and fro, lowered it to the ground then looked at the sky, in time to the percussion instruments. Several yards in front of the dragon pranced a man with a paper fish almost as big as himself on a pole, with which he teased the beast. Behind the head was a one-hundred-yard-long reptilian body constructed of coloured cloth painted in scales and stretched over a series of bamboo hoops. Under this danced several dozen men, only their legs showing and giving the dragon's body the appearance of a multicoloured circus centipede. The body curled in on itself, twisting across the road and generally behaving in a serpentine fashion. The crowds applauded, the cymbals clashed, the gongs clanged and then, with two police wagons driving side by side, it was all suddenly over.

'What did you think of that?' my father asked as we lined up for the launch on the wall of the dockyard basin.

'Very impressive,' I replied noncommittally, having just heard someone else in the queue make the same remark.

'Just think,' my father went on, 'all over the Empire, these celebrations will be going on today. All for one young woman, our new Queen.'

For a moment, I thought he was going to cry. Whatever else he was, my father was definitely a monarchist.

7

LIVING ON CLOUDS

WE DROVE ON TO THE VEHICULAR FERRY AT YAU MA TEI, THE RAMP
was raised and the vessel headed out across the harbour. My
mother and I stood at the front, a light spume blowing over us.
My father remained with the car at the back of the deck, industri-
ously wiping any hint of spray from the paintwork with a chamois
leather.

'Where are we going?' I asked insistently and not for the first
time.

'I've told you, I'm not telling you,' she retorted impishly.

Living in Kowloon, I rarely crossed the harbour to the island of
Hong Kong. My parents frequently visited friends for dinner
there, went to HMS *Tamar* for a mess night or to dine on a
visiting warship – and, of course, my father crossed the harbour
daily to go to his office in the dockyard – but I only accompanied
them on select occasions, such as an Open Day on an aircraft
carrier or submarine, or the annual Dockyard Fête, at one of
which I won first prize in the .22 rifle shooting competition, with
a score of 97/100. The first prize was a fully stocked blue-and-
white woven rattan and plastic picnic hamper which my mother

used for ten years before it finally unravelled. My success, over adults as well as children, had infuriated my father who scored only seventy-something, yet who regarded himself as a top shot. In front of his colleagues and inferiors, he had lost considerable face: Commodore Blimp had been beaten by his boy. At home that night, my father had roundly derided the prize, although I noticed he removed the two bottles of wine it contained as well as the cashew nuts to which he was – as was I – more than partial. I never got to eat a single one of them. That, my mother told me, was my punishment for being a crack shot.

On Hong Kong-side, we drove off the ferry and a short distance through the city streets before skirting the Bank of China building and starting to ascend a steep wide road. Ahead was verdant mountainside with low blocks of apartments on the gentler slopes but, as the mountain rose more precipitously, houses half hidden in trees. My father had to change down to third gear and then to second for the first corner on a junction. The car remained in a low gear to negotiate two sinuous hairpin bends and a long straight to a four-way junction in a pass.

'Magazine Gap,' my mother said as my ears popped and, looking out the rear window, I caught a glimpse of the harbour and Kowloon beyond and well below.

The car continued to climb through luxuriant forest, plants with leaves as big as elephants' ears crowding each other out in the shade. Lianas and aerial roots hung down like ropes while butter-flies flitted through the shadows and dappled light. Through gaps in the trees I caught snatches of open sea: at Magazine Gap we had crossed on to the south side of Hong Kong island.

Still we climbed. Edging the car into first gear, my father gunned the engine and we set off up an incline of at least 30 degrees called Mount Austin Road, moved round a right-hand corner in second gear and turned up another steep road that

looked as if it ran along a knife-edge ridge. At the end of this was a four-storey block of apartments. My father parked the car and we entered the building, climbing the wide stairs.

'Who lives here?' I asked my mother.

'We do,' she replied. 'From the day after tomorrow.'

On the top floor, my father produced a key and we entered Apartment 8, Mount Austin Mansions. Despite a few pieces of furniture, it echoed like a cathedral.

'Close your eyes,' my mother said as we went in.

I did so. She led me through the apartment. I heard another door open then the faint sound of birdsong, a cicada and the gentle shush of a mountain breeze.

'Open them.'

I was on the veranda. At my feet lay Hong Kong.

The view left me speechless. Down below was the central business district, the Bank of China and the Hongkong and Shanghai Bank next door little more than a child's building bricks. The harbour was a pool with small boats moving across it. Alongside HMS *Tamar* were two grey warships whilst, in mid-harbour, several others swung at anchor. Beyond lay the peninsula of Kowloon. A P&O liner was berthed in Tsim Sha Tsui, cargo vessels unloading at jetties further along the waterfront. The Yau Ma Tei typhoon shelter was a mere rectangle of water partly crammed with a brown wedge of junks and sampans. In the distance were the Kowloon hills and, further away still, a progression of hills disappearing towards China. Looking east was a sylvan ridge dotted with houses. Below them, beyond the eastern urban areas, were more hills and, far away, a scatter of islands.

The sun was now low and hidden behind a summit surmounted by a copse of radio aerials: the riot of neon in the streets to the east and on Kowloon-side started to come alive in readiness for the approaching twilight. The last rays of the sun

tinged the top of the Nine Dragons. In fifteen minutes, it was night, the lights of the colony shimmering in the heat. The walla-wallas and ferries were now trails of light upon blackened water, the warships decorated with white bulbs strung between their masts or lining their sides.

'So?' my mother asked.

'I don't know,' I replied.

'What do you mean, "I don't know"?' my father snapped. 'This is one of the most famous panoramas in the world and you are going to live on top of it. People would commit murder to live here. People sail halfway round the world to see this view for fifteen minutes and you're going to have it twenty-four hours—'

'Do stop harping on, Ken,' my mother muttered.

'Well, honestly . . .' my father replied, determined to have the last word. 'We give him the earth and—'

'We have not given him the earth,' my mother retorted. 'We have been allotted this as our quarters and he – and we – are bloody lucky. You had nothing to do with it.'

'I had nothing to do with it? My job – my rank – played no part in it?'

'You're a DNSO, Ken, not the First Sea Lord. You have a wife and son. That gives you X amount of housing points. This is an X-points quarter. It has been vacated. We were next in line for allocation. Now shut up!'

In truth, I was fully appreciative of the view. It was just that the enormity, the grandeur of it did not match my eight-year-old vocabulary. Fantastic or incredible or even stupendous seemed utterly devoid of the emotion I felt. It was, like the song, as if I really was sitting on top of the world.

As if that view were not enough, crossing through to the dining room, we looked south, out over the South China Sea. A fairly substantial island lay between Hong Kong and the horizon on

which there were other low strips of land with pinpricks of light bunched in one spot on them.

'The island close to is called Lamma,' my mother said. 'Those in the distance are Communist Chinese.'

Yet I was not looking that far. On the sea around and beyond Lamma twinkled tiny lights. There were perhaps a hundred of them. They did not seem to move but were drifting on the tide.

'What're those lights?' I asked, but I realized the answer before being told.

'Fishing sampans,' my mother explained.

We headed back to Boundary Street. As the ferry edged across the harbour, I asked my mother to show me the building in which we had just been. Distinguished by the lights in its windows, it was perched on the very top of a secondary promontory to the east of the Peak, the mountain that stood guardian over the colony.

'What's it called?'

'The little summit is called Mount Austin and we have Apartment 8, Block A.'

'That's lucky,' I declared.

'What do you mean?' my father asked, folding his chamois leather into a wad.

'Eight's a lucky number,' I said. 'The Chinese think eight brings riches.'

'He does pick up some drivel,' my father remarked to my mother.

Yet she winked at me. She was by now well down the *hutong* to becoming a dedicated sinophile: unbeknownst to my father, she had even enrolled herself in Cantonese classes.

Life on the Peak had as much in common with that in Kowloon as a bowl of fish soup at a *dai pai dong* had to a traditional English fried breakfast, with or without salad cream. First, there were no shops except for a small Dairy Farm general store. Second, there were hardly any people about except around an observation point where tourists with cameras mingled with touts trying to sell them packs of photographs of what they were themselves about to photograph. Third, there were no eating places except the Peak Café, a low, red-roofed building that I had spotted as my father halted to change gear on our first visit. Finally, there were very few buildings and those that did exist were either the houses of the rich *taipans*, secure behind walls topped with barbed wire or broken glass, or apartment buildings.

From a busy urban existence, I was suddenly catapulted into a pacific rural one, with a gamut of new experiences to undergo and new lessons to be learnt.

The morning of the move, we arrived at Mount Austin shortly after two dark-blue Bedford lorries with RN painted in white upon the sides. Half a dozen Chinese ratings leapt out, lowered the tailgate and began to carry all our belongings up to Apartment 8. To complement the general-issue furniture provided by the Navy, my parents had purchased a low Chinese coffee table with bow legs, reminiscent of an English bull terrier's, a Chinese dining-room suite and a bar – an essential for my inabstinent father.

As soon as the unpacking commenced, it was diplomatically suggested that I might like to go outside and play. With whom or at what was not an issue. Hardly believing my good fortune, I left the building and set off down the curving ridge road. At the T-junction I turned right and started to ascend to the summit of the Peak.

The road was steep and passed a derelict lot where the

foundations of a building were laid out in the ground with a few fragments of wall remaining. It was, in effect, a cleared bomb site: I had seen enough of those in Portsmouth to recognize it. Higher up, several rather fine houses stood to the right of the road with magnificent views of the city below. I walked on, my legs beginning to ache. A few hundred yards on there appeared at the side of the road a small stone building not much bigger than my grandfather's garden shed. The door was open and the sound of voices emanated from within. I knocked and looked in. Sitting at a desk was a policeman. Another sat to one side, his chair tilted back. In a corner, a kettle simmered on an electric ring. They nodded a greeting. I expected to be invited in for a bowl of tea. That would have been Mong Kok protocol. I wasn't.

Beside the police post were some stone steps. I descended them and found myself on a path that, after fifty yards, crossed a small tumbling stream. Tiny fish darted in the sandy-bottomed pools. It seemed amazing that, not three hundred feet from the top of a mountain, there was a flowing stream filled with fish. I stepped over the water by a small stone bridge and walked on. The path was narrow and clung to the not-quite-sheer side of the hill, keeping to more or less the same contour. It was obvious few people came this way, for the undergrowth met over the path and my legs were soon scratched and bleeding. Yet it was worth it. The views were breathtaking. Below me was a pale azure reservoir, Lamma Island across a narrow channel and the South China Sea beyond it. To the west, beyond the next, conical hill, were the distant islands of western Hong Kong and, beyond them, Lan Tau Island, the biggest in the territory. I did not realize quite how high I was until a kite, rising on a thermal, briefly hovered near me. It swivelled its head from side to side with avian wonderment at finding someone so close on the normally deserted mountainside.

The following morning, I woke to find my room bathed in an eerie, soft light. Getting out of bed, I opened the curtains to discover we were in the clouds. Unlatching the metal-framed window, a warm and invisible dampness drifted in, touching my face as a ghost might. It occurred to me that perhaps I was allowing demons to enter so I closed it quickly.

At breakfast, my mother announced, 'You're going to go to the Peak School now. It's much too far to go to Kowloon Junior every day. We've an appointment with the headmistress at eleven o'clock.'

By the time we set off for the school, the sun had burnt off the clouds and we began our walk under a blazing sky. The air, however, was cool, with zephyrs tickling the tall, sparse grass and wild flowers on the bomb site.

'What building stood there?' I asked my mother as we passed it.

'I don't know,' she said, 'but you'll find ruins here and there on the Peak, of buildings destroyed by the Japanese in the war.'

The Peak School was about twenty minutes' walk away on Plunkett's Road, but to get there meant descending the very steep hill to the café. My mother, wearing a smart cotton print dress and high-heeled shoes, attempted the descent, stopped after a few yards, removed her shoes and continued barefoot. We arrived at the school hot and harried. The headmistress showed us into her office, a few formalities were undergone, I was taken to a classroom and obliged to stand in front of my future classmates, declare my name and then sit down at a desk next to another *gweilo* with pre-pubescent acne and breath that smelt as if he had breakfasted on hundred-year-old eggs. It did not bode well.

The pupils were predominantly British with a few Chinese, Americans and others of European extraction. Many of them seemed particularly distant and snooty. I preferred to keep myself

to myself, get on with my work, read in break times and head for the door at the first chime of the bell. I ate my lunch on my own, rebuffed most approaches of friendship and worried my form teacher. As a consequence, when the school play was being cast, I was auditioned under duress and given a lead part, perhaps to bring me out of my shell. The play was *Toad of Toad Hall*. I was Mole.

The part was not too demanding. I learnt my lines with ease and only regretted being involved because it meant staying behind after school each day for over a month, rehearsing.

Only one memorable facet of my thespian adventure remains – the costume.

Each parent was asked to provide their child's outfit. My mother, not being adept with a needle and thread, asked Ah Shun if she could make it, but she admitted it was beyond her, too. My mother summoned her tailor.

Mr Chuk was a soft-spoken, elderly Chinese gentleman who came on occasion to the apartment to measure my mother. When this was done, the two of them would sit and drink bowls of jasmine tea whilst she went through his pattern books and material samples. He could make a midnight blue silk cocktail dress in five days, a lady's two-piece suit in seven. A mole costume was another matter.

I was taken into my parents' bedroom, stripped to my underpants and measured. My mother – no artist, she – then poured the tea and produced her drawing of a mole. The tailor studied it and shrugged.

'I no look-see dis an'm'l,' he said. 'Maybe dis no an'm'l China-side.'

'Maybe they've eaten them all,' my mother said to me as an aside.

She tried sketching it again. The result looked like a tailless,

earless, eyeless rat with copious whiskers and exaggeratedly large front feet.

'He no can look-see?' the tailor enquired, noticing the sketch had no eyes.

'He no can look-see,' my mother confirmed. 'Live under-ground.'

'*Loh siu* liff unner groun'. Can see plentee good,' the tailor responded.

'This is not *loh siu*,' my mother said, exasperation creeping into her voice. 'It is not a rat. It is a mole.'

The tailor cupped his ear. 'He no can . . . ?'

'Yes,' my mother declared firmly. 'Can hear very good.' She was getting fed up with discussing the physical disabilities of a mole. 'You can make?'

'Can do,' came the optimistic reply.

It was deemed I did not require a fitting and so, two days before opening night, the tailor arrived at the apartment carrying a bundle containing a dark chocolate-brown, one-piece cross be-tween a parachutist's jump-suit and a Glaswegian shipbuilder's boiler suit. I tried it on. It was as loose-fitting as a maternity smock and just as shapeless. My mother stifled a laugh, which was not a good sign.

The tailor had sewn whiskers (made of thin bamboo strips taken from a broom) on the top of the head. My face peered out through the mouth which was lined by white cloth teeth, serrated like a dragon's. What was more, the tailor had clearly taken pity on the mole's disabilities and given it two shiny glass eyes and a pair of cat-like ears. My mother paid the bill. On open-ing night, Rat (grey hairy costume, tail, beady eyes, bowler hat, waistcoat), Toad (grey-green painted mottled rubber attire made from a frogman's wet suit, a pair of cut-down plus fours and a deerstalker), Badger (tweed jacket and cut-down tartan golfing

trousers with a realistic black-and-white papier mâché head) appeared on stage alongside a mutant creature of indeterminate species and origin which, not wearing any human clothing, was, presumably, naked. At curtain call, I received resounding applause and was asked to step forward for an extra bow. It was not, I was certain, due to my acting abilities.

Once a month, a cylindrical package arrived for me by sea mail. It was rolled up tightly, wrapped in brown paper and had twine tied round it and running through the middle. It had been mailed by my grandfather. When the string was cut, the rolled-up contents opened out to show the previous month's issues of the *Eagle*, *Dandy* and *Beano*. Tucked somewhere in them would always be a ten-shilling postal order. Unrolling the comics, I envisaged Grampy walking to the newsagent's once a week, an aroma of tobacco following him down the street like an invisible shadow, buying the comics, keeping them safe in the cupboard under the stairs that smelt of ale and stale bread, then once a month making his way to the Post Office. This was, to me, the height of love and I promptly wrote back by blue air mail lettergram to thank him and give him my news.

I held no information back from him, telling him of all my escapades, even into Kowloon Walled City, in the sure and certain knowledge he would not report them to my grandmother and, through her, to my father. She could not be trusted with a pod full of peas. Not once did he betray my confidence and he always replied, although my questions were not always answered. He did not tell me what *jig-a-jig* meant so I assumed he did not know.

My grandfather was not alone in sending parcels. The comics

were certainly unobtainable in Hong Kong, but almost everything else was: in England, food, clothing, petrol and much more were in short supply and had been since the war. Some items were still on ration. An elderly maiden aunt called Olive assumed, despite many letters to the contrary, that we not only lived under rationing but also in pretty primitive conditions. Every two months for our first year in Hong Kong, a 'care' parcel arrived from her containing cotton handkerchiefs, soap, aspirin, adhesive and crêpe bandages, safety pins, Dettol, Reckitts' Blue laundry starch, thick woollen socks for my father, a lipstick for my mother and a Dinky toy car for me. She fell short of sending toilet rolls, presumably assuming we had plants with leaves large and soft enough for the job. (We had.) Eventually, my mother made up a parcel for Olive containing intricately embroidered napkin sets, silk handkerchiefs, brocade cushion covers, a cotton blouse, a tourist book of the sights of Hong Kong, a hand-painted lacquer dragon, a set of chopsticks (with instructions for use), a packet of jasmine tea (also with instructions) and a small jar of Tiger Balm ointment, the ubiquitous Chinese cure-all containing tiny quantities of opium and morphine which could fix, my mother claimed, anything from a wart to an unwanted pregnancy. Parcels from Olive ceased forthwith.

All expatriates referred to the country of their origin as 'home'. Even the old China Hands, those who had lived 'in-country' since the 1920s, did so. At first, my mother followed suit. However, by the winter of 1953, her outlook had subtly changed. She started to write to her mother that she wanted to remain in Hong Kong after my father's three-year-long tour of duty ended. In addition to learning Cantonese, she attended classes in Chinese history and culture, sought employment first on the local English-language radio station and then as a secondary school teacher of English and geography in a Chinese school, both without success. Her

problem was that she lacked a formal higher education, yet she more than made up for it in intelligence and intellectual curiosity.

Of the old China Hands, I was to come to know two.

The first was a friend of my mother's, an English woman called Peggy who had married a Dutchman in the 1930s. When war broke out in 1939, her husband may have returned to Holland to fight for his homeland but he may have also stayed in Hong Kong and been killed when the Japanese invaded in 1941. Certainly, Peggy was rounded up and thrown into the civilian camp, the pre-war high-security prison at Stanley. I think they had no children: whenever I met her, she spoiled me rotten. As every colonial housewife did, she employed servants. In her case, she had a traditional *saw hei* amah.

This amah was one of those who had risked her life over and over again smuggling food and Chinese herbal medicines into the camp for her missee. Indubitably, her clandestine activities saved Peggy's life and probably those of several of her fellow prisoners-of-war. After the Japanese surrender, Peggy remained in Hong Kong and the amah returned to work for her but now they had a different relationship. Both of approximately the same age, they were no longer missee and amah but two spinsters living together and looking out for each other. Peggy obtained employment with the Hongkong and Shanghai Bank and, in time, rose through its ranks to a position of authority and responsibility. The amah kept home for both of them in a small flat on Robinson Road which they shared with at least two dozen rescued stray cats that Peggy loved with almost religious intensity. She and the amah were to die in their late seventies within days of each other.

The other China Hand, whom I came to both like and loathe, was Sammy Shields. As a man, I adored him, but he was also my dentist.

His surgery was in Star House, a two-storey building facing the

Kowloon Star Ferry pier across the bus terminal. In actual fact, Sammy was not a qualified dentist. Before the war, he had been a dental technician, making and fitting dentures or braces. When he, too, was incarcerated in Stanley, it was found that he was the only person in the camp with any real dental know-how, so he became the camp dentist by default. After the war, with a large number of patients on his books – most of them ex-civilian prisoners-of-war – he set up in practice, his reputation growing, as it were, by word of mouth.

I visited his surgery with mixed feelings. The whine of his belt-driven drill could be heard in his tiny waiting room and was sure to send shivers of apprehension up the spine of the bravest man. His dentist's chair, the cantilevered arm of his drill and every other metal fitting were covered in cream enamel, chipped in places. It looked as if he had bought it second-hand, which was probably the case. It was certainly of pre-war vintage.

Sammy had a special technique with small boys such as myself, whose mothers he refused to allow into his chamber of tortures. Whenever my mother left the room, I felt suddenly terrified, but Sammy would soon put me at my ease . . .

'Right now, open wide. Ah! Let's see . . . a bit of plaque here . . . we'll chip that off in a tick . . . Good . . . wash out . . . Open wide again . . . a filling needed here, I'm afraid . . . just a little prick for the cocaine . . .' ('Aarrhh! Ah hurhs!') 'All done . . . wait for it to put your jaw to sleep . . . Did I ever tell you about my time as a guest of his Imperial Japanese Majesty?'

From then on, the sound of his drill and the abrupt jab of pain as he hit the nerve were mere momentary interruptions in a narrative of roasting rats on shovels over a fire of dried cow dung collected on Stanley beach, of boiling barnacles and steaming giant snails which had to be purged first in case they had been feeding on poisonous plants, of face-slappings and rifle buttings,

of outbreaks of diphtheria, of men dying of disease or being shot on the beach, of removing fellow prisoners' molars without any anaesthetics, of the Americans' bombing of two prison buildings, killing the occupants.

'Bloody fools, Americans,' Sammy would appendix this story. 'What I'd give for one of those pilots sitting where you are now . . .'

I heard these stories every six months. They never lost their potency and never failed to take the edge off what I was undergoing. It was, I thought, nothing compared to what he must have endured for four years.

A fortnight before my ninth birthday, Wong asked me, 'What you likee you burfday cake, young master?'

'A cake,' I replied, puzzled by the enquiry, 'with nine candles.'

'What shape you likee?'

My consternation multiplied. As far as I was concerned, cakes were round and that was an end to it.

'Maybe you likee house?' he suggested, seeing my bewilderment. 'Likee tempul? Wong can do tempul good for you.'

Without really thinking about it, I answered, 'I'd like a battle-ship.'

Several days later, I went to the kitchen to find my way barred. The swing door had had a wooden wedge jammed under it.

'You lo can come kitchen-side now,' Wong declared with an authority I had not previously seen in him. 'You wantee somef'ing, makee bell.'

'I only want a Coke,' I said, conscious of my parents' orders that I did not ring the servants' bell for petty demands.

He took one out of the fridge, opened it and handed it to me through a crack in the door, adding, 'Two week, you lo go kitchen-side. You go, Wong v'wy ang'wee.'

I complained to my mother. Her reply was that I was to obey Wong.

On my birthday, which fell on the second day of the new academic year, I arrived home in eager anticipation as it had been decided that I should not receive my presents until teatime. I burst into the apartment to be confronted by my mother.

'Tea first, prezzies second,' she announced.

I should have guessed something was up. Most unusually, my father was home two hours before normal. I was led into the dining room where Wong had laid out tea – sandwiches, bread and butter, scones, the teapot . . . Yet the moment I saw the table all thought of gifts and food evaporated.

In the centre of the table was a two-and-a-half-foot-long model of a Royal Navy destroyer, exact in every detail. It was painted battleship grey with its identification letter and numbers on the hull. At the bow hung the Union Jack, at the stern the White Ensign. On the bridge were the Aldiss lamp and searchlights, the wheel and a brass compass and engine room telegraph. On deck, the guns pointed fore and aft, the anchor chain lay on the deck and there were rope loops on the Carley floats and lifeboats. Even the rigging existed, thin lines of what I assumed to be fuse wire running from deck to mast.

Models such as this were only to be found in maritime museums. I was speechless. Wong stood by my side.

'Dis you cake, young master. Happy burfday for you.' In the background, Ah Shun smiled, bemused by the whole affair.

'Cake?' I replied.

'You say you wantee warship cake. Wong do for you.'

I just hugged him.

The cake had taken Wong a fortnight. He had worked every spare moment he could afford, often late into the night. The hull and superstructure were a rich fruit cake chock-full of glacé cherries and sultanas and covered in hard royal icing, the lifeboats made of marzipan and icing, the main armament and gun turrets of solid icing. Most astonishing of all was the rigging, made of spun sugar. To keep the cake as it was assembled, it had been hidden in the windowless dry room off my parents' bedroom where clothes and shoes were kept to avoid them going mouldy in the humid tropical air. Despite this precaution, they still quickly grew a hazy fur of fungus, and the cake would have grown a microscopic lawn in hours, but Wong knew a trick. A small charcoal burner was kept alight in the room which absorbed any humidity that got in.

I did not want to cut into it. Neither did my mother. At the end of the table was a smaller ordinary cake with candles on it. We ate that instead but, the following day, we started on the destroyer. I forget what presents I received.

The destroyer was not Wong's only artistic culinary masterpiece. He could carve chrysanthemum blooms out of raw carrots and decorative leaves out of cucumbers. Mashed potato was always served in small volcano shapes with the tops slightly browned under the grill. Crown roast New Zealand lamb arrived on the table with the rib ends culminating in parsnip, not paper, decorations. For cocktail parties, Wong prepared what was known as *small chow*, but which my father preferred to refer to as finger fodder, possibly a naval term. Mushrooms stuffed with anchovies, cheese and soy sauce sticks, thinly sliced fresh pineapple and shrimps on toast with home-made mayonnaise and a scattering of sesame seeds – his repertoire and penchant for ex-perimentation seemed inexhaustible.

At drinks parties, Wong being occupied in the kitchen, my

father delegated me to help him wait on the guests. My responsibilities were to see that no-one's glass was empty and to serve the trays of *small chow*.

At first, I regarded this as an onerous chore but I came to look forward to it. My father taught me how to mix drinks, I was able to consume Wong's delicacies on the sly and I became privy to the world of adult conversation which, on occasion, I found fascinating. It was by such eavesdropping that I learnt the true story of HMS *Amethyst*, attacked by Chinese forces on the Yangtze River in 1949 and the Rape of Nanking by the Japanese in the winter of 1937. Such parties also had their lighter side. On Christmas Eve morning, 1953, I went into my parents' bathroom to get a new tube of toothpaste only to discover a Royal Navy Commander, resplendent in mess uniform with gold braid and medals, asleep on his back in the bath, gently snoring, his arms crossed over his chest with a tiger lily thrust between his fingers. I tip-toed out and never saw him again.

That same winter, my father returned home in the early hours from a mess night with the Royal Air Force at Kai Tak airport. He was well oiled and humming tunelessly. This was most unusual, for my father was typically morose and self-pitying when the worse for booze. His dinner suit was caked in congealed blood.

I stood by as my mother, simultaneously concerned and furious, stripped my father to his vest and Y-fronts, sat him in the bath and washed him down. He had a nasty gash on the inside of his arm but it was insufficient to account for the quantity of blood all over him, even matted in his hair. When he was clean, my mother pulled the plug, sent him into the spare room, covered him with a sheet and went back to her own bed. I withdrew to mine.

In the morning, my mother held a breakfast inquisition.

'What the hell were you doing last night, Ken? Your dinner

jacket's ruined. So's your shirt. And you've lost two of the gold studs your father gave you.'

My father made no reply.

'That's not a rhetorical question, Ken.'

'Fan cricket,' my father admitted at length. He looked down at his arm, his wound covered by a large adhesive bandage.

What had happened was that, after the formal dinner, the RAF officers' mess members had decided on a game of fan cricket, mess vs. guests, which involved everyone present forming a circle around a ceiling fan. This was set at maximum speed and an empty beer can tossed into it. Wherever it flew out from the spinning propeller, it had to be caught. Of course, after the first toss, the metal was mangled into pieces as sharp as razor blades.

'You'd better visit the *Tamar* MO and have a tetanus shot,' my mother stated. 'God knows what bacteria were breeding on the can.'

My father got up to leave the table, his breakfast untouched.

'Sit down!' my mother commanded imperiously.

My father obeyed. I had never seen him so docile and compliant.

'What's more, your trousers are torn and the remnants of your jacket smell of petrol.'

'Better than perfume,' my father answered back, smiling sheepishly and hoping to bring some sense of levity to the breakfast table.

'What . . . !' said my mother, her jaw set and her eyes wide with rage.

My father confessed how the evening's jollity had ended. The mess piano had been carried outside and placed at the rear of a Hawker Hunter jet fighter parked on the apron. The engine was then fired up and the piano incinerated.

My mother listened to this in silence then commented, 'A fine example for Martin. Now eat your bloody breakfast.'

My father prodded his fried egg with his fork and made to stand up again.

'Wong gets up before six to see you have a breakfast,' my mother remarked, 'so kindly show him the respect he deserves and eat the bloody thing. And one more matter,' she continued, 'when the mess bill comes in, the cost doesn't come out of my housekeeping money.'

This was the second occasion during our years in Hong Kong when my father's drunken escapades had cost my mother dear. When stationed in Japan, one night he and a friend had gone into a saloon in Sasebo where there was an American naval rating shooting his mouth off about the Royal Navy, the Queen and the British in general. He made it abundantly clear that the Royal Navy was not worth the water it sailed on, the Queen was 'a nice piece of ass' and the British as a nation were spineless, gutless and worth less than their navy. My father and his friend agreed with him and kept his glass full until he was paralytic. They then carried him out of the bar and down the street to a tattoo artist who tattooed his entire chest in full colour with the White Ensign, the Union Jack and *God Save the Queen*. My mother's house-keeping allowance was somewhat short that month.

As time went by, my father's increasing delight in and reliance upon the company of Johnnie Walker, Messrs Justerini and Brooks and his namesake (but no relation) Mr Booth – not to mention his friend, Mr Gordon – grew. When he arrived home from the office, his first visit was to the drinks cabinet, Wong running in from the kitchen with a jug of water, a container of ice and a cold bottle of tonic, covering all the angles with them. Sometimes, my father returned late having, as he put it, *just popped into the wardroom*. His favourite snifter was pink gin,

popular in officers' messes on every warship afloat. It consisted of gin diluted with water, with a dash of Angostura bitters. My father took it without the water.

My father's drinking never got him truly, staggeringly, equilibriumly challenged, sad-song-singingly, punch-flingingly, bosom-friend-makingly drunk. Furthermore, he never suffered from a hangover. Consequently, my father never felt himself to be sozzled, as my mother termed it, trying to make light of the situation for her own sanity and self-respect. Worse still, he would never admit to being under the influence. No matter how much alcohol slid down his gullet, my father remained vertical, comparatively lucid and even able to drive without incident. The only obvious sign of intoxication other than his breath was his attitude towards my mother and me. He was psychologically abusive, skilfully criticizing or belittling us in front of our friends. His attacks were never short, sharp, soon-to-be-forgotten, even forgiven, episodes. They were calculated, long-term personal projects bent on undermining his subject's spirit and, as his drinking increased, these melded together into a continuous animosity which drove people – my mother, myself, my parents' friends – away in disgust. As a result, my father was tolerated rather than liked and became a lonely, disenchanted and bitter man.

He never praised but only criticized or admonished, muttering through clenched teeth that my mother and I did not come up to his standard – but then he never told us where the benchmark lay. After one confrontation with him, my mother declared to me that we had already exceeded his standard and that that was the problem, but I did not understand what she meant.

One Saturday lunchtime, not long after we moved to the Peak, my father arrived home in a foul temper. Something had gone wrong at the office.

'What's the matter, Ken?' my mother enquired, coming in from the kitchen.

'Don't you start!' he snapped as he mixed himself a quadruple pink gin.

'I was only asking—'

'Well bloody well don't!'

My mother let this roll over her and said, 'Let's have lunch. Philip and Ray'll be here at two.'

'I'm not going swimming,' my father replied. 'Bloody waste of time.'

Normally, this would have upset my mother. She did not drive and we were therefore reliant upon my father or public transport to take us everywhere. But Philip and Ray Bryant were close friends of my mother's and owned a huge pre-war grey Jaguar saloon with massive headlights and leather seats. I sensed Philip was critical of my father's naval pretensions and despised his treatment of my mother. A handsome and jovial man, he was a Royal Navy Commander, Ray a vivacious and pretty woman with black hair and the refined movement of a ballet dancer. They had met in Egypt during the war.

'Well, we're going swimming,' my mother rejoined firmly. 'You can do what you like. You can sleep all bloody day for all I care.'

At this, my father grabbed a cushion off the settee and hurled it at the glass doors to the balcony. It was a hot day. They were open. The cushion spun through them without touching the sides and sailed, like a brocade extra-terrestrial craft, out into the air. It disappeared from view on its way down the steep mountainside towards the city below. My mother and I rushed downstairs and out on to the lawn that surrounded the building. Arriving at the retaining wall, we looked down. Hong Kong and the harbour, with Kowloon in the distance, lay at our feet. The cushion was

lodged in some bushes about fifty yards down on a not quite sheer slope. A short distance beyond it, the angle of the hillside sharpened before dropping into a band of trees.

'You're right, Ken,' she said as we returned to the apartment, 'you're not coming. You're going down the bloody hillside and you're going to retrieve my bloody cushion.'

As we drove to the beach in Philip's Jaguar, my mother recounted what had come to pass. I asked what would happen if my father slipped.

'No need to worry,' Philip answered. 'Lugard Road'll break his fall.'

When we returned at dusk, the cushion was back on the settee, cleaned by Ah Shun. A filthy white shirt, shredded by thorns, lay on my mother's bed, a sort of trophy of war.

At home, when my father threw things, they were always items – books, the newspaper, cushions – that were sure not to make a dent in the wall or parquet flooring. In the office, it was a different matter. There, midway through berating a Chinese clerk or typist standing trembling before him, he would, to emphasize a point in his tirade, grab the black bakelite telephone and hurl it at the wall. It would smash to pieces. Women would burst into tears. The men would keep on quaking. If the telephone was not handy, he threw the office wall clock. In the end someone fitted a shorter cord to the telephone so that, when he flung it, it reached the extent of its flex and fell harmlessly on to the carpet. The Chinese staff called him *mok tau* (blockhead) and worse. They often used these names to his face but as he spoke no Cantonese, they were safe. I once heard a clerk call him *gai lun jai* (chicken penis boy): the clerk must have assumed that, as I was my father's son, I spoke no Cantonese either.

Having met one or two at school, I came to the conclusion that my father was a natural-born bully. On the other hand, I did grow

up mixing a mean cocktail. Maybe that was one of his benchmarks of a good son.

Although we now lived on the Peak, across the harbour from and over a thousand feet above all my mother's Chinese friends, she remained in constant touch with them, meeting the room boys from the Fourseas on their days off, going to tea houses with them, sometimes spending an afternoon with them and their girlfriends or wives at the beach. At other times, she went on picnics with them. These frequently took place on school days but when they occurred at a weekend or in the school holidays, I was invited along.

My father took a dim view of these outings. My mother ignored his opinion completely until one Saturday when she announced she was going out with 'the boys and girls', as she put it, the following day.

'I see,' my father remarked shirtily. 'So I'm left here with Martin.'

'No!' I chirped up. 'I'm going, too.'

'If you ask me, Joyce,' my father went on, giving me a filthy look, 'you should stay home at the weekends. To go off midweek is one thing, but . . . All this gallivanting about will get you a reputation.'

'Gallivanting with the natives will get me a reputation, will it, Ken?'

'You know what I mean.'

'I'm sure I don't.'

'Well, you should. Tongues'll wag.'

'I don't care if they flap in the wind like flags,' my mother

rejoined. 'And neither should you. If some old biddy with nothing better to do starts bad-mouthing me, it's up to you to defend my honour.'

'Drawn cutlasses at dawn?' my father replied ironically.

'Don't be ridiculous, Ken. Besides, what's the alternative? Spend the weekend watching you snore. Some live spark you are, Ken. About as bright as a NAAFI candle.'

For some reason I could never fathom, my mother assumed that candles purchased from the Navy Army and Air Force Institutes were always incapable of burning brightly and frequently used this metaphor.

'I work hard all week and—'

'So does everybody else, Ken, but they don't spend the weekend sleeping and snorting like a grampus.'

Half an hour later, we met up with Ching, Halfie and some of the other Fourseas staff at the Outlying Islands ferry pier in Central District. A black-and-white Hongkong Yaumatei Ferry company vessel pulled alongside and we boarded it with a throng of boisterous Chinese weekend picniceers, all bound for Cheung Chau and carrying rattan baskets or bags.

No sooner was the ferry underway than everyone produced an array of snacks – chicken's feet, pork spare ribs, *wah mui*, crystallized ginger, pomeloes, oranges and melon seeds. Vendors travelled the deck selling bottled drinks and sweetmeats. The bones, peel and shells were thrown over the side, as in any Hong Kong street, with scant regard for those below: the ferry had a bottom passenger deck.

After an hour, the ferry turned into the harbour of Cheung Chau, a dumb-bell-shaped island with an ancient village in the centre. Deepwater fishing junks rode at anchor, with sampans weaving between them like agile aquatic insects. A drift of joss-stick smoke indicated the location of a large temple.

As soon as the gangplank hit the jetty, a phalanx of passengers ran ashore to claim the best tables in a nearby restaurant. We followed but by-passed the eating place with its tanks of live fish and crabs destined for the table.

'What is the temple?' I asked Ah Tang, one of the room boys.

'Pak Tai,' he answered. 'Sea god temple. More old all Hong Kong.'

I wanted to visit it but it was not on our itinerary. Instead, we went south along the *praya*, passing fish vendors, sleeping cats and vociferous dogs, fishermen mending nets or baiting lines and houses with their windows shuttered against the fierce sunlight. At the periphery of the village, we struck out along a path running through a tunnel of trees and rocks.

'Where are we going?' I asked my mother.

'I haven't the slightest idea,' she replied. 'I'm just going with the general flow.'

The path was alive with tawny Rajah and delicate cream-and-black dragontail butterflies supping on fallen fruit. In the dry leaves, smooth skinks with black side stripes rustled and flashed out of sight. Birds sang and flitted through the branches of a sacred banyan tree upon which pictures of the gods had been pinned. Joss-sticks smouldered in the roots. Here and there were groves of yellow and green striped bamboo, many of the stems substantial enough to make a coolie's pole. All the while, the sea glinted away to my right through sparsely needled pine trees.

My mother was happy, walking with a jaunty step, swinging our picnic basket. Where the path widened, she took my hand.

'This is fun, isn't it?' she asked.

I agreed that it was but, after a short distance, posed a question that had long been bothering me.

'Why doesn't Dad come to places with us?'

She looked down at me.

'He's a stick-in-the-mud,' she responded. 'And he's got a chip on his shoulder.'

I asked what that meant.

'It's hard to explain. It's just – well, he thinks he's better than everyone else but they don't agree.'

'Was he always a stick-in-the-mud?' I enquired.

'No! We used to go for cycle rides in the country and go to the pictures or for walks on the Downs, and we'd have lunch in a little village pub at Cowplain . . .' She paused. I sensed she was sad but then she perked up. 'What the hell! It was all a long time ago.'

Up ahead, our companions were singing a Chinese song in time with their steps. My mother joined in.

The path descended a hillside towards the sea. We halted by a group of boulders. Within minutes, someone had a small primus alight and was boiling water for tea. A cloth was spread over a flat rock and weighted down with stones. With the others, my mother set about laying out our picnic.

I settled myself on a slab of pinkish granite, the sunlight dancing on the mica fragments as if on tinsel. To my left was a cove surrounded by low cliffs, gentle waves sucking at the rocks. My mother approached with Ah Tang.

'Martin, come and see this!'

We followed Ah Tang along a cliffside path and down towards the shore where there was a tumble of huge boulders.

'You come all same me,' he said beckoning to us.

We slithered down the boulders to find several of them had formed a sort of cave. He gestured us in. The entrance was narrow, the roof low and the floor sand.

Squatting on his haunches, Ah Tang said, 'This place for Cheung Po Tsai. He live here.'

'Who is Cheung Po Tsai?' I enquired.

'Long time before, more four hund'ed year, Cheung Po Tsai

big time py-rat. Got many junk, many men work for him, all same py-rat. He also got *gweipor* wife. Catch her on one ship one time. She love Cheung Po Tsai, no wan' go back Inglun'-side. Stay here.'

My mother gazed out of the entrance to the sea.

'Just imagine,' she said, 'living here with a pirate chief, thousands of miles from home and knowing you could never return.'

The romantic in her was working double-speed.

When the picnic was over, some of the room boys' girlfriends started to dance. It was a Chinese dance that involved tiny steps, moving in a circle, singing a song and, with arms raised, making a twisting motion with the hand, as if one were screwing in a light bulb. My mother was invited to join in, being taught the words and motions. I watched as she danced with these young Chinese women. She did not look, I thought, very different from them, except that her hair was blond not black. She was, as she would have put it, as happy as a sand boy.

We walked slowly back to the ferry jetty, the lowering sun warm on our faces. The butterflies on the path made no effort to fly off at our approach: Ching said they were drunk.

'How can a butterfly get drunk?' I said.

'The juice,' Ching explained, 'can make alcohol in the hot sun.'

As we sailed back to Hong Kong, my mother leant out of the ferry window, the warm wind ruffling her hair. The gleaming sun reflected gold off the sea and on to the ferry cabin ceiling. The Chinese day-trippers were mostly quiet now. A few played cards but most dozed or read a newspaper or magazine. Ching and Halfie faced each other over a set of *tin gau* tiles.

At the HYF pier in Central, we said our goodbyes and took a taxi home. My father was sitting with a gin and tonic listening to

the BBC World News on the radio. I went out on to the veranda and looked down on the city. The first neon lights were coming on, bright as coloured stars in the shadow of the Peak.

'Have a good time?' my mother asked.

I nodded.

'It's days like this you never forget, no matter how old you get,' she advised me. 'It's what life's all about. Warm sun, friendship and music.'

She did a little twirl, miming fitting a light bulb in the sky and went inside.

What first prompted the thought in my mother's mind I have no idea, but a fortnight after my ninth birthday, she warned me not to make any arrangements for the following Saturday morning. When I asked why not, she was uncharacteristically equivocal.

'Just wait and see,' she said, 'and don't – I repeat, don't – mention it to your father.'

On the morning in question, my mother waited until my father departed for the office then took me to the top terminus of the Peak Tram, the famous funicular mountain tramway. We descended nearly two thousand feet to the bottom terminus, hurriedly made our way past the cathedral and by banks and shipping line offices, crossing Statue Square to the Star Ferry pier. All this way, my mother hardly spoke, ignoring my enquiries as to our destination.

Once over the harbour and off the ferry, our pace slowed to a normal walk.

'What was all that rush about?' I asked.

'I didn't want to bump into your father. He thinks I'm having coffee with Biddy Binns.'

'So what we're doing—' I began to suggest.

'Is a secret,' my mother interrupted, confirming my thoughts. 'You must never tell your father. It's not that what we're doing is wrong but, if he found out, I'd never hear the last of it. And neither would you.'

Finally, we arrived at a tenement building, the ground floor of which was occupied by a camera and binocular shop. To one side was a narrow doorway closed by a galvanized metal door. My mother opened it and we started to ascend a staircase that smelt of cats and boiled rice. At last, we arrived at a door with a number painted upon it and a picture of Kwan Ti pasted beneath a spy-hole. On the wall to one side was a brass plate in Chinese characters such as one might find outside a doctor's surgery.

Immediately, my anxiety grew. I was in for some kind of treatment: but I was not ill. A boy I'd known at school had recently been circumcised and told all in graphic detail to his friends. Was this my fate? I felt my penis and testicles shrink with fear. Then it occurred to me: was my mother ill? A shiver went down my back. She looked healthy enough, yet . . . What if she died? A future of Dickensian proportions and misery spread ahead of me.

My mother knocked on the door. The spy-hole momentarily darkened before several bolts were drawn and we were confronted by a middle-aged Chinese woman wearing Western clothes.

'Good morning, Mrs Booth,' she greeted us in a slightly American accent. 'Please come in.'

She stepped aside and we entered a small and sparsely furnished tenement flat. Upon one wall were a number of mathematical charts and tables. In the window hung the almost

obligatory bird cage containing a lone zebra finch. A door opened and an elderly Chinese man entered wearing a long, dark-blue brocade gown, the character *sow*, meaning long life, woven into an almost invisible pattern. His face was lined and the nail of his left index finger was at least two inches long. This, I knew, signified he was a man of learning who never involved himself with manual work.

'Good morning. I am Mr Zhou,' he introduced himself. He shook my mother's hand then looked at me. 'And this is the subject?'

I felt instantly more apprehensive and wondered if I was here to receive some maths tutoring: the charts suggested that this might be the case and, indeed, I hoped that it was, preferring even maths coaching to circumcision. But then my father would have approved of maths coaching. This visit was to be kept secret. I was in a quandary.

'May I introduce my son, Martin?' my mother said.

'Hello, Martin,' Mr Zhou said without a trace of an accent. 'Tell me, when is your birthday?'

'I've just had it,' I replied.

'This I know,' said Mr Zhou, pulling over a stool, 'but tell me the date.'

'The seventh of September 1944.'

'You were born in the Year of the Monkey. It is a good year for you.' He started now to speak more to my mother. 'A male born in this year is very intelligent and good at solving mysteries or problems. Like a monkey, he can be devious or cunning. Very big-headed, I think you say. Maybe arrogant. Those born under this animal are always moving, have a quick mind. Now,' he positioned his stool directly before me, 'relax yourself.'

For the next five minutes, Mr Zhou thoroughly felt my head, studied my palms and looked intently at my face. All the while, he

muttered in an undertone, the lady taking notes. This done, he produced a highly polished tortoise shell from a drawer. It was complete except for the tortoise. He studied this, muttered some more then put it away.

Upon a writing desk, Mr Zhou set out a fan of cards with pictures on them. Taking down the bird cage, he stood it on the end of the desk and opened the door. The tenement window was open, the sounds of the street below and the warm, diesel-tinged air wafting in. The chances of the zebra finch doing a Joey were, I thought, pretty high.

Instead, the bird flew out of its cage, strutted along the cards, picked one out with its beak and flew straight back into the cage. Mr Zhou closed the door and gave the bird a small berry from a jar.

He studied the card and the lady's notes. We watched as he wrote a long document in black ink on coarse, buff-coloured Chinese paper. His brushstrokes were rapid. Every so often, he used another brush to draw a red circle. Finally, he waited for the ink to dry, folded the oblong sheet and slipped it in an envelope on which he wrote my name.

'In summary,' he announced as he handed it to me, 'you will be a clever man but sometimes very lazy. You will be a leader, a famous man in what you do. You will live to be sixty-four years old and you will be prosperous and have sons. You will have a good marriage. In your fifty-seventh year, you will have much illness but in the remainder of your life you will be healthy.'

With that, he stood up, shook my mother's hand, briefly put his hand in mine and left the room, closing the door behind him. My mother paid the lady with a cheque.

'So now we know,' my mother remarked as we reached the street. 'You'll have a good life.'

She seemed relieved, as if prior to this she had had her doubts.

'Mr Zhou is highly respected,' she continued. 'He's considered the best fortune-teller in the colony. They say the Governor's wife goes to him.'

I did not comment, but I saw little difference between him and those I saw outside the Tin Hau temple in Yau Ma Tei, except that he spoke English and operated from a tenement flat.

We walked to Tkachenko's for a mid-morning coffee and Black Forest gateau.

'Remember,' my mother warned me, 'not a single, solitary word to your father.' I nodded my agreement. 'If he finds out,' she went on, 'I'll be branded a witch, given a broomstick and sent to Coventry.'

'Why would he send you there?' I asked.

'It's just an expression.'

I sipped my drink and said, 'Well, at least I'm not going to be a dustman.'

My mother looked at me for a moment then broke out laughing. I liked it when she laughed. It was not that often that she did.

Christmas Day 1953 dawned bright. The sky was cloudless and blue, the air chill. At nine o'clock, we embarked upon the Christmas-morning ritual of present giving.

In the lounge, we had a Christmas tree, of sorts. Imported from California, it was about three feet high and had started to lose its needles somewhere around Hawaii. By now it was a tinsel-hung, glass-ball-strewn, fairy-lights-lit skeleton of near twigs with an embarrassed-looking angel on top. We gathered before it, shortly to be joined by Wong and his family. Tuppence held back. The master's side of the house was unequivocally out of bounds

to him and any excursion into it was bewildering. My mother took him by the hand and led him in. Whilst she appreciated the exclusion rule and agreed it was necessary, the egalitarian in her disapproved of it. Tuppence was seated on an armchair and showered with small presents which included clothing as well as Chinese sweets and toys. Wong and Ah Shun received their presents, coffee was served and then we got on with opening ours.

Lunch that day could have graced a monarch's table. The turkey, a gift from The Asia Provision Company, which presented all its customers with a hamper of gratitude every Christmas, was raised in Australia. Its skin, as highly polished and varnished as the table upon which it stood, looked like that on a whole Ho Man Tin pig. It was stuffed with cranberry, sage and thyme and the flesh fell apart like fish. The pudding was traditionally round and the size of a football, with a sprig of holly on top. We wondered where Wong had got it: holly was not indigenous to southern China. Then we found out. It was made of icing sugar. As for the pudding, it was so big we were still eating it fried in butter in the first week of January. The only thing that marred the meal was my father's half-hour fit of pique when he found out the thing had been set alight with his best armagnac.

Christmas afternoon was spent playing Dover Patrol on the lounge carpet, listening to the Queen's Speech (which my father considered obligatory) and settling the surfeit of food. Late in the afternoon, I walked down to a block of 1920s apartments near the Peak Café to visit a friend. We messed around a bit and I set off for home just before dark. It was a cool South China winter's night. A stiff breeze blew by the café, rippling the creepers on its roof.

Reaching the tourist observation point, I stood alone, the updraft of wind from the harbour below making my eyes water. The lights of the city glistened in the cold air. A lone vehicular ferry made its way towards Yau Ma Tei. In the middle of the

Kowloon peninsula, I imagined I could see the red, blue and green neon sign on the front of the Fourseas and immediately felt homesick for Soares Avenue and the *dai pai dongs* of Mong Kok: I doubted there was a single hundred-year-old egg anywhere on the Peak. Especially on Christmas night.

Feeling, as my mother would have put it, a little blue, I trudged on up the steep hill to Mount Austin, hauling myself along on the railing. My parents were playing canasta at the bull terrier coffee table when I arrived home. My mother had a gin and tonic at her side, my father a tumbler more than half full of neat whisky. I went into the kitchen and opened the fridge. Wong immediately appeared and poured me a glass of milk. Without asking, he then set to making turkey sandwiches. I took my milk into the lounge and settled down in an armchair to read the latest *Eagle* album, a Christmas present from Grampy, along with a five-pound postal order.

After a while, my father put a 78 record on the phonograph: the Original Dixieland Jazz Band playing 'Tiger Rag'. It was tentatively suggested that I might go to bed, but I pleaded turkey sandwiches and Christmas night and the subject was dropped.

At about half-past ten, my mother went out onto the veranda. This was a nightly ritual. She would stand there sometimes for fifteen minutes, just taking in the panorama. I was not to know it, and nor was my father, but she was beginning to scheme secretly how she might make Hong Kong her home for the rest of her life.

'Ken,' she called a few minutes later, her voice tight with urgency, 'get your binoculars.'

'What is it?' I enquired, joining my mother on the veranda.

'I don't know,' she replied, pointing across to the north-western end of Kowloon. 'What do you make of it?'

A dull ruddy blush glowed behind some low hills. My father

arrived and put his binoculars to his eyes, turning the focusing ring.

'Oh, my God!' he murmured.

My mother snatched them from his face.

'Can I see?' I insisted. I had to ask several times before she would relinquish them.

I adjusted the focus. It seemed as if a whole hillside was ablaze. It was the Shek Kip Mei squatter area going up in flames. The fire was intense. Even from a distance of five miles, individual flames could clearly be seen licking into the air. The highest must have reached fifty feet. I thought of my experience at Ho Man Tin, of the young man with only the photo of his family to link him to his former life back in China, before the Communists destroyed it.

My mother turned into the lounge, calling for Wong.

'Yes, you wanchee, missee?' he asked, expecting an order for more sandwiches or a fresh bottle of tonic water.

'Look!' she exclaimed, pointing once more at Kowloon.

He stepped on to the veranda and looked at the distant fire through the binoculars. His face showed no emotion whatsoever. To the Chinese, this was fate and it was his good luck to live and work in a comparatively non-flammable building, and the squatters' ill luck not to.

'No good for plenty people, missee,' he said.

My mother set to work.

'Wong, get all the blankets out of the camphor wood chest. Martin, you—'

'What are you doing, Joyce?' my father asked.

'What do you think I'm doing?' she snapped back. 'Go and get the car.'

'Get the car . . . ?' my father repeated. 'It's after eleven, Joyce! On Christmas night—'

'I know! Get the bloody car, cloth ears!' It was a derogatory expression my father often used on her.

In thirty minutes, all the bedding in the house was tied into individual bundles of one blanket and two sheets. My school Hong Kong basket was full of turkey sandwiches and there were two cardboard boxes of tonic and soda water. This was all loaded into the car and we set off. My father was all for leaving me behind but my mother would not have it.

We drove down the Peak and on to the vehicular ferry. There were only two other private vehicles on board, both large American saloon cars filled with raucous party-goers returning home. The remainder of the deck was occupied by several fire engines and ambulances.

Once landed at Yau Ma Tei, it was only a matter of a mile or so to Shek Kip Mei but we were halted by a road block at Prince Edward Road and forced to turn right. My father drove a short way and parked in the forecourt of an apartment block. My mother got out, piled me high with blanket and sheet bundles and, with as many as she could carry herself, set off in the direction of the fire. I followed. My father was forgotten in her rush: maybe she thought he would rather guard and polish the car.

We had not gone three hundred yards when a British police officer stopped us. Beyond him, crowds were gathering in the streets.

'You can't go beyond here,' he ordered my mother.

'St John Ambulance,' she replied, adding unnecessarily, 'blankets. More coming.'

Her bluff worked. He let us through. The side streets were thronged with hordes of people sitting down. What was unnerving was that they were virtually silent, unlike most Chinese crowds which usually chattered like a flock of migrating starlings. My mother handed out bundles to the first families she came

across. They took them, smiling at her. One man stood up, said, 'T'ankee you, missee,' and touched my hair. For his family, at least, things were not going to be so bad after all.

The air was contaminated with the foul smell of burning rubber and cloth. Ash blew past us like grey snow, some of the flakes still alight. A fire engine pumped water down a fat undulating hose from a street hydrant but it could not have had much effect. The sky was alight with sparks and flames, a thick column of smoke rising into the night sky then bending away on the wind. Spotlights played upon the havoc.

Next, we distributed the turkey sandwiches but carrying the boxes of bottles was beyond us so we returned home with them.

'Bloody long way to come to give away a dozen blankets and a picnic,' my father remarked irritably as we halted at the vehicular ferry pier.

'Shut up, Ken,' my mother said tartly and, curling up on the back seat, promptly fell asleep.

My father and I settled down to drink the tonic and wait at the car ramp for the next ferry departure, scheduled for two o'clock.

The following day, the full extent of the fire was broadcast on the radio. Ten thousand huts over an area of forty-five acres had been totally destroyed; sixty thousand people had been made homeless. The blaze, which had developed into a fire storm, had reached such high temperatures that aluminium cooking vessels had been completely burnt away. Incredibly, no-one was killed. This prompted the conjecture that the fire had been set deliberately to force the government into speeding up the squatter re-housing and rehabilitation programme. If this were the case, it worked. Within a year, the site of the Shek Kip Mei blaze was a brand-new refugee housing estate.

In weeks I had become more or less *au fait* with the geography of the Peak. The path I had taken that first day was called Governor's Walk. The near conical mountain was called *Sai Ko Shan* (or, in English, High West), *shan* meaning mountain. I attempted to climb it but it was too steep for me. At its base was a rifle range where I collected deformed .303 bullets, digging them out of the butts with my penknife.

To reach the rifle range, I had to take what must be one of the most spectacular walks on earth. It began – and ended – at the foot of Mount Austin Road and circumnavigated the Peak.

I would always set off clockwise, walking beneath overhanging trees alive with butterflies and the birds that ate them, passing a waterfall and arriving at the place where the soldiers lay down to shoot across a valley at the butts. On one occasion, my walk was halted by a police barrier. A young woman had been murdered on the shooting platform, which I thereafter avoided for fear of ghosts.

After visiting the butts, my pocket full of spent ordnance, I carried on around the mountain. At first, the road wound its way by several houses, one of which was empty because no servants would work there. It was, according to Wong, haunted by the spirits of previous amahs who had been raped and murdered there by Japanese troops in 1942. A short distance further on, the road narrowed and became unsuitable for vehicles.

Holding more or less to the same contour, it continued around the mountain, sometimes as a viaduct, at others cut into the rock. Bit by bit, an incredible vista unfolded, first the western harbour approaches with merchant vessels awaiting a docking berth or discharging cargo into junks and flat barges called lighters.

In the distance was Stonecutters' Island, a military signals base. Further on, Kowloon came into sight, the peninsula crammed with buildings, ships lying along the jetties, ferries ploughing across to the island, walla-walla boats little more than aquatic insects. In another hundred yards, the central business district and the eastern suburbs came into view, the lower slopes of the hills dotted with houses and the red-brick block of the Bowen Road military hospital. Beyond Kowloon were the nine dragon hills.

Yet it was not the view that captivated me. I took that for granted. My bedroom window afforded me the same panorama. It was the sound. At first, I did not hear it but, gradually, it impinged itself upon me. It was a faint humming noise, as a wild bee hive might make. One weekend, walking the two roads with my mother, I asked her if she could hear it.

'Oh, yes,' she said, 'I can hear it. Do you know what it is?'

'It's the city,' I replied, surprised that she did not realize it.

'No,' she answered, 'it's the sound of a million people working hard.'

Halfway down the western flank of the Peak, on a promontory 1,100 feet above sea level and approached by a cracked and overgrown concrete track called Hatton Road, was a large gun emplacement known as Pinewood Battery. During the war, it had been equipped with two 3-inch anti-aircraft guns but had been destroyed on the morning of 15 December 1941, during the battle for Hong Kong. The gun platforms still existed, as did the subterranean block houses, the command post, ammunition bunkers and sleeping quarters. The concrete walls of the buildings were still decorated with their camouflage paint, whilst in the sleeping quarters, the metal-frame bunk beds remained standing, the remnants of palliasses draped upon them.

Pinewood was a special place for me. The ruins were a purpose-built adventure playground in which a few friends and I could

enact the Japanese storming it and the British defending it, the latter always winning in strict contradiction of history. Yet it was when I went there alone that it was the most exciting. Just walking down to the battery made my spine creep and the hair on my neck rise. A man had died there during the four-hour-long bombardment of 15 December. Now, it was as if his ghost still inhabited the place, rode the breezes coming up the mountain, sighed in the stunted pine trees and whispered in the azalea bushes.

I would sit on one of the emplacement walls and watch the ferries far below me, heading for Lan Tau or Lamma islands or the smaller outlying islands of Cheung Chau and Peng Chau. They carefully avoided Green Island directly in front of me where, as red warning notices on the shore stated, Hong Kong stored its explosives. Only fishing sampans risked passing through Sulphur Channel between Green and Hong Kong islands. The shoreline was strewn with treacherous rocks, the currents fast and unreliable.

Tiring of the view, I would then start hunting for wartime relics. Most of all, I wanted a British cap badge or uniform button. The battery had been manned by Indian Army troops when it fell and a Rajput regimental emblem would have been a find indeed. My wish list also included a Japanese shell from a Zero fighter – I was sure the place must have been strafed and knew that bullets hitting soft earth did not necessarily deform – machine-gun cartridge cases and, best of all, a shell case from one of the AA guns. What I actually found outdid the lot.

I was working through the low, dense scrub below the battery, about twenty yards out from the concrete skirt, when I came upon a piece of khaki material sticking up from the ground. Hoping it might be a fragment of discarded uniform with a button on it, I grabbed it and tugged. It was firmly embedded in the earth

so I pulled harder. It would not shift. Kneeling, I set to work excavating it with my penknife. In less than a minute, I discovered the edge of a collar. Just beneath it was the smooth side of a skull, an eye socket filled with earth staring up at me.

Immediately, I knew what I had found and jumped backwards as if it had been a reared cobra, ready to strike. Scrambling through the undergrowth, I reached the battery, ran through it and headed up Hatton Road. It was a steep climb to Harlech Road. My legs ached as never before. I paused to gather my breath and wits and then ran on to the Peak Café where I asked someone to telephone the police for me.

An hour later, I was back at Pinewood with a dozen police officers and some coolies. They started to dig up the skeleton as I was asked questions by a British police officer who then took me home in a police car. My father was summoned from his office. I thought I was going to be for the high jump when he arrived, yet he was surprisingly mellow.

We were informed that the skeleton I had found was that of a Japanese soldier who had been shot in the back of the head. He had not, I was told, died in the war but afterwards, captured by local Chinese who had probably murdered him in retribution for what the Japanese had done to the local population.

'What's going to happen to him?' I asked. I toyed with the idea of asking if he had any badges on him but decided that was pushing my luck.

'His remains will be handed over to the Japanese authorities for return to Japan,' the police officer answered, 'where he can rest in peace.'

The next time I walked down Hatton Road, the hair on my neck did not prickle and I felt utterly alone.

This was not always the case during my Peak wanderings.

Whilst some of the mountain was covered in thick scrub, much

of it was densely forested. Where there was a road, path or clearing, the fringes of the forest were heavily overgrown with plants seeking the sunlight but, under the canopy of the trees, the undergrowth was comparatively open. In this universe of dappled light existed creatures rarely seen.

The first wild animal I saw appeared fleetingly to me about a month after we moved to Mount Austin. It was early dusk and I was returning from the rifle range. A little way ahead of me, there was a rustle in the undergrowth and what I took to be a miniature deer stepped daintily out into full view. I froze.

Not much bigger than a large dog, it was reddish-brown in colour, had a short tail, two swept-back antlers and, to my astonishment, tusks. I was enchanted by it. The only other deer I had seen were in England, in the New Forest, where they seemed as tame as the feral ponies. This one was different. It was a truly wild animal that had chosen to show itself to me. Except for its disproportionately big ears, it too did not move: then it uttered a brief dog-like yelp and vanished.

'It must have been a muntjak,' my mother explained when I got home. 'They're also known as barking deer because their call is like a dog's yap. You were very lucky. Few people ever see one. They only come out at night.'

Discovering that such creatures existed, I started to explore the forests. Several evenings later, I saw a bushy-tailed, cat-sized animal appear quite suddenly out of a burrow. With a badger-like striped face, the rest of it was otherwise a nondescript brown. It stood at the burrow entrance, sniffed the air then, spinning round, vanished back down the way it had come. It did not reappear and I was later told it was a ferret badger.

I soon realized that entering the forest was pointless. With the ground covered in dry leaves and twigs, walking silently would have been hard work for an experienced hunter, never mind me.

The denizens of the forest could see, hear, smell and locate me long before I did them. Furthermore, most of them were nocturnal, and I could not stay out after dark.

At the bottom of the valley that dropped away to the south of Mount Austin was Pokfulam reservoir, the first ever built in Hong Kong to provide water for the embryonic city. As 1953 had been the driest year on record, by December and the school holidays the reservoir was very low indeed. This implied two things to me: first, that whatever lived in the valley would probably have to visit it to drink and, second, that whatever lived in the reservoir was now restricted to shallow water and therefore easily seen.

Supplied by Wong with a picnic lunch, I set off one Saturday morning and settled myself down on the cracked-mud periphery of the reservoir, as near as I dared to the water's edge and the soft mud. To my surprise, there were very few footprints pressed into the softer mud. I pondered this, found a stone and tossed it down to the water's edge. It struck the mud and disappeared with a sucking noise. The muntjak knew what I had not: the mud was quick. I shivered at the thought of what might have happened had I stepped another ten feet across the reservoir bottom. There was no-one about who would have heard my calls for help. I took up my picnic, left the mud and sat on the dam wall.

The water lay below me, as still and transparent as green bottle glass. I could make out every detail of the bottom. Schools of tiny fish occasionally darted by. A frog swam along. Suddenly, there was a large flurry of mud. It took a while to settle but I knew that something had put paid to the frog. As the water cleared, I noticed an oval outline in the mud about the size of a large meat-serving dish. Very slowly, it detached itself from the bottom and rose towards the surface, trailing mud that spiralled down from it. It was a grey-coloured turtle. From one end, a white and grey

mottled head appeared, stretching out on a long neck which curved upwards towards me. It culminated in a prehensile nose that broke the surface for a moment before the head was retracted and the creature drifted back down to the mud. If I had not seen where it settled, I would never have known it was there.

Over the winter months, I also stumbled upon a pangolin feeding at an ants' nest in a wide crack in the concrete on Hatton Road, any number of giant African snails with shells the size of a whelk's, a dozing owl and, in a cave high up on the Peak, a colony of hibernating Japanese pipistrelle bats. Even the pangolin, normally nocturnal, paid me scant attention, feeding until I was almost upon it and even then just scurrying off.

Other encounters were not quite so benign.

The one warning my mother frequently issued was to beware of snakes. Hong Kong was home to over two dozen species of which at least four were venomous to man and potentially if not actually fatal. I kept an eye out for snakes but rarely saw one and, if I did, it was invariably heading away from me as fast as it might. Snakes in China appeared to know instinctively that there was a better than evens chance they might end up in a *wok*.

Walking to and from school, I daily passed along comically named Plunketts Road, at the side of which ran an open drain, or *nullah*, designed to shed heavy rainfall off the mountain as quickly as possible to prevent landslides. One afternoon, taking the path beside it, I heard what sounded like a hissing water leak. As a main water line ran along the side of the *nullah* and the public was being exhorted to save water and report wastage, I exercised my civic duty and went to investigate. The *nullah* was about eighteen inches wide and two and a half feet deep, sloping downhill in a series of steps.

In it was a common rat snake. Approximately three feet long, it was dark brown for its entire length with no pattern. A fangless

constrictor, I had seen them often enough in snake restaurants and had once watched as one crushed then swallowed a small bird on the Peak. This snake must have fallen into the smooth-sided *nullah* and could not get out. If it continued down the *nullah* it would reach a storm culvert and escape. If it headed uphill, it would arrive at several blocks of apartments and, I was certain, a place on the supper table in one of the servants' quarters. It was facing uphill.

A stick was needed to turn the snake. I found one of a sufficient length in the undergrowth, knelt down on the edge of the *nullah* and attempted to force the snake's head round to face the way to safety. I had given it a few prods when it reared up, spread its hood and spat at me.

This was no common rat snake. It was a cobra.

I recoiled, a smear of slimy venom on my shirt. Very carefully, so as not to touch it, I removed the garment and dropped it on the path. At this moment, two boys from my class arrived on the scene. We debated what to do. The primitive and illogical fear of snakes welled up in us. That cobras fed on rats and rats spread disease to humans was forgotten. This was the devil in serpent form, the creature that had tempted Adam – we had had Bible Studies in school – and seduced Eve, whatever that meant.

A decision was made. Like Stephen in the Bible, we would stone it to death.

Gathering as many large stones as we could find, we commenced hurling them at the snake. Some found their mark, most did not. All the while, the snake raised its head, the hood spread to show the black-and-white ghost-like pattern of a face on its surface.

We had been at this endeavour for five minutes or so when two coolies carrying poles over their shoulders came trotting down the hill. They looked over the edge of the *nullah*. The cobra seemed

slightly wounded. One coolie dangled a coil of rope in front of the cobra's head. It struck at it then pressed its head to the *nullah* floor. The other coolie, signalling us to stand back, reached down into the *nullah*, grabbed the cobra by its tail, swung it up in the air and slammed it down on the concrete pathway. It was dead. They coiled it up, tied it with twine, hung it from one of their poles and set off down the hill. I walked home, ashamed that I had taken part in this assassination and vowing never to kill a snake again. Except in self defence.

My only other dangerous and somewhat farcical encounter occurred one evening on the Old Peak Road, a very steep footpath that wound down the mountain to the city below. Until the Second World War, it had been used extensively by sedan chairs and coolies but had fallen into disuse, the undergrowth on either side encroaching upon it, sometimes covering it completely. My reason for going down it was that someone had told me a Tokay gecko lived in the vicinity of the junction with Barker Road and was best seen at sunset when it appeared to go hunting.

The world's biggest gecko, at seven inches in length when fully grown, the Tokay gecko was spectacular, a light brown with red, white and black spots. Its call, a distinctive *tock-aye*, gave it its name. It was also very rare, mainly because it was a highly prized local entrée.

I had descended as far as Barker Road when I heard a noise behind me that sounded like someone rattling several half-empty boxes of matches. Turning, I found a fully grown porcupine coming at me in reverse, all its quills upright and a-quiver. I stood my ground, not thinking it would press home its advance. Yet it did, accelerating in my direction. I clapped my hands and shouted – to no avail. I fled. The porcupine, although not overhauling me, at least kept pace. The angle of ascent soon told on me. I slowed. The porcupine continued its attack. Moving backwards up a 1 in 3

slope seemed not to bother it. I found a new lease of fear and reached the level ground by the observation point. The porcupine stopped at the roadside and faced me. Now that I could see it clearly, it was huge, three feet long and bulky. Its nose was blunt, like a beaver's, its quills black and white. It shivered. The quills rattled. Then it was off, running clumsily down Harlech Road and into the twilight. It was only later that a Chinese friend of my mother's told me that porcupines could kill a leopard cat with their quills.

I was not only grateful to have avoided a leopard cat's fate but also glad no-one had witnessed the confrontation. The loss of face would have been mortifying.

There were only two ways to reach the top of the Peak, discounting walking up the Old Peak Road which would test the stamina of a marine. One was by car or bus, the other by the Peak Tram.

Built in 1888, this was the world's steepest funicular railway and it operated on the simplest of systems. A long and well-greased steel cable was wrapped around a massive drum in the engine house at the top. On each end was a tram car. As one travelled down the mountain, so the other rose up it. At the halfway point, the track divided in two so that the cars might pass each other. The only snag was that there were more stations in the lower half of the route than the upper. Consequently, when the lower car stopped at one of the stations, the upper car would halt in the middle of nowhere, surrounded by sub-tropical forest and birdsong.

The tram car was of unique design. Constructed of varnished wood on a steel frame and chassis, the uphill portion was an

enclosed cabin. This was where Europeans or wealthy Chinese travelled. Other Chinese passengers, with the exception of baby amahs and their charges, were obliged to ride in the rear half which, although it was roofed, was otherwise open to the elements.

Whenever I could, I chose the rear portion. One just climbed on and sat down. There were no side walls, no restraining ropes, no safety bars. The only thing to hold on to was an armrest. Just before leaving the lower terminus on Garden Road, a tinny bell rang three times, there was a pause and the car edged forwards, running alongside a *nullah* and the Helena May Institute where, my mother frequently and convincingly but inaccurately remarked, Margot Fonteyn had taken her first ballet lesson. The single track then started to climb more steeply. To request it to stop, one pressed a labelled button; for boarding, one just put one's hand out to hail the brakeman.

All the while, the gradient increased. Above Bowen Road the angle of ascent was at least forty-five degrees. The May Road station, just below the halfway passing place, was at the steepest point. Here, when the car stopped, it yo-yo-ed alarmingly as the long steel cable flexed. Of necessity, it was elastic. This bouncing always set tourists chattering or American sailors chortling with alcohol-fuelled hilarity. Boarding or dismounting was difficult and one had to wait until the car stopped moving. Uphill from the May Road platform was a small signal box in which a man changed the points at the passing place. From here the tram car trundled steadily upwards, entering a cutting and turning a long bend in the middle of what was essentially sub-tropical jungle. This is where it would sometimes stop to accommodate the other car in a lower station. Huge butterflies would flit through the open rear, birds dance and jump in the tree branches. I once saw a small python sliding through the undergrowth, much to the

frustration of my fellow amah and coolie passengers who could not disembark and catch it for the pot.

I grew blasé about the Peak Tram, for I took it as commonly as most people might a bus. The view, the harbour a backdrop at the top of the windows, the slopes of the Peak and the buildings apparently leaning backwards at a bizarre angle, were everyday phenomena.

The comments made by the tourists and American sailors were as predictable as sunrise: 'Hey, you guys! You bin on the rides at Coney Island?' At a mid-jungle halt: 'OK! Y'all out 'n' push!' At the elastic stage: 'How many times you reckon this baby's snapped?' To the brakeman leaning on a dead man's handle, who spoke not a word of even pidgin English: 'Ya hold that baby real tight now, y'hear?' On any number of occasions, I was asked if I was the British Ambassador's son, to which I replied haughtily that Britain did not need a Hong Kong embassy because we owned the place.

The Peak Tram being one of Hong Kong's tourist attractions, it was also frequented by celebrities. I rode it with The Ink Spots, a famous black American jazz quartet; the film star Danny Kaye and the English actor Jon Pertwee who later became *Dr Who*. They never really impressed me: they were just people whose autographs my mother insisted I request. One day in 1954, however, was different. My mother met me after school at the Peak Tram terminus to take me down to the city. I forget why. As we waited for the next tram, a notice declared that Barker Road station was temporarily closed. When the car arrived, we boarded it, sitting in the open coolie section at my request, which was at the front of the car on its descent. My mother did not complain. It was a hot afternoon.

The tram set off. Barker Road station approached. It was thronged with people. A bright light switched on as we drew near.

The car stopped in the station. Someone appeared briefly with a clapper board. Another called, 'Action!' A man in a light-coloured suit detached himself from the crowd, walked down the platform and entered the cabin. The tram set off. The powerful light switched off. My mother put her hand on mine. It was quivering.

'That's Clark Gable!' she whispered.

And it was. He was shooting a film called *Soldier of Fortune*.

She scrabbled in my school bag, took out an exercise book, tore a page from it, fumbled in her handbag for a pen, then said the obvious.

'Martin, get his autograph.'

'You get his autograph.'

'I can't,' she fumed. 'I'm a grown up. You get it.'

'You tore a page out of my exercise book,' I complained. 'I'll get into trouble for that.'

'I'll square it with your teacher. Now get his autograph.'

'I don't want it.'

'He's one of the biggest film stars in the world.'

I remained unmoved. She grabbed my arm.

'Get his bloody autograph,' she threatened *sotto voce*, her lips tight. 'If you don't . . .'

'What if I do?' I parried. It seemed I might as well take advantage of the situation.

The Peak Tram reached May Road station and bounced on its cable for a minute. Clark Gable stood up, disembarked and walked off into a crowd of film people. The tram carried on down the mountain.

'Just for that,' my mother said peevishly, 'we're not going to Tkachenko's.' A thought then occurred to her. 'Maybe we'll be in the background as he got on.'

When it was released, we went to the cinema several times to see the film. We did not feature in it.

Apart from the vehicular ferry, and the walla-walla boats which were expensive, the only way to reach Hong Kong island from the mainland of Kowloon was by the Star Ferry, universally known as 'the ferry', which plied, every fifteen minutes for eighteen hours a day, across the mile-wide harbour from Tsim Sha Tsui to Central District, as the heart of Hong Kong's business world was called. As on the Peak Tram, the passengers were segregated, the wealthy and well-to-do – Chinese and European – travelling on the enclosed top deck, the rabble of coolies, amahs and others on the bottom – open to the elements – with their poles, boxes, bales and large, circular baskets of complaining chickens. To cross the harbour on the upper deck cost ten cents one way: the lower cost five.

I looked forward to taking the ferry. The craft would have to weave between warships at anchor, with Chinese women in rocking sampans painting the hulls or collecting the garbage. Cargo ships under a harbour pilot's control slid by like mobile cliffs of black metal, eager faces at open portholes. The ferry had to give way to sail and oar so it was common for it to slow to a crawl or change course mid-harbour to allow passage to an ocean-going junk in full sail heading for the open sea. On one occasion, the ferry on which I was riding had to stop for a massive junk flying the Communist Chinese flag and armed with two small cannon mounted on her stern. It really was a case of the eighteenth meeting the twentieth century.

Whilst the ferries themselves were perfectly safe, I had my doubts about the ferry piers. Constructed of a wooden deck on wooden piles, they creaked and swayed dizzily as a vessel came alongside. The piles screeched, the deck planking moaned like lost

souls and everyone waiting to board swayed unsteadily. What was more toe-curling was the fact that there were gaps between the planks. Twice, I accidentally dropped my pocket money down them, only to see the coins hit the water below and sink without trace. Not that I would have accepted them back, for the harbour was notoriously dirty – the Kowloon sewers emptied into it – and, one day, pushing through a crowd of Chinese peering down through the cracks between the planks, I saw a dead coolie floating under the pier. He was face down, bare to the waist, his arms rising and falling with the rhythm of the wavelets. In the centre of his back, halfway down his spine, was a hole, washed clean of blood by the sea. I could see his vertebrae. Schools of small fish hovered around him. A small crab rode on his shoulder. According to the Radio Hong Kong news that evening, he had been murdered with a baling hook.

My mother and I frequently rode the bottom deck.

'Let's rough it,' she would say, approaching the coolie turnstile. 'See how the other half live.'

We boarded the ferry, the gangplank moving to and fro as the vessel rocked on the waves. There were few seats on the lower deck and invariably, these were occupied by amahs who ran for them the minute they stepped on the deck. A running amah, dressed in her white jacket and black trousers, looked for all the world like an intoxicated penguin.

As the ferry set sail for the mile-long crossing, a mist of spume blew across the deck. Amahs carrying babies on their backs in cotton slings faced into the wind to protect their infants. Coolies removed the lengths of cloth they customarily wore like grubby cravats and rubbed their glistening muscles with them. My mother closed her eyes and let the spray cool her face. I, heedful of a bi-lingual notice on the bulkhead, watched out for pick-pockets.

Another notice bluntly stated, *No Spitting*. The 'other half' had a habit of spitting to clear their throats of phlegm or catarrh. They also blew their noses by thumbing one nostril shut and then, leaning forward over the gutter, blowing hard. Consequently, it was commonplace to see gobs of pale green snot lying by the side of the road alongside cracked melon seed shells and chewed wedges of sugar cane. The concept of a handkerchief was alien to the Chinese. It seemed utterly ridiculous to them to blow one's nose then put the contents in one's pocket. Whilst spitting and hawking were disgusting habits, I had to agree with their logic and tried blowing my own nose in a similar fashion, yet I never mastered the knack. The snot came out all right but it dribbled as slime down to my lips and chin instead of flying free.

Once, I tried to get my father to see how the common man travelled on the ferry but he steadfastly refused. I asked why.

'If God had intended me to be a coolie,' he replied tersely, 'he'd've given me a bamboo pole.'

'But God doesn't give the coolies poles. They buy them.'

'It's a metaphor,' my father replied.

'What's a metaphor?' I answered.

'Do shut up, Martin,' was my father's response. 'Remember, it's better to keep your mouth closed and be thought a fool than open your mouth and prove it.'

I shut up, boarded the top deck and moved the seat back over so we were facing forwards. The seating was designed so that whichever way the ferry was going, one could face the direction of travel.

Several weeks later, I informed a guest at one of my parents' cocktail parties that a coolie's pole was called a metaphor. He kindly put me right and I vowed henceforth not to trust my father's sketchy knowledge of matters Oriental.

Although there was both the local and BBC World Service radio, and the cinema, I tended to make my own entertainment. My imagination was sharp and I had the whole of the Peak on which to ramble. As long as I kept clear of steep drops, rock faces and slippery surfaces, I was safe. No-one would molest me or accost me unless it was to pass the time of day. One of the constables who did duty in the police post took to engaging me in conversation. He was keen to learn English in order, I presumed, to get a red number flash on his shoulder, which indicated he was reasonably fluent in it. Everyone else I met would greet me, from the coolies carrying massive sacks suspended from their poles to the briefcase-toting *taipans* walking down in the damp morning mist to the Peak Tram.

One elderly European, always dressed in a grey suit with a gold watch chain, would be carried to the Peak Tram in a sedan chair, probably the last to be used in Hong Kong. It was a curious-looking contraption, a sort of mockery of an ecclesiastical throne made out of dark varnished rattan. If it was raining, the rattan was encased in a black custom-made canvas cover. The square roof, rather like those found on small shrines, was curled at the corners. Supported on two long bamboo poles, the chair was carried by two coolies. They had to walk in step to prevent their passenger rocking from side to side. At each step, the rattan creaked rhythmically, the occupant moving slightly up and down as the poles bent. Arriving at the Peak Tram terminus, the coolies knelt on the road, the rear coolie first, and lowered the poles. Their passenger stepped out and, without a word to the two men who had just transported him, walked off to catch the tram. He would, however, greet everyone else who was not Chinese,

including me, with a gruff, almost begrudging, good morning. The Chinese he ignored as if they were made of vapour.

This I considered the height of ill manners and was of a mind to address the man on the subject, but he carried a gold-topped cane and I knew, from experience at home, what that could do to my buttocks or the backs of my thighs. And, on the other hand, the coolies seemed inured to his rudeness. Once, I followed them to see if I could have a ride and find out where they spent their day, but they disappeared through an imposing gate which was closed behind them. They were not for hire.

Public entertainment was limited, not through any law but because most people were too busy earning a living. Yet every Chinese New Year, temporary stages were erected on waste ground around Hong Kong for the presentation of Chinese operas.

The stages were marvels of Oriental ingenuity. Made of thousands of bamboo poles lashed together with strips of the same material, they could be a hundred feet wide, forty deep, fully roofed with canvas or *atap* panels and equipped with electric lights. The audience remained in the open, unprotected from the elements. Rather like the theatre in Shakespeare's day, the clientele talked, drank, ate (even cooked) during the performance, which could last six hours. The actors dressed in flamboyant classical Chinese costumes in primary colours and wore heavy, stylized make-up. They sang in very high-pitched voices, their movements exaggerated and carefully choreographed.

I enjoyed these spectacles, but not for too long. The falsetto singing prompted a headache in fifteen minutes and a migraine in thirty. What six hours would do beggared even my imagination. What I really enjoyed were the fights. Swords, pikestaffs and other weapons of bodily pain and torture were flashed and swung, the combatants whirling and ducking, thrusting and slicing while

all the time the orchestra was going frantic, cymbals clashing as swords met, gongs booming when the main protagonists struck each other a mortal blow. It was controlled mayhem and I loved it.

Bedlam could also be experienced, admittedly for a shorter period, at my favourite entertainment venue, The China Fleet Club in Wanchai, an infamous area of tenements, cheap hotels, tattoo parlours, Triad gangsters, bars and bordellos. It was the land of Suzie Wong.

Close to the naval dockyard, The China Fleet Club was a social club established, as the title page of its programme proudly stated, *with funds contributed by the men of the lower deck – to whom this club belongs*. It was operated by Royal Navy sailors for their comrades and incorporated several bars, a restaurant, sleeping accommodation, a barber's shop, billiards room and a cinema. As the offspring of a parent attached to the armed forces, albeit as a civilian worker, I was permitted to go to the club cinema for Saturday matinées.

The main feature seldom interested me. What I went for were the cartoon preliminaries, and one in particular – *Tom and Jerry*. I was not alone. Sailors, many of them hung-over from a night on the Wanchai tiles, crammed into the seats, jostling, arm-punching and ribbing each other. As soon as the lights went down, the National Anthem was played. They all stood up. It ended. They sat down and the noise and kerfuffle began again. The screen came alive with the Pathé news. For this, the audience fell silent. Newsreels showed the colonial uprisings Britain was facing – Cyprus, Kenya, Malaya – soldiers fighting, struggling through jungle, advancing through rubber plantations or sun-baked rocky hills, dying. The screen went black. For a minute or two, the memory of the pictures of war kept the peace. Then someone would shout out.

'Where's Fred?'

Other voices would join in.

'Give us Fred!'

'We want Fred! We want Fred!'

Feet would start to stamp, hands clap and mouths hoot like owls or bay like wolves.

If the screen lit up with a Donald Duck or Woody the Woodpecker cartoon, all hell would break loose. The floor would vibrate as if an army were marching over it, the air thick with whistles and indignation. If, however, the cartoon was *Tom and Jerry*, the sailors would fall silent until the captions gave the name of the producer, then they all yelled 'Good old Fred!' in unison. The producer's name was Fred Quimby. Throughout the cartoon, guttural, masculine, lower-deck mess laughter greeted every twist in the tale.

About noon, after the matinée ended, I sometimes strolled through Wanchai, passing the bars with their bamboo bead curtains, young women standing in the doorways with bottles of Coke, smoking Lucky Strikes. Once or twice, I tried to enter one of these bars but was rebuffed by the girls at the door, never mind the barmen within. Either they were brusque and ordered me out, sometimes all but manhandling me to the door, or they accepted my presence, asking me if I *wanted jig-a-jig*, which sent everyone but myself into paroxysms of hilarity. I thought it all a bit of a liberty. I meant no harm, only wanted a drink and a bit of conversation but found myself either an outcast or the butt of incomprehensible humour. What was more, they all touched my hair. I gave them luck. Yet they would not so much as sell me a Green Spot. It was some years before I understood how the young women in the beaded curtain doorways of Wanchai made their living.

This aside, Wanchai did not appeal to me. The streets were

sombre and lacked the vivacity of the rest of Hong Kong. Certainly, they were usually crowded, but there were few *dai pai dongs*, the streets were laid out in a severe, American-style grid pattern, the newer buildings square and characterless concrete blocks. There were no dried prawn or fish shops, no vendors of preserved eggs or rice, no little temples tucked away in back streets.

I mentioned to my mother that Wanchai seemed to lack soul.

'Maybe it's because it's on reclaimed land,' she remarked.

'Reclaimed land?'

'They knock a mountain down, pour it into the sea, let it settle and then build on it. Hong Kong hasn't got much land space, so they make more of it in this way.'

I could only wonder how they knocked down a mountain.

From the time my mother's mother was widowed in 1947, she had not left Portsmouth or, save to go to the shops, her tiny terraced house, and was living on a very meagre state pension. To give her a much needed holiday, my parents arranged for her to visit us, 'indulging' on an RFA vessel.

'Indulgence' was a quaint military arrangement dating back to the days when naval spouses accompanied their husbands aboard ship. By 1953, it meant that, if there was a spare cabin on a ship, it could be rented to a close relative of a serving officer for a nominal sum. The passenger had to take pot luck, however: departure and arrival dates were speculative. If the vessel was diverted *en route*, the passenger went with it. It was a potential military magical mystery tour.

My mother decided it would be best if my grandmother visited

in the spring. She was sixty-four and it was considered that she would find the heat and humidity of the high summer debilitating. A request was put in to the Admiralty in London and my grandmother was found a berth upon the RFA *Bacchus*, a tiny, shallow-draft ship with a crew of about forty, which had been built as a sea water distilling vessel but was now used as a freighter carrying naval stores. My grandmother was listed on the ship's manifest as super-cargo.

The *Bacchus* arrived alongside HMS *Tamar* on the morning of 14 March 1954. My grandmother walked unsteadily down the gangplank, holding on to both side ropes. She looked a lot older and more frail than when I had seen her last. She was wearing a dark blue dress, a cardigan, an overcoat and heavy, flat shoes. Even her leather handbag looked cumbersome. All the elderly women I had met in Hong Kong – even my headmistress – dressed in light clothing, in bright colours, and walked with a spring in their step.

'Nanny's not sick, is she?' I enquired of my father as my mother ran to the foot of the gangplank, tripping like a little girl and embracing her mother.

'No,' replied my father, who intensely disliked his mother-in-law. 'She's as fit as an old fiddle.' I detected a slight hint of wishful thinking.

'But she looks so old and ill,' I said.

'That's what England does to you,' he retorted bitterly.

For all his imperial, monarchist jingoism, my father loathed Britain – 'the lousy benighted weather . . . the bloody taxes . . . the blithering idiots running the unions . . . the bloody strikes . . . the blithering idiots running the government, the country . . .' – with a vengeance and yet he never felt really at home in Hong Kong.

Later that day, as my grandmother unpacked her suitcase, I related our brief conversation to my mother.

'Nanny's not ill,' she told me, 'but she's very tired. Living in England is not easy . . .' Her voice trailed off and she kissed me. 'Be nice to Nanny. She's had a rough time of it since Dan-Dan died.'

Staying for just under three weeks, my grandmother's time was filled with cocktail parties, Chinese banquets, shopping outings (which bedazzled her, coming from utilitarian Britain) and a drive round the New Territories, on which there was a near replay of my father's encounter with the duck farmer incident, this time involving a man with two huge sway-backed pigs, who refused to chivvy them on to the grass verge. I showed my grandmother the ancient Dragon Inn tortoise whilst the Dragon Inn monkey showed us a sizeable and bright pink erection which brought tears of mirth to my grandmother's eyes. My mother also took her in a rickshaw to Hing Loon where Mr Chan gave her a beer and she bought a string of pearls, to tea in the Pen (with sufficient funds this time), to Mr Chuk's establishment for new clothes, to the United Services Recreation Club for lunch, to the dockyard mess for dinner. It was a social whirl the likes of which my grandmother had never known.

One afternoon's excursion was to the Tiger Balm Gardens. These had been created in the 1930s by a Chinese multi-millionaire called Aw Boon Haw who had made his fortune from inventing and manufacturing Tiger Balm. What my grandmother had expected – as, indeed, had I – was a formal garden of flowerbeds, fountains, trees, lawns and notices keeping visitors off the grass. Instead, paths wound through rock grottoes, passing caves hacked out of the mountainside. Each cave housed a fantastical tableau featuring life-sized figures fashioned out of plaster or concrete and painted in garish colours. What made these tableaux even more bizarre was the fact that many of them depicted men being cast into Hell, their stomachs ripped open,

their hands cut off, the stumps of their wrists scarlet with blood, as well as executions and scenes of the most vile torture imaginable. In one, a man was being consumed by a tiger, his face contorted with pain.

'Why do they want to portray such beastly happenings?' my grandmother mused.

My mother shrugged and said, 'I suppose they're a warning of what will happen if you stray from the straight and narrow. And the Chinese can be a very brutal people.'

'And you've chosen to live amongst these people?' my grandmother finally asked, passing a larger-than-life statue of a man with a dog's head and huge ears.

'Don't be silly, Mum,' my mother retorted. 'All mankind's like that. Think of the Germans and the concentration camps. Think of the Brandenburg PoW camp Dad was held in during the first war.'

'I don't choose to live in Germany,' my grandmother replied tersely.

Towering over the gardens, and an opulent mansion once the home of Aw Boon Haw, was an exquisite white pagoda. Seven storeys high, it was visible from virtually anywhere in the harbour.

'And look at that,' my grandmother continued. 'Such beauty next to such an abhorrence.'

'Maybe that's to emphasize how beautiful life can be if you don't sin,' my mother suggested.

My mother greatly enjoyed sharing her colonial life with her mother. It was not that she wanted to brag about her new existence, in which she felt so at ease, but that she wanted to share it with someone she loved. For my father, Hong Kong was just another place in which to work: he might just as well have been posted to a supplies office in Chatham as China.

I too revelled in showing my grandmother the Hong Kong I

knew. Walking round Harlech and Lugard roads, I was quick to point out a butterfly, a blue-tailed skink, a giant snail. I took her to the rifle range and dug out a bullet for her. It had been my intention to take her to Pinewood Battery, but the walk was too much for her. I also took her on the Peak Tram, sitting in the open section. To my surprise, this frightened her. My parents drew the line at my taking her to eat out at a *dai pai dong*.

My grandmother's brief visit made me aware of how much I had changed. Sitting beside her on a bench along Harlech Road one afternoon, I recalled my life 'back home' in England, the cinder playground at Rose Valley School, the compost heap at the bottom of our garden which was my castle, the antiquated tractor that drew the gang mower on the nearby playing fields, the incessantly grey skies and that damp dog smell of drizzle-sodden pullovers. When a coolie trotted by and I returned his greeting in Cantonese, and my grandmother commented that I was now 'a proper little Chinese boy', I felt strangely proud. This was, I now understood, where I wanted to be. For me, 'back home' meant an apartment on the Peak with a world-famous view, not a semi-detached at the end of a cul-de-sac on the eastern fringes of London.

When the time came for my grandmother to depart, my mother was sad yet her mother was, I am sure, perplexed. She had arrived in Hong Kong to discover her daughter and grandson had in her eyes 'gone native' in all but clothing – and, even then, my mother occasionally wore a brocade cheongsam with modest side slits as a cocktail dress. It was light blue with pale green bamboo designs upon it, finches perching on the stems. I felt full of pride seeing her wear it. Most European women looked like a sack of sago pudding in a Chinese dress, with prominent bulges where there should most definitely not have been any, but my mother was petite, lithe and slim and fitted such clothing better than most *gweipor*.

I imagine that my grandmother realized, as the ship edged away from the dock, that she would rarely see her only child and grandchild again. Such was the lot of the colonial family whose existence was punctuated by partings. She knew that she was condemned to a lonely widowhood, looking out for the postman delivering a blue aerogramme or an envelope with exotic stamps upon it.

As the months went by, I came to learn a great deal more about the Peak, which for many years had been exclusively set aside as a European residential area. No Chinese was permitted to buy, rent or live there and the only Chinese allowed access were those who served the Europeans. By the time we lived there this law had been relaxed, but one clause, which forbade a Chinese from owning or operating a business on the Peak, was still in force.

There was, however, one exception to it. A Chinese lady owned and ran the café opposite the Peak Tram terminus.

A low, single-storey stone building with a tiled roof, originally erected in 1901 as a shelter for the sedan chair and rickshaw coolies, the Peak Café was an unpretentious place consisting of one large dining room under a roof criss-crossed with old wooden beams. The menu was unassuming, offering toast (naturally), sandwiches and eggs and bacon as well as Chinese food, soft drinks, sundaes, beer and tea and coffee, ice-creams and popsicles. The latter could also be purchased from itinerant Dairy Farm ice-cream sellers riding silver-painted bicycles with cold boxes mounted over the front wheel. The popsicles were made in fruit flavours as well as milk, soya milk and red bean paste, which looked enticing but was an acquired taste which I never acquired.

Every day during term time, my mother gave me a dollar bill with which to buy a drink on my way back from school. The temperature was often in the eighties Fahrenheit, the heat bouncing off the mirage-liquid road surface, so I frequently forewent a Coke and had two ten-cent 'popsies' instead, thereby saving eighty cents a day. However, by artful manipulation of human character, I was frequently able to save the money completely.

Although the Korean War was all but over, Hong Kong was still experiencing a very large through-put of military personnel, especially Americans. Like all tourists, they would head up the Peak Tram to marvel at the view.

The Peak Café did a roaring trade when the US fleet was in. As soon as the sailors had taken in the panorama, they seemed programmed to need a beer and there was only one place to go. Yet before they could order a bottle of the local San Miguel beer, I would ambush them, leaning on the wall by the entrance to the café and panting with thirst. My face would be conveniently flushed from the heat and the walk from my school, my shirt sticking to my back. Within a few minutes, an American sailor would pause at my side and say something like, 'Hey, kid! How ya doin'?'

'Tuckered,' I would reply, using a word picked up in the Fourseas with which they would be familiar. I wiped my brow with my forearm.

'Sure is hot! Ya wanna Coke, kid?'

And I was in, seated at a table under a ceiling fan with a condensation-coated bottle of Coke, a waxed straw and the dollar bill still secure in my pocket. Our conversation ranged widely. They wanted to know where I came from, where I lived, what my father did for a job and had I any big sisters. These preliminaries over, they would embark upon their own life stories. I listened

avidly. The sailors came from all over America, from every background. A black sailor told me how his grandfather had been a slave. A lieutenant – he pronounced it *lootenant* – from New York made me believe he was the son of a gangster. A Texan remembered the *corrida* and the *remuda*, and pined for the open range. Many may have told me tall stories, but I came to appreciate that a man may tell a stranger far more than he could his best friend.

This was not my only lesson in human nature. Ordinary sailors and non-commissioned officers were far more generous than commissioned officers who were usually only good for a drink – if that. Americans were by far the most generous. Next came the Australians, then Canadians and, finally, the British, who ignored me. No army squaddie ever offered me so much as a glass of water.

My sojourns at the Peak Café came to an abrupt end one day when the proprietor came out and shoo-ed me away.

'You no good boy,' she criticized me in very competent English. 'You like a beggar, always hanging round to get something from the sailors.' She shook her finger at me. 'But no more. You come here again, I tell your mother. I know where you live,' she threatened unnecessarily. The Peak community was not much more than a few thousand people and most of them used the Peak Tram on a very frequent basis. Accosting my mother would have been easy.

I apologized to her in Cantonese and thereafter took to buying a drink or a ten-cent popsy, if I needed one, from one of the bicycle vendors. She lost out on my custom yet I had saved over forty dollars in two terms.

My father's principal hobby, as my mother frequently declared with no small display of chagrin, was sleeping. He would return from the office at noon on Saturday and then, except for meals, the BBC World News and to replenish his glass of whisky or pink gin, he would essentially stay in bed until Monday morning. At first, my mother tried hard to get him to take an interest in life outside his work, but without success. On only a few occasions did he surrender to my mother's sense of adventure.

One of these was her desire to visit Sunshine Island, or Chow Kung Chau. To reach it, one had to take a ferry to Peng Chau then hire a *kai doh*, a sampan with a hunch-backed old woman and a long oar or a superannuated walla-walla past its best. Audacious my mother may have been but to risk life and limb drifting without a walkie-talkie in the open sea, towards a Communist Chinese-held shore, was another matter.

However, one winter Sunday, a naval launch was requisitioned by a party of my father's dockyard colleagues to visit Sunshine Island and have a picnic. Or so I was informed . . .

A hilly island about three-quarters of a mile long by a third wide, Sunshine Island had been settled by a few farmers, fishermen and, in the nineteenth century, pirates, but abandoned since 1941. It was now home to two European families, one headed by an eccentric, the other by a China Hand driven by God to help his fellow man.

I was reluctant to go but my mother persuaded me with embroidered tales of the pirates. My father was enticed along by the prospect of being on a boat, which brought out the sailor in him.

At the appointed time, we stepped on to the launch in the dockyard basin and cast off. The harbour was fairly calm but we had to cross open sea which was choppy. One or two of our party of fifteen started to look green about the gills but managed to

retain the coffee and biscuits that were served as we rounded Green Island.

My mother, dressed in an old shirt of my father's, a large pullover and a pair of jeans, enjoyed the crossing, as did my father, who, wearing a pair of neatly creased trousers with a cravat at his throat, persuaded the Chinese coxswain to relinquish the wheel to him once we were out of the harbour. The coxswain, assuming a naval *gweilo* would be familiar with the manoeuvring of a launch, agreed but soon regretted it when he noticed my father was heading straight for the wrong island. Not having the courage to admonish him, the coxswain mentioned it to Alec Borrie, a thin, tall, friendly man who was not only the trip's organizer but also my father's divisional superior – his Old Man.

'I think we need to go a few degrees to port, Ken,' he said quietly. 'You're on a heading for Peng Chau.'

My father looked extremely sheepish and altered course. A few minutes later, he surrendered the wheel once more to the coxswain and busied himself with his binoculars.

I noticed on these occasions that my father was often left out of the conversation and he seldom sought to join in. Sometimes, I felt sorry for him and wanted to go over and talk to him but, at the last moment, I would decide against it, knowing that I would be put down, dismissed or derided.

An hour out, we swung in to a small beach on the leeward side of a windswept, treeless island. The coxswain ran the bow of the launch up on the shore and a crew member sent out a gangplank. Boxes were unloaded and placed at the top of the beach. We all then went ashore and the launch reversed away. I felt marooned.

Carrying our boxes, we set off along a hint of a footpath across the island, coming first to an *atap*, a wood and straw hut. This was the home of Jack Shepherd, aka Jonathan Sly, of whom I had read in the newspaper. Formerly one of the managers of the Kowloon

YMCA, he now lived with his wife in this hovel, making a meagre living writing short stories for the local press. As we drew near, he appeared at the door. Skinny, with short hair and a trim beard, he was barefoot and wearing an ordinary shirt with a dark blue Chinese padded silk jacket. Wrapped around his waist was a multi-hued Malay *sarong*. This was a man who had really 'gone native'. Compared to him, I thought, the Queen of Kowloon was verging on normality. He greeted us in a gruff, monosyllabic voice and closed the door.

My father looked disparagingly at the figure as it disappeared.

'He's certainly letting the side down,' he remarked to no-one in particular. 'Thank God he's doing it out of sight.'

'Frankly,' piped up one of the women who had overheard him, 'I think individuality is a trait to be encouraged.'

My father was about to remonstrate but my mother got him first.

'You do realize, don't you, Ken,' she said, looking pointedly at his feet, 'that you've got on one of your best pairs of shoes? I hope you've got some others with you,' she added, knowing full well he had not.

'Standards,' he responded, glancing at what the rest of us were wearing. 'I'm not wearing pumps or clodhoppers. Or jeans trousers, come to that,' he added: there had been an argument over those before we left the apartment.

'On your own head be it, Ken.' My mother shrugged.

My father, determined to have the last word, said, 'This isn't the Western Front, Joyce.'

'I don't think our brave Tommies in either war wore denim jeans,' my mother retorted, grabbing the last word for herself.

My father silenced, we walked on, descending into the valley between the two hills where more *atap* huts stood amid some newly tilled plots. This, my mother informed me, was the home

and dream-child of a remarkable Christian activist called Gus Borgeest.

Like so many in Hong Kong, Borgeest, his Chinese wife and their small daughter had arrived in 1951 as penniless refugees, in their case from Hangzhou. A Quaker, he was a humanist, which is what had endeared him to my mother who was not religiously inclined at all. At first, Borgeest had worked for the Hong Kong government social services department and came to appreciate first-hand the plight of the thousands of squatters and street-sleepers. It dawned on him that many had been farmers in China who had lost their land and livelihoods to communization. In them, he reasoned, was a workforce that merely required a chance to rise up above poverty and contribute to society.

Agricultural land being at a premium in Hong Kong, Borgeest turned his attention to the outlying islands. Chow Kung Chau provided what he required. He took out a lease upon it from the government at an annual rent of $180, less than the average servant's monthly wage, moving there and renaming it Sunshine Island. By the time we walked into the valley, the embryonic community consisted of the Borgeests, two Chinese associates and several families of impoverished Chinese farmers.

We were all introduced to Borgeest and given a short talk on his aims and ambitions. This over, we were taken on a quick tour of the centre of the island, interrupted by such expressions as 'Here will be the piggery' or 'This is the site of the fish ponds'. All I could see was a bleak, rock-strewn, grassy hillside with, here and there, plots marked out with white-painted stakes.

Pondering on the contents of the picnic, not to mention evidence of the pirates' occupation, my day-dreaming was interrupted when two of the launch crew strode over the crest of the hill carrying shining new hoes, spades, forks and other implements of manual labour.

They put them down and returned to the launch. Mr Borrie assumed charge and briskly divided us into work parties. It was then I realized my mother had brought me to the island under false pretences. I spent the remainder of the day helping to dig a ditch, carting the soil away in a bucket. The only relief from this toil was a sparse supply of sandwiches and a bottle of lukewarm Coke. We left the island at five o'clock. My back ached, my arms and legs were sore, I had a blister on my palm the size of a ten-cent coin and another to match on my heel, which had burst.

'The strain of honest toil,' my mother remarked, rubbing the base of her spine as we waited for my father, who was limping, to bring the car. He had spent the afternoon in charge of a wheel-barrow. 'Doesn't it make you feel good?'

'No,' I replied pointedly. It was not just that my every muscle ached. I had been duped by talk of piracy into becoming a forced labourer. 'And I didn't see any trace of pirates.'

'But think of the good you've done. You've helped those far less fortunate than yourself to start rebuilding their lives.'

Put that way, I felt smugly self-righteous.

'You have to realize this,' my mother continued. 'We do not own Hong Kong. It's a crown colony. We merely administer it. A hundred and something years ago, we stole this land from the Chinese. Because of that, we owe an obligation to the people who live here. And think. Many of them have fled here from Communism. They are refugees. We must help them. In a tiny way, that's what you've done today. And,' she went on, 'even if you don't agree with me, at least we've ruined a pair of your father's best shoes.'

She put her arm round me and gave me a hug. It hurt.

I began to range further afield than the Peak. My mother's life was filled with Cantonese classes and her usual daily social whirl. My father, of course, was engaged in his office, often not returning until well into the evening.

Having been rebuffed from Wanchai, I decided to head in the opposite direction and see what Western District had to offer.

The oldest part of the city, it clung to the lower slopes of the Peak beneath an almost sheer rock face that glistened with water in all but the hottest and driest of summers. Many of the streets were narrow, built for coolie rather than car traffic, whilst many of those that ran north to south up the mountainside consisted of steps. Those vehicular roads that ran parallel to them were very steep indeed with sharp corners that tested many a clutch and burnt out not a few. The ladder streets, as the stepped thorough-fares were called, tested the calf muscles. Along all the streets, the buildings were ancient, some a century old, with ornate balconies from which projected the ubiquitous bamboo poles of dripping, freshly laundered clothes or from which hung tresses of plants. Some were almost entirely hidden by garishly painted shop signs hanging out over the pavement.

My first visit to the area was prompted by my wish to see a famous temple which stood on the curiously named Hollywood Road. Claiming to be the son of a guest, I acquired a tourist-guide map from the concierge of a hotel and made my way along Queen's Road West. At first, the buildings were modern office blocks and stores but, gradually, as if by some strange natural metamorphosis, they changed into narrow nineteenth-century buildings.

Dodging coolies slogging up the ladder streets with full loads hanging from their poles, I reached the temple. It was roofed in green-glazed tiles with a decorated ridge of warriors, gods, dragons and demons. I stepped into the forecourt to be

surrounded by a gaggle of wizened crones, with arms outstretched for *kumshaw*. My claim that I had no money – indeed, I only had my Peak Tram fare and enough for a drink – cut no ice with them. I was a *gweilo*. *Gweilos* were rich. They closed ranks. A few hands tugged at my shirt. Then one of them tentatively touched my hair, much as one might risk a quick stroke of a dog the temperament of which one was not quite sure. Seeing I did not react, they all started touching my head, giggling and cackling and wheezing amongst themselves.

I gave them a minute to build up their stock of good fortune, which, by their appearance, was pretty reduced, then, extricating myself from their company, entered the temple through two massive red-painted wooden doors.

Inside, it was sumptuous, rich scarlet banners hanging down with thick, black, dramatic characters upon them. The altar was pristine and the deities most impressive. On the right, just inside the door, sat an old man selling joss-sticks and candles: on the left were a table of *lai see* packets and some shelves of dusty books. The air was heavy with incense smoke. Apart from its grandeur, however, it was no different from any other temple I had visited.

I was about to leave when a voice asked, 'Do you like it?'

Turning, I came face to face with an elderly Chinese man wearing a long black robe to his ankles and a skull cap with a red button on the top. He sported a wispy beard and, in one hand, he held a closed fan. He resembled a character from a biography of Confucius. I just stared at him, dumbstruck, sure that he was either an apparition or a wizard.

'Can you not speak?' he went on. He spoke slowly, pronouncing each word exactly, as if imitating a teacher.

'Yes,' I stammered, 'and I like the temple very much.'

'But do you understand it?'

I shook my head and answered, 'No, sir. Not really.'

'So I will teach you.'

He led me up to the altar, joss-stick ash falling from one of the spiral coils hanging from the roof beams. This he brushed off with his fan which he then flicked open, quivering it in front of his face like the half wing of a huge black butterfly.

'This temple,' he enunciated slowly, 'is called the Man Mo temple. Man means literature and Mo means war. As you can see, there are two gods. Man Cheung, the god of literature, wears a green robe and Kwan Yu, who is also called Kwan Ti, wears a red robe. He is the god of war.'

I gazed up at their faces. They were powerful but impassive.

'Kwan Yu,' the man went on, 'was a real man. He lived two thousand years ago in the time of the Han dynasty when he was a general in the emperor's army. Now he is the saint of brotherhoods, especially policemen and gangsters.'

That cops and robbers worshipped the same god seemed obtuse in the extreme but I made no comment. China was, I had learnt well, a land of extremes and contradictions.

'Who is Man Cheung the saint of?' I asked.

'He is the god of civil servants,' the old man answered.

I bit my cheek to stop myself laughing. The thought that my father had a god looking specifically over him and his kind was too much to bear.

The elderly man then showed me the side altar to Pao Kung, the black-faced god of justice, and, to the right, that of Shing Wong, the god of the city. Elsewhere were several heavy sedan chairs used in religious processions, a huge bronze temple bell shaped like an inverted tulip and a massive drum.

'Now I must pay my respects,' the old man announced.

He walked unsteadily to the altar and bowed to the god of literature. I left the temple, wondering who he might be. He looked like one of the letter writers at the Tin Hau temple in Yau

Ma Tei yet there was somehow something more to him. He seemed to have the bearing of a learned man, rather than one who merely took down coolies' dictation. Who – or what – he really was I would never know. Perhaps he was a phantom after all.

Now that I had achieved my aim of finding the temple, I dropped the map in a drain grid. From here on, I was to wander without direction, discovering what I could. It was like being an explorer.

For two hours, I sauntered through the streets where Hong Kong had first begun, at least as far as the *gweilo* population was concerned. Many of the early buildings remained standing, in a dilapidated sort of way, their plaster cracked by the sun and eroded by typhoons.

From the narrow balconies projected the ubiquitous bamboo poles of laundry, small bamboo cages of song birds and, here or there, a larger cage containing a cockerel. Dogs slept out of the way under the arcades, cats slinking cautiously past them to investigate the latest fish bone thrown from an upstairs window. Some of the buildings had sprouted bushes from cracks in the walls. Bougainvillaea or jasmine trailed down from pots on balconies. All this was part and parcel of any Chinese street scene. What made this place different were the shops and businesses.

Whereas Mong Kok had its pavement *dai pai dongs*, Tai Ping Shan (as the Chinese called the area) had little cafés and restaurants inside the shop spaces under the buildings. They mostly sold noodles, *won ton*, soups and *dim sum*, the ingredients of some of which I could not identify, despite having attended and graduated from the Yau Ma Tei School of Street-Eating.

The ladder streets contained stalls balanced on the steps or constructed on platforms. These precarious entrepreneurial adventures sold buttons, thread and zips, cut keys or sharpened knives, repaired *wok* handles and swapped or sold secondhand

domestic appliances. One stall sold ancient Imperial Chinese dynastic bronze coins with square holes in the middle. Dating back in some cases several centuries, people bought them to ensure fiscal good fortune. The coins cost only a few cents each and, if one had a spare dollar or three, one could buy a hundred coins tied with red twine into the shape of a short sword, the better for fighting off ill luck and malevolent spirits.

I passed a door guarded by a be-turbaned Sikh armed with a shotgun. Behind him, the shop window was filled with gold, brilliantly illuminated by spotlights. It was all 24k fine gold – as near to pure as one could get it, soft, pliable and unsuitable for jewellery. Its colour was brash and it was not sold in blocks of bullion. Most of it had been fashioned into something – a crouching tiger, a fat Buddha, a Ming warrior or mandarin, a writhing dragon. I even saw intricate, solid gold sampans, junks, cars, pagodas, pandas and phoenixes. I knew the metal was sold by weight with only a nominal charge being added on for the exquisite workmanship. It seemed a waste of effort to me to fashion the metal into something when I knew the Chinese regarded it as merely an investment to be sold when times got tough. And, presumably, melted down. When I mentioned this to my mother, however, she gave me the explanation. To put a gold block on show in your house was in poor taste and arrogant, but to put on display a beautiful object not only indicated the owner's refinement but, at the same time, his wealth.

A short distance further on I came across a coffin-maker's workshop, open to the street. A carpenter was at work as I walked by, shaping the side of a coffin from a wide plank, curls of reddish wood peeling off from the blade. Another man was rounding off the clover-leaf end of a coffin, rubbing it with sandpaper. In the gloomy rear of the premises, completed coffins stood on racks. As I watched, the carpenter spied me and suddenly ran at me with a

chisel. I fled to shouts of rage behind me. A wood off-cut bounced on the road at my side. Once in the next street, I stopped to get my breath back and to glance round the corner to check I was not being followed. He was nowhere in sight.

This episode of sudden, wild rage was not only terrifying but also incomprehensible. I had blond hair. I was lucky. I brought good fortune. Apart from the skull-faced gardener at the Fourseas, who was in any case verging on the certifiable, I had never before seen the legendary sudden wrath to which the Chinese were prone. Later, I asked Wong if this had happened because it was considered bad luck for the dead to have their coffins peered at by a *gweilo*.

'No,' Wong replied. 'This man jus' no like you. Maybe he Communist.'

To gain my composure, I walked down the street to a tea shop. Entering it was akin to stepping back a hundred years. The walls were panelled, the sides lined with cubicles divided from each other by latticed screens, the fretwork cut in patterns of the characters for prosperity and longevity, and containing a dark wood table and benches. The brass tea urns steamed at the rear of the shop, next to a shrine and an elderly man sitting at a table with a cash box, an abacus and a book of receipts. I appeared to be the only customer.

A waiter approached me and jutted his chin at me.

'*Yum cha*,' I replied.

He looked at me for a moment then signalled me to sit in one of the cubicles. A minute later, he brought me a pot of gunpowder tea and a tea bowl. I filled the bowl and took a sip.

'*Ho sik!*' I exclaimed, adding in English, 'Very good!'

The waiter made no response whatsoever but walked away.

Although at first I was the only customer, over the next half hour, the place began to fill with elderly men, every one of them

carrying a small bird cage containing a finch. They were tiny
birds, some striped black, white and red, some yellow, some green,
some a nondescript fawn. As they sat down, the men hung the
cages from hooks suspended from beams in the ceiling directly
over their seats. Tea was served. More arrived until every seat was
occupied except the three in my cubicle.

Sipping their tea, the men conversed avidly amongst themselves. Overhead, the birds twittered and sang at each other.
There were, it dawned on me, two different sets of conversation
going on, human below and avian above. The tea house was like a
social club for both species.

The waiter came over to me, signalling that I should leave. He
was not antagonistic, but four men had entered with bird cages
and wanted my cubicle. I nodded and asked for the bill. He shook
his head and waved his hand from side to side, dismissing payment. I placed a fifty-cent coin under the teapot and left. I had not
gone ten yards when the waiter came running down the street
after me waving it.

'*Tipsee*,' I said. '*Kumshaw.*'

He looked at me and smiled broadly. It was then I saw
his silence was because he had no tongue. I made an effort to
ignore his infirmity. He made a throaty sort of laugh, pocketed
the coin and stroked my hair. I wished, as his hand touched my
head, that somehow I would not bring him wealth but return to
him the power of speech. When I got home, I told Wong about
him.

'Japanese cut plentee tongue wartime,' he said stoically.

As I walked along the street, a faint and unidentifiable herbal
smell reached me. The further on I walked, the stronger it became
until, finally, I arrived at the source. It was a shop unlike any
ordinary Chinese store, with a shop-front window and a glass
door bearing vermilion Chinese characters. A neon sign of a

six-foot-high snake coiling itself around a bamboo stake hung outside over the street.

The window display was most curious. It included bowls of seeds, what appeared to be bits of dry twig, desiccated bark, dried leaves, dehydrated roots, shrivelled fungi and flowers. Behind them were a dozen or so large ground-glass stoppered bottles containing preserved frogs, lizards, snakes and other less easily recognized pieces of flesh. Other reptiles lay on trays in front, dried out and stretched on frames of bamboo splints. Beside them were trays of what looked like black dried turds.

Going in, I found there was only one other customer, a woman with a florid birthmark on her neck the size of my outstretched hand. Behind the counter a man was busy writing on sheets of plain paper and opening drawers in a cabinet that reached to the ceiling and ran the length of the shop. From each he took a pinch or a handful of the contents, putting them into the sheets of paper. Every so often, he studied an old book. This done, he skilfully folded each sheet into a small, self-sealing parcel and placed it in the woman's rattan basket. When she had paid and left, the man turned his attention to me.

'Wha' you wan'?' he asked in pidgin English.

'What dis shop?' I replied.

'Dis Chilese med'sin shop,' he replied. 'Can do for *gweilo*, too. You sick by 'n' by, you come. I see you lo more sick.' He looked me up and down. 'You lo sick now?' he enquired optimistically.

'I lo sick.'

'You wan' see med'sin? Lo all same like *gweilo* med'sin.'

Never one to turn down an opportunity, I said I did and he showed me round the shop. In addition to a vast array of dried plant and fungal material, there were velvet-covered deers' antlers, tiny birds' nests, powdered pearls like grey talc shot through with stardust, the ghostly pale exoskeletons of sea-horses,

dried bears' spleens (the 'turds' in the window), an assortment of dried insects, a mummified tiger's penis ('. . . make you good wif you lady fr'en' . . .') and his *pièce de résistance*, a rhino's horn. When I asked for what these were cures, he reeled off a list of ailments, most of which I was ignorant of and hoped to so remain. When he was unable to give the English name, he mimed the symptoms, reminding me of the grotesque tableaux in the Tiger Balm Gardens.

Before I could leave, he mixed up a packet of dried plant matter for me.

'Good gen'ral med'sin for you. Like tonic. You put water, boiloo wung hour. Drink wung cup wung day. Make you st'ong.' He flexed his biceps and felt them. 'Lo ill for maybe t'ee mumf.'

When I got home, I gave the packet to my mother who was in the kitchen making a light supper, it being Wong's day off. She tipped the contents into a saucepan and boiled it for an hour. The apartment filled with such a noxious odour it woke my father, asleep in the bedroom. It also brought a shine to the interior of the saucepan not seen since it was new.

My mother and I let it cool then poured a cup. It tasted execrable. We left the remainder for Wong. When he returned, he was most grateful for it. As far as he was concerned, this was only a few drops short of being the elixir of life, its cost prohibitive on his wages.

The main mercantile district of Hong Kong, the city of Victoria, referred to by everyone as Central District – or just Central – held little interest for me. Most of the buildings were the offices of

banks, shipping lines, lawyers, insurance companies and import/
export firms. The Hongkong and Shanghai Bank towered over
the parked cars in what was known as Statue Square. To one side
were the law courts, a classical colonnaded building with a dome
on top. It could have been transported there from any European
city. Yet, for all that, the old China still impinged itself upon the
mid-twentieth century.

In rush hour, the chances of a rickshaw jam were greater than
one composed of vehicles, for many office workers and businessmen coming from Kowloon took rickshaws from the ferry pier to
their offices. Of those who chose to walk, many paused at the
shoe-shine 'boys'.

I could not understand why grown men were referred to
as boys. The Fourseas had had room boys: only the bellboy,
Halfie, had actually been a boy. Wong was our house boy; my
father employed a Chinese office boy who was at least twice his
age.

The shoe-shine boys bucked the trend. Half of them were
indeed boys, some of them my age, who squatted on the pavement
under the shade of an arcade, a box before them. If a customer
halted, tins of polish, brushes and cloths would appear from
within the box. Deft fingers rolled up trouser legs and, within
minutes, the shoes would appear pristine, scuff marks and dust
removed.

On one occasion, my father having withheld my pocket money
for some misdemeanour, I toyed with making a shoe-shine box of
my own, stocking it with polish and brushes from the kitchen and
setting up my pitch. At fifty cents a polish – the going rate –
I could earn a week's pocket money thrice over in a morning. I
mentioned my plan to my mother.

'You want to do what!' For a moment she looked at me, then
burst out laughing.

'It's not funny,' I defended myself. 'I've got to earn some pocket money.'

'Can you imagine your father coming along the street . . . ?' She grinned broadly at the prospect. 'Now that would be "going native" in no small measure. A definite plunge in standards. You'd be in the paper! Photo and all!' She extrapolated further. '*Gweilo Boy Sets New Trend. The Shoe-shine Entrepreneur. Son Sets Up Shoe-shine Box: Father Commits Hari-kiri.*'

'So, can I do it?' I asked, sensing the wind blowing my way and wondering what *hari-kiri* was.

'No,' my mother said. 'It's not because you'd cause a scandal. That would be hilarious. It's that, if you were to set up in business, you would be taking earnings from the other shoe-shine boys and they need all they can get.'

As usual, my mother's common sense prevailed and I put the idea out of my head. She surreptitiously reinstated my weekly allowance.

The shoe-shine boys shared the pavements with a small coterie of beggars. One was a tall, thin man who was totally blind, his face always turned up to the sky, his hand holding a begging cup and a length of bamboo painted as white as his sightless eyes. He was invariably accompanied by a child whose role was not to induce sympathy in passers-by but to act as a guide dog might, seeing him across the road or on to a tram. Another beggar was a woman whose body and limbs were twisted by deformity into a grotesque embryonic crouch. She got about on a small wooden platform to which had been affixed the wheels of an old baby's pram. For her, in her miserable condition, beggary must have been particularly demeaning, for every day she sold newspapers by Blake Pier, cradling her limited stock of copies of the *China Mail* and *Wah Kiu Yat Po* in her arms like the baby she would never have.

Perhaps the most obvious intrusion of ancient Cathay into

modern Hong Kong were the coolies. Throughout the day, swarthy Hakka women from the rural hinterland dressed in black, often wearing dust caps made out of folded newspaper, appeared down the street with bamboo poles over their shoulders from which were suspended anything from baskets of building rubble and bundles of waste paper to discarded wooden filing cabinets and office chairs. If it could be re-used, re-cycled or re-sold, it was.

These women were not restricted to carting débris. I once came to a hillside being blasted with dynamite and watched as the charges were laid by women, the detonator wire run out by women and the warning given by a woman with a gong. When the dust settled, it was women who carried away the dislodged rocks and earth. Not one man seemed to be involved.

Only one place in Central held me in awe and I visited it over and over again, like a rubber-necking tourist. It was the main banking hall of the Hongkong and Shanghai Bank headquarters. I had gone there first with my mother. Reluctantly.

On either side of the entrance was a life-size bronze lion. The left-hand one was growling.

'They're called Stephen and Stitt,' my mother said as we waited to cross the road.

'Which is which?'

'Stephen's growling,' was her reply.

'What's a stitt?'

'They're named after two bank managers, Mr Stephen and Mr Stitt.'

On reaching the lions, I was struck by their size, yet this was not all. They had bullet holes in them from the war and Stephen had a lump of shrapnel embedded in him. Both were covered in a dark brown patina except that Stitt's front paw shone like gold. I soon saw why. People walking by touched it. For luck.

'This,' my mother announced as we entered the bank and turned to climb a flight of stairs, 'is actually the back door. The front door, and the address, are on the other side.'

This seemed nonsensical and I said so.

'It's to do with the laws of necromancy,' my mother replied. 'The main door has to face the hills, away from the harbour, to keep the sea dragon out and to stop the money flowing out into the ocean.'

Explained thus, it made perfect sense to me.

The banking hall was vast. The sound of voices was muffled by its immensity. Huge, square, dark brown marble pillars held up the ceiling – and what a ceiling it was: barrel vaulted and covered in a gargantuan mosaic. In the centre was an elaborate golden starburst set against an azure backdrop, around the sides was a multicoloured frieze of figures engaged in all manner of Oriental and Occidental craftwork and industry. The ceiling never failed to stun me. I would often take a detour through the bank on my way from the Peak Tram to the Star Ferry just to pass under the reflected glow of the mosaic.

Once, accompanying my father to the bank, I announced my determination to be an artist.

'What on earth prompted that ridiculous idea?' he exclaimed, busying himself at the counter with his cheque book.

'That did,' I said, staring mosaicwards.

He did not look up.

'Well, put that notion out of your head. No-one gets rich by being an artist.'

'There's more to being rich than having a lot of money,' I answered.

The teller accepted his cheque. He turned to face me.

'No, there isn't,' he said succinctly, 'and anyone who says there is is a bloody fool.'

'Mum told me there is,' I said.

'Yes, well your mother doesn't have to earn it,' he rejoined.

When he had collected his money and put it in his wallet, I said, 'Look up at the ceiling, Dad.'

He did so, briefly.

'Very impressive,' he remarked offhandedly.

Once outside, as we walked to the car parked in Statue Square, I mused, 'I bet the artist was paid a lot of money to make that ceiling.'

'Probably drank it all and never did another thing in the rest of his life.'

That, I considered, was ripe coming from an experienced pink gin downer but refrained from saying as much. I was fast learning the art of knowing when, as my father put it, to keep my trap shut.

Not long after the forced-labour day on Chow Kung Chau, another trip was arranged by launch to the adjacent island of Hei Ling Chau. It was sparsely populated and consequently the location of a leper colony – and it was this we were to visit.

My mother heard of the trip from a newsletter sent out to naval wives and immediately announced we were going. My father was reluctant in the extreme. He and disease were not close relations, he declared, and he was damned if he was going to spend his Sunday leisure time wandering around staring at those who were.

'What's a leper colony?' I asked.

'It's where they lock away the poor buggers who've caught leprosy,' my father replied, hoping this would deter me from joining my mother.

I asked what leprosy was.

'Leprosy,' my mother answered, giving my father a look that precluded his interrupting, 'is a disease caused by bacteria. There are two kinds – dry leprosy and wet leprosy. If you have the dry sort, your nerves die off bit by bit and you become paralysed. Or, because they have no nerves in them, parts of your body wither and drop off. Most common is you lose your nose and fingers and toes, but you can have a whole arm drop off. If you have wet leprosy, your entire body is covered in running sores and ulcers. That kind is dangerously contagious, meaning you can get it just by touching someone with it, but the dry is very hard to catch indeed—'

'And your mother wants to take you to meet some people who've got it,' my father butted in, no longer able to contain himself. 'Really, Joyce, sometimes you take the bloody biscuit. Anyway, you're not going. I shall simply refuse to allow it. I'm not having our son exposed—'

'Don't talk such bloody bosh. We'll be perfectly safe. You think the people who run the leprosarium will put visitors at risk?'

'Why do you think they lock all the poor bastards away on a ruddy island?'

'They don't lock them away. They look after them and cure them.'

'And once they're cured, they just become beggars,' my father retorted. 'You can't do much with only one arm and half a leg. Better to let them die.'

My mother pursed her lips and replied, 'Sometimes, Ken, I wonder what I saw in you.'

A fortnight later, on a Sunday of bright sun and high scudding clouds, we were all three of us cutting through a choppy sea aboard a naval launch heading for Hei Ling Chau. On arrival at a short jetty, we were met by a Chinese man who helped us to

disembark under an archway of gold and scarlet bunting. A dozen other private launches rode at anchor.

'Welcome to our fête!' the Chinese man said as we stepped on to dry land.

'How do you spell that?' my father muttered. '*F a t e* or *f ê t e*. I really do not see why they don't just have a bloody flag day like anybody else. This really is bloody madness, Joyce.'

Ahead of us were some low buildings surrounded by stalls. Everything was decorated with strips and banners of gold and scarlet crêpe paper, catching the sunlight as they rippled in the breeze. Several hundred people milled about, trying their luck at a coconut shy, a roll-a-ten-cent-coin table and other attractions such as might have been found at any church bazaar anywhere in rural Britain. The only difference was that some of the helpers were British Army privates and naval ratings and there was a .22 rifle range set up for those who fancied their hand as a dab shot.

'Well,' my mother replied, 'it seems to be a pretty bloody widespread madness.'

We joined the crowd, tried the lucky dip, bought some raffle tickets and visited the tombola stall. My father hung back, smoking his pipe, his teeth clenched in anger on the stem. I wondered if he smoked to enjoy the tobacco or to fumigate the air around him. After a short time, we saw him strolling off southwards.

'Wouldn't it be funny,' my mother mused, 'if he missed the boat back? Marooned on a desert island with a colony of lepers and that bloody pipe . . .'

It was then I saw my first leper. He was sitting behind a trestle table upon which were arranged a number of home-made wooden objects such as bookends, desktop pen holders and paperweights shaped like the outline of the island, its name burnt into the surface with a hot poker. From the front of the table hung a sign

in English and Chinese stating *Woodworks made by inmats. Please by. Garuntee very clean.*

As my mother had predicted, the leper had no nose, only a ragged hole surrounded by flaps of skin. He had also lost several fingers and an ear. Apart from this, he looked quite normal and healthy, certainly in better shape than many of the beggars I saw on the streets. I searched my pockets. I had ten dollars left from a postal order sent by Nanny for my birthday.

Walking up to the stall, I studied the wares on offer. They were simple items but very well made. The leper smiled at me but did not speak, his upper lip curling like a snarling dog's, his lower hanging loose. I picked up a pair of bookends.

'We get our wood from a timber yard,' a voice said over my shoulder. 'They're left-overs. Mahogany, teak, sandalwood.'

I turned. A European man stood behind me dressed in slacks and an open-neck cotton shirt. He only differed from the rest of the Sunday crowd in that a stethoscope hung round his neck to denote his office.

'Having fun?' he enquired.

'Yes, sir,' I answered then, seizing the moment, asked him a question that had been bothering me for days. 'Is it true you only cure the lepers so they can become beggars?'

'Who on earth told you that nonsense?' he exclaimed, quite clearly taken aback. 'We don't just cure their illness, we cure their souls, too. We train them to do jobs. This man here's going to be a carpenter. Once he has a job, which we'll find for him, he'll get his dignity and his life back.' He smiled down at me. 'You don't want to believe everything you hear, sonny Jim.'

I pointed to the bookends and asked, '*Gai doh cheen?*'

The leper sort-of chortled and raised five assorted digits.

'*Ng mun?*' I questioned, to be sure of the price.

He nodded, his eyes bright at the thought of a sale. I gave him

five dollar notes and he handed me the bookends, bound together by several rubber bands. As I parted with the money, our hands met, his skin blotched, warped and stretched by leprosy, mine smooth with health.

'*Dor jei*,' I thanked him. He chortled again and I saw he had only half a tongue.

As I was about to go, he reached out with one hand, nodding enthusiastically at me, his eyes pleading for something. His index and middle finger were missing. Going round the back of his stall, I stood next to him. Fleetingly, so that I hardly felt it, he touched my hair.

On the return launch trip, I took my mother aside, out of my father's earshot. 'I let a leper touch my hair,' I admitted, hurriedly adding, 'but he was a dry one.'

I expected a scolding, or at least an admonishing, but neither materialized.

'Well then,' my mother replied with a smile, 'let's hope to God it brings the poor man luck, shall we?'

When we got home, however, I accidentally mentioned my encounter with the leper to my father. He went apoplectic.

'You did what?' he bellowed. 'Joyce! Do you know what this stupid little sod has done?'

'Lots of things, I expect,' my mother urbanely replied.

'He allowed a bloody leper to stroke his hair. It's bad enough in the bloody street with the entire bloody population of China, but in a benighted leper colony . . .' His face was red with anger, going towards puce. He put down his pink gin. 'Go into your bedroom and stay there.'

I did as I was told. There were raised voices in the sitting room followed by a slammed door. My father entered my room carrying a red leather slipper.

'Bend over the side of the bed.'

'Why? I haven't done anything wrong.'

I was amazed at my defiance. Always in the past, I had meekly succumbed to a beating, accepting it much as a miscreant dog might a kick or a rolled-up newspaper. Yet now, I thought, I would not. I had not been disobedient or insolent, the usual crimes levelled at me, not always without reason. A paddling now would be an injustice. My father clenched his teeth.

'Bend over, damn you—'

'No.'

He swung the slipper at my buttocks. I side-stepped.

'And they don't cure them to be beggars. You were wrong. They find them proper jobs so they get their dignity back.'

I had no idea what dignity was but it had to be a good thing.

'What?' my father exploded.

'The leper doctor told me.'

'I'll give you bloody dignity, you little sod!'

My father's left hand struck quicker than a cobra. Grabbing me by the back of the neck, he forced me to bend over, then, with all his might, he hit me four times in quick succession on the buttocks. I did not cry: I would not give him the satisfaction.

'Now get into bloody bed.' He was grinding his teeth with rage.

It was from that moment that I hated my father, truly abhorred him with a loathing that deepened as time went by and was to sour the rest of both our lives.

8

IDA, SU YIN, THE LIGHT OF TIN HAU AND THE WRATH OF YEN LO

MY MOTHER AND I HAD PLANNED TO GO SWIMMING AT REPULSE BAY on the afternoon of Sunday, 27 August 1954. My father reluctantly said that he would drive us there, returning home to indulge in his usual weekend pastime of pink gin and sleeping. As Wong set the table for an early lunch, my father stood legs apart on the veranda as if on the rolling deck of his own battleship, surveying the harbour through his binoculars.

'Lunch 'edy, missee, master,' Wong announced.

My father stepped into the lounge and announced, 'Beach is off, Joyce. Number One signal's up.'

By this, he meant that he had looked at the Hong Kong Observatory on Kowloon through his binoculars and seen a storm warning on the signal mast.

My mother, not to be done out of an afternoon's swimming, replied, 'Are you sure? It's a lovely day and One is only a stand-by . . .'

'Tropical storms can gather very quickly,' my father opined.

'Surely not between now and five o'clock,' my mother

came back. 'I don't think we need to be concerned.'

To win the argument, my father telephoned HMS *Tamar*. The meteorological officer on duty confirmed it: they expected to raise the Number Five some time in the early evening. We sat down for lunch.

'What do the signals actually mean?' I asked.

My father, ever the knowledgeable maritime obfuscator, replied, 'Number One is a standby signal, Number Five to Eight predicts winds up to sixty miles per hour and designates the direction they will come from, Number Nine is winds up to gale or storm force and Number Ten hurricane force, over sixty with gusts up to a hundred and thirty.'

'What's this one going to be?'

'*Tamar* says a near hit, so Nine, possibly Ten.'

My mother called Wong and gave him the news. He immediately went out on to the veranda and brought in my mother's potted plants. After lunch, we prepared for what was coming, removing ornaments from window sills, parking the car well under the adjacent block of apartments, putting old towels along window sills and external door lintels. In her bedroom, my mother stored away all her make-up jars, hairbrushes, ring stand and my father's cufflink tray. Wong, meantime, emptied the bathroom shelves and placed the contents – and the glass shelves – in the dry room. In my bedroom, I removed my ornaments from the window sill – a pile of High West bullets, my carved wooden camel and a detailed model of a junk – placing them in my cupboard with my books.

I had experienced several severe tropical storms and one typhoon before, but we had been living in the Fourseas or Boundary Street at the time and only suffered a few leaking windows. Now we were positioned on the fourth floor of a block of apartments erected on the very pinnacle of a summit secondary

only to the Peak. With no protection on all sides, we were perched at about fifteen hundred feet above sea level.

'What's this typhoon called?' I enquired.

Every typhoon was allotted a girl's name, for a reason I could not fathom but which Philip Bryant had confided was because all females were like typhoons: impulsive, destructive, exciting, dangerous, single-minded, determined and immovable.

This one was called Ida. We had a spinster relative of the same name, but she was a mousy, quiet woman who lived in a rural shire town, spent her life baking scones and lovingly scolding an old cat. Perhaps we were not in for a bad typhoon after all.

I was wrong.

By the time I went to bed, the sky was covered with dense cloud, the lights of the city reflecting off it. I read my comics, recently arrived, and went to sleep to be woken just after dawn by the booming gusts of wind. Each time one hit the building, the air within seemed to contract. I could feel the pressure on my ears. It was like living inside a bass drum.

I switched on my bedside light and crossed to the window. The cloud base had dropped to not much above the roof of our building. I could still see the city below in a monochromatic dawn light but under a metallic sky that seemed to glower with rage and rob the view of colour. Kowloon was invisible. Intermittently, squalls of heavy rain blew by. They did not strike the window full on but sprayed off the corner of the stonework as if it were the bow of a ship. A substantial tree branch blew by – vertically.

Yet what was most frightening, although at first I did not recognize its significance, was my reflection in the window. When a gust hit the glass, it distorted like a circus Hall of Mirrors, the distortion lasting only seconds.

'Martin, get away from the window!' It was my mother in her nightie and dressing gown. 'Now!'

'Why? I was only looking—'

'The glass is bending. If we get a really hard knock, it'll implode and you'll be cut to shreds. Go to the front door.'

Suddenly, I felt vulnerable. This, I imagined, was what it must have been like in the war, never knowing if a bomb was going to hit your house. In the entrance hall to the apartment were piled suitcases filled with everything moveable and of value.

'Are we going away?' I asked.

'Don't be so bloody stupid!' my father retorted.

He was fully dressed and ready for action. By his side was Wong, armed with a mop, his weapon at the barricade in the battle against the typhoon.

'Use your bloody brain,' my father continued. 'How the hell do you think we'll get down the bloody drive?'

I had to admit he had a point. The curving driveway up to the building was completely exposed. We were marooned.

Over the morning, the wind increased. It howled, fizzed, whined, whistled and hummed. Water seeped in through the galvanized steel Crittal window frames which were allegedly typhoon proof, keeping Wong busy soaking it up with his mop to prevent the parquet floor from getting sodden and warping. My mother helped him, emptying the bucket and wringing out the old towels. All Hong Kong business was suspended, the ferries were in the typhoon shelters and radio messages warned everyone to stay inside. Scaffolding was blowing down, live electricity cables were lying in urban roads, shop signs were falling like ninepins, there were a number of landslides blocking major roads and flooding was reported in the New Territories. Social events – the Hong Kong Cricket Club whist night, Such-and-such a company's annual dinner at the Pen – were postponed by radio announcements.

Nevertheless, my father still thought he should be at work. The

Royal Navy, he insisted, counted on people like him to keep things going. That there was not a single warship in the harbour, all of them having put to sea to ride out the storm, was neither here nor there. It was Monday: he should be at work. Consequently, he spent two hours on the telephone trying to organize supplies for a destroyer that had sailed to safety in international waters. Then the line went dead. He slammed the receiver down and cracked it.

'Intelligent,' my mother remarked bluntly. 'We're stranded on a mountain top in a typhoon and you break the bloody phone.'

'The perishing line's down,' he replied sourly. 'Fat lot of bloody use the phone is.'

'Yes,' my mother agreed, 'but they'll soon fix the line. It'll take days to get a replacement phone.'

'I'm military, an essential user,' my father said. 'They'll bring us a new one PDQ.'

The telephone line was operational by late the following morning. The telephone, which my mother fixed with Elastoplast strips, worked. A new telephone arrived four weeks later, when my mother remarked caustically it was a good job China had not invaded since Ida.

The Number Nine signal was raised at half-past eleven. By now, the wind was terrifying. Each gust curved the windows. The building creaked like a galleon under sail. According to the radio, the sustained wind speed was reaching sixty-five miles per hour with gusts at 130. The rain turned squally, lashing the windows. The veranda became an inch-deep pool. In the servants' quarters, rain sprayed through the lattice brickwork as if the building were forging ahead through a heavy sea.

Suddenly, over the space of fifteen minutes, the wind died to less than a summer zephyr and the rain let up.

'Eye of the storm,' my father announced. 'You come with me.'

He and I left the building and made our way down the drive. Leaves and branches were littered everywhere. At the bottom, we turned left and went beneath the next block of apartments. There, at the back, was my father's car, bespattered with leaves that were adhering to the entire surface. It might have been custom decorated by a miscreant sylvan elf or a wallpaper designer with a naturalistic bent.

'Get those leaves off the paintwork,' my father ordered. 'They'll discolour it.'

I started at the trunk. It seemed an utterly pointless exercise. I knew all tropical cyclones – we had done the topic in geography – were circular and that, in the middle, was the eye, a place of calm around which the storm revolved. Once that passed by, the winds would blow again, but from the opposite quarter. The leaves we removed would soon be replaced.

'Not the bloody windows, cloth ears!' my father said, breaking into my thoughts. 'The glass won't discolour, will it? We haven't got all bloody day.'

Indeed, the wind was already beginning to pick up again so we made our way back up the drive. It took my breath away. I could feel the gusts tugging at my lungs as it had the window glass. By the time we reached our apartment block my father – as he was keen to prove – could physically lean on the wind. Behind him, struggling up the drive, was one of our neighbours who had taken advantage of the eye to walk his wife's dachshund. The dog was being lifted as much as four inches off the concrete, a bemused look on its face. But for its lead, it could have blown away.

In the early evening, the Number Eight signal was raised and remained in force through the night. By noon the following day, the typhoon was gone, leaving behind squally showers and a gunmetal sky, and the clear-up began. My father revisited his car.

It was, as before, heavily bestrewn with leaves. Worse, another car in the parking space had been blown against the rear of my father's, denting the bumper and nicking the paintwork.

'Bloody hell!' my father fumed. 'Why can't other benighted drivers . . . ? That one over there tied his car to the bloody pillars. Why couldn't this cloth-eared individual . . . ?'

I set about removing the leaves but the bonnet and front of the car were devoid of them. A downpipe had broken free and sprayed rainwater continuously over the car for hours. My father unlocked the door, got in and attempted to start the engine. The starter motor turned over asthmatically but nothing else happened. My father opened the bonnet. The engine was sodden, a deep puddle beneath it covered in a rainbow film of oil.

'Buggeration!' my father exclaimed and slammed the bonnet down. A piece of trim fell off.

We had got off comparatively unscathed. An apartment at the top of the adjacent building had lost a window, setting off a chain reaction with three or four others. The wind sucked out anything lighter and smaller than a coffee table, splintering them to pieces as they struck the window frames.

The wind having died down a good deal, I walked up the road to the police post. The bushes in some places had been stripped of leaves as if attacked by locusts. All the hibiscus bushes had lost their blooms, which lay in the road like sodden purple scraps of tissue paper. And yet the birds were singing and, when the sun came out between the squalls, the tarmac was alive with all manner of butterflies drying their wings in the warmth. I wondered where they had weathered the storm.

My mother and I went to the Peak School for an interview with the headmistress. I had been playing hookey from games lessons and she wanted to know why. So did my mother. Education was important to her because her own had been so minimal. I had my argument ready and expressed anathema for the concept of team sports because they destroyed one's individuality. This left both women momentarily flabbergasted. I was told to join in more, in lessons, in sports, in the social extra-curricular life of the school. I could hardly reply I preferred a *dai pai dong* to country dancing.

On the walk back, my mother was silent. Several times, she started to speak then thought the better of it. I guessed she felt torn. On the one hand, she had to back the school. On the other, she would rather have had an independently minded sinophile than a soccer player for a son.

We entered the apartment to find Ah Shun sitting on the settee, a duster in her hand and Tuppence disconsolately perched by her side. This was, to put it mildly, unusual. If servants ever did sit down on the furniture, they were sure to be swift in getting to their feet as soon as the key rattled in the lock.

'Are you all right, Ah Shun?' my mother enquired with a concerned look on her face.

'Lo, missee,' Ah Shun replied. It was about as far as her knowledge of English went.

'Go and get Wong,' my mother ordered me.

'Wong go,' Ah Shun said.

'Wong go? Go where?'

It was no use speaking Cantonese to Ah Shun. She only spoke Shanghainese.

'Go, missee.'

Wong was not in the kitchen or the servants' quarter. I reported his absence, admitting selfishly to myself that this diversion could not have come at a handier time.

'Oh, my God!' my mother exclaimed, jumping to conclusions. 'He's left her.'

A frantic phone call to my father drew a blank. Predictably, he could not get away. Looking out of the window, I could see an aircraft carrier riding at a buoy off *Tamar*. He would try and return early that evening.

My mother sat next to Ah Shun and put her arm round her. A short time later, we heard a movement in the kitchen. My mother rushed out to find Wong depositing the shopping bags on the floor.

'Thank God!' she said. 'Wong, Ah Shun is sick.'

'Lo sick, missee,' he answered calmly.

'Wong, she can barely get up. She's tired. I'm going to call the doctor.'

'Lo call, missee. Ah Shun no sick. Ah Shun got baby come.'

My mother stared at him for a long moment. I looked at Ah Shun. By now, I knew a fair amount about the birds, the bees and babies. She certainly did not look fat but then the uniform she wore was hardly close fitting.

'When?' my mother asked.

'Lo long time,' Wong replied. 'Maybe wung week.'

'One week!' my mother exclaimed. 'Wong, you cannot let Ah Shun carry on cleaning, doing the laundry.'

'Lo p'oblum, missee. Ah Shun can do.'

'Ah Shun cannot do!' my mother replied.

'Must do,' Wong said. 'Dis her job. Mus' work for money.'

'Never mind the money!' my mother replied. 'You help Ah Shun to her bed. I'll call a doctor and then put the shopping away. You find another amah to help you.'

It didn't occur to my mother until later that, in China, Ah Shun had probably delivered herself of her other children. I was told to ring my father and tell him what was happening.

'Ah Shun's having a baby,' I stated bluntly.

'Jolly good!' my father replied offhandedly.

'Now,' I added, feeling he had missed the point.

'Now? You mean this very bloody moment?'

'Soon. The doctor's coming.'

'Oh, bloody hell! Can't your mother cope? I've got HMS—'

'Can you cope?' I called out.

'Is that what he said?'

I nodded. She stomped over to the telephone table.

'Give me the phone. Ken? Yes, I can cope. Marriage to you is all about bloody coping. It's also supposed to be about sharing bloody problems.' She held the receiver three inches above the cradle and let it drop. 'I hope that's given him a bloody headache.'

An hour later, a naval midwife in attendance, Ah Shun's waters broke. I was told to stay in my room and amuse Tuppence. He had never, at least not to my knowledge, been in my room and we played with my toy soldiers and military Dinky toys.

Ah Shun gave birth to a little girl whom they named Su Yin. My mother was appointed 'godmother' and relished the role. Not only was she proud to be asked, but here was another link to China.

My father, who never broke any law, by-law, rule or regulation that might even vaguely apply to him, read his tenancy agreement and informed the naval quartering officer of the event. A month or so later, a letter came to the effect that the servants' quarters did not cater for four, that babies were not allowed in quarters as their crying might *discommode other residents*, that fire regulations were being breached and that, in general, the Royal Navy did not approve. It was tactfully but firmly stated that either the servants be dismissed or the amah be let go, or the infant be sent to live with relatives.

My mother went incandescent with rage.

'Sack my servants! Put them out on the streets! With a new-born baby! Remember, Ken, they've already got children lodging elsewhere.'

'Wong shouldn't be so fecund,' my father answered.

'What does fecund mean?' I enquired.

'You keep your bloody nose out of this.'

'They're not going, Ken.'

'I mean, don't the Chinese take precautions?'

'Against what?' I asked.

My mother went into the bedroom and slammed the door. The key turned in the lock. My father poured himself a pink gin. I decided it politic to keep my mouth shut.

An hour later, my mother reappeared, poured herself a gin and tonic, sat down and announced, 'Ken, get me an interview with the Commodore.'

'Under no circumstance whatever,' he answered.

'Either I have an interview or I have a ticket for myself and Martin on the next P&O liner to come into port.'

I knew this was a bluff – ny mother would pull her own teeth out rather than leave Hong Kong before she had to – but my father begrudgingly said he would see what he could do. The outcome was that it was not a naval matter but a civilian one to do with fire regulations and suchlike.

'In that case,' my mother declared, 'I'm going to see the Governor.'

'That, Joyce, I certainly will not allow.'

'Allow?' my mother responded, her eyes narrowing. 'I'm not asking your bloody permission. I'm telling you what I'm going to do. Out of bloody courtesy.'

An exchange of letters with Government House followed, culminating in my mother being granted an audience with His Excellency, Sir Alexander Grantham KCMG. She demanded I

accompany her partly, I suspect, because she was scared witless now that her persistence had paid off and I was acting as a sort of hip flask of Dutch courage, or perhaps she wanted me along to demonstrate that she was also a mother who would not be parted from her offspring.

My father refused even to drive us to the meeting – perhaps he was afraid his car licence plate might be noted down as belonging to a subversive – so we went to Government House by taxi. We were met by the Governor's ADC under the portico to the front door.

'His Excellency is fully acquainted with the situation,' he said as he guided us in to a large lobby. 'I'm afraid he can only give you ten minutes.'

The Governor appeared, shook my mother's hand, then mine. He asked my name.

'Martin, sir,' I admitted.

'Good name. Strong name,' he replied. 'Do you know who I am?'

'His Excellency the Governor, sir,' I answered.

He smiled and led us into a room furnished like an English country house, indicating we all sit down. A steward came in with a tray of Chinese tea.

'Would you like an orange juice, Martin?' the Governor asked.

'I would prefer tea, sir,' I answered.

'It's Chinese tea,' the Governor warned me.

'That all right, sir,' I replied. 'I drink lots of tea at the *dai pai dongs*.'

His Excellency raised an eyebrow, smiled and said, 'Do you, indeed? A real little China Hand. Do you like Hong Kong?'

'Yes, sir. Very much.'

'I'm afraid,' he apologized, 'this tea might not be up to the standard of a *dai pai dong*.'

The tea was poured into cups, not bowls, and my mother and the Governor then got down to business. I minded my own, sipped the tea and studied the paintings hanging in the room. In less than the ten allotted minutes, the matter was settled. So long as the landlord did not object and the fire escapes were acceptable, servants' families would no longer be arbitrarily split up. The matter would take some months to go through Legislative Council. In the meantime, as far as he was concerned, Wong, Ah Shun, Tuppence and Su Yin were to remain where they were pending a change in the law. We shook hands again and my mother and I were shown to the porch where a government car had been hailed for us.

That evening, when my father returned from work, my mother waited until he had a drink in hand then told him of the meeting.

'So the landlord has to agree,' he commented. 'That's the Navy.'

'I'm sure they will,' my mother responded sweetly.

'I wouldn't count on it,' my father forewarned her.

'I'm not,' she said mildly. 'I'm counting on you. You let me down and I will go to the Commodore, with or without your bloody say-so.'

And, now, my father knew, she would.

Several months later, the law was changed and the Wong family's tenure was secure. My mother felt she had struck a blow for Chinese rights – which she had. My father admitted defeat. And, as I heard my mother say to a friend, 'We'll still have Wong's marvellous sponges.'

One Sunday, my parents and I were invited to lunch on Stone-cutters' Island in the western half of Hong Kong harbour. A

colleague of my father's, a Mr Newton, lived there with his wife and son, Andrew, whom I liked. Even better was the fact that, near their house, there was a large anti-aircraft gun left over from the war. It was still operable, the gearing well greased. We could rotate it on its base and elevate or lower the barrel. It was the ultimate boys' plaything.

To reach Stonecutters', which was a closed military site on account of the signals station on it, one had to take the naval launch from HMS *Tamar* to the island. Once there, we walked to the Newtons' bungalow along narrow paths, the undergrowth encroaching over the wartime concrete. It was said that unique species of rare snakes lived on the island, escapees from a Japanese wartime laboratory that had sought to use their venom in biological weapons. All I ever saw there was a dead, red-necked keel-back water snake on the shingle beach, being voraciously picked over by dark blue and red rock crabs.

There had been a landslip on Garden Road caused by recent rain, so my father had to take a longer route to HMS *Tamar* via Happy Valley then through Wanchai. In Hennessy Road, a coolie on a tricycle suddenly appeared from a side street, pedalling hard. My father, used to demon-dodging pedestrians, slammed on his brakes. The road was wet. The car skidded and hit the front of the tricycle, the coolie jumping clear at the moment of impact.

One of the two front wheels of the tricycle was buckled but the vehicle had otherwise suffered no discernible damage. The coolie, however, was livid. He waved his hands in the air, appealed for justice to the inevitable crowd of onlookers (which was swelling by the minute) and harangued my father who, not understanding a word but capturing the general gist of the diatribe, just stood staring at the infinitesimal dent in the Ford's chrome bumper.

Finally, my father drew himself up and roared at the shouting coolie, 'Who do you think you're screaming at?'

The coolie fell silent.

'It was your own bloody fault,' my father bellowed. 'You didn't look, you blithering idiot. You just came swanning out with not a care in the world. Now look what you've done . . .'

He pointed to the bumper. The coolie took a cursory look, waved his hand in the general direction of his tricycle and let off a stream of invective in a high-pitched squeal. This, I knew, was bad. When an angry Chinese voice rose an octave, there was soon going to be physical action. My father knew as much about street fighting Hong Kong-style as he did Cantonese. Or astrophysics. It was plain before it started who would win a punch-up.

My mother got out of the car, as did I. She was about to muster all her command of Cantonese to defuse the situation but, at that moment, a police paddy-wagon appeared, the crowd melting away. A Chinese sergeant told off the coolie for the dangerous driving of a tricycle. The coolie argued for money to cover the repair to his wheel but the policeman denied his appeal and sent him on his way. A European police inspector then had a brief word with my father and it was all over.

'He could've made that bloody coolie pay for the damage to the bumper,' my father complained as we set off again. 'It'll need re-chroming.'

'The cost of repairing a barely visible dent might equal a week's coolie wage,' my mother pointed out. 'You could've offered to pay to straighten his wheel. He could be out of work until it's fixed. That would have been the gentlemanly thing to—'

'What?' my father retorted. 'It wasn't my bloody fault. He . . . and you side with . . .' He was left spluttering for words.

The outcome of this minor traffic accident was that my father became an unnecessarily over-cautious driver. He would, for example, be driving along a wide road in the New Territories, in the high heat of midday, with nobody and nothing moving on it

– no buffaloes, pigs, hens, farmers, duck-herds, ducks or dogs. We would pass, say, a country temple set well back from the road. Seated on a stool by the door would be an old crone smoking a thin silver pipe.

A hundred yards further on, my father would ask, not taking his eyes from the road ahead, 'Was that old woman back there OK, Joyce?' The sub-text was, Did I hit her?

For the first few occasions, my mother or I would be truthful and reply that we had not seen the old woman. At this, my father would do a U-turn and go back to ensure she was still smoking her pipe – or, as my mother put it out of my father's earshot, to have another go at missing her. Thereafter, my mother and I learnt to say automatically, 'Yes, Ken/Daddy, he/she/it's OK.' It was the only way to arrive at our destination on time, with our sanity intact.

Typhoons were not the only natural force with which Hong Kong had to contend. Heavy rain invariably caused landslides, avalanches of rock and soil sliding down the hillside taking trees, bushes, boulders, squatter shacks and even substantial buildings with it. People were frequently buried alive or crushed to death. Hundreds were made homeless. Roads were blocked, sometimes for several days.

Despite the prevalence of typhoons and tropical storms, droughts were not uncommon either. The reservoir levels would plunge, brush fires spring up and smoulder for days, a terrible threat to the squatter areas. The wind, when it blew, was hot and dry, the only humidity in it picked off the sea. In such times of water shortage, restrictions were enforced, the mains water only

being switched on for a few hours a day – or even every other day. When the taps were running, every receptacle in the house would be filled – baths, basins, saucepans, woks, empty bottles. It was common colonial practice to retain Gordon's gin bottles for, being flat on one side, they were ideal drinking-water containers which fitted in the fridge on their sides. In a drought, up to two dozen stood on the kitchen floor, filled to the brim and awaiting their turn to be chilled.

With the baths being used for water storage, and showers redundant, many people went to the beach in the evening to wash. It became an everyday sight to see bathers lathering their hair or soaping every inch of flesh not covered by a swimming costume. Sweetmeat vendors caught on to the exodus from the city, and soon the beaches were lined with purveyors of everything from sweet pickled turnip and sugar cane to Dairy Farm popsies. There would be almost a party atmosphere at the bigger beaches, especially at Repulse Bay where the Chinese occupied the strand whilst the Europeans, once they had bathed, dressed in smart casual clothes and decamped to the bar of the famous Repulse Bay Hotel.

My parents chose to drive further afield, to a wide sandy beach at the eastern extremity of Hong Kong island called Shek O. To one side, a tiny fishing (and once notorious pirate) village stood on a promontory. The bay, facing straight out into the South China Sea, was frequently visited by deep-water-dwelling sharks, and although they very rarely came close into shore, a lifeguard seated on a tall bamboo lookout tower kept watch for them.

At weekends, Shek O beach was crowded, all the beach tents rented by half-past nine, but on mid-week and 'personal hygiene' evenings (also known as sweat 'n' swim nights), the beach was usually all but deserted. The bus service ceased at dusk so only those with cars could reach it.

Shek O was my mother's favourite beach. The water in the bay was usually calm, there was no undertow and the sea floor shelved gently. By her own admission, my mother was a recreational swimmer, 'pootling about like a mermaid on holiday', as she put it, but despite his naval pretensions, my father hardly ever went in the water. Indeed, he could not really swim. His excuse for not swimming was that someone had to guard the tent containing our clothes, watches and so on, yet this was unnecessary. There were no thieves.

Late one afternoon, we drove to Shek O armed with swimming costumes, towels, shampoo and soap. Offices tended to close early on sweat 'n' swim days to allow staff to see to their maritime ablutions before it got dark. By the time we arrived, the beach was occupied by no more than a dozen parties, mostly Europeans. We rented a tent, bought a pannier of fresh water and, wading in up to our waists, my mother and I washed ourselves. Small fish, undeterred by the lather and unused to legs that were not thrashing about, nibbled at our shins and feet. Feeling clean – if salty – we then returned to the tent and sat in deckchairs while my father washed.

By now, it was dusk. The tent boy brought round two oil lanterns and placed them on the sand in front of the tent. The air was warm, the sea black and the world seemingly at peace. From the direction of the café beneath a huge awning of tangled vines on the beach before the village, came the distant clatter of mahjong tiles, the only sound other than the lap of waters. The only lights were our oil lamps, those of the café and perhaps the lanterns on a sampan fishing south of the islet.

'It's time we were going, Joyce,' my father suggested, studying the luminous hands on his gold Cyma.

'Not quite yet, Ken. It's a wonderful evening.'

'It's already night. I don't like driving on the twisting roads—'

'It's hardly the Khyber Pass under snow,' my mother interrupted. 'No highwaymen or wily Pathans. No black ice.'

At this point, my mother stood up from her deckchair, tugged
the hem of her swimming costume down round her buttocks and
announced, 'I'm going to have another quick dip before we go.'

'Don't be ridiculous, Joyce,' my father said. 'No-one swims in
the dark. It's dangerous.'

'Rubbish!' she retorted.

'And I think it's against the law.'

'So call a policeman.'

'You'd never see an attacking shark,' my father continued. 'Or a
jellyfish. What if . . . ?'

'I'd never see an attacking shark in broad daylight. In any case,'
my mother came back at him, 'they don't stalk you, you know. As
for a jellyfish, I'd feel the stings long before it drifted my way.'

It was truly dark by now. My mother set off for the water's
edge. My father, abandoning his sentry post, followed her. I sat on
a deckchair to watch.

'Joyce! Do not go in the water.'

My mother walked on, her tanned back glowing in the light of
the lamps.

'Joyce! I'm telling you not to go in the water.'

There was no moon. The sky was a carpet of stars. Far out to
sea were the lights of a cargo ship hove to until morning.

'Joyce! I forbid you to go in the water.'

'Forbid all you want, Ken,' she replied merrily over her
shoulder and stepped into the sea.

My father returned to the tent, sat down next to me and said, 'Do
you know, the stings from a jellyfish can give you a heart seizure.'

He got up, moved the lanterns behind us and, standing by a guy
rope, squinted into the sea.

'I can't see her,' he murmured. 'If the tide's going out . . .'

To my surprise, he appeared to be genuinely concerned.

Then a voice called out urgently, 'Martin! Come here!'

'I forbid you to go,' my father said.

I got out of my deckchair.

'If you go down there, you'll get no pocket money for a month.'

I headed for the water's edge, my father keeping pace just behind me. My mother was the one who doled out my pocket money now and obeying her could hardly be construed as disobedience. It was, although I did not know how to express it, a conflict of interests. My mother's won.

'If you go into the water, I'll write to Grampy and tell him not to send any more *Eagles*.'

That I knew, as the water lapped at my ankles, was a bluff. My father enjoyed reading them too.

'Walk slowly,' my mother called. She was standing up to her waist in the sea, not ten yards from the beach. 'You too, Ken,' she added.

'I think two corpses at Shek O are enough to make the headlines in the *South China Morning Post*,' my father replied sourly and, somewhat nonplussed by his family's rebellion, returned disconsolately to the tent.

I stood next to my mother.

'Watch!' she said.

She splashed the water. Suddenly, all around her radiated with a ghostly, pale green light.

'You do it!'

I brought my hands down on the sea. A fire of pale light spread out from my hands, dancing on the surface. The splashes on my body glimmered briefly.

I was entranced. Every movement I made produced an eruption of luminosity. China, I considered, was a land of spirits and spectres and this was incontrovertible proof.

'It's called phosphorescence,' my mother said. 'Isn't it marvellous?'

'Is it made by ghosts?' I enquired, feeling my toes dig into the sand. Whenever I felt uneasy, especially approaching dog shit on the pavement, they curled.

'No,' she answered, 'it's made by millions of microscopic organisms called plankton. When the air touches them, a chemical called phosphorus in their body glows. Look!' She pointed to some breaking wavelets approaching us. They were not white but an unearthly pale green, as if touched by death.

'Maybe,' I suggested, 'it's the light of Tin Hau come to save her brothers.'

'Maybe,' my mother replied, adding ironically, 'she's protecting us from sharks and jellyfish.'

I did not question how my mother had come to acquire such information. I accepted it as I did all she said, for she was knowledgeable in the world whereas my father was only conversant with the ways of military chandlery.

We splashed around for a few more minutes then waded in to rejoin my father. He sat in the deckchair, smoking his pipe and staring out to sea as we took turns in the tent to dress.

'That was one of the bloody stupidest things I've ever known you to do, Joyce. And that's from a pretty bloody comprehensive catalogue of benighted stupidities. As for taking Martin with you . . .'

'Tell me, Ken,' my mother asked as we reached the car, 'have you ever, in your entire bloody life, done anything out of the norm, on the spur of the moment, because you suddenly felt the urge?'

My father did not answer. He got in the car, started the engine and waited for us to get in. We drove the length of Hong Kong island in silence. Back at the apartment, my mother turned on the

radio while my father headed for the drinks cabinet. Ten minutes later, my mother came into my room to tuck me up although, in the hot weather, this involved nothing more than making sure the cotton sheet I slept under was pulled up. She had heard an old colonial wives' tale that, if the stomach was not covered at night, one could be dead by morning. Of what, it was never stated. Assured that my belly was protected from the diseases of darkness, she leant over and kissed me.

'Goodnight, Martin. That was fun, wasn't it?'

'Yes,' I confirmed. 'It was.'

'Don't ever tell,' she whispered, 'but if it weren't for you, I'd leave him . . .'

I did not at the time understand what she was talking about and closed my eyes.

'Goodnight, Joyce,' I said: I had taken on occasion to addressing my parents by their given names, although my father insisted I called him *sir* when we were in company.

She touched my head then. Perhaps for luck.

Close to Pinewood Battery there was a narrow road that ran down the north side of High West. It led nowhere, just petering out on the hillside, and it was extremely steep. Consequently, few people ever went down it and the wildlife that inhabited the undergrowth was undisturbed. I sometimes went that way in the late afternoon, the sun warm off the rocks, the sky hazy and tired to the west. Skinks rustled in the leaf litter or scurried ahead of me, their azure tails swinging from side to side to counteract their movement. Butterflies sunned themselves on the cracked concrete of the road bed or fluttered over the lantana florets.

Balmy breezes blew up from the docks and narrow streets of Sai
Ying Pun, carrying the sounds and smells of the city. Every now
and then, the bellow of a cow in the Kennedy Town abattoir
might lift up to me, to be abruptly cut short. All around me,
unseen in the cover, birds caroused as they mapped out their
territories for the night.

One particular afternoon, I went that way straight from school,
hiding my Hong Kong basket full of games kit and homework
under a bush a few yards from a boulder with the inscription:
25th. Battn Middlesex Regt. "Tyndareus" Feb. 6th 1917. It was in
memory of soldiers who had died when their troopship, bound for
Hong Kong, struck a German mine off South Africa.

Setting off down the road, I had no specific purpose in mind. It
had been a bad day at school. I had scored poorly in a maths test,
been awarded fifty lines for sucking a *wah mui* in class ('It helps
me concentrate, Miss') and been given a severe ticking off for
putting the wire seal on my statutory mid-morning third of a pint
of milk ration back in the empty bottle.

A little way beyond the *Tyndareus* memorial, I suddenly
felt strangely ill at ease. It was not the maths test result nor
was it the fact that I would have to own up to getting lines. The
feeling was far more primeval, coming from the pit of my soul,
from that part of the brain that has no apparent function. I looked
back in case I was being followed, yet there was no-one – and
no thing – in sight. I could see over a hundred yards in both
directions.

Then, from the undergrowth, a small rodent appeared on the
concrete not five paces ahead of me. It stopped, stared at me
and then ran directly towards me, skittering between my legs and
on down the road. In a few seconds, it was followed by two
others which behaved in exactly the same way. I reasoned they
were running from a snake and stood quite still. Yet no snake

showed itself so, after a few minutes, I went back up the hill, collected my school basket and set off towards the Peak Tram terminus.

I had gone barely two hundred yards when a muntjak bounded out of the trees and down a steep bank. It stood in the middle of the road then, with one leap, was gone downhill in the direction of the reservoir. I could mark its progress through the forest by the noise it made. To see the creature in albeit by now fading daylight was rare enough. For it to make such a shindig as it fled was quite extraordinary. These were animals which could walk silently over a three-inch-deep layer of fresh cornflakes.

About fifty yards further on, the road narrowed, the trees growing over to form a tunnel that was always alive with birds. Used to people walking beneath their roosts, the dusk chorus was strident and melodic as I drew near.

Yet I was a short way into this sylvan subway when, all of a sudden, all the birds fell silent simultaneously. It was as if the current to them had been switched off. It was eerie and I felt apprehensive again, once more looking over my shoulder. There was no-one there. I quickened my pace and was soon at the junction by the Peak Café, heading as fast as I could up the steep road home.

When I recounted the experience to my mother, she replied that there had probably been a snake in the trees. I was not satisfied. When birds saw snakes they did not fall silent, they took to the wing.

After supper, my parents listened to the BBC World Service. I went to my room, wrote out my lines and hid them inside a textbook. Around nine o'clock, my father came in demanding to see my maths test paper. I reluctantly handed it to him. His face set as he saw the grade.

'Is there any point in us paying for you at the Peak School?' he

asked in a sullen tone. 'It seems to me you must pass half your day gazing out the bloody window.'

'I don't understand maths,' I replied.

'If you don't pay attention, it's no bloody wonder.' He tore the test paper up and dropped the pieces on my bed. 'Pull your bloody socks up or, next September, you'll find yourself boarding at Hilsea College.'

As soon as he made the threat, I knew I was safe. He could not afford the fees at Hilsea College. Furthermore, my mother would never allow it. He was all bluster and I had seen through him.

'When's the next test?'

'Next month,' I admitted.

'Well, you'd better do a bloody sight better in that one or you know what . . .'

I knew what. This threat was not bluster. I would be paddled by the flat of my mother's hairbrush or one of my father's slippers.

I got into bed, pulled up the sheet to cover my stomach, switched off the bedside lamp and turned over to face the wall. I could not understand elementary algebra or fathom the difference between the discriminant and the coefficient and was sure I never would. And why substitute letters for numbers? It seemed particularly obtuse to me and I could see no purpose to it at all.

The door opened quietly. I knew it was my mother and feigned sleep. She left and I wallowed in my self-pity and fear of the next inevitable paddling. After a while, I drifted off into a troubled sleep.

Some time in the early hours, I woke. The room was in a faint half-light cast through the slats of the venetian blinds by the glow of the city below my window. Everything looked unreal and colourless. Even the bright cover of the *Eagle* annual on my table seemed leached of hue.

Quite suddenly, I heard a deep boom. It was not loud, more like a single peal of thunder far out to sea. I gave it little thought: summer lightning over the distant islands sometimes created a resonant, far off thunderclap.

Then, the sound fading, the venetian blinds started to ripple as if an unseen hand was running over them. The *Eagle* annual began to move across the table. At the same time, my bed edged away from the wall. The air filled with a strange vibrating hum. My model junk slid along the bookshelf. The books were starting to fall.

Instantly, I conjured up mental visions of the ghosts that inhabited China, the evil gods, the cruel war-lords of heaven and hell to whom I had burnt no joss-sticks or paper money.

Screaming, I leapt from my bed and grabbed the junk before it could fall and break, putting it on the bed. I was fully awake now yet I was certain this was a dream.

My bedroom door slammed back. I jumped, the next scream frozen in my mouth. My mother rushed in, snatched me off my feet and ran with me to the front door of the apartment. My father was holding it open. Behind him, the occupants of the apartment across the landing were hurrying for the stairs.

Then it stopped. All was silent. My mother put me down. I pulled my pyjama trousers up. They had slipped halfway down my thighs and there was a girl my age living in the opposite apartment who was in my class at school.

Wearing assorted night attire, we joined the residents of the other seven apartments on the drive outside. The servants stood in a group near by talking urgently amongst themselves.

'Well, that was interesting,' my father commented with as much insouciance as he could muster.

'What happened?' I asked my mother.

'It was an earth tremor,' she replied. 'A small earthquake. It's

all over now. There may be what they call after-shocks for a few days, but we'll probably not even feel them.'

It occurred to me that the strange behaviour of the muntjak, the birds and the rodents might have been a premonition. Could the animals have been aware it was coming? Yet, although convinced this was so, I held my peace. My father, I knew, would ridicule the assumption. It was not logical, just another example of the bloody boy's vivid imagination.

We returned to our apartment to be met by Wong carrying a tray of tea, biscuits and a glass of milk.

'No p'oblum, master, missee, young master. Happen all time China-side,' he greeted us with a placatory smile.

My father took a cup of tea and started lecturing us about the earth's crust, the western Pacific earthquake zone, volcanoes and continental drift. It meant as much to me as quadratic equations. I went out into the kitchen to refill my glass of milk. Wong was sweeping up the shattered remains of some rice bowls which had slid off the draining board.

'What you think make this trouble?' I asked him.

'Yen Lo,' he said significantly and without any hesitation. 'He ang'wee. No like what man do. Tomowwow, Ah Shun go tempul-side. Maybe burn some money. Make him happy one more time.'

I preferred Wong's supernatural reasoning to my father's logic. Yen Lo was the chief god of the underworld.

9

HIKING TO BUDDHA, SWIMMING WITH COLONEL NOMA

ANOTHER OUTING ORGANIZED BY MR BORRIE PROMISED, FROM THE outline sent to my mother, to be a two-phase forced march. My father was once again reluctant to go but, as Mr Borrie was his Old Man, he was more or less faced with a three-line whip. Consequently, one winter's Saturday afternoon at thirteen hundred hours sharp, we and a party of about two dozen set off in a naval launch for the fishing village of Tung Chung on the northern coast of Lan Tau. I was the only child present. The outing guidelines had precluded those under sixteen because a good deal of walking would be involved, but my mother said I was probably fitter than half the adults and won the argument. This inevitably annoyed my father.

'It states quite clearly in the rules, Joyce—'

'Bugger the rules!' my mother retorted.

'Well, if the boy lags behind,' my father declared, 'you'll be the one to stay with him. If the two of you get lost in the mountains, be it on your own head.'

'I'll take that risk,' my mother retorted. 'It's hardly the

Himalayas. We're not likely to get caught out by a blizzard.'

Progress had passed the village of Tung Chung by. The low buildings, most well over a century old, looked out across a valley of rice paddies, banyan, paper bark and lychee trees. Behind every house or farmstead was a stand of huge yellow, green-striped bamboos, some of the stems as thick as my thigh. These, I discovered, had been deliberately planted in times past to attract snakes. When I first heard it, this information astounded me. I asked if the snakes were there to be caught for the pot, but was told that the occupants of the houses were farmers who stored their rice in the settlement. And rats ate rice. And snakes ate rats.

Stepping from our naval launch on to a rickety wooden pier, we congregated on dry land to be addressed by Mr Borrie.

'Now, have you all your maps and directions?' he asked. 'After we leave the paddyfields, there are only two places where you might get lost. One is at the nunnery, the other as you reach the pass. Be sure to consult your maps at these points. Needless to say, do not enter the nunnery.'

'What's a nunnery?' I whispered to my mother.

'Another word for a convent.'

'Why can't we enter it?' I wanted to know. Such adamant exclusion had aroused my curiosity.

'The nuns don't like men entering their houses.'

'I'm not a man,' I argued. 'I'm a boy. Neither are you. Can't we go in?'

My father, overhearing this conversation, said, 'Don't ask so many damn questions. You can't go in and that's an end to it.'

As he spoke, he fought with the straps of a military knapsack. Unaccustomed to anything larger or more complicated than an attaché case, my father was finding it hard knowing which

strap went where. My mother, who had already slipped hers on, watched impassively.

'Well don't just stand there, Joyce,' he muttered under his breath. 'Help me get this benighted thing on.'

'Didn't they show you how in the war?' she replied genially.

'I wasn't in the bloody Army.'

'Nor the bloody Navy,' she responded and set about untangling him.

'Where exactly are we going?' I asked my mother as my father tried to ease his shoulders and settle his pack.

'Ngong Ping,' my mother answered.

'What's at Ngong Ping?'

'Wait and see.'

'Where is it?'

She pointed two thousand feet or more up the mountainside and said, 'See that little dip to the left of that ridge? It's a mile the other side of that.'

We crossed a tidal creek on an uneven timber footbridge and went through the little village of Ma Wan Chung. The houses were ancient, their roofs covered with black glazed tiles. Dogs barked half-heartedly at us and chickens scattered under our feet. A large sway-backed pig lay in a patch of dust in front of a small temple, suckling a copious litter of squealing piglets. Out of the village, we set off along a wide, well-beaten track surrounded by fallow paddyfields. In another half a mile, we arrived in front of a small, derelict, grey-stone fortress covered in creepers. One of our party, armed with a *kukri*, sliced a path through to the battlements on which stood six cannon dating to the early nineteenth century. A short lecture by the *kukri* wielder informed us that the fortress was erected about 1830 in the Q'ing dynasty. It was not actually a fort *per se* but a *yamen* and centre for the administration of a number of other forts in the area. My mother whispered to me

that, had my father been Chinese and alive then, he might have been posted here as a civil servant to supply war junks. At this notion, we broke out into giggles which my father attempted unsuccessfully to stifle with narrowed eyes.

We walked indian file across more paddyfields, keeping to the paths that ran along the tops of the narrow dykes dividing the fields. On either side, rice stubble projected from hardened mud into which the hoof- and footprints of buffalo and humans had been impressed. Coming to the end of the valley, the path started to rise into the mountains, rough rocks making the going hard.

I left my parents and moved to the head of the line where Mr Borrie was making good progress.

'Hello, young Booth,' he addressed me. 'Full of beans?'

'Yes, sir.'

'Being held up by the old fogeys?'

I was not quite sure how to respond but he saved me the effort.

'Go on ahead,' he invited. 'Scout out the way. But,' he paused for effect, 'when the path branches at a Y-shaped junction, the right-hand path consisting of steps, you stop and wait for the rest of us. You savvy?'

I savvied and set off up the mountain. The path grew steeper but I swung my arms, measured my breathing and was soon several hundred yards ahead of the party. It was not long before I came to the Y junction. A small rill tumbled down the mountain-side and I wet my face in it but did not drink. One never knew if the water had already served a multitude of purposes in a settlement at a higher altitude. I crossed the path and sat on the steps to let the rest of the party catch up. Behind me stood a small group of buildings from which, when the breeze temporarily shifted direction, I could smell joss-sticks.

There came a soft shuffling sound from over my shoulder. I turned to find myself being observed by two Buddhist nuns. They

wore grey, long-sleeved, ankle-length habits and their heads were
shaven, so it was quite impossible to judge their ages. Around
their necks hung simple necklaces of wooden beads. Not sure
what to do, and heedful of Mr Borrie's warning, I stood up and
stepped back on to the path. They watched me go, impassive looks
upon their faces. I sensed that perhaps they were young and
wanted to talk to me, this strange, small *gweilo* from the other
world of which they occasionally heard talk but had not seen for
many years, nor perhaps ever would again.

The remainder of the party arrived and I rejoined my parents
to find my father in a mood.

'What do you think you were doing, you blithering little idiot?'
my father demanded to know.

'Let him be, Ken,' my mother remonstrated.

'That's rich, coming from someone who took him swimming at
night with the tide going out.'

'He's come to no harm.'

My father ignored these entreaties and directed his full attention to me. Keeping his voice, which was breathless from the
climb, low he said, 'Where were you? Your mother and I were
worried stiff.'

'No, I wasn't,' my mother chimed in. 'If Martin can find his
way through the streets of Kowloon, he can sure as eggs is eggs
find his way on a mountainside with only one path on it.'

'And if he had fallen?' my father replied.

'He has the run of the Peak, Ken, for God's sake,' my mother
said with a hint of exasperation. 'I think he's intelligent enough to
know a sheer drop when he sees one. Besides, do you notice any
precipices, Ken? Cliffs? The worst he can do is slip on the path
and slide down on his bum.'

She looked at me pointedly then at the rear of my father's
trousers. They were covered in dust and I regretted having gone

ahead. My father sliding downhill on his arse must have been a sight to behold.

'I had permission. I was asked to scout ahead as far as the nunnery.'

'By whom?' my father answered, in the tone of voice that suggested he was convinced I was lying.

'Ken—'

'No, Joyce, I'm getting to the bottom of this . . .'

At that moment, Mr Borrie called back from the head of the line, 'Hello, Ken, Joyce. Well, young Booth, ready for some more scouting?'

My father gave me a thunderous look. I had not been lying. My mother gave me a smile and a sly wink.

The path grew steeper as it approached the high flanks of Lan Tau Peak. I started to get breathless, my head spinning with the exertion, and was about to pause for a rest when the path levelled out and I could see, some way ahead, a ceremonial archway, or *pi lau*. Curiosity overcame exhaustion.

The *pi lau* was made of stone and stood silhouetted against the sky. The Chinese characters engraved over its span had once been painted red but the mountain wind had all but wiped them clean. From the *pi lau*, the path followed the contours of a hill to a plateau of neatly tended vegetable fields. I was surprised to find any agriculture going on at such an altitude but what really amazed me were the number of pagoda-like structures that dotted the landscape. They too were made of stone, about twelve feet high, painted white and resembling several iced doughnuts placed one on top of the other, getting consecutively smaller as the structure got higher. On the top was a finial painted imperial Chinese yellow.

'What are they, sir?' I asked Mr Borrie who had caught up with me.

The remainder of the party was strung out behind him. The rearguard, which consisted of my father, had only just reached the *pi lau*.

'I believe they're either the graves of abbots,' Mr Borrie replied, 'or receptacles for holy scriptures. This is Ngong Ping, our destination. You've done very well getting up the mountain. Put the rest of us to shame.' He glanced back. My father was leaning against the *pi lau*. 'Your poor old dad's a bit out of shape.'

'What's an abbot?' I enquired.

'The head of a monastery,' came the reply.

'But why do they bring them all the way up here to bury them?'

'Step forth, young Booth,' Mr Borrie answered, 'and all shall be revealed.'

We walked on together. The path widened. Ahead, surrounded by low trees, was a group of stone buildings.

'Here we are,' Mr Borrie announced. 'This is the Po Lin monastery. *Po Lin* means Precious Lotus, so that should tell you what religion is worshipped here.'

It did and I replied, 'Buddhism, sir.'

'Well done!' he congratulated me. 'Now, as the others arrive, you tell them to wait here.'

Mr Borrie hurried on to the monastery. I felt adult and important with my responsibility. In fifteen minutes, he returned and led us along a path through carefully tended vegetable plots, past an area of tea bushes and into the monastery complex, the buildings tucked under a low ridge. It was by now late afternoon. The sun was already down below the montane horizon and the temperature dropping fast.

Gathered together by a circular moon gate, we were introduced to a monk whom we were told was the guest master. Like the nuns I had seen, he wore a grey-coloured robe and his head was shaven. He welcomed us in broken English, informed us of the

monastic timetable, invited us to join the monks in prayer around dawn and reminded us that this was a tranquil place so we were not to 'make big noise'. Our party was then divided into two groups by gender. The women were allotted a dormitory some way off, the men another in a two-storey building immediately behind the temple.

I was placed with the men. The room in which we were to sleep was on the second floor, had a low ceiling with beams that were nothing more than tree trunks supporting the roof. The beds were plain wooden *kangs* surrounded by screens, each one covered by a woven mat and a thin cotton quilt with a hard Chinese traditional pillow. Lighting was provided by three guttering oil lanterns which cast a timeless orange glow on the dark wood. It reminded me of the opium den in Kowloon Walled City.

My father, having struggled to escape the clutches of his knapsack, unpacked it. He had brought a dressing gown, flannel pyjamas and the slippers that doubled as instruments of summary justice back home. These neatly laid out on his *kang*, he took out his red leather wash bag and a towel, placing them beside his clothing. When he was done, his possessions looked like a naval rating's bunk in a lower-deck mess awaiting a daily kit inspection. No-one else bothered to unpack.

'Here's your stuff,' my father said, producing a wash bag from the knapsack. He rummaged further. 'I can find your towel . . .' he said at length, handing it to me '. . . but I'm damned if I can find your pyjamas. Your mother seems to have forgotten them.'

A sonorous bell, almost as deep as a bass drum, boomed in a nearby building. I went outside to discover Mr Borrie standing by the moon gate.

'Excuse me, sir,' I asked, breaking into his thoughts, 'but why are we allowed to stay here when we aren't monks?'

'Good question, young Booth,' he replied. 'Buddhist monks

take a vow of hospitality. That means, they are obliged to give succour – food and shelter – for free, to anyone who demands it. But when people like us come to stay here we make an offering to the monastery and pay the cost of our food and lodging.'

'Why?'

'Because we are rich *gweilos* and they are poor Chinese monks,' Mr Borrie replied. 'A dollar to us is a pack of cigarettes, but to them . . .' He paused then went on, 'Tonight, you'll live like a Buddhist monk, just as they have for a thousand years.'

'I've not got any pyjamas,' I admitted. My mother's omission was worrying me.

'Don't fret,' Mr Borrie reassured me. 'Neither have any of us. Except perhaps your father.' He winked at me and went on, 'We'll be having supper soon. Don't be late.'

I left him and went into the temple. It was like all the other temples I had visited, with an ornate altar, smouldering incense, embroidered tapestries, offerings, lanterns and censers. The one difference was the statue of Buddha. In the curio shops and gold dealers of Hong Kong, Buddha was represented by a fat, grinning man with a paunch of obese proportions. This Buddha, by contrast, was a benign seated figure with a peaceful expression, its right hand raised in blessing. There were no demon warriors or guardians of heaven. I lit a joss-stick, genuflected – after checking my father was not about to enter – and placed it in the sand-filled urn. Had my father, who professed Christianity but never went to church, caught me worshipping false gods and idols, I dared not think of the consequences. He would probably have personally condemned me to eternal damnation.

Returning through the moon gate, I followed the sound of the bell and came upon a hall in which lines of monks sat at a square of low tables finishing a meal. At one end of the room, a monk stood at a simple lectern reading a collect as his brothers ate. The

only sounds were his chant-like reading and the tolling of a bronze bell which was shaped like an inverted tulip. It was rung by a log of wood suspended horizontally by two ropes from a ceiling beam.

I lingered in the doorway. The monks paid me not the slightest attention and, after a few moments, I slipped away.

'You forgot my pyjamas,' I said to my mother as I came upon her by a small pond in which a number of red-eared terrapins floated in the water or lay on a rock in the centre.

'Do you know why they keep terrapins?' she rejoined.

'To eat?' I ventured.

'No,' she replied. 'It's because terrapins and turtles – especially marine turtles – are considered very lucky and stand for longevity. That means long life. The turtle supports the elephant upon whose back rests the world. A long time ago, the Chinese believed the world was a giant turtle's shell. Besides,' she finished, 'what do you want pyjamas for? It's going to be far too cold for py-jams. When you go to bed, just take your shoes off, keep all your clothes on and wrap yourself up in the quilt.'

'But Daddy's got his,' I argued, ignoring the homily on the universal and divine turtle which I already knew from my visits to numerous back-street temples.

'Well, he would, wouldn't he?' was my mother's response.

We ate by lamplight in a large room at the other end of the monastery from the monks' hall. The food was delicious, the flavours subtle and the textures exquisite. Yet, although I was an experienced *dai pai dong* diner, I was unable to recognize many of the dishes and asked my mother what meat was in them.

'None,' she answered.

With my chopsticks, I picked up a piece of what looked like and tasted like braised duck's breast.

'I know what you're thinking,' my mother said, 'but it's not

duck. It's against the Buddhist religion to take life. All the food is made out of *dofu*, fungi and herbs. The vegetables are grown in the plots we saw as we arrived. The monastery is virtually self-sufficient in everything except paraffin, candles and joss-sticks.'

At nine o'clock, we turned in. There were eight of us in the dormitory. My *kang* was in a cubicle on its own, my father's the far side of the screen separating my space from the others'. I removed my shoes and snuggled under the quilt fully clothed. Outside, a cold wind had sprung up, rattling the shutters of the window by my head. My father came round the end of the screen to say goodnight. He was wearing his dressing gown over the flannel pyjamas. His slippers clicked on the wooden floor.

The boards of the *kang* were hard, as was the pillow block, but I soon fell asleep, a cold draught blowing over my face.

During the night, I was woken by a strange noise. It sounded like castanets being played in slow motion or a convention of geckoes. On consideration, I knew it could not be the latter. One rarely saw geckoes in the winter: it was too cold for them. It then occurred to me that it might be the skeleton of a lonely spirit wandering the earth. If there were spirits anywhere, they would surely be in a monastery high in the mountains.

Then a muted voice said, 'For heaven's sake, Ken, put your clothes back on. Your shivering's keeping us awake.'

Around dawn, I was woken again but this time by muffled chanting. Slipping my shoes on, I tiptoed down the stairs and went outside. The sound was coming from the temple. I went to the main door and stepped inside. The monks were kneeling in front of the altar, chanting prayers. Their shaven heads shone in the lamplight. Buddha seemed to hover in mid-air in the semi-darkness, the lamps glinting off the brass cups. The joss-stick smoke hung marbled in the air, moving only when a finger of breeze blew in. It was an unearthly experience. I felt I was

wrapped in the pure essence of divinity. Somehow, I had tran-
scended the ordinary in my life and was now in what an adult
might have termed a state of grace.

By the time the prayer session ended, it was fully daylight. I left
the temple to find the men from my dormitory sluicing their faces
at a water trough fed by a small stone-lined gully. A few had
loosened their shirts and were rubbing their armpits. I followed
their example. The water was only a few degrees above freezing
and tightened my skin the moment it touched it, stealing my
breath. The cold breeze chilled my wet skin until it hurt.

I was pondering on whether or not to fetch my towel when my
father appeared, fully dressed but dishevelled, his towel around
his neck. Not greeting me, he balanced his wash bag on the edge
of the trough and removed from it a razor, shaving brush and a
bowl of shaving soap. He wet his face with a flannel, soaped
himself without being able to build up much of a lather, and
started shaving. Several of the other men gave each other knowing
glances.

It must have been hell. Over the sound of the wind, I could hear
the blade of his safety razor rasping at his stubble. More than once,
he winced but kept his jaw set and his razor hand firm. He had
just finished his chin when the towel slipped from his neck,
caught his wash bag and the two of them fell into the water. His
shaving brush followed, the weight of its ivory handle sinking it to
the bottom of the trough. My father had no alternative but to strip
to the waist and immerse himself to the shoulder to retrieve it.

An hour later, warmed by a bowl of tea and a serving of *congee*,
we bade the guest master farewell by bowing to him and left
the monastery. We headed for Mui Wo, otherwise known as
Silvermine Bay, seven and a half miles away over the mountains.
It was quite heavy going in places but, by mid-morning, the sky
was cloudless and blue, the sunlight sharp and warm on the skin.

As on the day before, I forged ahead of the party and thought over my brief stay in the monastery. I could never, I decided, adapt to the life of a monk, yet it certainly held a distinct attraction. The monastery had been so peaceful, my father's chattering teeth apart, and the chanting had somehow lifted my soul. I knew, there and then, that I would return to the monastery one day.

On Hong Kong-side, in addition to rickshaws, taxis and buses, there was a double-decker tram system that ran from Kennedy Town in the west to Shau Kei Wan at the eastern extremity of the city. A branch line veered off to Happy Valley where it went in a circuit round the racecourse and was diverted to the tram depot. The newer trams were made of metal panelling on a steel chassis, the seats were wooden slats and the windows went up and down on a sash. Power was supplied by overhead poles connecting to wires, the trams driven by electric motors. On those that were older, the front and rear upper decks were open whilst one or two very old models had upper decks that were completely open to the sky.

The trams were slow and noisy as they rattled and ground their way along tracks set in the metalled surface of the streets, yet they were also almost romantic, a means of locomotion from another age. Furthermore, they were cheap. The fare was ten cents, no matter how far one travelled. This was ideal for me. I would walk towards Kennedy Town and mount a tram heading east. If I got on near the start of the journey I was assured a top-deck front seat.

The vehicle seemed to clatter and clank its way through a history of urban Hong Kong. From Western District with its

narrow nineteenth-century streets lined with traditional Chinese buildings as old as the colony itself, the tram tracks entered Central District, swaying by the plush prestige stores such as the Dragon Seed Company. Running down the centre of Des Voeux Road, it went along the edge of Statue Square, by the façades of the Hongkong and Shanghai Bank and the Bank of China – under the impassive bronze gaze of Stephen and Stitt – before skirting the Hong Kong Cricket Club pitch.

From my vantage point on the top deck I could look down on the pedestrians, coolies and rickshaws, old crones pushing wheeled trolleys piled with bags of laundry, Chinese school children in pristine uniforms, amahs immaculate in black and white, policemen in their khaki uniforms, with their black Sam Browne belts and revolvers in holsters, directing the traffic from their pagoda-like platforms. Conservative-looking British and brash American cars drove by. Cyclists wove in and out of the traffic.

Next, the tram would enter Wanchai, sliding past bars, tea houses, mahjong schools and restaurants. Passengers boarded or alighted at tram stops on small traffic islands, getting on the tram at the front and off at the rear. Onwards then along the edge of the Causeway Bay typhoon shelter, North Point, Quarry Bay and Sai Wan Ho. Eventually, after more than an hour, the tram would reach Shau Kei Wan where, turning in a circle by a junk-building yard, it would set off on the return journey. I would break my journey here, sit on the sea wall over which I knew the invading Japanese Imperial Army had swarmed in 1941, drink a Green Spot and watch the carpenters shaping planks to make a junk before me, the keel laid and the air scented with the perfume of teakwood shavings.

One summer's afternoon, I was sitting on the upper deck of an eastbound tram when an elderly European woman carrying a

silver-topped walking cane and a bunch of yellow roses wrapped in cellophane sat next to me.

'Excuse me, young man,' she said, 'but can you tell me if this tram is for Happy Valley?'

'No,' I replied, 'this tram goes to North Point.'

'Oh, dear!' she exclaimed, suddenly clearly distressed. 'I need to get to Happy Valley. It's all most confusing.'

I realized then that she was not a *gweipor* and offered to take her there. She readily accepted and, after changing trams at the Percival Street switch-over, we proceeded around the race course perimeter.

'Where exactly are you going?' I enquired.

'To the cemetery,' was her answer.

The Happy Valley cemetery was the second oldest in Hong Kong, the earliest graves dating to the foundation of the colony.

As we approached the tram stop by the cemetery entrance, she asked, 'You wouldn't help me, would you, young man? I'm afraid my legs aren't what they used to be.'

I helped her down the stairs and across the road into the cemetery. The graves were arranged on a series of stepped terraces running up the side of the valley.

'I need to find a grave,' she said as we entered the cemetery.

I looked in dismay at the serried ranks of perhaps a thousand tombstones. Those higher up the cemetery were overgrown with creepers. Ideal snake terrain, I thought. And I was wearing shorts, short socks and sandals.

'Could you help me find it?'

I was beginning to think I had been suckered by this sweet old lady but decided to assist her nevertheless.

'What is the . . . ?' I was not sure how to refer to a corpse.

She gave me the surname, adding, 'He died in 1879.'

While the elderly lady perched on a grave, leaning on her cane

and wiping her brow, I started to trot methodically along the lines of graves. In three-quarters of an hour I had viewed all the graves except those in the cover which I was most loathe to approach.

All the graves were of Europeans, predominantly men under the age of thirty. Some were military graves, others civilian. Yet what astonished me was their causes of death. Diseases I had expected, but not 'fell from the rigging', 'lost overboard', 'murdered in the pursuance of his duty', and 'killed by pirates off Cheefoo'. Many of the memorials had been erected 'by his shipmates' or public subscription.

The elderly lady was disappointed I had not found her grave but she gave me a ten-dollar note.

I thanked her and asked why she was seeking the grave.

'It's my great-grandfather,' she replied. 'He was one of the first British people to live here.'

I thought for a minute then said, 'The oldest graveyard is in Stanley. I go swimming near there.'

'And how might I get to Stanley?'

'There's a bus,' I told her, 'but I don't know where to catch it.'

She bent down and kissed me on my cheek. 'You are a little angel,' she praised me.

At that, she picked up her roses and hailed a taxi.

'Can you tell the driver where I want to go?'

I leant through the window and said, '*Chek Chue.*'

With that, she was gone. The last I saw of her were her yellow roses on the back parcel shelf of the taxi.

When I arrived home, I told my mother what I had been up to.

'Well, you did your best for the poor soul,' she remarked.

'But the graves . . .' I said. 'No-one died of old age.'

'No, I'm sure they didn't,' my mother replied. 'That was their sacrifice. Those people founded Hong Kong. They set the ball

rolling for all of us.' She was pensive for a moment before adding, 'I wonder what they'd think of it now.'

That evening, I sat on the balcony with all of Hong Kong spread out at my feet and tried to imagine it without streets and buildings and ferry boats. Instead of grey British and American warships I attempted to visualize men-o'-war and opium clippers and war junks. And it came to me that I was a descendant of those men, keeping the ball rolling merely by my being there.

My father had a fierce hatred of the trams based upon the facts that they had no brake lights, they caused traffic jams at tram stops where vehicular traffic had to give way to alighting or embarking passengers, and they had a right of way over the traffic lights. Worse, however, was their inability to stop as quickly as a car.

The first incident happened on Yee Wo Street. My father wished to turn right into Kai Chiu Road. Disregarding a tram coming up behind, he pulled smartly into the centre of the road – where the tram tracks lay – and waited for a break in the traffic. There was the sound of tearing metal. Sparks flew from the tram wheel. A North Point bound tram slid into the back of the Ford at an impact speed of about three miles an hour. I was mildly jolted in the back seat. My father got out to survey the damage. The rear offside lights of the Ford were smashed, the bumper and rear wing dented and deformed. The tram driver alighted, surveyed the situation then gesticulated for my father to get his car out of the way. On the tram, all the passengers were leaning out of the windows.

My father refused to move. My mother and I joined him. A

crowd began to gather on the pavement expectantly awaiting what was an inescapable confrontation.

'Move the car towards the kerb, Ken,' my mother suggested.

'No, Joyce! Not until the police have seen it.'

'You've got me and Martin as witnesses.'

'No!' my father repeated bluntly. 'I want independent third-party verification. The law clearly states that the driver of any vehicle that goes up the back of another vehicle is liable. I'm not at fault here . . .'

My mother sought to placate my father. 'No-one says you are, Ken.'

'He's culpable,' my father said, pointing an accusatory finger at the tram driver, who took umbrage at being pointed at and let off a stream of invective in Cantonese that even I could not translate.

'Don't you speak to me like that!' my father retorted. 'You should have kept your bloody distance . . .'

At this, the driver decided not to keep any distance at all and closed on my father.

'Don't you come on to me like that!' my father muttered loudly and he removed his blazer, putting it in the car.

'Ken, I don't think this is helping matters,' my mother observed. 'Just let it go.'

'I'm damned if I will!' my father exclaimed over his shoulder. 'I'm not in the wrong here.'

The passengers in the tram, like schoolboys in a playground seeing a fight in the offing, started to egg the tram driver on. He commenced bouncing about on his heels like a boxer warming up.

This, I knew as a spectator at any number of coolie arguments, did not bode well, yet there was nothing I could do to defuse the situation.

Suddenly, the tram driver lunged at my father who blocked

the blow. My mother tried to step between the combatants, safe in the knowledge that no-one would dare hit a *gweipor*. The tram driver dodged round her and took another swing. My father blocked it once more and managed to land a clout around his opponent's ear. The passengers on the tram and the audience on the pavement gave vent to a loud *Whoa!* intermingled with an undertone of *Ayarhs!*

Needless to say, this enraged the driver further. He had lost face in front of at least two hundred onlookers.

Feeling I should do something, I stepped forwards and yelled at him, *'Wei! Lei! Heui la! Diu nei lo mo!'* (literally, Hey, you! Get lost! Go fuck your mother!).

At the time, I was ignorant of the exact meaning of the phrase but knew it was pretty expressive. My knowledge of the language of the streets exercised, I then stepped forward and shook my finger at him in a school-ma'amish fashion.

The crowd on the pavement broke out into hoots of hilarity. So did the passengers. The driver just stared at me, taken aback by this little *gweilo* who spoke at least a smattering of colloquial Cantonese.

A police traffic patrol arrived.

As the Ford was now askew across both the east- and west-bound tram lines, it was quickly causing a backlog to build up in both directions. A traffic patrol had come to see what was creating gridlock half a mile down the road.

'This bloody fool—' my father began.

'I can see what's happened, sir,' a European police inspector interrupted him. 'Now, with your permission . . .'

A Chinese constable drove the Ford to the kerb whilst four others directed the traffic. The westbound trams started moving again. After a few words from a Chinese police corporal, the tram driver returned to his place and the tram went on its way.

The inspector took out a notebook and pencil then came over to my father.

'Not very lucky, are we, sir?' He opened the notebook. 'First the tricycle . . .'

He took down the details. The tram company paid for the damage. They also accepted liability for the next two, identical accidents. On the fourth, they sued for remuneration of income lost due to delayed services. They did not win the case. As a result, however, my father – like my mother before him – was the cause of a change in the law. It was henceforth illegal to stop a vehicle on the tram lines.

For as long as we lived in Hong Kong, my mother had attempted to get me to swim. She was a fairly competent swimmer herself and wanted me to be likewise, ostensibly as a life skill such as playing tennis or bridge or being able to ballroom dance, but actually so as to have someone to swim with.

At least once a week throughout my school holidays and often at a weekend during term, my mother and I would go to the beach together, sometimes in the company of friends, sometimes just the two of us. Her favourite spot when we lived at the Fourseas and on Boundary Street in Kowloon was 11½ Mile Beach. It lacked any amenities whatsoever and the only shelter was three or four ruined beach houses destroyed in the war and a row of trees. However, a Dairy Farm popsicle seller was usually to be found in the vicinity.

The beach was of sand with a freshwater stream cutting through it at one end. Transport was provided by the Navy, which ran a daily families' bus service to Kadoorie Beach, seven

miles further on with beach toilets, deckchairs, ice-cream sellers and a *dai pai dong* or two. Whereas the latter was frequently crowded, *sap yat bun* (Cantonese for 11½), as my mother called the beach, rarely had two dozen people on it.

As soon as her foot touched sand, my mother undressed. Wearing only a pair of shorts and a blouse over her swimming costume, she was stripped for action in seconds. I took longer out of a reluctance to join her. I would rather have spent my afternoon catching fish in the stream or hunting for tree frogs in the ravine down which it ran. Finally, unable to dismiss my mother's entreaties any longer, I would take off my clothes and, grudgingly be-trunked, wade out to join her.

The sea was always warm and lapped at my stomach. The sandy bottom was firm with only a few rocks here and there to which clung barnacles, minuscule sea anemones that packed a vicious sting and urchins with long black spines as sharp as hypodermic needles. A crevice in a large submarine rock was the residency of a small octopus which could be lured out with a dead fish or a piece of meat. It never completely quit its shelter but I often managed to encourage its tentacles and head into the open.

Yet we were not there to enjoy the wonders of marine nature. My mother would take my hands and, towing me as she walked backwards, attempt to get me to kick my legs. I watched as the water rose up her body and knew that once her bosom was submerged I was out of my depth. At this point, she would let go of one hand and tell me to move it breast-stroke fashion. I would obey but grip her other hand so tightly she could not cast me adrift. All the while, I would be breathing hard in panic and begging her not to let me go. She promised she would not and she never did. As a consequence she didn't betray a trust nor did I learn to swim. I possessed plenty of theory but precious little courage.

After a while, she would give up and swim out to the swimming platform where she would sit absorbing the sub-tropical sun, her head tilted back, her short blond hair golden in the light and her eyes closed, day-dreaming.

I would sit on the beach and look out at her, often wondering how life would be if it were just her and me. I think it was at those moments I came to love her rather than just rely upon her as children do their mothers. I was becoming independent and my feelings for her were altering – maturing – as a consequence.

At five o'clock, the grunting horn of the Bedford bus would summon us from the beach and we would climb the concrete steps to the road and board it. Because the seats were wooden and slatted we did not even need to change out of our wet costumes.

After our move to the Peak we frequented Tweed Bay, a secluded sandy beach set aside for the exclusive use of the members of the Prison Officers' Club at Stanley, of which my parents were curiously members. It lay in a tiny bay under the very walls of Hong Kong's top security jail and was reached by passing through several guarded gates. No-one had ever escaped from the place: only one prisoner had ever scaled the walls and he had broken his legs in the process. Every bather was a turnkey, his superior or their families.

I liked Tweed Bay the least of all the beaches we visited. There were no food or popsicle sellers, no streams or woods to explore – and if there had been, they would have been out of bounds as I found out when I tried to climb the hill behind the beach to get a look into the prison. I had not gone fifty yards before I was apprehended by two warders. In short, Tweed Bay was boring.

It was here I finally learnt to swim.

One Saturday afternoon, my mother and I drove to Tweed Bay with Philip and Ray as our club guests, riding in their Jaguar. Both the Bryants were good fun and, as they had no children of

their own, I became a surrogate son whenever we were together. In retrospect, I think Philip appreciated how my father regarded me with indifference and decided to fill in a few of the cracks in his non-existent paternity.

We parked by the prison walls and walked to the beach. There were no changing facilities but, as usual, we wore our swimming costumes in lieu of underwear. In next to no time, the adults were in the sea and I was paddling in the shallows.

Eventually, tiring of this, I sat on the beach, absent-mindedly and unsuccessfully digging for the small opaque crabs that lived in holes in the sand. After a while, Philip left the sea and walked up to me.

'I think it's time,' he said.

'Time for what?' I rejoined.

'To swim. Before we go home, I'll have you frolicking like a porpoise.'

This I very much doubted but I trusted Philip and agreed he could have a go where my mother had failed. I was not to know that she and Ray were in on it too.

Philip and I walked out until the water was up to my chest. He then held his arms out and I lay across his hands, face down. The wavelets broke in my face, stinging my eyes.

'Now,' Philip said, 'kick your legs like frogs do.'

I did as he suggested.

'Now, don't stop kicking and move your arms, fingers closed, as if you were pushing the water behind you.' Again, I complied.

Suddenly, I sensed his hands were no longer touching my stomach. Indeed, he was at least ten feet away and treading water. I panicked, stopped kicking, tried to stand up and sank vertically. I was going to drown. I knew it. I opened my mouth to scream. At that moment, my head broke the surface, strong hands under my armpits.

'I want to get out!' I spluttered, clinging to his neck.

'If you want to get out,' he answered calmly, 'you'll have to swim to the beach. I'll come with you.'

'I can't swim,' I pleaded.

'Yes, you can,' he declared, smiling at me. 'The human body is less dense than seawater. It floats. Look at your mother and Ray.' Sure enough, they were holding hands and floating on their backs. 'Now, let's try again.'

I wanted to trust Philip. I liked him and I knew he would never let me come to harm, but . . . He put his hands on my stomach again, held me horizontal in the water and off we went. He removed his hands and, with much splashing and gasping, I made it to the beach.

My mother and Ray kissed me; Philip shook my hand, man to man.

'You see,' he said when the clamour of female congratulation had died down, 'in life we can do anything within our physical power if only we have the courage. You could climb Mount Everest if you genuinely wanted to.'

That hot Saturday in the South China Sea, I learnt more than how to swim. Philip had shown me that much more was possible if one pushed the limits a bit and, from then on, I did.

As my mother and Ray got changed behind a towel, Philip and I did the gentlemanly thing and looked out beyond Tweed Bay into the greater Ty Tam Bay beyond.

'A good place to learn to swim,' he remarked offhandedly. 'Not much current, and if you knew about the place you'd never let your feet touch the bottom.'

'Why not?' I asked, picturing giant clams or beds of sea urchins.

'Do you know who Colonel Noma was?'

I shook my head.

'Well,' Philip told me, 'after the war, the Japanese in Hong

Kong who had murdered a lot of our chaps – and local Chinese, too – were rounded up and tried in a court of law for what were called war crimes. That was not just killing people in the fighting, which is what happens in war, but afterwards. Killing wounded soldiers instead of treating them, unarmed prisoners, women and children. That sort of thing. Those that were found guilty were hanged in the prison behind us. There were nine of them in all. The most senior were Colonels Noma and Tamura. When they were dead their bodies were weighted with chains and dumped in the sea.'

'What did they do?' I asked.

'Noma was head of the gendarmerie. He killed and tortured many people.'

'How many?'

'Certainly hundreds, probably thousands.'

'Why didn't they dig graves for them?'

'Because the British and Chinese wanted to punish them for ever. The Japanese believe a man's soul cannot go to heaven if he is drowned or buried at sea.'

'Where did they dump them?' I asked.

'Here,' Philip answered, taking his pipe out of his mouth and pointing with it. 'In Ty Tam Bay.'

Immediately, my toes curled into the damp sand.

'Touch bottom here and you might be standing on the bones of Colonels Noma and Tamura themselves.'

I am sure Philip told me this to make certain I continued to swim and, over the coming months, I came to do so quite well, but never again at Tweed Bay.

Not long after my grandmother's departure back to England, my mother's health had begun to deteriorate. She had previously contracted jaundice whilst my father was away in Japan. At the time, I was bundled off to stay with a Mr and Mrs Everett who lived at Magazine Gap and my mother was admitted to the Royal Naval Hospital at Mount Kellett. Now, a year or so later, her illness was less immediate but more insidious. She started to suffer pains in her joints, periods of weakness and migraine headaches. There seemed to be no apparent cause for this but the diagnosis was the onset of rheumatoid arthritis, the prognosis (which fortunately turned out to be erroneous) being that she would be crippled by the age of fifty and probably dead by fifty-five. As she was then thirty-four, this promised a bleak and brief future with considerable pain. It was noticed that she felt worse when our apartment was in the mist which, being the better part of fifteen hundred feet above sea level, it was quite frequently. Particularly during the hot season, the top of the Peak could become shrouded in warm mist. It was not polluted but simply water vapour that had condensed around the summits, cooled by the rising breezes and rock faces.

I found walking to school in this mist an exhilarating experience. When the mountain was in the mist, the pace of life slowed. Birds ceased to sing so much, people moved with a measured speed. In the servants' quarters, fingers of mist inveigled themselves through the lattice stone work and laundered clothes had to be brought in to the kitchen to dry. By the Peak Tram terminus, all would be quiet, no tourists thronging the observation point, no American sailors patronizing the Peak Café. Cars crept along in low gear, their headlights dipped, the drivers peering through the windscreen to follow the line of the road. Often I would not meet another living soul. It was as if I had the Peak to myself. Sounds were suppressed, my footsteps barely

audible to me. Shadows loomed up in the mist, boulders and trees with which I was more than familiar taking on alien shapes. My over-active imagination tinkered with them. It was a scary time. On rare occasions, I woke in the morning to find the apartment above the mist. The view from the windows was much as I expected it might be from a high-flying aircraft, the solid-looking billows of cloud beneath bathed in pristine sunlight.

Due to my mother's adverse reaction to the mist, her doctors suggested we leave the Peak and move back down to the city or at least to Mid-Levels, the band of housing halfway up the mountain and usually below the cloud line. The problem was that there were no available quarters.

Throughout the summer term, I hurried home from school every day to be with my mother. Those few friends I had were obliged to come to my home to play. She liked meeting them but there were times when our boisterousness tired her quickly and we had to leave. She and I would also go for walks, my mother strolling rather than striding out as she was wont. I shared my places with her – the rifle range where she dug for bullets with me, Governor's Walk where she marvelled as had I at the fact that tiny fish lived at the top of a mountain and the ruins of Mountain Lodge and Pinewood Battery.

It was when we were sitting on the wall of one of the gun emplacements at Pinewood late one afternoon that she first broached the subject with me that had clearly been in her mind for a while.

'Martin,' she began, 'do you like living in Hong Kong?'

'Yes,' I answered, wondering where the conversation was going.

'More than England?'

'I think so,' I said. 'I can't really remember it except Nanny's house, and Granny and Grampy's house . . .'

'You know that in less than six months we have to go back to England, don't you?'

I had not really given this much thought.

'Your father's tour of overseas duty ends and he's being posted to a naval stores depot at Corsham, near Bath. You'll be going to a prep school to cram for the eleven-plus examination. If you pass, you'll go to the Royal City of Bath Boys' Grammar School.'

'And if I don't,' I said glumly, 'I suppose I'll be a dustman.'

'Like hell you will!' she retorted. 'Whatever you choose to do, you'll succeed. Isn't that what the fortune-teller predicted? Don't listen to your father. He's a plodder. Twenty years before the typewriter and he hasn't even made Commander . . .'

She fell silent for a while. I watched the kites soaring over Sai Ying Pun. On the slopes of Mount Davis, the most westerly high point of the island, the squatters' cooking fires were visible as sparks in the shadow of the hill.

'I don't want to go back,' my mother said emphatically, breaking our silence. 'England is dreary, colourless, down-in-the-mouth. Lifeless. Just look at this.' She turned and faced distant Lan Tau, the rays of the setting sun fingering between the mountains. 'How can I live in Romford or Woking or Basingstoke after this?'

'Or Bath,' I suggested.

She laughed ironically and stood up, suggesting, 'Let's go back via Lugard Road.'

As we walked slowly round the mountain, the city unfolding beneath us, my mother said, 'I want to stay here. In Hong Kong. And I've been thinking. Your father will have to resign from the Admiralty and get a job here. In the government, perhaps. Tax is much lower here than in Britain and the salaries are a good deal higher.'

I noticed she did not say 'Back home' as so many of her friends did.

'Will he change jobs?' I wondered aloud.

'Oh, yes!' my mother replied quietly and with a cast-iron confidence. 'Maybe not this week, maybe not next month, but he will. You mark my words!'

My mother adored the apartment at Mount Austin. It was spacious and had views from every window for which any Hollywood star would have inserted bamboo splinters under their fingernails, she had Wong and Ah Shun to attend to the chores, Su Yin to cosset and Tuppence to spoil. Her Chinese circle of friends, larger than her crowd of *gweipor* acquaintances, regularly visited for tea, often staying on into the evening, much to my father's chagrin: as long as my mother had guests he had to ease up on the pink gins and whisky sodas.

At other times, she continued to go for picnics with them, swimming parties or *chow*, which meant a meal in a Chinese restaurant. To her friends' children, she was universally known as Auntie Joy. When festivals came round, she was invited along to the celebrations as an ersatz relative.

The *gweipor* in her only came out in the mornings when she went to play canasta and drink coffee with other European women. She went swimming as much as she could, the exercise keeping her joints flexible. When that was not feasible, she wrote letters and poetry and knitted baby clothes either for Su Yin, the various new-born of friends or a squatter charity. Yet both she and I knew the time was coming when we would be presented with the opportunity to leave the Peak. And we would have to take it.

Finally, after six weeks of intermittent mist and continuous painkillers, with no quarters becoming available, my parents decided there was only one thing they could do. Just in time for the beginning of the new academic year in September, we packed

up the apartment, put our furniture in store, reluctantly dismissed Wong and Ah Shun with much shedding of tears (but with references so glowing Wong could have landed a job in the Savoy or the Ritz had he so chosen), signed me off the roll at the Peak School and moved across to take up residency once more in the Fourseas Hotel.

10

MONG KOK REVISITED

LITTLE HAD CHANGED IN THE STREETS AROUND THE FOURSEAS HOTEL during my Peak-side sojourn. Mr Tsang, the shopkeeper, remembered me and greeted me with a stroke of my hair. The Communist Chinese school still held its patriotic morning assembly but with the stirring music now blaring from loudspeakers rather than the scratchy phonograph. The late-morning quayside at Yau Ma Tei was still slick with fish scales and entrails and the rickshaw coolies still slept with their machines in Soares Avenue at night. Ah Sam was not amongst them. I was told he had died of a weak heart, weakened no doubt by his rickshaw and the *nga pin*. His number 3 hat was being worn by another now.

When I went up there, I found the Ho Man Tin squatter area had been rebuilt but now it had a rudimentary sewage system and was provided with standpipes and a concrete laundry area. The thoroughfares between the houses were wider in order to serve as fire breaks.

The Queen of Kowloon still lived in her cockloft and was still tormented by the local children. Yet, now, I did not join in their mockery or railway gravel throwing. I had learnt much about the

world since I had last seen her, learnt to differentiate between fun and cruelty, humour and contemptuous laughter, love and hate. On one occasion, I approached her with the intention of buying her a meal at a *dai pai dong*. I wanted to see if I could extract some of her life story. I knew enough of adults now to be aware that they all possessed incredible tales – if only one could get at them. I was taller now than when she had first seen me but, otherwise, I was little altered in appearance.

It was early one evening in Mong Kok that I saw her for the last time. She was being chased by a woman who owned a fruit stall, with a stiff bamboo broom. The Queen was shuffling along as fast as she could go, dropping apples and oranges in her wake. At the sight of me, the stallholder immediately gave up the chase and started to retrieve her stolen merchandise. I went up to the Queen and addressed her in Cantonese.

'Good evening, madam,' I began politely. 'You should not have to steal. I would like to buy you food.'

She squinted at me, her eyes beady slits under a fringe of dishevelled, badly trimmed and matted hair. For a moment, I thought I was going to get a lucid answer. I was wrong.

She recoiled from me. Her hands rose over her head to the complementary stench of her armpits and general rank body odour.

'*Kwai! Kwai!*' she screamed in a falsetto voice that could have cracked a wine glass.

With that, she fled with far greater speed than she had to avoid the broom. A month later, I risked approaching her cockloft. It was occupied by a Chinese family. I felt guilty then. Had I, I thought, unwittingly driven her away? It was only later I realized she must have thought I was the ghost of the young heir to the Russian throne, returned from the dead to haunt her in her opium- and alcohol-befuddled dreams.

Things had changed, however, inside the Fourseas. Mr Peng was still the manager, but Ching had left, along with at least half the other room boys I had known. Ah Kwan was still the third-floor captain, but the whores had been moved out, the clientele now predominantly tourists or expatriates waiting for housing. The latter were exclusively British, the former almost exclusively American. The skull-faced gardener was no longer employed, his place taken by a kindly, elderly man who wore a battered trilby hat at all times and spoke to the plants in undertones of affection. Rumour had it that Skull-face had been 'chopped' – attacked with a meat cleaver – and done a runner for China. It was also discovered that he was more than just a card-carrying member of the Communist party. As such, he must have fallen foul of the fiercely patriotic and anti-Communist local Triad society and narrowly escaped a traditional execution of death by a thousand cuts.

Politics did not really enter into the lives of the Hong Kong Chinese. They were presided over by gods not governments. They had no vote, for elections were never held: members of the Legislative Council, Hong Kong's parliament, were appointed by the Governor. However, once a year, the spiritual world stepped aside momentarily and the population could display their political allegiances.

10 October was known as the Double Tenth, a public holiday celebrating the anniversary of the Wuhan uprising which sparked the 1911 Chinese Revolution and was the foundation of modern China. Strings of firecrackers were exploded. Buildings were decked out with huge and often badly executed portraits of Generalissimo Chiang Kai-shek. They were surrounded by red and gold bunting and the Chinese Nationalist Kuomintang flag, which was then the national flag of Taiwan, whence Chiang had fled on losing mainland China to the Communists. The flag also

fluttered in squatter areas and from tenement roof tops, washing poles, trees and even bicycle handlebars.

Not every building was so decked out, however. Some carried defiant Communist Chinese flags and a picture of Chairman Mao. This sometimes resulted in scuffles and street fights, observed by a large crowd of detached onlookers until broken up by the riot squad which arrived on grey-painted, open-sided police vehicles. Armed with long truncheons and rattan shields, they formed a phalanx and moved into the fray in complete silence save for the thump of their boots and a *gweilo* officer barking orders in fluent Cantonese through a loudhailer. After a few skulls were cracked and arrests made, the remaining assailants melted away. The onlookers followed them in suppressed mood, like football fans leaving a stadium after their side had been trounced. The fun was over until another Chiang supporter tore down a red flag or a Mao supporter desecrated a picture of the Generalissimo.

Street fights in general were often spectacles to behold, little short of urban, outdoor theatre. Normally docile, when the Chinese lost their temper they did it in style, shouting abuse with astonishing intensity and originality before eventually resorting to blows. Sometimes, the fighting consisted of little more than face slaps and the occasional artless punch, but if the protagonists possessed even a modicum of martial arts knowledge, the fights would involve back kicks and short leaps, stabs with fingers, and rabbit punches with hands shaped into hard blades. The injuries in the *kung-fu* type fights were always the worst unless a knife appeared from a sleeve: then the pavement would be spattered with blood before the police arrived. After a bloody fight, the street dogs would lick the pavement clean.

I came to realize that the Chinese were a nation of spectators. From a full-scale riot to two rickshaw coolies squabbling over a parking space, they would gather to watch. On one occasion, I

even saw bets being made on the outcome, with side bets being placed on spin-off likelihoods.

Gambling and being Chinese were synonymous. Apart from mahjong, they indulged in *tin gau*, a strategy game played with tiles vaguely similar to dominoes. It was the first Chinese game I learnt to play and, in time, I became sufficiently proficient as to risk a part of my pocket money on it with the rickshaw coolies and mechanics in the Fourseas garage. I seldom left a session down.

Other gaming pastimes included heads 'n' tails and coin tossing. Played with ten-cent coins, the players stood in a line facing a wall. The first player threw a coin at the wall. It bounced off and settled on the ground. The idea was to throw one's coin so that it would land as near to the bottom of the wall as possible, but not touching it. He who succeeded took all the money but there were strategies. One could hit another's coin away from the wall or one could partly cover it, in which case, your coin took its place.

Although by law gambling was illegal unless conducted in a licensed mahjong club or through official Royal Hong Kong Jockey Club horse betting offices, it went on everywhere. To eradicate gambling was akin to prohibiting the eating of rice. I not infrequently saw policemen on the beat call into a tea house for a bowl of gunpowder tea and a few hands of *tin gau* and, for all his gentility, the new Fourseas gardener kept a stable of fighting crickets in minute, ornate bamboo cages. He fed them grass and chrysanthemum sprouts but, despite my attempts to bribe him, he never took me to a match.

The fact that anyone in Hong Kong could support the Communist cause seemed beyond me. They had butchered, dispossessed and robbed millions. Not a single squatter had avoided Communist brutality and yet even some of the squatter shacks flew the scarlet flag of mainland China with its five gold stars.

One of the hotel staff, although not a Communist sympathizer,

had fought as a partisan with them during the Japanese occupation. His name was Ah Lam. When I discovered his past, I sought him out and asked him why.

'Japanese more bad Communist,' was his pragmatic response.

'But why do people support the Communists now?'

'They wan' China one country. No like Taiwan, China, Hong Kong, Macau. Wan' China be one place for all Chinese.'

This seemed reasonable to me but I could not equate it in my mind with the atrocities of the recent civil war.

'But the Communists were very bad to the people.'

'All pe'pul bad to all pe'pul in war,' Ah Lam stated bluntly.

'Were you bad in the war?' I enquired.

'Me ve'y bad in war. One day, I show you.'

A few days later, as I was in my room doing my homework, there came a knock at my parents' door. It was Ah Lam asking to see them. I put down my pen and went through the adjoining door into my parents' suite.

'Master and Missee Bo Fu,' Ah Lam began, 'I wan' ask you for me take Martin New Te"ito'ies-side, show him some t'ing from the wartime. In wartime, I fighting Japanese for English. I East 'iffer B'igade man. Not Communist. Fight for England.'

He fumbled in his pocket and took out a small, brown cardboard box. On the lid were printed the letters *OHMS* and a crown with the words *Official Paid* round it. He handed it to my father who opened it and took out a medal. Cast in silver and attached to a red, white and blue ribbon, one side showed a lion standing on a dragon whilst on the other was the head of King George VI.

'Governor give me,' he continued, 'for fight Japanese. If Martin can come, I look-see him ve'y good. No p'oblem.'

My father had a we'll-let-you-know look on his face but my mother immediately acceded to the request, saying, 'Yes, I'm sure that's fine, Ah Lam.'

That Saturday afternoon, Ah Lam and I set off in the hotel
Studebaker bound for Sai Kung, a fishing village at the far eastern
end of the New Territories famous for its seafood and the
distinctly Communist leanings of its populace. Ah Lam told me
that the narrow road to Sai Kung, known as Hiram's Highway,
had been built by the British military but had been much improved by the Japanese, using allied and Chinese slave labour. It
was the only road that penetrated the Sai Kung peninsula, an area
of mountains, forests and isolated villages approached only by
remote footpaths and known to the Japanese as a hotbed of
sedition.

As we drove over the airport runway, he said, 'We go Sai
Kung-side, you no talk-talk about Communist. You just no talk,
boy.'

Sai Kung was quiet. Fishing junks lay three deep at the
quayside. On a few, children or women were washing down the
decks. The nets hung from the masts, drying in the sun like giant
furled spiders' webs. Scattered here and there on the dock were
dead fish or their remnants, the leftovers from the catch landed
that morning. Outside the quayside buildings stood buckets of sea
water containing live fish or lobsters, their massive claws secured
by wedges rammed into the claw joints, jamming them closed.
Crabs clicked in other buckets, ten deep, their claws manacled by
pliable bamboo twine. Seated on a low stool, a fisherman was
tying them in bunches of three with a loop to act as a carrying
handle.

Ah Lam parked the Studebaker in the shade of a wide-
spreading tree and we walked through the village to a tea house,
sitting at an outside table under an awning. He entered into a long
conversation with the proprietor whom he obviously knew well. I
sipped my tea and kept quiet. At length, Ah Lam introduced me
to the tea house owner.

'How do you do?' he said, shaking my hand.

'*Ho! Ho! Nei ho ma?*' I replied.

He laughed at this, but I sensed the threat of malice hiding behind his laughter.

'You don't need to speak Cantonese with me. I speak English. So,' he went on, 'you are going with Lam here to see something in the hills. Do you know what you will see?' I said I did not. 'You will see what Lam and I did in the war. Lam is my good friend and old comrade.' He put his hand on my shoulder. 'Are you a strong boy?'

I considered the question and said, 'I think so. I can walk a long way. I walked from Tung Chung to Ngong Ping without—'

'I do not mean strong in your legs but . . .' his hand shifted to my head '. . . in your mind.'

I did not quite understand what he meant but answered that I thought I was. He grinned.

'It is a long walk. Maybe two miles. And it is a hot day.'

He put four bottles of Coke in a small string bag and handed me a tiny bottle opener in the shape of a Coke bottle. Thus provisioned, Lam and I set off along a wide path across paddy-fields of waving green rice, the pale white grain hanging down like cascades of tiny opals, ready to ripen. As we walked, frogs leapt from the path into the paddy. Where there were stone bridges over watercourses, lizards ran helter-skelter ahead of us making for the security of a crevice.

'Who was that man?' I enquired.

'He my boss in war,' Ah Lam replied.

'Your boss?' I repeated.

'He East 'iffer B'gade off'sser.'

'What is the East River Brigade?'

'In war,' Ah Lam explained, 'many Chinese pe'pul wan' fight Japanese but he no can do. Got no gun. But some pe'pul got gun.

Communist got gun. They make small-small army, liff in mountungs . . .' He pointed to the east where the land was mountainous
with narrow wooded valleys between grass- or bush-covered
ridges. 'Dis mountungs. He call East 'iffer B'igade. He fighter, not
sol-jer. Sometime Communist, sometime Kuomintang, sometime
just man no like Japanese.'

'But what did you do?'

'Make trubbul for Japanese.'

After about half a mile the path, now narrower and cut into
earth steps, left the paddyfields and started up a hillside carved
into terraces upon which was growing a variety of vegetables.
Here and there between the terraces were small platforms bearing
rows of golden pagodas and one or two graves.

'What sort of trouble did you make?' I asked.

'Big trubbul. You know Watah-loo Road, near hotel, is a b'idge
for t'ain. Kowloon-Canton . . .' he struggled with the word '. . .
Wailway? One time, we blow up. Put plenty PE under b'idge.
Phoom! No t'ain can go China-side long time.'

'What is PE?' I enquired.

'In English he call plas-tic ex-plo-sif,' he enunciated slowly.
'B'itish sol-jer come China-side, giff us.'

We carried on up the hill to a point where the path ran
horizontally along the hillside, following the lie of the land. It was
easier going now and, in twenty minutes, we reached a steep-sided
wooded valley. Just as we were about to enter the trees, Ah Lam
froze. I did likewise. Crouching down, he signalled me to move to
his side and pointed ahead. Not twenty yards away was a wild
boar, his tusks like old ivory, his back bristled. He did not look in
our direction and, after a moment, moved off into the undergrowth. I began to stand up, but Ah Lam held me down. In less
than a minute, the boar's sow crossed the path followed by seven
piglets with light brown coats and thick, dark horizontal stripes.

No sooner were they gone than Ah Lam stood up and, in a loud voice, said, '*Ho sik!*'

At the sound of his voice there was a crashing in the undergrowth as the boars fled.

'In war,' Lam went on, 'we eat dis pig. Taste ve'y good! Much more better farm pig.' We crossed a dry watercourse in the centre of the valley then began to follow the ever diminishing path through the remainder of the trees. Halfway to the edge of the woodland, however, Al Lam stopped by a huge boulder, so big it had created a clearing for itself. He sat down on it and gave me two of the bottles of Coca Cola which I opened, handing him one. The Coke was warm but quenched a thirst I did not realize I had until then.

When he had drained his bottle Ah Lam, with characteristic Chinese disregard, tossed it into the trees. I heard it smash on a rock. This done, he slithered down the boulder, crossed the path, squatted down and started to clear away the leaf litter with his hands.

'You come see,' he said.

I joined him. A few steps from the path, he had uncovered six dull white stones. Each was about the size of a small watermelon and decorated by a similar series of thin, jagged cracks. They were in a line about three feet apart.

'You know dis one?' he asked.

'No,' I answered. The stones were a puzzle to me, all the more so for their being in a line.

Ah Lam patted the top of his pate. His hair was cut short, not much longer than a well-used toothbrush.

'Japanese sol-jer head,' he declared matter-of-factly. 'Six piece. We kill him here. Hide behind rock, jump on him. Very quick! No noise.'

My toes curled involuntarily as I looked down on the tops of the

soldiers' skulls. It seemed incredible to me that there were dead people at my feet, buried in the earth with no coffin, no headstone, no epitaph. Then it occurred to me. Why could I see the tops of their heads? Dead people lay down in their graves.

'Did you bury them?' I asked.

Ah Lam nodded, grinning. 'Mus' do or Japanese come fin', take away, maybe kill pe'pul in Sai Kung for punish.'

'But why are they . . . ?' I mimed upright as opposed to supine.

Ah Lam's grin extended further as he replied, 'Japanese man no like die up.' He stood to attention to emphasize the point. 'If no lie down no can go to heaven.'

My father did not like having to return to the hotel. In part, I sympathized with him. He could no longer live as he had done in an apartment, with servants, entertaining in style, enjoying as prestigious an address as one could get in Hong Kong without living in a house on the mountain.

There was another reason for his dislike of the hotel. My mother was back in close contact with her Chinese friends amongst the staff. In my father's eyes, it was beneath her to befriend what were in effect her servants.

'In my opinion, Joyce,' he said frostily one evening as he waited for her to dress to go out to dinner, 'you're going native.'

I could hear the conversation through the adjoining door which was ajar.

'Letting the side down,' my mother replied.

'Precisely!'

'Don't be such a bloody fool, Ken!'

'I don't like it.'

'In that case,' my mother said, 'you can lump it.'

At this juncture, I knocked and went into their room.

'I've gone native,' I announced proudly.

My father stared at me for a moment then addressed my mother again. 'And that!' He pointed at me. 'Your son's more Chinese than a coolie. He'll have a bloody pole and a rattan hat next. Is this what you want?'

'Yes!' my mother replied emphatically. 'It is just what I want. I want a child who knows the world, knows the value of people whatever their race or rank and can appreciate what he sees.' She picked up her evening bag: it was black with silver beads sewn on to it. 'What I don't want is a boring, narrow-minded bigot with a drink problem.' She smiled amiably. 'Shall we go?'

Bit by bit, my parents grew even further apart. My mother maintained her gradually increasing coterie of Chinese friends, seldom inviting my father into this circle but, whenever she could, including me in her excursions. I particularly loved going with her to festival celebrations.

Some, such as the Moon Festival, involved little more than a slap-up meal taken *al fresco* with the moon high in the sky and the children carrying multi-coloured lanterns shaped like rabbits, birds, butterflies, dragons and fish. If clouds threatened to obscure the moon, everyone made a loud noise by banging saucepans together or letting off a short string of firecrackers to drive the clouds away. The only aspect of the festival I just could not abide was the moon cakes, one of the very few Chinese foods I found it impossible to swallow. They came in a variety of sizes and looked vaguely like English pork pies. The dough was made of flour, syrup or honey, rice wine and eggs. After some hours, it was rolled out and a filling made of lotus seed paste and whole duck egg yolks, care being taken not to break them. Once filled and shaped in a ball, they were pressed in wooden moulds, glazed

and baked. The Chinese adored them but most *gweilos* found them inedible. The glutinous contents had the unpleasant habit of sticking to the roof of the mouth.

Other festivals, like Ch'ing Ming (or the Hungry Ghosts' Festival) in the spring, were a more exclusive matter and it was a sign of the regard in which my mother was held by her Chinese friends that, after only three years in Hong Kong, we were invited to attend this most personal of ceremonies.

On the morning of the appointed day in early April, we rendezvoused with a noisily joyful gaggle of thirty Chinese in a hundred-yard-long queue at the railway station in Tsim Sha Tsui. Everyone was weighed down by a parcel, wicker basket or string bag. After twenty minutes, we were herded aboard a train which set off immediately.

The train trundled through Kowloon and entered a tunnel in the hills. When it emerged in the Sha Tin valley, it was as if I were riding a time machine. At one end of the tunnel was a mid-twentieth-century city, on the other a timeless landscape of tiny villages, paddyfields, salt pans and fishing junks. If a British man-o'-war had sailed into the cove, cannons blazing, it could have still been the Opium War.

Following the coast to Tai Po, the train then headed north to Fanling, where we disembarked. Once we were all gathered together, the party headed into the low hills to the south. It was a long walk, first up a disintegrating concrete road then along a path through brush and scattered trees. Finally, we arrived at our destination: three graves and a row of a dozen or so golden pagodas. The women – including my mother – swept the semicircular platforms before the graves. A man with a tin of red paint touched up the characters on the grave doors. This done, josssticks were produced and burnt with everyone, including my mother and me, kow-towing to the ancestors.

After this, food was produced, including, incredibly, a whole suckling pig. Bowls of hot rice ladled from a thermos were placed before the entrance to each grave with a piece of the pig, some steamed vegetables and a little bowl of rice wine. The label on the bottle read *Sam Sheh Jau* – Three Snake Wine. Pickled in the bottle was a small nondescript snake. On the top of the graves, thick wads of Hell's Banknotes were weighted down with a stone. Next to them was placed a car made out of tissue paper stretched over a split bamboo frame. This was set alight, the ashes blowing away on the breeze and adhering to the crackling on the pig.

'The money is to pay the ancestors' bills in heaven,' my mother whispered in explanation.

'And the car?'

'They haven't got one in heaven, so . . .'

Two of the men approached with armfuls of human bones. Behind them, one of the golden pagodas was open. The bones were placed on the ground where several women dusted them down and set about buffing them up with light tan Cherry Blossom shoe polish. I watched utterly mesmerized, wondering what it would be like to dig up my grandfather and give him a shine.

While the contents of all the nearby ossuaries were cleaned, a picnic was laid out. The human bones were then arranged around the picnic cloth. Every skeleton was set a place. I found myself sitting between my mother and a skull carefully balanced on a heap of its associated bones, the lower jaw dropped as if the ancestor who owned the bones was having a damned good laugh at the rest of us.

'What happens to their food?' I asked my mother, not letting my eye off my neighbour's rice bowl. I think I half expected to see it gradually disappear, consumed by the ghost of the skeleton.

'The ancestors in heaven soak up the essence of the food, then it's thrown away,' my mother informed me.

'Including the pig?' I enquired, my mouth watering at the thought of it.

'No,' my mother answered. 'Only the food in the bowls. We eat the rest.'

No-one spoke to the bones and, when the picnic was eaten, we indeed threw the ancestors' food into the bushes for the ants and birds. With the bones returned to their golden pagodas, we set off for the railway station. As we descended the hills, I saw other families scattered across the slopes of the hills doing as we had done.

Arriving home, we found my father sitting on the balcony of my parents' room reading a month-old copy of an English newspaper and puffing on his pipe. He had temporarily grown a full beard, partly, I suspected, because naval officers were permitted to do so. Indeed, he had unnecessarily asked Mr Borrie's permission.

'So, feel you've done your bit for someone else's forebears?' he asked acerbically.

There was, however, one festival my father was actually prepared to attend, despite the fact that it contained much that he abhorred – joss-stick smoke, firecrackers, dense jostling crowds and (to him) inedible delicacies. This was the birthday of Tin Hau and my father tolerated it because it entailed a boat trip.

The primary festival of the sea-going folk of Hong Kong, it was held not only at all the Tin Hau temples around Hong Kong but also at the ancient temple in Tai Miu Wan, named – literally – Joss House Bay by early European settlers who referred to temples as joss houses.

The journey to Tai Miu Wan was explained to me by my father, who insisted I sat at a table in the hotel lounge with him as he pored over our impending nautical experience with military

precision, plotting it with dividers and a navigational ruler on a naval chart. He might have been preparing an invasion.

'It'll take us about ninety minutes to get there from HMS *Tamar*,' he began. 'Our party will be taking one of the larger, faster launches. At first, we head towards the eastern harbour, then – pay attention – go on to a bearing east-south-east through Lei Yue Mun and into . . .' he jabbed the point of the dividers into the map '. . . the Tat Hong Channel. We change to a north-easterly bearing here . . .' he moved the dividers '. . . once clear of the island of Tit Cham Chau.'

I looked at the map and said, 'It's not very far.'

'Dangerous waters,' my father replied. 'Rocky shores, rip tides.'

'How far is it?'

He spun the dividers round in his fingers and said, 'Seven-and-a-half nautical miles, give or take.'

'Don't you have to be very accurate?'

My father did not reply and rolled up the map.

The naval launch had been decked out in signal flags and pennants including a huge scarlet triangular Chinese one at the bow with a black serrated edge and black characters in the centre.

We cast off and joined a veritable flotilla of vast fishing junks, motorized sampans, walla-wallas and pleasure craft, all extravagantly decked out in the same fashion. By the time the launch reached its destination, it was reduced to barely moving, jostling with the other craft. A hundred yards off shore, the bos'n dropped anchor and prepared to lower a dinghy. It had not been readied on its derricks before two sampans arrived alongside, a vociferous argument ensuing between the Chinese naval launch crew and the women in the sampans. It seemed no-one was allowed to organize their own landing arrangements, the sampans being the only permitted 'ship-to-shore' craft. They had fixed a monopoly so, in the name of colonial expediency and not wanting

to arouse the anger of the Triads on the beach, we all clambered into the sampans and were oared ashore.

I had never been in a sampan before and was fascinated at how it was propelled by its single stern oar, twisted on the out-stroke to give forward momentum then twisted back on the in-stroke to avoid drag. The woman driving the boat stood barefoot on what my father called the stern flat, wearing a loose jacket and baggy trousers cut of a shiny black material that seemed to be steeped in tar. Her face was wrinkled and tanned by a life at sea.

We reached the pebble beach, went ashore down a plank extended from the bow of the sampan and joined the dense throng of celebrants. Entering the temple itself was impossible.

'Can't see why you wanted to come, Joyce,' my father grumbled. 'We can't get in the damn temple. Why couldn't we come on a day . . . ?'

'For the atmosphere,' my mother replied in a weary tone.

'Atmosphere!' my father retorted. 'Smoke more like.'

As he spoke, an elderly lady pushed past him carrying a bundle of lit joss-sticks, three feet long and as thick as Churchillian cigars. My father got the full benefit of the drift of their smoke right in his nostrils. He let out a gargantuan sneeze which had the lady turn round and briefly give him a piece of her mind.

In front of the temple, to appease those who could not get in to pay their homage, a secondary shrine had been set up on the beach. The image of Tin Hau was made of tissue stretched over a bamboo frame and surrounded by red and gold paper and small brightly coloured plastic propellers that spun like miniature windmills in the sea breeze. Before the image was arrayed a number of fully grown roast pigs, cooked chickens and ducks, bowls of pink bread buns, cakes, a large pile of pink-coloured boiled eggs and joss-sticks of all sizes. In the temple, gongs

clanged and a deep bell continuously rang. Several bands played against each other from opposite ends of the temple.

Many of the junks riding at anchor were of the huge, deep-sea variety, vessels from another century. Every so often, the crews let off strings of firecrackers hanging from the masts, the blue smoke and fragments of paper drifting over the sea towards land. I half closed my eyes and imagined they were war junks fighting off pirates or East Indiamen running opium up the Pearl River to Canton.

After an hour at the festival, we returned to the launch and sailed three miles across open sea to the Ninepins, a group of four uninhabited islands with a natural rock archway on one. The water was as clear as – as my father put it – chilled vodka and we could see the rocks of the sea bottom six fathoms down. Every so often a dark shadow drifted over them and was the reason no-one swam. Due to a confluence of currents, this place was notorious for its sharks.

As the adults drank, ate and talked, I lay on the deck at the bow and looked down, watching the sharks glide by and thinking all the while that an instant and terrible death moved by only twenty feet below me. I only had to roll off the deck . . .

'What're you up to?' my mother asked, kneeling on the deck beside me.

'Watching the sharks,' I replied.

At that moment, a vast shape like that of a delta-wing bomber passed beneath me.

'What's that?' I almost shouted.

Everyone looked up and some came over to stand by me. Something broke the surface a short distance off. It floated just beneath the light waves as a sodden face flannel might.

'It's a manta ray!' someone exclaimed.

The launch crew quickly raised the anchor and started the

engines. The ray began to move away. We set off in slow pursuit. The creature had a wingspan of at least fifteen feet and was, someone reckoned, over twenty feet from its bizarre, horseshoe-shaped snout to the tip of its long, quite rigid tail. It was dark grey in colour with a few cream patches and did not so much swim as gracefully fly under the water, its vast wings beating like a great bird's but in slow motion. It looked the epitome of marine beauty and yet simultaneously exceptionally sinister and dangerous.

'I wouldn't like to meet him when I was swimming,' I said to no-one in particular.

A man clutching an expensive German camera and kneeling on the deck next to me replied, 'You'd have nothing to fear. All they eat is plankton.'

I considered this information. That such a huge creature could live only by consuming the microscopic creatures that made phosphorescence was, at that moment, one of the wonders of my world.

'That ray was astonishing,' my mother remarked as my father drove our car on to the vehicular ferry that evening.

'Not really,' he commented dismissively. 'I saw bigger in west Africa during the war.'

'Well, you would have had to, wouldn't you, Ken?' my mother answered. 'If I had a boil on my bum, you'd have had a bigger one during the war.'

She leant back in the passenger seat and winked at me. My father glanced in the driving mirror to see my reaction. I kept my face deadpan. Had I been caught grinning, I would have been belted for some misdemeanour, trumped up or otherwise, by bedtime.

1 1

'HOMEWARD' BOUND

AS 1955 ADVANCED, THE WEATHER HEATING UP AND THE DAILY humidity rising, my parents' life became increasingly frenetic and fraught. At his office, my father was preparing to hand over to his successor. This caused him frequently to return to the Fourseas in a flaming temper.

'I don't know how they do it!' he would mutter. 'The oldest bloody civilization on earth and they can't file. I've put a chart up. What goes where. Anchor butter is not the same as anchor chains. Dear God! My life is blessed with blithering idiots.'

This tirade made, he would pour himself a pink gin and sit on the balcony, watching the traffic go by and the setting sun illuminate the hill opposite.

My mother spent much of her time packing for the voyage 'home', which she no longer considered her home – or mine. Our larger possessions – furniture and the Ford – had already been sent ahead by cargo ship. When she was not packing or visiting friends, my mother quietly wept to herself. She did this in private, but I heard her through the door between our rooms. On just one occasion, my father found her wiping her eyes.

'What's the matter, Joyce?' he enquired as he poured himself a gin and tonic, the hotel being temporarily out of Angostura bitters, much to his vexation.

'Nothing.'

He sat down in one of the armchairs, rolling the ice round in his glass.

'Must be something.'

'I got some dust in my eye.'

'Right,' he said and sipped his drink.

My mother gave him the sort of look she might have afforded a street cat that had just regurgitated the half-digested intestines of a rotten garoupa on her bed.

'What?' he asked, catching the look.

'You're an unfeeling bastard, Ken.'

My father, having no direct response to this, replied, 'I've had a hell of a day in *Tamar*, Joyce, and I didn't come home to have to take this display of petulance.'

He put his half-finished drink down and walked to the door.

'Off to the wardroom?' my mother called out to his receding back.

He slammed the door and returned at midnight.

My preparations for leaving Hong Kong consisted of stocking up on *wah mui*, packets of joss-sticks and dried melon seeds, and buying presents for my grandparents. For my father's mother, I bought a table linen set embroidered with Chinese scenes, whilst for Nanny, who had stocked up on table linen during her visit, I bought a folding octagonal waste-paper basket with little Chinese figures of playing children appliquéd to its sides. For Grampy, a seafaring man, I bought a rosewood model of a sampan which cost me three weeks' pocket money.

My mother was invited by her Chinese friends to a number of farewell banquets as the date of our departure drew nearer. My

father was not always invited and, when he was, he more often than not declined.

'Silly old sod!' my mother said to me one day after he had rejected yet another invitation. 'He's not happy unless he's bloody miserable.'

I accompanied my mother to a few of these banquets, the best of which was given by the hotel room boys. We met at a restaurant in Tsim Sha Tsui just as night fell. The neon shop signs were coming on, the air was warm and moths were beginning to flicker around the lights. In the trees that lined Nathan Road, birds squabbled noisily over roosting perches.

The banquet was superb and went on well past midnight, the dishes appearing with a mouth-watering regularity: sharks' fin soup, abalone, quails' eggs and hundred-year-old duck eggs (which my mother tasted for the first time and was amazed to discover I not only knew of but also liked), chickens' feet, braised duck, soft-shelled hairy crabs cooked in salt and sugar, chicken wrapped in pickled cabbage and baked in clay, various fish, pork and beef with chillies and garlic . . . We were showered with farewell gifts. They were simple things, like sets of chopsticks, chopstick rests, decorated porcelain bowls and soapstone figurines, but to my mother they were as precious as gems and she prized them for the rest of her life.

After the banquet my father, who had attended on this occasion, returned to the Fourseas in a taxi, but my mother elected to walk. It was at least two miles but this did not deter her. I walked at her side, holding her hand despite the fact that I considered myself too mature now to do such a thing. In the circumstances, it just seemed right.

The air was warm. From the windows of the tenements came the sounds of everyday Chinese life – the song of caged birds, the clack of mahjong tiles, the raucous chorus of a Cantonese opera

playing on the radio. The shops were shuttered. Under the arcades sat old men in their pyjamas with the legs rolled up to the knee, reading Chinese comic books or the past day's papers, talking to each other, smoking cigarettes of Chinese tobacco, some mixed with opium.

My mother and I did not speak. In our own ways, we were letting Hong Kong impinge itself upon us.

'Will you be sad to leave?' she asked, finally breaking our silence as we turned into Waterloo Road.

'Yes,' I admitted. 'Very.'

'Would you like to come back?'

'For a holiday? Yes!'

'No. For good.'

I thought about it. I had been happy in Hong Kong. It had been an exciting place in which to live and I was sure it had much to offer that I had yet to uncover. However, there was more to it than that. I felt I had grown up in Hong Kong. I could recall little of my life prior to the *Corfu*. It was as if my memory – my actual existence – had begun the minute my foot had touched the dock in Algiers. England was as strange a place to me now as Hong Kong had been on that June morning in 1952. In short, I felt I belonged there.

'Yes,' I said at last. 'Definitely.'

'In that case,' my mother replied, 'we'd best see what we can do about it.'

On my last night in Hong Kong, I went down Soares Avenue bidding farewell to the shopkeepers. Mr Deng, the seller of cherry bombs, gave me a ten-cent biro and ruffled my hair. Mr Tsang cut open a pomelo.

'You can buy in Ing-lan'-side?' he enquired, handing me a piece and taking one for himself.

'Lo can buy Inglan'-side,' I confirmed, biting into it and spitting

the flat pips on to the pavement. This, I thought at the same moment, was a habit I would have to lose. And quick!

'*Ayarh!*' he exclaimed. 'You mus' come back Hong Kong-side!' He too stroked my head for a last fix of luck. 'You come back. I low. One day, no long time, you come see me one more time.'

Halfway down Nathan Road, my mother said suddenly, 'Ken . . . ! Stop the car!'

My father, sitting in the front passenger seat next to a young naval rating with a flat Birmingham accent and a badly sunburnt neck, ordered the driver to pull into the kerb.

'Give me the boarding passes, will you, Ken? Mine and Martin's.'

For the briefest of moments, I saw a sense of intense fear pass over my father's face. My mother had always been an expert at timing. If she really were going to leave him, and I assumed it was possible, this would be the supremely appropriate moment. And he knew it. Yet he reached into his jacket pocket, removed his wallet and handed her two pieces of folded green-tinted paper.

'How long will you be?' he asked.

'How long is a piece of string?' she replied evasively.

It was one of her stock answers and she knew it infuriated my father, whose life was filled with certainties to which there was never any string attached.

'Depends on the size of the parcel,' I said, aping my mother's usual response to further interrogation.

My father gave me a scathing look and went on, 'Well don't be long, that's all.'

We stepped out of the car and it drove away. I briefly saw my father's face through the front passenger door window. He looked crestfallen, defeated and scared. I felt strangely, guiltily jubilant.

Directly across Nathan Road was Whitfield Barracks, two sentries with cockades in their berets and Lee Enfield .303 rifles in their hands standing either side of a gateway. Through it I could see an armoured scout car of which I had an exact Dinky replica.

Without any haste, my mother and I walked down Nathan Road. Ahead of us, between the buildings, rose the Peak, hazy in the mid-afternoon sun. It was hot, the humidity high. Rickshaws passed us, carrying people, boxes and bales of cloth. Red and cream Kowloon buses sped by, washing hot air over us. My mother looked at them and I wondered if she was watching out for Her Russian Majesty.

At the southern end of the barracks, we crossed Nathan Road, entered Haiphong Road and took the second left into Hankow Road. Hing Loon Curio and Jewellery Company was open but we did not go in for a chat or a free drink. We had already said our goodbyes.

My mother, who had not spoken twenty words since we got out of the car, said, 'Well, what do you say?'

I made no answer. We both had the same thought in mind and entered the Pen. We were shown to a table and my mother ordered tea for two. She specifically requested Chinese tea. It soon arrived at our table in a bone china teapot accompanied by wafer thin sandwiches and a silver stand of dainty cakes. On a balcony above, a string quartet started up, playing tunes from recent hit musicals.

'This is living,' my mother said after a long silence. 'Really living . . .' She looked about her. 'Haven't we been the lucky ones!'

'Yes,' I said, 'we certainly have. And,' I added, 'we will be again.'

My mother reached across the table and took my hand in both of hers.

'Too bloody right!' she said with characteristic defiance. 'You can bet your bottom dollar on it.'

She looked at her watch and summoned a waiter Chinese style, her palm downwards and all her fingers beckoning together.

'*Mai dan, m'goi*,' she said as he drew near. Her accent was almost perfect.

The bill was presented. My mother paid it, smiling at me with the memory of our first tea here. We left through the grand front entrance as if we were minor royalty, a Chinese boy in the hotel livery holding the door open for us, another asking if we required a rickshaw or taxi. That tart – I understood the meaning of the word now – the Duchess of Windsor could not have been better treated.

Beside the Tsim Sha Tsui fire station was a short concrete slope to the hillside on the top of which stood the marine police head-quarters. A tree hung over it. In its shade, as usual, was the old grasshopper man seated on a folding stool, a rattan basket of bamboo splints and leaves by his side. With them, he skilfully wove grasshoppers, arranging them around his feet or along the top of a culvert. As we approached, he held one out.

'You wan' g'asshoppah, missee? B'ing you plenty good luck. Only one dollar.'

I bought two and gave my mother one.

'You good boy for you muvver,' the old man said and, getting up, stroked my hair.

We walked on, past Sammy Shields' dental surgery and into the Kowloon Docks. Alongside the first pier was the P&O liner *Carthage*, the sister ship of the *Corfu*. Her white hull towered over

us, gleaming in the sunlight. Smoke drifted from her funnel. Signal flags flew from her mast. The Blue Peter announced she was soon to sail.

The dock was crowded with baggage coolies, rickshaw pullers, cars, trucks and well-wishers. Along the hull, sampans bobbed on the waves. Junks sailed by out in the harbour and walla-wallas puttered about, tossing in the wake of a Star Ferry leaving its jetty. I glanced at the Peak across the shimmering water. Block A, Mount Austin stood out, silhouetted against the sub-tropical sky and I thought that, no matter what, I could always claim I once lived there.

Plank by plank, hand in hand, clutching our lucky grass-hoppers, we slowly climbed the gangway. My mother was crying.

It was the afternoon of Monday, 2 May 1955, and I was ten.

Four years later, exactly as my mother had predicted, my father was a colonial civil servant and we were back. For good.

GLOSSARY

THE SPELLING OF CANTONESE WORDS DOES NOT NECESSARILY FOLLOW the accepted Pin Yin or other linguistic systems (such as Wade-Giles) but is the roughly phonetic spelling of how Cantonese was spoken by the average European (*gweilo*) at the time. It may well be inaccurate, for which I apologize. The spelling of pidgin English is also phonetic.

atap a woven bamboo and/or rice straw matting used to cover bamboo windbreaks, peasant buildings and temporary structures

ayarh! a common expletive: it has no literal meaning

baksheesh alms (of Middle Eastern origin) cf. *kumshaw*

cash ancient Chinese copper coins with round or square holes in the centre

chau island

cheen money

chop noun: an ivory carved seal; verb: to attack with a meat chopper or knife

chop! chop! pidgin English for *get a move on/hurry up*

chow   food: a generic word (*small chow* means canapés)

congee   a form of rice gruel-cum-porridge eaten for breakfast

dai   big – e.g. *dai fung* (typhoon) means big wind

dai pai dong   a street-side cooked-food stall (not a fast-food purveyor)

dim sum   small steamed dumplings containing bite-sized lumps of shrimp, pork, beef and other ingredients

diu nei lo mo   Literally *go fuck your mother* but often used coarsely as an epithet the equivalent of *You don't say!* or *Well, I'll be damned*; also used vindictively or pejoratively

dofu   known in the West as tofu or soya bean curd

dor jei   *thank you* (for an item or gift)

Fide! Fide!   literally *Quick! Quick!* but implying the more impolite *Get a move on!*

fung shui   pronounced *fong soy*, it is the art (or science) of achieving harmony in one's surroundings by balancing the influences of wind (*fung*) and water (*soy*)

gai doh cheen   *how much?* Literally, *how much money?*

Gai duk toh   a Christian

garoupa   a large sea fish, a delicacy frequently served in Chinese cuisine

godown   a warehouse

golden pagoda   an ossuary urn

heui la!   *go!/let's go!*

ho   *good* or *yes*

Ho! Ho! Nei ho ma?   *Good! Good! How are you?* (a common polite greeting)

ho pang yau   good friend

Ho sik!   Good to eat/eating/food

hutong   alley or passageway

kai fong associations   Chinese social charities

kam taap   golden pagoda: see above

kang a traditional Chinese sleeping bed or platform made of wood or stone, the latter often having a fire beneath it for warmth

kukri an exceedingly sharp, curved fighting knife used by Nepalese Gurkha troops

kumshaw alms (of Cantonese origin)

kwai a ghost; more accurately a disembodied spirit

Kwan Ti the god of war and literature, and the patron god of secret brotherhoods, the police and many others

lai see packet a red paper envelope printed with gold lettering and containing money: usually given as a gift at Chinese New Year

loh siu a rat (or mouse)

mai dan the bill

Mat yeh? *What?* (rudely implying *What do you want?*)

m'ho bad or no

m'ho cheen Literally, *no money*

m'koi *thank you* (for a service or act); also, on occasion by implication, *please*

muntjak a small, indigenous deer, also known as a barking deer on account of its dog-like call

Nei wui mui gong ying mun? *Do you speak English?*

Nei giu mut ye meng? *What is your name?*

Nei ho ma? *How do you do?* – a common greeting

nga pin opium

ng mun five dollars

Ngo giu jo *My name is . . .*

nullah an open drain, varying in size from two feet wide and three deep up to sixty feet wide and fifteen deep; usually built to cope with heavy rain or effluent

pi lau a ceremonial archway

praya a stone-fronted dock or esplanade

pu-erh a variety of Chinese tea

roorkee chair a folding camp chair used in India and rather like a film director's chair

sarong a Malay (usually Tamil) ankle-length cotton skirt worn by men

saw hei combed or combed back (of hair)

Sei Hoi Jau Dim Fourseas Hotel

shadouf an ancient Egyptian crane-like irrigation mechanism for raising water

shéh snake

skink a common lizard

suq an Arab market or bazaar

taipan a wealthy businessman, traditionally the expatriate head of a major trading company or 'noble house'

ushabti a small ancient Egyptian funerary sculpture

wan bay or inlet

wei! *hey!* or, if used on the telephone, *hello*: the American equivalent would be *Yoh!*

wok a type of cooking pot, used especially for shallow frying or searing

won ton a deep fried dumpling of minced beef and pork, water chestnuts and onions

yamen a building housing the home and office of a mandarin, magistrate or other regional administrator in dynastic times

yat, yee, sam, sei, ng, lok . . . one, two, three, four, five, six . . .

yum cha literally *drink tea*

DUE